The transcriber Margaret Bird has been an honorary research fellow in the History department of Royal Holloway, University of London since 2006.

Born in central London in 1946, she read Modern History at St Anne's College, Oxford and gained her master's degree in Modern History at Royal Holloway. For both degrees she specialised in aspects of English history in the eighteenth century.

She has lived in Kingston upon Thames since 1970 and was a partner with her husband Tony in the economic consultancy they founded and ran for 22 years.

She has a deep love of the landscape and waterways of the Norfolk Broads in eastern England. All her life she has spent as much time as possible on the family boat, at first with her parents and later with her husband and three sons

[*cover photographs Margaret Bird 2011; portrait of Mary Hardy in 1785 by Huguier, from the Cozens–Hardy Collection*]

The
Remaining Diary of
Mary Hardy
1773–1809

The
Remaining Diary of
Mary Hardy
1773–1809

Entries 1781–1809
not included in
the four-volume
edition of the diary

transcribed by
MARGARET BIRD

BURNHAM PRESS
KINGSTON UPON THAMES
2013

BURNHAM PRESS
2013
❊ KINGSTON UPON THAMES ❊

www.burnham-press.co.uk

Published by
  Burnham Press, Burnham Lodge,
  193 Richmond Road, KINGSTON UPON THAMES,
  Surrey, KT2 5DD, United Kingdom

First published April 2013
Second impression May 2013

Transcription of diary text copyright
  © Margaret Bird 2013 from original manuscripts
  held privately in the Cozens-Hardy Collection
Copyright of illustrations as specified under each caption

Design and typesetting in Adobe InDesign
  by Margaret Bird

www.biddles.co.uk

MIX
Paper from
responsible sources
FSC   FSC® C018575
www.fsc.org

Printed and bound in the UK by Biddles,
  part of the MPG Books Group, Bodmin and King's Lynn,
  24 Rollesby Road, Hardwick Industrial Estate,
  KING'S LYNN, Norfolk, PE30 4LS, United Kingdom
  on 115 gsm Vancouver matt-coated paper
  woodfree and FSC accredited

Mary Hardy websites
maryhardysdiary.co.uk
and
maryhardysworld.co.uk

ISBN 978-0-9573360-5-6

A CIP record for this title is available from the
  British Library

facing page Late-mediaeval sound hole in the ringing chamber
of Whissonsett's church tower which Mary Hardy's father
helped to restore during her childhood
[*photograph Margaret Bird 2011*]

Contents

The text of the remaining entries

North Norfolk

Mary Hardy's Letheringsett years 1781–1809

Some places named in the diary

TOWNS AND VILLAGES WITH PUBLIC HOUSES SUPPLIED WITH BEER
BY THE HARDYS IN THESE YEARS ARE SHOWN IN ITALIC

N

NORTH SEA

MILES
0   3   6

0   5   10 KM

Cley-Next-the-Sea

WELLS-NEXT-THE-SEA

R. STIFFKEY

R. BURN

R. GLAVEN

R. WENSUM

R. BURE

R. WENSUM

Wells-Next-the-Sea

Burnham
Overy Staithe

**BURNHAM
MARKET**

Holkham

Pit

Blakeney

Morston

Stiffkey

Langham

Warham
All Saints

Wighton

West
Rudham

Syderstone

Raynham

Godwick

**LITTLE
WALSINGHAM**

*Great
Snoring*

*Little
Snoring*

Alethorpe

Hindringham

Thursford

Kettlestone

FAKENHAM

R.
WENSUM

Hempton

Toftrees

Colkirk

Whissonsett

Pudding
Norton

Ryburgh

Brisley

North
Elmham

*East
Bilney*

Stanfield

Horningtoft

Wiveton

Glandford

Bayfield

Saxlingham

Field Dalling

Binham

Bale

Sharrington

Gunthorpe

Brinton

Stody

Thornage

Burgh Parva

Briston

Melton

Brininghem

Swanton
Novers

Stibbard

Twyford

Guestwick

Hindolveston

Bintree

REEPHAM

Sparham

Whitwell

Lenwade

Cawston

LETHERINGSETT

HOLT

Hempstead

Edgefield

Hunworth

Saxthorpe

Itteringham

Irmingland

Corpusty

Blickling

Heydon

Hevingham

AYLSHAM

NAVIG-
ATION

Brampton

Swannington

Salthouse

Kelling

Weybourne

Sheringham

*East
Runton*

Beeston
Regis

Beckham

Bodham

Baconsthorpe

Gresham

Bessingham

Aldborough

Aylmerton

CROMER

Overstrand
(Beckhithe)

Southrepps

**NORTH
WALSHAM**

Tunstead

Great
Haut-
bois

Coltishall

Horstead

Hoveton

R. BURE

NℳB13
20

Introduction: even chaff has its worth

by Margaret Bird

THIS WORK REPRESENTS THE REMAINDER of the text of Mary Hardy's manuscript which I chose not to include in the three published volumes of her Letheringsett diary.

Those volumes were brought out by Burnham Press in 2013, under the overall title *The Diary of Mary Hardy 1773–1809*, as *Diary 2* (1781–1793), *Diary 3* (1793–1797), and *Diary 4* (1797–1809). The full text of the diary written at Coltishall is published as *Diary 1* (1773–1781). The full diary text (1793–1797) of the apprentice brewer Henry Raven is included in *Diary 3*.

This book contains the chaff, or screenings—the husks and debris of harvested corn and malted barley. Such by-products have their value, as does this book. Mary Hardy's 36-year record paints an extraordinarily detailed panorama of daily life in a world hitherto glimpsed with little clarity. The four volumes of *The Diary* set out to open that world to our eyes, as will the companion volumes of commentary and analysis under the title *Mary Hardy and her World 1773–1809*. But some of the manuscript's usefulness is lost in the process of abridgment. We need the full story.

The unabridged 36-year record has its own fascinations. In the household we follow the course of the various illnesses suffered by family and friends, and the frequency with which the heavy washing is undertaken. We hear the full account, where rendered, of work in the fields and visits by innkeepers; and we can compile a daily weather chart. We monitor the changing pattern of the diarist's church attendance and that of her family. We also learn of all the Sunday school sessions at which she teaches, of the full complement of the Methodist and other Nonconformist meetings attended, and where; and the names of those accompanying her, and whom they heard preaching.

At the social level these extracts record the daily round of personal and professional calls, with all the associated hospitality: calls by lawyers, surgeons, merchants, shopkeepers, excise officers' families, surveyors, travelling players. Looking further afield, the entries amplify the record of visits to family and friends, listed on page ix as digressions from the daily record.

The entries in this volume will make no sense unless consulted with the other *Diary* volumes to hand. They do not furnish a stand-alone account. Instead they proffer comprehensive evidence for those building up a carefully constructed argument or compiling their own databases.

The 161,742 words of manuscript entries transcribed here represent 44 per cent of Mary Hardy's text spanning the period from 1781, when she and her family moved to a new world at Letheringsett, to her death in 1809 at the age of 75. The style of presentation and the transcription method adopted for the individual entries, summarised in the editorial conventions (overleaf), is the same as that for *The Diary of Mary Hardy*. Unlike the Diary volumes there are no marginal notes and almost no illustrations; nor is there is a glossary, bibliography or index.

However almost all the people, places and subjects in these extracts feature in the indexes at the end of each Diary volume. Readers who wish to know more about the editorial method will find it explained at the beginning of each Diary volume.

The purpose of this book is to serve as an adjunct to the Diary volumes, to answer any unresolved questions which readers may have over the excluded entries, and to spare them an encounter with the complete photocopied manuscript which was lodged in the county repository, the Norfolk Record Office, in April 2013 on the publication of *The Diary of Mary Hardy 1773–1809*.

These extracts are taken from the original manuscript held in the private archive known as the Cozens-Hardy Collection. I am extremely grateful to its custodians, the members of that family, for allowing me to work on their papers and for permission to reproduce the transcription.

Kingston upon Thames
2 May 2013

These websites give further information:

maryhardysdiary.co.uk
   for *The Diary of Mary Hardy 1773–1809*
   (the four-volume edition of the text, and this book)

also
maryhardysworld.co.uk
   for *Mary Hardy and her World 1773–1809*
   (the four volumes of commentary and analysis,
   also by Margaret Bird, for future publication)

and
www.burnham-press.co.uk
   (the publishers of all nine volumes)

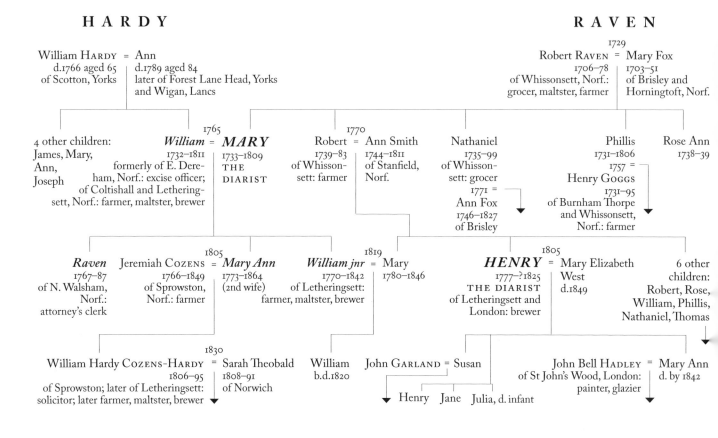

The diarists Mary Hardy (writing 1773–1809) and Henry Raven (writing 1793–97)
are shown in capitals in italic type. Mary Hardy's husband and three children
all made entries in her diary and are also shown in italic

$\mathcal{M}_{20}^{B13}$

Editorial conventions

(Young Smith preach'd)	diarist's text in her own parentheses	{ at work }	superfluous words: diarist's repetitions
[ ]	diarist has left text blank	⟦ Inserted text ⟧	text entered in the MS by others, the writer being identified in editorial italics
[. . . . .]	MS is illegible		
. . .	editor's excision from the MS those entries being in the *Diary* edn	Display type **Bold type**	editorial heading, subhead
[at the third act]	editor's explanation or correction		
«with»	editor's conjecture, where text omitted		

Digressions from the daily record

The Letheringsett years 1781–1809

above Letheringsett Hall's east front, viewed in 1892 from the
meadow at Hall Farm. The River Glaven flows out of sight, con-
cealed by the dip in the ground. Mary Hardy wrote her diary in
this house from 1781, when the family moved from Coltishall,
north-east of Norwich, until her death here in 1809.

Many of the Hall's features seen in this view are the result
of her son William's remodelling; he died in June 1842 in his
ground-floor study to the right of the porch. The stables (centre
right) were built by his nephew William Hardy Cozens-Hardy
in the mid-19th century.

This panorama remains very largely the same 120 years later
[*photograph Gerald Cozens-Hardy Willans 1892: Cozens-Hardy
Collection*]

inset Mary Hardy in 1798 aged 64, by Immanuel
[*Cozens-Hardy Collection*]

facing page Raven Hardy, the diarist's 13-year-old son, busies
himself with copying this long extract from the newspaper
during the bustle of settling in. The Hardys had moved from
Coltishall to Letheringsett on 5 Apr. 1781.

The daily Letheringsett entries are transcribed in full in the
published volume *Diary 2* from 5 Apr. to 7 Aug. 1781.

The editorial abridgment then begins, the first of the omitted
entries, for 8 Aug., appearing in this volume on page 4

1781

Manuscript ledger 2 (*cont.*)
7 January 1778–22 September 1782

[LETHERINGSETT]

From the newspaper
The trial of John Donellan 1781 [*cont.*]

APRIL 12, THURSDAY [*by Raven Hardy, cont.*]

[[. . . The first witness that was call'd for the prosecution was Mr Powell, an Apothecary at Rugby. The witness said that Rugby, the place where he lived, was within 3 Miles of Lawford hall where the late Sir Theodosius Boughton resided at the time of his death. He was employd by the Deceas'd to cure him of a Venereal Complaint which he had contracted immediately before his application to him; but it was very slight, & by no means a continuation of any old disorder of that kind, as had been, he believed, represented. He administered cooling Physic to him for 3 weeks; after which, supposing his patient was in no further need of medicine, he suspend^d this application; but in about a fortnight afterwards, on a trifling swelling in his groin, he again administred some draughts, which however were of the most gentle & inocent kind, consisted of 4 doses, & were compos'd, 2 of Manna of Salts only & 2 of rhubarb & jalap, 15 grains each. The last dose which he sent him was on the 29th of August, the day before Sir Theodosius died. He also saw the deceased the same day, who was then in perfect health & spirits.

The day following he was sent for by Lady Boughton, to Lawford hall. It was 9 O Clock when he arrived there, & when he went into Sir Theodosius's room, which he did immediately on his arrival, he found that he had been dead above an hour. Captain Donellan accompanied him into the room, but though a medical man askd him no questions concerning the event which had taken place; but on being interrogated as to the nature of his death by the witness, Capt Donellan said that Sir Theodosius had died in Convulsions, & wished to make the Witness believe that the cause of it was cold, for that he was a very imprudent young man & took no care of himself. The body bore no appearance of distortion when he saw it, & the bottles which contain'd the draughts were not then in the Room. The witness then produced 2 bottles in the Court, exactly of the same colour, but differing very much in smell & taste, & in the effects of their ingredients. The one was composd of rhubarb &c as above describ'd, the other had the same ingredients in it but had also an infusion of Laurel water, a water distill'd from the Laurel Leaf. The first of these perfectly innocent, the other the strongest poison that could be administred.

Lady Boughton was next calld; she said that her son, Sir Theodosius, was 20 years of age on the 3^d of August, the month in which he died; when he should have attain'd the age of Maturity the Estate which he was entitled to was £2000 per Ann^m, but in case of his death the principal part was to go to his sister, the wife of the prisoner at the bar; that Capt Donellan came to Lawford hall in 1778, & Sir Theodosius quitted school in 1779, & had been with her ever since. She & the prisoner had several conversations concerning the deceas'd's health, & the preisoner described him to be in such a bad state with a particular disorder, that it would not be proper for her to take an excursion to Bath, which she intended, as she did not know what might happen.

A Mr Fonnereau was expected at Lawford hall, who was to have staid a week, her son was then to have accompanied him to Northamptonshire & to have staid a considerable time. Mr Fonnereau came in September, 3 days after her sons death; that Sir Theodosius us'd to lock up his Physic, but on his forgetting one day to take it, the prisoner advised him to leave it in some open place, where he could run no hazard of missing it, & from that time it was placed on an open shelf.

On the evening preceding the death of her son, Capt Donellan came to her in the garden, & said he had been seeing Sir Theodosius fish, & had persuaded him to return home lest he should catch cold; that he was in good health that night, as also he was this morning at 7 oClock. After the witness had had some conversation with the deceas'd about a net he intended to take with him fishing, he asked her for his Physic, & shewed her where the bottle stood. He first requested her however to get him a bit of cheese which she accordingly did. Having taken down the bottles, & read the Labels, which were, 'Purging draughts for Sir Theodosius Brougton,' she pour'd one of them into a tea cup; but Sir Theodosius observing she had not shaken it, requested it might be return'd into the bottle, in order that it might be shook. Having done so, he drank it, saying it was very nauseus; to her the smell of it appear'd like bitter almonds. Here the 2 different bottles which had been produced by Mr Powell were presented to her, when she pointed out the one in which the decoction of Laurel was contain'd, & said, 'This is it which resembles the smell of that which I gave my son'.

She further declared, that the deceas'd observed he did not think he should be able to keep it in his stomach, he strugled very much, gurgled in his Throat, and appear'd in Convulsions. In about 10 Minutes he appear'd more compos'd, & she left him. In about 5 Minutes she return'd again to his room, & to her great astonishment found him in a dreadful & alarming situation, with his eyes fixd upwards, his teeth clench'd, his stomach heaving violently, & froth issuing from his mouth, when she immediately dispatch'd a Messenger for Mr Powell.

In about 5 Minutes the prisoner at the bar came in, & she inform'd him of the Melancholy & unfortunate accident which had happend, on which he said he would go into Sir Theodosius's room with her. They went together, & when there she told him what had happen'd from what had been given in the bottle, the contents of which were strong enough to have «?killed» a dog. On her saying this, the prisoner asked where the bottles were. She told him; upon which he seized one of them, & immediately «?poured» some water into it, rins'd it, & then pour'd it into a Bason of dirty water. She asked him why he did this, & said it was very improper to touch the bottles or anything in the room till the Apothecary arrived, that he might see the true state of every thing & judge accordingly. He did not take notice of what she said, but snatched the other bottle also, & rins'd it in like manner. On her asking him the reason of this conduct again, & urging it more strongly, he replied, he only did it to taste of its contents, & afterwards put his finger to the bottle & then to his mouth.

2 servants Sarah Brundell & Catherine Amos coming into the room, the prisoner order'd Sarah Brundell to take away the bottles & clean the room. The witness took the bottles out of her hand when she was going to remove them, & bid her let them alone. The Prisoner however insisted that the room should be cleand, & the bottles & other things were at last removed. Sir Theodosius was not quite dead when this altercation took place between her & the prisoner. The Witness & Capt Donellan meeting soon after in the parlour, the latter observed to his wife that Lady Boughton had been pleas'd to take notice of his washing the bottles, & if it had not come into his head to have said that he did it only to taste its contents, he did not know what he should have done. The prisoner, receiving no answer from the witness, soon after rung the bell for a servant. The coachman came in, upon which Capt Donellan said to him, William, don't you remember my going out this morning through the iron gate? I have not been at the other side of the house today. Yes, Sir, says William, I do remember it. Then, resumed the Capt, you William are my evidence.

Lady Boughton said that Sir Theodosius died on Wednesday the 30th day of August, & was buried on the Wednesday following; & that she was present with Capt Donellan at an examination held by the Coroner's Inquest. When she mentioned the circumstance about washing the bottles, Capt Donellan pulled her by the sleeve & seem'd to wish her not to mention it. When they return'd home, Capt said to Mrs Donellan that Lady B. had been forward in mentioning the circumstance concerning the washing of the bottles, which she had no occasion to do.

Lady B. being asked if she recollected a quarrel her son had at Bath & another at Rugby, & whether Capt D. did not interpose on both occasions to prevent the consequences she said she did remember that at Bath, & she believed the same at Rugby. Being question'd how the Capt & her son generally agreed she said they were always haggling with each other.

Catherine Amos was next calld. She said she was cook maid to Lady B. She corroborated part of Lady Boughton's evidence with respect to the effects of the poison on Sir Theodosius, & added that a few days after his death the prisoner brought her a still to clean, & desir'd it might not be suffer'd to rust. She had seen the prisoner work at this still. He us'd to lock himself up in a room which was calld his room, though he did not sleep in it excepting only when Mrs D. was lying in, & was known to be at this still for hours together.

Dr Ratteray, physician, Mr Wilmer, surgeon, Dr Ash, physician, & Dr Parsons, professor of anatomy in Oxford, all gave their opinion that the deceased had died of the poison contained in the bottle which contained the laurel water—the most deadly of all poisons.

Dr Ratteray in particular, being interrogated as to his knowledge of the effects of laurel water, said he derived it from repeated experiments, of which he gave the following instances to the Court: His first experiment, he said, was upon a dog. He held it between his legs & gave it 2 ounces. It died in less than a minute without one convulsion, unless a tremulous motion of the under jaw might be so called. He afterwards tried it upon an aged mare, to which he gave a pint and a half. She fell instantly, continued in manifest convulsions for 15 Minutes, & then expired: she tried to rise during this interval, but could not effect it otherwise than by just raising her forefeet like a dog, from which he inserted [inferred] that the poison had depaved [deprived] her of the power of her hind legs. He repeated his experiment upon a horse; he gave it 2 hornfuls. The horse fell immediately on having received the first hornful, he made an attempt however to get up; as he was rising he administred his second hornful, which knock'd the poor animal flat down, & in 28 minutes after it expired.

The effect of this poison, he said, appears to be different from that of almost all others: it does not seem to impede the circulation, & so produce death, but appears to drive the blood entirely from the centre of the exterior parts or extremities, & by that means leaves to [too] little for conducting the important & vital parts of the animal machine. He was asked if he thought there was a sufficient quantity of this poison in the phial that had been shewn him to kill a man. He replied there certainly was.

The evidence for the prosecution ceasing, the prisoner was called upon for his defence, which was nearly as follows. That many false & injurious reports had been circulated concerning him in the various newspapers in town & country, equally injurious to his honour & dangerous to his safety, & that he had most undeservedly labourd under a load of prejudice, which he believed no man before him had ever sustained, or had at least been tried under. He hoped however that the integrity & justice of the Judge & Jury would interpose to relieve him from the effects of those unprovoked aspersions, & that he should receive from their hands that justification which he was conscious he had the most indisputable right to.

When he first married into the family of the Boughtons, he did it on the most liberal principles & in the most generous manner in the world, for he bound himself under restrictions to his wife,

that he could not receive even a life enjoyment in any estate of hers, either actual or in expectancy; what inducement therfore could he have for the perpetration of so cruel & horrid a deed when no advantage could be derived to himself from it. He had always lived in the most perfect harmony & freindship with the late Sir Theodosius Boughton, & had given many proofs of it, by having interfer'd to reconcile his differences & keep him out of danger. This was not the conduct of a person who wished to deprive another of his life. The prisoner proceeded to state some instances of his amicable disposition, & afterwards went into a description of his conduct with respect to his supposed unwillingness for suffering the dissection of the body. He concluded with expressing a firm assurance of innocence, & a sanguin hope that his character would be shewn in its proper light by the decision of that day & prove his innocence to the world, prejudiced as it at this time undoubtedly was against him.

Mr John Hunter, the celebrated anatomist, being called, deposed that in his judgement the appearances of the body as described by the various gentlemen of the faculty proved nothing, for all those described symptoms are the usual concomitants of putrefaction, & have no necessary tendency to demonstrate the Deceas'd to have Died by Poison. If he had died of an apoplexy the symptoms might have been exactly similar, of an epilepsy, or any other disorder which produces instant death, when the person was in previous health. This able anatomist, after having by plain & simple reasoning considerably weaken'd, if not subverted, the elaborate doctrine of his more technical brethren, was now solemnly appealed to by the judge to answer this question, whether he would take upon him]] [*Mary Hardy takes over briefly before Raven resumes*] to pronounce it as his Opinion that the Deceasd had actually Died through some other means than Poison. Mr Hunter with a very laudable caution replied to this home-put Interrogatory that he could pronounce nothing with certainty or decision. Natural causes might have produced the appearances which had been describ'd, Poison might be the same thing. It was therefore utterly out of his pow'r to give a decided opinion from which of the two possible sources the decided appearance had Originated.

The Evidence on both sides was now concluded & the Judge enterd upon his Charge, which he delivrd with eaqual neatness, perspicuity & penetration. The Jury withdrew after the Charge was [[finished, & having retired about 6 minutes, returned their Verdict, pronouncing the prisoner guilty of the charge «of» which he stood accused.

The Judge then arose, put on his cap, & addressed him as follows: John Donellan, You now stand convicted, on the clearest evidence that could be produced, of the crime of murder which of all crimes, next to those against the state, the government, or the constitution, is the most atrocious. Of all murders, poisoning is the most horrible; & if there may be degrees allowed in that species of guilt, that of which you are now convicted surpasses all others of the kind that went before yours, as much as murder itself surpasses all other crimes. The place, the manner, & the person on whom you committed this murder greatly enhance your guilt. It was committed in a place where you had an opportunity of freindly intercourse with the deceased & was little expected to commit an Act of so horrid a nature. But your ambition has made you commit what every honest mind must shudder at. You have cut the rising offspring of an antient & respectable family. In the commission of this cruel act, avarice seems to be your motive & hypocrisy your cloak. The greatness of his fortune has caused the greatness of your crime. You saw him likely to be in possession shortly of an Ample fortune, equal to support the antient dignity of the family. You saw that his death would put you into the enjoyment of that fortune, & therefore wickedly determined to sacrifice the devoted youth who stood between you & your ambitious designs.

The blackness of your crime is the deeper still from the consideration that the unhappy youth stood in so near a relation to you & that you took away his life under the treacherous mask of freindship & a pretended care of his health. The instrument too which you made choice of for this detected purpose is an additional aggravation to your offence. It was not sufficient for you to sacrifice the son, but you must pitch upon his unhappy mother to be the inocent instrument of your foul purpose . . .

The Copy of a letter which John Donellan wrote to his wife the night preceding his execution: My once esteemed Wife, Do not think that I am about to reproach you for declining your visits to me in my present ignominious situation; I am beter satisfied that you did not even attempt it. Brought together by the hand of indifference, it would be a mockery of feeling to affect a concern for our separation, disgracefull as it is about to prove. To argue with you on the score of those dark arts which have undone me would be fruitless; because I know your conjugal has ever been subservient to your filial affection. As to your mother— but I will suppress my indignation; if however you would wish to know my dying sentiments of her ask our freind W—son, the mournful bearer of this, & he will not hesitate to impart them to you, because I shall charge him with my last breath not to refuse you such a request. Were he to advise your immediate separation from her, it would have no weight: for my little influence over you has long been at an end! M^{rs} H—, you well know, has for a series of years treated me with a tender & disinterested regard; let it not surprize you then to learn that I have bequeathed her my gold watch & miniature picture as the last & strongest token I can give of my gratitude. As to our 2 poor children, if you deem pledges of our love, cherish them as such, but try to conceal from them their unhappy father's fate. I have been long combating with unnumber'd wishes that pressed me to clasp them in my fond arms, & bid them a last adieu! Thank god however, I have at length subdued them: the whole world, except my own offspring, are welcome to become the spectators of my ignominious, though unmerited exit!

If I have omitted any thing that I should have said to you your own heart, I trust, will urge it for me, when I shall be no more: Farewell!

    John Donellan
    Warwick Gaol, Sunday night
    April 1st 1781

Immediately after the conviction of Capt Donellan a Divine, accompanied by a particular friend of the prisoner's, went to see him, & to all appearance he was perfectly resigned to his unhappy fate. It was urged to him that as the evidence had been so clear, a denial of the fact would be look'd on by the world as mean prevarication, & would induce people to throw additional insult upon his memory. To this observation he answer'd, he could not help any man's conclusions; he knew his own heart, & would, with his last breath, assert his innocence. Some few unguarded & unpremeciated [?unpremeditated] expressions, aggravated by falsehoods of the most flagrant kind, which were sworn at his trial, had induced a jury to take his life; but time would do him justice, and prove him an injur'd man, ruined by those who ought to have been his friends. Perceiving the gentlemen in astonishment at this conversation, he added that he should dedicate to morrow (Sunday) to the purpose of drawing up an answer to & a refutation of the evidence & should leave it with a friend, that he had no doubt would comply with the last request he should make, that of seeing it correctly published. He was asked whether he had not a desire to see his wife & take a last farewell. To this he hastily replied, I do beseech thee, let me not hear again of this; if she does not come I shall die composed.

On Sunday evening he deposited his case with a gentleman of Coventry, who assisted him in his trial, with an earnest request that he would print & publish it. He then gave some directions relative to the adjustment of the sad operation which was to take place in the morning, & appeared remarkably composed.

At 7 o'clock next day he was carried to the place of execution in a mourning coach, followed by a hearse, & the sheriff's officers in deep mourning; as he went on, he frequently put his head out of the coach, & earnestly desired the prayers around him. On his arrival at the place of execution, he alighted from the coach, & ascending a few steps of the ladder, prayed for a considerable time, & then joined in the usual service with the greatest appearance of devotion; he then in an audible tone of voice addressed the spectators in the following terms: That as he then was going to appear before God, to whom all deceit is known, he solemnly declared that he was innocent of the crime for which he was to suffer; that he had drawn up a vindication of himself which he hoped the world would believe, for it was of more consequence to him to speak truth than falsehood, & had no doubt but that time would reveal the many mysteries that had arisen in his trial, & prove that he fell a sacrifice to the malice & black designs of his— .

After praying fervently for some time, He let his handkerchief fall, a signal agreed on between him & the executioner, & was launched into eternity. After hanging the usual time, the body was put into a black coffin & conveyed to the town hall to be dissected. He was dressed in a suit of deep mourning.

Sketch of the life & character of the late John Donellan, Esq.:

Capt Donellan, who was executed on Monday near the city of Warwick for the inhuman murder of his brother-in-law, Sir Theodosius Boughton (by poison), was formerly distinguished by the appellation of Diamond Donellan; an addition derived from a remarkable fine brilliant Diamond which he obtained in the East Indies & used to wear in a ring on public occasions. He was said to be the reputed son of a Gentleman in the army, who is still alive & confined in a private madhouse, in consequence of an attempt made upon a state officer. This unhappy gentleman had been long urging a suit at the Treasury, & being in the end totally disappointed, his reason & his hope deserted him in the same instant.

During a considerable residence in India, Capt Donellan distinguished himself on many occasions; & indeed the wounds he received in action left no room to doubt his personal bravery. Many however pretend to know certain facts, & did not scruple to rank them in the black catalogue of Asiatic enormities; he returned to Europe with a large sum of money & many valuable gems; but in what manner they were obtained is not, even at this day, generally known. To his companions he used to boast of secret services, & openly accused the East India Company of ingratitude & injustice.

Ambition was improperly said to be his ruling passion; for when we consider the known objects of his pursuit, in London, Bath, & other fashionable places, we are rather inclined to think, that an extravagant vanity was the principal bias of his nature. His dress was generally gaudy without elegance, & his ideas & conversation were contracted. Under the absolute controwl of irregular propensities, his fortune in a short time became greatly injured; however, he reserved a sum which enabled him to purchase a share or two in the Pantheon, from whence, upon its original institution, great advantages were expected; &, to which place of polite rendezvous, he was appointed Master of the Ceremonies. Although he possessed endowments that strongly recommended him to that station, he did not long retain it. Embarrassments of a pecuniary nature surrounded him; &, it is said, he was obliged to sell his shares under great disadvantages.

Play & gallantry, the ultimate subterfuges of dissipation, were the next objects which presented. His universal intercourse with polite prostitutes, though sufficiently known, was too often the subject of his egotism; & the recommendations of his consequence. His inclination, however, was not confined to pleasurable intercourses. His connexion with the married M^{rs} H—, in the vicinity of Rathbone place, is in the recollection of most people. The house, the table, the servants, the carriages &c of this Lady were at the Captain's constant disposal, & it is suspected that his attendance was rewarded in that liberal way, which enabled him to continue his appearance in public; & gave him an opportunity of being acquainted with the unhappy family into which he married]] . . .

[LETHERINGSETT] [*Mary Hardy resumes*]

AUGUST 8, WEDNESDAY A fine Day. Bricklayers & Carpenters at work. Mr Hardy at home all Day.

AUGUST 9, THURSDAY A very Hot Dry Day. Bricklayers & Carpenters at Work. Mr Hardy went with Mr Burrell to Bowling Green Even 3, came home Even past 8. I & Mary [Mary Ann] took a Walk to Holt after Tea . . .

AUGUST 16, THURSDAY A fine Day, Showr in Even. M^r & Mrs Springthorp went away Even 2. Mr Hardy went to Bowling Green Even 4, came home past 8. Bricklayers & Carpenters at Work.

AUGUST 17, FRIDAY A fine Day, some small Showrs. Bricklayers & Carpenters at Work. Mr Hardy at home all Day . . .

AUGUST 22, WEDNESDAY A fine Day. Bricklayers & Carpenters «and» Plumer [plumber] at work. Mr Hardy at home all Day.

AUGUST 23, THURSDAY A fine Day. Bricklayers & Carpenters «and» Plumer at work. Mr Hardy at home all Day . . .

SEPTEMBER 5, WEDNESDAY A very Wet Day. Bricklayers & Carpenters at Work. Mr Springthorp, J Rolfe & Childr^n went to Cley M10, came home Even 4. Mr Hardy at home all Day .

SEPTEMBER 6, THURSDAY A very Wet Day. Bricklayers & Carpenters at Work. Mr Hardy at home all Day. Mr Springthorp & J Rolfe went away after Dinner.

SEPTEMBER 7, FRIDAY A fine Day. Bricklayers & Carpenters at Work. Mr Hardy at home all Day . . .

SEPTEMBER 9, SUNDAY A very warm Day. I & Childr^n went to our Church Afternoon, Mr Burrell Preachd. Mr Hardy set of Even 2 for Fakenham & Whissenset.

SEPTEMBER 10, MONDAY A fine Day. Bricklayers & Carpenters at Work. Mrs Custance of Fakenham calld here as she was going to Holt. I went to se the Childr^n Dance Afternoon, drank Tea at Mr Bakers. Mr Hardy came home Even 8, heard Mrs Case of Patesly [Pattesley, near Oxwick] Dyed Yesterday . . .

SEPTEMBER 12, WEDNESDAY A fine Day. Bricklayers & Carpenters at Work. Mrs Custance, Mrs Raven, I & Childr^n drank Tea at Mrs Bakers. Mr Hardy at home all Day. A Tempest in the Night.

SEPTEMBER 13, THURSDAY A fine Morn, Showers Afternoon. Bricklayers & Carpenters at Work. Mrs Custance, Mrs Raven, I & Childr^n dind, drank Tea & Supt at Mr Bakers. Mr Hardy came for me in the Chaise & Supt there, came home Even past 10.

SEPTEMBER 14, FRIDAY A very fine Day. Bricklayers & Carpenters at Work. Mr Hardy went to Cromer M10, came home Even 9. Mrs Custance & Mrs Raven went to Wickmer [Wickmere] from Holt & came back to our House Even past 8 . . .

SEPTEMBER 16, SUNDAY A Showry Day. All went to our Church foornoon, Mr Burrell preachd. Mr Raven & John came to Dinner & then went to Cley and all came back & Supt & Slept here.

SEPTEMBER 17, MONDAY A fine Morn, Showry Afternoon. Mr Custance went away M5. Mrs Custn^e, M^r & Mrs Raven & Childr^n went to Mr Bakers to Din^r & then went home, Miss Baker went with them. Mr Hardy at home all Day. Bricklayers & Carpenters at Work.

SEPTEMBER 18, TUESDAY A fine Day. Bricklayers & Carpenters at Work. M^r & Mrs Moy Dind & drank Tea here then went to Mr Johnsons of Holt. Raind in the Night . . .

SEPTEMBER 21, FRIDAY A fine Day. Bricklayers & Carpenters at Work. Mr Goggs & Sister & B Ginby & Wife went away after Dinner. Mr Hardy at home all Day.

SEPTEMBER 22, SATURDAY A fine Morn, Close Cold Aftrn. Bricklayers & Carpenters at Work. Mrs Custance went from Holt Even 2. Mr Hardy, I & M Ann walkd to Holt Even 3, I drank Tea at Miss Leaks & came home Even 7. Mastr Burcham here to Play . . .

SEPTEMBER 25, TUESDAY A very Wet Cold Day, Wind very high. Bricklayers & Carpenters at Work. Mr Hardy at home all Day.

SEPTEMBER 26, WEDNESDAY A very Wet Cold Day, Wind very high. Bricklayers & Carpenters at Work. Mr Hardy at home all Day . . .

SEPTEMBER 29, SATURDAY *New Michalmas Day* A fine Morn, Close Aftern. Bricklayers & Carpenters at work. J Bays & his Wife went away M11. I & M Ann walkd to Holt Even 3, a Petty Sessions there, came home Even 7, Mr Hardy went Even 5, came home Even 10.

SEPTEMBER 30, SUNDAY A Wet Day. I & Childr^n went to our Church foornoon, Mr Burrell preachd. Mr Hardy & Mr Baker of Holt set of in our Chaise Even 1 for Coltishall & Yarmouth & Norwich. Mrs Rouse & Childrn drank Tea here.

OCTOBER 1, MONDAY A tolerable dry day. Bricklayers & Carpenters at Work. Mr Hardy not at home. Mr Dunthorn drank Tea here, M^r N [Neale] Raven of N Walsham calld here.

OCTOBER 2, TUESDAY A Showry Close Day. Bricklayrs & Carpenters at Work. Mr Hardy not at home.

OCTOBER 3, WEDNESDAY A Cold Dry Day. Bricklayers & Carpenters at Work. Mr Hardy not at home.

OCTOBER 4, THURSDAY A very fine Day. Bricklayrs & Carpenters at Work. Mr Hardy & Mr Baker came home Even 10.

OCTOBER 5, FRIDAY A fine Day. Bricklayers & Carpenters at Work. Mr Hardy at home all day. Mrs Baker & Mrs Miles drank Tea here.

OCTOBER 6, SATURDAY A Close Dry Day. Bricklayers & Carpenters at Work. Mr Hardy at home all Day. I & M Ann & Mrs Rouse walkd to Holt Even 3, drank Tea at Miss Leaks, came home Even 8 . . .

OCTOBER 9, TUESDAY A very fine Day. Bricklayrs & Carpenters at Work. Mr Hardy went to Cley Afternoon, came home Ev 10. I walkd to Holt Afternoon, drank Tea at Mrs Bakers . . .

OCTOBER 14, SUNDAY A fine Day. M Ann went to Miss Alps M9 on a Visit, came home Even 6. Mr Hardy, I & Childr^n went to our Church foornoon, Mr Burrell preachd.

OCTOBER 15, MONDAY A very fine Day. Bricklayers & Carpenters at Work. Mʳ Hardy set of M10 for N Walsham, Coltishall & Norwich & several other places. I took a Walk to Holt Aftrn, came back to Tea . . .

OCTOBER 17, WEDNESDAY *New Moon* A very fine Day. Bricklayers & Carpenters at Work. Mʳ Hardy not at home.

OCTOBER 18, THURSDAY A fine Day. Bricklayer & Boy at Work. Mʳ Hardy came home Even 3 . . .

OCTOBER 20, SATURDAY A cold Windy Morn, fine Afternoon. Mʳ Hardy, I «and» Childrⁿ went to Cley M9 to see the high Tide, came back Even 1. I & M Ann walkd to Holt Even 4, drank Tea at Miss Leakes, home E7. Mʳ Hardy went to Markᵗ, came home 10 . . .

OCTOBER 22, MONDAY A very Cold Stormy Day, wind high. Mᵉˢˢʳˢ Oakes & Neve went away M past 7. Mʳ Hardy at home all Day.

OCTOBER 23, TUESDAY A very fine Day. Mʳ Hardy walkd to the Breck Farm [?Thornage] to speak to Mʳ Kerrison but he was gone away, came back Even 5 & went to R Mays s with Mʳ Balls, came home Eve 10 . . .

OCTOBER 27, SATURDAY A fine Morn, foggy Afternoon. Mʳ Hardy went to Cley foorn, came back to Dinner, Phillip Ponten [?Ponting] Dind here. I & M Ann walkd to Holt Afternoon, drank Tea at Mʳˢ Harcourts, came home Even 7. Mʳ Hardy & Raven went to Holt Even 4, came back Even 9.

OCTOBER 28, SUNDAY A fine Day. All went to our Church foornoon, Mʳ Burrell preachd. Mʳ Hardy at home all day.

OCTOBER 29, MONDAY A Close Dry Day. Carpenters & Bricklayers at Work. Mʳ Hardy at home all Day. Holt Assembly.

OCTOBER 30, TUESDAY A Showry Day & Cold. Maids & Goody Ram Washd. Mʳ Hardy at home all Day. Bricklayers & Carpenters at Work.

OCTOBER 31, WEDNESDAY A very fine Day. Bricklayers & Carpenters at Work. Mʳ Hardy at home all Day. Miss Pearmain drank Tea here . . .

NOVEMBER 2, FRIDAY A very Wet Day. Bricklayers & Carpenters at Work. Mʳ Hardy at home all Day, spent the Even at R Mays.s, came home Even 10.

NOVEMBER 3, SATURDAY A very fine Day. Bricklayers & Carpenters at Work. Mʳ Hardy went to Markt Even 4. Mʳ Howard of Walsingham came home with him Even 9, Slept here.

NOVEMBER 4, SUNDAY A very fine Day. Mʳ Howard went away M11. All went to our Church Afternoon, Mʳ Burrell preach'd . . .

NOVEMBER 7, WEDNESDAY A very Wet Day. Bricklayers & Carpenters at Work. Mʳ Hardy at home all Day . . .

NOVEMBER 10, SATURDAY A Close foggy Day. Bricklayrs & Carpenters at Work. Mʳ Hardy at home all Day. I & MA walkd to Holt Aftrn, came home to Tea.

NOVEMBER 11, SUNDAY A very Wet Day. All went to our Church foornoon, Mʳ Burrell preachd. From the News Paper, Lady L Estrange Died last Sunday.

NOVEMBER 12, MONDAY A Close Mild Day. Carpenters at Work. Mʳ Hardy at home, spent the Even at R Mays s, came home Even 8.

NOVEMBER 13, TUESDAY A fine Day. Carpenters at Work. Mʳ Hardy went to Clay M10, came home Even 5, then went to Mays s & came home Even ps [past] 9. Ellen Mason came & staid all Day. Heard Robᵗ Allison Died last Week . . .

NOVEMBER 15, THURSDAY *New Moon* A fine Day. Carpenters at Work. Mʳ Hardy at home all Day . . .

NOVEMBER 17, SATURDAY A Close Day, raind in Even. Bricklayers & Carpenters at Work. I & M Ann walkd to Holt Aftern, drank Tea at Mʳ Davys, came home Even 8 . . .

NOVEMBER 20, TUESDAY A fine Day but Cold. Bricklayers & Carpenters at Work. Maids & [   ] Washᵈ. Mʳ Hardy at Mays in Even & at Supper, came home past 11. Labʳ [labourer] in Garden . . .

NOVEMBER 24, SATURDAY A very fine Day. Carpenters at Work, 2 Gardiners & Labʳ in Garden. Mʳ Hardy at home all Day.

NOVEMBER 25, SUNDAY A fine Day. I & Childrn went to our Church foorn, Mʳ Burrell preachd. Mʳ Hardy at home all Day . . .

NOVEMBER 27, TUESDAY A Dry Close Day. Carpenters at Work. Mʳ Hardy set of for N Walshm & Coltishall &c M9. I & MA & Ellen Mason walkd to Holt foornoon, came back to Dinner.

NOVEMBER 28, WEDNESDAY A Close Dry Day. Bricklayers & Carpenters at work. Mʳ Hardy not at home. Labrʳ in Garden . . .

NOVEMBER 30, FRIDAY A very fine Day. Carpentrs at Work. Mʳ Hardy came home Even 6.

DECEMBER 1, SATURDAY *full Moon* A Close Cold Day. Carpntrs & Bricklayrs at Work. Mʳ Hardy went to Holt Market Even 4, came home Even 11.

DECEMBER 2, SUNDAY A Cold Day. All went to our Church Afternoon, Mʳ Burrell preachd. Mʳ Cole drank Tea & Supt here, Miss Johnson & Miss & Mastrs Bakers drank Tea here . . .

DECEMBER 6, THURSDAY A Close Dry Day. Carpenters at Work. Brothˢ went away Even 2. Mʳ Hardy at home all Day.

DECEMBER 7, FRIDAY A Close Cold Day. Carpenters at Work. Mʳ Samˡ Nash came to Dinner, a Sale at Breck Farm. Myles Raven & George Custance went away after Dinner. Mʳ Hardy went to Mays's Even 3, came home Even 10.

DECEMBER 8, SATURDAY A Close Day & very Cold. Carpenters at Work. I & MA went to Holt, drank Tea at Miss Alps. Mʳ Hardy went to Market, came home Even 10.

DECEMBER 9, SUNDAY A Close Cold Dry Day. All went to our Church foornoon, Mʳ Burrell preachᵈ. J Neve came Even 6, Slept here.

DECEMBER 10, MONDAY A fine Dry Day. Carpentrs at Work. I went up to Holt with M Ann, came back directly. Mʳ Hardy went to Cley Aftrn, home E6 . . .

DECEMBER 15, SATURDAY A Close Dry Day. Carpntrs at Work. Mʳ Hardy at home all Day. I & Mʳˢ Rouse walkd up to Holt Aftrn, drank Tea at Miss Leakes. Mʳ Custance of Yarmouth Died.

DECEMBER 16, SUNDAY A fine Day. All went to our Church Afternoon, Mr Burrell preachd.

DECEMBER 17, MONDAY A Close Wet Morn, foggy Day. Maids Washd. Mr Hardy & Chilrⁿ walkd to Holt Aftrn to View Downans [Nicholas Downing's] Hushold Furniture, came home Even 6.

DECEMBER 18, TUESDAY A Close foggy Day. 2 Gardiners at Work. Mr Hardy & Childrⁿ went to Mr Downings Sale Morn 10, came home Eve 8 . . .

DECEMBER 20, THURSDAY A fine day. Mr Hardy, I & W^m went to the Auction at Holt M10, bought some trifles. I came home Eve 4, Mr Hardy came home Morn past 1 . . .

DECEMBER 22, SATURDAY A Close Mild Day. Gardiner at Work. I poorly. Mr Hardy went to Market Even 3, came home Even 7.

DECEMBER 23, SUNDAY A Close Mild Day. All went to our Church foornoon, Mr Burrell preachd.

DECEMBER 24, MONDAY A fine Day. Gardener at Work. Mr Hardy at home all Day. Mr Alsop here . . .

DECEMBER 26, WEDNESDAY A Close Mild Day. Childrn at Mr Rouses in Even. Mr Hardy at home all Day. Wet Night . . .

The visit to Whissonsett
27 December 1781–4 January 1782

DECEMBER 28, FRIDAY A Dry Day, Wind high. Went to Church foornoon. Mr Hardy came home Afternoon. We all drank Tea & Supt at Bro^t Robts. Wet Night.

DECEMBER 29, SATURDAY A Close Dry Day. Dind at Sister Goggs's, drank Tea at Mrs Ratclifs, Supt & Slept at Mr Goggs.

DECEMBER 30, SUNDAY A rough Day. All went to Church foornoon, Mr Bird Preachd. Dind, drank Tea, Supt & Slept at Sister Goggss. Stormy Night.

DECEMBER 31, MONDAY A Stormy Day. Went to Brot^{hs} Nathl [Brother Nathaniel's] after Dinner. M^r & Mrs Moy, M^r & Miss Fox there in the Eveng, I Slept there. Wm Goggs of Dunham Died.

1782

[WHISSONSETT, *cont.*]

JANUARY 1, TUESDAY A very Cold Day, some Storms of Snow & Rain. Went «to» Church foornoon, drank Tea & Supt at Sister Goggs. Heard Mr Case of Franshm [Fransham] was Dead.

JANUARY 2, WEDNESDAY A Windy Day. Drank Tea, Supt & Slept at Mr Moys. Wet Eveng.

JANUARY 3, THURSDAY A Dry Windy Day. Drank Tea at [and] Supt at Bro^t Robt^s, M^r & Mrs Moy there. Mr Hardy came with Mr Fox Even 7. Slept at Bro^t Nath^{ls}.

JANUARY 4, FRIDAY A Dry Windy Day. Set of Morn past 11 for home, came by Melton & look'd into the Church, home Even 4.

[LETHERINGSETT]

JANUARY 5, SATURDAY A fine Day. Mr Hardy & Raven went to Holt Even 3, came home past 8 . . .

JANUARY 10, THURSDAY A Cold Day. Storms of Snow & Hail. Mr Hardy at home all Day. Mr Burrell Junr drank Tea here.. . .

JANUARY 12, SATURDAY A Sharp frost. Mr Hardy went to Holt Market Even 4, came home Even 7.

JANUARY 13, SUNDAY A Close foggy Day. I & Childrⁿ went to our Church Aftrn, Mr Burrell Preach^d. 2 Men from St Faiths at Dinner. Mr Baker & Childrn drank Tea here.

JANUARY 14, MONDAY A Close foggy Day. Maids & Goody Greves [Greaves] Wash^d. Mr Hardy at home all Day. Mrs Ratcliff of Whisenset Died . . .

JANUARY 16, WEDNESDAY A Cold Stormy Day. Childrⁿ at School, Mr Hardy at home all Day. 2 Mill Wrights at Work.

JANUARY 17, THURSDAY A fine Day. Childrⁿ at School, Mr Hardy at home all Day. 2 Millwrights at Work. Mr Hardy at Holt Club E7, came home Even 12.

JANUARY 18, FRIDAY A Sharp frost. Childrⁿ at School, Mr Hardy at home all Day. 2 Millwrights at Work . . .

JANUARY 20, SUNDAY A Dry Morn, very Wet Aftern. All went to our Church foornoon. Mr Hardy went to Clay Afternoon to see after some Coales, Calld at Mr Fosters [Forster's] & came home past 8.

JANUARY 21, MONDAY A Close Dry Day. Childrn at School, Mr Hardy at home all Day . . .

JANUARY 23, WEDNESDAY A fine Day. Childrn at School. Mr Hardy went to Briston Afternoon, came back E5. Mrs Redden [Catherine Readwin] drank Tea here.

JANUARY 24, THURSDAY A Close Cold Day. Childrⁿ at School. Mr Hardy went to Holt M11, came back Even 6, went to Mr Forsters, drank Tea & Supt there, I & Raven went Even 5, came home Even past 12. The Quarter Sessions at Holt. Old M^r [Adam] Custance of Holt Died Aged 68.

JANUARY 25, FRIDAY A fine Day. Childrⁿ at School. Mr Hardy at home all Day.

JANUARY 26, SATURDAY A Cold Stormy Day. Mr Hardy & 2 Boys went to Clay M11, came home E9. I went up to Holt E3, drank Tea at Miss Alpes, came home Even 8.

JANUARY 27, SUNDAY A fine Morn, Stormy Aftern. All went to our Church Afternoon, Mr Burrell preachd. Mr Custance of Holt Burried.

JANUARY 28, MONDAY A very Cold Day. Childrn at School, Mr Hardy at home all Day. Edm [Edmund] Beck Dind here. Holt Assembly this Night. A good deal of Snow fell in the Night.

JANUARY 29, TUESDAY A frosty Morn, thawd in Day & froze again at Night. I & M$_r$ Hardy & Childrn drank Tea at Mr Bartles [Bartell's]. J Jeckell here, Mr Cole Dind here. Childr^n at School.

JANUARY 30, WEDNESDAY A Close Cold Day, raind towards Night. Children at School. Edmd Gray came with a Letter from Mr Ives of Coltishall, staid all Night. Mr Athow of Holt & Mr Franklin of Bodham here in the Afternoon. Mr Hardy at home all Day.

JANUARY 31, THURSDAY A Cold Day. Childr^n at School. Mr Hardy at home all Day .

FEBRUARY 1, FRIDAY A fine Day. Childr^n at School. Mr Hardy Went to Edgefield, Dind & spent the Day at Mr Theordoricks [Theodorick's], came home Even 11.

FEBRUARY 2, SATURDAY A very Cold Stormy Day. Childr^n at School. Mr Hardy went to Briston M10, came back by Holt, Supt at Mr Bakers, home Even past 9.

FEBRUARY 3, SUNDAY A fine Day. All went to Church foornoon, Mr Burrell preach^d. M^r & Mrs Rouse & Childr^n drank Tea here.

FEBRUARY 4, MONDAY A Dark foggy Day. Childr^n at School. Mr Hardy went to Clay M11, came home Even 11.

FEBRUARY 5, TUESDAY A Cold Stormy Day. Mr Hardy at home & at Mays in the Eveng. Childr^n at School . . .

FEBRUARY 10, Shrove Sunday Frost & Squales of Snow. All went to our Church Afternoon, Mr Burrell preachd . . .

FEBRUARY 12, Shrove Tuesday, New Moon Excesive Sharp frost, frequent Squarles of Snow. Childr^n at School, Mr Hardy at home all Day. Carpenters at Work . . .

FEBRUARY 15, FRIDAY A frosty Morn, Thawd Aftrn & froze again at Night. Childr^n at School, Mr Hardy at home all day. Carpenters at Work.

FEBRUARY 16, SATURDAY A very Sharp frost, Snowd a good deal in the Morn & again in the Eveng. Raven & W^m at School. I & M Ann walkd to Holt Afternoon, drank Tea & Supt at Mrs Bakers, came home E10 with Mr Hardy & Raven.

FEBRUARY 17, SUNDAY A Sharp frosty Morn, Thaw^d all day. All went to our Church foornoon, Mr Burrell «preached» . . .

FEBRUARY 19, TUESDAY A {A} Thaw, some rain. Childr^n at School. Carpenters at Work, Mr Hardy at home all Day.

FEBRUARY 20, WEDNESDAY A Close Wet Morn, fine Afternoon. Childr^n at School, Mr Hardy at home all Day. Mr Bensley of Holt & Mr Burrell drank Tea here.

FEBRUARY 21, THURSDAY Wet Morn, fine Afternoon. Childr^n at School, Carpenter at Work. Mr Hardy went to the Club at Holt Eve 7, came home Eve 12. Took a walk to the Meadows with MH [Mr Hardy].

FEBRUARY 22, FRIDAY A Wet Morn, fine Aftern, wind very high. Childr^n at School. Mr Hardy at home all Day, Carpenters at Work . . .

FEBRUARY 24, SUNDAY A Wet Morn, fine Afternoon. All went to our Church Afternoon, Mr Burrell preachd. Mr Hardy, Mr Rouse & Mr Cole drank Tea at Mr Burrells . . .

FEBRUARY 27, WEDNESDAY A fine Day. A Carpenter at Work. Mr Hardy & Raven came home Even 7. M Ann at School.

FEBRUARY 28, THURSDAY A very fine Day. Childrn at School. Mr Hardy & Mr Burrell went to the Club at Holt Even 7, came home Eve past 12.

MARCH 1, FRIDAY A Dry Cold Day, Wind rough. Childr^n at School, Mr Hardy at home all Day.

MARCH 2, SATURDAY A very Wet Day. Childr^n at School. Mr Hardy & Raven went to Holt Market Even 4, came home Even 9. Maids went to Holt Even 5.

MARCH 3, SUNDAY A fine Day. All went to our Church foornoon, Mr Burrell preachd. We all drank Tea at Mr Rouses, M^r & Mrs Bartell there.

MARCH 4, MONDAY A Close dry Day. Childr^n at School. Mr Bensley of Holt came M10, took a walk to his Meadow with Mr Hardy, Dind & drank Tea here, went with Mr Hardy Even 6 to the Town Meeting at Richd Mays s. Mr Hardy came home abt 12.

MARCH 5, TUESDAY A Cold dry Day. Childrn at School. A Frollick at R Mays s, Mr Hardy went Even 6, came back past 11 . . .

MARCH 7, THURSDAY A Dry Cold Day. Childrn at School, Mr Hardy at home all Day . . .

MARCH 15, FRIDAY A very Cold Day with Squarles of Snow & Hail. Bricklayers & Carpenters at Work. Mr Hardy at home all Day. A great deal of Snow fell in the Night . . .

MARCH 17, SUNDAY Thawd all Day, frequent Storms of Snow & Hail. All went to our Church foornoon, Mr Burrell preach^d. M^r & Mrs Rouse & Childr^n drank Tea here. A great Deal of Snow fell in the Night & froze . . .

MARCH 21, THURSDAY A very Cold Stormy Day. Childr^n at School. Mr Hardy at home all Day, at Mays s in Even. Bricklayers & Carpenters at Work.

MARCH 22, FRIDAY Excesive Cold, Snowd all Day. Childr^n at School. Bricklayers & Carpenters at Work, Mr Hardy at home all Day. M Anns new Stays came home.

MARCH 23, SATURDAY A very Sharp frost {Day}. Childr^n at School, Bricklayers & Carpenters at Work. Mr Hardy at home all Day & at Mays s in the Even. I & MA & Mrs Rouse walkd to Holt Afternoon, drank Tea at Mr Davys. A good deal of Snow fell in the Even.

MARCH 24, SUNDAY A Cold Dry Day. M^r & Mrs Baker & Childr^n came Aftrn, went to Church with us & drank Tea here . . .

MARCH 26, TUESDAY A very Cold Windy Day. Childr^n at School. Bricklayers, Carpenters & Plumbers at work. Mr Hardy at home all Day, at Mays s in the Even . . .

MARCH 28, THURSDAY A very Wet Day, Wind very high. Childr^n at School. Mr Hardy at home all Day, went to Holt Club Even 8, came home Even past 12.

MARCH 29, FRIDAY A Cold Stormy Day, Childrn not at School. Carpenters at Work. Mr Hardy at home all Day . . .

MARCH 31, SUNDAY A fine Day, Wind rough. All went to our Church foorn, Mr Burrell preachd, had a Comunion. MA poorly. M^r & Mrs Bartle & Childr^n, 2 Miss Alpes & Miss Burcham [?Bircham] drank Tea here.

APRIL 1, MONDAY A Close dry Morn, Wet Aftrn. MA & W^m went to Dancing. Mr Hardy up to Holt foorn, home to Dinner, went to Town meeting at Mays Even 6, came home Even past 12.

APRIL 2, TUESDAY A very Wet Cold Day. Mr Hardy up to Holt foornoon, back to Dinner. Mrs Rouse & Childrn drank Tea here, Mr Rouse here in the Eveng.

APRIL 3, WEDNESDAY A fine Morn, Wet Afternoon. Childr^n at School, 1 Carpenter at Work. T Erwin of Corpusty here. Mr Hardy at home all Day . . .

APRIL 5, FRIDAY A Wet Day. Childr^n at School. Mr Alexander & Mr Mays Dind here. Mr Hardy went to Mays s all the Aftern, came home Even 8.

APRIL 6, SATURDAY A fine Day. Childr^n at School. Mr Hardy, I & M Ann went to Holt Even 3, I & MA drank Tea at Miss Leakes, came home Even 8. Raven at Clay & Holt Afternoon.

APRIL 7, SUNDAY A Showry Day. All went to our Church Afternoon, Mr Burrell preachd. Miss Girdleston & Miss Pearmain drank Tea here . . .

APRIL 9, TUESDAY A Cold Dry Day. MA at School, Mr Hardy & Raven at Coltishall . . .

APRIL 13, SATURDAY A Showry Day. Childr^n at School. Sarah Goodman here all Day. Mr Hardy went to Market Even 3, came home Even 11, Raven at Cley Afternoon.

APRIL 14, SUNDAY A very Wet Day. No service at our Church. We all drank Tea at Mr Rouses.

APRIL 15, MONDAY A tolerable Day. Childr^n at School. I walkd up to Holt Afternoon to se the Childr^n Dance, drank Tea at Mr Bartles. Mr Hardy at home all Day. Boy had the Ague.

APRIL 16, TUESDAY A very Wet Day. Raven & MA at School. Mr Hardy & W^m went to Fakenham & Gresenhall & Whisensett.

APRIL 17, WEDNESDAY A very Wet Day. Childr^n at School, Mr Hardy & Raven [William] not at home.

APRIL 18, THURSDAY A Wet Day. Childr^n at School. Mr Hardy & W^m came home Even past 4. M^r & Mrs Bartle, Mrs Baldin [Baldwin] & Mrs Raven from Norwich drank Tea here. Kill«ed» the Pold [polled] Cows Calf.

APRIL 19, FRIDAY A Cold Dry Day. Childr^n at School. Wm Groom Dind here. Mr Hardy went to Clay Afternoon, came back to Holt Club, came home Even past 12.

APRIL 20, SATURDAY A fine Day. Childr^n at School. Carpenters at Work, Mr Hardy at home all Day. I & MA went up to Holt Afternoon, drank Tea at Mr Bakers.

APRIL 21, SUNDAY A fine Day. All went to our Church Afternoon, Mr Burrell preachd . . .

APRIL 24, WEDNESDAY A Cold Close windy Day. Childr^n at School, Mr Hardy at home all Day.

APRIL 25, THURSDAY *St Mark* A very Wet Day. Holt Fair, but no Company there. Mr Hardy, I & Childr^n drank Tea & Supt at Mr Bartles, came home Even 11.

APRIL 26, FRIDAY A Wet Cold Day. M^r & Mrs Wilson & Child Dind & drank Tea here. Mr Simonds of Yarmouth came Morn 11. Mr Hardy at home all Day.

APRIL 27, SATURDAY A Stormy Day. Mr Hardy went to Clay Even 2, came back by Holt Market, home Even 8. 2 Maids went up to Holt to buy some things.

APRIL 28, SUNDAY A very Cold Dry Day. All went to our Church foornoon, Mr Burrell preachd, Miss Baker & Miss Custance came to Church. Mr Hardy & Mr Rouse went to Mr Coles of Hunworth Even 4, came home Even past 11. I & Childr^n drank Tea at Mrs Rouses.

APRIL 29, MONDAY Excesive Cold Windy Day, Wind East. Childr^n at School, Mr Hardy at home all Day. I & Mrs Rouse walkd to Holt Afternoon to see the Childr^n Dance, drank Tea at Miss Alpes.

APRIL 30, TUESDAY A very Cold Day. Childr^n at School. Ellen Mason came. Mr Hardy went to Blakeney, Clay & Salthouse Afternoon, came home Even 11.

MAY 1, WEDNESDAY Dry Day, something Milder, Wind North. Childr^n at School. Mr Hardy & I rid to Salthouse Afternoon to Mr Hunts, Bought a Compleat Sett of Buirston [?burstone, ?Burslem] China at £3 3s 0d, A Sett of Dishes & 2 Doz. Plates at £1 5s 0d.

MAY 2, THURSDAY A fine Day, Wind Cold. MA at School, Childr^n went to Salthouse foornoon for China. Mr Hardy went Even 4 to the Bowling Green Club at Holt, came home Even past 8.

MAY 3, FRIDAY A very Cold Windy Day. Childr^n at School, Mr Hardy at home all Day.

MAY 4, SATURDAY A Dry Cold Day. Childr^n at School. Mr Hardy went to Justice Sitting at Holt, Dind there, came home Even 8. I & MA went to Holt Aftern, drank Tea at Miss Pearmains, heard M^r [James] Moody of Coltishall was Dead . . .

MAY 6, MONDAY A Wet Morn, Cold Close Day. Childr^n at School, Mr Hardy at home all Day. Wind North . . .

MAY 9, THURSDAY A fine Dry Day, Wind East. Childr^n at School. Mr Hardy went to Blakeny M10, came back to Dinner, went to Bowling Green Even 3, came home Even 8, went to Mays Even 9, to A Mr Green of Holt, came home Morn past 1 . . .

MAY 11, SATURDAY A fine Day, Wind rough, Raind towards Even. Mr Hardy at Markt, came home Even 9. I & M Ann walkd up to Holt Aftrn, drank Tea at Mrs Bacons, came home in the Chaise because of the rain.

MAY 12, SUNDAY A Showry Day. All went to our Church foornoon, Mr Burrell preachd. From the News paper, Coales sold at London at £4 4s pr Chaldrn . . .

MAY 14, TUESDAY A very Wet Day. Childr^n at School, Mr Hardy at home all Day.

MAY 15, WEDNESDAY Showry Day. Childr^n at School, Mr Hardy at home all Day. I Irond . . .

MAY 17, FRIDAY A Showry Cold Day. Childr^n at School, Mr Hardy at home all Day.

MAY 18, SATURDAY A Showry Day. Mr Hardy at home all Day. I & Raven rid to Holt Aftrn, drank Tea at Mr Bartles, came home past 8 . . .

MAY 21, TUESDAY A Tolerable Dry Day but very Cold. Mr Hardy & MA at home. I & Childrⁿ went to Mr Custance's at Fakenham, walkd up to Hempen [Hempton] Green Fair with Sister Raven.

MAY 22, WEDNESDAY A Showry Day. Sister Goggs came to me at Mr Custances Morn 11, Dind & drank Tea there, as did M^r & M^{rs} [Henry] Raven of Bramerton, M^{rs} [Neale] Raven of Walsham, M^r & Mrs Barrett [Baret] of Horstd. I & Childrⁿ set of for home Even 7, got home Even 9. Ann Chalders came home Even 6.

MAY 23, THURSDAY A very Wet Day. Childrⁿ at School. Mr Hardy at home all Day . . .

MAY 26, SUNDAY A Cold Dry Day. I & Childrⁿ at Church foornoon, A Communion. Mr Burrell preachd. Mr Hardy poorly. Mr Baker came Even 6 . . .

MAY 28, TUESDAY A very fine warm Day. Childrⁿ at School. Mrs Dunthorn & Childrⁿ drank Tea here. 2 Gardeners at Work.

MAY 29, WEDNESDAY A fine Morn, very Wet Aftrn. Childrⁿ at School. Mr Hardy & Willm came home from Coltishall Eve 10. 2 Gardiners at Work, left at 4 on Acct of Rain.

MAY 30, THURSDAY A Windy dry Day. Childrn at School, Mr Hardy at home all day. 2 Gardiners at Work.

MAY 31, FRIDAY A fine Day. Childrⁿ at School, Mr Hardy at home all Day. M^r & Mrs Bartle & Mrs Rouse drank Tea here. 2 Gardiners at work.

JUNE 1, SATURDAY A Wet Morn, Cold Afternoon. Childrn, I & Mrs Rouse & MA walkd to Holt, drank Tea at Mr Davys. Mr Hardy went to Market Eve 3, came home Even 9. 2 Gardiners at Work.

JUNE 2, SUNDAY A Cold Dry Day. All went to our Church Afternoon, Mr Burrell preachd.

JUNE 3, MONDAY A tolerable Day. Childrⁿ at School. I walkd up to Holt Afternoon to see the Childrⁿ Dance, drank Tea at Mr Bakers. Mr Hardy at Mays Afternoon, came home Even 9.

JUNE 4, TUESDAY *Kings Birth Day* A fine Day. Childrⁿ at School foornoon. Mr Hardy, I, Raven & M Ann, M^r & Mrs Rouse & 2 of their Childrⁿ drank Tea at Mr Davys. Mr Hardy went to the Gentlemen [?Volunteers] at the Feathers Even 8, came home M1.

JUNE 5, WEDNESDAY A fine Day. Childrⁿ at School. Mr Hardy at Mayss foornoon, went to Cley Afternoon, came home Even 8. Mrs Baker drank Tea here.

JUNE 6, THURSDAY A fine Day. Childrⁿ at School. Mr Hardy went to Briston Afternoon & came back by Bowling Green, home Eve 10. Mrs Wilson of Briston brought to Bed of a Girl.

JUNE 7, FRIDAY A fine Day. Childrⁿ at School. Carpenters & Bricklayers at work. Mr Hardy at home all day. Raven poorly.

JUNE 8, SATURDAY A Wet Morn, fine Day. Childrⁿ at School, Mr Hardy at home all day. I & M Ann walkd to Holt Afternoon, drank Tea at Miss Alpes. W^m taken Ill, Raven poorly . . .

JUNE 10, MONDAY A Showry Morn, fine Aftern. R & MA at School, W^m poorly. Mr Hardy at home all Day. Bricklayers at Work . . .

JUNE 12, WEDNESDAY A fine Day. Raven & MA at School, W^m poorly. Mr Hardy at [and] Mays came home Even 10.

JUNE 13, THURSDAY Very high Wind. Childrⁿ at School. Mr Hardy went to Bowling Green Even 4, came home Even 9. Mr Smith of Holt broke up for the Holydays.

JUNE 14, FRIDAY A very high wind. Miss Alpe broke up for the Holydays. Mr Hardy at home all Day.

JUNE 15, SATURDAY A very warm Day. Mr Hardy at home all Day. I & MA walkd to Holt Afternoon, drank Tea at Mr Bakers.

JUNE 16, SUNDAY A fine Warm Day. All went to our Church Afternoon, M [Mr] Burrell preachd. M^r & Mrs Foster of Bayfield Drank Tea & Supt here, Mr Cole Supt here . . .

JUNE 20, THURSDAY A Close Cool Day. Mr Hardy at home all Day . . .

JUNE 23, SUNDAY A Hot Dry Day. I & Childrⁿ went to our Church foornoon, 2 Maids went out Afternoon.

JUNE 24, MONDAY Hot Dry Day. Mr Hardy went to Bowling Green with Mr Burrell in the Chaise Even 3, came home Even 9, I & Nanny walkd to Holt After Tea. Old Duke in Garden.

JUNE 25, TUESDAY Very Hot Dry Day. Raven came from Wisenset M8 & Henry Goggs and Robt Raven with him. Old Duke in Garden . . .

JUNE 29, SATURDAY A Dry Day. Mr Hardy at home all Day, I walkd to Holt after Tea. Old Duke in Garden.

JUNE 30, SUNDAY A Dry Day. All went to our Church Afternoon, Mr Burrell preachd. M^r & Mrs Rouse came after Tea, took a Walk. Thos Watterson of Holt Died . . .

JULY 2, TUESDAY A fine Dry Day. Mr Hardy at home all Day. Old Duke in Garden.

JULY 3, WEDNESDAY Some very small Showers. Mr Hardy on ten pin Ground all the Afternoon. Old Duke in Garden.

JULY 4, THURSDAY Some very small Showers. Mr Hardy at home all Day. M^{rs} & Miss & Mast^r Baker & 2 Miss Custances drank Tea here . . .

JULY 6, SATURDAY A Dry Morn, wet Even. I & MA & Miss Custance went to Holt Afternoon, drank Tea at Mr Bartles.

JULY 7, SUNDAY A Wet Day. Mr Hardy very Ill. I & Childrⁿ at Church . . .

JULY 9, TUESDAY A fine Day. Mr Hardy very poorly . . .

JULY 11, THURSDAY Showry Day. Mr Hardy something better, at home all Day. Dr Girdlestone came to see Mr Hardy.

JULY 12, FRIDAY A Showry Afternoon. Mr Hardy poorly.

JULY 13, SATURDAY A fine Day, Wet Night. Mr Hardy something better, Dr Girdlestone came. I & MA walkd to Holt after Tea.

JULY 14, SUNDAY A very Wet foornoon, Dry Afternoon. All went to our Church Afternoon, Mr Burrell preachd. M^r & Mrs Bartle & Childrⁿ drank Tea here. M^r & Mrs Springthorp came Even 8 . . .

JULY 18, THURSDAY A very fine Day. Childr^n at School. Mr Hardy at home all Day & poorly . . .

JULY 25, THURSDAY A very Hot Day. Childr^n at School, Mr Hardy at home all Day . . .

JULY 28, SUNDAY Showry Day. Mr Martin went away Morn 10. All went to our Church Afternoon, Mr Burrell preachd.

JULY 29, MONDAY A Showry Day. W^m & M Ann at Dancing School. I & Mr Hardy rid up to Holt Afternoon to see the Childr^n Dance. I drank Tea at Miss Leakes, Mrs Rouse there, he went to Bowling Green . . .

AUGUST 1, THURSDAY A fine Day. 2 Childr^n at School, Mr Hardy at home all Day.

AUGUST 2, FRIDAY A Showry Day. 2 Childr^n at School. Mr Withers & Mr Elgood of Horning came to Dinner, went away Eve 6. Mr Hardy at home all Day.

AUGUST 3, SATURDAY A fine Day. 2 Childr^n at School foorn, Miss Burch«a»m came to play with M Ann Afternoon. Mr Hardy at home all Day .

AUGUST 4, SUNDAY A fine Day. All went to our Church foornoon, Mr Burrell preachd.

AUGUST 5, MONDAY A fine Day. W [William] & MA at Dancing School, Mr Hardy went to Bowling Green with Mr Browne. I & Mrs Rouse went to see the Childr^n Dance, drank Tea at Mrs Bartles.

AUGUST 6, TUESDAY A Close foornoon, Showry Afternoon. M^r & Mrs Goggs of Whisensett came to Dinner . . .

AUGUST 10, SATURDAY A Close Day, raind towards Even. Raven at School. Mr Hardy went to Markt Even 5, came home Even past 8, I walkd up to Holt after Tea . . .

AUGUST 15, THURSDAY A Showry Day. 2 Childr^n at School. I something better. Mr Hardy at home all Day . . .

AUGUST 17, SATURDAY A Showry Day. 2 Childr^n at School. I much better. Mr Hardy at home all Day. Very Wet Night. Mrs Davy brought to Bed with a Girl Namd Margeret . . .

AUGUST 19, MONDAY A fine Day. W^m & MA at Dancing School. Mr Hardy went to Bowling Green E4, came home Even 9. Mrs Burrell at Holt.

AUGUST 20, TUESDAY A Showry Day. 2 Childr^n at School, Mr Hardy at home all Day . . .

AUGUST 24, SATURDAY A dry Windy Day. MA at School. I went to Holt Aftr, drank Tea at Miss Leakes. Mr Hardy at Market, came home Even 9. Mr Boggis from London came Even 8.

AUGUST 25, SUNDAY A fine Day. All went to our Church Afternoon, Mr Burrell preachd. Mr Boggis & we all drank Tea at Mr Rouses . . .

AUGUST 28, WEDNESDAY A Cold Dry Day. MA at School. Mr Hardy & Raven came home Eve 8.

AUGUST 29, THURSDAY A Showry Day. 2 Childr^n at School. Mr Hardy went to Bowling Green Even 4, came home Eve 8. Carted some Pease.

AUGUST 30, FRIDAY A fine Day. 2 Childr^n at School, Mr Hardy at home all Day . . .

SEPTEMBER 1, SUNDAY A fine Dry Day. I & Childr^n went «to» our Church foornoon, Mr Burrell preachd. I &

Childr^n went to Holt Church Afternoon, came back to Tea.

SEPTEMBER 2, MONDAY A very fine Day. W & MA at Dancing School. Mr Hardy went to Brinton Club Even 6, came home past 10.

SEPTEMBER 3, TUESDAY A fine Day. 2 Childr^n at School. Mr Hardy went to Gressenhall, Slept at Mr Croffts. I & MA drank Tea at Mr Davys.

SEPTEMBER 4, WEDNESDAY A very fine Day. 2 Childr^n at School. Mr Hardy went from Gressenhall to Massenham [Massingham] & Whisensett, Slept at Brot Nathl.

SEPTEMBER 5, THURSDAY A very fine Day. 2 Childrn at School. Mr Hardy came home Even 9 . . .

SEPTEMBER 8, SUNDAY A Hot Day. All went to our Church Afternoon, Mr Burrell preachd. M^r & Mrs Bartle, M^r & Mrs Rouse & Childr^n drank Tea here.

SEPTEMBER 9, MONDAY Very fine Day. 2 Childr^n at Dancing School. Mr Hardy & I went to Holt Aftrn, drank Tea at Mr Bartles . . .

SEPTEMBER 13, FRIDAY A Close Cold Day. R at School. Mr Hardy, I & MA Dind & drank Tea at Mr Wilsons of Briston, M^r & Mrs Bartle there at Tea.

SEPTEMBER 17, TUESDAY A fine Day. 2 Childr^n at School, Mr Hardy at home all Day. I & Mrs Rouse walkd up to Holt Afternoon, drank Tea at Mr Davys . . .

SEPTEMBER 20, FRIDAY A very Showry Day. 2 Childr^n at School, Mr Hardy at home all Day.

SEPTEMBER 21, SATURDAY A Showry Day. 2 Childr^n at School, Mr Hardy at home all Day. I & MA drank Tea at Miss Leakes . . .

Manuscript ledger 3

23 September 1782–20 July 1790

SEPTEMBER 23, MONDAY A Showry day. 2 Childr^n at School, Mr Hardy at home all Day. M^r & Mrs Burcham calld here.

SEPTEMBER 24, TUESDAY A fine Day. Mr Hardy, I & Jo^s Hardy went Morn 6 to Mr Croffts of Gressenhall, came home Even 9.

SEPTEMBER 25, WEDNESDAY A Dry windy Day. Mr Hardy at home all Day, 2 Childr^n at School. Jo^s Hardy went to Mr Wilsons of Briston Afternoon . . .

SEPTEMBER 27, FRIDAY A Showry Day. Mr Hardy at home all Day. Miss Gay, Miss Fisher & Miss Howard drank Tea here . . .

SEPTEMBER 29, SUNDAY A very Wet Day. MA very Ill. All went to our Church foornoon, Mr Burrell preachd.

SEPTEMBER 30, MONDAY A fine Day. R at School, Mr Hardy at home all Day . . .

OCTOBER 2, WEDNESDAY A Showry Day. Raven at School, Mr Hardy at home all Day . . .

OCTOBER 4, FRIDAY High wind & Showers. Mr Hardy at home all Day . . .

OCTOBER 6, SUNDAY A very Wet Day. All went to our Church Afternoon, Mr Burrell preachd. Mr Cole of Hunworth drank Tea here.

OCTOBER 7, MONDAY Showry Day. Raven «and» MA at School. Mr Hardy went to Clay & Blakeney M9, came back by Holt, home Even past 9 . . .

OCTOBER 9, WEDNESDAY A Showry Cold day. MA at School, Mr Hardy not at home . . .

OCTOBER 11, FRIDAY A very Cold Showry Day. MA at School. Mr Hardy came home E10.

OCTOBER 12, SATURDAY A Showry Day. Mr Cole Dind here. Mr Hardy, I & Raven went to Holt Market Even 3, drank Tea at Mr Girdlestones.

OCTOBER 13, SUNDAY A wet Day. All went to our Church foornoon, Mr Burrell preachd. Miss Girdlestone, Miss Leake & Miss Pearmain drank Tea here, Mr Browne of Walsingham Dind here . . .

OCTOBER 17, THURSDAY A fine Day. 2 Childrn at School. Mr Hardy & I drank Tea at Mr Bakers at Holt.

OCTOBER 18, FRIDAY A Cold Close Day. R & MA at School, Mr Hardy at home all Day . . .

OCTOBER 20, SUNDAY A Cold Dry Day. All went to our Church Aftrn, Mr Burrell preachd. We all drank Tea at Mr Rouses.

OCTOBER 21, MONDAY Wet Morn, Dry Day. R & MA at School. Mr Hardy went to Cromer M9, came home Even 1 . . .

OCTOBER 26, SATURDAY A Mild Dry day. I & MA walkd up to Holt Afternoon, drank Tea at Mr Bartles. Mr Hardy at Mark^t, came home Even past 8. 2 Gardiners at Work Edgn [edging] the Walks.

OCTOBER 27, SUNDAY A close damp Day. All went to our Church foornoon, Mr Burrell preachd. Mr Hardy, Mr Rouse & Mr Burrell went to Mr Coles, Hunworth, Aftr, came home E8 . . .

OCTOBER 29, TUESDAY A Cold Stormy Day. Ravn & MA at School, Mr Hardy at home all Day. Maids & Goody Greves Washd.

OCTOBER 30, WEDNESDAY A very fine Calm Day. R & MA at School, Mr Hardy at home all Day. Wet Windy Night . . .

NOVEMBER 3, SUNDAY A Close foggy Day. All went to our Church Afternoon, Mr Burrell preachd. M^r & Mrs Rouse & Childr^n drank Tea here.

NOVEMBER 4, MONDAY A very Cold Stormy Day. R & MA at School, Mr Hardy at home all Day . . .

NOVEMBER 6, WEDNESDAY A Cold Stormy day. R & MA at School. Mr Hardy went to Edgefield M10, came back Even 6. Miss Baker of Holt Dind & drank Tea here.

NOVEMBER 7, THURSDAY A Cold Stormy day. R & MA at School. Mr Hardy went to Weyborn & Plumstd M9, came back Even 6.

NOVEMBER 8, FRIDAY A Cold Stormy Day. R & MA at School. Mr Hardy went to the Justice Sitting at Holt M10, came home Even 8. Susan [Sarah] Nicholds went to her Grandmothers Funeral M11, came home Even 6.

NOVEMBER 9, SATURDAY *Ravens Birth Day «aged» 15* A Cold Stormy day. Mr Hardy at home all Day. I walkd up to Holt Aftrn, drank Tea at Mr Seales's, Raven came for me.

NOVEMBER 10, SUNDAY A Cold Wet Day. All went to our Church, Mr Burrell preachd.

NOVEMBER 11, MONDAY A Close Cold day. R & MA at School, Mr Hardy at home. Mr Howard of Walsingham Dind here.

NOVEMBER 12, TUESDAY A Close Cold Day. R & MA at School, Mr Hardy at home all Day.

NOVEMBER 13, WEDNESDAY A Sharp rime frost. R at School, Mr Hardy at home all Day . . .

NOVEMBER 15, FRIDAY A Close Stormy Day. R & MA at School, Mr Hardy at home all Day. M^{rs} [Jane] Burrell continue very bad . . .

NOVEMBER 18, MONDAY A Cold Stormy Day. R & MA at School, Mr Hardy at home all Day.

NOVEMBER 19, TUESDAY A Cold foggy day. R at School. I very poorly. Mr Hardy at home all day. Mrs Burrell Burried Even 5. Maids & Goody Greves Wash^d 3 Weeks Linnen.

NOVEMBER 20, WEDNESDAY A very fine Day. MA at School, Mr Hardy at home all Day . . .

NOVEMBER 23, SATURDAY A fine Day. Mr Hardy came home from Norwich Even 9 . . .

NOVEMBER 26, TUESDAY A Sharp Frost. Mr Hardy at home all day. Mr Hewit, Mr Browne of Wicton [Wighton], Mr Drake & friend Dind here, went away Even 3 . . .

DECEMBER 7, SATURDAY A Cold foggy day. I & Mrs Rouse walkd to Holt Afternoon, Mr Hardy at Market.

DECEMBER 8, SUNDAY A Cold foggy day. All went to our Church foornoon, Mr Smith preachd. Mr Hardy poorly.

DECEMBER 9, MONDAY A Cold foggy Day. R & MA at School, Mr Hardy at home all Day. [[[*by Mary Ann, in error*] Ravens birthday aged 15 years]] . . .

DECEMBER 12, THURSDAY Chearly Day. R & MA at school, Mr Hardy at home all Day .

DECEMBER 13, FRIDAY A Chearly day. R & MA at School, Mr Hardy at home all day. Mr Paul Myles came to Dinner & Slept here.

DECEMBER 14, SATURDAY A Wet Morn, froze Aftrn. I & Mr Hardy & P Myles went to Holt Aftrn, I drank Tea at Mr Bartles. A little Snow fell in the Night.

DECEMBER 15, SUNDAY A Cold Stormy Day. All went to our Church Afternoon, Mr Paul Johnson preachd. M^r & Mrs Baker & Childr^n came to our Church & drank Tea here.

DECEMBER 16, MONDAY A Close foggy Day. R & MA at School, Mr Hardy at home all Day. P Myles went away . . .

DECEMBER 23, MONDAY A fine Dry Day. Mr Hardy at home all Day . . .

DECEMBER 26, THURSDAY A very fine Day. Mr Hardy went to Clay Afternoon, drank Tea at Mr Mans [Mann's], came home Even 11. Paul Myles came again. I & MA walkd to Holt Afternoon, came back to Tea.

The visit to Whissonsett
27 December 1782–4 January 1783

DECEMBER 27, FRIDAY A fine Day. Paul Myles here. Mr Hardy, I & MA set of for Whisensett M9, went by Walsingham, Dind at Mr Howards & reachd Whisensett Even 5, Slept at Mr Goggs's.

DECEMBER 28, SATURDAY A very fine day. I, Mr Hardy, Bro^t Nathl & Miss [Elizabeth] Goggs walkd to Horningtoft foornoon, went to M^r [Thomas] Ravens & Mr Moys & back to Dinner, drank Tea & Slept at Mr Goggs's.

DECEMBER 29, SUNDAY A Cold fair Day. All went to Church foornoon, Mr Bird preachd. Dind, drank Tea, Supt & Slept at Bro^t Nathl.

DECEMBER 30, MONDAY A Close foggy Day. Mr Hardy went away Morn 10. I went to speak to Uncle Nathl & Sister Goggs foornoon, came back to Bro^t Nathl to Dinner. M^r & Mrs Goggs, M^r & Mrs Moy spent the Even with us there.

DECEMBER 31, TUESDAY A Close Day. Raven came Even past 1. We all spent the Even at Bro^t Robts.

1783

[WHISSONSETT, *cont.*]

JANUARY 1, WEDNESDAY A very Sharp Frost. I poorly. We all spent the Even at Mr Goggs, Robt Goggs Child Christnd [Phillis].

JANUARY 2, THURSDAY A Sharp frost. We all drank Tea & Supt at Old M^r [Nathaniel] Ravens. I poorly. Paul Myles went away.

JANUARY 3, FRIDAY *New Moon* A Sharp frost. Sister Goggs Dind with us at Bro^t Nathl. Bro^t & Sister & I walkd to Mr Moys Afternoon, spent the Even there, Mr Hardy met us there.

JANUARY 4, SATURDAY Thawd. We set of from Bro^t Morn past 11, Dind at Mr Custances at Fakenham & got home Even 5. Henry Goggs & Robt Raven came home with us.

[LETHERINGSETT]

JANUARY 5, SUNDAY A Mild damp Day. No service at our Church, Childr^n went to Holt Church. MA poorly.

JANUARY 6, MONDAY A Close damp Day. Mr Hardy set of for N Walshm & Coltishall Morn 11. Paul Myles Dind here.

JANUARY 7, TUESDAY A Close damp Day. Childr^n drank Tea & Supt at Mr Rouses . . .

JANUARY 11, SATURDAY A fine Day. Mr Hardy went to Holt Markt Even 3, came home Even 10. Paul Myles here.

JANUARY 12, SUNDAY A Close Dry Day. I poorly. Paul Myles went away. All went to our Church afternoon, Mr Burrell preachd. Mr Cole of Hunworth drank Tea here . . .

JANUARY 15, WEDNESDAY A very fine day. Mr Hardy at home all Day . . .

JANUARY 18, SATURDAY *full Moon* A very Cold Snowy Day. I & Mr Hardy went to Holt Afternoon in the Chaise, drank Tea & Supt at Mr Bartles, came home Even 12, M Ann came home with us from Mr Davys. W^m came home from Whisensett.

JANUARY 19, SUNDAY Very Cold Snowy Day. I & Childr^n at our Church foornoon, Mr Burrell preachd. Mr Hardy poorly.

JANUARY 20, MONDAY A Sharp frost. MA began going to School after the Holydays. Mr Hardy at home all Day, spent the Even at Mr Rouses.

JANUARY 21, TUESDAY Thawd. MA at School, Mr Hardy at home all day. Maids & Goody Greves Washd 5 Weeks Linnen.

JANUARY 22, WEDNESDAY A Cold damp day. M Ann at School, Mr Hardy at home all day . . .

JANUARY 25, SATURDAY A Close cold Day, raind towards Even. Mr Hardy went to Holt Market Even 3, came home Even 8. MA Scalt [scalded] her foot.

JANUARY 26, SUNDAY A fine Chearly Day. All went to our Church Afternoon, Mr Burrell preachd. Mr Hardy, I & M^r & Mrs Rouse drank Tea at Mr Burrells . . .

JANUARY 29, WEDNESDAY A fine Day. MA at School, Mr Hardy at home all Day. M^r & Mrs Mays drank Tea & Supt here. 2 Gardiners at Work.

JANUARY 30, THURSDAY A Cold Windy Day. MA at School. Thos Erwin Dind here. 2 Gardiners at work. Mr Hardy went to Holt Club Even 6.

JANUARY 31, FRIDAY A fine Day, Wet Eveng. MA at School, Mr Hardy at home all Day. Mr Playford of Yarmouth came to Dinner & Slept here. Raven & W^m drank Tea & Supt at Mr Bakers. 2 Gardiners at Work . . .

FEBRUARY 2, SUNDAY A Wet day. All went to our Church foornoon, Mr Burrell preachd. Mrs Rouse here alittle while in the Eveng.

FEBRUARY 3, MONDAY A Close mild Day, raind in the Even. MA at School. Mr Hardy went to Wroxham & Coltishall Morn 11.

FEBRUARY 4, TUESDAY A very fine Morn, Wet Afternoon. Expected Mr Hardy home to Dinner, did not come all day. Mr Garret came, would not stay «to» Dinner. MA at School.

FEBRUARY 5, WEDNESDAY A fine Morng, Wet Aftern. MA at School. Mr Hardy came home Eve 5, Myles Raven with him. Mr Hardy, I, Myles & Raven went to Mr Bakers, drank Tea & Supt there, Lawyer Girdlestone & his Daught^r there, came home Morn 2.

FEBRUARY 6, THURSDAY A fine Day. MA at School. Mr Bensley calld here Aftr, Mr Hardy went with him to Mr Burrells, drank Tea there, came home Even 8 . . .

FEBRUARY 8, SATURDAY A Wet Day. Myles Raven & Myles Custance went away M10. Mr Hardy bought Small Piggs of Hareson [off Harrison].

FEBRUARY 9, SUNDAY A Showry Day. All went to our Church Afternoon, Mr Burrell preachd. We all drank Tea at Mr Rouses . . .

FEBRUARY 14, FRIDAY A fine Day. MA at School, Mr Hardy at home all day. Raind towards Eveng.

FEBRUARY 15, SATURDAY A Close Dry Day. MA & I walkd to Holt Afternoon, drank Tea at Miss Leakes, Mr Hardy at Market, we Supt at Mr Bartles & came home past 12 . . .

FEBRUARY 19, WEDNESDAY A Sharp frost, fine day. MA at School, Mr Hardy at home all day. Carpenters at Work parting the yard . . .

FEBRUARY 21, FRIDAY A Close Cold Day. MA at School. Mr Hardy, I, M^r & Mrs Bartle drank Tea & Supt at Mr Ballss in this Town.

FEBRUARY 22, SATURDAY A fine Morn, Wet Aftrn. Mr Hardy at home all Day . . .

FEBRUARY 26, WEDNESDAY A very Sharp frost. MA at School. Paul Myles came M11, went away Even 6. Mr Hardy & Raven came home from Walsham Even 7.

FEBRUARY 27, THURSDAY A Close Cold Day. MA at School, Mr Hardy at home all Day. Bro^t Robt & Thos Fox came Even 7, Slept here.

FEBRUARY 28, FRIDAY A Chearly Day but Cold. MA at School. Bro^t Nathl came to Dinner. Mr Garthon of Norwich & another Gentleman came & Dind here, brought a Letter from Messers Gurneys. M^r & Mrs Bartle drank Tea & Supt here. A Deal of Snow fell in the Night.

MARCH 1, SATURDAY Thawd. Broth^s & Mr Fox went away Even 2. Mr Theordoric came after Dinner. Mr Hardy & I walkd to Holt, drank Tea & Supt at Mr Bakers, came home Eve 10. Sharp frost at Night.

MARCH 2, SUNDAY Cold Bright day. All went to our Church foornoon, Mr Burrell preachd . . .

MARCH 4, TUESDAY A very Sharp frost. Mastr Bartle came to Dinner, Slept here, Miss & John Baker drank Tea here. Mr Hardy at home all Day.

MARCH 5, *Ash Wednesday* Excesive Sharp frost & Snowd a little Afternoon. Mr Hardy walkd up to Holt foornoon, came back to Dinner. W^m came home Even 6 . . .

MARCH 7, FRIDAY Very Close Stormy Day. Mr Hardy walkd to Holt foornoon, spoke for Mrs Sheppards Post Chaise to go to Norw^h, came back to Dinner . . .

MARCH 10, MONDAY A very fine Day. MA at School. Mr Hardy went to Briston & Hilderveston [Hindolveston] & met me at Mr Bartells of Holt, drank Tea & Supt there . . .

MARCH 13, THURSDAY A very Sharp Windy day. MA at School. Mr Hardy very poorly. Mr Forster of Bayfield drank Tea & Supt here.

MARCH 14, FRIDAY A Sharp windy Day. MA at School, Mr Hardy reather better. Thetford Assizes began.

MARCH 15, SATURDAY A Sharp bright Day. Mr Hardy much better.

MARCH 16, SUNDAY Bright Day, somthing Milder. All went to our Church foornoon, Mr Burrell preachd.

MARCH 17, MONDAY A very fine Day. MA at School, Mr Hardy at home all Day. I walkd up to Holt Afternoon to look at Mr Custances Furniture, drank Tea at Mr Bakers . . .

MARCH 19, WEDNESDAY A Close Dry Day. MA poorly. I went to Holt Morn past 11 to Sale, Dind at Mr Bartells, drank Tea at Miss Leakes, home Even 7.

MARCH 20, THURSDAY A fine Day. Mr Hardy at home all Day.

MARCH 21, FRIDAY A very fine day. Mr Hardy at home all day. I & MA walkd to Holt Afternoon, M^r & Mrs Bartell came back with us. M^rs & Miss Baker drank Tea & Supt here . . .

MARCH 27, THURSDAY A fine Day but Cold. Mr Hardy at home all Day. M^r & Mrs Bartell drank Tea & Supt here.

MARCH 28, FRIDAY A very Cold Stormy Day. I poorly. Mr Hardy & I drank Tea & Supt at Mr Bartells . . .

MARCH 30, SUNDAY A Showry Morng, Mild Aftern. All went to our Church foorn, Mr Burrell preachd. M^r & Mrs Rouse & all the Childr^n drank Tea here . . .

APRIL 2, WEDNESDAY A very fine day. MA at School, Mr Hardy at home all Day. 2 Gardiners at Work . . .

APRIL 4, FRIDAY A very fine Warm Day. MA at School, Mr Hardy at home all Day. 2 Gardiners at Work.

APRIL 5, SATURDAY A Cold Dry Day. MA at School foornoon. Mr Hardy, I & M^rA [MA] walkd to Holt Aftrn, drank Tea at Mr Bakers, Supt at Mr Bartells, came home Even 11 . . .

APRIL 8, TUESDAY A fine warm day. MA at School. Paul Myles came Even 7, Slept here.

APRIL 9, WEDNESDAY A very fine warm Day. MA at School. M^r & Mrs Bartell drank Tea & Supt here, Mr Baker Supt here. Mr Hardy came home Even past 11.

APRIL 10, THURSDAY A very warm dry day. MA at School, Mr Hardy at home all day.

APRIL 11, FRIDAY A Close cool Day. MA at School, Mr Hardy at home all Day. Mrs Prior came.

APRIL 12, SATURDAY A Close foggy Day. MA at School. Mr Hardy went to Market Even 3, came home Even 11 . . .

APRIL 14, MONDAY A very fine Day. MA & W^m went to Dancing School. Mr Hardy went to Weyborn Even 2 to look at some repairs, came home Even past 8.

APRIL 15, TUESDAY A Cold Close drisley Day. MA at School, Mr Hardy at home all day. Mrs Prior & I walkd up to Holt after Tea. Maids & Goody Greves Wash^d.

APRIL 16, WEDNESDAY A fine Day. MA at School, Mr Hardy at home all Day. Carpenter at Work.

APRIL 17, THURSDAY A very fine Day. MA at School, Mr Hardy at home all day. Mr Paul here afternoon. Mrs Bartell sent for to Mr Dowsons of Shotsham [Shotesham], he being like to Die . . .

APRIL 19, SATURDAY A very fine Day. MA at School foornoon. I walkd to Holt Afternoon, drank Tea at Mr Bartells. Mr Hardy went round by Clay to Holt Market, came home Even 8.

APRIL 20, SUNDAY A Cold Dry Day. All went to our Church Afternoon, Mr Burrell preachd . . .

APRIL 22, TUESDAY A very Cold Windy stormy Day. Mr Hardy at home all Day. 2 Gardiners at work ½ a Day, weather bad, could work no longer.

APRIL 23, WEDNESDAY A very Cold Day. MA at School, Mr Hardy at home all Day. M^r & Mrs Bartell drank Tea & Supt here. Mr Howard of Walsingham drank Tea & Supt here, Slept here. 2 Gardeners at Work. J Davison came Even 7, Slept here.

APRIL 24, THURSDAY A Close Cold Windy day. MA at School. Mr Howard went away M11. Mr Hardy at home all Day. 2 Gardiners at Work.

APRIL 25, FRIDAY A Cold Dry Day. MA at School, Mr Hardy at home all day. Mr Thos Hewit Dind & drank Tea here.

APRIL 26, SATURDAY A fine day. I & MA walkd up to Holt Afternoon, drank Tea at Mr Bakers. Mr Hardy at Mark^t.

APRIL 27, SUNDAY A very fine Day. All went to our Church foornoon, A Comunion. Mr Burrell preachd. We all walkd to Holt Church Afternoon, drank Tea at Mr Bakers . . .

APRIL 29, TUESDAY A very fine Day. Mr Hardy up to Holt foornoon, home to Dinner. Mr Hardy & I drank Tea & Supt at Mr Bartells.

APRIL 30, WEDNESDAY A Cold Dry Day. MA at School. Mr Hardy went to Fakenham M11, came home by Snoring Even 8 . . .

MAY 2, FRIDAY A very Cold Windy day. MA at School, Mr Hardy at home all day . . .

MAY 4, SUNDAY A fine Day. All went to our Church Afternoon, Mr Burrell preachd. We all drank Tea at Mr Rouses . . .

MAY 7, WEDNESDAY A very Cold Day, Wind high. MA at School. I poorly. Mr Hardy at home all Day. Old Duke in Garden . . .

MAY 9, FRIDAY A Milder Day, Wind rough. MA at School. Mr Bartell Bled me, my Eyes still poorly. Mr Hardy, Mr Burrell, I & MA drank Tea at Mr Bensleys . . .

MAY 11, SUNDAY A very fine Day. All went to our Church foornoon, Mr Burrell preach^d. M^r & Mrs Baker & Childrn & Paul Myles drank Tea here. Old Dukes Son came to see him . . .

MAY 16, FRIDAY A very Dry warm Day. MA at School. Men at work in the River, Mr Hardy at home all day. M^r & Mrs Bartell & Mr Burrell drank Tea & Supt here.

MAY 17, SATURDAY A very Warm Day, a Small Show^r Afternoon. MA at School foornoon. MA & I walk^d to Holt Afternoon, drank Tea at Mr Bartells. Mr Hardy at Mark^t, came home Even 10. Men in river.

MAY 18, SUNDAY A Cold windy Day. All went to our Church Afternoon, Mr Burrell Preachd. We all drank Tea at Mr Rouses, M^r & Mrs Bartell, M^r & Mrs Davy there.

MAY 19, MONDAY A very Cold Day. MA & W^m at Dancing School, Mr Hardy at home all Day. I walkd to Holt Aftrn, drank Tea at Mr Bartells. Men at Work in River.

MAY 20, TUESDAY A dry Day, something milder. MA at School. Mr Hardy walkd up to Holt Even 5 to Overtons Bowling Green, Supt at Mr Johnsons, came home Even 11.

MAY 21, WEDNESDAY A Dry Day but Cold. MA at School. M^r & Mrs Moy came to speak to us M9, went back to Holt to Dinner. Mr Hardy & I drank Tea at Mr Johnsons at Holt.

MAY 22, THURSDAY A Cold dry Day. MA at School. Mr Hardy & I drank Tea & Supt at Mr Bartells.

MAY 23, FRIDAY A very Cold Day, wind very high. M^r & Mrs Bartell drank Tea & Supt here.

MAY 24, SATURDAY A Cold Chearly Day. MA at School. MA & I walkd to Holt Afternoon, drank Tea at Mr Bartells. Mr Hardy at Markt, came home past 8. Men finished in river.

MAY 25, SUNDAY A Cold dry Chearly Day. All went to our Church Forenoon, Mr Burrell preachd. Mr Cock of Hempton Dind here . . .

MAY 27, TUESDAY A very Wet Cold Day. Mr Hardy at Coltishall.

MAY 28, WEDNESDAY A Cold Wet Day. MA at School. Mr Hardy came home Even 9 . . .

MAY 30, FRIDAY A fine Day. MA at School, Mr Hardy at home all Day.

MAY 31, SATURDAY A very fine warm Day. MA at School. I & MA walkd up to Holt Afternoon, drank Tea at Mr Davys. Mr Hardy at Markt, came home Even past 10.

JUNE 1, SUNDAY A very fine warm Day. All went to our Church Afternoon, Mr Burrell preachd. M^r & Mrs Bartell, M^r & Mrs Davy & Childrn, M^r & Mrs Rouse & Childr^n drank Tea here.

JUNE 2, MONDAY A Cold Windy Day. W^m & MA at Dancing School, Mr Hardy at home all Day. I & Mrs Rouse walkd to Holt Afternoon to see the Childr^n Dance, drank Tea at Miss Leakes.

JUNE 3, TUESDAY A fine warm Day. Mr Hardy at home all day. M^r & Mrs Bartell drank Tea & Supt here.

JUNE 4, WEDNESDAY A very fine dry Day. MA at School foornoon, Kings Birth Day. Mr Hardy Dind & Supt at the Feathers at Holt, came home Morn 1.

JUNE 5, THURSDAY A finc Dry Day. MA at School, Mr Hardy at home all Day.

JUNE 6, FRIDAY A very fine Day. MA at School, Mr Hardy at home all day. Expected M^r & Mrs Wilson of Briston, did not come.

JUNE 7, SATURDAY A very fine Day. MA at School. I & MA went to Holt Aftrn, drank Tea & Supt at Mr Bartells. Mr Hardy at Mark't . . .

JUNE 12, THURSDAY A fine Day. MA at School. Mr Hardy came home E11 . . .

JUNE 14, SATURDAY A fine Day, very Warm. Mr Hardy at home all Day. MA & I drank Tea at Mr Bartells. A small Thunder Storm abt 8 O Clock in the Even . . .

JUNE 16, MONDAY A very fine Day. Mr Hardy at home all day. I walkd up to Holt after Tea with Mrs Rouse.

JUNE 17, TUESDAY A Showry day. Mr Hardy at home all day. I Bathd . . .

JUNE 19, THURSDAY A Showry Day. Mr Hardy at home all day. I Bathd . . .

JUNE 22, SUNDAY A very fine Day. Had no service at our Church. M^r & Mrs Forster drank Tea & Supt here. M^r & Mrs Bartell came after Tea.

JUNE 23, MONDAY A very fine Day. Mr Hardy at home all Day. I Bathd . . .

JUNE 27, FRIDAY A Hot Dry Day. Mr Hardy at home all Day. Expectd M^r & Mrs Bartell, did not come on Acct of Mrs Bald«w»in & Mrs Raven of Norwich coming. I bathd . . .

JUNE 29, SUNDAY A very Hot Day. All went to our Church Aftrn, Mr Burrell preachd. I bathd . . .

JULY 1, TUESDAY A Hot Day. M^r & Mrs Bartell, M^r & Mrs Wymer, Mrs Baldin & Mrs Raven Dind, drank Tea & Supt here. Mr Hardy went up to Mr Jewells foornoon, at home all Day. I bathd . . .

JULY 4, FRIDAY A Cooler Day then Yesterday. M^r & Mrs Bartell drank Tea here. I bathd. M^r & Mrs Wymer, Mrs Baldin & Mrs Raven went away from Mr Bartells.

JULY 5, SATURDAY A moderate Day. I bathd. I & MA drank Tea at Mr Bartells. Mr Hardy at home all Day . . .

JULY 9, WEDNESDAY Very Hot Day. I poorly. Mr Hardy came home Even 11. Ellen Mason came. {M^r Hardy came home Eve 11.}

JULY 10, THURSDAY A very hot dry Day. Mr Hardy at home all Day.

JULY 11, FRIDAY A very hot Day. I bathd. Mr Hardy at home all Day. Henry Goggs & Robt Raven went away Even 6 . . .

JULY 13, SUNDAY Very hot & dry. M^r & Mrs Wymer came M11 to speak to us. We all went to our Church Aftrn, Mr Burrell preachd. We all drank Tea at Mr Rouses . . .

JULY 23, WEDNESDAY A Showry day. MA & W^m at School, Mr Hardy at home all day . . .

JULY 25, FRIDAY A hot Dry Day. W & MA at School, Mr Hardy at home all Day.

JULY 26, SATURDAY A hot Dry Day. Mr Withers of Horning & Elgood & J Jeckell of Edgefield Dind here, went away Even 4. I & W^m went to Holt Aftrn, drank Tea & Supt at Mr Bartells, Mr Hardy Supt there. I bathd.

JULY 27, SUNDAY Excesive hot Day. No service at our Church, we all went to Holt Church Afternoon, Mr Burrell preachd there. We all drank Tea at Mr Davys. I bathd . . .

JULY 29, TUESDAY Excesive hot Day. W^m & MA at School, Mr Hardy at home all day. I bathd . . .

AUGUST 2, SATURDAY Excesive hot Day. W & MA at School, Mr Hardy at home all Day. I & MA walkd up to Holt Aftern, drank Tea at Mr Bartells. I & M^{rs} & Miss Rouse bathd.

AUGUST 3, SUNDAY A very hot Day. All went to our Church foorn, Mr Burrell preachd. M^r & Mrs Rouse drank Tea here. I & M^{rs} & Miss Rouse bathd.

AUGUST 4, MONDAY A Moderate Day. W^m & MA at Dancing School, I & Mrs Bartell went to see them Dance, I & Mr Hardy drank Tea at Mr Bartells. Began Harvest . . .

AUGUST 7, THURSDAY Some small Showers. W & MA at School, Mr Hardy at home all Day. M^{rs} & Miss Baker drank Tea here . . .

AUGUST 9, SATURDAY A Close dry Day. I bath^d. MA & I drank Tea at Mr Seales. Mr Hardy at Market.

AUGUST 10, SUNDAY A Showry Day. I bathd. All went to our Church Afternoon, Mr Burrell preachd. We all drank Tea at Mr Rouses, M^r & Mrs Bartell there.

AUGUST 11, MONDAY A fine day. I bathd. W^m & MA at Dancing School, Mr Hardy at home all Day. Men caried Barly. M^r & Mrs Bartell drank Tea & Supt here. Showr in the Night . . .

AUGUST 16, SATURDAY A very hot Day. Men shearing. Mr Hardy at home all Day. I bathd. I & MA drank Tea at Mr Chaplins.

AUGUST 17, SUNDAY A hot Dry Day. I bathd. All went to our Church foornoon, Mr Burrell preachd. Miss Gay, Miss Wymer & Miss Howard drank Tea here.

AUGUST 18, MONDAY A very hot Dry Day, Thunderd Afternoon but no rain. I bathd. W & MA at Dancing School, Mr Hardy at home all Day . . .

AUGUST 20, WEDNESDAY Sultry hot Day. W & MA at School, I bathd. Nathl Burrell came from Ipswich . . .

AUGUST 22, FRIDAY A hot Day, a large Showr Afternoon. I bathd. Mr Hardy came home Even past 11. W^m & MA at School.

AUGUST 23, SATURDAY A fine Day. I bathd. W^m & MA at School. Mr Hardy, I & W^m & MA walkd to Holt Afternoon. I drank Tea at Mr Bakers, Mr Hardy drank Tea at Mr Davys, MA drank Tea at Mrs Jewells.

AUGUST 24, SUNDAY A Close Showry Day. I bathd. All went to our Church Aftrn, Mr Burrell preachd. Mr Cole, Mr Rouse & Sons drank Tea here.

AUGUST 25, MONDAY Showers with Thunder. I bathd. W^m & MA at Dancing School. Mr Burrell & 2 Sons drank Tea here, Mrs Bartell & Son drank Tea & Supt here. Mr Hardy at home all Day . . .

AUGUST 27, WEDNESDAY A fine Day. W & MA at School, Mr Hardy at home all Day.

AUGUST 28, THURSDAY *Cawston Sheep shew* A fine Day. I Bathd. W & MA at School, Mr Hardy at home all Day. Mrs Lawrence & Mrs Squires from Norwich came Even 3.

AUGUST 29, FRIDAY A very Wet Morn, somthing dryer Afternoon. Mrs Larrence & Mrs Sqires, Mr Hardy, I & MA drank Tea at Mr Bartells. Mr Drosier of Blakeney Died this Afternoon.

AUGUST 30, SATURDAY A fine dry Day. I bathd. W & MA at School. Mrs Lawrence & Mrs Sqires went away M8. I & MA drank Tea at Mr Bartls [Bartell's].

AUGUST 31, SUNDAY A fine dry day. All went to our Church foornoon, Mr Burrell preachd . . .

SEPTEMBER 2, TUESDAY A very fine Day. W & MA at School. Mr Hardy at Mr Bartells & Mr Bakers Afternoon. Maids & Goody Gidney Washd a months Linnen.

SEPTEMBER 3, WEDNESDAY A fine Morn, Wet Even. W^m & MA at School, Mr Hardy at home all day. M^r & Mrs Bartell & a Mr Larrod [?Larwood] drank Tea & Supt here . . .

SEPTEMBER 5, FRIDAY A Cool Windy Day. W^m & MA at School. Messrs Boggis & Cole went away Even 4. Mrs Baker drank Tea here . . .

SEPTEMBER 7, SUNDAY A Showry Day, Wind high. All went to our Church Afternoon, Mr Burrell preachd. Young Edwd Davy drank Tea here. I bathd.

SEPTEMBER 8, MONDAY A Close Cold Day. W^m & MA at Dancing School, Mr Hardy at home all day. I bathd . . .

SEPTEMBER 10, WEDNESDAY A Cold Showry day. W^m & MA at School. Mr Hardy went to Wells MIO, came home Even 7. Miss Bartell here.

SEPTEMBER 11, THURSDAY A Dry Day. W^m at School, Mr Hardy at home all day. Mr Pike of Foulsham Dind here. Miss Bartell went away Even 6. I bathd.

SEPTEMBER 12, FRIDAY A Dry Day. W^m & MA at School. Mr Hardy went to Clay Afternoon, came home Even 7. I bathd. Mr Jennis Buried . . .

SEPTEMBER 14, SUNDAY A fine Day. All went to our Church foornoon, Mr Burrell preachd. Miss Pearmain & Miss Leake drank Tea here.

SEPTEMBER 15, MONDAY A fine Day. W^m & MA at Dancing School, Mr Hardy at home all day. I drank Tea at Mr Davys, Holt. I bathd.

SEPTEMBER 16, TUESDAY Fine Morn, Wet Afternoon. Mr Hardy at home all Day, W^m & MA at School.

SEPTEMBER 17, WEDNESDAY A fine day. W at School, Mr Hardy at home all day. Mrs Davy & 2 Childr^n drank Tea here.

SEPTEMBER 18, THURSDAY A Close mild Day. W at School, Mr Hardy at home all Day. I bathd.

SEPTEMBER 19, FRIDAY A very fine Day. W^m at School. I & Mr Hardy & MA drank Tea at Mr Burrells, M^r & Mrs Rouse there. I bathd.

SEPTEMBER 20, SATURDAY A Wet Morn, dry Aftern. Mr Hardy, I & MA went to Holt Afternoon, drank Tea & Supt at Mr Bartells. I bathd.

SEPTEMBER 21, SUNDAY A fine day. All went to our Church Afternoon, Mr Burrell preachd. I bathd.

SEPTEMBER 22, MONDAY A very Wet Day. Mr Hardy at home all Day . . .

SEPTEMBER 26, FRIDAY A fine Day. Mr Hardy at Justice Sitting at Holt, Dind at Mr Bartells. M^r & Mrs Bartell, Mrs Wymer, M^r & M^{rs} & Miss Baldin & a Mr Page from London drank Tea & Supt here . . .

SEPTEMBER 28, SUNDAY A very fine Day. All went to our Church foornoon, Mr Burrell preachd. I poorly.

SEPTEMBER 29, MONDAY A very fine Day. I poorly, rid up to Holt foornoon, Mr Bartell Bled me. M^{rs} & Miss Baker & Mrs Davy drank Tea here . . .

OCTOBER 3, FRIDAY A fine Day. Mr Hardy poorly.

OCTOBER 4, SATURDAY A fine Day. Mr Hardy poorly. A Petty Sessions at Holt . . .

OCTOBER 9, THURSDAY Sharp frosty Morn, A fine Day. Mr Hardy somthing better.

OCTOBER 10, FRIDAY A fine Day. Mr Hardy poorly. MA at School . . .

OCTOBER 12, SUNDAY A very fine Day. W^m & MA went to our Church foornoon, Mr Burrell preachd. M^r &

Mrs Baker & all their Childr^n drank Tea here. Mr Hardy much as yesterday.

OCTOBER 13, MONDAY A very fine warm Day. Mr Hardy very finely. MA at School . . .

OCTOBER 16, THURSDAY A dry Day. MA at School. Mr Hardy poorly, at home all Day . . .

OCTOBER 19, SUNDAY A Close dry Day. Mr Hardy poorly. All went to our Church Aftern, Mr Burrell preachd. Mastr Bartell drank Tea here . . .

OCTOBER 22, WEDNESDAY A fine Day. MA at School, Mr Hardy at home all Day . . .

OCTOBER 24, FRIDAY A Windy Morn, Wet Aftern. MA at School, Mr Hardy at home all Day & poorly. Mr Burrell drank Tea here, Mr Mathews & Mr Bolton here in the Even'g.

OCTOBER 25, SATURDAY A fine Day. MA at School, Mr Hardy at home all Day. I & MA walkd up to Holt Afternoon, I drank Tea at Miss Leakes, MA drank Tea at Mrs Garlands . . .

OCTOBER 28, TUESDAY A fine Day. MA at School, Mr Hardy at home all day. Maids & Goody Gidney Washd.

OCTOBER 29, WEDNESDAY A very fine Day. Mr Hardy at home all Day. J Burrell went to Cambridge.

OCTOBER 30, THURSDAY A very fine day. MA at School, Mr Hardy at home all Day.

OCTOBER 31, FRIDAY A fine dry Day. MA at School, Mr Hardy at home all Day . . .

NOVEMBER 2, SUNDAY A fine Day. All went to our Church Afternoon, Mr Burrell preachd. Mr Curle went away Even 3. Mr Burrell here in the Even . . .

NOVEMBER 4, TUESDAY A fine Day. I, Mr Hardy & MA drank Tea & Supt at Mr Bartells.

NOVEMBER 5, WEDNESDAY A very Close cold Day. M^r & Mrs Bartell drank Tea & Supt here . . .

NOVEMBER 7, FRIDAY A very fine Day. MA at School, Mr Hardy at home all Day. M^{rs} & Miss Baker drank Tea & Supt here, Mr Baker here in Even.

NOVEMBER 8, SATURDAY A very fine Day. MA at School, Mr Hardy at home all Day. I & MA walkd up to Holt Aftern, drank Tea at Mr Davys . . .

NOVEMBER 12, WEDNESDAY A Dry Day. Mr Hardy at home all Day . . .

NOVEMBER 14, FRIDAY A very Wet & Windy Morn, fine Afternoon. Mr Hardy at home all Day.

NOVEMBER 15, SATURDAY A Dry Day. I & MA & M [Mr] Hardy walkd to Holt, drank Tea & Supt at Mr Bartells, W^m came for us with the Cart.

NOVEMBER 16, SUNDAY A Close Dry Day. All went to our Church Afternoon, Mr Burrell preachd.

NOVEMBER 17, MONDAY A Close Day, wind high. MA at School, Mr Hardy at home all Day.

NOVEMBER 18, TUESDAY Very fine Mild Day. MA at School, Mr Hardy at home all Day. Mr Dew of Swanton [Novers] drank Tea here. Maids & Goody Gidney Washd 3 Weeks Linnen.

NOVEMBER 19, WEDNESDAY A very Wett Morn, dry Windy Afternoon. Mr Hardy at home all Day, MA at School.

NOVEMBER 20, THURSDAY A very fine Day. Mr Hardy at home all Day, MA at School.

NOVEMBER 21, FRIDAY A fine Day. MA at School, Mr Hardy at home all Day . . .

NOVEMBER 24, MONDAY *New Moon* A Showry Day. MA at School. I & W^m went to Holt Even past 3 to speak to Mrs Bartell, She being very ill. Came home to Tea . . .

NOVEMBER 27, THURSDAY A very fine bright Day. MA at School. Mr Hardy went to Overtons Club at Holt Even 7, came home Eve past 12.

NOVEMBER 28, FRIDAY A very fine Day. MA at School, Mr Hardy at home all Day.

NOVEMBER 29, SATURDAY A very fine Morn, Close hasy Afternoon. MA & I walkd up to Holt, so did Mr Hardy after us. Drank Tea at Mr Seales's & reckd [reckoned] & paid our bill, playd at Cards at Mr Bartells & came home to Supper.

NOVEMBER 30, SUNDAY A very Close hasy Day. All went to our Church Afternoon, Mr Burrell preachd. We all drank Tea at Mr Burrells . . .

DECEMBER 4, THURSDAY A very fine Day. Mr Hardy at home all Day.

DECEMBER 5, FRIDAY A Close Day. MA at School, Mr Hardy at home all Day .

DECEMBER 6, SATURDAY A Close hasy Day. Mr Hardy, I & MA drank Tea & Supt at Mr Bartells.

DECEMBER 7, SUNDAY A Wet Day. All went to our Church foornoon, Mr Burrell preachd.

DECEMBER 8, MONDAY A Close Day. Mr Hardy went to Clay foornoon & drank Tea at Mr Hipkins of Salthouse, came home Even 9 . . .

The visit to Whissonsett
9–22 December 1783

DECEMBER 10, WEDNESDAY A fine Day. At Sister Goggs all Day . . .

DECEMBER 16, TUESDAY A Close Day. Mrs Custance went home after Dinner. Sister Raven at the Hall & Sister N Raven drank Tea with us Aftern.

DECEMBER 17, WEDNESDAY A Close Day. Sister N Raven drank Tea & Supt with us . . .

DECEMBER 20, SATURDAY A Close Day. I drank Tea at Sister Goggs Aftern. Mr Hardy at Mr Bartells . . .

[LETHERINGSETT]

DECEMBER 24, WEDNESDAY A Close Cold Day. Mr Hardy at home all Day.

DECEMBER 25, THURSDAY *Chrismas Day* A very Sharp rime frost. I & Childr^n at Church foorn, Mr Burrell preachd & Administerd the Communion. Mr Hardy at home all Day. A great deal of Snow fell in the Night.

DECEMBER 26, FRIDAY A Sharp Frost, & some Snow fell. Mr Hardy at home all Day. M^r & Mrs Bartell drank Tea & Supt here.

DECEMBER 27, SATURDAY A Sharp Frost & deep Snow. Mr Hardy went to Holt Market Even 3, came home Even 7.

DECEMBER 28, SUNDAY A Sharp Frost, a deal of Snow fell. All went to our Church Afternoon, Mr Burrell preachd.

DECEMBER 29, MONDAY A very Sharp Frost. Mr Hardy at home all Day. I & Mrs Prior walkd up to Holt Afternoon, came back to Tea.

DECEMBER 30, TUESDAY Excesive sharp Frost. I & Mr Hardy drank Tea & Supt at Mr Bakers, Willm Supt there . . .

1784

JANUARY 1, THURSDAY A Slow thaw. I & Ravn & MA went up to Holt, drank Tea at Mr Davys, Mast^r Bartell came home with us.

JANUARY 2, FRIDAY Thawd a little & Snowd, but Excesive Cold & Wind high. We all drank Tea & Supt at Mr Bartells, came home Morn 2. A very Stormy Night & Wind high. Raven Slept at Mr Bartells.

JANUARY 3, SATURDAY A very Coarse Day, Thawd a little. Mast^r House went to Holt M10 for Raven, came home Even 6. Mr Hardy & Willm went to Holt Mark^t Even 4, came home Even 6 . . .

From the newspaper
William Pitt's Government 1784

[[JANUARY 4, SUNDAY . . . [*by William Hardy*] Duke of Richmond, M^r^t Genl of Ordenance; Sr Geo Howard, Comm^n in Ch [Commander-in-Chief] of Forces; Lords of the Treasury, Ld Graham, Edwd Ja^s Elliot, John Buller, John Aubrey; Lords of the Admiralty, Levison Gower, C G Perceval, Lord Apsley, Chas Brett, J M Heywood, J J Pratt; Lord [Lloyd] Kenyon, Attorney General; Richd Pepper Arden, Soliciter Genl; Earl of Salisbury, Ld Chamberlain; Duke of Chando{i}s, Ld Stew^d of H Hold [Household]; Lord De Ferrars, Cap of band of Pensioners [Captain of the Band of Gentlemen Pensioners]; Wm Windh^m Grenville, Joint pay^r of Forces; Hen Dundas, Treas^r of the Navy; Sr Geo Young [Yonge], Secretary at War; Wm Smith, Treas^r of Ordenance; Gibb{e}s Crawford, Clark of D^o; John Aldridge, keeper of D^o; Thos Balee [Baillie], Cl^k to deliverer of D^o [Clerk of the Deliveries of the Ordnance]; Lord Clarendon, Chanceler of Dutchey [Duchy of] Lancast^r; Earle Bathurst, Rang^r of St James s & Green Park; Duke of Dorsett, Ambasador to France; Daniel Ha«i»les, his Secretary; Geo Aug Selwin, Surv^r of Crown Lands; Sam Eastwick, Secr^y & Reg^r of Chelsea Hosp^l; Mr Rose & Mr Steel, Secr^ys to Treasury; Mr Banks, private Secr^y to Mr Wm Pitt; Lord Mahon, Master of the Mint]] . . .

[LETHERINGSETT]

JANUARY 9, FRIDAY A Sharp frost. Mr Hardy at home all Day. Miss Baker & her Bro^t drank Tea here. Jame [James Cornwell] broke down the Wagon.

JANUARY 10, SATURDAY A Close frosty Day. I & MA walkd up to Holt, drank Tea at Miss Leakes, Mr Hardy at Market, came home in Little Cart.

JANUARY 11, SUNDAY A Close frosty Day. All went to our Church Afternoon, Mr Burrell preachd. M^r & Mrs Davy & 4 of their Childr^n drank Tea here & Mr Burrell . . .

JANUARY 14, WEDNESDAY A Slow Thaw & foggy. Mr Hardy at home all Day, 3 Mill Wrights at work.

JANUARY 15, THURSDAY A Wet Morn, dry Windy Afternoon. Mr Hardy at home all Day, 3 Mill Wrights at work . . .

JANUARY 23, FRIDAY A Sharp Frost, Deep Snow. I poorly. Raven went away Even 2, Mr Hardy at home all Day.

JANUARY 24, SATURDAY A Sharp frost, very Chearly Day. Deep Snow. Mr Hardy went to Mark^t Even 4, came home Even 7 . . .

JANUARY 26, MONDAY A very Sharp rime frost & very Close, Deep Snow. Mr Hardy at home all Day . . .

JANUARY 28, WEDNESDAY A very Sharp frost, Deep Snow. 2 Millwrights at work. Mr Hardy went to Overtons Club Even 7, came home Eve 12.

JANUARY 29, THURSDAY A Sharp Frost, wind high. Deep Snow, Snowd a considerable deal. 2 Mill Wrights at Work. Mr Hardy & I walkd up to Holt, drank Tea & Supt at Mr Bartells, home Even 12.

JANUARY 30, FRIDAY A Sharp frost & Chearly, Deep Snow. 2 Mill Wrights at Work foornoon, 1 in Afternoon. Mr Hardy at home all Day, Mr & Mrs Bartell drank Tea & supt here.

JANUARY 31, SATURDAY A Sharp Frost, deep Snow & frequent Storms of Snow. Mr Hardy, I & MA walkd up to Holt, drank Tea at Mr Davys . . .

FEBRUARY 3, TUESDAY A very Sharp Frost, deep Snow & very much driftd. Maids & Goody Gidney Washd 3 Weeks Linnen . . .

FEBRUARY 5, THURSDAY A Wet foornoon, Thawd very fast but very Cold. 2 Mill wrights at Work. Mr Hardy at home all Day. Snowd a great deal in the Night.

FEBRUARY 6, FRIDAY Snowd great part of the Day, very deep & very Cold. 2 Mill wrights at Work. Mr Hardy at home all Day.

FEBRUARY 7, SATURDAY Snow dccp, a very Stormy coarse Day. 2 Mill wrights at work. Mr Hardy went to Markt Even 3, came home Morn 3. A deal of Snow fell in the Night . . .

FEBRUARY 9, MONDAY Deep Snow, very Sharp Stormy Day. 2 Mill Wrights at work. Mr Hardy at home all Day . . .

FEBRUARY 11, WEDNESDAY A very Severe frost, Bright Day. Deep Snow. M^r & Mrs Bartell drank Tea & Supt here.

FEBRUARY 12, THURSDAY Deep Snow & very Severe Frost & very Close. Mr Hardy at home all Day, Mr Burrell drank Tea here. 2 Mill Wrts at Work, Taylor Westby [Westby the tailor] at work. {2 Mill Wrights at Work.}

FEBRUARY 13, FRIDAY Deep Snow, very Severe frost & very Close, wind reather high. Mr Hardy, I & MA drank Tea at Mr Burrells. Taylor Westby at work, 2 M Wrights . . .

FEBRUARY 15, SUNDAY A very deep Snow, Close cold day. All went to our Church foornoon, Mr Burrell preachd.

FEBRUARY 16, MONDAY A Deep Snow much drifted. A very Sharp frost, wind rough. Mr Hardy at home all Day. Paul Myles here Afternoon, brought a Letter & Writing from Mr Bucks.

FEBRUARY 17, TUESDAY A Deep Snow & very Sharp frost. Mr Hardy at home all Day. 2 Mill wrights at work.

FEBRUARY 18, WEDNESDAY Much such weather as Yesterd«ay». 3 Mill Wrights at Work. Mr Hardy at home all Day. Mr Hewit of Thornage came Even 1, drank Tea & Supt here. Heard Mr Goggs was very Ill again . . .

FEBRUARY 21, SATURDAY A Slow Thaw all Day. Mill Wrights went away at Noon. Mr Hardy & W^m went to Holt Market Even 2, came home Even 8.

FEBRUARY 22, SUNDAY A Slow Thaw, Raind a little Afternoon. All went to our Church Afternoon, Mr Burrell preachd & drank Tea here.

FEBRUARY 23, MONDAY A very fine Chearly Day. Thaw continue, Snow very much wasted, a Large Flood. Roads exceeding bad, in many places unpasable. M^r & Mrs Bartell drank Tea & Supt here.

FEBRUARY 24, TUESDAY *Matthias* A Close Day, raind a little Afternoon, Water very high in River. Mr Hardy at home all Day . . .

FEBRUARY 26, THURSDAY A Close Day, rain towds Even. Mr Hardy at home all Day, 2 Mill Wrights at work. Messrs Foster & Balls here in Even . . .

FEBRUARY 29, SUNDAY A fine Dry Day. All went to our Church foornoon, Mr Burrell preachd. M^r & Mrs Baker & 2 Childrn drank Tea here. A Frosty Night . . .

MARCH 3, WEDNESDAY A very Cold Close Day. 2 Mill Wrights at Work. Ratt Catcher here. Mr Hardy at home all Day, went to Holt Club Even 7, came home Even past 11.

MARCH 4, THURSDAY A Showry Morn, Mild Day. 2 Mill Wrights at Work. Ratt Catcher went away. Mr Hardy set of for Fakenh«a»m & Whisinsett Morn 10. MA & I walkd up to Holt Afternoon, drank Tea at Miss Leakes . . .

MARCH 11, THURSDAY A Cold Dry Day, Snowd in Morng. 4 M Wrights at Work, Mr Hardy at home all Day. Miss Baker drank Tea here, Miss Custance Slept here. M^r & Mrs Bartell drank Tea & Supt here.

MARCH 12, FRIDAY A very Cold Dry Day. 4 M Wrts at Work, Mr Hardy at home all Day. W^m, MA, Phillis & Miss Custance went up to Holt Aftr in L Cart, drank Tea at Mr Bakers . . .

MARCH 15, MONDAY Very Sharp frost, Chearly Day. 4 M Wrights, 3 Gardiners at Work & Old Duke in Gardn. Mr Hardy at home all Day . . .

MARCH 17, WEDNESDAY A very Sharp Day. 4 M Wrights at work. Mr Hardy rid to Briston, spoke to Mendham abt a Bond of Shores, came home Even 6 . . .

MARCH 20, SATURDAY A Stormy Day. 4 M Wrts at work, Mr Hardy at home all Day. I & W^m & MA rid up to Holt Afternoon, drank Tea at Mrs Bartells.

MARCH 21, SUNDAY A Chearly Day. All went to our Church Afternoon, Mr Burrell preachd. We took a walk after Church, Mr Baker & P Myles came in the Eveng . . .

MARCH 26, FRIDAY Excesive Sharp Stormy Day. Mr Hardy at home all day. 4 M Wrights at Work.

MARCH 27, SATURDAY A tolerable Day. H Goggs & R Rav^n went away after Dinner. MA & I walkd up to Holt, Mr Hardy & Raven follow'd us, drank Tea & Supt at Mr Bartells. W^m came for us in Little Cart.

MARCH 28, SUNDAY A very Cold Windy Day. All went to our Church foornoon, Mr Burrell preachd. Rav^n went up to Holt Aftern, drank Tea at Mr Bartells. Fisget [?] Thompson drank Tea here . . .

MARCH 31, WEDNESDAY A Sharp frost, wind high & very Stormy. Mr Hardy at home all Day. J Davison came, Slept here. A deal of Snow fell in the Night. Our Boy Carried a Letter to Mr Smiths, Tenninham [? Trimingham] . . .

APRIL 2, FRIDAY A Sharp frost in Morng & deep Snow but thawd all Day. Mr Hardy at home all Day.

APRIL 3, SATURDAY A very Cold close Day. I & W^m rid up to Holt in L Cart, drank Tea at Mr Bakers. Mr Hardy at home all Day . . .

APRIL 10, SATURDAY A tolerable Day but Cold. I walk^d up to Holt with Mrs Rouse, drank Tea at Mr Davys. Mr Hardy walkd up to Markt, drank Tea at Mr Bakers, came home past 7.

APRIL 11, SUNDAY A Dry Morng, Wet Stormy Aftern. All went to our Church foornoon. Mr Burrell preachd & had a Communion . . .

APRIL 15, THURSDAY A very fine Day. 2 M Wrights at work. Mr Hardy came home from Norwich Even 8.

APRIL 16, FRIDAY A Wet Morng, close Aftern. 2 M Wrights at work, Mr Hardy at home all Day.

APRIL 17, SATURDAY A fine Chearly Day. Mr Ram of Swannington Dind here. I & Mr Hardy walkd up to Holt Mark^t, I & Mrs Rouse drank Tea at Miss Leakes. Mrs Bartell came home from Norwich . . .

APRIL 20, TUESDAY A fine Day. Mr Hardy at home all Day. Raind a good deal in the Night . . .

APRIL 22, THURSDAY Wet Morn, Wind high, fine Aftern. Mr Hardy at home all Day . . .

APRIL 24, SATURDAY A Cold Showry Day. Mr Hardy went to Holt Mark^t Even 3, came home Eve past 10.

APRIL 25, SUNDAY *St Mark* A fine Day. All went to our Church foornoon, Mr Burrell preachd. Raven came from N Walshm to Dinner. Mast^r Bartell drank Tea here . . .

MAY 1, SATURDAY A Close cold Showry Day. Mr Hardy went to Mark^t Even past 2, drank Tea at Mr Bartells, came home Even 8, I & W^m walkd up after Tea . . .

MAY 7, FRIDAY A Dry Windy Day. Mr Erwin Dind here, Mr Hardy at home all Day.

MAY 8, SATURDAY A Close windy Day. I & Mr Hardy walkd up to Holt Afternoon, drank Tea at Mr Bakers, W^m came for us in L Cart.

MAY 9, SUNDAY A fine Warm Day. All went to our Church foornoon, Mr Burrell preachd. Mr Bartell came & Bled me After Noon . . .

MAY 13, THURSDAY A fine Dry Day, brisk wind. Old Duke & 2 Men at work in Shrubry. Mr Hardy at home all Day. W^m sett of for Whisinsett Morn half pst 4, came home Even 9.

MAY 14, FRIDAY A Showry Day. Mr Hardy at home all Day. Carpenter & 2 Men at Work in Shruberry.

MAY 15, SATURDAY A very warm Dry Day. I & Mr Hardy walkd up to Holt Afternoon. I drank Tea at Mr Bartells, Mrs Bartell gone to Norwich. Bay Mare had Horse . . .

MAY 17, MONDAY A Hot dry Day. Mr Hardy at home all Day. Men at Plow & some in Garden. I walkd up to Holt after Tea . . .

MAY 19, WEDNESDAY A Hot Dry Day. Mr Hardy went to Hildonveston Afternoon, home Even 8. Mrs Baker drank Tea here. N Walsham Fair . . .

MAY 22, SATURDAY A very hot dry Day. Mr Hardy went to Mark^t Afternoon, I walkd up after Tea. I poorly in the Eveng.

MAY 23, SUNDAY Exessive Hot dry Morn, some Showers with Thund^r towards Even. M^r & Mrs Buck & Raven came to Dinner, M^r & Mrs Bartell & 2 Childr^n drank Tea here.

MAY 24, MONDAY A Showry Morn, very fine Day. M^r & Mrs Buck & Rav^n went away Even past 3. Mr Hardy went to Baconsthorpe Aftern, drank Tea at Mr Hewits, home past 8. W^m went to Holt after Tea.

MAY 25, TUESDAY A very fine Hot Day. Maids & Goody Gidney Wash^d 3 Weeks Linnen. Mr Hardy at home all Day. Some Showers in the Night.

MAY 26, WEDNESDAY Very Hot, wind blustering. Mr Hardy at home all day. Bro^t Nathl & Robt Fox came Even 4, Slept here. A good deal of rain with Lightning in the Night.

MAY 27, THURSDAY A very fine Day. Mr Hardy & Bro^t at Holt foornoon, came back to Dinner. Bro^t & Robt Fox went away after Tea.

MAY 28, FRIDAY Fine Day, a great Showr ab^t Noon. Mr Hardy went to Mr Thos Hewits foornoon, came home to Dinner. Sent the Boy to Fakenham with M Anns things.

MAY 29, SATURDAY A dry Morn, Wet Aftern. Mr Hardy poorly, did not go to Mark^t. I & W^m walkd up to Holt after Tea. Mr Davys Child Alice Died Sudenly this Morng.

MAY 30, SUNDAY A Wet Morng, dry Aftern. All went to our Church Afternoon, Mr Burrell preachd. We walkd up to Furr Closes after Tea . . .

JUNE 3, THURSDAY A Cold Close Day. I & Mr Hardy went to Holt Afternoon, drank Tea & Supt at Mr Bartells, W^m came in Eveng . . .

JUNE 5, SATURDAY A very fine Day. Mr Hardy at home all Day. I & W^m walkd up to Holt after Tea.

JUNE 6, SUNDAY A small rain great part of the Day. All went to our Church foornoon, Mr Burrell preachd, had a Communion . . .

JUNE 8, TUESDAY Wet Morn, cold hasy Day. Mr Hardy at home all Day . . .

JUNE 13, SUNDAY A very fine Morn, Showry Day. All went to our Church Afternoon, Mr Burrell preachd . . .

JUNE 16, WEDNESDAY Showry Day. Mr Hardy at home all Day.

JUNE 17, THURSDAY {A} some small Showers. Mr Hardy at home all Day.

JUNE 18, FRIDAY A fine Morn, Showry Aftrn. M^r & Mrs Moy, M^r & Mrs Johnson & 3 Childr^n drank Tea here. Mr Hardy at home all Day.

JUNE 19, SATURDAY A tolerable Day. I & Mr Hardy & MA walkd up to Holt Afternoon, drank Tea at Mr Davys. W^m came for us in L Cart.

JUNE 20, SUNDAY A fine Day. All went to our Church foornoon, Mr Burrell preachd. M^r & Mrs Bartell at Mr Rouses.

JUNE 21, MONDAY A fine Morn, very Showry Afternoon. Mr Hardy at home all Day. M^r & Mrs Bartell & Miss Wymer drank Tea & Supt here. Miss Brantwait, the two Miss Chicheleys, Miss Rouse & 2 Miss Davys drank Tea here . . .

JUNE 23, WEDNESDAY A Showry Day. Mr Hardy at home all Day. MA at Mr Rouses to meet some young Company to Dance.

JUNE 24, THURSDAY Dry Morn, very Wet Day. MA drank Tea at Mr Bartells. Mr Hardy set of for Walsingham Even 2, staid all Night at Mr Howards . . .

JUNE 26, SATURDAY A dry Morn, Wet Aftern. I & MA walkd to Holt Afternoon, MA drank Tea at Mrs Davys, I drank Tea at Mr Bartells & all Supt there, came home Even 11.

JUNE 27, SUNDAY A Wet Day. All went to our Church Afternoon, Mr Burrell preachd . . .

JUNE 29, TUESDAY A Close Dry Day. Mr Hardy at home all Day. Sister Raven, Childr^n & I walkd up to Holt after Tea.

JUNE 30, WEDNESDAY A Close Dry Day. Peter Allexander & Thos Erwin Dind here. Sister Raven, Childr^n & I & Mr Hardy drank Tea at Mr Bakers.

JULY 1, THURSDAY A Close Dry Day. Mr Hardy at home all Day. M^r & Mrs Bensley, M^r & Mrs Baker drank Tea here.

JULY 2, FRIDAY A fine Day. Sister Raven & I rid up to Holt foornoon. Raven came from N Walsham, M^r & Mrs Bartell drank Tea & Supt here.

JULY 3, SATURDAY A fine Dry Day. Mr Hardy, I, Sister Raven & 4 of the Childr^n walkd up to Holt Afternoon, drank Tea at Mr Bensleys, home Even 8. Bro^t & Robt Raven came Even past 7 . . .

JULY 5, MONDAY A very hot dry Day. Mr Hardy at home all Day. Bro^t & Sister Raven & Childr^n went away Even 6, Raven set off at the same time . . .

JULY 7, WEDNESDAY Excesive hot Day. Mr Hardy, I & M Ann rid to Briston after Tea. Men carried Hay. A Tempest with rain in the Night. Taylor Westby at work.

JULY 8, THURSDAY A fine dry Day. Mr Hardy at home all Day. W^m & M Ann rid to Clay & Salthouse Afternoon, came back to Tea. Taylor Westby at work.

JULY 9, FRIDAY A fine Day. Mr Hardy at home all Day. Taylor Westby at work.

JULY 10, SATURDAY A very fine Day. I & MA walkd up to Markt Aftern, drank Tea at Mr Bartells, Mr Hardy there. Taylor Westby at Work . . .

JULY 16, FRIDAY A fine Day. Mr Hardy at home all Day . . .

JULY 18, SUNDAY A very fine Dry Day. All went to our Church foornoon, Mr Burrell preachd. M^r & Mrs Seales drank Tea here Afternoon . . .

JULY 22, THURSDAY A very Wet Day. 2 Gardiners came to work, were oblidgd to leave of at 10 oClock on Acct of the rain. Mr Hardy at home all Day.

JULY 23, FRIDAY A very fine Day. Mr Hardy at home all Day. We Supt at Mr Burrells . . .

JULY 25, SUNDAY A Showry Day. All went to our Church Afternoon, Mr Burrell read a Lecture. M^r & Mrs Seales at Church & drank Tea at Mr Balls s, Mr Burrell & Son drank Tea here.

JULY 26, MONDAY A Showry Day. Mr Hardy at home all Day, Robt Jeckell of Hayden [Heydon] here. I & Mrs Rouse walkd up to Holt Afternoon, drank Tea at Mr Davys. W^m at Dancing School, came for me in L Cart.

JULY 27, TUESDAY Very Wet foornoon, dry Afternoon. Mr Hardy went to Overtons Bowling Green Afternoon, came home Even 8 . . .

JULY 31, SATURDAY A Close dry Day. I & Mr Hardy walkd up to Holt Afternoon, drank Tea at Mr Bartells. Myles Raven came home with us & Slept here . . .

AUGUST 4, WEDNESDAY A fine Dry Day. Mr Hardy at home all day. M^r & Mrs Bartell & Mrs Baker & 2 Childrn drank Tea here. Norwich Assises began . . .

AUGUST 6, FRIDAY A Showry Morn, very Wet Afternoon. Expected Mr Hardy home, did not come.

AUGUST 7, SATURDAY A fine Day. Mr Hardy did not come home. I & Mrs Rouse walkd up to Holt Afternoon, drank Tea at Miss Leakes. Raind in the Night . . .

AUGUST 11, WEDNESDAY A dry Day. Mr Hardy at home all Day.

AUGUST 12, THURSDAY A Dry Day, very warm. Mr Hardy & I drank Tea & Supt at Mr Bartells.

AUGUST 13, FRIDAY Very hot Day, Cloudy Aftern but did not rain. Mr Hardy went to Mr Harris s of Hildonveston Even 4, came home Even 10.

AUGUST 14, SATURDAY A Hot dry Day. I & Mr Hardy walkd up to Holt Mark^t, drank Tea at Mr Bartells.

AUGUST 15, SUNDAY Very Hot dry Day. All went to our Church foornoon, Mr Burrell preachd. Miss Leake & Miss Pearmain & a young Girl drank Tea here. Mr Shore & Mr Clarke here, Jo^s Baker Dind here & reckd.

AUGUST 16, MONDAY A fine dry Day, cooler then yesterday. W^m at Dancing School, Mr Hardy at home all Day. Mrs Davy & Miss Bacon calld in the Eveng.

AUGUST 17, TUESDAY A Close Cool Day. Fanny Gidney & Maids Washd. Mr Hardy at home all Day.

AUGUST 18, WEDNESDAY A very Cold Day, Wind high. Mr Hardy at home all Day . . .

AUGUST 21, SATURDAY A Close Windy Day, Showers Afternoon. I & Mr Hardy walkd up to Holt Afternoon, drank Tea & Supt at Mr Bartells, came home Even 12, M^r & Mrs Wymer of Norwich there.

AUGUST 22, SUNDAY A very Close Windy Morng, Wet Afternoon. I taken poorly with [ ] in my Head & Eyes. Mr Wymer & Mr Bartell call«ed» foornoon. All went to our Church Aftern, Mr Burrell read a Lecture. M^r & Mrs Bartell, M^r & Mrs Wymer & George Wymer Junr, Mrs Baldin & Daught^r, M^r & Mrs Raven of Norwich, M^r J Johnson of Clay & Mr Bartells 3 Childrn drank Tea here . . .

AUGUST 24, TUESDAY A tolerable Morn, Dark Drisly Afternoon. Mr Hardy at home all Day. Mrs Balden & Daugh^tr, Mrs Raven, M^r & Mrs Bartell Dind, drank Tea & Supt here . . .

AUGUST 26, THURSDAY A very Wet Day. Mr Hardy at home all Day . . .

AUGUST 28, SATURDAY A dry Morn, very great Showr abt 6 oClock. I walk'd up to Holt Aftrn, drank Tea at Mr Davys. Mr Hardy went to Clay Afternoon, came home Even 8. I saw Miss Borne [Boorne] at Holt . . .

SEPTEMBER 6, MONDAY Excesive Hot Day. Mr Hardy at home all Day. M^r & Mrs Bartell drank Tea & Supt here.

SEPTEMBER 7, TUESDAY A fine Day. I & Mr Hardy walkd up to Holt Afternoon, drank Tea at Mr Bakers. Mrs Baker sent for to Mrs Man of Clay, she being very Ill.

SEPTEMBER 8, WEDNESDAY Excesive Hot Day. Mr Boorne of Coltishall Dind here. Mr Hardy at home all Day.

SEPTEMBER 9, THURSDAY Very hot Day, hosy [hazy] towards Even. Mr Hardy at home all Day.

SEPTEMBER 10, FRIDAY Fine Day but not so hot as Yesterday. I walkd up to Holt Afternoon, drank Tea & Supt at Mr Bartells, W^m came for me. Mr Hardy should have come, did not . . .

SEPTEMBER 12, SUNDAY A very Hot Day. All went to our Church foornoon, Mr Burrell preachd . . .

SEPTEMBER 16, THURSDAY A fine Day. Men carried Barly. Mr Hardy at home all Day. M^r & Mrs Bartell drank Tea here . . .

SEPTEMBER 19, SUNDAY A very fine Day. All went to our Church Afternoon, Mr Burrell read a Lecture . . .

SEPTEMBER 22, WEDNESDAY A tolerable Day. Bricklayers & Carpenters at Work in Counting House. I & Mr Hardy went to Holt, drank Tea & Supt at Mr Bartells . . .

SEPTEMBER 27, MONDAY A very cold Showry day. Mr Hardy at home all Day.

SEPTEMBER 28, TUESDAY A very Wet foornoon, Close Showry Afternoon. Mr Hardy at home all Day. I & Mrs Boorne & W^m rid up to Holt foornoon, went up in Afternoon & drank Tea at Mr Bartells . . .

OCTOBER 1, FRIDAY A fine Day. Raven & I & MA drank Tea at Mr Bartells, Raven went home ½ past 6. Mr Hardy came for us in Even, came home Even 9 . . .

OCTOBER 3, SUNDAY A Close Cold Day. All went to our Church Afternoon, Mr Burrell preachd. Mr Baker call^d in the Even . . .

OCTOBER 6, WEDNESDAY A very fine Day. Maids & Goody Gidney Washd 3 Weeks Linnen. Mr Hardy set of for Norwich after Dinner . . .

OCTOBER 8, FRIDAY A very fine Day. Mr Hardy at home all Day.

OCTOBER 9, SATURDAY A Close cold Day. I & Mr Hardy walkd up to Holt Sessions Aftrn. I drank Tea at Mr Bartels, Mr Hardy drank Tea at Mr Davys, home Eve 8 . . .

OCTOBER 17, SUNDAY A very fine Day. All went to our Church Afternoon, Mr Burrell preachd. Miss Leake, Mr Rowe & another Gentleman drank Tea here. M Anns Foot Sore.

OCTOBER 18, MONDAY A very fine Day. Mr Hardy at home all Day. M^rs & Miss Baker drank Tea & Supt here. M Ans foot very bad . . .

OCTOBER 21, THURSDAY [at North Walsham] A very fine Day. After Brkfst walkd to M^r [Neale] Ravens, went back & Dind at Mr Bucks, set of for home Even 3, got home Even pst 7.

OCTOBER 22, FRIDAY A Close Cold Day. Mr Bensley here foornoon & recknd. Mr Hardy & Messrs Burrell drank Tea at Mr Bensleys. M^r & Mrs Bartell drank Tea & Supt here.

OCTOBER 23, SATURDAY A Close Morn, Showry Day. Mr Hardy walkd up to Holt Afternoon, drank Tea & Supt at Mr Bartells.

OCTOBER 24, SUNDAY A very Showry Day. All went to our Church foornoon, Mr Burrell preachd . . .

OCTOBER 26, TUESDAY A Cold Stormy Day. Mr Hardy at home all Day . . .

OCTOBER 29, FRIDAY A Cold Close Day. Mr Hardy at home all Day.

OCTOBER 30, SATURDAY A fine Morn, Close Showry Afternoon. Mr Hardy sett of for Coltishall Even 1. I & MA walkd up to Holt Afternoon, drank Tea at Mr Bartells, came home E8. MA taken very poorly.

OCTOBER 31, SUNDAY A Wet Day. I & W^m went to our Church Afternoon, Mr Burrell preach'd. MA very poorly, could not go to Church . . .

NOVEMBER 4, THURSDAY A Close cold Day. MA very bad, sent for Mr Bartell. Mr Hardy at home all Day.

NOVEMBER 5, FRIDAY A Close cold day. MA very bad. Mr Hardy at home all Day.

NOVEMBER 6, SATURDAY A Cold windy Day. MA something better. Mr Hardy went to Holt Mark^t Even 3, came home Even 8.

NOVEMBER 7, SUNDAY A Stormy Day. All went to our Church foornoon, Mr Burrell preachd. MA finely. Mr Baker drank Tea here, Mr Howard of Walsingham drank Tea, Supt & Slept here.

NOVEMBER 8, MONDAY A Cold Chearly Day. Mr Howard went away after Breakfst. Mr Hardy at home all Day. MA finely . . .

NOVEMBER 11, THURSDAY A very Stormy Day. M^r & Mrs Moy & M^r & Mrs Raven calld here Morn past [ ] as they were going home. Mr Hardy at home all Day.

NOVEMBER 12, FRIDAY A Dry Day. Mr Hardy at home all Day . . .

NOVEMBER 14, SUNDAY A Close drisley Day. All went to our Church Afternoon, Mr Burrell preachd. Paul Miles Dind & Slept her«e». Wind high at Night.

NOVEMBER 15, MONDAY A Close Windy Morng, very Wet Afternoon. I & Mr Hardy walkd up to Holt Aftrn to see Mr Jewell Burried, drank Tea at Mr Bakers, came home Even past 9.

NOVEMBER 16, TUESDAY A fine Day. Mr Hardy at home all day. Thos Westby at work.

NOVEMBER 17, WEDNESDAY A fine Day. Mr Hardy at home. T Westby at work . . .

NOVEMBER 19, FRIDAY A fine Day. Mr Hardy went up to Holt M11 to the Justice Sitting, came home Even 4. Thos Westby at work.

NOVEMBER 20, SATURDAY A very Cold Day, Stormes of Hail & Snow. Mr Hardy walkd up to Holt, drank Tea at Mr Bartells. I & MA walkd up, drank Tea at Mr Seales's, came home Eve 9. Thos Westby at Work . . .

NOVEMBER 27, SATURDAY A Close dry Day. I & M Ann walkd to Holt Afternoon, drank Tea at Miss Leakes, Mr Hardy drank Tea at Mr Bartells, came home Even 8.

NOVEMBER 28, SUNDAY A Close Day. All went to our Church Afternoon, Mr Burrell preachd. We drank Tea at Mr Burrells. Raind in the Night.

NOVEMBER 29, MONDAY A Chearly Day. Mr Hardy at home all Day . . .

DECEMBER 2, THURSDAY A Chearly Day. Mr Minns here foornoon & Mr Baker, Mr Hankenson of Lynn here afternoon. Mr Hardy at home all Day . . .

DECEMBER 5, SUNDAY A rime frost, Wet Afternoon. All went to our Church foorn, Mr Burrell preachd. Wind very high in the Night . . .

DECEMBER 7, TUESDAY A very Cold Wet Day. Mr Hardy at home all Day. Wind high . . .

DECEMBER 9, THURSDAY A Sharp frosty Air & Snowd all the Foornoon, Clear Aftrn. Mr Hardy at home all Day. Paul Myles here Afternoon.

DECEMBER 10, FRIDAY A very Sharp frost. M^r & Mrs Bartell drank Tea & Supt here. Mr Hardy at home all Day . . .

DECEMBER 12, SUNDAY A very Stormy Day & Thawd. All went to our Church Afternoon, Mr Burrell preachd.

DECEMBER 13, MONDAY A very Cold Close Day. Mr Hardy sett of for Coltishall & Norwich Morn 10 . . .

DECEMBER 15, WEDNESDAY A very Stormy Day. Mr Hardy came from Norwich Even 7.

DECEMBER 16, THURSDAY A very Cold Stormy Day. Mr Hardy at home all day . . .

DECEMBER 18, SATURDAY A very Close Day. I & Mr Hardy walkd up to Holt Afternoon, drank Tea & Supt at Mr Bartells.

DECEMBER 19, SUNDAY A close Dry Day. All went to our Church foornoon, Mr Burrell preach^d.

DECEMBER 20, MONDAY A Frost, fine Day. I & Mr Hardy, M^r & Mrs Bartell drank Tea at Mr Emmerys, M^r & Mrs Bartell Supt here. A good deal of Snow fell in the Night.

DECEMBER 21, TUESDAY A very Stormy Day. Maids & F Gidney washd. I & Mr Hardy rid up to Holt, I drank Tea at Mr Davys, Mr Hardy at Mr Bartells.

DECEMBER 22, WEDNESDAY A Sharp wind frost. Mr Hardy went to Overtons Club in Eveng, came home pst 11. Recd a Letter from T Neve. Snow fell in the Night . . .

DECEMBER 26, SUNDAY A frosty Morn, reather thawd Afternoon. All went to our Church Afternoon, Mr Burrell preachd . . .

1785

JANUARY 1, SATURDAY A very Sharp Wind frost. Mr Hardy, I, Rav^n & M Ann walk'd up to Holt Afternoon, drank Tea at Mrs Bartells, went to Play at 3^d Act, W^m & Robt Raven came.

JANUARY 2, SUNDAY A Slow Thaw. No Service at our Church, Childr^n went to Holt Church Afternoon . . .

JANUARY 5, WEDNESDAY A very Close foggy Day. Mr Hardy walkd up to Holt foornoon, came back to Dinner. M^r & Mrs Bartell, Mr Yarington & Mr Scraggs drank Tea & Supt here . . .

JANUARY 7, FRIDAY A Sharp Frost. Mr Hardy at home all Day. Mr Bensley & Mr Baker of Holt drank Tea & Supt here, Miss Ann Davy here.

JANUARY 8, SATURDAY A very Close drisly Day. Mr Hardy walkd up to Mark^t, sent MA & Miss Davy up in L«ittle» Cart. W^m & I went to Play After Tea, Mr Hardy & MA there.

JANUARY 9, SUNDAY A very Close Day. All went to our Church Afternoon, Mr Burrell preachd & drank Tea here. I very poorly with a Cold . . .

JANUARY 12, WEDNESDAY A Sharp rime frost. Mr Hardy at home all Day. MA went to Mr Davys of Holt on a Visit. Mr Hardy went to the Play, it was Witmans [Whitman's] benefit.

JANUARY 13, THURSDAY A Close Cold Day. M Ann came home Even 4. Mr Hardy at home all Day, Mr Baker & Old Lawyer Girdlestone Supt here . . .

JANUARY 16, SUNDAY A very Close Day. All went to our Church foornoon except W^m, Mr Burrell preach'd . . .

JANUARY 18, TUESDAY A Close Mild Day. Maids & Fanny Gidney Wash^d 4 Weeks Linnen. Mr Hardy at home all Day.

JANUARY 19, WEDNESDAY A very Close mild Day. Mr Hardy at home all Day. M^r & Mrs Pearsons benifit, heard they had a very full House.

JANUARY 20, THURSDAY A very Mild Foggy Day. Mr Hardy went to Holt Quart^r Sessions Morn past 10, came home Eve past 10 . . .

JANUARY 21, FRIDAY A very fine Day. Mr Hardy at home all Day . . .

JANUARY 23, SUNDAY A very fine Day. All went to our Church Afternoon, Mr Burrell preachd. M^r & Mrs Davy & 3 of their Childr^n drank Tea here.

JANUARY 24, MONDAY A very fine bright Day. Mr Hardy at home all Day. M^r & Mrs Bartell drank Tea & Supt here . . .

JANUARY 27, THURSDAY A very fine bright Day. I & Mr Hardy drank Tea & Supt at Mr Bartells. I poorly . . .

JANUARY 29, SATURDAY A fine Morng but Cold. Mr Hardy walkd to Holt Markt Even 3, drank Tea at Mr Bartells & came home Even 8 . . .

FEBRUARY 1, TUESDAY A Cold Day, wind not so high. Mr Hardy went to Holt MII, Dind at Mr Huguers, drank Tea at Mr Bensleys, home Eve 8 . . .

FEBRUARY 3, THURSDAY A Close Day. I went to Mr Huguers Afternoon & we all drank Tea at Mr Bartells, came home Even 9, Mr Hardy came home at the same time . . .

FEBRUARY 5, SATURDAY A Clear frosty Day. Mr Hardy went to Holt Mark^t Even 3, went to Play & came home pst 12 . . .

FEBRUARY 11, FRIDAY A Close Mild Day. Mr Hardy walkd up into Holt Morn 11 to justice Sitting, Dind at Mr Bakers & came home Even 5 . . .

FEBRUARY 13, SUNDAY A very fine Day. All went to our Church foornoon except W^m, Mr Burrell preachd. M Ann went to Holt Church Afternoon.

FEBRUARY 14, MONDAY *Valentine Day* A Close Cold Day. Mr Hardy at home all day. M^r & Mrs Huguier call«ed» in Even as they came home from Fakenham . . .

FEBRUARY 17, THURSDAY A Sharp frost, frequent Squarles [squalls] of Hail & Snow. Mr Hardy at home all Day.

FEBRUARY 18, FRIDAY Sharp frost with frequent Storms of Snow. Mr Hardy at home all Day. Thos Youngman had the Ague . . .

FEBRUARY 20, SUNDAY Excesive Sharp rime frost. Thos had the Ague. We all went to our Church Afternoon, Mr Burrell preachd. Mr Hardy, I & MA drank Tea at Mr Burrells, M^r & Mrs Emmery there. A great deal of Snow fell in the Night.

FEBRUARY 21, MONDAY Very Sharp Day, Snow very deep, a great deal fell in the Day. Mr Hardy at home all Day.

FEBRUARY 22, TUESDAY Excesive Sharp frost. Mr Hardy at home all Day. M^r & Mrs Huguier drank Tea & Supt here. Snow fell in the Night.

FEBRUARY 23, WEDNESDAY A very Stormy Morn, something better Afternoon. I & Childrⁿ went to our Church foornoon, Mr Hardy at home all Day. John Burrell came home from Cambridge last Night . . .

FEBRUARY 27, SUNDAY A very Sharp Frosty Day. I & MA at our Church foornoon, Mr Burrell preachd.

FEBRUARY 28, MONDAY A Terible Sharp Day. I & Mr Hardy walk'd up to Holt Afternoon, drank Tea & Supt at Mr Bartells . . .

MARCH 3, THURSDAY A Frosty Morn, thawd in Day. Mr Hardy, I & MA went to Mr Forsters of Bayfield, drank Tea & Supt there, M^r & Mrs Huguier there.

MARCH 4, FRIDAY A Frost, Chearly Day. Mr Hardy at home all Day .

MARCH 5, SATURDAY Frosty Morn & very Cold Day. I & Mr Hardy & MA walk^d up to Holt Afternoon, drank Tea & Supt at Mr Huguiers.

MARCH 6, SUNDAY A Sharp frost, Chearly Day. Raven came from N Walsham Even 2. All went to our Church

except W^m, Mr Burrell preach^d & went to preach at Holt afterwards. Mr Baker calld in Eveng . . .

MARCH 8, TUESDAY A Close Cold Day. M^r & Mrs Huguier went away Morn 9. Mr Hardy at home all Day.

MARCH 9, WEDNESDAY A Sharp frost, Stormes of Sleet Afternoon. I, MA & Mrs Prior walkd up to Holt Afternoon, I & MA drank Tea at Mr Huguiers. Mr Hardy came to us in Even, Supt here. Thos had the Ague.

MARCH 10, THURSDAY A Sharp frost, Chearly Day. Mr Hardy at home all Day. M^r & Mrs Huguier drank Tea & Supt & Slept here. Thos had the Ague.

MARCH 11, FRIDAY A very fine Chearly Day. M^r & Mrs Huguier went away after Breakfast. Raven came MII, went away Even past 5, I went up to Holt after Tea. Raind in Even & very dark. Thos had the Ague.

MARCH 12, SATURDAY Sharp frost, frequent Stormes of Snow. I & Mr Hardy walkd up to Holt Even 5, drank Tea & Supt at Mr Bartells. Thos had the Ague.

MARCH 13, SUNDAY A Sharp frost, Chearly Day. All went to our Church foornoon, Mr Burrell preachd. Thos had the Ague.

MARCH 14, MONDAY A Sharp frost. Mr Hardy at home all Day but poorly. M^r & Mrs Huguier drank Tea & Supt here . . .

MARCH 17, THURSDAY A Cold Dry Day. Mr Hardy poorly. M^r & Mrs Bartell, Mrs Baker, Miss Baker & Miss Custance drank Tea & Supt here.

MARCH 18, FRIDAY A fine Chearly Day. Mr Hardy something better. M^r & Mrs Huguier drank Tea & Supt here.

MARCH 19, SATURDAY A very fine Day but Cold. Mr Hardy much worse. I walkd up to Holt Aftern, drank Tea at Mr Huguiers, came home with M^{rs} Fo«r»ster.

MARCH 20, SUNDAY A very Sharp frost, Chearly Day. All went to our Church except Mr Hardy who was very poorly . . .

MARCH 22, TUESDAY A Sharp frost, bright Day. Mr Hardy very poorly. Maids Wash^d. Miss Davys drank Tea here. M^r & Mrs Huguier went to Mr Forsters to Tea, Slept there. A Stormy Night.

MARCH 23, WEDNESDAY A Sharp frost & frequent Stormes of Snow. Mrs Huguier came Morn 10, went to Church with me & Dind here . . .

MARCH 25, *Good Friday, New Lady Day* A very Coarse Cold Day. M^r & Mrs Huguier Breakfstd, Dind & drank Tea here then went home, Mr Burrell drank Tea here.

MARCH 26, SATURDAY A tolerable Day. I & Mr Hardy & M Ann rid up to Holt Aftern, drank Tea at Mr Huguiers. Snowd in the Night . . .

MARCH 28, MONDAY A very Sharp frost, bright Day. Mr Hardy something better. Mr Huguier calld foornoon going to Bayfield, Mrs Huguier drank Tea here & then went to Bayfield. A flight of Snow fell in the Night . . .

MARCH 30, WEDNESDAY A Sharp frost. Mr Hardy at home all Day . . .

APRIL 1, FRIDAY *Wm Birth Day agd 15* A very Sharp frost with frequent Storms of Snow &c. M^r & Mrs Huguier went to Norwich. Bro^t & Mr Fox went away Morn 9, left Robt Raven. Mr Hardy at home all Day. Mrs Bartell went to Norwich.

APRIL 2, SATURDAY A very Cold Day, frequent Stormes of Snow &c. I & Mr Hardy rid up to Holt Eveng 4, I drank Tea at Mr Davys, he drank Tea at Mr Bensleys, came home Eve 7.

APRIL 3, SUNDAY A very Sharp frost with frequent Storms of Snow &c. I & W^m went to our Church Afternoon, Mr Burrell preachd.

APRIL 4, MONDAY A Chearly Day. Mr Hardy at home all Day.

APRIL 5, TUESDAY A very mild Chearly Day. Mr Hardy at home all Day.

APRIL 6, WEDNESDAY A fine Chearly Day. Mr Hardy at home all Day, Mr Bartell drank Tea here . . .

APRIL 8, FRIDAY A fine Chearly Day. Mr Hardy at home all day.

APRIL 9, SATURDAY A fine Chearly Day, Cold in Even. I & Mr Hardy rid up to Holt Afternoon, I drank Tea at Mr Bartells, Mr Hardy drank Tea at Mr Davys, came home Even past 7. Mrs Bartell came from Norwich in Stage Coach . . .

APRIL 11, MONDAY A very fine Day. I & Mr Hardy rid up to Holt Afternoon, drank Tea & Supt at Mr Bartells, came home ½ past 10 . . .

APRIL 13, WEDNESDAY A very bright dry Day. Mr Hardy at home all Day.

APRIL 14, THURSDAY A very bright dry Day. Mr Hardy at home all Day.

APRIL 15, FRIDAY A very dry bright Day. Mr Hardy walkd up to Holt foornoon, Dind & drank Tea at Mr Bartells, home Even 7 . . .

APRIL 17, SUNDAY A very fine Day. All went to our Church Afternoon, Mr Burrell preachd. Mrs Emmery, Mr Burrell & Son drank Tea here . . .

APRIL 19, TUESDAY A Moist Morng, Dry Windy Day. Maids & Fanny Gidney Wash^d. Mr Hardy at home all Day.

APRIL 20, WEDNESDAY A Dry windy Day. Mr Hardy at home all day . . .

APRIL 23, SATURDAY A fine Mild Day. Mr Hardy & I walkd up to Holt Afternoon, I drank Tea at Miss Leakes, he drank Tea at Mr Bartells, home Even 8 . . .

APRIL 26, TUESDAY A very Dry bright Day. I & Mr Hardy drank Tea & Supt at Mr Bakers, Raven & Wm Supt there . . .

MAY 1, SUNDAY A fine Day. All went to our Church Afternoon, Mr Burrell preach^d. We afterwards drank Tea at Mr Burrells, Mr Lyons there.

MAY 2, MONDAY A very Dry Day. Mr Hardy at home all Day. I & W^m walk^d up to Holt after Tea to see Lyons Shell work.

MAY 3, TUESDAY A very Dry Day. Mr Hardy at home all day . . .

The visit to North Walsham
4–6 May 1785

MAY 5, THURSDAY A bright Dry Day. Breakfst^d & Dind at Mr Bucks, drank Tea at Mr Ravens, Supt & Slept at Mr Bucks.

MAY 6, FRIDAY A very Dry bright Day. After Breakfst went to Mr Ravens & set of for home Morn past 11, got home Even 4. Mr Hardy at home all Day . . .

[LETHERINGSETT]

MAY 8, SUNDAY Very Dry Day. All went to our Church foornoon, Mr Burrell preachd.

MAY 9, MONDAY A very Dry Day. Mr Hardy at home all Day. A very great want of rain.

MAY 10, TUESDAY Dry Windy Day. Maids & Goody Gidney Washd 3 Weeks Linnen. Mr Hardy at home all Day . . .

MAY 18, WEDNESDAY A Cold Windy Day, small Showrs. Mr Hardy at home all Day.

MAY 19, THURSDAY A Showry Day. Mr Hardy at home all Day. Mr Bartell & Mr Yarrington drank Tea here, Mr Burrell here aftr Tea. Mary, Wife of W^m [Thomas] Hall, Died agd 62.

MAY 20, FRIDAY A Cold Windy Day. Mr Hardy at home all day.

MAY 21, SATURDAY A Bright Dry Day. Mr Hardy & I walkd up to Holt Mark^t Afternoon, he drank Tea at Mr Davys & came home Even past 10, I drank Tea at Mr Bartells & came home with Willm Even 8. M^rs [Amy] Mays, Mother to David Mays, Died aged [ ].

MAY 22, SUNDAY A very fine Dry Day. All went to our Church foornoon, a Comunion, Mr Burrell preachd. Rav^n came from N Walsham Morn 12. Thos Youngman & Wife went out this Morng . . .

MAY 28, SATURDAY A Dry Day but Cold. I & Mr Hardy walkd up to Holt Afternoon, I drank Tea at Mr Bakers & Supt at Mr Bartells, M^r H drank Tea & Supt there . . .

MAY 30, MONDAY A Showry Cold Day. I & Mr Hardy walkd up to Holt Aftern, drank Tea & Supt at Mr Bartells, home Even 11 . . .

JUNE 3, FRIDAY A fine Day. Mr Hardy at home all Day. M^r & Mrs Baker, Mrs Stangroon [Stangroom], M^r & Mrs Bartell & M^r T Hewit drank Tea here. Bricklayers Building a Bath . . .

JUNE 5, SUNDAY A Wet very Close Day. All went to our Church Foornoon, Mr Burrell preachd.

JUNE 6, MONDAY A Close dry Day. I & Mr Hardy drank Tea at Mr Bakers, M^r & Mrs Bartell there . . .

JUNE 9, THURSDAY A fine Day. Mr Hardy at home all Day.

JUNE 10, FRIDAY A very Hot Day. Mr Hardy at home all Day.

JUNE 11, SATURDAY A very hot Day. Mr Hardy & I walkd up to Holt Aftern, I drank Tea & Supt at Mr Bartells, Mr Hardy Supt there. Thos Father & Mother came to see him . . .

JUNE 14, TUESDAY A very warm Dry Day. Mr Hardy at home all Day. Raven came Even 4 from Foulsham, drank Tea & went away Even pst 7. Young Bullock was Buried, Mr Burrell drank Tea here.

JUNE 15, WEDNESDAY A Sultry Hot Day. M[r] Hardy at home all Day. W[m] set of for Whisensett Even 2 in L [little] Cart to bring his Sister home to Morrow . . .

JUNE 17, FRIDAY A very Cold Windy Day. Bro[t] went away Even 4. I taken poorly with Dimness in my Eyes. M[r] & M[rs] Bartell drank Tea & Supt here.

JUNE 18, SATURDAY A Close Cold Day. I & Childr[n] walkd up to Holt after Tea. Raven came from N Walsham Morn 10. M[r] Hardy walkd up to Holt Markt . . .

JUNE 21, TUESDAY A fine Day. I Bathd & was better then Yesterday. I & Childr[n] walkd up to Holt Afternoon, drank Tea at M[r] Bartells. M[r] Hardy at home all Day . . .

JUNE 24, FRIDAY A very Hot Day. M[r] Hardy at home all Day. Bro[t] & Childrn went away Even 3. M[rs] & Miss Baker & Adam drank Tea here.

JUNE 25, SATURDAY A hot Day. M[r] Hardy, I & M Ann walkd up to Holt aftern, M & I drank Tea at Miss Leakes, M[r] H at Mr Bensleys. I bathd.

JUNE 26, SUNDAY A Hot dry Day. All went to our Church Afternoon, M[r] Burrell read a Lecture.

JUNE 27, MONDAY A very Hot Day. M[r] Hardy, I & MA Dind, drank Tea & Supt at M[r] Bartells, M[r] & M[rs] Wymer from Norwich there, Miss Clara Wymer came home with us. I bathd.

JUNE 28, TUESDAY A Hot Day. M[r] & M[rs] Wymer, M[r] & M[rs] Bartell Dind, drank Tea & Supt here. M[r] Hardy at home all Day.

JUNE 29, WEDNESDAY A very Hot dry Day. M[r] Hardy at home all Day. Miss Wymer & MA Dind at M[r] Bartells, came home to Tea. I bathd . . .

JULY 1, FRIDAY Excesive Hot Day, A Shower with Thunder Afternoon. M[r] Hardy came home from Dereham Even 9. Miss Wymer & MA drank Tea at M[r] Seales. I bathd . . .

JULY 3, SUNDAY A fine Day. All went to our Church foornoon, a M[r] Bulwer preachd.

JULY 4, MONDAY A very fine Day. I & MA & Miss Wymer drank Tea at M[r] Bakers, Miss Wymer left us to go to M[r] Bartels. M[r] Hardy went to Kettleston after Dinner, came home Even 7. I bathd.

JULY 5, TUESDAY A fine Day. Maids & Goody Ram wash[d]. M[r] Hardy, I & MA drank Tea at M[r] Emmerys, M[r] Burrell there. I bathd.

JULY 6, WEDNESDAY A Close drisley Morn, Dry Day. M[r] Hardy, I, MA & M[r] Burrell drank Tea at M[r] Bensleys . . .

JULY 8, FRIDAY A Hot Dry Day. Miss Wymer at Dinner, M[r] Hardy, I & MA drank Tea at M[r] Forsters . . .

JULY 10, SUNDAY A very fine Day. M[r] & M[rs] Bensley & Child, M[r] & M[rs] Seales & Miss Wall came to our Church Afternoon & drank Tea here, & the 2 M[r] Burrells . . .

JULY 12, TUESDAY A very Dry Day. M[r] Hardy, I & MA walkd up to Holt Afternoon, MA & I drank Tea at M[r] Bartells. M[r] Hardy went to Overtons Bowling Green, home Even pst 8. I bathd.

JULY 15, FRIDAY Close Day, a small Showr abt Noon. I & M[r] Hardy walkd up to Holt, drank Tea & Supt at M[r] Bartells. I bathd.

JULY 16, SATURDAY Very Hot dry Day. M[r] Hardy did not go up to Market. I & W[m] walkd up, drank Tea at M[r] Bakers. I bathd.

JULY 17, SUNDAY Dry Morn, Showry Afternoon with Thunder. All went to our Church Foornoon, M[r] Burrell preachd.

JULY 18, MONDAY A Showry Day with Thunder. M[r] Hardy at home all Day. I bathd.

JULY 19, TUESDAY Fine Morn, Showry Aftern with Thunder. M[r] Hardy at home all Day. I bathd . . .

JULY 21, THURSDAY A Showry Day with Thunder. M[r] Hardy at home all Day. M[rs] Custance of Fakenham, M[rs] & Miss Baker & Miss Custance of Yarmouth Dind & Supt here. I bathd.

JULY 22, FRIDAY A moist Morn, fine Day. M[r] Hardy & I dind & Supt at M[r] Bakers. I Bathd.

JULY 23, SATURDAY A fine dry Day. M[r] Hardy at home all Day. M[r] Scott Dind here, M[r] T Hewit calld. Young Groom came Aftern.

JULY 24, SUNDAY A very fine Dry Day. All went to our Church Afternoon, M[r] Burrell read a Lecture. M[rs] Forster & a Miss Riches & M[r] Burrell drank Tea here. I bath[d] . . .

JULY 27, WEDNESDAY A Showry Morn, very Wet Aftern. M[r] Hardy at home all Day. I bathd, should have gone to M[r] Bensleys at Holt but the Weather prevented us . . .

JULY 29, FRIDAY A fine Morn, very Showry Day. After Breakfst M[r] Hardy & I set of from Walsingham & got home Even 4 . . .

JULY 31, SUNDAY A fine dry Day. All went to our Church foornoon, M[r] Burrell preachd. M[r] Hardy sett of Even 2 for N Walsham & Norwich. M[r] & M[rs] Baker & their 3 Child[r], Myles Rav[n] & Sister [Elizabeth], M[r] Cook of [Sco] Ruston & 2 Sisters & Mastr Bartell drank Tea here . . .

AUGUST 2, TUESDAY A fine Day. Goody Ram & Maids Wash[d]. M[r] Hardy came home from Norwich Even past 11. I bathd.

AUGUST 3, WEDNESDAY A Stormy Windy Day. M[r] Hardy at Mays Afternoon . . .

AUGUST 5, FRIDAY A very fine Day. I bath[d]. M[r] Hardy at home all Day.

AUGUST 6, SATURDAY A very Showry Day. M[r] Hardy & I rid up to Holt Afternoon, drank Tea at M[r] Bensleys. I bathd.

AUGUST 7, SUNDAY A Showry Morn, fine Day. All went to our Church Aftr, M[r] Burrell preachd. M[r] & M[rs] Davy drank Tea here. I bathd.

AUGUST 8, MONDAY A Wet Morn, fine Day. M[r] Hardy at home all Day. I bathd . . .

AUGUST 10, WEDNESDAY A Hot dry Day. M[r] Hardy & I dind, drank Tea & Supt at M[r] Bartells. I Bathd . . .

AUGUST 12, FRIDAY A Showry Day, wind high. M[r] Hardy & I went to Sheringham Afternoon with M[r] & M[rs] Bartell & M[rs] Baldin & M[rs] Raven, drank Tea there & Supt at M[r] Bartells.

AUGUST 13, SATURDAY A Showry Day. I & M[r] Hardy rid up to Holt Afternoon, drank Tea at M[r] Davys & reckd.

AUGUST 14, SUNDAY A Wet Morn, fine Day. All went to our Church foornoon, Mr Burrell preachd. M^r & Mrs Bensley & Child, Mr Baker & 2 Boys drank Tea here . . .

AUGUST 16, TUESDAY A Showry Day. I Bathd. Mr Hardy at home all Day. M^r & Mrs Bartell drank Tea & Supt here. Heard John Coe of Dalling Died last Night . . .

AUGUST 17, WEDNESDAY A Showry Day. I bathd. Mr Hardy at home all Day & poorly.

AUGUST 18, THURSDAY Showry Morn, Close Windy Day. I & Mr Hardy rid [rode] to Edgefield, drank Tea at Mr Theordericks, came home Even 8. I bathd.

AUGUST 19, FRIDAY A Showry Day. Mr Hardy at home all Day & poorly. I bathd.

AUGUST 20, SATURDAY A Showry Day. I Bathd. Mr Hardy & I rid up to Holt Afternoon, drank Tea & Supt at Mr Bartells. Mr George Wymer [?junior] came home with us & Slept here.

AUGUST 21, SUNDAY A very Wet Day. Mr Wymer went away Even 3. I & W^m went to our Church Afternoon, Mr Burrell read a Lecture . . .

AUGUST 23, TUESDAY A Showry Close Day. I Bathd. Mr Hardy at home all Day.

AUGUST 24, WEDNESDAY A Dry Morn, very Wet Afternoon. Mr Hardy at home all Day. Mr Bensley, Mr Baker & Old Lawyer Girdlestone drank Tea here. Mr Hardy at Mays a little while in the Even.

AUGUST 25, THURSDAY A very Wet foornoon, Dry Aftern. M^r & Mrs Bartell, Mr Hardy & I drank Tea at Mr Burrells, they Supt here. I Bath'd.

AUGUST 28, SUNDAY A very fine Day. All went to our Church foornoon, Mr Burrell preach'd.

AUGUST 30, TUESDAY A Close Drisley foornoon, dry Afternoon. Mr Hardy at home all Day. Maids & Goody Ram Washd. I Bathd.

AUGUST 31, WEDNESDAY A fine Morn, Wet Afternoon. Mr Hardy at home all Day. I Bathd . . .

SEPTEMBER 4, SUNDAY A fine Day. Mr Hardy & I went to our Church Afternoon, Mr Burrell read a lecture. Miss Leake & Miss Pearmain & Miss Atthow [Athow] drank Tea here . . .

SEPTEMBER 7, WEDNESDAY A Wet Morn, dry Windy Day. Mr Hardy at home all Day. M^r & Mrs Bartell & Mrs Baldin Dind & drank Tea here. I Bathd . . .

SEPTEMBER 10, SATURDAY A fine Day. I Bath^d. Mr Hardy & I walk^d up to Holt Afternoon. I drank Tea at Mr Davys, M^r H drank Tea at Mr Bensleys, Mr Bensly very Ill.

SEPTEMBER 11, SUNDAY A fine Day except a Small Showr ab^t 4 o Clock Aftern. We all went to our Church foornoon, Mr Burrell preach^d. Mr Hardy & W^m went to Holt Church Afternoon & drank Tea at Mr Bensleys. I poorly with pain in Stomach.

SEPTEMBER 12, MONDAY Some Small Showrs. Mr Hardy sett of for Dereham Morn pst 9. I poorly.

SEPTEMBER 13, TUESDAY Small Showrs in Morn, fine Aftrn. I poorly. Expect^d Mr Hardy home, did not come.

SEPTEMBER 14, WEDNESDAY A fine Day. I bathd. Mr Hardy came home from Whisinsett Even pst 6 . . .

SEPTEMBER 18, SUNDAY A Showry foornoon, Dry Aftern. Mr Boggis went away after Dinner. We all went to our Church Afternoon, Mr Burrell preachd.

SEPTEMBER 19, MONDAY A very fine Day. I bathd. Mr Hardy at home all Day. M^r & M^{rs} & Miss Sippings [Seppings] from Holt drank Tea here & Miss Baker. M^r & M^{rs} & Mr Ben Croffts [Crofts] & Miss [?Penelope] Cobb call'd in Eveng . . .

SEPTEMBER 23, FRIDAY A very Wet Day. Mr Hardy at home all Day. Raven came from N Walsham Even 1 very Wet. Thos Youngmn at Plumste«a»d . . .

OCTOBER 2, SUNDAY A fine Day. All went to our Church Afternoon except W^m . . .

OCTOBER 4, TUESDAY A fine Day. Mr Hardy at home all Day. The General at Holt. I bathd.

OCTOBER 5, WEDNESDAY A fine Morn, Drisley Aftern. Mr Hardy went to Clay Aftrn, came home Even past 11. I bathd.

OCTOBER 6, THURSDAY A fine Day. I Bathd. Mr Hardy at home all Day. Very Wett Even.

OCTOBER 7, FRIDAY A fine Day. I Bathd. Mr Hardy at home all Day. A Wet Eveng.

OCTOBER 8, SATURDAY A Close Day. Mr Hardy, I & MA walk'd up to Holt Aftern. I & MA drank Tea at Mr Davys, M^r H drank Tea «at» Mr Bartells.

OCTOBER 9, SUNDAY A fine Day. All went to our Church foornoon, Mr Burrell preach^d. M^r & M^r [?Mrs] Baker & all the Childr^n drank Tea here. Showry Night . . .

OCTOBER 14, FRIDAY A very fine Day. I Bath'd. Mr Hardy at home all Day . . .

OCTOBER 19, WEDNESDAY A fine Day. I Bathd. Mr Hardy at home all Day. Maids Washd small Linnen.

OCTOBER 20, THURSDAY A Close Cold Day. I Bathd. Mr Hardy at home all Day.

OCTOBER 21, FRIDAY A Close Dry Day. I Bathd. Mr Hardy at home all day, went to Mr Mays to Town Meeting in Even, home Even 9.

OCTOBER 22, SATURDAY A Close Dry Day. I Bathd. Mr Hardy, I & M Ann walkd up to Holt Afternoon, Drank Tea & Supt at Mr Bakers . . .

OCTOBER 24, MONDAY A Close Dry Day. I Bathd. Mr Hardy sett of for Whisinsett Morn 10. Wet Eveng.

OCTOBER 25, TUESDAY A fine Day. I Bath'd. Mr Hardy came home Even 10 by Foulsham. Rain'd in Eveng.

OCTOBER 26, WEDNESDAY A fine Day. I Bath'd. I & Mr Hardy & MA drank Tea & Supt at Mr Bartells, Mr Yarrington there, he went away after Tea . . .

OCTOBER 28, FRIDAY A Close Cold Day, Wind high. I Bathd. Mr Hardy walkd up to Holt Aftrn, Drank Tea at Mr Bakers, came home Even 8. Mr Baker bad with a Sore Leg.

OCTOBER 29, SATURDAY A Close Cold Day. I Bathd. Mr Hardy, I & MA walkd up to Holt Mark^t, drank Tea at Mr Bensleys. W^m came up for us in L Cart.

OCTOBER 30, SUNDAY A fine Day. All went to our Church Afternoon, John Burrell Preach^d, Mr Burrell at Mrs Jodrills. 3 Mastr Davys & Mastr Bartell drank Tea here . . .

NOVEMBER 1, TUESDAY A fine Day. I Bathd. Mr Hardy at home all Day. M^r & Mrs Bartell drank Tea & Supt here, Raind in Even . . .

NOVEMBER 3, THURSDAY A very fine Day. I Bathd. I & W^m rid up to Holt foorn, came back to Dinner, W^m & MA rid [   ]. [[[by Mary Ann] MAs birth Day, 12 Years Old]] . . .

NOVEMBER 5, SATURDAY A Close Dry Day. I Bathd. Mr Hardy, I & MA & W^m walkd up to Holt Aftern. I & M drank Tea at Miss Leakes, Supt at Mr Bartells.

NOVEMBER 6, SUNDAY A Dry Morn, Wet Aftern. All went to our Church foorn, Mr Burrell preachd. M^r H & W^m went to Holt Church Afternoon, John Burrell preachd there. M^r H drank Tea at Mr Bensleys, W^m drank Tea at Mr Davys, Miss Leake & Miss Pearmain drank Tea here.

NOVEMBER 7, MONDAY A very Cold Stormy Day. We all drank Tea & Supt at Mr Bartells . . .

NOVEMBER 11, FRIDAY A fine Day. I Bathd. Mr Hardy at home all Day. 2 Gardiners at work.

NOVEMBER 12, SATURDAY A fine Day. I Bathd. Mr Hardy, I & W^m & MA walkd up to Holt Afternoon, drank Tea at Mr Davys, rid home in L Cart.

NOVEMBER 13, SUNDAY A very fine Day. All went to our Church Afternoon, Mr Burrell preach'd . . .

NOVEMBER 17, THURSDAY A very fine Day. I Bathd. Mr Hardy at home all Day. We took a walk after Noon.

NOVEMBER 18, FRIDAY A fine Day. I Bathd. Mr Hardy at home all Day. M^r & Mrs Bartell drank Tea & Supt here.

NOVEMBER 19, SATURDAY A fine Day. I Bathd. Mr Hardy, I & MA walk'd up to Holt Afternoon. I & MA drank Tea at Mr Davys, came home Even 8. A Windy Night.

NOVEMBER 20, SUNDAY A fine Day. All went to our Church Foornoon, Mr Burrell preach'd.

NOVEMBER 21, MONDAY A heavy Show^r in Morn, fine Day. I Bathd. Mr Hardy at home all Day . . .

NOVEMBER 23, WEDNESDAY A very fine Day. I Bathd. Mr Hardy came home ½ past 9 at Night.

NOVEMBER 24, THURSDAY A Sharp rime frost, Day turnd hasy. Mr Hardy at home all Day . . .

NOVEMBER 26, SATURDAY A Dry Morn, Wet Day. I Bathd. Mr Hardy did not go to Holt Mark^t.

NOVEMBER 27, SUNDAY A fine Day. All went to our Church Afternoon, Mr Burrell preachd . . .

NOVEMBER 29, TUESDAY A Cold Dry Day, Wind frost. I Bathd. Mr Hardy at home all Day. Miss Balls & Miss Bartell went away foornoon . . .

DECEMBER 2, FRIDAY A very Stormy Cold Day. Mr Hardy at home all Day.

DECEMBER 3, SATURDAY A Stormy Day, not very Cold. I Bath'd. Mr Hardy went to Holt Mark^t, came home 8.

DECEMBER 4, SUNDAY A very Wet Day. All went to our Church foornoon, Mr Burrell preach'd.

DECEMBER 5, MONDAY A fine Day. I Bathd. Mr Hardy at home all Day. M^r & Mrs Bartell drank Tea & Supt here.

DECEMBER 6, TUESDAY A Wet Windy Day. Mr Hardy & I rid up to Holt Afternoon, drank Tea & Supt at Mr Bartells, Mr Wymer of Norwich there . . .

DECEMBER 8, THURSDAY A Mild Day. I Bathd. Mr Hardy at home all Day.

DECEMBER 9, FRIDAY A Cold Stormy Day. I Bathd. Mr Hardy at home all Day .

DECEMBER 10, SATURDAY A Close Cold Day. I Bathd. Mr Hardy, I & MA walkd up to Holt Mark^t, drank Tea at Miss Leakes, home Eve 7.

DECEMBER 11, SUNDAY A Cold Stormy Day. All went to our Church Afternoon except Mr Hardy, Mr Burrell preachd.

DECEMBER 12, MONDAY A Close Cold Day. I Bathd. Mr Hardy, I & MA walkd up to Holt Afternoon, drank Tea at Mr Seppings's.

DECEMBER 13, TUESDAY A Close Cold Day. I Bathd. Mr Hardy, I & MA drank Tea at Mr Burrell.

DECEMBER 14, WEDNESDAY A Close Dry Day. I Bathd. Mr Hardy at home all Day & went to Overtons Club Even 7, came home Eve 11 . . .

DECEMBER 16, FRIDAY A Close moist Day. I Bath'd. Mr Hardy at home all Day. M^r & Mrs Bartell came Even pst 6, Supt here.

DECEMBER 17, SATURDAY A Close Day. I Bathd. I & MA walkd up to Holt Afternoon, drank Tea & Supt at Mr Bartells. Mr Hardy came to us Even 7, W^m came up for us in L Cart. A Wet Night . . .

DECEMBER 20, TUESDAY A Close Cold Day. I Bathd. Maids & Goody Ram Wash'd. Mr Hardy at home all Day. Mr Theoderick Dind here, went away Even 4.

DECEMBER 21, WEDNESDAY A Close drisley Day. I Bathd. Mr Hardy at home all Day . . .

DECEMBER 23, FRIDAY A Close foggy Day. I Bathd. Mr Hardy at home all Day. I & W^m & M Ann rid up to Holt Afternoon, came home to Tea . . .

DECEMBER 26, MONDAY A Snowy Day. Mr Hardy at home all Day . . .

DECEMBER 28, WEDNESDAY A Sharp Frost in Morn, Thawd in Day. Mr Hardy at home all Day. Mr Bartell drank Tea here . . .

DECEMBER 30, FRIDAY A very Sharp frost, Stormes of Snow. Mr Hardy & Family at home all Day.

DECEMBER 31, SATURDAY A Sharp frost & Stormes of Snow. Mr Hardy, Ravⁿ & W^m walk'd up to Holt afternoon. M^r H drank Tea at Mr Bartells, R & W^m drank Tea at Mr Bakers, home Even 8. A deal of Snow fell in the Night . . .

═1786═

JANUARY 3, TUESDAY A very Sharp frost. Miss Davy went away after Breakfst. Mr Hardy at home all Day. A very Sharp Night . . .

JANUARY 5, THURSDAY A very Sharp Day, Snow very deep & drifted. W^m carried Mrs Baker home after Brkfst [breakfast], left Miss Custance here. Mr Hardy at home all Day.

JANUARY 6, FRIDAY Began to Thaw but very Cold. Mr Hardy at home all Day. Rain'd in Eveng . . .

JANUARY 14, SATURDAY A very Sharp frost. I & Mr Hardy walkd up to Holt Afternoon, I drank Tea at Mr Bakers, walk'd home Even past 8, W^m up in Even'g. Rain & Snow in Night . . .

JANUARY 18, WEDNESDAY A very Sharp frost. Mr Hardy at home all Day.

JANUARY 19, THURSDAY A very Sharp frost. Mr Hardy walkd up to Holt abt Noon to Qrtr Sessions. I walkd up Afternoon, drank Tea & Supt at Mr Bartells, M^r & Mrs Baker there . . .

JANUARY 22, SUNDAY A Wet Day. R Stafe went away Morn 11. We all went to our Church Afternoon, Mr Burrell preachd . . .

JANUARY 24, TUESDAY A Mild Close Day. Mr Hardy went to Walsingham to take Care of Browns things Morn 10, came home Even 7.

JANUARY 25, WEDNESDAY A Mild Day. Mr Hardy at home all Day. 2 Gardeners at Work . . .

JANUARY 28, SATURDAY A very fine Day. I & Mr Hardy walkd up to Holt Mark^t, I drank Tea at Mr Davys, W^m came for us in Little Cart. Recd a Letter from M Ann.

JANUARY 29, SUNDAY A fine Day. We all went to our Church foornoon, Mr Burrell preachd. Mr Burrell & Son here a little while in Eveng . . .

JANUARY 31, TUESDAY A fine Day. Mr Hardy at home all Day.

FEBRUARY 1, WEDNESDAY A fine Day. Mr Hardy at home all Day.

FEBRUARY 2, THURSDAY A Cold Stormy Day. Mr Mindham [Mendham] call«ed» here in Afternoon, Mr Hardy at home all Day .

FEBRUARY 3, FRIDAY A fine Mild Day. Mr Hardy at home all Day. Mr Buck of No«rth» Walsham came Even past 5, M^r & Mrs Bartell drank Tea & supt here.

FEBRUARY 4, SATURDAY A Mild Chearly Day. Mr Buck went away after Dinner. I & Mr Hardy & W^m walkd up to Holt Mark^t, drank Tea & Supt at Mr Bartells.

FEBRUARY 5, SUNDAY Fine Morn, close Showry Aftern. All went to our Church Aftern. M^r & Mrs Davy & 3 Sons & Miss Baker & Miss F [Frances] Custance drank Tea here . . .

FEBRUARY 7, TUESDAY A Cold Windy Day. Expected Mr Hardy home, did not come. I very poorly.

FEBRUARY 8, WEDNESDAY A Cold Windy Day. Mr Hardy came home Even 8. I something better.

FEBRUARY 9, THURSDAY A tolerable Day. Mr Hardy at home all Day. Mr Burrell & his Son Nathl drank Tea here. Snowd in the Night.

FEBRUARY 10, FRIDAY Thawd & snowd & raind great deal in foornoon. I & Mr Hardy rid up to Holt Afternoon, Drank Tea & Supt at Mr Bartells, M^r & Mrs Ives of Glanford & Miss Baker & Miss Custance there to Tea.

FEBRUARY 11, SATURDAY A Chearly Day. Mr Hardy & W^m rid to Blakeney foornoon, came back to Dinner. We walk'd up to Holt Markt Afternoon, I drank Tea at Mr Davys, Mr Hardy drank Tea at Mr Bartells. W^m came for us in Little Cart.

FEBRUARY 12, SUNDAY A Chearly Day, Wind very high. All went to our Church foorn.

FEBRUARY 13, MONDAY A very fine Day. Mr Hardy at home all Day.

FEBRUARY 14, TUESDAY A very fine Day. Mr Hardy at home all Day . . .

FEBRUARY 18, SATURDAY A Close Day & a little rain. Mr Hardy went to Dawling [Field Dalling] Foornoon, came home Even 4, then walkd to Mark^t. I & MA walkd up to Holt, drank Tea at Mr Davys, M^r H drank Tea at Mr Bartells, came home Even 8.

FEBRUARY 19, SUNDAY A Cold Close dry Day, Sharp frost. All went to our Church Afternoon, M^r N Burrell drank Tea here.

FEBRUARY 20, MONDAY A Cold Dry Windy Day, Sharp frost. I & M^r H drank Tea & Supt at Mr Bartells . . .

FEBRUARY 23, THURSDAY A very Cold Windy Dry Day, Sharp frost. Mr Hardy at home all Day. W^m set of for Whisensett M10.

FEBRUARY 24, FRIDAY Very Sharp frost, Wind high. Mr Hardy at home all Day. W^m came home Even 7. M^r & Mrs Bartell drank Tea & Supt here.

FEBRUARY 25, SATURDAY A Sharp frost, Wind very high. Mr Hardy, I & M Ann walkd up to Holt Afternoon, drank Tea & Supt at Mr Bartells. A little Snow fell in the Night . . .

FEBRUARY 28, *Shrove Tuesday* A very Sharp Frost, Wind high at East. Mr Hardy, I & MA drank Tea at Mr Burrells.

MARCH 1, WEDNESDAY A very Sharp Frost, Wind high at East. Mr Hardy, I & MA went to our Church Foornoon.

MARCH 2, THURSDAY A very Sharp Frost, Wind high at East. Mr Hardy, I & MA walk'd up to Holt, drank Tea & Supt at Mr Bakers, W^m came Even 8 with Little Cart. A little Snow fell in the Night . . .

MARCH 6, MONDAY A very Sharp frost, Wind high with frequent Squarls of Snow. Mr Hardy drank Tea at Mr Burrells, Mr Bensley there. Raven came in little Cart with Cook Even past 2.

MARCH 7, TUESDAY A very Sharp frost, Wind high at North. Rav^n went to Saxlingham with Cook Morn 9, came back to Dinner. I & W^m walkd up to Holt with him Even 3, he went from Holt ½ past 4. I & W^m drank Tea at Mr Davys.

MARCH 8, WEDNESDAY A very Sharp frost, Snowd all the foornoon. Mr H, I & Wm went to our Church Foornoon. Mr Hardy at home all Day . . .

MARCH 12, SUNDAY A fine Chearly Day, Wind Cold. All went to our Church foornoon, Mr John Burrell preachd.

MARCH 13, MONDAY A very fine Day. Mr Burrell poorly. Mr Hardy at home all Day.

MARCH 14, TUESDAY A very fine Day. Mr Hardy at home all Day. Mr & Mrs Bartell drank Tea & Supt here, Mrs & Miss Baker drank Tea here.

MARCH 15, WEDNESDAY A very Cold Stormy Day, Wind high. Mr Hardy at home all Day . . .

MARCH 18, SATURDAY Close Showry Day. Mr Hardy, I & MA walkd up to Holt Afternoon, MA & I drank Tea at Mr Seales, Mr H drank Tea at Mr Bartells, Mr Howard of Hingham came home with us & Slept here. Mr Burrell very bad.

MARCH 19, SUNDAY A very fine Day. All went to our Church Afternoon, Mr Burrell very bad. Mr Howard went away after Dinner, Mr John Burrell drank Tea here.

MARCH 20, MONDAY A fine Day. Mr Hardy at home all day. Mr Hewit of Thornage, Mr Paul of Stody, John Davy [junior] & 3 of the Miss Davys drank Tea here. The Jubilee began at Holt.

MARCH 21, TUESDAY A Close Dry Day. J Davy Junr set of for London. Mr Hardy went to Saxthorpe & Aylsham with Mr Bensley M past 8, came home Even 8. Maids & Goody Ram washd a Months Linnen. Brot Raven from Whisensett & Son came Even 6 . . .

MARCH 23, THURSDAY A Showry Day & Mild. Mr Hardy at home all Day. Brot Ravn [Brother Raven] & Son went away after Dinner. Mr Burrell something better.

MARCH 24, FRIDAY A Fine Day. Mr Hardy at home all Day, set some Pease in Gardn.

MARCH 25, SATURDAY A Fine Morn, very Showry Afternoon. Mr Hardy, I & MA walkd up to Holt Afternoon, drank Tea & Supt at Mr Bartells. Mr Burrell better.

MARCH 26, SUNDAY A very Cold Day, Stormes of Snow. All went to our Church Foornoon, Mr J Burrell preachd . . .

MARCH 29, WEDNESDAY A Close Cold Day. Mr Hardy at home all Day. I & MA went to our Church foornoon.

MARCH 30, THURSDAY A Close Day & very Cold. MA walkd up to Holt Foornoon & came back to Dinner. Mr Hardy, I & MA walkd up to Holt Afternoon, drank Tea at Mr Bakers, Mr & Mrs Bartell there . . .

APRIL 8, SATURDAY A Close Cold Morn, began to rain abt 9 o Clock, continued till Even 4. Mr Hardy walkd to Markt, drank Tea at Mr Bartells, came home Even 10. I & Wm rid up after Tea.

APRIL 9, SUNDAY A Cold Chearly Day, Wind high. No Service at our Church, I & Wm walkd to Holt Church, came home to Tea. Mr J Burrell drank Tea here . . .

APRIL 15, SATURDAY A very fine Mild Day. I & Mr Hardy walk'd up to Holt Afternoon, drank Tea at Mr Davys, came home Even past 8 . . .

APRIL 18, TUESDAY A Close Cold Windy Day. Maids «and» Goody Ram Washd. Mr Hardy & I walkd up to Holt Aftern, drank Tea & Supt at Mr Bartells. Mr Baker there, Miss Baker very Ill. Wm came up for us in Eveng in L Cart.

APRIL 19, WEDNESDAY Dry Windy Day. Mr Hardy at home all Day. Mr Nathl Burrell drank Tea here . . .

APRIL 24, MONDAY Small Showers in Morn, fine Mild Day. Mr Hardy at home all Day. Mr & Mrs Bartell drank Tea & Supt here. A very Wet Night . . .

APRIL 27, THURSDAY A Cold Windy Day. Mr Hardy at home all Day. Mr N Burrell drank Tea here . . .

APRIL 29, SATURDAY A fine Morn, Close cold Aftern. Mr Hardy & I walkd up to Holt, drank Tea & Supt at Mr Bakers, home Even 11 . . .

MAY 1, MONDAY A Cold chearly Day. 2 Gardiners at work. Mr Hardy at home all Day. Mr & Mrs Bartell drank Tea & Supt here, Mr John Burrell Supt here . . .

MAY 3, WEDNESDAY A dry cold Morng, a very heavy Showr abt 2 o Clock. Mr Hardy & I walkd up to Holt, met Mr & Mrs Baker at Mr Bartells, drank Tea & Supt there . . .

MAY 5, FRIDAY A Cold Showry day. Mr Hardy at home all Day . . .

MAY 7, SUNDAY A Cold Windy Day. No service at our Church. Mr Hardy, I & Wm walkd to Holt Church Afternoon, drank Tea at Mr Bakers, Mr Hdy went to speak to Mr Burrell after he came home. A small rain in Eving . . .

MAY 9, TUESDAY A dry Morng, Wet Afternoon. Mr Hardy went up to Holt Morn 11 to the Generall, Dind at the Feathers, drank Tea at Mr Davys & came home Even 8.

MAY 10, WEDNESDAY A Showry Cold Day, Wind high. Mr Hardy & I drank Tea at Mr Seppings at Holt, met Mr & Mrs Baker & Old Mrs Girdlestone & Daughtrs there. Sender Leake & a Young Man with him came to Se our Organ. Mr Kendle of Thornage calld Aftern, pd him for the Cow £6 10s 0d . . .

MAY 13, SATURDAY A Wet cold Day. Mr Hardy walkd up to Holt Markt Even 3, drank Tea at Mr Bartells, home Even 9, I & Wm rid up after Tea. Raven came from No Walsham round by Cromer & came home with us. Miss Leake home from London.

MAY 14, SUNDAY A very fine Warm day. Ravn & Wm went to Holt Church Foornoon. All went to our Church Aftern, Mr Burrell preach'd. Mr & Mrs Baker & all their Family, 2 Mastr Davys, Mastr Bartell & Mastr Leacy [Lacey] drank Tea here. Raven went away Even past 7 . . .

MAY 18, THURSDAY A Fine day. Mr Hardy at home all Day. Mr & Mrs Bartell & the 2 Mr Burrells drank Tea & Supt here. Mrs Youngmans Sister came.

MAY 19, FRIDAY A fine Day. Mr Hardy at home all Day. Mrs Davy & Nanny [Ann Davy] & Mrs Baker drank Tea here . . .

MAY 21, SUNDAY A Fine Day. All went to our Church foornoon, Mr Burrell preachd. Mrs Bartell went to Norwich . . .

MAY 23, TUESDAY A very fine Morn, Windy cold Day. Mr Hardy at home all day. Mr J Burrell sett of for Holsworth [Halesworth] this Morng . . .

MAY 26, FRIDAY [*at North Walsham*] A very Hot Day. After Breakfst went to M^r [Neale] Ravens, Dind & drank Tea at M^r Bs [Buck's] & sett of for home Even past 5, got home a little before ten. Mr Hardy at home all Day.

MAY 27, SATURDAY A very fine Day but Cooler then Yesterday. Mr Hardy & I walkd up to Holt Afternoon, drank Tea at Mr Bartells. I Bathd.

MAY 28, SUNDAY A very fine Day. All went to our Church Afternoon, Mr Burrell preachd, he came home this Morng from Suffolk. We took a little walk after Tea.

MAY 29, MONDAY A very warm dry Day. Mr Hardy at home all Day. Nathl Burrell drank Tea here. I Bathd...

JUNE 2, FRIDAY A Hot dry Day. I Bathd. Mr Hardy went to Blakeney & Langham Morn 10, came home Even 7...

JUNE 6, TUESDAY A very hot Morn, Cool close Day. Mr Hardy set of for Fakenham with Mr Baker, dind at Mr Custances, drank Tea at Mr Brutons, went to Whisensett with Bro^t Rav^n.

JUNE 7, WEDNESDAY A Small Showr in Morng, dry Day. Expected Mr Hardy home, did not come.

JUNE 8, THURSDAY A dry Day, not hot. Mr Hardy came home from Whisinsett by Fakenham Even 9.

JUNE 9, FRIDAY A dry day, not very hot. Mr Hardy & I walkd up to Holt Afternoon, drank Tea & Supt at Mr Bartells...

JUNE 11, SUNDAY *Full Moon* A very dry Day, wind Cold. All went to our Church Afternoon, Mr Burrell preachd...

JUNE 13, TUESDAY A Close dry Day & Cold. Maids & Lydia Youngman Washd. Mr Hardy at home all Day. I Bathd.

JUNE 14, WEDNESDAY A dry cool Day. Mr Hardy at home all day...

JUNE 16, FRIDAY A cold Day, Wind high. Mr Hardy at home all Day. M^r & Mrs Bensley, M^r & Mrs Paske & Squire Paske & 2 Young Ladies, Mr Garrett of Norwich & Mastr Paske drank Tea here. I Bathd.

JUNE 17, SATURDAY A Showry Morng, close dry Aftern. Mr Hardy & M Ann walkd & I & W^m rid up to Holt Afternoon, all drank Tea at Mr Davys. I Bathd.

JUNE 18, SUNDAY A fine bright Day. All went to our Church foornoon, Mr Burrell preachd.

JUNE 19, MONDAY A very fine Day. Mr Hardy went to Clay Afternoon, drank Tea at Mr Mans, home Even 9. I & M Ann walkd up to Holt after Tea. I Bathd.

JUNE 20, TUESDAY A hot dry Day. Mr Hardy, I & MA drank Tea at Mr Bensleys. Raind in the Night. I Bathd...

JUNE 22, THURSDAY A Hot dry Day. Mr Hardy at home all Day, MA drank Tea at Mrs Girlings at Holt. I Bath«ed».

JUNE 23, FRIDAY A Hot Day. Mr Hardy at home all Day. M^r & Mrs Bartell & 2 Childr^n drank Tea & Supt here.

JUNE 24, SATURDAY A Tempest with a fine moderate rain in foornoon, Showrs Aftern. Mr Hardy at home all Day. I, W^m & M Ann rid up to Holt After Tea. I Bath^d...

JUNE 27, TUESDAY A very Showry Day. Mr Hardy, I & M Ann rid up to Holt Afternoon, drank Tea at Mr Bakers. I Bath^d...

JUNE 29, THURSDAY A Windy Showry Day. Mr Hardy at home all Day. I Bathd...

JULY 4, TUESDAY A Close Cool Day. Mr Hardy at home all Day. I, W^m & MA walkd up to Holt after Tea. Mr Hardy at Town meeting. I Bathd...

JULY 6, THURSDAY A very fine Day. Mr Hardy at home all Day. I, MA, W^m, Miss Wall & H Goggs rid to Bell View [Belle Vue, Briningham] after Dinner, came back to Tea. H Goggs went home. Mr Harrold call^d Aftern. I Bathd.

JULY 7, FRIDAY A Showry Day. Mr Hardy at home all Day. W^m & M Ann drank Tea at Mr Theordericks at Edgefield. I Bathd.

JULY 8, SATURDAY A fine Day. I & MA walkd up to Holt, drank Tea at Miss Bacons. Mr Hardy & W^m walkd up to Holt...

JULY 10, MONDAY A very fine Day. Mr Hardy, W^m & M Ann went in L Cart to Mr Barnwell of Bale & drank Tea there, home Even 9. I Bathd.

JULY 11, TUESDAY A fine Day. Mr Hardy, I & MA drank Tea at Mr Burrells. We Iron^d & finishd our Linnen. I Bathd.

JULY 12, WEDNESDAY A very fine Day. M^r J Crofts, Mr Elwin, M^r [   ] & 2 young Ladies paid us a Morng Visit. Mr Hardy went to Edgefield Aftern & pd the Excise at Holt, came home Even 9. I & M Ann walkd up to Holt afternoon, intended to drink Tea at Miss Leakes, heard Mrs Baker was come to Lethr [Letheringsett], came home to Tea. Attend^d the School from E7 to past 8. I Bathd.

JULY 13, THURSDAY A Showry Morn, dry Cool Afternoon. I & MA walkd up to Holt Afternoon. Mr Hardy followed us, drank Tea & Supt at Mr Bartells. I Bathd...

JULY 15, SATURDAY A fine Day. A Justice Sitting at Holt. Mr Hardy walkd up to Mark^t Even 2, MA & I walk^d up after Tea. I Bathd...

JULY 17, MONDAY A Hot dry Day. Mr Hardy at home all Day. I & MA walkd up to Holt after Tea...

The visit to Whissonsett
18–22 July 1786

JULY 19, WEDNESDAY A fine Day. W^m & Bro^t Raven went to Fakenham after Breakfst for Mrs Custance. I went to speak to Sister Goggs, Dind at Bro^t Ravens, drank Tea at the Hall, Supt & Slept at Bro^t Ravens.

JULY 20, THURSDAY A Wet Morng, dry Afternoon. Mrs Custance & I dind & drank Tea at Sister Goggs, Supt & Slept at Bro^t Ravens.

JULY 21, FRIDAY A Cold Stormy Day. At Bro^t Ravens all Day, Sister from the Hall & Mrs Mason came to us Afternoon...

[LETHERINGSETT]

JULY 25, TUESDAY A very Dry Day. Mr Hardy at home all Day. I & MA drank Tea at Mr Davys.

JULY 26, WEDNESDAY A very dry Day. Mr Hardy at home all day. I Bathd...

AUGUST 1, TUESDAY A fine Day. Mr Hardy at home all Day. I Bathd. Maids Wash^d Small Linnen.

AUGUST 2, WEDNESDAY A very Showry Day. Mr Hardy at home all Day. Mr Bensley Dind here, Mr Barnwell drank Tea here. I attended the School.

AUGUST 3, THURSDAY A fine Day. Mr Hardy at home all Day. I & W^m rid up to Holt after Tea. I Bathd . . .

AUGUST 5, SATURDAY A Showry Day. I walkd up to Holt Aftern, drank Tea at Mr Bartells, Mr Hardy followd me walking. W^m came up in L Cart for me. I Bathd . . .

AUGUST 13, SUNDAY Dry Morn, very Wet Aftern. All went to our Church foorn, Mr Burrell preachd. I attend'd the School all the Aftern. Lucy went out, could not get home the rain being so violent.

AUGUST 14, MONDAY A very Wet Day except abt 2 hours. Mr Hardy, I & Raven Dind, drank Tea & Supt at Mr Bartells, M^r & Mrs Wymer came Even 7.

AUGUST 15, TUESDAY A very wet Morn, fine Aftern. M^r & Mrs Wymer, M^r & Mrs Bartell dind, drank Tea & Supt here . . .

AUGUST 17, THURSDAY A Close dry Day. Mr Hardy, I & Raven drank Tea at Mr Bakers. I Bathd.

AUGUST 18, FRIDAY A fine Day. Mr Hardy at home all Day. I attendd the School in Eveng. I Bathd . . .

AUGUST 20, SUNDAY A very Showry day. I attendd the School both foornoon & Afternoon, all went to our Church Aftern. Matt & Jo^s Davy & a Young Gentleman from Mr Breertons of Brunton [Brinton] & Edmd Bartell drank Tea here.

AUGUST 21, MONDAY A fine day. Mr Hardy, I & Rav^n walkd up to Holt Afternoon, drank Tea at Mr Davys. Mr Hardy went to Bowling Green after Tea. I Bathd. Heard Mr Cremer of Beeston [Regis] was Dead . . .

AUGUST 23, WEDNESDAY A fine Morn, Showrs Aftern. Mr Hardy at home all day. I attend^d the School in Eveng. I Bathd.

AUGUST 24, THURSDAY A very fine Day. Mr Hardy at home all Day. W^m rid to Fakenham After Dinner to see M Ann, came home Even pst 9. I Bathd . . .

AUGUST 27, SUNDAY A Moist Morn, fine Day. All went to our Church foornoon, Mr Burrell preachd. I attendd the School Aftern.

AUGUST 28, MONDAY Moist Morn, fine Day. Mr Hardy at home, he & I walkd up to Holt Afternoon, drank Tea at Mr Johnsons. I Bathd . . .

AUGUST 31, THURSDAY A Dry Day. Wind very high. Mr Hardy at home all Day. Raven poorly.

SEPTEMBER 1, FRIDAY A Cold Day, Wind high. Mr Hardy at home all Day. I & Raven walkd up to Holt after Tea. I Bathd . . .

SEPTEMBER 3, SUNDAY A fine Foornoon, began to rain Even 3, Continued all the Afternoon & part of the Night. I attended the School Foornoon & Afternoon. All went to Church Afternoon, Mr Burrell preachd. Nanny Davy & Frances Chichely drank Tea here & staid all Night on Acct of the Rain. Raven very poorly.

SEPTEMBER 4, MONDAY A fine day except a Small Shower afternoon. Mr Hardy & I walkd up to Holt Afternoon,

drank Tea & Supt at Mr Bartells, M^{rs} & Mr Chaplin & Mrs Baldero there. I Bathd.

SEPTEMBER 5, TUESDAY A very fine Day. Maids & Ann Humph«r»y washd. Mr Hardy at home all Day. I Bathd.

SEPTEMBER 6, WEDNESDAY A fine Day. Mr Hardy at home all Day. Wm Chastney Died this Morng . . .

SEPTEMBER 9, SATURDAY A Showry Day. Mr Hardy & I rid up to Holt after Tea, W^m walkd up. I Bathd.

SEPTEMBER 10, SUNDAY A tolerable Day. All went to our Church foornoon, Mr Burrell preachd. I attendd the School all the Afternoon. N Burrell drank Tea here.

SEPTEMBER 11, MONDAY A fine Day, wind rough & Cold. Mr Hardy, I & Rav^n set of for Fakenham in Mrs Sheppards post Chaise Morn 10, Dind & drank Tea at Mr Crofts, came home Even past 8.

SEPTEMBER 12, TUESDAY A Wet Day, wind rough. Mr Hardy at home all Day. Thos [Youngman] spraind his Ancle. I Bathd.

SEPTEMBER 13, WEDNESDAY A Wet day, Wind high. Mr Hardy at home all Day, Mr Bensley drank Tea here. I attendd the School in Eveng.

SEPTEMBER 14, THURSDAY A Stormy day, Wind very high, severall Coombs of Apples blown down. Mr Hardy at home all Day. M^r & Mrs Bartell drank Tea & Supt here . . .

SEPTEMBER 17, SUNDAY A fine Day. I attendd the School foornoon & Afternoon, Mr Burrell attendd after Church. M^r & Mrs Baker & John, Mr Lacy & Matt Davy drank Tea here.

SEPTEMBER 18, MONDAY A fine Day. Mr Hardy at home all Day. I & W^m rid up to Holt after Tea, carried Mrs Davy some Apples.

SEPTEMBER 19, TUESDAY A very fine day. Mr Hardy at home all day. M^r & M^{rs} [Benjamin] Crofts from Gresenhall & M^r & M^{rs} [John] Crofts of Fakenham came to Dinner. Sent Thos Youngm to Fakenham for Mary Ann. I Bathd . . .

SEPTEMBER 22, FRIDAY A very fine day. M^r & Mrs Crofts set of for Gressenhall Morn 10, M^r J Crofts & Wife went for Booton. Mr Hardy at home all day.

SEPTEMBER 23, SATURDAY A Close Cold day. Mr Hardy went up to Holt MII to meet the Justices, dind at Mr Bartells, drank Tea at Mr Bakers. I, MA & Rav^n walkd up to Holt aftern, drank Tea at Miss Leakes . . .

SEPTEMBER 25, MONDAY A Cold close day, Wet Night. Mr Hardy & I dind, drank Tea & Supt at Mr Bartells, M^{rs} & Miss Wymer & Mrs Baldin there. I Bathd.

SEPTEMBER 26, TUESDAY A dry Morng, Wet afternoon. M^{rs} & Miss Wymer, Mrs Baldin, M^r & Mrs Bartell dind, drank Tea, Supt & Slept here. Mr Hardy at home all Day. Mr Dye Seppins Married to Miss Athell [Atthill].

SEPTEMBER 27, WEDNESDAY A Cold dry day. Our Company went away after breakfst. Mr Hardy at home all Day. I Bathd . . .

SEPTEMBER 30, SATURDAY A fine day. I, MA & Rav^n drank Tea at Mr Davys, Mr Hardy at Markt. I Bathd.

OCTOBER 1, SUNDAY A fine Day. I attendd the School Foornoon & Aftern, all went to our Church Afternoon,

Mr Burrell preachd. 2 Miss Davys, Miss Wymer, Miss Bartell & Miss Fanny Chichely at Church & drank Tea here . . .

OCTOBER 5, THURSDAY A fine Day. Miss Wymer Dind & drank Tea here. I poorly with A Cold . . .

OCTOBER 9, MONDAY A Close Mild Day. Sent our Boy to Norwich with the Cart. Mr Hardy at home all Day. . .

OCTOBER 11, WEDNESDAY A Close Showry Day. Mr Hardy at home all Day . . .

OCTOBER 13, FRIDAY A fine Day. Mr Hardy at home.

OCTOBER 14, SATURDAY A Close Day, began to rain Even 4, continued all Night. Mr Hardy, I & Rav^n walkd up to Holt Markt Afternoon, drank Tea at Mr Bartells. I Bathd . . .

OCTOBER 16, MONDAY A Close Day. Mr Hardy at home all Day. I Bathd. Henry Goggs came.

OCTOBER 17, TUESDAY A fine Day. Mr Hardy at home all Day, Henry Goggs went away after Dinner.

OCTOBER 19, THURSDAY A Close Mild Day. W^m set of for Fakenham Morn 10, Dind at Mr Custances, came home past 7. Mr Hardy at home all Day, Mr Bensley drank Tea here. I Taken with Dimness in my Eyes.

OCTOBER 20, FRIDAY A Close Day. Mr Hardy at home all Day. I Bathd.

OCTOBER 21, SATURDAY A Close Day, a small drisley rain Afternoon. Mr Hardy went to Markt Even 2, came home Eve 8. I Poorly with dimness in my Eyes. I Bathd.

OCTOBER 22, SUNDAY A Close Day, a small rain in Eveng. All went to our Church Foornoon, Mr Burrell preachd, I attendd the School Afternoon. Old Francis Jeckell was buried.

OCTOBER 23, MONDAY A Close foggy Day. I Bathd, poorly with dimness in my Eyes. Mr Hardy at home all Day . . .

OCTOBER 25, WEDNESDAY A very fine Day. Maids Washd small Linnen. Mr Hardy at home all Day. I & Raven rid up to Holt in L Cart Aftern, came back to Tea. I attendd the Schooll.

OCTOBER 26, THURSDAY A very fine Day, sharp frost. Mr Hardy at home all Day. I Bathd.

OCTOBER 27, FRIDAY A Sharp frosty Morn, Close foggy Day. Mr Hardy at home all Day, I attend'd the Schooll. M^r & Mrs Bartell drank Tea & Supt here.

OCTOBER 28, SATURDAY A very Cold close Day. Mr Hardy went to Markt Even past 2, came home Even 8. I Bathd . . .

OCTOBER 30, MONDAY A fine Day. Mr Hardy at home all Day. I & Rav^n rid up to Holt, came back to Tea. I Bathd.

OCTOBER 31, TUESDAY A Cold dry Windy Day. Maids & Ann Humphry washd. Mr Hardy at home all Day.

NOVEMBER 1, WEDNESDAY A Cold Stormy Day. Mr Hardy at home all Day . . .

NOVEMBER 3, FRIDAY A fine Morn, Showry day. Mr Hardy at home all Day, I attendd the School in the Even. I Bathd. [[[by Mary Ann] MAs birth day, aged 13.]]

NOVEMBER 4, SATURDAY A Showry Day. Mr Hardy & MA walkd up to Holt Mark^t Even 3, MA drank Tea at Mr Davys. Sent the Cart for them Even 7 . . .

NOVEMBER 6, MONDAY A very Cold dry Day. I Bathd. Mr Bartell came to see Rav^n. Mr Hardy & I drank Tea & Supt «at» Mr Bartells, Miss Stannard from Norwich there. Mr Jno [James, not John] Hewit & Mrs Hogg of Holt was Married. I Bathd . . .

NOVEMBER 11, SATURDAY A Close cold Day. Bro^t Rav^n & Mr Moy Dind here & went away Even 3. Rav^n something better. Mr Hardy went to Holt Markt Even 3, came home to Tea, Miss Stannard Dind here. Mr Bartell came to see Rav^n . . .

NOVEMBER 14, TUESDAY A very Sharp frost. Mr Hardy at home all Day. Miss Stannard came to see M Ann, staid all Night.

NOVEMBER 15, WEDNESDAY A very Sharp frosty Day. Mr Hardy at home all Day. Mr Bartell Visited Raven. {M^r Bartell Visited Raven.}

NOVEMBER 16, THURSDAY A Cold drisley Day. Mr Hardy at home all Day. Sent Miss Stannard to Mr Bartells before Dinner. Sister N Raven & her 2 Daughtrs & Rose Raven came to Dinner.

NOVEMBER 17, FRIDAY A Cold Stormy Day. Childr^n rid up to Holt before Dinner. Mr Hardy at home all Day. Mr Bartell Visited Raven, he was very bad.

NOVEMBER 18, SATURDAY A very Cold Wet Day. Mr Hardy at home all Day. Mr Bartell & Mr Burrell Visited Raven, he was very bad . . .

NOVEMBER 22, WEDNESDAY A Close Day. Mr Hardy went to Overtons Club Even 7, came home Even past 11. Raven something better, Mr Burrell calld to see Raven.

NOVEMBER 23, THURSDAY A Close Day. Mr Hardy at home all Day. Mr Bartell visited Raven, he was much as Usual . . .

NOVEMBER 25, SATURDAY A Close Dry Day. Mr Hardy rid up to Holt Mark^t & came back to Tea. MA & Mrs Youngman walkd up to Holt . . .

DECEMBER 2, SATURDAY A fine Morn, close Afternoon. Mr Hardy walkd up to Holt Mark^t Even 3, came home Eve 8. Rav^n very poorly, just walkd into Garden foornoon, Mr Bartell visited him.

DECEMBER 3, SUNDAY A Wet Day. Mr Hardy & MA at our Church foornoon, Mr Burrell preach^d. Mr Massingham of Holt call^d to see Raven. Mr Bartell visidd [visited] him, a Bottle of fever Mixture.

DECEMBER 4, MONDAY A fine Dry Day. Mr Hardy at home all Day. Mr Bensley calld Aftern, Mrs Baker & 2 Sons drank Tea here. Raven very poorly. Mrs Jay of Holt Died this Morn Aged [   ]. M Ann went to Mr Bartells Aftern.

DECEMBER 5, TUESDAY A Close dry Day. Rav^n something better. Mr Hardy at home all day . . .

DECEMBER 7, THURSDAY A Close Morn, fine Afternoon. Miss Stannard & MA walkd up to Holt Afternoon, came back to Tea. Mr Hardy at home all Day. Edmd Bartell came for Miss Stannard in the Even.

DECEMBER 8, FRIDAY A Close dry Day. Mr Hardy at home all Day. M^{rs} & Nanny [Ann] Davy drank Tea here. Raven very poorly . . .

DECEMBER 10, SUNDAY A Close Cold Day, Wind high towards Night. Mr Bartell visited Raven, he was finely. I & M Ann went to our Church Afternoon, Mr Burrell preach'd. Matt Davy & Mark Massingham of Holt drank Tea here, MA drank Tea at Mr Burrells . . .

DECEMBER 13, WEDNESDAY A dry Day. Mr Hardy at home all Day. Doct^r Pleasence came in the Eveng to see Rav^n. A very Stormy Night, Wind very high.

DECEMBER 14, THURSDAY A Chearly Day. Mr Hardy at home all Day, Rav^n reather better.

DECEMBER 15, FRIDAY A Chearly Day. Rav^n somthing better, Mr Bartell Visited Raven.

DECEMBER 16, SATURDAY A Sharp rime frost. Rav^n reather better. Mr Hardy walkd up to Holt Markt Even 3, W^m & MA rid up in L Cart Even 4 . . .

DECEMBER 20, WEDNESDAY Sharp frost, frequent Stormes of Snow. Mr Hardy at home all day. Mr Bartell visited Raven & drank Tea here . . .

DECEMBER 22, FRIDAY A rime frost. Mr Hardy at home all Day . . .

DECEMBER 26, TUESDAY A very Sharp frost, Close Day. Mr Hardy Dind & drank Tea at Mr Bensleys at Holt, had Venison for Dinner, came home Even 8. Miss Baker & Miss Custance came foornoon, M Ann went to Holt with them to stay 3 or 4 Days at Mr Bakers. Mr Bartell calld to see Raven.

DECEMBER 27, WEDNESDAY A thaw & rain. Mr Hardy went to Overtons Club Even 5, came home Even 11 . ..

DECEMBER 29, FRIDAY A very Wet Morn, fine Aftern. Mr Hardy at home all day. Rav^n very poorly . . .

DECEMBER 31, SUNDAY A Close foggy Day. Mr Hardy, W^m & MA went to our Church foornoon, Mr Burrell preachd. W^m went to Holt Church Afternoon.

1787

JANUARY 1, MONDAY A foggy Day. Mr Hardy at home all Day. Mr Forster of Bayfield drank Tea & Supt here & reck'd . . .

JANUARY 3, WEDNESDAY Sharp rime frost. Bro^t & Robt Ravn went away Even 3, MA & Miss Davy went to Holt Even 4. Mr Bartell calld to see Raven.

JANUARY 4, THURSDAY Close dry Day. Mr Hardy drank Tea & Supt at Mr Bakers of Holt, Boy went for him in Little Cart, home Eve 12 . . .

JANUARY 6, SATURDAY A very fine bright Day. Mr Hardy went to Markt Even 3, sent the L Cart for him & MA & Ann Davy, came home Even 8.

JANUARY 7, SUNDAY A Sharp frost, bright Day. All went to our Church Afternoon, Mr Burrell preachd. M^r & Mrs Baker & Miss & Ad^m [Adam] Baker & Miss Custance at our Church. M^r H & I drank Tea at Mr Burrells with M^r & Mrs Davy «and» M^r & Mrs Thompson.

JANUARY 8, MONDAY A Sharp rime frost, very foggy. Mr Hardy went to Mr Bartells, drank Tea & Supt there . . .

JANUARY 10, WEDNESDAY A Cold foggy Day. M Ann & Miss Davy walkd up to Holt afternoon . . .

JANUARY 13, SATURDAY A frost, very fine Day. Raven much the same. M^r H, I & Miss Custance & M Ann took a walk before Dinner. Mr Hardy walkd to Holt Markt Afternoon, came home Even 8. Mr Stangroom of Langham Died. Miss Baker went away . . .

JANUARY 16, TUESDAY A rime frost, fine Day. Rav^n somthing better. Mr Hardy at home all Day. Mr Theorderic calld. Mr Stangroom was buried at Holt . . .

JANUARY 21, SUNDAY A Close Morn, fine Day. MA & W^m at our Church Aftern. Mr Hardy poorly, & I poorly with Deafness . . .

JANUARY 24, WEDNESDAY A moderate rime frost, fine Day. Rav^n much as yesterday. Mr Hardy came home Even past 6. Miss Custance went away to Mr Bakers at Holt, MA walkd with her to Holt & came back to Tea.

JANUARY 25, THURSDAY A fine Day, small frost. Rav^n much as yesterday. M^rs & Nanny Davy & Mark Massingham drank Tea here. Mr Bartell calld to see Rav^n . . .

FEBRUARY 3, SATURDAY A Showry Morn, tolerable Afternoon. Mr Hardy walkd up to Holt Afternoon, W^m & M [Mary Ann] rid up Even 4.

FEBRUARY 4, SUNDAY A fine Day. Mr Hardy, W^m & MA went to our Church Afternoon, Mr Burrell preachd. M^r N Burrell drank Tea here.

FEBRUARY 5, MONDAY A rime frost, close Day. Rav^n reather worse. Mr Hardy at home all Day . . .

[*Raven Hardy died on 12 February 1787 aged nineteen and was buried at Letheringsett on 16 February*]

FEBRUARY 28, WEDNESDAY A tolerable Day, Wind rough. Mr Hardy, I & MA went to our Church foornoon. M^r H & I rid up to Holt Afternoon & drank Tea at Mr Bartells.

MARCH 1, THURSDAY Close mild Day, Wind high. Mr Hardy at home all Day. M^r & Mrs Burrell here a little while in the Even.

MARCH 2, FRIDAY Wind high & very Stormy. Mr Hardy at home all Day. 2 Gardiners at Work . . .

MARCH 4, SUNDAY A Wet Morn, Wind high. All went to our Church Afternoon, Mr Burrell preachd, M^r N Burrell here in Even. ⟦ [*by Mary Ann*] Thos whent to Whissonsett for my Uncles Chase [chaise]. ⟧

MARCH 5, MONDAY Close Morn, Wet Aftern. Mr Groom Dind here, Mr Burrell & Ben Emmery here after Dinner. Mr Hardy walkd up to Holt Even past 3, drank Tea at Mr Davys, home Eve 9. ⟦ [*by Mary Ann*] Thos came home Even 2.

The visit to Whissonsett
6–10 March 1787

MARCH 6, TUESDAY A very]] Wet [[[*Mary Ann continues*] bad Day. Father & Mother went to Whissonsett, got there past 2 O Clock, drank Tea and Suped and Slept at Uncles Ravens.]]

MARCH 7, WEDNESDAY A fine dry Day. All went to Whissensett Church, Mr Bird read prayers. Went to Sister Ravens at the Hall, drank Tea & Supt there.

MARCH 8, THURSDAY A fine Day. Mr Hardy & Bro^t Raven & M^r R Fox went to Fakenham by Rainham Morn 11. I dind, drank Tea & Supt at Mr Goggs, Mr Hardy came back to Tea & Supt there.

MARCH 9, FRIDAY A fine Day but Cold. All went to Church foornoon. Mr Hardy walkd with Mr Goggs after Dinner to Colkirk to Robt Goggs s, we all drank Tea at Mr Cases. M^r & Mrs Moy Supt with us at Bro^t Ravens.

MARCH 10, SATURDAY A Close Morn, some rain foornoon, dry Afternoon. Mr Hardy & I set of from Whisinsett Morn ½ past 10, got home Eve past 2. Mr Hardy & W^m walkd up to Holt Mark^t Even 4.

[LETHERINGSETT]

MARCH 11, SUNDAY A fine Day. All went to our Church foornoon, Mr Burrell preachd. Thos went to Whisensett with Bro^t Ravens Chaise, came home Even 8 . . .

MARCH 13, TUESDAY A Close Mild Day. Mr Hardy at home all Day. Mrs Burrell here in Eveng, 2 Gardiners at work . . .

MARCH 16, FRIDAY A very fine Day. Nanny Davy & I walkd up to Holt foornoon, came back to Dinner. Mr Hardy & MA came home Even past 9. Miss Boston of Holt Died.

MARCH 17, SATURDAY A very fine Day. Mr Hardy, I & W^m walkd up to Holt Afternoon, drank Tea at Mr Davys, Nanny Davy went home. Old Duke Choping thorn bulls.

MARCH 18, SUNDAY A very fine Day. Mr Hardy & W^m at our Church Aftern, Mr Burrell preachd. MA Ill with pain in her teeth & Cold, I could not go to Church. 2 Mastr Davys, Mastr Bartell & young Starling drank Tea here.

MARCH 19, MONDAY A very fine Day. MA something better. Mr Hardy & I met M^r & Mrs Bartell at Mr Bakers, drank Tea there. Old Duke choping thorn bulls.

MARCH 20, TUESDAY A very fine Day. Maids & Ann Humphry washd 4 Weeks Linnen. W^m walk^d up to Holt Afternoon, drank Tea at Mr Bakers. MA poorly. Old Duke choping thorn bulls.

MARCH 21, WEDNESDAY A very fine Day. Mr Hardy, I & MA went to our Church foornoon. We went to Bale Afternoon, drank Tea at Mr Barnwells. Old Duke choping thorn bulls . . .

MARCH 23, FRIDAY A Showry Morn, fine Aftern. Mr Hardy at home all Day.

[[MARCH 24, SATURDAY [*by Mary Ann*] A fine Day. Mother, Father and Brother & I went up to Holt Market. Mother & Father drank Tea at Mr Bartells, I drank Tea at Mr Davys, came home Even 7.

MARCH 25, SUNDAY Wind high, it rained in the Evening. We all went to our Church Morning, W^m went to Holt Church Afternoon . . .

MARCH 27, TUESDAY Fine Day. My Father at Home all Day. Ann Davy and I walked up to Holt after Tea, I came home Even 8 . . .]]

MARCH 31, SATURDAY A very fine Day. Mr Hardy, I & MA & W^m walkd up to Holt Mark^t Afternoon. I drank «tea» at Miss Leakes, MA drank Tea at Mr Davys, came home Even 7 in L Cart . . .

APRIL 4, WEDNESDAY [*at Whissonsett*] A fine Day. After breakfst walkd up to the Hall to speak to Sister Rav^n then went to Church. Dind at Bro^t then went to Fakenham, attend'd the Sale, drank Tea at Mr Custances & came home ½ past 8, brought Nathl Raven home with us.

APRIL 5, THURSDAY A Dry Day, Wind Cold. Mr Hardy rid to Clay Aftern, came home Even 8. I & W^m rid in L Cart with the Colt to Mr Boltons of Thornage, came back to Tea.

APRIL 6, *Good Friday* A very Cold dry Day. All went to our Church Afternoon, Mr Burrell preachd. M^r & Mrs Bartell drank Tea here.

APRIL 7, SATURDAY A Cold Windy day. We all walkd up to Holt Afternoon. I & MA drank Tea at Mr Davys, M^r H & W^m drank tea at Mr Bakers . . .

APRIL 9, MONDAY A Cold windy day. Mr Hardy at home all Day. I & MA walk«ed» up to Holt after Tea . . .

APRIL 11, WEDNESDAY A [   ]. Mr Hardy at home all Day, I attend d the School in Even.

APRIL 12, THURSDAY A dry Day. Mr Hardy at home all Day. I & W^m took a ride after Tea round by Thornage & Holt with the Colt . . .

APRIL 14, SATURDAY A Cold close day, raind towards Even. M^r & Mrs Burrell walkd up to Holt with us, we all drank Tea at M^r N Burrells, came home in L Cart . . .

APRIL 16, MONDAY Small rain in Morng, fine Day. W^m & MA sett of for Whisensett m ½ past 10 in L Cart with Colt. Mrs Stangroom, M^rs & Miss Baker drank Tea here.

APRIL 17, TUESDAY A dry windy Day. Maids & Ann Humphry washd. Mr Hardy at home all Day.

APRIL 18, WEDNESDAY [

                                                    ] . . .

APRIL 21, SATURDAY A fine Day but Cold. M^r H, I & W^m & Nathl walkd up to Holt Mark^t, drank Tea at Mr Bakers. Old Mrs Fisher of Holt Died Aged [   ].

APRIL 22, SUNDAY A Cold close Day. All went to our Church foornoon, Mr Burrell preachd. I attendd the School foornoon & Aftern. Mrs Davy & 2 Daughtrs & Son, Miss Riches & Mr Starling came after Tea. W^m at H«olt» Church.

APRIL 23, MONDAY A fine foornoon, began to rain Even 6, raind all Night. Mr Hardy at home all Day. W^m set of for Whisensett Morn past 5. M^r & Mrs Bartell, Miss & Robt Bartell & Miss Barnwell drank Tea & Supt here, the young ones staid all Night.

APRIL 24, TUESDAY A fine Day. We all drank Tea at Mr Burrells. W^m & MA came home Even 7 . . .

APRIL 28, SATURDAY A very Wet Day & Wind high. Mr Hardy & I walkd up to Holt, drank Tea & Supt at Mr Bartells. W^m came for us in L Cart.

APRIL 29, SUNDAY A very Wet Morn, Stormy Day. I attend'd the School foornoon & Aftern. All went to our Church Afternoon, Mr Burrell preach^d, M^r & Mrs Burrell came after Tea.

APRIL 30, MONDAY A very Sharp Day, Wind high & Stormy. Mr Hardy at home all Day. I poorly with dimness in my Eyes.

MAY 1, TUESDAY A very Cold Stormy day, Wind high. Mr Hardy at home all Day. Edm^d Bartell drank Tea here . . .

MAY 3, THURSDAY A very fine mild Day. Mr Hardy at home all Day. Mrs Davy & Bett & Miss Riches, M^r & M^rs & Robt Bartell drank Tea here, M^r & Mrs Burrell came after Tea.

MAY 4, FRIDAY A very fine day. Miss Riches & Bett Davy came for a walk in Morng. Mr Hardy at home all Day.

MAY 5, SATURDAY A Cold Stormy windy day. We all went up to Holt Aftern, drank Tea at Mr Davys, W^m drank Tea at Mr Bartells . . .

MAY 8, TUESDAY A fine day. Mr Hardy at home all Day.

MAY 9, WEDNESDAY A fine Morn, turnd Cold & hasy afternoon. Mr Hardy, I & MA rid up to Mr Bartells Aftern, drank Tea there, Matt, Mrs Davy, Mrs Baker &c there. Raind a little in the Night . . .

MAY 12, SATURDAY A fine Day. All walkd up to Holt Afternoon. I & MA & W^m drank Tea at Mr Bartells, M^r H drank Tea at Mr Bakers.

MAY 13, SUNDAY A very fine Day. All went to our Church Afternoon, Mr Burrell preachd. I attend^d the School foornoon & Aftern.

MAY 14, MONDAY A Chearly Morn, Close Cold Afternoon. Mr Hardy at home all Day. Sister Goggs & Henry came ab^t Noon. W^m poorly with a Cold & pain in his teeth.

MAY 15, TUESDAY A Chearly Day but cold & Wind rough. Sister Goggs, I & MA rid up to Holt before Tea. Mr Barnwell drank Tea here. Mr Hardy at home all Day, W^m very poorly.

MAY 16, WEDNESDAY A Chearly day but very Cold. Sister Goggs, I & Mr Hardy drank Tea at Mr Burrells, W^m very poorly.

MAY 17, THURSDAY A Chearly Day but Cold. Sister Goggs, I & W^m rid up to Holt foornoon, came back to Dinner. Mr Hardy at home all Day. M^r & Mrs Bartell & Charlotte, Mrs Davy, Miss Riches, J Davy & Mary & Sarah Davy, M^r & Mrs Garret, M^r & Mrs Burrell drank Tea here . . .

MAY 19, SATURDAY A fine Day. All walkd up to Holt Mark^t Afternoon, drank Tea at Mr Bartells . . .

MAY 27, *Whit Sunday* A fine day but Cold. All went to our Church Afternoon, Mr Burrell preachd. I attendd the School foorn & Afternoon.

MAY 28, MONDAY A Cold Showry day. Mr Hardy at home all day.

MAY 29, TUESDAY A Cold Showry «day». Mr Hardy at home all Day, Mrs Burrell drank Tea here. Mr Burrell went to bury Mr Pauls Child at Study [Stody], came here Even 8 . . .

MAY 31, THURSDAY A fine dry day. Mr Hardy at home all day. Tinker at Work . . .

JUNE 2, SATURDAY A dry day but Cold. Mr Hardy & W^m walkd to Holt Mark^t Aftern, drank tea at Mr Bartells. MA very Ill with a Cold. Tinker at Work.

JUNE 3, SUNDAY A fine day but cold. Mr Hardy very poorly, MA poorly. I & W^m at Church foornoon & at the Comunion, Mr Burrell preachd. I attendd the School Aftern. Mr Cooper of Holt drank Tea here, M^r & Mrs Davy & Childr^n walk'd down after Tea . . .

JUNE 5, TUESDAY A very fine day, a small Shower after Noon. Mr Hardy & W^m sett of for Yarmouth & Norwich after Dinner. Tinker at Work. A small Show^r Afternoon.

JUNE 6, WEDNESDAY A Cold Day, small Showrs. Miss Riches & John Davy drank Tea here. Tinker at work . . .

JUNE 8, FRIDAY A dry Chearly day. Attend'd the School in Even . . .

JUNE 11, MONDAY A Close Cold Day. Mr Hardy poorly. Tinker at work . . .

JUNE 13, WEDNESDAY A Cold hasy day. Mr Hardy very poorly. One Carpenter, Mr Cooper & 2 Bricklayers at work . . .

JUNE 15, FRIDAY A small Showr in Morn, Hot dry day. Mr Hardy very bad, sint [sent] for Mr Bartell, had 6 powders, a bottle of Deaphorche [?] & an opening Drft [draught]. One Carpenter «and» Mr Cooper at work.

JUNE 16, SATURDAY A very fine day. Mr Hardy very bad with the Gout, Mr Bartell visited him, orderd no Physic. W^m went to Holt Mark^t. One Carpenter & 2 Bricklayers at work.

JUNE 17, SUNDAY A very fine Day. Mr Hardy very poorly. W^m & MA at our Church foornoon, Mr Burrell preachd. I attend'd the School After & Lectures in Eveng, W^m at Holt Church After. Mr Bartell here, orderd no physic.

JUNE 18, MONDAY A fine Day. Mr Hardy very poorly. One Carpenter, Mr Cooper & 2 Bricklayers at Work.

JUNE 19, TUESDAY Fine Morn, some small Showrs in the Day. Mr Hardy very poorly, Mr Bartell visited him foornoon, no physic orderd. M^r & Mrs Bartell drank Tea here Aftern. Maids & Ann Humphry washd 4 Weeks Linnen. One Carpenter, Mr Cooper at [and] 2 Brick^l at work. A good deal of rain in the Night . . .

JUNE 21, THURSDAY A very fine day. Mr Hardy poorly. No Carpenter but Thos & 2 bricklayers at work.

JUNE 22, FRIDAY A drisley Morn, hot dry Aftern. Mr Hardy something better. No Carpenter but Thos, 2 Bricklyrs [bricklayers] at Work. Mr Keeler & Miss Billings drank Tea here. Mrs Custance, M^rs [Hannah] Raven & Miss [Elizabeth] Raven came to Holt, W^m & MA rid up to Holt Foornoon.

JUNE 23, SATURDAY A very fine day. Mr Hardy reather better. M^r & Mrs Rav^n &c & Mrs Custance & M^r & Mrs Baker paid us a Morning Visit. I & W^m rid up to Holt in our Chaise, drank Tea at Mr Bakers . . .

JUNE 25, MONDAY A fine Morn, Showry Aftern. Mr Hardy, I & MA Dind & drank Tea at Mr Bakers with M^r & Mrs Rav^n & Mrs Custance . . .

JUNE 27, WEDNESDAY A Showry day. I & W^m rid up to Holt before breakfst in Chaise. M^r & Mrs Baker & son,

Mrs Custance & Son & Miss Rav^n Dind, drank Tea & Supt here. Mr Hardy much as Yesterd, Mr Bartell calld to ask Mr Hardy how he did as he went past. One Carpenter & 2 bricklayers at work . . .

JUNE 29, FRIDAY A very fine dry day. Mr Hardy at home, much as yesterd. I attend'd the School in Even. 1 Carpenter & 1 Bricklayer at work. . .

JULY 1, SUNDAY A very fine dry day. All went to our Church foornoon except Mr Hardy, Mr Burrell preach'd. Mr Hardy much as Yesterday. I attend'd the School afternoon, all attendd Lectures in the Eveng. Mr Barnwell call'd, staid ab^t an hour . . .

JULY 4, WEDNESDAY A Sultry dry day. Mr Hardy much as Yesterday. 1 Bricklayer & 1 Carpenter at work.

JULY 5, THURSDAY A very hot dry day. Mr Hardy much as Yesterday. I & W^m went to Fakenham Aftern in our Chaise to speak to Mr Danl Jones, he was not at home, drank Tea at Mr Custances, came home Even 9. MA went to Bale with Mr Barnwell.

JULY 6, FRIDAY A hot day, some small Showers Afternoon. Bro^t & Robt Raven came Even 2, went away Even 7. I attend'd the School in Even. Mr Hardy much as Yesterd. 1 Bricklayer & 1 Carpenter at work, began the back Stair Case.

JULY 7, SATURDAY A very fine day, not too hot. Mr Hardy much as usual. 1 Carpenter & 1 Bricklayer at work.

JULY 8, SUNDAY A fine Day. Mr Hardy poorly. W^m went to our Church Afternoon, Mr Burrell preachd. W^m went to Mr Barnwells after Tea for M Ann. Mrs Baldin & «Mrs» Rav^n & M^r & Mrs Wymer came to Mr Bartells.

JULY 9, MONDAY A fine day. Mr Hardy something better, we rid up to fur Closes after Tea. 1 Bricklayer & 1 Carpenter at work.

JULY 10, TUESDAY A Showry Day. 1 Bricklayer & 1 Carpenter at work. M^r & Mrs Wymer calld here in Eveng coming from Mr Barnwells, Mrs Bartell &c went to the Play at Walsinghm with him.

JULY 11, WEDNESDAY A fine morn, Showry Aftern. Mr Hardy, I & M Ann dind & drank Tea at Mr Bartells, came home Even 9. 1 Carpenter & one Bricklayer at work.

JULY 12, THURSDAY A very Showry Day. 1 Carpenter & one bricklayer at work. Mrs Baldin, Mrs Wymer, Mrs Raven, M^r & Mrs Bartell & 2 Childr^n Dind & drank Tea here.

JULY 13, FRIDAY A very Close Showry Day. One Carpenter & one bricklayer at work. Mrs Baker & Miss Miss [? Mrs and Miss] Raven & Miss Custance dind & drank Tea here . . .

JULY 17, TUESDAY A very Showry Day. Maids & Ann Humphry Washd. Mr Hardy at home all Day. One Bricklayer & one Carpenter at work, 2 Gardiners at work half a Day.

JULY 18, WEDNESDAY A fine day except a small Showr towards Even. Mr Hardy & MA rid up to Holt after Tea, paid Excise.

JULY 19, THURSDAY A very fine day. Mr Hardy & I rid up to Holt after tea to change some Cloth of Mr Smith. One Carpenter & one bricklayer at work.

JULY 20, FRIDAY Showry day. Mr Hardy, I & MA drank Tea at Mr Davys with Miss Raven. One Carpenter & one bricklayer at work.

JULY 21, SATURDAY A fine day except a very heavy Showr ab^t 2 oClock. Mr Hardy, I & M Ann rid up to Holt, drank Tea at Mr Davys, their Childr^n better. One Carpenter & one bricklayer at work . . .

JULY 23, MONDAY A Showry day. Mr Hardy at home all Day. 1 Bricklayer at work, no Carpenter . . .

JULY 26, THURSDAY A very Showry Day. Mr Hardy at home all Day. One Bricklayer & one Carpenter at work.

JULY 27, FRIDAY A fine Day. Bro^t Raven came Morn 9, went away Even 6 with Mr Moy. Mrs Davy, Mrs Bolton, Miss Riches & 3 of Davys Childr^n drank Tea here.

JULY 28, SATURDAY A fine Day. Mr Hardy poorly, did not go to Mark^t, rid out Afternoon. One Carpenter & one Bricklayer at work.

JULY 29, SUNDAY A fine Day. All went to our Church foornoon, Mr Burrell preachd. Mrs Sheppard from Norwich came. M^rs & Mr Davy & Family came after Dinner, drank Tea at Mr Burrells . . .

JULY 31, TUESDAY Showry Morn, fine Aftern. Mr Hardy at home all Day. One Carpenter & one bricklayer at work. Mrs Sheppard went away by Wade.

AUGUST 1, WEDNESDAY A fine day, reather hot. One Carpenter & one bricklayr at work. Mr Hardy & I rid to Clay after Tea.

AUGUST 2, THURSDAY A hot dry Day. One Carpenter & one bricklayr at work. M Ann poorly, we shd have gone to Whisensett . . .

AUGUST 5, SUNDAY A very Sultry dry Day. I attendd the School a little wile foornoon & Afternoon, all went to our Church Afternoon & attendd Lectures in Eveng.

AUGUST 6, MONDAY A Close Morn, fine Afternoon. One bricklayer & 2 Carpenters at work. Mr Hardy, I & M Ann, M^r & Mrs Burrell went to Mr Barnwells at Bale, met M^r & Mrs Elvin [Elwin], M^r & Mrs Bulcock, drank Tea & Supt there, came home M2 . . .

AUGUST 9, THURSDAY A Hot dry Day. Mr Hardy something better. One bricklayer & 2 Carpenters at Work. A tempest in the Night.

AUGUST 10, FRIDAY A very hot Sultry Day. Mr Hardy very poorly, Mr Burrell call^d to see him, he rid out foornoon & Afternoon to take the Air. M^r & Mrs Burrell drank Tea here, Mrs Forster & 3 other Ladies came after Tea. [[[by Mary Ann] 1 Mason, 2 Carpenter]] . . .

AUGUST 14, TUESDAY A Showry Day. Washd. One Carpenter, 2 bricklayers at work. Mr Hardy much as yesterday.

AUGUST 15, WEDNESDAY A Showry day. Mr Hardy & I went to Northreps to Mrs Brookes Sale in Mrs Sheppards post Chaise, bought nothing, Dind at Alsops at Cromer, got home Even 7. One Carpenter & 2 bricklayrs.

AUGUST 16, THURSDAY A fine Day. One Carpenter, no bricklayers at work. Mr Hardy & I went to Mr Dews of Swanton [Novers] to Tea.

AUGUST 17, FRIDAY A fine Day. One Carpenter at work. M^r & Mrs Bartell, Mrs Davy & Bett drank Tea here, M^r & Mrs Burrell here in Eveng.

AUGUST 18, SATURDAY A fine Morn, wet Aftern. Mr Hardy poorly. W^m & MA rid up to Holt after Tea. Thos Nash & Ja^s Fitt of Hobis [Hautbois] came after Tea. One Carpenter at work.

AUGUST 19, SUNDAY A very fine Day. M^r & M^rs & Miss Wymer, M^r & Mrs Bartell, Dind, drank Tea & Supt here, M^r & M^rs & Miss Wymer Slept here. Our service at the Church After, did not go but all of us went to Le«c»tures . . .

AUGUST 21, TUESDAY A fine Day. Mr Hardy at home. Mrs Geo^r Wymer & Mast^r Bartell drank tea here, M^r & Mrs Burrell drank Tea & Supt here. One Carpenter at work.

AUGUST 22, WEDNESDAY A very fine Day. M^r & Mrs Geo^r Wymer here foornoon. M^r & M^rs & Miss Wymer, Mr Hdy, I & MA drank Tea & Supt at Mr Burrells. One Carpenter at work.

AUGUST 23, THURSDAY Close Morn, a Showr ab^t Even 2. M^r & M^rs & Miss Wymer, M^r & Mrs Burrell, Mr Hardy, I & MA went to Sheringham Afternoon, drank Tea at Mrs Scoots [Scott's]. 2 Carpenters at work.

AUGUST 24, FRIDAY A Close dry Day. M^r & Mrs Wymer went away after Breakfst. Mr Hardy at home all day. One Carpenter at work. M^r & Mrs Burrell & young Mr Daglass here in Even, playd at Cards. 2 Carpenters at work.

AUGUST 25, SATURDAY A very Wet Day. Mr Hardy at home all Day. M^r & Mrs Burrell here after Tea, playd at Cards. Wet Night, wind very high. 2 Carpenters at work.

AUGUST 26, SUNDAY A Showry Day. All went to our Church foornoon, Mr Burrell preachd. I attend'd the School afternoon, we all attend^d Lectures.

AUGUST 27, MONDAY A Close drisley Day. Mr Hardy, I & Miss Wymer & MA drank Tea at Mr Davys at Holt. 2 Carpenters at work. . .

AUGUST 29, WEDNESDAY A Close Morn, fine in medle [middle] part of the Day & raind towards Even. Mr Hardy, I & Miss Wymer & M An drank Tea at Mr Bartells, M^rs B poorly. 2 Carpenters at work. . .

AUGUST 31, FRIDAY A Close Morn, drisley Aftern. Mr Hardy, I, Miss Wymer & MA drank Tea at Mr Bakers. 2 Carpenters at work.

SEPTEMBER 1, SATURDAY A Close drisley Day. Mr Hardy at home all Day, I & W^m & Miss Wymer rid up to Holt after Tea. 2 Carpenters at work . . .

SEPTEMBER 5, WEDNESDAY A Close drisley Day. Mr Hardy at home all Day. 2 Carpenters at work.

SEPTEMBER 6, THURSDAY A fine dry Day. Mr Scot went away by the Mail Cart from Holt. Mr Hardy at home all Day. I, Miss Wymer & MA walkd up to Holt, drank Tea at Mr Bartells. 2 Carpenters at work.

SEPTEMBER 7, FRIDAY A fine Day. Mr Hardy at home all day, men at harvest work. 2 Carpenters at work.

SEPTEMBER 8, SATURDAY A fine Day. Mr Hardy rid to Study & to Holt after breakfst to the Justice sitting, Dind at the Feathers, drank Tea at Mr Bartells, home Even 8. I, Miss Wymer & MA walkd to Holt Aftern, drank Tea at Miss Leakes. 2 Carpenters at work . . .

SEPTEMBER 10, MONDAY A very fine Day. Mr Hardy set of for Whesenset Morn 9. Thos Theoderick from London calld.

SEPTEMBER 11, TUESDAY A very fine Day. Mr Hardy came home Even 7. 1 Carpenter at work . . .

SEPTEMBER 18, TUESDAY A fine Day. Ann Humphry, L Young^m [Lydia Youngman] & Maid washd 5 weeks Linnen. M^rs & Miss Baker, Mrs Bartell & 2 Childr^n, Miss Wymer & Miss Hipkins drank Tea here, Mr Bartell & Mr Baker came for them Even 7. My Arm poorly. One Carpenter at work, 1 bricklayer.

SEPTEMBER 19, WEDNESDAY Windy day. Mr Hardy rid to Salthouse & Keeling [Kelling] Aftern, came home Even 7. Mr Bartell came to see me, had a bottle of bathing Embrocation for my Arm.

SEPTEMBER 20, THURSDAY A fine Day. Mr Hardy at home all Day. 1 Carpenter, 2 Bricklayrs at work.

SEPTEMBER 21, FRIDAY A Wet Morn, Close windy Day. 1 Carpenter & 2 bricklayers at work. Mr Hardy at home all day. Miss Wymer & Edm^d Bartell drank Tea here.

SEPTEMBER 22, SATURDAY A Wet Morn, tolerable aftern. 1 Carpenter & 2 Bricklayers at work. Mr Hardy rid up to Mark^t abt Noon, drank Tea at Mr Bartells. I & MA walkd up to Holt Aftern, drank Tea at Mr Bartells, walkd home Even 8. Mr Bartell came to see me in Morn, my Arm very poorly . . .

SEPTEMBER 25, TUESDAY A very fine Day. Mr Hardy better & at home all Day. I & MA walkd up to Holt after Dinner, came home to Tea. Mr Bartell came to look at my Arm.

SEPTEMBER 26, WEDNESDAY A very fine day. Mr Hardy at home all Day. I attend^d the School in Eveng . . .

OCTOBER 16, TUESDAY A very Wet Morn, Showry Day. Mr Hardy at home all Day. Maids & Ann Humphry Washd. Mr Bartell drank Tea here.

OCTOBER 17, WEDNESDAY Wet Morn, some small Showrs in the Day. Mr Hardy at home all Day . . .

OCTOBER 20, SATURDAY A very Wet Morn, Showrg all Day. Mr Hardy walkd up to Holt Morn 11 to Justice sitting, Dind with them. I & W^m & MA rid up in L Cart Afternoon, drank Tea at Mr Davys, home before 8 . . .

OCTOBER 22, MONDAY A very Wet Morn, dry Afternoon. Mr Hardy at home all Day, W^m went up to Holt after Tea.

OCTOBER 23, TUESDAY A very fine Morn. Miss Baker & Miss Custance came to speak to us in Morng. Duke in Garden . . .

OCTOBER 25, THURSDAY A very Wet Day. Mr Hardy at home all Day. W^m could not git home on acct of the rain. Old Duke in Garden.

OCTOBER 26, FRIDAY A Close showry day. Mr Hardy at home all day. W^m came home Even 6. Goody Woods was buried. Old Duke in Garden . . .

OCTOBER 29, MONDAY A Close moist Day. Mr Hardy at home all Day. T Youngman Ill. Old Duke in Garden. A Wet Night. { Thos Youngman Ill } . . .

OCTOBER 31, WEDNESDAY A very fine Day. I & MA walkd up to Holt afternoon, came back to tea. Mr Barnwell calld. Mr Hardy came home Even past 8. Old Duke in Garden.

NOVEMBER 1, THURSDAY A Close Morn, raind a little Afternoon. Mr Hardy at home all Day. 2 Gardiners at work & Old Duke.

NOVEMBER 2, FRIDAY A Close Day. Mr Hardy at home all day. 2 Gardiners at Wo{o}rk & Old Duke in Garden.

NOVEMBER 3, SATURDAY A very fine Day. Mr Hardy & I walkd up to Holt Aftern, drank Tea at Mr Bakers, Wm came for us Even 8 in L Cart.

NOVEMBER 4, SUNDAY A Close frosty Morn, wet Aftern. All went to our Church foorn, Mr Burrell preachd. I attendd the School forn [forenoon] & Aftrn. Wm went to Holt Church & drank Tea at Mr Bartells . . .

NOVEMBER 8, THURSDAY A very Wet Day. Mr Hardy at home all Day. Old Duke in Garden. Mr Baker came foornoon & reckond . . .

NOVEMBER 10, SATURDAY A fine Day. We all walkd to Holt Markt Afternoon. Mr H & I drank Tea at Mr Bartells, Wm & MA drank Tea at Mr Davys. Mr Hdy taken very poorly with pain in the teeth, Wm came home for L Cart for Mr H & I, Bett Davy came home with MA . . .

NOVEMBER 14, WEDNESDAY A Cold Showry Day. Mr Hardy something better. Mr Bartell visited him, sent him a small box of Pills. Gardiner removing the Greens, Old Duke at Plow.

NOVEMBER 15, THURSDAY A tolerable dry Day. Mr Hardy Wnely. Old Duke at Plow. Miss Harpley & 2 Miss Theorderics calld to speak to M Ann.

NOVEMBER 16, FRIDAY A Wet Day. Mr Hardy better, Mr Bartell came to see him & drank Tea here.

NOVEMBER 17, SATURDAY A very fine Morn, close aftern. Mr Hardy & MA rid up to Holt in L Cart, I & Wm walkd, all drank Tea at Mr Bartells except Wm who drank tea at Mr Davys, all rid home Eve 8.

NOVEMBER 18, SUNDAY Very Stormy Morn, fine aftern. All went to our Church foorn, Mr Burrell preachd. Wm went to Holt Church Afternoon . . .

NOVEMBER 21, WEDNESDAY A Close cold Day. Mr Hardy finely, went to Holt Even 5, drank Tea at Mr Bartells then went to Overtons Club, came home Eve past 11.

NOVEMBER 22, THURSDAY A calm morn, a showr abt 2 oClock then fine towards Even. Mr Hardy finely.

NOVEMBER 23, FRIDAY A fine Day. Mr Hardy at home all Day. Mr Youngman went home aftcr Dinner. Mr Custance of Fakenham came, Dind & drank Tea here.

NOVEMBER 24, SATURDAY A fine Day. Mr Hardy set of for Norwich Morn 8. I & MA walkd up to Market aftern, drank Tea at Mr Davys, home Even 8 . . .

NOVEMBER 27, TUESDAY A Sharp rime frost, beautifull Day. Mr Hardy at home all day. MA went to Mr Davys of Holt with Bett Davy after Breakfst.

NOVEMBER 28, WEDNESDAY A Sharp rime frost, beautifull Day. Mr Hardy at home all Day. I walk'd up to Holt after Dinner for MA, came home to Tea. Old Duke in Garden . . .

NOVEMBER 30, FRIDAY A very sharp rime frost, beautifull Day. Mr Hardy at home all Day.

DECEMBER 1, SATURDAY A sharp Morn, began to thaw about 10 o Clock, continued to Thaw all «day», raind alittle aftern. Mr Hardy walkd up to Holt Market Eve 2, came home Eve 8. Old Duke in Garden.

DECEMBER 2, SUNDAY A Close Day. All went to our Church foornoon, Mr Burrell preachd, I attendd the School Aftern. Young Starling, Mat & Jos Davy drank Tea here, Bett Davy staid all Night. Wm came home to Dinner, Robt Raven with him . . .

DECEMBER 6, THURSDAY A Close drisley Day. Mr Hardy at home all Day. Old Duke in Garden.

DECEMBER 7, FRIDAY A fine Chearly Day. Mr Hardy at home all Day. Old Duke in Garden. M Ann walkd up to Holt foornoon to go to a Ball at Mrs Sheppards . . .

DECEMBER 9, SUNDAY A very damp Day. I poorly with dimness in my Eyes. Wm only went to our Church Afternoon. Mr Scott from Yarmouth came Even 8 upon our Colt from Norwich. Mr Jeary [Robert Jary] of Holt Died.

DECEMBER 14, FRIDAY A Close dry Day. Mr Hardy at home all Day. Old Duke in Gardn . . .

DECEMBER 16, SUNDAY A very wet Day. Mr Scott went away Morn 10. All went to our Church foornoon, Mr Burrell preachd, I attendd the School Afternoon. Wm went to Holt Church Afternoon . . .

DECEMBER 18, TUESDAY A fine Morn, very Wet Aftern. Expected Brot Raven to Dinner, did not come. Mr Dew of Swanton Dind here & stayd till Night, Mr Hardy at home all Day.

DECEMBER 19, WEDNESDAY A Close foggy Day. Mr Hardy at home all Day. MA very Ill with pain in her teeth & swelld face. Old Duke in Garden . . .

DECEMBER 22, SATURDAY A Sharp frost, fine Day. Brot & Robt went away after Dinner. Mr H, I & Wm walkd up to Holt, drank Tea at Mr Bakers.

DECEMBER 23, SUNDAY A Sharp frost, Storms of Hail & Snow. All went to our Church Afternoon, Mr Burrell preachd. Miss Leake drank Tea here. . .

DECEMBER 27, THURSDAY A fine Day. Mr Hardy at home all Day. Mr Forster of Bayfield drank Tea & Supt here & reck'd . . .

DECEMBER 29, SATURDAY A Close Day. Brot went away Morn 10. Mr Hardy went to Blackeney MII & came home by Holt Markt Even 9. I & MA walkd up, drank Tea at Mr Davys, left MA there, home Even 9. Wm came up . . .

DECEMBER 31, MONDAY A Close Mild Day. Mr Hardy at home all Day. MA came from Mr Davys Afternoon, Wm came from Norwich Even 6.

1788

JANUARY 1, TUESDAY A Dry Day. Mr Hardy rid to Blakeney foornoon. Maids & Ann Humphry Washd 4 Weeks Linnen.

JANUARY 2, WEDNESDAY A Wet Morn, cleard up a little while & raind again in Eveng. Mr Hardy at home all Day . . .

JANUARY 5, SATURDAY A fine day. Mr Hardy & I walk^d up to Holt afternoon, I came home to Tea, Mr Hardy came hom Even past 8. Miss Chicheley & a Miss Johnson came home with MA, staid all Night. The Ship Sail^d from Blakeney for Liverpool.

JANUARY 6, SUNDAY A Wet Day. Miss Chichely & Miss Johnson went away at Noon. We all went to our Church Afternoon, Mr Burrell preachd. I attend^d the School Afternoon . . .

JANUARY 11, FRIDAY A Close mild Day. W^m & MA went to a Dancing Frollick at Mr Bartells Even 4, came home Even past 11.

JANUARY 12, SATURDAY A very fine bright Day. I & W^m walk^d up to Holt Mark^t Aftern, drank Tea at Mr Davys. W^m drank Tea at Mr Bartells.

JANUARY 13, SUNDAY A Close dry Day. All went to our Church foornoon, Mr Burrell preachd. M^r & M^rs & Bett Davy drank Tea here. Frose at Night. . .

JANUARY 16, WEDNESDAY A Sharp frost, chearly day. W^m rid to Holt foornoon & to Thornage Afternoon with Edmd Bartell, he drank Tea here.

JANUARY 17, THURSDAY A frost, bright Day. W^m rid up to Holt foornoon to Invite Miss Chichely to a Dance next Tuesday.

JANUARY 18, FRIDAY Thaw^d, a close stormy day. MA Ill with pain in her teeth, sent for Mr Bartell to draw it, he & Mrs Bartell were gone to Norwich, Edm^d came down.

JANUARY 19, SATURDAY A very Cold close day, Wind high at North. MA better. W^m went to Holt Market Afternoon, came home Eve 7 . . .

JANUARY 23, WEDNESDAY A very Cold Windy Day. Edmd Bartell went away before breakfst, the 3 Davys & Miss B [Bartell] went away after Dinner. Mrs Jewell & M^r B & Miss Baker & Miss Chichely drank Tea here.

JANUARY 24, THURSDAY Cold dry Day, Wind very high. Henry Goggs came Morn 11, he & W^m went up to Holt to the Quarter sessions, came back. Henry went away after Tea . . .

JANUARY 26, SATURDAY A very fine day, roads dry. W^m rid up to Holt Market, I & MA walkd up, drank Tea at Mr Davys, home ½ past 6.

JANUARY 27, SUNDAY A Close mild day. All went to our Church foornoon, Mr Burrell preachd, I attend'd the School Afternoon. W^m went to Holt Church.

JANUARY 28, MONDAY A beautifull Day. Miss Chicheley walkd down. MA walkd up with her to Holt & came back to Dinner. Mrs Thos Hewit & Miss Loyd came for a Morng Visit . . .

JANUARY 31, THURSDAY A beautifull Day but cold. W^m set of for Fakenham Mark^t ½ past 11, came home Even pst 7 . . .

FEBRUARY 2, SATURDAY A Sharp Wind frost, close day. I & W^m & MA walk^d up to Holt Afternoon. I & MA drank Tea at Mr Davys, W^m at Mr Bartells, home Even 7 . . .

FEBRUARY 6, *Ash Wednesday* A clear frost. W^m at home all Day, I & MA at Church foorn.

FEBRUARY 7, THURSDAY A fine Morn, foggy afternoon. M^r A [Mary Ann] walk'd up to Holt foorn, Bett Davy came home with her to Dinner. I irond all Day.

FEBRUARY 8, FRIDAY A Close cold Day. Bet Davy went away after Dinner . . .

FEBRUARY 10, SUNDAY A Close «day», a small Snow all Day. All went to our Church foorn, Mr Burrell preachd. W^m went to Holt afternoon to go to Church, was no service, drank Tea at Mr Davys. I attendd the School Afternoon.

FEBRUARY 11, MONDAY A Thaw, Close Day. W^m rid to Blackney foornoon, came home Even 1. Recd a Letter from Mr Hardy from Liverpool.

FEBRUARY 12, TUESDAY A Close foggy Day. W^m at home all Day . . .

FEBRUARY 15, FRIDAY A very foggy Morn, Wet aftern. W^m at home all Day.

FEBRUARY 16, SATURDAY A very Close Wet Day. W^m went to Holt Mark^t Eve pst 3, came home Even past 7.

[[FEBRUARY 17, SUNDAY [*by Mary Ann*] A Fine Day. We all went to our Church Afternoon, Mr Burrell Preached. The two Davys and Young Bartell drank Tea here.]] Recd a Letter from Mr Hardy . . .

[[FEBRUARY 19, TUESDAY A vary Close Rainy Day.]] W^m at home all Day.

FEBRUARY 20, WEDNESDAY A tolerable Day. I & MA went to Church foornoon, we walk'd up to Holt Aftern, drank Tea at Mrs Jewells, W^m came for us in the Eve, got wet coming home.

FEBRUARY 21, THURSDAY A very dark Wet Day. W^m at home all Day . . .

FEBRUARY 23, SATURDAY A Chearly Morn, drisley afternoon. We all walk'd up to Holt Afternoon, drank Tea at Mr Bartells . . .

FEBRUARY 26, TUESDAY A fine Chearly Day. Maids Washd 3 Weeks Linnen alone. Mr Hardy & W^m took a walk after Dinner. W^m went to Holt Ball Even 7, came home Morn 3.

FEBRUARY 27, WEDNESDAY A very chearly Day. I & MA went to our Church foornoon. Mr Hardy at home all Day.

FEBRUARY 28, THURSDAY A Close foggy Day. MA poorly with a Cold, I taken poorly Afternoon. Mr Hardy at home all Day.

FEBRUARY 29, FRIDAY A Close Cold Day. Mr Dennis Din^d here, Mr Hardy at home all Day. I something better.

MARCH 1, SATURDAY A cold chearly Morn, close Afternoon. Mr Hardy, I, MA walk'd up to Holt Afternoon. M^r H & I drank Tea at Mr Davys, W^m drank Tea at Mr Bartells & MA at Mrs Jewells, home E 8 . . .

MARCH 4, TUESDAY A sharp frost, reather showry Afternoon. W^m rid to Blackney foornoon. Mr Hardy at home all Day. Edm^d Bartell drank Tea here.

MARCH 5, WEDNESDAY A sharp frost. I & MA went to our Church foornoon & walkd up to Holt Afternoon, drank Tea at Miss Leakes. Mr Hardy walkd up to Holt Afternoon, drank Tea at Mr Bensleys & recknd & went to Overtons Club & came home Even 11. Began Snowing Eve 4 . . .

MARCH 7, FRIDAY A very sharp frost, wind high. Mr Hardy at home all Day. MA walk'd up to Holt foorn, Mrs Davy & Bett drank Tea here. A good deal of Snow fell in the Night.

MARCH 8, SATURDAY Sharp frost, chearly Day. I taken poorly with dimness in my Eyes. Mr Hardy & MA walk^d up to Holt Mark^t Even 4, came home Even 9, MA staid at Mr Davys all Night.

MARCH 9, SUNDAY A sharp frost, chearly Day. I poorly all Day with dimness in my Eyes. W^m & MA went to our Church Afternoon . W^m went to Holt Church, Mr Burrell preachd there . . .

MARCH 13, THURSDAY A sharp Chearly Morn, Close afternoon. Mr Hardy at home all Day .

MARCH 14, FRIDAY A Cold Windy Day. Mr Hardy at home all Day. M Ann walk'd up to Holt foornoon to stay a Day or 2 with Bett Davy.

MARCH 15, SATURDAY A Close Windy Day. M^r H & I walkd up to Holt Mark^t Even past 3, drank Tea at Mr Davys, came home Even 9. A very wet Eveng . . .

MARCH 18, TUESDAY A Close cold Day. Mr Hardy at home all Day. M^r & Mrs Bartell & Edmd drank Tea & Supt here . . .

MARCH 20, THURSDAY A Close cold windy Day. Mr Hardy at home all day . . .

MARCH 23, *Easter Sunday* A very Wet Windy Morn, very Close & Cold all Day. I went to Church foornoon, Mr Burrell preachd & then went to Holt Church. Mr Ives was buried . . .

MARCH 28, FRIDAY A Mild Showry Day. Mr Hardy at home all Day . . .

MARCH 30, SUNDAY A Close Mild Day. All went to our Church Afternoon, Mr Burrell preach'd & then preach'd at Holt. W^m went to Holt Church & drank Tea at Mr Davys, recd a Letter from MA by Mast^r Bartell . . .

APRIL 1, TUESDAY *Wms Birth Day Aged 18 Years* A very Wet Morn, Wind very high at West all day. Maids Wash'd 3 Weeks Linnen. Mr Hardy at home all Day, W^m went to Armingland Hall with Lamb to bring home some of the Stuff, home Even 6.

APRIL 2, WEDNESDAY A Close Showry Day. Robt & Henry Raven from Whisinsett came M9, brought us a young Pea Hen, they went away Even 6. Mr Hardy at home all Day . . .

APRIL 4, FRIDAY A very Stormy Day, Wind very high. Mr Hardy & W^m at home all Day, Mr Theoderic Dind here & reckn^d.

APRIL 5, SATURDAY A very Stormy Day, Wind high. Mr Hardy & I walkd up to Holt Afternoon, drank Tea at Miss Leakes. W^m rid up, drank Tea at Mr Bartells, came home Even past 8.

APRIL 6, SUNDAY A tolerable fine day but Cold. All went to our Church foornoon, Mr Burrell preach'd, Mrs Letton [Lytton] at Church. W^m went to our Church & came back to Tea.

APRIL 7, MONDAY A Wet Morn, close mild Day. Mr Hardy at home all Day. Mr Davy call^d after Dinner, Mr Cock of Hempton came.

APRIL 8, TUESDAY A very fine bright Day. Mr Hardy at home all Day. M^rs & Bett Davy, M^r & Mrs Bartell drank Tea here. 2 Gardiners at Work.

APRIL 9, WEDNESDAY A very fine Day. Mr Hardy & I walkd up to Holt, drank Tea at Mr Bartells. Mr Hardy staid at the Club, came home Morn 3. 2 Gardiners at Work . . .

APRIL 11, FRIDAY A very fine Day. Mr Hardy at home all day, Ginby & Boy at Work. Mrs Baker drank Tea here, Mr Baker came in the Eve . . .

APRIL 14, MONDAY A Wet foornoon, dry Aftern. Ginby at work here, Mr Hardy at home all Day.

APRIL 15, TUESDAY A Cold windy Day. Mr Hardy at home all day. { Mr Hardy at home all Day.}

APRIL 16, WEDNESDAY A Close cold Day, a little shower in Afternoon. Mr Hardy at home all day, Edm^d Bartell drank Tea here.

APRIL 17, THURSDAY A fine Day. Mr Hardy, I & Miss Baker walk«ed» to Bayfield & drank Tea at Mr Forsters, home Even 9 . . .

APRIL 19, SATURDAY A very fine Day. I & Miss Baker walkd up to Holt Afternoon, Mr Hardy followed us, drank Tea & Supt at Mr Bakers.

APRIL 20, SUNDAY A beautifull Day. Mr Hardy & I went to our Church foornoon, Mr Burrell preach^d, I attend d the School Afternoon. W^m came home from Whisensett Even past 8 . . .

APRIL 28, MONDAY A very fine warm Day. Mr Hardy rid to Armingland Hall Morn 10, Dind at Mr Theordericks, came home Eve 8. The Blind Mare Died.

APRIL 29, TUESDAY A very warm Day. Mr Hardy, I & MA walkd up to Holt Afternoon, drank Tea & Sup^t at Mr Bartells . . .

MAY 1, THURSDAY A very Hot dry Day. Mr Hardy at home all Day, I & MA walkd up to Holt after Tea.

MAY 2, FRIDAY A Close cold Day. Mr Hardy at home all day . . .

MAY 4, SUNDAY A dry Windy Day. I & MA went to our Church foornoon, Mr Burrell preachd. W^m & Starling went to Holt Church Afternoon, drank Tea at Mr Davys, M^r & Mrs Davy & Childr^n came after Tea.

MAY 5, MONDAY A dry windy day. I & MA drank Tea at Mr Bartells, Mrs Jewell, Mrs Bell & Mrs Wilson there. Mr Hardy came for us in Eveng.

MAY 6, TUESDAY Very fine Day. Maids Washd. Mr Hardy, I & MA walkd up to Holt, drank Tea at Mr Davys & reconed.

MAY 7, WEDNESDAY A Moist Morn, fair Afternoon. Mr Hardy at home all day, I & M [Mary Ann] Irond.

MAY 8, THURSDAY A dry warm day. Mr Hardy reather lame with the Gout. I & MA finishd ironing.

MAY 9, FRIDAY A Showry Day. Mr Hardy much as yesterday . . .

MAY 11, *Whit Sunday* A very fine warm Day. All went to our Church Aftern, M^r H something better. Mrs Forster & Jo^s Davy drank Tea here.

MAY 12, MONDAY A very fine Day. Mr Hardy reather better.

MAY 13, TUESDAY A very fine day. M^r H much as yesterday. M^r & Mrs Bartell & Mrs Stannard drank Tea here.

MAY 14, WEDNESDAY A dry windy Day. I & MA walkd up to Holt Aftern, drank Tea at Mr Bartells. Mr Hardy lame with Gout.

MAY 15, THURSDAY A Close cold Windy Day. Mr Hardy but poorly. M^r & Mrs Bartell & Mrs Stannard drank Tea here.

MAY 16, FRIDAY A Shower in Morn, fine Day. Mr Hardy finely.

[[MAY 17, SATURDAY [*by Mary Ann*] A fine Day. Father much the same. Mother, W^m & I Walked up to Holt, Drank Tea at Mr Bartells, came home Even^g 8. MAH [Mary Ann Hardy].

MAY 18, SUNDAY A Close Day, small Rain in the Afternoon. Mrs Bartell, Mrs Stannard & Miss Stannard Drank Tea here. MAH.

MAY 19, MONDAY A vary fine Day. I walked up to Holt in the Morning, came home to Dinner. Mrs Jewell, Miss Chicheley, Mrs Davy and Mr Roxby from London drank Tea here. MAH . . .

MAY 21, WEDNESDAY A vary fine Day. Father, Mother and I walked up to Holt, Drank Tea at Mr Bakers, came home Even^g 9. MAH.

MAY 22, THURSDAY A vary fine day. Mother Ironed in the Morning, Mr Hardy at home all Day. We heard Mr Hipkins of Salthouse Dyed this Morning. MAH . . .

MAY 24, SATURDAY A Hot Dry Day. Father, Mother, Brother and I went up to Holt, drank Tea at Mr Bartells, came home Even 9.

MAY 25, SUNDAY A vary Hot Day. We all went to our Church in the Aftern. M^r and Mrs Davy, Joseph and Mary and Sarah drank Tea here, went away Evening 8. MH [MAH] . . .

The visit to Whissonsett
26–31 May 1788

MAY 28, WEDNESDAY A Drisly Day. Father and Mother {went to} Dined and drank Tea at Mrs Ravens at the Hall, slept as usual.

MAY 29, THURSDAY A vary Rainy Day. Father and Mother Dined and Drank Tea at Mr Goggs.

MAY 30, FRIDAY A fine Day. Father and Mother Drank Tea at Mr Fox, Brisley . . .]]

[LETHERINGSETT]

JUNE 2, MONDAY A very pleasant Day. M^r H, I & MA walkd up to Holt Afternoon, drank Tea at Mr Bakers, MA drank Tea at Mrs Jewells . . .

JUNE 4, WEDNESDAY A fine Day. Bro^t Raven went away after Tea, Mr Hardy at home all Day . . .

JUNE 6, FRIDAY A very hot Day. I & MA & Childr walkd up to Holt foornoon, came back to Dinner. Mr Hardy at home all Day, Robt Raven went away after Tea.

JUNE 7, SATURDAY A Close cold Windy Day. I & MA & Childr^n walkd up to Holt, Childr^n drank Tea at Mr Davys, I & M [Mary Ann] drank Tea at Miss Leakes. M^r H & W^m at Market.

JUNE 8, SUNDAY A Windy cold Day. All went to our Church Afternoon, Mr Burrell preachd. I attendd the School foornoon & Afternoon. [[[*by Mary Ann*] E^dm Bartell walked down after Tea . . .]]

JUNE 10, TUESDAY A dry windy Day. Mr Hardy at home all Day . . .

JUNE 13, FRIDAY A dry windy day. Mr Hardy at home all Day. Sister Goggs & Son came foornoon.

JUNE 14, SATURDAY A small rain in Morn, Cold Close Day. M^r H, Sister Goggs, I & Childr^n walkd up to Holt Afternoon, drank Tea at Mr Bartells.

JUNE 15, SUNDAY A dry cool Day. All went to our Church foornoon. I attendd the School a little time in Aftern. M^r & Mrs Baker & Son drank Tea here, M^r & Mrs Davy came after Tea . . .

JUNE 17, TUESDAY A warm dry Day. Maids Washd 1 Weeks linnen. Mr Hardy at home all day. I & MA & Childr^n walk'd up to Holt after Tea.

JUNE 18, WEDNESDAY A very hot Day, a small Show^r at Even 8. Mr Hardy at home all day.

JUNE 19, THURSDAY A fine day. Mr Hardy at home all Day.

JUNE 21, SATURDAY A Clos«e» cold day. All walkd up to Holt Aftern, Sister & I & M^r H drank Tea at Mr Bakers, the young people at Miss Leakes . . .

JUNE 26, THURSDAY Rain great part of the day. Mr Hardy at home all Day . . .

JUNE 28, SATURDAY A very Wet day. Mr Hardy walkd up to Holt Mark^t Aftern, came home Even 9.

JUNE 29, SUNDAY A fine Day. All went to our Church foornoon, Mr Burrell preachd, I attended'd the School Afternoon . . .

JULY 6, SUNDAY A fine day. All went to our church Afternoon, Mr Burrell preachd, I attend'd the School foornoon & afternoon. M^r & Mrs Davy came after Tea.

JULY 7, MONDAY A Showry Morn, dry aftern. I & MA walkd up to Holt after Tea. Mr Hardy at Town meeting at R Mays, home Even 9.

JULY 8, TUESDAY A fine Morn, Showry Aftern. Maids Washd 3 Weeks Linnen. Mr Hardy at home all day. Mr Betts of Gresenhall here in the Morng . . .

JULY 13, SUNDAY A fine Morn, Excesive hott & raind Afternoon. All went to our Church foornoon, Mr Burrell preach'd, I attendd the School foornoon & Afternoon. P Myles came again after Tea . . .

JULY 15, TUESDAY A fine Day. Mr Hardy at home all day. M^r & Mrs Burrell drank Tea here. M^r H should have gone to Sheringham . . .

JULY 19, SATURDAY A moist Morn, fine Day. I & Mr Hardy walk'd up to Holt Afternoon, drank Tea at Mr Davys, W^m drank Tea at Mr Bartells.

JULY 20, SUNDAY A fine Day. Mr Starling went to Mr Pauls of Study, Dind & drank Tea there. We all went to our Church Afternoon, Mr Burrell preachd, I attend'd the School foornoon & afternoon. Took a walk to Fir Closes after Tea.

JULY 21, MONDAY A Wet morn, fine Day. M^r H & I walkd up to Holt Afternoon, he went to Mrs Sheppards bowling green, I drank Tea at Miss Leakes.

JULY 22, TUESDAY A fine Day. Maids Washd 2 Weeks Linnen. M^{rs} & Miss Baker & Mrs Davy drank Tea here, Mr Davy & Mr Bartell came for them in the Eveng.

JULY 23, WEDNESDAY A very fine Day. Mr Hardy & I sett of for Fakenham Morn 10, Dind with Mr Croffts at Mr Brutons, drank Tea there, went to Mr Rayltons Sale, went to Whisensett in the Eveng with Bro^t Raven . . .

JULY 26, SATURDAY A fine Day. Mr Hardy, I & W^m walk'd up to Holt Mark^t Afternoon, drank Tea at Mr Bartells. 2 Miss Leakes & Mr Bullcock on a Visit at Mr Burrells . . .

JULY 30, WEDNESDAY A Showry Morn, very hot Day. Mr Hardy & I rid up to Holt Afternoon, calld «on» Mrs Davy & drank Tea at Mr Chas Kendles. Mrs Baldin came to Mr Bartells.

JULY 31, THURSDAY Very hot Day. Mr Hardy went to Quarter Sessions at Walsingham with Mr Burrell Morn 9, came home Even past 9 . . .

AUGUST 3, SUNDAY A fine Day. All went to our Church Afternoon, Mr Burrell preachd, I attend'd the School Foornoon & Afternoon.

AUGUST 4, MONDAY Excesive hot Day. Mr Hardy at home all Day . . .

AUGUST 6, WEDNESDAY A dry Day, wind blustering. Mr Burrell began Harvest. Mr Hardy at home all Day, W^m sett of for Whisensett Even 2 to look at some repairs doing at Horningtoft.

AUGUST 7, THURSDAY A close cool Day. Mr Hardy went to Sheringham M11 to look at the repairs doing at the Clifft, came home Even 9, W^m came home Even 8. M^r & Mrs Baker & George Custance, M^r & Mrs Bartell drank Tea here.

AUGUST 8, FRIDAY A Close cool Day. Mr Hardy at home all Day. Mr Starling went to Cawston Morn 5, came home Even 9. M^{rs} & Miss Ann Johnson of Holt drank Tea here.

AUGUST 9, SATURDAY A drisly Morn, close Day. Mr Hardy & I set of for Whisensett in our new post Chaise Morn 10, got to Mr Goggs ab^t 1, Dind, drank Tea & Slept there.

AUGUST 10, SUNDAY A small Showr in Morn, fine day. We all went to Whisensett Church Afternoon, Mr Bird preach'd. Drank Tea at Sister Goggs & sett of for hom Even ½ past 5, got home a little after 8 . . .

AUGUST 12, TUESDAY A fine Day. Mr Hardy at home all Day, Men Shearing Wheat in 6 Acres. A good Shower in the Night . . .

AUGUST 14, THURSDAY Showry Day. Mr Hardy at home all Day. I taken poorly with dimness in my Eyes. Edm'd Bartell drank Tea here . . .

AUGUST 17, SUNDAY A very wet Morn, tolerable Aftern. All went to our Church Afternoon, Mr Burrell preachd,

I attendd the School foornoon. MA came home from Holt Even 8 . . .

⟦ AUGUST 24, SUNDAY [*by Mary Ann*] A vary fine Day. We all went to our Church in the Morn. Miss Stannard and Miss Bartell drank Tea here, Willm walked home with her . . . ⟧

SEPTEMBER 3, WEDNESDAY A very Hot dry Day. Mr Hardy at home all Day. W^m went up to Holt Aftern, drank Tea with John Davy . . .

SEPTEMBER 6, SATURDAY A fine Morn, Showry Afternoon. Men carrying Barly till the rain prevented them abt 3 Aftern. I walkd up to Holt after Tea for MA, she & the Davys came home with me & MA returnd to Holt again with them.

SEPTEMBER 7, SUNDAY A very fine Day. All went to our Church foornoon, Mr Burrell preachd, I attend'd the School Afternoon. MA came home & the Davys with her after Tea. W^m went to Holt Church Afternoon, drank Tea at Mr Davys, Starling Dind there.

SEPTEMBER 8, MONDAY A very fine Day. Mr Hardy at home all Day. I & MA walkd up to Holt after Tea.

SEPTEMBER 9, TUESDAY A very fine Day. Mr Hardy at home all Day .

SEPTEMBER 10, WEDNESDAY A very fine Day. Mr Hardy at home all Day.

SEPTEMBER 11, THURSDAY A Showry Morn, fine Day. Love came to teach MA. Mr Hardy & W^m sett of for Norwich Morn 10. Francis Wymer was Married to Miss Owers. Mr Bartell, Miss Stannard & Miss Davy drank Tea here. Maids & Mrs Durant Washd.

SEPTEMBER 12, FRIDAY A very fine Day. Mr Hardy & W^m came home Even past 11.

SEPTEMBER 13, SATURDAY A fine Day. I & MA walkd up to Holt Afternoon, drank Tea at Mr Bartells, M^r H & W^m walkd up after Tea.

SEPTEMBER 14, SUNDAY A very fine Day. All went to our Church except W^m who went to Holt Church Afternoon. I attendd the School both Mo{o}rn & Afternoon. M^r & Mrs Burrell came after Tea.

SEPTEMBER 15, MONDAY A fine Day. Mr Davy came a Shooting, Dind & drank Tea here. Mr Burrell drank Tea here.

SEPTEMBER 16, TUESDAY Dry windy Day. Mr Hardy at home all Day, I walkd up to Holt after breakfst. Raind in the Night. W^m went to a Ball at Holt, home M1 . . .

SEPTEMBER 18, THURSDAY A Close Showry Day. Bro^t Raven went away Morn 11, left Nathl. M^r H & W^m went to Horse race after Dinner. Mrs Baldin, «Mrs» Raven & 4 friends, M^r & M^{rs} & Miss Bartell drank Tea here.

SEPTEMBER 19, FRIDAY A Close Morn, Wet afternoon. M^r H, I & MA walkd up to Holt foornoon, there was a Raffell [raffle] at Mr Pages, came home to Dinner, Bett Davy came home with us.

SEPTEMBER 20, SATURDAY A Close dry Day. Mr Hardy & W^m went to Justice sitting at Holt, Dind at the Feathers. Bett Davy went home after breakfst. I & MA walkd up to Holt Aftern, drank Tea at Mr Davys, Lamb came up for us with the Carr«i»age . . .

SEPTEMBER 23, TUESDAY A fine Day. Mr Hardy at home all Day.

SEPTEMBER 24, WEDNESDAY A tolerable Day. Mr Hardy at home all Day . . .

SEPTEMBER 26, FRIDAY A Wet Morn, fine afternoon. Mr & Mrs Foster [Forster] came to the Sale & drank Tea here, Mr & Mrs Bartell drank Tea here.

SEPTEMBER 27, SATURDAY A fine Day. Mr H, I & MA walkd up to Holt petty Sessions, drank Tea at Mr Bartells, Mr H drank Tea at Mr Bakers. Wm went up after Tea . . .

OCTOBER 4, SATURDAY Dry Morn, Wet Afternoon. Mr Hardy & Wm walkd up to Holt Markt, Wm came home Even past 7. Mr Hardy went to play 3d Acct [at the third act], came home Even past 11.

OCTOBER 5, SUNDAY A fine Day. All except Starling (who went to Holt foornoon to see his Father) went to our Church foornoon, Mr Burrell preachd. Wm went to Holt Church Aftern. I attendd the School Afternoon.

OCTOBER 6, MONDAY A Dry Windy Morn, very Wet Aftern. Mr Hardy at home all Day .

OCTOBER 7, TUESDAY A dry Windy day. Mr Hardy at home all Day. Maids & Mrs Durrant Washd 4 Weeks Linnen . . .

OCTOBER 10, FRIDAY A very fine Day. Mr Hardy at home all Day. Betty Mirham went away. Carpenters & Brickl at work.

OCTOBER 11, SATURDAY A fine Day. We all walk'd up to Holt Markt, drank Tea at Mr Davys, came home Even 8.

OCTOBER 12, SUNDAY A fine Day. No service at our Church, Mr Burrell poorly with a Cold. I attend«ed» the School foornoon & Afternoon . . .

OCTOBER 14, TUESDAY A Close day. 3 Carpenters & Gardiners at work. Mr Hardy, I & MA walkd up to Holt, drank Tea at Mr Seales. {Gardiner at work} . . .

OCTOBER 18, SATURDAY A fine Day. Mr Hardy at home all Day. 2 Carpenters at work, Gardener at Work . . .

OCTOBER 25, SATURDAY A Showry Morn, dry day. I walkd up to Holt Aftern, came back to Tea. Mr Hardy walkd up to Holt MII to Justice Sitting, Dind at Feathers, came home, went to Play . . .

OCTOBER 28, TUESDAY A fine Day. Brot Raven & Daught came to Dinner, we all walkd up to Holt Afternoon, came home to Tea. Mr Baker & Mr Playford came in the Eveng.

OCTOBER 30, THURSDAY A fine day. Mr Hardy at home all Day. Bett Davy & Miss Paul Dind here . . .

NOVEMBER 1, SATURDAY A fine day. I & MA & cousin M [Mary Raven] walk'd up to Holt Afternoon, drank Tea at Miss Leakes.

NOVEMBER 2, SUNDAY A fine day. All went to our Church foornoon, Mr Burrell preachd, I attend'd the School Afternoon. Wm went to Holt Church. Edmd Bartell drank Tea here.

NOVEMBER 3, MONDAY A dry day but windy. Maids & Mrs Durrant washd. Mr Hardy at home all Day. Wm rid to Holt & Blakeney foornoon. I & 2 Girls walkd up to Holt Afternoon, drank Tea at Miss Leakes . . .

NOVEMBER 7, FRIDAY A fine day. Mr Hardy at home all day. Mrs Baker, Mr & Mrs Bartell, Mrs Davy & Bett Davy drank Tea here . . .

NOVEMBER 9, SUNDAY A fine day. I attend'd the School a little while foornoon, all went to our Church Afternoon, Mr Burrell preach'd. 3 Miss Johnsons, Jos Davy & Bett & Mr Roxby drank Tea here. Mr & Mrs Davy & 2 Girls drank Tea at Mr Burrells . . .

NOVEMBER 11, TUESDAY A fine day. Mr Hardy & Wm at home all day. I & Cousin M Raven & MA walk'd up to Holt after Dinner, came back to Tea . . .

NOVEMBER 13, THURSDAY A Close day. Mr Hardy at home all Day. Brot Raven & Son came Even past 6 . . .

NOVEMBER 15, SATURDAY A Stormy day. I & MA walkd up to Holt Aftern, drank Tea at Miss Leakes. Mr Hardy drank Tea at Mr Bartells & went to the Play, I & MA went in at 3d Act. Lamb came for us with the Carriage.

NOVEMBER 16, SUNDAY A fine day. All went to our Church foornoon, Mr Burrell preach'd. Wm went to Holt Church Afternoon. I attended the School Afternoon . . .

NOVEMBER 20, THURSDAY A Close dry day. Mr Hardy at home all Day. Mr & Mrs Bartell drank Tea & Supt here . . .

NOVEMBER 22, SATURDAY A Close dry day. Mr H, I & MA walkd up to Holt Aftern, drank Tea at Mr Davys, MA went to the Play with Bett Davy. Wm came up in Eveng, went to Play with us at 3d Acct, Lam«b» came for us with the Carriage.

NOVEMBER 23, SUNDAY A Close dry Day. I attendd the School a little while foornoon, all went to our Church Aftern. Mr & Mrs Davy, Bett, Jos [Davy] & Edmd Bartell came to our Church & drank Tea here . . .

NOVEMBER 27, THURSDAY A very sharp close day, Snow & Sleet. Mr Hardy went to Overtons Club in Eveng, came home past 12.

NOVEMBER 28, FRIDAY A Close cold Day. Mr Hardy at home all day . . .

NOVEMBER 30, SUNDAY Close damp weather. All went to our Church foornoon except Mr Hardy who was poorly with a Cold. Wm & Starling went to Holt Church Aftern, drank Tea at Mr Davys. I attended the School Afternoon . . .

DECEMBER 3, WEDNESDAY A Sharp frost, a great deal of Snow fell in Storms. Mr Hardy & Wm came home Even 8 . . .

[[DECEMBER 6, SATURDAY [by Mary Ann] A Cold chearly Day. Mr Hardy and Wm went up to Holt Market, came home Even 9.]] I poorly with dimness in my Eyes.

[[DECEMBER 7, SUNDAY A bright forenoon, close Aftern and vary Cold. We all went to Church in the Afternoon. Mother Attend«ed» the School]] . . .

DECEMBER 9, TUESDAY A bright Cold Day. Mr Hardy at home all day, Wm rid to Study Afternoon. Wm poorly with a Cold.

DECEMBER 10, WEDNESDAY A chearly day but cold & reather Stormy. Wm took some physics from Mr Mathews. Mr Hardy went to Holt to pay the Excise, came home Even 7, Mr Errington came instead of the Collector . . .

[[DECEMBER 11, THURSDAY [*by Mary Ann*] A Sharp frost, Chearly Day. Mother and W^m went up to Holt After-noon, came home to Tea. Mr Hardy at Home all Day.

DECEMBER 12, FRIDAY A Sharp frost and fine Morn, Stormy Afternoon. W^m took some mor Physic of Mr Mathews and was vary poorly. Mr Hardy at Home all day . . .]]

DECEMBER 14, SUNDAY Sharp frost «at» Night, Wind rose M8 & Snowd very much all the foornoon, no Snow fell Aftern but wind continued high & very sharp. No serv-ice at our Church, Mr Burrell preachd for Mr Johnsons [Revd William Tower Johnson] of Holt. W^m & Starling went to Holt Church Afternoon . . .

DECEMBER 16, TUESDAY A very Sharp frost. I & W^m walkd up to Holt M11 to Wymarks Sale. I Dind at [and] drank Tea at Mr Bartells, W^m came home & Mr Hardy came up to Tea. Lamb came for us with the Carriage Even 8. Bro^t Raven & Robt came from the Audit.

DECEMBER 17, WEDNESDAY A Sharp frost & storms of Snow. I & MA walkd up to Holt to the Sale after Dinner, did not drink Tea any were [anywhere], came home Even 9, Edmd Bartell with us. M^r H at home all Day taken poorly with the Gout. Bro^t & Robt went away after Dinner.

DECEMBER 18, THURSDAY Sharp frost & snow. I & MA walkd up to Holt after Dinner to the Sale, drank Tea at Miss Leakes, Lamb came for us with the Carriage. Mr Hardy better & at home all Day . . .

DECEMBER 20, SATURDAY Weather the same. Mr Hardy went to Holt Mark^t Even 3, came home Even 9.

DECEMBER 21, SUNDAY Weather the same. All went to our Church Afternoon, Mr Burrell preachd. Miss Stan-nard, Edmd Bartell & Jo^s Davy drank Tea here.

DECEMBER 22, MONDAY Very Sharp frost. I & MA walkd up to Holt foornoon, came home to Dinner. Mr Hardy at home all Day . . .

DECEMBER 26, FRIDAY Thawd foornoon, froze sharp agn [again] Afternoon. Mr Hardy walkd up to Holt After-noon, drank Tea at Mr Bensleys & went to Overtons Club & came home Even 12.

DECEMBER 27, SATURDAY A very Sharp frost, wind high & Stormes of Snow. Mr Hardy walkd up to Holt Mark^t Afternoon, came home Even 7 . . .

DECEMBER 30, TUESDAY Excesive severe frost. W^m set of for Whisinsett Even pst 2. Mr Hardy, I & MA drank Tea at Mr Burrells. Maids & a Woman from Holt Washd 4 weeks Linnin. M^r H poorly with the Gout . . .

1789

JANUARY 3, SATURDAY Prodigious sharp rime frost. Mr Hardy something better. MA & Mr Starling walkd to Holt Markt, MA drank Tea at Miss Leakes. W^m came home Even 5.

JANUARY 4, SUNDAY A very severe frost. Mr Hardy some-thing better. All except Mr Hardy went to our Church Afternoon, Mr Burrell preachd. M^r & Mrs Davy, M^r T Raven Junr of Fakenham & a young Man with him drank Tea here . . .

JANUARY 6, TUESDAY A very severe frost, wind high. Mr Hardy much as Yesterday. Mr Baker, Mr Davy & Mr Burrell here foornoon. Miss Baker & Bro^t, Miss Stan-nard & Edmd Bartell drank Tea here. M^r & Mrs Bur^l [Burrell] here in Eveng . . .

JANUARY 8, THURSDAY A very severe frost but Chearly. Mr Hardy poorly.

JANUARY 9, FRIDAY A Close sharp frost, some Snow fell in Eveng. Mr Hardy somthing better then Yester^d. I & MA walk'd up to Holt Aftern, drank Tea & Supt at Mr Bartells, Mr Baker & Family there. Lamb came for us with the Carriage E12, Miss Stannard came home with us. Edmd Bartell went to Norwich in his way to Cam-bridge . . .

JANUARY 11, SUNDAY Sharp frost, Chearly Day. Mr Hardy better. No service at our Church. I attend d the School alittle while in foornoon. W^m & Starling drank Tea at Mr Pauls of Study . . .

JANUARY 15, THURSDAY A very slow thaw, roads very slippery. Mr Hardy, I, Miss Stannard & MA drank Tea & Supt at Mr Burrells, W^m came to Supper. The mome-tor 35 M10.

[*The diarist has muddled the dates 15–18 January 1789 and appears in so doing to have spread the events of Friday 16 January across two days*]

JANUARY 16, FRIDAY A Chearly Day, reather frosty in Morn, Th^r [thermometer] 33 M10. Mr Hardy finely. Lamb went to Blackney for Coales. A Close Day, slow thaw. Lamb went to Blakeny for Coales foornoon, drove us up to Holt in Carr^g [carriage] & came for us again Even past 12. We drank Tea & Supt at Mr Bakers.

JANUARY 17, SATURDAY Weather much as Yesterday. Mr Hardy rid up to Holt foorn to Justice Sitting, Dind at Mr Bakers, drank Tea at Mr Davys & came home Even 9. W^m went up Afternoon.

JANUARY 18, SUNDAY Thaw, wind high, some snow fell in Morn. All went to our Church Afternoon. I attend-«ed» the School a little time in Aftern. Jo^s Davy drank Tea here.

JANUARY 19, MONDAY A fine chearly Day, The^r 39 Morn 10. Mr Hardy & W^m at home all Day. Raind a great deal in Night & then froze & Snowd . . .

JANUARY 21, WEDNESDAY A cold close day, roades very bad. Mr Hardy & W^m at home all Day. M^r & Mrs Burrell, M^r & Mrs Bartell, M^r & Mrs Baker & Family & Mrs Stangroon [Stangroom] drank Tea & Supt here, Mrs Bartell & Miss Baker Slept here . . .

JANUARY 24, SATURDAY A fine foornoon, Wet Aftrn. Mr Hardy rid up to Holt Morn 11 to Justice Sitting, came home Even 7 . . .

JANUARY 26, MONDAY A very wet Morn, close dry Aftern. Mr Hardy at home all Day.

JANUARY 27, TUESDAY A very fine Mild Morn, close Afternoon, began to rain Even 4, wet Eveng. Mr Hardy at home all Day. I & Miss Stannard & MA walkd up to Holt Aftrn, drank Tea at Mr Davys, Lamb came for us Even 8 with Carriage.

JANUARY 28, WEDNESDAY A fine mild Day. Mr Hardy at home all day. Miss Stannard & MA walkd up to Holt Afternoon, drank Tea at Miss Johnsons, Lamb went up for them Even 8 with the Carriage . . .

JANUARY 30, FRIDAY A wet day. Mr Hardy at home all day, The^r 52.

JANUARY 31, SATURDAY A very fine mild day. Mr Hardy walkd up to Holt Morn 11 to Justice sitting. W^m, MA & Miss Stannard rid to Salthouse foornoon. We all walkd up to Holt Afternoon, drank Tea at Mr Bartells, Lamb came for us.

The visit to Whissonsett
1–7 February 1789

FEBRUARY 1, SUNDAY A close mild day. Mr Hardy & I sett of for Whesinsett Even 2 in our own Carriage, Lamb & Ned went with us, we took up our Lodging at Bro^t Ravens.

FEBRUARY 2, MONDAY A fine bright day. Lamb & Ned went home early. M^r & Mrs Moy & Miss Case drank Tea & Supt with us at Bro^t Ravens, we went to Church foornoon . . .

FEBRUARY 4, WEDNESDAY A Stormy Day, Wind very high. We all drank Tea & Supt at Sister Ravens at the Hall. Mr Hardy very poorly.

FEBRUARY 5, THURSDAY A Stormy day, Wind high. Mr Hardy very poorly. We both Dind & drank Tea & Supt at Mr Goggs, M^r H rid on Bro^t [brother's] Mare.

FEBRUARY 6, FRIDAY A tolerable Day. Bro^t & Sister & I went to Mr Moys in his Chaise {to Mr Moys}, drank Tea & Supt there, Mr Hardy so bad could not go.

FEBRUARY 7, SATURDAY A dry Morn, very Wet Aftern. Lamb & Boy came for us M7. We left Whisenset half after 2 oClock & got home Even 6. Mr Hardy very poorly & very much tired with coming home.

[LETHERINGSETT]

FEBRUARY 8, SUNDAY A dry Morn, Wet Afternoon. Mr Hardy very poorly, all went to our Church foornoon except him, Mr Burrell preachd. W^m & Starling went to Holt Church & drank Tea at Mr Davys.

FEBRUARY 9, MONDAY A fine Day. Mr Hardy somthing better. Miss Stannard came foorn, dind & drank Tea here. W^m, MA & I went to the Assembly, came home M2.

FEBRUARY 10, TUESDAY Fine day. Miss Bar^t [Bartell] & Miss Stannard drank Tea here, M^r & Mrs Burrell here in Eveng . . .

FEBRUARY 12, THURSDAY A Close day, Snowd a deal. Mr Hardy at home all day & but poorly.

FEBRUARY 13, FRIDAY A close dry day. Mr Hardy better. Mr Baker drank Tea here . . .

FEBRUARY 16, MONDAY A Windy, bright Day. Mr Hardy at home all Day. MA walkd up to Holt aftern with M^r & Mrs Burrell, drank Tea at Miss Trotters, Lamb went for them with the Carr^{ge}.

FEBRUARY 17, TUESDAY A Wet & windy Day. Mr Hardy at home all day.

FEBRUARY 18, WEDNESDAY A fine day. Mr Hardy at home all day. Miss Stannard came foornoon & went from Mr Bartells Even 5 in a return post Chaise . . .

FEBRUARY 20, FRIDAY A fine day. Mr Hardy at home all day, M^r & Mrs Burrell here in the Eveng.

FEBRUARY 21, SATURDAY A very wet foornoon, dry Aftern. We all walkd up to Holt Aftern except M [Mr] Hardy & he rode up, we all drank Tea at Mr Davys & walkd home.

FEBRUARY 22, SUNDAY A Wet Morn, fine Aftern. Mr Hardy poorly. I taken poorly with dimness in my Eyes, could not go to Church, MA & W^m at Church foornoon.

FEBRUARY 23, MONDAY A fine Day, very stormy Eveng & wind high. Mr Hardy poorly with the Gout. We drank Tea at Mr Burrells, Lamb came for us with Carriage . . .

[[MARCH 3, TUESDAY [by Mary Ann] A fine Day. Mr Hardy at Home all Day. M^r and Mrs Forster drank Tea and Suped here.

MARCH 4, WEDNESDAY A vary Stormy Day. I and MA went to Church, Mr Burrell preach'd. Mr Hardy at Home all Day.

MARCH 5, THURSDAY A fine Morn, Stormy Afternoon. Mr Hardy, I and MA walked up to Holt, drank Tea at Mr Bakers. M^r H and M^r B went to the Club, I and MA Sup^t at M^{rs} B^s, Lamb came for us Ev^{ng} 10.]]

MARCH 6, FRIDAY A Sharp frost with Storms of Snow all day. M^r H, I & MA with M^r & Mrs Burrell drank Tea at Mr Cobens, Lamb came for us with the Carriage.

MARCH 7, SATURDAY A very Stormy day. M^r H, I, W^m & MA walkd up to Holt, drank Tea at Mr Davys, Lamb came for us Even 8 with the Carriage.

MARCH 8, SUNDAY A very Cold day with Storms of Snow. All went to our Church foornoon, Mr Burrell preachd, I attendd the School Afternoon. W^m & Starling went to Holt Church, came home to Tea . . .

MARCH 10, TUESDAY Sharp frost & Snow. Mr Hardy at home all Day .

MARCH 11, WEDNESDAY Sharp frost with frequent Storms of Snow. Mr Hardy at [and] W^m at home all Day. Excise paid. M^r & Mrs Bartell drank Tea here. I & MA at Church foornoon . . .

MARCH 16, MONDAY A Sharp frost. Mr Hardy, I & MA walkd up to Holt Aftern, drank Tea at Mr Bartells, Lamb came for us with the Carriage.

MARCH 17, TUESDAY A frost but very fine day. Mr Hardy at home all Day, M^r & Mrs Burrell here in Even.

MARCH 18, WEDNESDAY Wet Morn, close Afternoon. Mr Hardy at home all day, M^r & Mrs Burrell drank Tea here.

MARCH 19, THURSDAY A tolerable day. Mr Hardy went to Overtons Club, came home Even pst 11 . . .

MARCH 21, SATURDAY A tolerable day. Mr Hardy, I & MA walkd up to Holt Mark^t, drank Tea at Mr Davys, walkd home before 7. I poorly with dimness in my Eyes M9.

MARCH 22, SUNDAY A very Wet day. All went to our Church Afternoon, Mr Burrell preachd. I poorly with a Cold . . .

MARCH 26, THURSDAY A sharp frost, chearly day. Mr Hardy, I & MA walk'd up to Holt with Bett Davy, drank Tea there. M^r H went to Overtons Club & MA & I walkd home Even 8.

MARCH 27, FRIDAY Sharp frost, very chearly Day. M^r H, I & MA, M^r & Mrs Burrell drank Tea at Mr Bakers, walkd home Even past 9.

MARCH 28, SATURDAY A Cold dry day. Mr Hardy, I, MA & W^m walk'd up to Holt Mark^t, I & MA drank Tea at Miss Leakes, M^r H at Mr Bartells, W^m at Mr Davys, all walkd home.

MARCH 29, SUNDAY A dry cold day. All went to our Church foornoon, Mr Burrell preach'd. Mrs Stodderd [Stoddart] & Mrs Raven from Norwich, M^r & Mrs Bartell & Children drank Tea here. W^m at Holt Church Aftern.

MARCH 30, MONDAY A very cold stormy Day. Mr Hardy, I & MA walkd up to Holt foornoon, Din'd & drank Tea at Mr Bartells. Mrs Stoddard & Mrs Raven went away Even 2 . . .

APRIL 1, WEDNESDAY A Wet Morn, dry windy day. Mr Hardy at home all Day, I & MA at Church foornoon . . .

APRIL 3, FRIDAY A very cold close day. Mr Hardy at home all Day.

APRIL 4, SATURDAY A very chearly day but cold. All walkd to Holt Aftern, I & MA drank Tea at Miss Leakes, M^r H & W^m drank Tea at Mr Davys, all walk'd home Even 7.

APRIL 5, SUNDAY A chearly day but Cold. I attend d the School a little time foornoon & Afternoon before service. All went to Church Afternoon, Mr Burrell read a Lecture. Miss Leake & «Miss» Pearmain drank Tea here & Jo^s Davy. Mr Hardy went to Mr Burrells after Tea, Mr Cooper of Holt there.

APRIL 6, MONDAY A Chearly day but Cold. Mr Hardy at home all Day . . .

APRIL 8, WEDNESDAY A Frost & fine day. I & MA & W^m went to our Church foornoon. M^r & Mrs Temple, M^r & Mrs Burrell & Mrs Davy drank Tea here. M^r H at home all day . . .

APRIL 10, *Good Friday* A very fine day. All went to our Church Afternoon, Mr Burrell preachd. Mr Davy drank Tea here.

APRIL 11, SATURDAY A fine Day. Mr Hardy walkd to Holt Mark^t, drank Tea at Mr Bartells. I & MA & W^m walkd up after Tea, home Even 8.

APRIL 12, SUNDAY A very fine Day. All went to our Church foornoon, A Comunion, no Sermon. I attend'd the School Afternoon, W^m & Starling went to Holt Church Afternoon. We all took a walk to Fir Closes after Tea.

[[APRIL 13, MONDAY [*by Mary Ann*] A vary fine Day. Robt Raven came in the Morning. Miss Trotter, Miss Ann & De^{by} [Debby] Johnsons, Miss Adcock and Bett Davy drank Tea here. Mr Hardy went to the town meeting in the Evening.]] Hunters Ball at Holt, none of us went . . .

APRIL 15, WEDNESDAY A very fine dry day. Robt Raven went away Morn pst 6. Mr Hardy at home all Day, M^r & Mrs Burrell came after Tea.

APRIL 16, THURSDAY A very mild dry day. Mr Hardy went to Overtons Club Even 6, came home Even past 12.

APRIL 17, FRIDAY A Wet Morng, fine Aftern. Mr Hardy at home all Day, M^{rs} & Miss Baker drank Tea here.

APRIL 18, SATURDAY A fine day. All walkd up to Holt Mark^t Afternoon. I & MA & W^m drank Tea at Mr Bartells, home Even 8 . . .

APRIL 20, MONDAY A very fine day. Mr Hardy, I, MA & W^m drank Tea at Mr Burrells . . .

APRIL 24, FRIDAY A very Wet Morn, cold windy day & some Showers. Mr Hardy at home all Day.

APRIL 25, SATURDAY A fine day. Mr Hardy went to Justice sitting at Holt M11. I & W^m & Mrs Burrell walkd up Aftern, I & W^m drank Tea at Mr Davys, walkd home Even 8. Some rain in the Night . . .

APRIL 27, MONDAY A very cold Windy Day with Showers. Mr Hardy walkd up to Holt Fair Morn 10, Dind at Mr Bakers, drank Tea at Mr Davy. I & W^m went up Even past 3 in our Carriage, took Mrs Bream with us. We drank Tea at Mr Bakers & Supt there. W^m walkd home, Lamb came for us in Carriage Even pst 9.

APRIL 28, TUESDAY A cold chearly Day, Wind high. Mr Hardy at home all Day. Mrs Bream, Mrs Brerton & Mrs Burrell calld to speak to us in Morng . . .

APRIL 30, THURSDAY A very fine day. 2 Miss Theordericks & Miss Harpley dind & drank Tea here. Mr Hardy at home all Day . . .

MAY 2, SATURDAY A Moist Morn. Mr Symonds & Child went away Even 3. Mr Hardy & W^m went to Mark^t Even past 3, I walkd up after Tea.

MAY 3, SUNDAY A drisley cold day. All went to our Church Afternoon, Mr Burrell preach'd. I attend d the School a little time foornoon & Afternoon. W^m & Starling went to Thornage Aftern & drank Tea at Mr Kendles.

MAY 4, MONDAY A drisly Morn, fine Aftern. Maids & Goody Ram began washing afternoon 5 weeks Linnen. Mr Hardy at home all Day .

MAY 5, TUESDAY A very fine dry day. Mr Hardy at home all day. Maids & Goody Ram finishd washing, dryd & fold'd Linnen . . .

MAY 9, SATURDAY A very warm dry day. Bricklay^r mendg Garden Wall. Mr Hardy, I & MA walkd up to Holt Aftern, drank Tea at Mr Bartells, M^r H & W^m drank Tea at Mr Davys, home Even 8 . . .

The visit to Norwich and Great Yarmouth
10–24 May 1789

MAY 13, WEDNESDAY A Hot Day. Walkd into Town [Norwich] foornoon, at home Afternoon. Mrs Bartell Dind & drank Tea at Doct^r Dacks. I poorly with my Eyes twice. We walkd into Town after Tea . . .

MAY 18, MONDAY A close windy day. Took a walk after breakfst, dined & drank Tea at Mr Stannards, went to the Play with Mrs Stoddard & Mrs Raven, Supt at Mr Ravens, Slept at Mr Stoddards.

MAY 19, TUESDAY A fine day. Took a walk into Town foornoon. All drank Tea at Mrs Heaths Afternoon . . .

MAY 22, FRIDAY A fine Morn, began to rain Even 4 & continued till Eveng. I & MA Breakfstd at Mr Wilkins with Bro^t Raven & 2 of his Childrⁿ. Went to Guildhall with them After, drank Tea & Supt at Mr Wymers.

MAY 23, SATURDAY A very warm Day. We took a walk into Town Foornoon. Mr Hardy came to Town Morn 11, took a walk into Quantrils [Quantrell's] Gardens Afternoon, went to the Play at 3^d Acct, Roben Hood & the Divorce . . .

[LETHERINGSETT]

MAY 26, TUESDAY A fine day. Mr Hardy & W^m at home all Day. Old Duke in Garden . . .

MAY 28, THURSDAY A dry day. Mr Hardy poorly with the Gout, I poorly.

MAY 29, FRIDAY A Close showry day. Mr Hardy very bad with the Gout, I poorly.

MAY 30, SATURDAY A Showry day. Mr Hardy at home all Day very bad with the Gout in both feet, I very poorly. W^m & M [Mary Ann] walkd up to Holt Aftern, M drank Tea at Miss Trotters . . .

JUNE 1, MONDAY A Showry Day. Mr Hardy very poorly, I reather better . . .

JUNE 4, THURSDAY Showry Day. Mr Hardy much as yesterday . . .

JUNE 7, SUNDAY A Showry day. Mr Hardy much as yesterday. I, W^m & MA went to our Church foornoon, A Comunion, I attendd the School Afternoon. Mr Burrell began reading Lectures Eveng 6. Robt Raven came for Nathl Eveng 7 . . .

JUNE 9, TUESDAY A fine day. Robt & Nathl went away Morn 9, W^m went with them to Whisinsett. MA walkd up to Holt after Tea, was caught in a Shower coming home, raind very hard in the Eveng . . .

JUNE 11, THURSDAY A close dry day. Mr Hardy somthing better, Mr Bartell calld to see him. W^m came home Eveng 8.

JUNE 12, FRIDAY A Close cold day. Mr Hardy much as yesterday.

JUNE 13, SATURDAY A close cold day. Mr Hardy much as Yesterday. W^m went to Holt Mark^t & drank Tea at Mr Davys, I & MA walkd up to Holt after Tea. Mr Bartell calld.

JUNE 14, SUNDAY A very fine day. All went to our Church Afternoon except Mr Hardy, Mr Burrell preach^d. I attend'd the School foornoon & Afternoon. Bett & Jo^s

Davy drank Tea here. M^r B [Burrell] read a Lecture in Eveng. M^{rs} & Miss & Adam Baker, M^r & Mrs Davy & 2 Childrⁿ, Miss Alpe & a young Lady came down after Tea.

JUNE 15, MONDAY A very fine warm Day. Mr Hardy got out & into Garden upon his Crutches. Mrs Bartell & young Mr Kendle of Thornage drank Tea here. Durrant the Gardiner at work. Mr Bartell calld.

JUNE 16, TUESDAY A very hot dry Day. Mr Hardy somthing better, MA walkd up to Holt after Tea. Gardiner Durrant at Work . . .

JUNE 18, THURSDAY A very hot Day. Mr Hardy much as usial, Mr Bartell calld.

JUNE 19, FRIDAY Very hot Day. Mr Hardy somthing better. M^r & Mrs Burrell came after Tea & Miss A Johnson, playd a pool at Quidril [quadrille] . . .

JUNE 22, MONDAY Fine Morn, very heavy showrs afternoon. Mr Hardy finely. Mrs Jewell, Miss Chichely & Miss Girdleston drank Tea here . . .

JUNE 24, WEDNESDAY A fine day, no rain. M^r H much as Yesterday, rid out in Little Cart foornoon . . .

JUNE 26, FRIDAY Showry Day. Mr Hardy, I & MA drank Tea at Mr Bartells, rid up in L Cart, Lamb came for us Even 9 with the Carriage. Mrs Letten [Lytton] come to Bayfield . . .

JUNE 30, TUESDAY A fine warm day. Mr Hardy, I & MA drank Tea at Mr Bakers, M^r & Mrs Playford there. Lamb came for us with the Carriage. M^r & Mrs Burrell went to Beetly . . .

JULY 4, SATURDAY A very hot day. Mr Hardy at home all Day. W^m went to Markt & drank Tea at Mr Davys, I & MA walk'd up after Tea.

JULY 5, SUNDAY A very wet day. All went to our Church foornoon, Mr Burrell preachd. I attend'd the School foornoon & Afternoon, the Singers came in Eveng to teach the Children.

JULY 6, MONDAY A very fine Day. Mr Hardy, I & MA went to Mr Theorderics of Edgefield to Tea in the Carriage, W^m went on Horse back. Miss Ann Harply there.

JULY 7, TUESDAY A fine day. W^m went to Blakeney & Clay Afternoon. M^r H, I & MA took a walk into the Field Afternoon, I attend'd the Sunday School Childrⁿ at Church in Eveng . . .

JULY 9, THURSDAY A very fine Day. Mr Hardy at home all Day. Robt & Rose Raven came Aftern. Met the Childrⁿ at Church in Eveng, Henry Goggs went away Even 9 to Edgefield.

JULY 10, FRIDAY A Showry Day. Mr Hardy at home all Day. Lamb went to Sheringham. Robt Raven went away after Tea. I attendd the School at Church in the Eveng, I taken with dimness in my Eyes Eveng 9 . . .

JULY 13, MONDAY Dry Morn, Wet Afternoon. Mr Hardy at home all Day, Mrs Burrell drank Tea here.

JULY 14, TUESDAY A Showry Day. Mr Hardy, I, MA & Rose Raven drank Tea and Supt at Mr Forsters, we went in Carriage, M^r H on Horse back . . .

JULY 16, THURSDAY A fine Day. 2 Miss Theorderics & Miss Ann Harply drank Tea here. Raind in the Eveng. W^m rid to Study Aftern, home to Tea.

JULY 17, FRIDAY Fine Morn, Showry Aftern. I, MA & Rose Raven walkd up to Holt, drank Tea at Mr Bakers. Mr Hardy rid up & did not come home till past 11 o Clock.

JULY 18, SATURDAY A fine day. Mr Hardy went up to Holt foornoon to Justice sitting, came back to Dinner, went up to Mark^t Aftern. I & MA & Rose Rav^n & W^m walkd up to Holt, drank Tea at Mr Bartells.

JULY 19, SUNDAY Very Showry Day. All went to our Church foornoon, Mr Burrell preachd, I attendd the School foornoon & Aftern. Mr Burrell read a Lecture . . .

JULY 22, WEDNESDAY A Wet Morn, tolerable Aftern. Mr Hardy at home all Day.

JULY 23, THURSDAY A fine Morn, Showry Aftern. Mr Hardy at home all Day. I attend'd the School in Eveng . . .

JULY 27, MONDAY Dry day, wet Eveng. Mr Hardy at home all Day . . .

JULY 29, WEDNESDAY A fine Morn, Close Aftern. Mr Hardy, I, MA & Rose Raven drank Tea at Mr Press's. Carpenters at Work . . .

JULY 31, FRIDAY A fine Morn, Wet Aftern. Mr Hardy at home all Day. Carpenters at Work. Clay fair. Lamb came from Stalham Morn 8.

AUGUST 1, SATURDAY A dry Morn, Wet Aftern. Mr Hardy, I, MA & Rose Raven walkd up to Holt after Tea, W^m drank Tea at Mr Davy .

AUGUST 2, SUNDAY A fine Day. All went to our Church foornoon, Mr Burrell preach'd, I attendd the School foornoon & Afternoon. Mr Burrell read a Lecture in Even. M^r & Mrs Winn & Mrs Breerton came into our Garden in Eveng. W^m & Starling drank Tea at Mr Coopers at Holt Lawn.

AUGUST 3, MONDAY A very fine Day. Ann Raven & Deb^r Johnson come down from Holt to speak to us foornoon & drank Tea here Afternoon. Miss & Mr Riches, Bett & Jo^s & M [?Margaret, ?Mary, ?Matthew] Davy drank Tea here. Mr Hardy & W^m at home all Day . . .

AUGUST 7, FRIDAY A fine Day. Miss Deb^r Johnson & Ann Raven drank Tea with me Afternoon. Lamb sett off for Helsdon [Hellesdon] with the Horses to bring his Mast^r &c home Morn 11, the«y» came home Even past 10.

AUGUST 8, SATURDAY A fine Day. All walkd up to Holt, drank Tea at Mr Bartells except W^m who drank Tea at Mr Davys. I Bathd.

AUGUST 9, SUNDAY A very fine Day. All went to our Church Afternoon, Mr Burrell preachd & read A Lecture in Even, I attend'd the School foornoon & Aftr. Mr Davys family, Miss Deb^r Johnson & Ann Raven drank Tea at Mr Burrells . . .

AUGUST 14, FRIDAY A fine day. Mr Hardy at home all day, W^m at home . . .

AUGUST 16, SUNDAY A fine Day. Mr Custance & R Rav^n went away after breakfast. I poorly with pain in my Stomach. All went to our Church foornoon, Mr Burrell preachd & read a Lecture in the Eveng. I attendd the School Afternoon. W^m & Starling went to Holt Church & drank Tea at Mr Davys. M^r & Mrs Stoddard & Mrs Rav^n from Norwich & M^r & Mrs Bartell Dind at Mr Rouses, Glanford . . .

AUGUST 19, WEDNESDAY A fine day. M^r H at home all Day. M^r & Mrs Bartell, Mrs Stoddard, Mrs Raven & Miss Rouse dind & drank Tea here. Ann Raven & Deb Johnson call«ed» in Morng. My Stomach no better. W^m came home Even past 6 . . .

AUGUST 21, FRIDAY A fine day. M^r & Mrs Stoddard & 3 Gentlemen from London, M^r & Mrs Bartell, Mrs Rav^n & Miss Rouse dind, drank Tea & Supt here. Mr Hardy at home all Day.

AUGUST 22, SATURDAY A fine Morn, a small Showr ab^t 2 oClock Afternoon & after that very fine the rest of the day. Mr Hardy walkd up to Holt & Dind at Mr Bartells. I & MR [Mary Raven] rid up to Holt after Dinner & went with Mr Bartells company to Sheringham, drank Tea there, came back to Holt Even 9, Supt & spent the Eveng there, came home past 11. Stomach somthing better.

AUGUST 23, SUNDAY A very fine Day. All went to our Church Aftern, Mr Burrell preachd & read a Lecture in the Eveng. I attend'd the School a little time in foornoon & all the Afternoon. Ann Rav^n & Deb^r Johnson came after Dinner, did not go to Church. My Stomach much as yesterday . . .

AUGUST 25, TUESDAY A very fine Day. Mr Hardy & W^m at home all day. Maids & Goody Ram washd 5 Weeks Linnen . . .

AUGUST 28, FRIDAY A fine day. Mr Hardy at home all Day, W^m at home all Day. Mrs Davy & Miss Riches drank Tea here . . .

SEPTEMBER 2, WEDNESDAY A very fine day. Mr Hardy & W^m at home all Day. M^r & Mrs Burrell, M^r & Mrs Burrell [?Bartell] drank Tea here . . .

SEPTEMBER 6, SUNDAY A fine Day. All went to our Church Afternoon, Mr Burrell preachd & read a Lecture in the Eveng. I attendd the School a little time in foorn & Afternoon . . .

SEPTEMBER 8, TUESDAY A fine day. Mr Berry tund'd [tuned] the Organ foornoon, Dind here, taught the Childr^n to Sing Afternoon then went to Mr Burrells, we all drank Tea at Mr Burrells, M^r & Miss Baker there. I bathd.

SEPTEMBER 9, WEDNESDAY A Close Morn, fine Day. I Bathd. Mr Hardy walkd up to Holt foornoon to pay the Excise, dind at Mr Bakers. Mr Horsefall & Berry Dind here & went away after Dinner. M^r & Miss Baker, M^r & Mrs Bartell drank Tea here.

SEPTEMBER 10, THURSDAY A fine day. I Bathd. Mr Hardy at home all Day. I & MA walkd up to Holt Aftern with M^r & Mrs Burrell, drank Tea at Miss Trotters, Lamb came for us with the Carriage.

SEPTEMBER 11, FRIDAY A Shower in the Morng early, fine Day. Mr Hardy at home all Day. I poorly with pain in my Stomach . . .

SEPTEMBER 13, SUNDAY A fine day. All went to our Church foornoon, Mr Burrell preachd & read a Lecture in Eveng. I attend«ed» the School foornoon & Afternoon.

SEPTEMBER 14, MONDAY A fine Morn, Wet Afternoon. Miss Riches, Miss Bett & Mary Davy drank Tea here. Mr Hardy Dind & drank Tea at Mr Chaplins, Blakeney. Mr Berry came to teach the Childr^n & went to Holt to Sleep . . .

SEPTEMBER 17, THURSDAY A fine dry Day. Mr Davy & Son John from London Dind & drank Tea here, M^r & Mrs Burrell drank Tea here.

SEPTEMBER 18, FRIDAY A dry Morn, Wet Aftern. Mr Hardy at home all day. [[[by Mary Ann] Willm din'd at Mr Davys, came home Even 8.

SEPTEMBER 19, SATURDAY A dry Day, A vary wet Eve^{ng}. The Justices Sitting at Holt, Mr Hardy and W^m din'd with them. I & MA walkd up to Tea at Mr Davys, Lamb came for us Even^g 9.

SEPTEMBER 20, SUNDAY A wet Morn, dry Afternoon. Mr Berry and a Company of Girls came here to Dine, all went to Church Afternoon, Mr Burrell Preached. Mrs Jewell, Miss Chichely, Miss Hardey from Norwich, the 2 Miss Hewhits [Hewitts], M^r and Mrs Davy drank Tea here. Berry Slep^t here . . .

SEPTEMBER 22, TUESDAY A Close Dry day. Maids and Goody Ram washed. MA took a ride with M^r and Mrs Burrell in the Morn^g, came back to Dinner. Willm went and dined with Mr Purdy of Keeling. M^r H, I and MA drank Tea at Mr Bartells, came home Even 9 . . .]]

SEPTEMBER 26, SATURDAY A fine day. Mr Hardy, I, MA & W^m walk'd up to Holt Sessions, drank Tea at Mr Davys, walkd home Even 8. I bathd.

SEPTEMBER 27, SUNDAY A fine Day. Mastr Stannard came to stay a few Days, Robt Bartell dind here. All went to our Church foornoon, Mr Burrell preachd & read a Lecture in Eveng. I attendd the School foorn & Aftrn. W^m & Starling went to Thornage Afternoon, drank Tea at Mr Kendles . . .

SEPTEMBER 29, TUESDAY A Stormy Day, wind high. Mr Hardy came home Eve 8. Mr Berry taught MA and W^m, Dind here & went away Even 4. I & MA walkd up to Holt, drank Tea at Mr Burtells [Bartell's], Miss Baldin there. Lamb came for us with the Carriage. I Bathd.

SEPTEMBER 30, WEDNESDAY A fine Day. Mr Hardy at home all Day. I & MA walk'd up to Holt Aftern, drank Tea at Mrs Girlins [Girling's], Lamb came for us with the Carriage.

OCTOBER 1, THURSDAY A very Wet Morn, dry Aftern. Mr Hardy walkd up to Holt Aftr, drank Tea at Mr Bakers.

OCTOBER 2, FRIDAY A fine Day but Cold. Mr Hardy & Mr Burrell went in Mrs Sheppards Chaise to [   ] & Cromer & came home Even 8. Miss Baldin & Miss Rouse dind & drank Tea here. M^r & Mrs Bartell & Robt, Mrs Davy & 2 Childr^n drank Tea here. I Bathd . . .

OCTOBER 4, SUNDAY Showry foornoon, dry Aftern. All went to our Church Afternoon, Mr Burrell preachd, I attend'd the School foornoon & Aftern. A Lecture Eve 7 . . .

OCTOBER 6, TUESDAY A Close drisley Day. Maids & Goody Ram washd 2 Weeks Linnen. Mr Hardy at home all Day. F Wymer came Even 7, Slept here. I bathd.

OCTOBER 7, WEDNESDAY A drisley Morn, Showry Day. Mr Hardy set of on Horseback Morn 7 to Norwich Quartr Sessions on Acct of Joshua Yarum [Yarham's] Setlement «(»which was found to be at Gresham). M^r F Wymer went away M9. M^r H sent his Horse home by Mr Breertons Servt . . .

OCTOBER 11, SUNDAY A fine day. All went to our Church foornoon, I attend'd the School foorn & Aftern. Miss Baldin went home from Mr Rous's, Glanf'd. M^r & Mrs Robt Wymer, M^r & Mrs Bartell & 2 Childr^n & Miss Barnwell, Miss Leak & «Miss» Pearmain & a Miss Brown from Norwich drank Tea here. Eliz Coe came as upper Servt.

OCTOBER 12, MONDAY A very Wet foorn, dry Aftern. Mr Hardy, I & MA went up to Holt Aftern in Carriage, drank Tea & Supt at Mr Bartells, Lamb came for us Even 11. Pleasance Gidney came as Cook.

OCTOBER 13, TUESDAY A fine Day. Mr Hardy at home all day. M^r & Mrs Wymer, M^r & Mrs Bartell Dind, drank Tea & Supt here.

OCTOBER 14, WEDNESDAY A fine Morn, Wet Afternoon. Berry came to teach the Childr^n abt Noon, Dind here. Mr Hardy at home all Day. «Berry» gave MA a Lesson & W^m.

OCTOBER 15, THURSDAY A Wet day. Mr Hardy & W^m walkd up to Holt foornoon to the Qrtr Sessions, W^m came home Even 3. Mr Hardy Dind at the Feathers, drank Tea at Miss Leakes, came home Even 9 . . .

OCTOBER 17, SATURDAY A fine Day. I taken with dimness in my Eyes foornoon. Mr Hardy walk'd up to Holt Foornoon to Justice sitting, Dind at the Feathers. I, MA & W^m walkd up Afternoon, I & MA drank Tea at Miss Leakes. W^m drank Tea at Mr Davys & went home Eve 7 & sent Lamb with the Carriage for us, we supt at Mr Bartells & came home before Eve 10 . . .

OCTOBER 21, WEDNESDAY A fine Day. Mr Hardy at home all Day, paid Excise. We shd have met M^r & Mrs Temple at Mr Burrells but M^r & Mrs Burrell [? Bartell], Mr Vestber & Mrs Raven from Norwich came, drank Tea & Supt here.

OCTOBER 22, THURSDAY A Close dry Day. Mr Hardy at home all Day . . .

OCTOBER 24, SATURDAY A Close dry Day. We all walkd up to Holt Aftern, drank Tea at Mr Bakers, walkd home. Starling went to his Fathers in Even.

OCTOBER 25, SUNDAY A very fine bright Day. All went to our Church foornoon, Mr Burrell preachd. Mr Hardy & W^m went to Holt Church Aftern, Mr Astley of Thornage preachd there. I attend'd the School foornoon & Aftern, Mr Burrell read a Lecture in the Eveng . . .

OCTOBER 28, WEDNESDAY A Close Morn, Wet Afternoon. Mr Hardy at home all Day . . .

NOVEMBER 3, TUESDAY A Wet Morn, cleard alittle towards Eveng. Maids & Goody Ram Washd 4 Weeks Linnen. Mr Hardy at home all Day . . .

NOVEMBER 5, THURSDAY A Close foggy Day. Lydia Youngman came to help to Iron. Mr Hardy walkd to Holt Aftern, drank Tea at Mr Bartells & went to Overtons Club, came home Even past 12 . . .

NOVEMBER 7, SATURDAY A fine day. We all walkd up to Holt Afternoon, drank Tea at Mr Davys, M^r H drank Tea at Mr Bartells, M Davy came home with us Even 9.

NOVEMBER 8, SUNDAY A fine day. All went to our Church foornoon, Mr Burrell preachd. Jo^s Davy Dind here. W^m & Starling walkd to Clay & Weybon to see the Shipwreck, drank Tea at Mr Davys, came home E8. I attend'd the School foorn & Aftern, Mr Burrell read a Lecture in the Eveng . . .

NOVEMBER 11, WEDNESDAY A fine day. Mr Hardy & W^m both at home all Day. M^r & Mrs Temple, M^r & Mrs Davy drank Tea here. Mr Burrell went to Walsingham for 2 Miss L«e»akes. Mr Berry here, taught MA.

NOVEMBER 12, THURSDAY A Close foggy day. Mr Hardy at home all Day. W^m rid to Thornage after Dinner . . .

NOVEMBER 15, SUNDAY A Close drisly Day. I attend'd the School foornoon & Aftern. All went to our Church Aftern Even 4, Mr Burrell preachd, he had preachd at Holt before in the Afternoon.

NOVEMBER 16, MONDAY A fine Day. Mr Hardy, I & MA walk'd up to Holt Aftrn, drank Tea at [and] Supt at Mr Bartells, Lamb came for us with the Carriage Even 9. Mr Berry came & taught the Childr^n to Sing.

NOVEMBER 17, TUESDAY A fine Morn, Showry Aftern. Mr Hardy at home all Day. M^r & M^{rs} & Miss Baker & M^r & Mrs Bartell drank Tea here . . .

NOVEMBER 20, FRIDAY A Close drisly day. Mr Hardy & W^m at home all day. Raind in the Night.

NOVEMBER 21, SATURDAY A Close Morn, drisly Aftern, very Wet Eveng. Mr Hardy, I & MA walkd up to Holt Aftern, drank Tea at Mr Davys, Lamb came for us with the Carriage Even 9. W^m went to Whesinsett [Whissonsett] Even 3.

NOVEMBER 22, SUNDAY A Close dry Day. All went to our Church foornoon, Mr Burrell preachd. Mr Starling Dind & drank Tea at Mr Davys. I attend^d the School foornoon & Afternoon.

NOVEMBER 23, MONDAY A fine Morn, Showry After. Mr Hardy at home all Day. I & MA walkd up to Holt Afternoon, drank Tea at Miss Leakes & walkd home Even 8. Mr Berry came & taught the Childr^n to Sing . . .

NOVEMBER 25, WEDNESDAY A fine Morn, very Wet day. Mr Hardy, H Goggs & W^m went to the Horse fair foornoon, came home to Dinner, walkd up after Noon, drank Tea at Mr Davys. Mr Hardy, I & MA rid up in Carriage, drank Tea at Mr Bartells, Lamb came for us with the Carriage Even past 9.

NOVEMBER 26, THURSDAY A fine day. W^m & H Goggs rid to Weybon foornoon, came home to Dinner & [Henry Goggs] went away after dinner. Mr Hardy at home all day. Mr Berry came to teach MA in Morn, Breakfstd here.

NOVEMBER 28, SATURDAY A bright day, not much frost. Mr Hardy walkd up «to» Holt Aftern, I and MA walkd up towards Night, we all drank Tea at Mr Davys, walkd home. W^m at home all Day . . .

DECEMBER 1, TUESDAY A very fine day. Mr Hardy & W^m at home all day, Mr Baker Dind here . . .

DECEMBER 3, THURSDAY A very fine day. Mr Hardy & W^m went to Clay foornoon to look at some Deales [deals], did not buy any, came home Even 6. John Davy drank Tea here.

DECEMBER 4, FRIDAY A close Morn, Wet Aftern. Mr Hardy at home all Day. M^r & M^{rs} & Miss Purdy, Mrs Davy, John and Matt & Mary Davy drank Tea here, MD [Mary Davy] staid all Night.

DECEMBER 5, SATURDAY A very fine day. Mr Hardy walkd up to Holt, drank Tea at Mr Bartells. I, MA & W^m walkd up to Holt, drank Tea at Mr Davys, John & Matt Davy walkd home with us & Slept here.

DECEMBER 6, SUNDAY A fine day. All went to our Church foornoon, Mr Burrell preachd, I attend'd the Schooll Aftern. W^m & Starling Dind & drank Tea at Mr Davys, came home Even 8 . . .

DECEMBER 8, TUESDAY A Close foggy day. Maids & goody Ram washd 5 weeks Linnen. Mr Hardy did not come home, W^m at home all day. J Bolton went away aftern, Starling spent the Even at Mr Pauls of Study.

DECEMBER 9, WEDNESDAY Fine Morn, very foggy day. J Davy Dind & drank Tea here, W^m & Starling spent the Eveng at Mr Davys.

DECEMBER 10, THURSDAY A very fine day. Mr Hardy came home from Norwich Eve past 5, W^m dind & drank Tea at Mr Purdys of Kelling with John & Matt Davy.

DECEMBER 11, FRIDAY A close dry day. Mr Hardy at home all day. Mr Keeler & Miss Billings came Afternoon, drank Tea here, left Miss Billings here. J [John] & Matt Davy came after Tea, W^m & Starling went home with them to spend the Eveng, Matt goes away in the Morng.

DECEMBER 12, SATURDAY A fine day. We all walkd up to Holt Afternoon, drank Tea at Mr Bartells, W^m drank Tea at Mr Davys. Lamb came for us with the Carriage E8.

DECEMBER 13, SUNDAY A close dry day. I attend'd the School foornoon & Aftern, had service Even 6. W^m, MA & Miss Billings at Church, Mr Burrell preachd . . .

DECEMBER 15, TUESDAY A Wet Morn «?and» Day. Mr Hardy & W^m at home all day.

DECEMBER 16, WEDNESDAY A Wet Morn, fine Aftern. Mr Hardy & W^m at home all day. J Davy drank Tea, Supt & Slept here. Mr Berry came foornoon, taught W^m & MA & Dind here.

DECEMBER 17, THURSDAY A very Showry day. Mr Hardy Dind at the Feathers at Holt at the School feast. I, MA & Miss Billings walkd up to Holt, drank Tea at Miss Leakes, Lamb came for us Eve 8 . . .

DECEMBER 28, MONDAY A fine day. Mr Hardy went to Wells Morn 9, came home Eveng 7. My foot very poorly.

DECEMBER 29, TUESDAY A very Wet Morng, dry Aftern, Wind high. I very lame with my Foot. M^r & Mrs Baker & Adam, M^r & Mrs Bartell drank Tea & Supt here.

DECEMBER 30, WEDNESDAY A fine day. Mr Hardy & W^m at home all Day. My toe gathered to a Sore & very bad.

DECEMBER 31, THURSDAY A very fine day. My foot somthing better. Mr Hardy & W^m at home all day . . .

1790

JANUARY 2, SATURDAY A rime frost, close day. My foot better. Mr Hardy & MA walkd up to Holt Afternoon, drank Tea at Mr Davys & walkd home.

JANUARY 3, SUNDAY A fine day. All went to our Church Afternoon, Mr Burrell preach'd. I took the Names of the Sunday Schollars. Mrs Prior & Kinsman from Mileham came Eveng 6 . . .

JANUARY 7, THURSDAY A very fine day. Lamb & W^m went to Weybon for a Ship Mast, came home E4, drove us & Mrs Bartell to Mr Temples at Thornage, drank Tea & Supt there. Lamb came for us Eve 12.

JANUARY 8, FRIDAY A beautifull day. Mr Hardy at home all day. Lamb went [

] . . .

JANUARY 10, SUNDAY A Close cold day. All went to our Church foornoon, Mr Burrell preach'd, I attend'd the School Aftern.

JANUARY 11, MONDAY A Close dry day, Wet Eveng. Mr Hardy at home all Day . . .

JANUARY 13, WEDNESDAY A Wet Day. Mr Hardy at home all Day. M^r & Mrs Burrell & Miss Leak, M^r & Mrs Temple «of» Thornage, M^r & Mrs Forster of Bayfield drank Tea & Supt here . . .

JANUARY 15, FRIDAY A fine Mild day. Mr Hardy at home all day. Mr Berry came Even 6, gave MA a Lesson, drank Tea, Supt & Slept here . . .

JANUARY 21, THURSDAY A Sharp rime frost, fine Day. Mr Hardy went to qr^{tr} Sessions at Holt Morng 11, Dind at Mr Bartells, came home Even 7 . . .

JANUARY 30, SATURDAY A Close Morn, Wet Afternoon. Mr Hardy went to Market Even 3, Lamb went for him with Carriage Even 7. Robt Raven came Even past 5.

JANUARY 31, SUNDAY A Wet Morn, dry Afternoon. All went to our Church Afternoon, Mr Burrell preach'd. I attend'd the School foornoon & Afternoon . . .

FEBRUARY 3, WEDNESDAY A fine day. Mr Hardy at home all day, W^m & MA came home from Guestwick Even 6. Mr Tooby drank Tea here, Paul Myles came to Dinner & Slept here . . .

FEBRUARY 7, SUNDAY A Close day. All went to our Church foornoon except Mr Hardy, Mr Moore went away ab^t Noon. I attend'd the School Afternoon, W^m went to Holt Church Aftern.

FEBRUARY 8, MONDAY A fine day. Maids & Goody Ram Washd 5 Weeks Linnen. Mr Hardy at home all Day. Lamb at muck Cart . . .

FEBRUARY 10, WEDNESDAY A very fine day. Mr Hardy at home all day. We Irond linn^n [linen]. Mr Cooper of Holt drank Tea & Supt here.

FEBRUARY 11, THURSDAY Some Snow fell in Morn, tolerable day. Mr Hardy at home all day. W^m rid to Blakney Afternoon after some timber, drank Tea at Mr Harrolds [?Hurrell's], came home E7.

FEBRUARY 12, FRIDAY A dry Windy day. Mr Hardy at home all day. Bett Davy came home from Woodbridge.

FEBRUARY 13, SATURDAY A very fine day. All walk'd to Holt Mark^t Afternoon, drank Tea at Mr Davys, MH [Mr Hardy] drank Tea at Mr Bartells. Lamb came for us with the Carriage E past 8.

FEBRUARY 14, SUNDAY A very fine day. I look'd into the School foornoon. M^r & Mrs Davy, Bett, Jo^s & Mary Davy & Miss M Riches drank Tea here. M^r & Mrs Stoddard came to Mr Bartells.

FEBRUARY 15, MONDAY A very fine day. Mr Hardy, I & MA drank Tea & Supt at Mr Bartells, W^m came in Eveng, Lamb came for us with the Carriage Even 12. Mr Davy went up to London.

FEBRUARY 16, TUESDAY A Drisly Morn, close dry Aftern. M^r & Mrs Stoddard, M^r & Mrs Bartell Dind, drank Tea & Supt here. M^r & Mrs Burrell & Miss Leak came in the Eveng, Supt here . . .

FEBRUARY 20, SATURDAY A very fine day. Mr Hardy, I, MA & W^m walkd up to Holt Mark^t Aftern, all drank Tea at Mr Davys except M^r H & W^m. Lamb came for us with the Carriage Even past 9, left MA at Mr Davys.

FEBRUARY 21, SUNDAY A beautiful Day. All went to our Church foornoon, Mr Burrell preachd. W^m went to Holt Aftern, drank Tea at Mr Davys. I attend'd the School Afternoon . . .

FEBRUARY 23, TUESDAY A very fine day. Mr Hardy & W^m not at home. I & Sarah Davy walkd up to Holt after Dinner, met Mrs Baker, M^{rs} & Bett Davy & Miss Riches & MA coming down, they drank Tea here, Mr Baker came to Tea.

FEBRUARY 24, WEDNESDAY A Close foggy Morn, fine Aftern. I & MA went to our Church foornoon. Mr Hardy & W^m came home Even 8 . . .

FEBRUARY 26, FRIDAY A very Windy day. Mr Hardy at home all Day.

FEBRUARY 27, SATURDAY A fine day. M^r H, I, MA & W^m walkd up to Holt Markt, M^r H drank Tea at Mr Bartells, we at Mr Davys. Lamb came for us Even 8.

FEBRUARY 28, SUNDAY A fine day, reather Windy. I & MA sett of for the Woodrow [at Cawston] alittle after 12 in our Carriage to meet Miss Wymer, got home Even 6. Mr Hardy & W^m at our Church after Noon . . .

MARCH 3, WEDNESDAY A very fine day. Mr Hardy at home all day. I, Miss Wymer & MA walkd up to Holt Aftern, came back to Tea.

MARCH 4, THURSDAY A fine day. Mr Hardy at home all day.

MARCH 5, FRIDAY A very fine day. Mr Hardy, I, Miss Wymer & MA drank Tea at Mr Burrells.

MARCH 6, SATURDAY A fine day. M^r H, I, Miss Wymer & MA walkd up to Holt Afternoon, drank Tea at Miss Leakes except Mr Hardy who drank Tea at Mr Bakers.

MARCH 7, SUNDAY A fine day. All went to our Church foornoon except Miss Wymer, Mr Burrell preach'd. I attend'd the School Afternoon.

MARCH 8, MONDAY A very fine day & beautifull Even. M^r H, I, Miss Wymer & MA drank Tea at Mr Temples of Thornage, met Mr Kendle & Mrs Lewis, Bett Davy & Miss M Riches there. Lamb came for us Even past 8.

MARCH 9, TUESDAY A fine «day», wind blustering. Maids & Neb Ram washd 4 Weeks Linnen. Mr Hardy at home all day. Mr Smith, Attorney from Wells, drank Tea here Afternoon.

MARCH 10, WEDNESDAY Wind high, some Storms of Hail. MA & Miss Wymer din^d, drank Tea & Supt at Mr Bartells, Mr Hardy & I drank Tea & Supt there, Lamb came for us Even 11. I & 2 Girls went to our Church foorn, Mr Burrell read Prayers.

MARCH 11, THURSDAY A beautifull day. Mr Hardy & we at home all Day.

MARCH 12, FRIDAY A very fine day. Berry dind here & taught MA a Lesson. Miss Wymer & MA walkd up to Holt Afternoon, drank «tea» at Mr Davys, Lamb went for them Even 9. M^r & Mrs Bartell drank Tea & Supt here . . .

MARCH 16, TUESDAY A fine day. Mr Hardy & W^m at home all Day. M^r & Mrs Burrell & Miss Leek drank Tea here . . .

MARCH 19, FRIDAY A very fine day. Mr Hardy at home all Day.

MARCH 20, SATURDAY A fine day. I, MA, Miss Wymer walkd up to Holt Mark^t, we drank Tea at Mr Bartells, M^r H drank Tea at Mr Bakers, walk^d home Even 8 . . .

MARCH 22, MONDAY A very fine day. MA poorly with a Cold. Mr Hardy at home all day. M^r & Mrs Temple of Thornage drank Tea here.

MARCH 23, TUESDAY A fine Morn, close Aftern. 3 Carpenters at work. Mr Hardy & I walkd up to Holt, drank Tea at Mr Davys they being a going to London to Morrow, came home Even past 7. MA very poorly . . .

MARCH 26, FRIDAY A close cold day. M^r H, I & MA, M^r & Mrs Burrell & Miss Leek walk'd up to Holt Aftern, drank Tea at Mr Bakers, walkd home. Ann Davy came in Morn & walkd up to Holt with us Aftern. Berry here, taught MA . . .

MARCH 28, SUNDAY A chearly day but Cold. All went to our Church Aftern. Bett, Jo^s, M & Susan Davy, Miss M Ritches & M^r R Starling drank Tea here, Ann Davy Slept here.

MARCH 29, MONDAY A close cold Day. Mr Hardy at home all Day. M^r & Mrs Bartell call«ed» Afternoon as they were going to Mr Temples of Thornage.

MARCH 30, TUESDAY A Close blustering day. Maids & old Neb Ram wash'd 3 Weeks Linnen. M^r & Mrs Wymer of Wroxham came Even 5, drank Tea, Supt & Slept here. M^r & Mrs Bartell drank Tea & Supt here . . .

APRIL 1, THURSDAY A Cold dry Windy day. M^r & Mrs Wymer went away M past 10. M^r H & W^m walkd up to Holt Aftern, came home to Tea.

APRIL 2, FRIDAY A dry Windy day. All went to our Church foornoon, Mr Burrell preachd. Mr Hardy at home all day. Berry here, taught MA . . .

APRIL 4, SUNDAY A fine day. All went to our Church foornoon, A Communion, no Sermon. I attend'd the School Aftern. W^m went to Holt Church Aftern, drank Tea at Mr Kings. The Davys walkd down after Tea, MA walkd up to Holt with them. Miss Rouse went to Norwich with Mr Raven.

APRIL 5, MONDAY A Cold Windy day. W^m walkd up to Holt Afternoon, came home to Tea. Mr Hardy, I & MA drank Tea at Mrs Jewells, Mrs Chrismas there. Mrs Bartell went to Norwich this Afternoon in Mr Ravens Chaise. Ann Davy came this Afternoon. A Town meeting at Mr Mays's, W^m there.

APRIL 6, TUESDAY A Cold Windy day. Mr Hardy & W^m at home all day. Ann Davy here . . .

APRIL 11, SUNDAY A very Cold day, Wind high. Our White fac'd Cow died. All went to our Church Aftern, Mr Burrell preachd. My Eye somthing better. Did not attend the School.

APRIL 12, MONDAY Som small Showers of rain, wind rough. Mr Hardy at home all Day. Ann Davy & M Riches came foorn, dind & drank Tea here. Mr Cooper of Holt drank Tea here. MA & W^m walkd up to Holt after Tea, W^m came home Even 10, MA staid all Night. Mr Playford & Mr Baker came Even 7, supt here, went away Eve past 10.

APRIL 13, TUESDAY A Cold windy day, began to rian [rain] moderately Even 6, continued all Night. Mr Hardy at home all Day. Ann Davy & MA walkd down Aftern & went back to Tea. Miss Temple, Daughtr of Robt Temple of Weyborn, was Married to Mr Robinson of Norwich. A Town meeting.

APRIL 14, WEDNESDAY A Cold Showry day. Mr Hardy went to Overtons Club Even 7, came home Even past 12.

APRIL 15, THURSDAY A dry Morn, began to Snow M11, Continued all the Aftern very fast, Wind at N East & very Cold. Mr Hardy & W^m at home all Day. Miss Jesup [? Jessop] & Mrs Page from Woodbridge came from Fakenham to Mr Davys . . .

APRIL 17, SATURDAY A fine day but cold. Mr Hardy walkd up to Holt foornoon, Dind at Mr Bakers, drank Tea at Mr Davys. Miss Davy & MA came down to dinner. We all walkd up to Holt Aftern, drank Tea at Mr Davys, Lamb came for us Even 9. Berry here, did not teach MA . . .

APRIL 20, TUESDAY A fine day. Mr Hardy at home all Day. I & MA walkd up to Holt after Tea, M^r & Mrs Davy came home this After from London.

APRIL 21, WEDNESDAY A Close cold day. Mr Hardy at home all Day. Mrs Holman from Downham, Mrs Wm Custance from Norwich & Mrs Priest from Do [ditto] came to Mr Bakers. W^m came home from Coltishall Even 7.

APRIL 22, THURSDAY A Showry day. Mr Hardy, I & MA walk^d up to Holt Aftern, drank Tea & Supt at Mr Bakers, Lamb came for us Eve past 11. Berry here, did not teach either MA or W^m . . .

APRIL 24, SATURDAY A very Showry day. M^r H walkd up to Holt foornoon, came back to Dinner. Mrs Hollman, Mrs Priest, Mrs Custance of Fakenham, Mrs Custance of Norwich, M^rs & Miss Baker dind, drank Tea & Supt here, Mr Baker came to Supper. Sent them home in our Carriage.

APRIL 25, SUNDAY A very fine Morn, some heavy Showers Afternoon. W^m walk'd to Kelling Aftern to meet Mr Davys Family. M^r H, I & MA went to our Church Aftern, Mr Leak preachd. Mr Hardy walkd up to Holt, drank Tea & Supt at Mr Bakers, M^r & Mrs Forster drank Tea here. Robt Raven came Even 7 by Holt . . .

MAY 2, SUNDAY A fine day. All went to our Church foornoon, Mr Burrell preachd. Mr Hardy somthing better. W^m walkd to Holt Church Afternoon, drank Tea at Mr Bakers, they walkd home with him. I attendd the School foorn & Aftern . . .

[[MAY 4, TUESDAY [by Mary Ann] A fine Day. Father & Mother went to Bale after dinner in little Cart, came back to Tea. Mr Hardy better.

MAY 5, WEDNESDAY Fine Day, rather drisly. Mr Hardy at home and finely. Willm rode to Bale after Tea, M^r H went to town meeting in the evening. We Iron'd]] . . .

MAY 7, FRIDAY A small rain all day. Mr Hardy at home all day. W^m walkd up to Holt after Tea.

MAY 8, SATURDAY A fine day but cold. Mr Hardy rid up as far as Mr Smiths [at Holt Rectory] in L Cart then walkd up to Holt Market. I & MA walkd up, drank Tea at Miss Leaks, M^r H drank Tea at Mr Davys. W^m walkd up after Tea. Lamb came for us Even 8 . . .

MAY 10, MONDAY A Close drisley day. Mr Hardy at home all day .

MAY 11, TUESDAY A Chearly day, Wind Cold at North. Mr Hardy at home all Day, M^r & Mrs Bartell drank Tea here.

MAY 12, WEDNESDAY A Chearly day, Wind rough. Lamb drove us to Kelling Afternoon, we drank Tea at Mr Purdys.

MAY 13, THURSDAY A Chearly day, wind rough & Cold. Mr Hardy at home all Day. W^m rid to Bale after Tea to look at the Timber fillers [fellers]. I & MA walkd up to Holt after Tea . . .

MAY 15, SATURDAY A Close Morn, fine Afternoon. I & MA walkd up to Holt Afternoon, drank Tea at Mr Bartells, came home Even 7. Mr Hardy came home Even 9.

MAY 16, SUNDAY A very fine Day. All went to our Church foornoon, Mr Burrell preachd, I attend'd the School Afternoon. M^r & Mrs Burrell & Miss Leak came into Garden after Tea . . .

[[MAY 18, TUESDAY [by Mary Ann] A fine Day. Mr Hardy & W^m went to see the Timber fellers After Dinner, came back to Tea. Mrs Hardy and I walked up to Holt after Tea.

MAY 19, WEDNESDAY A fine Day, some showrs in the Evening. Mr Hardy at home all Day. Mrs Sales and Miss Wall, M^r, M^rs & Miss Baker drank Tea here. Young Theodorick painting the best parlour . . .

MAY 21, FRIDAY A fine Day. Mr Hardy at home all Day. Mother poorly. Painter here.]]

MAY 22, SATURDAY A fine day. Painter here & finish'd the Parlour. Mr Hardy went to Bale Morn 8 to Measure the Timber, came home Even 6. I & MA walk'd up to Holt Afternoon, drank Tea at Mrs Davys, W^m walkd up Even 8 & Supt there. Raind in the Eveng.

MAY 23, SUNDAY A close hasy Morn, fine Afternoon. I poorly with pain in my side. All went to our Church Afternoon, I attend'd the School alittle while after Service. John Kendle drank Tea here, Mrs Davy & Family calld in Eveng.

MAY 24, MONDAY A Wet Morn, close Afternoon. Mr Hardy at home all Day. W^m sett of for Whisensett Even ½ past 2. I very poorly with pain in my Side. M^r T Temple drank Tea here.

MAY 25, TUESDAY A drisly Day. Mr Hardy at home all Day.

MAY 26, WEDNESDAY A Close dry Day. Mr Hardy at home all Day. M^r & Mrs Moore, Miss Ann Johnson & Miss Leek drank Tea here. W^m came home from Whisensett Even 9.

MAY 27, THURSDAY Drisly Morn, close foggy day. Maids & Goody Ram Washd 3 Weeks linnen. Mrs Bartell came down after Tea . . .

MAY 29, SATURDAY A fine Day. Irond up all our Linnen. All of us walkd up to Holt after Tea. Miss Ritches & M Davy & Mr Berry drank Tea here . . .

JUNE 1, TUESDAY A fine Day. Mr Hardy, I & MA met M^r & Mrs Moore at Mr Bakers, drank Tea there . . .

JUNE 3, THURSDAY A close Morn, Showers Aftern. M [Mr] Hughes, Dru«g»gist from London, Dind here. M^r, M^rs & Miss Baker calld us to go to Mr Temples of Thornage, we drank Tea there, M^r & Mrs Moore there . . .

JUNE 5, SATURDAY A fine day, Wind very high. We all walkd up to Holt Afternoon, I & MA drank Tea at Miss Leaks, M^r H & W^m drank Tea at Mr Davys. Miss Ritches & M Davy came home with us & Slept here.

JUNE 6, SUNDAY A very fine day. I attend'd the School foornoon. All went to our Church Afternoon, James Winn not at home. Jo^s Davy drank Tea here. Took a walk after Tea.

JUNE 7, MONDAY A fine day. Mr Hardy at home all Day. M^r & Mrs Wymer of Wroxham came Afternoon, M^r & Mrs Bartell drank Tea & Supt here . . .

JUNE 9, WEDNESDAY Showry Morn, fine day. M^r & Mrs Wymer, I & W^m walk^d up to Holt foornoon. We all went to Sheringham Afternoon, drank Tea there & came home Eve p 9.

JUNE 10, THURSDAY A very fine day. M^r & Mrs Wymer went away after Dinner. Mr Hardy at home all Day. Mr Wright very poorly. W^m went to Salthouse Afternoon with J Kendle & Jo^s Davy, came home Even 9.

JUNE 11, FRIDAY A very fine day. Miss Leek, Mrs Brearton [Brereton] & Mrs Best came after breakfast. Mr Theorderick the younger & Miss Sebs [?Sibbs] calld foornoon. Mr Hardy at home all «day». W^m rid to Brinton, Blakney & Langham Afternoon, came home Even past 8.

JUNE 12, SATURDAY A fine day. Mr Hardy, I & MA walkd up to Holt Afternoon, drank Tea at Mr Davys. M^r & Mrs Moy at Holt, W^m went up to Holt Even 7, Mrs Stoddard & Mrs Raven came to Mr Bartells of Holt.

JUNE 13, SUNDAY A fine day. All went to our Church foorn, Mr Burrell preachd. Mrs Stoddard & Raven went home about Noon. W^m went to Thornage Church Afternoon & drank Tea at Mr Kendles . . .

JUNE 16, WEDNESDAY A fine Day. Mr Hardy & W^m at home all Day. I & MA walkd up to Holt Afternoon, drank Tea «at» Mr Davys, Mrs Bell of Wells & Mrs Baker there.

JUNE 17, THURSDAY A fine day. {We Irond.} Mr Hardy at home all Day. We Irond 3 Weeks Linnen . . .

JUNE 19, SATURDAY A Hot day. Miss Riches & M Davy Dind here. I & MA walkd up to Holt Afternoon, drank Tea at Mr Davys. Mr Hardy & W^m came home Eveng 7, drank Tea at Mr Bartells. Miss Baker came home with us & Slept here . . .

JUNE 23, WEDNESDAY A dry Day, not so excesive hot as Yesterday. We were all at home all Day.

JUNE 24, THURSDAY A very dry day, wind blustering. Sister Goggs, I & Miss Harpley & Nathl Raven rid in our Carriage to Sheringham, Mr Hardy & MA on Horseback, drank Tea there & came home Even 10 . . .

JUNE 26, SATURDAY A dry close Morn, Showry Afternoon. We all walkd up to Holt after Tea.

JUNE 27, SUNDAY A Wet day. All went to our Church foornoon, Mr Burrell preach^d, I lookd into School Afternoon. Mr Burrell read a Lecture Even 7 . . .

JUNE 29, TUESDAY A fine day. I, Sister Goggs, Miss Harpley & MA walkd up to Holt Afternoon, drank Tea at Mr Bakers. Mr Hardy came home from Gresenhall Even 6, came up to Holt for us, came home Eve 10.

JUNE 30, WEDNESDAY A Close dry Day. Mr Hardy at home all Day. M^r & Mrs Davy, M^r & Mrs Baker, M^r & Mrs Burrell & the 2 Miss Leakes drank Tea here.

JULY 1, THURSDAY A fine day. Mr Hardy at home all Day. We all drank Tea with the Miss Leaks at Mr Burrells.

JULY 2, FRIDAY A fine Morn, very heavy Showers Afternoon with Thunder. Sister Goggs, I & Miss Harpley & M Ann went to Salthouse in Carriage, Mr Hardy on Horseback, drank Tea there, came home Even 9. H Goggs came Eve 9.

JULY 3, SATURDAY A very fine day. Sister Goggs, I, Miss Harply & MA drank Tea at Mr Davys, Mr Hardy drank Tea at Mr Bartells. W^m & H Goggs walkd up to Holt after Tea . . .

JULY 6, TUESDAY A very cold Day, wind very high. Mr Hardy & W^m rid to Bale & Blackney Afternoon, came home Eve 9.

JULY 7, WEDNESDAY A very fine Day. Mr Hardy, I, Rose & M Ravn & MA Dind, drank Tea & Supt at Mr Bartells, Lamb came for us with the Carriage.

JULY 8, THURSDAY A very fine day. Mrs Stoddard, Mrs Raven & 3 Childr^n, M^r & Mrs Bartell & Robt dind, drank Tea & Supt here . . .

JULY 10, SATURDAY A fine day. Mr Hardy walkd up to Holt Afternoon, drank Tea at Mr Davys. I, MA, Rose & M Raven drank Tea at Miss Leakes, all came home Eve past 9. Robt Raven came Even 11 . . .

JULY 13, TUESDAY Showry Day. Maids & Goody Ram Wash'd 4 Weeks Linnen. Mr Hardy at home all Day. Painter at work.

JULY 14, WEDNESDAY A Wet Morn, Showry Day. Mr Hardy at home all Day, Mr Temple drank Tea here. Painter & Gardiner at work.

JULY 15, THURSDAY A fine day. Mr Hardy at home all Day. Painter & Gardiner at work.

JULY 16, FRIDAY A fine Day. Mr Hardy at home all Day. Painter & Gardiner at work. Mr Hardy, I & MA drank Tea at Mr Seales^s, Lamb came for us.

JULY 17, SATURDAY A fine Day. Mr Hardy, I & M Ann walkd up to Holt after Tea, home Eve 9 . . .

Manuscript ledger 4

21 July 1790–7 May 1800

JULY 23, FRIDAY A fine Day. Mr Hardy at home all Day. MA poorly.

[[JULY 24, SATURDAY [*by Mary Ann*] A fine day. MA vary poorly. Mr Hardy and I walk'd up to Holt after Tea . . .

JULY 27, TUESDAY A fine Day. Mr Bartell visited me, I vary bad, MA much as yesterday. Mr Hardy at home all Day . . .

JULY 29, THURSDAY Vary wet Morn, fine Afternoon. The two Miss Leek's drank Tea here Afternoon . . .

AUGUST 1, SUNDAY Showry Morn, fine Afternoon. No service at our church, I attended the School a little while foornoon & Afternoon. Miss Trotter and Mr Whithers [Withers] drank Tea here. Mr Coke of [Pudding] Norton Died vary suddenly this Morn . . .

AUGUST 6, FRIDAY A wet day. Mr Hardy and W^m at home all Day.

AUGUST 7, SATURDAY A close dry Day. I, Mr Hardy & MA walk'd up to Holt, drank Tea at Mr Davys. W^m at home all Day . . .

AUGUST 12, THURSDAY A hot dry day. Mr Ransome & Bolton went away Morn 10, W^m went up to Holt with them. Mr Hardy at home all Day. M^r & Mrs Bartell, Mr Barnham and Mr Harvey, an Attorney from London, came after Tea. Rain'd in the Night.

AUGUST 13, FRIDAY A close hot day. Mr Hardy at home all day. MA went to speak to Mrs Burrell. It Lightened in the evening and rained a good deal.

AUGUST 14, SATURDAY A close Morn, fine Afternoon. Mr Hardy, I, MA & W^m went up to Holt Afternoon. I & MA drank Tea at Miss Bacons, came home even ½ after 8.

AUGUST 15, SUNDAY A Hot Day. Mr Hardy, I & MA went to our Church Afternoon, Mr Burrell preach^d. W^m rode to Edgfield Afternoon, drank Tea at Mr Theodoricks, came home even 9 . . .

AUGUST 18, WEDNESDAY A vary fine Day. M^r & Mrs Oxenborough & M^r & Mrs Smith went to Clay & Blakeny Morn 11 and from thence to Wells. M^r & Mrs Crofts dined & drank Tea here, M^r T Theodorick came to Tea. Mr Crofts 2 Children from Miss Alpes came Even 2, we all walk'd up to Holt After Tea, left the Children with Miss Alpe.

AUGUST 19, THURSDAY A fine day. M^r & Mrs Crofts, M^r H & I, W^m & MA rode to Salthouse to Tea, came home even 9.

AUGUST 20, FRIDAY A vary hot Day. M^r & M^rs C, M^r H & I & MA walk'd up to Holt, M^r & M^rs C drank Tea at Miss Alps, we drank Tea at Mr Bartells, came home even 9 . . .

AUGUST 22, SUNDAY A fine Day. We all went to our Church foornoon, Mr Burrell preach'd. W^m went to Holt Church Afternoon. I & MA went to the Lecture in the Evening . . .]]

SEPTEMBER 5, SUNDAY A very Wet foornoon, dry close Windy Afternoon. All went to our Church foornoon, Mr Burrell preachd. W^m went to Holt Church Afternoon, came back to Tea. I attend'd the School Afternoon. Jo^s & Bett Davy came home from London . . .

SEPTEMBER 7, TUESDAY A fine Morn, Showry Day. Maids & Goody Ram Washd 4 Weeks Linnen. Mr Hardy at home all Day . . .

SEPTEMBER 12, SUNDAY A fine Day. Bett Davy went home after breakfast. All went to our Church Aftern, Mr Burrell preachd, I attend^d the School Afternoon. Robt Raven went away after Tea. M^r & Mrs Davy & Childr^n walkd down after, Mary Davy went home with them. W^m walkd up to Holt after Tea . . .

SEPTEMBER 20, MONDAY A dry Day, Wind high. Mr Hardy at [and] W^m at home all Day. M^r & Miss Bartell drank Tea here. Heard [Prince Henry Frederick] the Duke of Cumberland was Dead . . .

SEPTEMBER 23, THURSDAY A very Wet foornoon, close Aftern. Mr Hardy at home all Day & W^m. Sister Raven & Robt & Phillis came Even 7.

SEPTEMBER 24, FRIDAY A fine Day. Mr Hardy went up to Holt about Alsops business, dind at the [White] Lion, drank Tea at Mr Baker. We walkd up to Holt Afternoon, Sister Raven & I drank Tea at Mr Bakers, MA & Phillis drank Tea at Mr Davys, home Even 9.

SEPTEMBER 25, SATURDAY A fine Day. Walkd up to Holt foornoon with Sister Raven, came home to Dinner. Mr Hardy went up to Holt in Morng to meet the Commisioners on Alsops Bankrupcy, din'd at Mr Moores. Sister Raven went away Even 4. I & MA walkd up to Holt after Tea, home Even 8.

SEPTEMBER 26, SUNDAY A fine Day. All went to our Church Afternoon, Mr Burrell preachd, I attend^d the School foornoon & Afternoon. A General Mourning began for the late Duk«e» of Cumberland. W^m at home all Day . . .

SEPTEMBER 28, TUESDAY A fine Day. Maids & Neb Ram washd 3 Weeks Linnen. Mr Hardy at home all Day, went to Mays in Even to Town meeting, home Even 8 . . .

OCTOBER 2, SATURDAY A fine Day. Mr Hardy walkd up to Holt foornoon to Justice Sitting, dind at Mr Davys, we all drank Tea there except W^m who went up after Tea. Lamb came home from Stalham Even 8 . . .

OCTOBER 7, THURSDAY A Wet Morn, close dry Aftern. Mr Hardy & W^m at home all Day. M^r & M^rs & Miss Baker & Mrs Stangroom drank Tea here. M^r & Mrs Smith of Wells came from Norwich Even 5, staid all Night.

OCTOBER 8, FRIDAY A very fine Day. Mr Hardy at home all Day. Mrs Smith & MA walkd up to Holt foornoon, came back to Dinner, M^r & Mrs Smith went away after Dinner. M^r & Miss Bartel drank Tea here.

OCTOBER 9, SATURDAY A chearly Day but Cold. We all walk'd up to Holt Petty Sessions Afternoon, Mr Hardy drank Tea at Mr Bakers, I & MA drank Tea at Mr Bartells, W^m at Mr Davys, all walkd home Even 9.

OCTOBER 10, SUNDAY A fine Day. All went to our Church Afternoon, Mr Burrell preachd. Jo^s, Bett, Mary & Susan Davy & John Kendle drank Tea here. Maids & Boy went away . . .

OCTOBER 12, TUESDAY A fine Morn, Wind high & very Stormy Afternoon. Mr Hardy rid to Bale Afternoon, calld at Mr Temples of Thornage & drank Tea, home Even 7. The rain prevented the new Maids coming . . .

OCTOBER 15, FRIDAY A fine Day. Mr Hardy & I drank Tea & Supt at Mr Forsters, met M^r & Mrs Temple there. W^m drove me to Bayfield in our L Cart, Lamb came for us with the Carriage . . .

OCTOBER 18, MONDAY A dry Morn, began to rain Morn 10, Continued the greatest part of the Day. Mr Hardy, I & MA set of for Norwich in our own Carriage Morn 8, baited at Caston [Cawston] Woodrow & got to Norwich ½ after twelve, Dind at Mr Wymers. M^r H & MA sett of for London in the heavy Coach Even 9. I left Norwich Even 5, stopt at the Wood row at 8, baited & set of Even 9, got home Even 12.

OCTOBER 19, TUESDAY A very fine Day. W^m at home all Day. M^r & Mrs Bartell drank Tea here, Bett Davy came after Tea to stay with me some Days. {W^m at home all Day.}

OCTOBER 20, WEDNESDAY A Sharp frosty Morn, close Windy Cold Day. I taken with dimness in my Eyes. I & Miss Bett Davy walk'd up to Holt Afternoon, drank Tea at Mr Bartells, met M^r & M^rs & Miss Baker there, W^m came for us in Eveng.

OCTOBER 21, THURSDAY A very fine day. W^m at home all Day. M^rs & Miss Baker drank Tea here, Mr Baker calld for them Even 7, had been at Walsingham. Recd A Letter from Mr Hardy from London . . .

OCTOBER 24, SUNDAY A fine Day. Jo^s & M Davy dind here, I & Bett & M Davy went to our Church Afternoon. John Rolfe came & prevented W^m going, he [William] went Even 5 to Mr Kendles of Thornage to Tea, came home Even 8. Bett & M Davy went away Even p 8. M^r, M^rs & Miss Baker came in Eveng, Miss Baker staid all Night . . .

OCTOBER 28, THURSDAY A fine dry day. Maids & Goody Ram Washd a few Linnen. Lamb went with R Stafe as far as N Walsham in Little Cart Morn 10, came back Even 9. Miss Baker & W^m drank Tea at Mr Bakers.

OCTOBER 29, FRIDAY A fine day. I & Miss Baker walkd up to Holt Afternoon, drank Tea at Mr Davys, came home Even 9. W^m went to the Assembly at Holt Even 8, came home Morn 2 . . .

NOVEMBER 1, MONDAY A very Wet Day. W^m at home all Day, Miss Baker & I drank Tea at Mr Burrells. A very Wet Stormy Night . . .

NOVEMBER 3, WEDNESDAY A fine Day. Mr Hardy & W^m at home all Day. M^rs & Bett Davy, Miss Grist, Miss Sheppard & Miss Bartell drank Tea here. A Wett Night.

NOVEMBER 4, THURSDAY A Chearly Day. Mr Hardy at home all Day. W^m sett of for Fakenham Morn 10, came home Even 9.

NOVEMBER 5, FRIDAY A very fine Day. Mr Hardy walkd up to Holt foornoon, came home to Dinner. I went to our Church foornoon, Mr Burrell preachd. Mr Hardy, I & MA walkd up to Holt Afternoon, drank Tea at Mr Moores, Mr Bakers & Mr Temples Familys met us there. Lamb met us coming home with the Carriage.

NOVEMBER 6, SATURDAY A Close dry Day. Wm sett off for Whisensett Even 4. Mr Hardy, I & MA walkd up to Holt Afternoon, drank Tea at Mr Davys, walkd home Even 9.

NOVEMBER 7, SUNDAY A fine Day. All went to our Church Afternoon. M^r & M^rs & Miss Baker at our Church, did not stay at Tea. Mr Cooper at the Lawn was Married to Miss Dersley of Norwich.

NOVEMBER 8, MONDAY A fine Day. Maids & Goody Ram began Washing 6 Weeks Linnen. Mr Hardy at home all Day. W^m came home by Gresenall Even 6, Mr Smith of Wells calld here Even 6 going to Holt.

NOVEMBER 9, TUESDAY A Close dry Day. Maids & Goody Ram Washd. Mr Hardy at home all Day.

NOVEMBER 10, WEDNESDAY A Close Cold dry Day. W^m walkd up to Holt Mill Afternoon, came home to Tea. Mr Hardy, I & MA walkd up to Holt Afternoon, drank Tea at Mr Bakers, walkd home Even 9.

NOVEMBER 11, THURSDAY A Close dry Day. We Irond. W^m walkd to Holt Mill Afternoon, Mr Hardy at home all Day . . .

NOVEMBER 14, SUNDAY A very chearly Day. All went to our Church except MA who had a bad Cold. Mr Bolton calld Aftern. Miss Leake & M Davy drank Tea here . . .

NOVEMBER 17, WEDNESDAY A Close cold Day. Mr Hardy at home all Day & went to Overtons Club in Even, came home Eve p 11.

NOVEMBER 18, THURSDAY A fine Day. Mr Hardy & W^m at home all day . . .

NOVEMBER 24, WEDNESDAY A fine Day. Mr Hardy at home all Day. Bricklayers at work at the Copper. M^r & M^rs & Miss Baker, Mrs Man of Clay, M^r & Mrs Bartell drank Tea here . . .

NOVEMBER 29, MONDAY A Close Cold Day. Mr Hardy, I & MA walkd up to Holt Aftern, drank Tea at Mr Bakers, met Mrs Jewell & Mrs Thompson there, Lamb came for us Even past 9 with the Carriage. A little Snow fell in the Night . . .

DECEMBER 7, TUESDAY A very Wet Day. Mr Hardy & W^m at home all Day.

DECEMBER 8, WEDNESDAY A Close Morn, dry windy Aftern. Mr Hardy walkd up to Holt Afternoon, paid the Excise, went to Overtons Club & came home Even past 11.

DECEMBER 9, THURSDAY A close foggy Morn, fine Day. Mr Hardy & W^m at home all Day, Carpenters at Work. We Irond.

DECEMBER 10, FRIDAY A fine Day. Carpenters at work. Mr Hardy, I & MA rid up to Holt Afternoon in L Cart, drank Tea at Mr Bartells, Lamb came for us Even 9 with the Carriage.

DECEMBER 11, SATURDAY A Wet Morn, fine Afternoon. Mr Hardy went to Holt Mark^t Afternoon, we sent the L Cart for him Even 8.

DECEMBER 12, SUNDAY A fine Day. W^m set of for Whisensett Morn 9. Service at our Church foornoon, we did not go, Lamb drove us to Holt Church Afternoon, came home to Tea.

DECEMBER 13, MONDAY A very Wet Day, Wind very high. Mr Hardy at home all Day. W^m came home from Whisenset Even 4 . . .

DECEMBER 15, WEDNESDAY A very dry Day, Wind very high. Mr Hardy & W^m at home all Day. M^r & Mrs Croffts of Fakenham calld here having been to Holt for the Children. Mr Hardy went to Overtons Club Even 5, came home Even 11 . . .

DECEMBER 17, FRIDAY A fine Day, very wet Night. Mr Hardy & W^m at home all Day. M^r & Mrs Bartell & Miss Stannard drank Tea & Supt here. Miss Stann^d staid all Night, M^r & M^rs B went home in our L Cart.

DECEMBER 18, SATURDAY A very Wet cold Day, Wind high. Mr Hardy at home all Day, W^m walk'd up to Holt Markt Afternoon. I, MA & Miss Stannard went up in our Carr«i»age Even 4, drank Tea at Mr Bartells, came home Even 8.

DECEMBER 19, SUNDAY A Sharp frost. We all walkd to Holt Church Afternoon. It raind in Eveng . . .

DECEMBER 26, SUNDAY A frost, very fine Day. Mr Hardy, I & MA went to Holt Church Afternoon in our Carriage, W^m & Sheppard walkd, came home to Tea.

DECEMBER 27, MONDAY Sharp frosty Morn, thaw Aftern, raind in Eveng. Mr Hardy & W^m at home all Day. I & MA walk'd up to Holt afternoon, came home to Tea . . .

DECEMBER 29, WEDNESDAY A Sharp rime frost. Mr Hardy, I & MA walkd up to Holt in Even. M^r H went to Overtons Club, came home past 12, I & MA came home Even 9. W^m came home from Whisensett Even 9.

DECEMBER 30, THURSDAY Thawd, A very wet Afternoon & Eveng. Mr Hardy & W^m at home all Day. M^r & Mrs Foster, M^r & Mrs Temple, M^r & Mrs Bartell, Charlot [Charlotte Bartell] & Miss Stannard, M^r & M^rs & Miss Baker drank Tea & Supt here, went home Morn 1. Miss Stann^d, Miss Baker & Miss Bartell Slept here.

DECEMBER 31, FRIDAY A fine Day, a frosty Air. Mr Hardy & W^m at home all Day. The young Ladies went away before Dinner . . .

1791

JANUARY 2, SUNDAY A fine Day. Mr Hardy, I & MA & Miss Stannard rid to Holt Church Afternoon, W^m walkd.

JANUARY 3, MONDAY A Sharp frost. I, MA & Miss Stannard rid up to Mr Bakers in our Carriage, drank Tea & Supt there. Mr Hardy & W^m came to Sup^r [supper], came home Even past 12. Maids & Ann Lamb Wash^d.

JANUARY 4, TUESDAY A Sharp rime frosty Morn, thawd & Snowd Afternoon, raind in Eveng. Mr Temple came Even 2, drank Tea & Supt here . . .

JANUARY 6, THURSDAY A fine day for the time of year. Mr Hardy & W^m at home all Day.

JANUARY 7, FRIDAY A Wet Morn, tolerable Afternoon. Mr Hardy & W^m at home all Day. MA went up to Holt in L Cart foornoon for Miss Stannard, came home to Dinner.

JANUARY 8, SATURDAY A Windy Day. Mr Hardy, I & Miss Stannard & MA walkd up to Holt Mark^t Afternoon, drank Tea at Mr Bartells, walkd home Even 8. W^m went to the Play at the 3^d Acct.

JANUARY 9, SUNDAY A dry Morn, began to rain abt Noon, cleard up at Even 3. Mr Hardy, I, MA & Miss Stannard went to Holt Church in our Carrig^e, W^m did not go to Church . . .

JANUARY 11, TUESDAY A fine Day. Jo^s & Bett Davy went home before breakfast. Mr Hardy & W^m at home all Day. Mrs Jewell, Miss Chichely, M^r & Mrs Bartell, M^r & M^rs & Miss Baker drank Tea here . . .

JANUARY 16, SUNDAY A dresly foornoon, dry Afternoon. I & W^m went to our Church foorn, Mr Burrell preachd. Mr Hardy & W^m walkd to Holt Church Afternoon, W^m drank Tea at Mr Davys, Mr Hardy came home to Tea.

JANUARY 17, MONDAY A fine Day. Mr Hardy & W^m at home all Day . . .

JANUARY 19, WEDNESDAY A Wet Day. Mr Hardy at home all Day. W^m & his 2 Cousins went «to» the Play in the Even, it was Pattersons benifit, came home near 12 oClock . . .

JANUARY 22, SATURDAY Stormy Day. I & Mr Hardy walkd up to Holt Afternoon, drank Tea at Mr Bartells, came home Even 8. W^m drank Tea at Mr Davys. Bought Sister Goggs a Tea Urn . . .

The visit to Whissonsett
23–30 January 1791

JANUARY 24, MONDAY A fine Day, Windy. Sister R Rav^n came & drank Tea & Supt with us at Mr Goggs's.

JANUARY 25, TUESDAY A fine Day. Rose Raven came & drank Tea & Supt with us at Mr Gogg's . . .

JANUARY 27, THURSDAY A Wet foornoon, dry Afternoon. Dind at Sister Ravens & went back to Mr Goggs' Afternoon.

JANUARY 28, FRIDAY A small frost, very chearly Day. Sister Goggs & I walkd Afternoon to speak to Mrs Dix. Sister Raven came to Mr Goggs^s in Even, Supt there . . .

[LETHERINGSETT]

JANUARY 31, MONDAY A fine chearly Day. M^r and Mrs Baker, M^r & Mrs Bartell drank Tea here.

FEBRUARY 1, TUESDAY A fine dry Morn, Windy & Stormy Afternoon. MA & Miss Custance went to Mr Bakers foornoon to stay a Day or two. Mr Hardy at home all Day. Maids & Ann Lamb Washd 4 Weeks Linnen. Wind very high in the Night . . .

FEBRUARY 5, SATURDAY A Cold Day, Stormes of Snow & Sleet. Mr Hardy, I & MA & W^m walkd up to Holt Afternoon, I & MA drank Tea at Mr Davys, M^r H & W^m drank Tea at Mr Bartells, we all went to the Play at the 3^d Acct, Supt at Mr Davys & Lamb came for us with the Carrage.

FEBRUARY 6, SUNDAY A Mild close Day. Mr Hardy walkd to Mr Temples of Thornage Aftern to look at some thorns, drank Tea there, came home Even 8. We all went to our Church Afternoon, Mr Burrell preach^d.

FEBRUARY 7, MONDAY A Close Morn, Wet Afternoon. Mr Hardy & M^r T Temple of Thornage went to Wells in our L [little] Cart, Slept at Mrs Richardsons. W^m at home all Day.

FEBRUARY 8, TUESDAY A Close Day. W^m at home all Day. Mr Hardy & Mr Temple came home from Wells Even 8 . . .

FEBRUARY 13, SUNDAY A Mild Showry Day. I, W^m & MA went to our Church foorn, Mr Burrell preachd. Mr Hardy & W^m went to Holt Church Afternoon, came home to Tea. Young Theorderic came to Tea . . .

FEBRUARY 15, TUESDAY A Showry Day, wind blustering. Mr Hardy at home all Day. Mrs Patterson here all Day, Mr Patterson at Supper. W^m at Salthouse all Day, came home by Kelling Even 9.

FEBRUARY 16, WEDNESDAY A fine dry Day. Mrs Patterson here all Day, Mr Patterson came to Tea & Supper. Mr Hardy at home all Day, W^m at Salthouse all Day. Mr Ellis of Clay drank Tea & Supt here.

FEBRUARY 17, THURSDAY A fine Day, raind in Eveng. Mrs Patterson here, went home Even 4. Mr Hardy at home all Day, W^m at Salthouse all Day . . .

FEBRUARY 19, SATURDAY A Cold windy Day. Henry Goggs came to Diner, walkd up to Mark^t with us. I & MA drank Tea at Miss Leakes, Mr Hardy & Mr Goggs drank Tea at Mr Bartells. W^m went to Salthouse Afternoon, came home by Holt Even 7, we all walkd home Even 8 . . .

FEBRUARY 21, MONDAY A drisly Morn, fine Afternoon. Mr Hardy at home all Day, M^r & Mrs Bartell drank Tea & Supt here . . .

FEBRUARY 23, WEDNESDAY A Wet Windy Day. Mr Hardy at home all Day . . .

FEBRUARY 26, SATURDAY Wind very high, Storms of rain foorn. Mr Hardy & W^m went to Mark^t Afternoon, came home Even pst 8. The Theordericks went away Eveng 4.

FEBRUARY 27, SUNDAY A Stormy Day, Wind high. I & MA went to our Church foornoon, Mr Burrell preach^d. Mr Hardy & W^m went to Holt Church Afternoon, drank Tea at Mr Bartells, home Even past 6.

FEBRUARY 28, MONDAY A tolerable Day. Mr Hardy at home all Day & W^m. Expectd Mrs Baker to Tea, did not come.

MARCH 1, TUESDAY A Cold Stormy Day. Maids & Ann Lamb washd. Mr Hardy at home all Day. W^m went to Salthouse Afternoon & came home by Kelling, drank Tea at Mr Purdys, home E8 . . .

MARCH 3, THURSDAY A fine Dry Day. Mr Hardy & W^m at home all Day . . .

MARCH 6, SUNDAY A very fine Day. I & MA went to our Church Afternoon, Mr Hardy & W^m went to H [Holt] Church Aftern. Miss Baker & Miss Custance came after Tea to stay a week.

MARCH 7, MONDAY A dry Windy Day. M^r H, I & MA & the 2 young Ladies walkd up to Holt Afternoon, drank Tea at Mr Bartells, Lamb came for us with the Carriage. W^m at home all Day.

MARCH 8, TUESDAY A close dry Day, wind Cold. M^r H, I, MA & Miss Custance & Miss Baker drank Tea & Supt at Mr Temples of Thornage, home Even 10. W^m rid to Clay & Salthouse afternoon, came home Even 9.

MARCH 9, WEDNESDAY A very fine Day. I, MA, Miss C & Miss B went to our Church foornoon. M^r & Mrs Forster & Miss Wingfield drank Tea here. Mr Hardy & W^m at home all Day. 2 Gardeners at Work.

MARCH 10, THURSDAY A very fine Day. Miss Baker went home after breakfst to Iron. Mr Hardy & W^m at home all Day, Miss Baker came agn Even 9. 2 Gardeners at Work . . .

MARCH 12, SATURDAY A very fine Day. We all walkd to Holt Afternoon, drank Tea at Mr Bakers.

MARCH 13, SUNDAY A very fine day. I, W^m, MA, Miss C & Miss B went to our Church foornoon, Mr Burrell preachd. The 2 young Ladies went away Afternoon, MA with them to stay a Week at Mr Bakers. M^r H & W^m went to Holt Church Afternoon, came home to Tea. Mr Tooby drank Tea here . . .

MARCH 16, WEDNESDAY A very fine Day. Mr Hardy went to Sheringham Morn past 7 to see to the Labourers at the Clif, came home Even 9. W^m at home all Day.

MARCH 17, THURSDAY A very fine Day. Mr Hardy & W^m set of for Sheringham Morn past 8 in L Cart. W^m came home Even past 8, lcft M^r H there all Night.

MARCH 18, FRIDAY A very fine Day. Miss Custance & MA came down from Mr Bakers, Holt, to speak to me, MA have a very bad Cough, went back to Dinner. Sent the boy to Sheringham Afternoon for Mr Hardy . . .

MARCH 20, SUNDAY A Wet foornoon, dry Aftern & raind again in Eveng. MA very bad with a Cold. I went to our Church Aftern, Mr Burrell preachd. Mr Hardy & W^m went to Holt Church Aftern, W^m came home to Tea, M^r H drank Tea at Mr Bartells . . .

MARCH 24, THURSDAY A fine Day. Mr Hardy & W^m at home all Day. Robt Raven went away Even past 6. Mealy Cow taken very Ill. Mrs Davy, Jo^s & Ann came home from London.

MARCH 25, FRIDAY A fine Day. Mr Hardy & W^m at home all Day. Mealy Cow very Ill.

MARCH 26, SATURDAY A Wet Day. Mr Smith Dind here. Mr Hardy walkd to Holt Mark^t Aftern, drank Tea at Mr Davys. W^m went up after Tea, came home Even 9.

MARCH 27, SUNDAY A Showry Day. I, W^m & MA went to our Church foornoon, Mr Burrell preachd. Mr Hardy & W^m went to Holt Church Afternoon, W^m drank Tea at Mr Davys.

MARCH 28, MONDAY A Close Mild Day, raind towards Eveng. Maids & Ann Lamb Washd 4 Weeks Linnen. Mr Hardy & W^m at home all Day . . .

MARCH 30, WEDNESDAY A very fine Day. W^m at home all Day. We Irond. M^r H walkd up to Holt Afternoon, drank Tea at Mr Bartells, went to Overtons Club, came home past 12 . . .

APRIL 2, SATURDAY A very fine Day. The Davys stayd till Afternoon, we all walkd up to Holt Afternoon. I, MA, W^m, Robt & Wm Raven drank Tea at Mr Bakers, Mr Hardy drank Tea at Mr Davys, all walkd home Even past 9.

APRIL 3, SUNDAY A beautiful fine Day. Robt Raven & Miss Custance went away Even 3. M^r & M^rs & Miss Baker came to our Church Afternoon & drank Tea here. Mr Hardy went to Holt Church Afternoon, came home to Tea.

APRIL 4, MONDAY A dry Day, wind blustering & Cold. Mr Hardy & W^m at home all Day. Mr Purdy of Kelling, Mr Temple of Thornage, Mr Cook & Mr Sturly of Thornage Dind & drank Tea here, drew of [off] a Pipe of Wine . . .

APRIL 9, SATURDAY A very Mild bright Day. Mr Hardy, I, W^m & MA walkd up to Holt Afternoon. I & MA drank Tea at Mr Bartells & came home Even 7, M^r H & W^m came home Even 9. MA very poorly . . .

APRIL 12, TUESDAY A fine Day. W^m at home all Day. Mr Hardy at home all Day. 2 Gardiners at Work.

APRIL 13, WEDNESDAY A very fine Day. W^m walkd to Corpusty foornoon, came home Even 8. M^rs & Miss Baker, M^r & Mrs Bartell drank Tea here. 2 Gardiners at work. Francis Wymer calld here foornoon. M^r H taken with the Gout in knee.

APRIL 14, THURSDAY A fine Day. W^m walkd to Corpusty foornoon, came home Even 8. Mr Hardy poorly with the Gout in his right knee, M Ann very poorly with a Cough . . .

APRIL 17, SUNDAY A fine Day. Mr Hardy better, MA reather better. I, MA & W^m & [[[by Mary Ann] Wm Raven went to our Church Afternoon, W^m walk'd up to Holt after Tea. Mr Baker walk'd down to speak to M^r H.

APRIL 18, MONDAY A fine Day. Mr Hardy & W^m at home]] all Day . . .

APRIL 20, WEDNESDAY A Windy Showry Day. W^m walkd to Corpusty foornoon to see the Workmen, I & MA went to our Church foornoon. Mr Hardy, I & MA rid up to fir Closes in L Cart after Noon.

APRIL 21, THURSDAY A fine Day. Mr Hardy & W^m at home all Day.

APRIL 22, *Good Friday* A Wet Day. Mr Hardy at [and] W^m at home all Day. I & MA went to our Church Afternoon, Mr Burrell preach'd . . .

APRIL 24, SUNDAY A Wet Morng, Showry Afternoon. I & W^m at our Church foornoon, I staid at the Communion. Mr Hardy & W^m went to Holt Church Afternoon. Henry Goggs came Even past 6. We went to Church to hear a Lecture . . .

APRIL 26, TUESDAY A fine Day but wind Cold. H Goggs went away Morn 6. Mr Hardy & W^m went to Corpusty in L Cart Morn 10, came home Eve 7 by Holt & took I & MA home, we «had» walkd up to Holt & drank Tea at Mr Davy.

APRIL 27, WEDNESDAY A Wet Cold Day. Mr Hardy & W^m at home all Day . . .

MAY 1, SUNDAY A very Close Cold Day. I & MA & L W^m [Little William—the brewing pupil] went to our Church Afternoon, Mr Burrell preach'd. Mr Hardy & W^m went to Holt Church Afternoon, M^r H came home to Tea, W^m drank Tea {Tea} at Mr Davys. Bett & M Davy came to speak to MA, She was poorly. Wind North.

MAY 2, MONDAY A Cold Wet Day. Mr Hardy walkd up to Holt Afternoon, drank Tea at Mr Davys, came home Even past 9. W^m at home all Day. Wind North . . .

MAY 4, WEDNESDAY A Cold chearly Day, W [wind] north. Mr Hardy, I & MA rid up to Holt in L Cart, drank Tea at Mr Bakers. Raind in Eve.

MAY 5, THURSDAY A Chearly Day, wind Cold at North. Mr Hardy & W^m at home all Day. Jo^s, Ann & Bett Davy drank Tea here Afternoon . . .

MAY 7, SATURDAY A fine Day. Mr Hardy walkd up to Holt foornoon, came home to Dinner, he & MA rid up in L Cart Afternoon, I & W^m walkd. Ann Davy came home with us . . .

MAY 9, MONDAY A very fine Day. Wind N West till Even 6 then shifted to S West. W^m did not come home . . .

MAY 13, FRIDAY A fine Day. Sisters, I, MA & W Raven rid up to Holt foorn, came home to Dinner. Mrs Davy drank Tea here, Mr Davy came after Tea.

MAY 14, SATURDAY A very fine Day. W^m & Robt Raven went to Corpusty foornoon in our L Cart, came home to Dinner, Sisters went away Even 3. I & W^m & MA walkd up to Holt Afternoon, drank Tea at Mr Davys, rid home in L Cart . . .

MAY 16, MONDAY A fine Day. W^m went to Blakney foornoon & to Corpusty & Norwich Afternoon . . .

MAY 19, THURSDAY A Cold blustering Day with small Showers foornoon. W^m at home all Day . . .

MAY 21, SATURDAY A Cold windy Day. I, MA & Miss Baker walkd up to Holt Afternoon, drank Tea at Mr Davy^s, Ann Davy walkd home with us, W^m did not go. H Raven came Even 2.

MAY 22, SUNDAY A fine Day. I, Miss Baker, MA & W^m & H Raven went to our Church foornoon, Mr Burrell preach^d. W^m went to Holt Church Aftern, drank Tea at Mr Davys . . .

MAY 24, TUESDAY A very fine Day. W^m at home all Day, open'd the Ditch in Shrubbery. I & MA walk'd up to Holt Aftern, drank Tea at Mr Davys. Miss Baker went home.

MAY 25, WEDNESDAY A very fine Day. W^m went up to Holt in Morng, breakfstd at Mr Davy^s. Jo^s Davy came home with him, Dind here, they rid in L Cart to Corpusty Afternoon. Miss Davy sett of for London in Mrs Sheppards post Chaise . . .

MAY 28, SATURDAY A Dry Cold Day, wind high. I, MA & W^m walk'd up to Holt Afternoon, drank Tea at Mr Davy^s, rid home in L Cart.

MAY 29, SUNDAY A very Cold windy Day. All went to our Church Afternoon except Sheppard, Mr Burrell preach'd.

MAY 30, MONDAY A Close cold Day. W^m at home all Day.

MAY 31, TUESDAY A Warm Day, weather very dry. W^m went to Corpusty Afternoon in L Cart, came home by Thornage, brought Jo^s Davy home with him Even 8, he Slept here . . .

JUNE 3, FRIDAY A Hot dry Day. Jo^s Davy went home Even 8, W^m walkd with him & Supt there, came home Even p 10 . . .

JUNE 5, SUNDAY A hot dry Day. I, W^m & MA went to our Church foornoon, Mr Burrell preach'd. Mr Hardy at home all Day. J Kendle drank Tea here. A Lecture in the Even . . .

JUNE 12, *Whit Sunday* Some rain in Morn, very Cold Day. I went to our Church Aftern, Mr Burrell preachd. Mr Hardy went to Holt Church Afternoon, came home to Tea . . .

JUNE 17, FRIDAY A Close Cold Day. Mr Hardy at home all Day. W^m walkd up to Holt Aftern, drank Tea at Mr Davys.

JUNE 18, SATURDAY A Close Morn, fine Afternoon. Mr Hardy walkd up to Holt Morn 9 to speak to Mr Breerton, Dind at Mr Bakers, drank Tea at Mr Davys, went to the Black Boys with Mr Keeler, Everitt & others, came home Even pst 12. I, W^m & Nathl walkd up to Holt after Tea, came home Even 9.

JUNE 19, SUNDAY A very Cold Day. W^m went to Thornage Church Afternoon, drank Tea at Mr Kendles. Mr Hardy & N Raven went to Holt Church Afternoon, came home to Tea. I went to our Church Even past 6, Mr Burrell preach'd.

JUNE 20, MONDAY A cold Day. Mr Hardy & W^m at home all Day. Mr Smith, Attorny of Wells, Dind here . . .

JUNE 23, THURSDAY A very fine Day. The Bishop^s Visitation at Fakenham. Mr Hardy & W^m at home all Day.

JUNE 24, FRIDAY A very fine Day. Mr Hardy & W^m at home all Day, Mr Bartell Dind here.

JUNE 25, SATURDAY A very warm Day. Mr Hardy & I walkd up to Holt Mark^t Even 4, came home Even 9. Mr Bartell had 6 people came [come] from London.

JUNE 26, SUNDAY A Hot Day. I & N Rav^n went to our Church Afternoon, Mr Burrell preach'd. Mr Hardy & W^m went to Holt Church Aftern, drank Tea at Mr Bartells. M^r & Mrs Bartell & their London Friends, 5 Gentlemen & A Lady, came home with them after Tea to take a walk in our Garden.

JUNE 27, MONDAY A very hot dry Day. Mr Hardy & W^m at home all Day. 2 Gardiners at Work.

JUNE 28, TUESDAY A hot dry Day. Mr Hardy & I rid to Mr Temples Aftern, met Mr Bakers family, Mrs Davy & some others. 2 Gardiners at work.

JUNE 29, WEDNESDAY Excisive hot Day. Mr Hardy & W^m at home all Day. M^r & Mrs Temple drank Tea here. Tempest came up Even past 8, Continued till Eve 12, some rain.

JUNE 30, THURSDAY A very hot Day. Mr Temple Dind here, Mr Hardy & he went to look at some Hay at Mr Kendles of Thornage, did not agree, drank Tea at Mr Temples & came home Even 8. W^m went to Corpusty Afternoon, came home Even 8.

JULY 1, FRIDAY A Cool Day. Mr Hardy & W^m at home all Day, M^r H bought a piece of Hay of R Mays. Mrs Davy walkd down after Tea . . .

JULY 3, SUNDAY A very fine Day. M^r & Mrs Davy & 3 of their Young people, M^{rs} & Miss Baker came to our Church Afternoon & drank Tea here. Mr Allison of Dalling preachd here . . .

JULY 6, WEDNESDAY A fine Day. Mr Hardy & W^m at home all Day making Hay. M^r & Mrs Bartell & A Lady from Norwich with them drank Tea here.

JULY 7, THURSDAY A fine Day till Even 5 then a Show^r of rain. Our people Carring & Mak^n Hay. Mr Hardy & I drank Tea at Mr Bartells, rid up in L Cart . . .

JULY 9, SATURDAY A fine Day. Our people gittn [getting] up Hay all Day, none of us went to Holt.

JULY 10, SUNDAY A Showry Day. I & Nathl Raven went to our Church Afternoon, Mr Burrell preachd. Mr Hardy & W^m went to Holt Church Afternoon. M^r H came home to Tea, W^m drank Tea at Mr Davys. A Wet Night . . .

JULY 13, WEDNESDAY A fine dry Day. Mr Hardy & W^m at home all Day.

JULY 14, THURSDAY A very fine dry Day. Mr Hardy at home all Day. W^m & N Raven walkd to Blakney & Clay foornoon, came back to Dinner . . .

JULY 16, SATURDAY A fine day. Mr Hardy, I, MA & R Rav^n walkd up to Holt Afternoon, drank Tea at Mr Davys.

JULY 17, SUNDAY A Hot Day. I, MA & Rose Rav^n went to our Church foornoon, Mr Burrell preachd. W^m went to Holt Church Afternoon, came home to Tea . . .

JULY 19, TUESDAY A hot Day. W^m, MA & R Rav^n sett of for Sheringham in L Cart Morn 9, Mr Hardy & I sett of at Noon, Dind & drank Tea there. M^r & Mrs Crofts of Fakenham, M^r & M^{rs} & Miss Theorderic, M^r & Mrs Moore, 2 Miss Jennis's & Mr Cremer met us there, we came home Eve 10 . . .

JULY 21, THURSDAY A fine Day. Mr Hardy & W^m at home all Day. Mr Kendle of Thornage, Mrs Lewis & Bett Davy drank Tea here, Mr Davy calld in Eveng . . .

JULY 23, SATURDAY A Wet Morn, dry Afternoon. Mr Hardy went to Holt Mark^t, drank Tea at Mr Davys. I, MA & R Raven walkd to Holt Afternoon, drank Tea at Mr Bakers, W^m walk'd up after Tea.

JULY 24, SUNDAY A Showry Day. All went to our Church except Mr Hardy Afternoon, Mr Burrell preach'd, M^r & Mrs Sales at our Church & drank Tea here. Mrs Davy went to Wells.

JULY 25, MONDAY A Showry Day. Mr Hardy & W^m at home all Day . . .

JULY 28, THURSDAY A fine Day. Mr Hardy, I, MA & R Raven walkd up to Holt Afternoon, drank Tea at Mr Davy^s. W^m at home all Day . . .

The visit to Whissonsett
2–4 August 1791

AUGUST 2, TUESDAY A fine Day. Mr Hardy & I set of for Whisonset in L Cart Morn past 9, got to Mr Goggs Even 1, Dind, drank Tea & Supt there.

AUGUST 3, WEDNESDAY A fine Day. Mr Hardy, I, Sister Goggs & Henry drank Tea at Sister Ravens at the Hall.

AUGUST 4, THURSDAY A very fine Day. We set of for Fakenham Even 3, H Goggs & Mrs Skinner went with us. We drank Tea at Mr Custances, sett of Even past 6 & got home Even 9. Miss Mendham came this Afternoon, Slept here, Mr Paul Myles came Yesterday.

[LETHERINGSETT]

AUGUST 5, FRIDAY A very Hot Day. Mr Hardy & W^m at home all Day, Paul Myles went away Even 2. M^r & M^{rs} & Edm^d Bartell drank Tea here, Miss Mendham went away Even 7.

AUGUST 6, SATURDAY A very hot Day. Mr Hardy & I walkd up to Holt Mark^t, W^m & MA rid up in L Cart with the New Mare, we all drank Tea at Mr Davys.

AUGUST 7, SUNDAY A Hot Day. Mr Moore of Gressenhall & his Niece Breakfstd here, went away Morn 11. I & MA went to our Church Afternoon, Mr Burrell preachd. Mr Hardy & W^m went to Holt Church Afternoon, came home to Tea.

AUGUST 8, MONDAY A fine Day. Mr Hardy went to Cromer Morn 10, came home [   ]. Mr Smith, Attorny from Wells, Dind here. M^r & Mrs Tooby & 3 Child^{rn} dran«k» Tea here.

AUGUST 9, TUESDAY A beautiful Day. Mr Hardy drank Tea & Supt at Mr Temples of Thornage. Maids & Ann Lamb Washd 4 Weeks Linnen. W^m at home all Day. Mr Davy & 2 Daug^{trs} & Son came down in Eveng.

AUGUST 10, WEDNESDAY A very fine Day. Mr Hardy & W^m at home all Day.

AUGUST 11, THURSDAY A fine day. Mr Hardy & W^m at home all Day . . .

AUGUST 13, SATURDAY A Close Sultry Day. Mt Chaplin of Blakney & Mr Mann of Clay here foornoon. Mr Hardy walkd up to Holt Mark^t Aftern, drank Tea at Mr Bartells, came home Even 9. I, W^m & MA rid up in L C after Tea.

AUGUST 14, SUNDAY A hot dry Day. I & MA at our Church foornoon. Mr Hardy & W^m went to Thornage Church Afternoon, drank Tea at Mr Kendles. M^r & M^{rs} & Miss Bartell & Miss Leak drank Tea here. Showr in the Night with Thunder . . .

AUGUST 21, SUNDAY A very pleasant Day. No service at our Church. I somthing better. Mr & Mrs Davy & their 4 Daughtrs drank Tea here, Mr Bartell visited me . . .

AUGUST 27, SATURDAY A Wet Morn, fine Afternoon. Mr Hardy at home all Day, Sheppard went out. W^m & MA came home Even 9.

AUGUST 28, SUNDAY A Close cool Day. I, MA & W^m went to our Church foorn, Mr Burrell preachd, read a Lecture in the Eveng. Mr Hardy & Wm went to Holt Church Afternoon, W^m drank Tea at Mr Bartells, Edm^d Bartell Supt here. Raind in Eveng . . .

AUGUST 30, TUESDAY A Close cold Day. Our Men finishd Shearing Wheat in fir Close. W^m set of for Coltishall Even 1. Mr Hardy, I & MA walk'd up to Holt After-noon, drank Tea with Edm'd Bartell, walk'd home Even 8 . . .

SEPTEMBER 3, SATURDAY Wet Morn, dry close Aftern. Mr Hardy walkd up to Holt Afternoon. I, W^m & MA rid up in L Cart, drank Tea at Mr Bartells. Men mowing Barly.

SEPTEMBER 4, SUNDAY Showry day. We all went to Holt Church Afternoon, W^m & MA drank Tea at Mr Bakers.

SEPTEMBER 5, MONDAY A dry Day. Maids & Ann Lamb Washd 4 weeks Linnen. Mr Hardy rid to Clay After-noon to meet Mr Smith of Wells . . .

SEPTEMBER 7, WEDNESDAY A fine dry Morn, A very heavy Showr Afternoon. Our Men Carring Bary [carry-ing barley] till the rain came & prevented them. Mr Hardy & W^m at home all Day . . .

SEPTEMBER 9, FRIDAY A very fine Day. Mr Hardy went up to Holt foornoon to look at the workmen, came home to Dinner, W^m at home all Day. Men finishd Car^g all the Sheafe Corn. M^r & M^rs & Miss Baker & Mrs Moore drank Tea here, Mr Bartell call«ed» to se me . . .

SEPTEMBER 11, SUNDAY A very fine Day. I & MA at our Church foornoon, Mr Burrell preach^d & read A Lec-ture in Eveng. Mr Hardy went to Holt Church After-noon, drank Tea at Mr Bartells, they walkd home with him. W^m came home Even 9.

SEPTEMBER 12, MONDAY A fine Day. Mr Hardy at home all Day. W^m up to Holt foornoon, home to Dinner, he & MA rid to Edgefield Afternoon, drank Tea at Mr Theordericks . . .

SEPTEMBER 14, WEDNESDAY A fine day. Mr Hardy walk^d up to Holt foornoon, came home to Dinner. I, W^m & MA rid up to Holt Afternoon in L Cart, drank Tea at Mr Davys . . .

SEPTEMBER 16, FRIDAY A very fine day. Mr Hardy at Walsingham Justice sitting, came home Even 9. Bett Davy & Charlot Bartell drank Tea here, L Youngman here Afternoon. Wm Dind at Mr Davys.

SEPTEMBER 17, SATURDAY A Close cold day. Mr Hardy at Justice sitting at Holt, Dind there, came home Even 9. W^m up to Holt Afternoon, drank Tea at Mr Davys. Mr Bartell call^d foornoon.

SEPTEMBER 18, SUNDAY A Cold Stormy day. I & W^m & MA went to our Church Aftern, Mr Burrell preachd. Mr Hardy went to Holt Church Afternoon, came home to Tea. M^r T Temple & J Kendle drank Tea here . . .

SEPTEMBER 22, THURSDAY A Close cold Day. Mr Hardy up to Holt Afternoon, home to Tea. M^r & M^rs & Miss Baker drank Tea here. Lidia [Youngman] here After-noon, finishd W^ms Shirts.

SEPTEMBER 23, FRIDAY A very fine day. Mr Hardy at home all Day. W^m & MA went to Mr Kendles of Thorn-age to Tea. I walkd to M^r T Temples after Tea, they came home that way & I rid home . . .

SEPTEMBER 25, SUNDAY A very fine Day. I & MA at our Church foornoon, Mr Burrell preachd. Mr Hardy & W^m went to Holt Church Afternoon, came home to Tea. Jo^s Davy drank Tea here . . .

SEPTEMBER 28, WEDNESDAY A fine Day. Mr Hardy went to Holt foornoon, came home to Dinner. Young M^r [? Christopher] Stannard came Afternoon, went back to Mr Bartells to Tea . . .

OCTOBER 1, SATURDAY A very fine Day. Mr Hardy, I & Mr Snape walkd up to Holt Petty Sessions Afternoon, drank Tea at Mr Bakers, I hired a Maid Servt.

OCTOBER 2, SUNDAY A very fine Day. Young Mr Stan-nard Dind here. I, MA & he went to our Church After-noon, Mr Burrell preach^d. Mr Hardy & Mr Snape went to Holt Church Afternoon. M^r, Miss & Robt Bartell drank Tea here . . .

OCTOBER 6, THURSDAY A little rain foornoon, dry Aftrnoon. Mr Hardy at home all Day. M^r F Wymer went away M10.

OCTOBER 7, FRIDAY A Close dry day. Mr Hardy at home all day, Mr Keeler & Mr Newstead dind here.

OCTOBER 8, SATURDAY A very fine day. Mr Smith, Attorney of Wells, Dind here. Mr Hardy at Holt Markt Aftern. I & MA walkd up, drank Tea at Mr Davys, rid home Eve 8 in L Cart . . .

OCTOBER 14, FRIDAY A fine Day. Mr Hardy at home all Day. Miss Baker, Miss Custance, 2 Miss Davys, Miss Jinnis, Miss A & D Johnson & Ann Raven from Whisen-sett drank Tea here.

OCTOBER 15, SATURDAY A fine Day. All walk'd up to Holt Mark^t, drank Tea at Mr Davys, rid home in L Cart.

OCTOBER 16, SUNDAY A Wet Day. I & MA went to our Church Afternoon, Mr Burrell preach'd. Mr Hardy walkd up to Holt Church to go to Church, was no serv-ice, drank Tea at Mr Bakers . . .

OCTOBER 21, FRIDAY A dry Windy Day. Mr Hardy at home all Day . . .

OCTOBER 23, SUNDAY A Wet Day. All went to our Church except Mr Hardy foornoon, Mr Burrell preachd. Mr Hardy, W^m & [Robert] Raven went to Holt Church Af-ternoon, came home to Tea, M^r H drank Tea at Mr Bar-tells. RR went home after Tea. I poorly . . .

OCTOBER 27, THURSDAY A Dry Cold Day. Mr Hardy & W^m at home all Day. I something better.

OCTOBER 28, FRIDAY A Stormy cold Day. Miss Bacon here foornoon to fit on MAs old Gown. Mr Hardy & W^m at home all Day . . .

OCTOBER 30, SUNDAY A Showry Day. W^m walkd up to Holt foornoon to Quak^rs meeting, Dind at Mr Bakers, went to Church Afternoon, drank Tea at Mr Davys. Mr Hardy walk'd to Holt Church Afternoon, came home to Tea . . .

NOVEMBER 1, TUESDAY Showry Day. Mr Hardy set of for Cromer & N Walsham Morn 10, W^m at home all Day. Maids & Goody Ram washd 4 Weeks Linnen.

NOVEMBER 2, WEDNESDAY A Showry Day. W^m at home all Day. Expected Mr Hardy home, did not come.

NOVEMBER 3, THURSDAY A Showry Day. W^m at home all Day, Mr Hardy return^d Even 5 from Cromer.

NOVEMBER 4, FRIDAY A Showry Day. Mr Hardy & W^m at home all Day.

NOVEMBER 5, SATURDAY A tolerable Day. We all walkd up to Holt Afternoon, drank Tea at Mr Bartells, Mr Hardy drank Tea at Mr Moores, all walk'd home Even past 8.

NOVEMBER 6, SUNDAY A fine Day. All went to our Church foornoon, M^r H exceptd, Mr Burrell preach^d. Mr Hardy & W^m went to Holt Church Afternoon, came home to Tea. John Davy from London came to his Fathers . . .

NOVEMBER 9, WEDNESDAY A dry Morn, Wet Afternoon. Mr Hardy & W^m at home all Day. Mr Davy, John & Jo^s Davy & Mr Temple Dind, drank Tea & Supt here.

NOVEMBER 10, THURSDAY A fine Morn, raind Even 4, Showry all Night. W^m went «with» Jno & Jo^s Davy to Mr Kendles of Thornage, Dind, drank Tea & Supt there. Mr Hardy, I & MA drank Tea & Supt there. Mr Moy & A Raven calld here going home . . .

NOVEMBER 12, SATURDAY A Close cold Day. MA & W^m walk'd up to Holt, Dind, drank Tea, Supt at Mr Davys. Mr Temple of Weybon Dind here. H Goggs came MII, we all drank Tea & Supt at Mr Davys . . .

NOVEMBER 16, WEDNESDAY A very Showry Day. M^rs & Miss Baker went away after breakfst. Mr Hardy & W^m at home all Day . . .

NOVEMBER 26, SATURDAY A fine Day. Mr Hardy, I & MA rid up to Holt in L Cart, drank Tea at Mr Davys, W^m rid up in Eveng. I taken with dimness in my Eyes, came home Even 8.

NOVEMBER 27, SUNDAY A fine Day. Mr Hardy & W^m went to Thornage Church foornoon. Miss Bartell Dind & drank Tea here. I, MA & Miss B went to our Church Afternoon, Mr Burrell preachd & preachd at Holt Afterwards. Mr Berry Slept here . . .

NOVEMBER 29, TUESDAY A very fine Day, finish'd Washing. Mr Hardy & W^m at home all Day, M^r J Kendle drank Tea here.

NOVEMBER 30, WEDNESDAY A fine Morn, Wet Afternoon. Mr Hardy & W^m at home all Day . . .

DECEMBER 2, FRIDAY A fine Day. Mr Hardy & W^m at home all Day.

DECEMBER 3, SATURDAY A frosty Morn, finc Day. Mr Hardy, I & MA walkd up to Holt Mark^t Afternoon, drank Tea at Mr Bakers, W^m came up in Eveng, came home in L Cart Even 9. A very Wet Night, Wind high.

DECEMBER 4, SUNDAY A very Wet windy Day. I & MA went to our Church Afternoon qrtr before 2, Mr Burrell preachd & then went to Holt Church. W^m went to Holt Church, came home to Tea.

DECEMBER 5, MONDAY A Sharp rime frost, fine Day. Mr Hardy at home all Day. W^m went to Sidiston [Syderstone] & Fakenham Morng 9, came home Even 8. M^r & M^rs & Miss Bartell drank Tea here, Mr Temple drank Tea & Supt here. Miss Bartell Slept here . . .

DECEMBER 7, WEDNESDAY A close Morn, Rainy Day. MA poorly with A Cold. Mr Hardy & W^m at home all Day . . .

DECEMBER 9, FRIDAY A Sharp frost, fine Day. Mr Hardy & W^m at home all Day. Mrs Davy, Bett & Sarah drank Tea here, Miss Bartell went away. A little Snow fell in the Night . . .

DECEMBER 11, SUNDAY A very severe Wind frost, Wind NW. I, W^m & MA went to our Church Afternoon, Mr Burrell preachd & then preachd at Holt {& preachd there}. Mr Hardy went to T Temples of Thornage Afternoon, drank Tea & Supt there.

DECEMBER 12, MONDAY Excesive Sharp wind frost, Snowd Aftern. Mr Hardy went to Wells Afternoon, W^m at home all Day. Holt Assembly. Thawd in Eveng . . .

DECEMBER 14, WEDNESDAY A very sharp frost. Mr Stoddard call«ed» here in Morng. Mr Hardy, I & MA went to Clay Afternoon in the Carriage, drank Tea at Mr Smiths, Attorny, came home Even past 10. W^m at home all Day.

DECEMBER 15, THURSDAY A very Sharp frost. Mr Hardy, I, MA drank Tea & Supt at Mr Bartells, W^m came in Even, Stoddards, Ravens, Burchams & drosier [Drosier] there. Lamb came for us with the Carriage, came home Morn 2 . . .

DECEMBER 17, SATURDAY A Sharp frost. Mr Hardy & M^r T Temple walkd up to Holt Mark^t Aftern, drank Tea at Mr Bartells. I & MA walkd up, drank Tea at Mr Davys, walkd home Even 9, M^r T supt here.

DECEMBER 18, SUNDAY A Sharp «?frost» in Morng, began to thaw Afternoon. I & MA went to our Church Afternoon, Mr Burrell preach'd & then preach'd at Holt. Mr Hardy & W^m went to Thornage Church Afternoon, came home to Tea . . .

DECEMBER 20, TUESDAY A Close day. Mr Hardy & W^m at home all Day . . .

DECEMBER 22, THURSDAY A very Sharp frost. W^m at home all Day, Jo^s Davy drank Tea here. Mr Hardy, I & MA walk^d up to Holt Afternoon, drank Tea at Mr Seales's, met Mrs Baker there, walk'd home . . .

DECEMBER 24, SATURDAY A very Sharp frost with Storms of Snow. Mr Hardy walkd to Market Afternoon, drank Tea at Mr Kendles, came home Even past 12 . . .

DECEMBER 26, MONDAY A Sharp frost, bright Day. Mr Hardy & W^m at home all Day. M^r & Mrs Bartell drank Tea here . . .

DECEMBER 29, THURSDAY A frost, fine Day. We Irond our Linnen. Young Stannard & young Elvin [Elwin] Dind here. W^m at home all Day, Mr Hardy came home from Norwich Even 10.

DECEMBER 30, FRIDAY A Sharp frost, thawd in the Day. Young Stannard Dind, drank Tea & Supt here. M^r & Mrs Bartell & Mr Temple drank Tea & Supt here.

DECEMBER 31, SATURDAY A very Showry Day. Mr Hardy walk'd up to Holt Markt Afternoon, drank Tea at Mr Bartells. I & W^m rid up to Holt in L Cart after Tea, came home Even past 9. Paul Myles came Even 6.

1792

JANUARY 1, SUNDAY A very showry Day. Mr Hardy & W^m went to Holt Church Afternoon. I, MA & P Myles went to our Church Afternoon, Mr Burrell preach'd . . .

JANUARY 4, WEDNESDAY A Close foggy Day. W^m at home all Day, Mr Hardy & Robt Raven came home Even 4. M^r & Mrs Forster, M^r & Mrs Temple, M^r & Mrs Bartell, M^r & Mrs Baker & Family & P Myles drank Tea & Supt here.

JANUARY 5, THURSDAY A Close foggy Day. Mr Hardy at home all Day. W^m & Robt Raven went up to Holt foorn, Robt went home Afternoon. P Myles went away.

JANUARY 6, FRIDAY A Close dry Day. Mr Hardy & W^m at home all Day . . .

[[JANUARY 8, SUNDAY [by Mary Ann] A Chearly Morn^g, Stormy Afternoon. I and MA went to our Church foornoon, Mr Burrell preach'd. Mr Hardy and W^m went to Holt Church Afternoon (Young Smith [Revd Joshua Smith jnr] preach'd), home to Tea . . .]]

JANUARY 11, WEDNESDAY A very sharp rime frost. We all spent the Eveng at Mr Bartells, met M^r & Mrs Forsters, M^r & Mrs Temple, M^r & Mrs Bakers & Family. Lamb came for us with the Carriage.

JANUARY 12, THURSDAY Excesive sharp frost & frequent Storms of Snow. W^m & MA drank Tea & Supt at Mr Bartells, Mr Hardy at home all Day.

JANUARY 13, FRIDAY A very Sharp frost. Mr Hardy & W^m at home all Day.

JANUARY 14, SATURDAY Excesive Sharp frost. We all walk'd up to Holt Mark^t. I & MA drank Tea at Mr Davys, M^r H & W^m drank Tea at Mr Bartells, came home in L Cart Even past 10 . . .

JANUARY 17, TUESDAY A foggy Day, raind towards Even. Mr Hardy & W^m at home all Day. We all drank Tea & Supt at Mr Temples, Lamb came for us in Carrge, met M^r & Mrs Forster, M^r & Mrs Bartel, M^r & Mrs Davy.

JANUARY 18, WEDNESDAY A frost, fine Day. Mr Hardy at home all Day. W^m & MA went to Mr Kendles of Thornag«e» Afternoon, drank Tea there, came home Even 8 . . .

JANUARY 20, FRIDAY A sharp frost. We all with Bro^t Raven & Robt Raven drank Tea & Supt at Mr Bakers with M^r & Mrs Temples & Mr Bartells Familys, Lamb came for us with the Carriage Morng past one . . .

JANUARY 24, TUESDAY A foggy Day. Maids & Neb Ram wash'd 4 weeks linnen. M^r & Mrs Bartell drank Tea here . . .

JANUARY 28, SATURDAY A very Wet day. Mr Hardy walk^d to Holt Mark^t Afternoon, drank Tea at Mr Davys, came home Eve 12. W^m at home all day.

JANUARY 29, SUNDAY A fine mild day. I & MA went to our Church foornoon, Mr Burrell preach'd. M^r B preach'd at Holt Afternoon, Mr Hardy & W^m went to Thornage Church Aftern. W^m drank Tea at Mr Kendles,

M^r H came home to Tea. M^r & Mrs Davy & 3 of their family drank Tea here. Toby [Tooby] had our LC [little cart] & Horse to go to Thorpe [? Thorpe Market].

JANUARY 30, MONDAY A fine mild day. W^m & MA set of for Whisensett Morn 9 in L Cart. Mr Hardy at home all day. A very Wet Night.

JANUARY 31, TUESDAY A very fine day. Mr Hardy at home all day.

FEBRUARY 1, WEDNESDAY A fine day. Mr Hardy walkd up to Holt foornoon, dind at Mr Bakers, drank Tea at Mr Coopers, came home Even pst 8 . . .

FEBRUARY 5, SUNDAY A rime frost, close day. I & N & M [Nathaniel and Mary] Raven went to our Church foornoon, Mr Burrell preach'd. W^m & NR went to Holt Church Afternoon, Mr Burrell preach'd there, they drank Tea at Mr Davys . . .

FEBRUARY 8, WEDNESDAY A dry foornoon, Showry Afternoon. Mr Hardy, I & M Raven walkd up to Holt Afternoon, drank Tea at Mr Bakers, rid home in L Cart. W^m came up in Eveng.

FEBRUARY 9, THURSDAY A fine day. Mr Hardy, I, MR walk'd to Mr Forsters, Bayfield, drank Tea & Supt there, met M^r & Mrs Temple, M^r & Mrs Kendle, M^r & Mrs Bartell. Lamb came for us with the Carriage . . .

FEBRUARY 11, SATURDAY A fine day. M^r H, I & M Raven walkd to Holt Mark^t Afternoon, drank Tea at Mr Davys, W^m came up to Tea, walkd home.

FEBRUARY 12, SUNDAY A very fine day. I & W^m at our Church foornoon, Mr Burrell preach^d. Mr Hardy walk'd to Thornage Church Afternoon, drank Tea at Mr Kendles. W^m went to Holt Church afternoon, drank Tea at Mr Davys . . .

FEBRUARY 16, THURSDAY A very sharp frost, wind high at N East, small storms of Snow. W^m at home all day. Mr Hardy, I & M Raven walkd up to Holt Aftern, drank Tea at Mr Bartells, met Mrs Thompson & Mr Bakers Family there, walk'd home . . .

FEBRUARY 19, Shrove Sunday A very bad day. A great deal of snow fell in afternoon & drifted very much, the wind being high at N East. Our service foornoon, I taken with dimness in my eyes, could not go to Church. W^m walk'd to Holt Church Afternoon & drank Tea at Mr Davys, Mr Burrell preach'd at Holt . . .

FEBRUARY 23, THURSDAY A sharp frost, beautifull day. Mr Hardy & W^m at home all day. Jo^s & M Davy & M^r T Temple drank Tea here. Lamb came from N Walshm . . .

FEBRUARY 26, SUNDAY A close foggy day. All went to our Church Afternoon except Mr Hardy. J Kendle came to our Church & drank Tea here . . .

MARCH 2, FRIDAY A fine morn, wet afternoon. Mr Hardy & W^m at home all day.

MARCH 3, SATURDAY A close dry day. Mr Hardy, I & MA walkd up to Holt afternoon. I & MA drank Tea at Mr Bartells, M^r H drank Tea at Mr Davys, walk'd home. A wet night . . .

MARCH 6, TUESDAY A showry foornoon, fine afternoon. M^r H rid to Blakney foornoon, dind at Mr Chaplins, drank Tea at Mr Smiths at Clay, came home Even 10. I & MA walk'd up to Holt afternoon, drank Tea at Mr Davys, home eve 6 . . .

MARCH 10, SATURDAY A sharp frost, frequent storms of snow. Mr Hardy & W^m walk'd to Holt Mark^t afternoon, W^m drank Tea at Mr Davys, M^r H at Mr Bartells, came home Even past 11.

MARCH 11, SUNDAY A sharp frost, chearly day. I taken with dimness in my eyes. Mr Hardy & W^m walk'd to Thornage Church afternoon, M^r H came home to Tea, W^m drank Tea at Mr Kendles. No service at our Church, Mr Burrell gone to Cambridge . . .

MARCH 13, TUESDAY A sharp frost. Mr Hardy & W^m at home all day. Gardiner at work. Thaw'd & raind in eveng . . .

MARCH 15, THURSDAY A close day. Mr Hardy & W^m at home all day. Gardener at work & finishd . . .

MARCH 17, SATURDAY A close day. Mr Hardy walkd to Holt Mark^t afternoon, drank Tea at Mr Bartells. W^m walkd up after Tea.

MARCH 18, SUNDAY A very fine day. I & MA went to our Church foornoon, Mr Burrell preachd. W^m went to Holt Church Afternoon, Miss Baker & Adam came home with him to Tea. Mr Baker came from Thetford assises, drank tea here, M^r & Mrs Davy & family came after tea . . .

MARCH 20, TUESDAY A dry chearly day, wind blustering. W^m at home all day. Mr Hardy, I & MA walk'd to Mr Temples, Thornage, afternoon, drank Tea there.

MARCH 21, WEDNESDAY A fine day. I & MA went to our Church foornoon. Mr Hardy & T Temple went to Clay Morn 8 to measure some timber bought at the Sale last week, dind at the tavern, drank Tea at Mr Ellis's, came home even 8.

MARCH 22, THURSDAY A moist morn, fine day. Mr Hardy & W^m at home all day . . .

MARCH 24, SATURDAY A dry windy day. Mr Hardy & W^m walkd to Holt Mark^t afternoon, drank Tea at Mr Davys. M^r H came home even 9, W^m staid to a Ball made by the young people & slept at Mr Davys.

MARCH 25, SUNDAY Showry Morn, A fine afternoon. I & MA & W^m went to our Church foornoon, Mr Burrell preach'd. Mr Hardy & W^m went to Thornage Church afternoon, came home to tea. Sarah Clark calld here aftern, the Davys &c calld. Mr Baker & Dr^{tr} [daughter] calld after tea . . .

MARCH 27, TUESDAY A cold stormy day. Maids & Neb Ram washd 4 weeks linnen. Mr Hardy & W^m at home all day . . .

MARCH 29, THURSDAY A dry windy day {day}. Mr Hardy & W^m at home all day. F Wymer from Norwich Dind here, J Kendle drank Tea here. Mr Foker rid Minor to Fakenham.

MARCH 30, FRIDAY Showry Morng, windy day. Mr Hardy & W^m at home all day. Mr Foker rid Minor out morng 9, came home even 7. A Wet eveng . . .

APRIL 1, SUNDAY A close windy day. I & MA went to our church foornoon, Mr Burrell preachd. Mr Hardy & I

took a little ride in L Cart afternoon. W^m went to Holt church afternoon, drank Tea at Mr Bartells . . .

APRIL 3, TUESDAY A Windy day. Mr Hardy & W^m at home all day, Minor at home all Day. A Wet Night . . .

APRIL 6, *Good Friday* A cold morn, fine day. Mr Hardy at home all day. I & MA went to our Church foornoon, Mr Burrell preach^d. W^m came home from Whisonsett even past 7 . . .

The visit to Whissonsett
9–14 April 1792

APRIL 10, TUESDAY A very fine warm day. Went to Church foorn, dind at Sister Goggs, drank tea & supt at the Hall, went back to Mr Goggs & slept there.

APRIL 11, WEDNESDAY A very warm day. Went to Brother Ravens afternoon, drank tea, Supt & Slept there . . .

APRIL 13, FRIDAY A very warm day. Walkd to Mr Goggs's foornoon, Miss Case & Rose Raven drank tea & Supt there . . .

[LETHERINGSETT]

APRIL 20, FRIDAY A chearly day but cold. Mr Hardy & W^m at home all day.

APRIL 21, SATURDAY A fine day. Mr Hardy, I & MA & W^m walkd up to Holt, drank tea at Mr Davys, walkd home even 8.

APRIL 22, SUNDAY A fine day. I & MA at our Church foornoon, Mr Burrell preach'd. Mr Hardy & W^m went to Thornage Church afternoon, drank tea at Mr Kendles. Brinded Cow calv'd.

APRIL 23, MONDAY A very fine day, windy. Brinded Cow very ill. Maids & Neb Ram washd. Mr Hardy walkd up to Holt afternoon, home even 9 . . .

APRIL 28, SATURDAY A fine day. Mr Hardy, I & MA walkd up to Holt market, drank tea at Mr Davys, M^r H drank tea at Mr Bartells, walkd home.

APRIL 29, SUNDAY A very fine warm day. I & MA at our Church afternoon, Mr Burrell preach'd. Mr Hardy & W^m at Holt Church afternoon, M^r H came home to tea, W^m drank tea at Davys, Jo^s & Bett came home with him . . .

MAY 2, WEDNESDAY A cold stormy day, Wind North. Mr Hardy at home all day. M^r & Mrs Smith & Miss Atthow dind & drank tea here, Mr Ellis of Cley drank tea here . . .

MAY 4, FRIDAY A very cold stormy day, Wind north. Mr Hardy at home all day. M^r & Mrs Temple, Miss Fisher & Miss Leeds drank tea here.

MAY 5, SATURDAY A cold stormy day, Wind north. Mr Hardy walkd to Holt Mark^t afternoon. W^m came home from his journey even 4 & walkd up to Mark^t, came home even 8. Mrs Riches call«ed» here going to Holt, Mrs Flower & Miss Wymer came after tea. Robt Raven from Whisonsett came even past 9.

MAY 6, SUNDAY A cold dry day, Wind North. I, MA, W^m & R Raven went to our Church foornoon, Mr Burrell preachd. M^r & Mrs Baker & Son & daughtr, Mr Custance of Fakenham & Miss Custance drank tea here, RR & M^r & MC [Miss Custance] went home even 8. Mr Dexter went to see his Wife.

MAY 7, MONDAY A cold dry day, Wind north. Mr Hardy at home all day, W^m walk'd up to Holt after tea.

MAY 8, TUESDAY A cold windy day, Wind North. Mr Hardy & W^m at home all day. M^r & Mrs Bartell & Miss Stannard drank tea & Supt here. Mr Dexter came home.

MAY 9, WEDNESDAY A cold windy day, North wind. W^m went to Corpusty morn 10, came home even past 7, Mr Hardy at home all day. T Temple Supt here.

MAY 10, THURSDAY A cold day, wind North. Mr Hardy at home all Day. W^m went to Sheringham & Cromer Morn 10, came home even 9. Messrs Bartells & Miss Stannard breakfstd here. I & MA walk'd up to Holt afternoon, drank tea & Supt at Mr Bartells, Mr Hardy walkd up to supper, home even past 10 . . .

MAY 12, SATURDAY A cold dry day, wind north. All walk^d up to Holt afternoon. I & MA drank tea at Mr Bakers, M^r H & W^m drank tea at Mr Davys, walk'd home even 9.

MAY 13, SUNDAY A fine mild day, wind South. I, W^m & MA went to our Church Afternoon, Mr Burrell preach'd. Mr Hardy went to Holt Church Afternoon, drank tea at Mr Bartells, John Kendle drank tea here.

MAY 14, MONDAY A mild dry morn, drisly afternoon. W^m at home all day. Mr Hardy went with Mr Moore to Mr Ellis^s of Cley, drank tea there & came home even 9. Miss Stannard came foornoon, staid all day & Slept here . . .

MAY 17, THURSDAY A Showry Morn, dry afternoon. Mr Hardy & MA rid up to Holt in L Cart, the Visitation at Holt. M^r H dind at Mr Davys, drank tea & Supt at Mr Bartells, MA there all Day. I & W^m walkd up to Holt Aftern, drank tea & Supt at Mr Bartells. Mr Jo^s Booth died . . .

MAY 20, SUNDAY A fine day. Mr Hardy went to Holt Church aftern. I, W^m & MA went to our Church foornoon, Mr Burrell preach'd. W^m went to Thornage Afternoon, drank tea at Mr Kendles.

MAY 21, MONDAY A fine day. Mr Hardy at home all day, W^m at home all day . . .

MAY 27, *Whit Sunday* A fine day. Mr Hardy & W^m went to Holt Church afternoon. I & MA went to our Church ½ after 5, no Sermon. Mr Acres [?Akers] from Norwich & a relation with him calld here.

MAY 28, MONDAY A Windy day, a Shower even 7. Mr Hardy at home all day. W^m rid to Mr Gro«o»ms of Briston afternoon, came home even 7 . . .

MAY 31, THURSDAY A tolerable day. Mr Hardy & W^m at home all day.

JUNE 2, SATURDAY A dry cold day. We all walk'd up to Holt afternoon, I & MA drank tea at Mrs Bacons, M^r H drank tea at Mr Bartells, W^m & H Raven drank tea at Mr Davys. T Temple supt here.

JUNE 3, SUNDAY A cold windy day. All except Mr Hardy went to our Church foornoon, Mr Burrell preach'd. Mr Hardy, W^m & Henry went to Thornage Church afternoon & drank tea at Mr Kendles. Mr Dexter went to Dereham.

JUNE 4, MONDAY A close cold day. Mr Hardy & W^m at home all day. Dexter did not come home as expectd . . .

JUNE 7, THURSDAY A cold chearly day. Mr Hardy & W^m went to Sheringham Morn 9, came home even 9. Mrs Page of Holt Died.

JUNE 8, FRIDAY A Wet day. Mr Hardy at home all day. W^m went to Sheringham Afternoon, came home even 9.

JUNE 9, SATURDAY A dry cold day. Mr Hardy & H Raven went to Sheringham foornoon, came home eveng 8. I & MA & W^m walk'd up to Holt Mark^t afternoon, drank tea at Mr Bartells, home eveng 8, R Raven came even 8.

JUNE 10, SUNDAY A tolerable day. I, W^m, MA, R Raven & Henry went to our Church foornoon, Mr Burrell preachd . . .

JUNE 12, TUESDAY A Showry cold day. Mr Hardy & H Raven went to Sheringham foornoon in L Cart, came home even 9. W^m at home all day.

JUNE 13, WEDNESDAY A cold showry day. Mr Hardy & W^m went to Sheringham foornoon, came home even past 9. Mrs Daniel from Holt altering a Gown for MA . . .

JUNE 16, SATURDAY A very fine day. Mr Hardy at home all day, W^m went to Holt Mark^t after tea.

JUNE 17, SUNDAY A fine warm day. I & MA & H Raven went to our Church foornoon, Mr Burrell preach'd. W^m & H Rav^n went to Holt Church Afternoon, drank tea at Mr Bartells, M^r B came home with them.

JUNE 18, MONDAY A Showry day. Mr Hardy went to Sheringham in L Cart foornoon, came home even past 9. W^m at home all day.

JUNE 19, TUESDAY A Showry day. Mr Hardy at home all day. W^m went to Sheringham foornoon, came home even 9. Norwich Mayors Feast.

JUNE 20, WEDNESDAY A Showry day. Mr Hardy & Mr Davy of Holt went to Shering^m Afternoon, came home even 10. W^m went to Cley Afternoon, came home to tea. H Raven went home Afternoon.

JUNE 21, THURSDAY A close Morn, fine afternoon. Mr Hardy walk'd to Holt afternoon, drank tea at Mr Bakers, came home even past 10. W^m went to Sheringham afternoon, came home even 9. Maids & F Gidney wash'd.

JUNE 22, FRIDAY A fine day. Mr Hardy & W^m went «to» Shering^m afternoon, came home even 9. We Irond. M^r & M^{rs} & Miss Bartell drank tea here . . .

JUNE 24, SUNDAY A Showry day. I, W^m & MA went to our Church afternoon, Mr Burrell preachd & then went to preach at Holt. Henry Goggs came even 7, Mr Bartell & young Stannard came after tea.

JUNE 25, MONDAY A fine day. Mr Hardy at home all day. H Goggs went away Eveng 3. W^m at home all day.

JUNE 26, TUESDAY A fine day. Mr Hardy at home all day. W^m rid to Sheringham afternoon, came home eveng 9.

JUNE 27, WEDNESDAY A very fine day. Mr Hardy at home all day. W^m went to Holt afternoon to look at the grass, drank tea at Mr Davys. Mrs Davy, Mary, Sarah & Susan, Miss Stannard & Miss Bartell drank tea here.

JUNE 28, THURSDAY A hot day. Mr Hardy, I & MA rid to Sheringham Afternoon in L Cart, came home eveng past 8. W^m set of for Whisonset half past 8. A Showr Eveng 6 . . .

JUNE 30, SATURDAY A fine day. Mr Hardy went to Sheringham Afternoon. W^m came home from Whisonsett Even 9, H Raven came with him. Miss Stannard & Miss Bartell drank tea here.

JULY 1, SUNDAY A fine day. I & MA at our Church foornoon, Mr Burrell preach'd. Mr Hardy & W^m went to Holt Church Afternoon, came home to tea . . .

JULY 3, TUESDAY A Close day. Mr Hardy & W^m at home all day. Sister Goggs & Sister Raven came to Dinner.

JULY 4, WEDNESDAY A close day. Mr Hardy at home all day. W^m up to Holt afternoon, drank tea at Mr Davys. Sister Raven & MA walkd up to Holt foornoon, came back to dinner. W^m & Har^y [Harry, ie Henry Raven] at Clay & Binham foornoon, came home to dinner . . .

JULY 8, SUNDAY A fine day. I, MA, W^m & J Kendle at our Church Afternoon, M^r [John] Astley preach'd. Mr Hardy & Nathl went to Holt Church afternoon, Mr Bell preach'd. Miss Bartell drank tea here, Mr Bartell & Mr Baker came after tea.

JULY 9, MONDAY A close day, riand [rained] towards eveng. Mr Hardy & W^m at home all day, I & MA walk'd up to Holt after tea.

JULY 10, TUESDAY A Wet foornoon, fine afternoon. Mr Hardy, I & MA walk'd up to Holt After, drank tea at Mr Bartells. Miss Bartell & Miss Stannard came home with us, Slept here . . .

JULY 12, THURSDAY A very fine warm day. Mr Hardy & W^m went to Sheringham afternoon, came home even 8. Miss Bartell went home after tea, Miss Stannard & MA walkd up to Holt after tea.

JULY 13, FRIDAY A Wet Day. Mr Hardy at home all day. W^m went to Sheringham aftern, came home even 9. Mr Pask died at Mr Bensleys.

JULY 14, SATURDAY A fine day. Mr Hardy, MA «and» Miss Stannard went to Sheringh^m Afternoon, came home even 9 . . .

JULY 16, MONDAY A very hot Day. Mr Hardy at home all day. W^m & MA went to Mr Seales^s afternoon to tea, Miss Wall there. Raind in the Night.

JULY 17, TUESDAY A hot day. Mr Hardy drank tea at Mr Davys, W^m went to Sheringham. Maids & Fanny Gidney Wash'd 4 weeks Linn^n . . .

JULY 21, SATURDAY A very wet day, wind high & cold. Mr Hardy at home all day. H Goggs went away after dinner, W^m went to Holt Mark^t after tea.

JULY 22, SUNDAY A fine day. No service at our Church. Mr Hardy, W^m & Nathl went to Holt Church afternoon, came home to tea . . .

JULY 25, WEDNESDAY A fine Morn, wet afternoon. Mr Hardy at home all day. W^m walkd up to Holt afternoon to look at the Hay, drank tea at Mr Davys . . .

JULY 28, SATURDAY A fine day. We all went to Holt Mark^t afternoon. I, MA & Nathl drank tea at Mr Davys, Mr Hardy drank tea at Mr Bartells, W^m at Mr Kendles, home even past 8.

JULY 29, SUNDAY A Show^r foornoon, fine afternoon. All went to our Church foornoon except Mr Hardy, Mr Burrell preach'd. I, MA, H & N Raven went to Holt Church afternoon, came home to tea. W^m went to thornage Church & drank tea at Mr Kendles. H & N Raven went home after tea . . .

AUGUST 2, THURSDAY A very hot dry day. Mrs Moy from Horningtoft & 2 Miss Johnsons came foornoon, did not dine here. Bett & Mary Davy drank tea here.

AUGUST 3, FRIDAY A very hot dry day. W^m at home all day. Expected Mr Hardy home from Norwich, did not come.

AUGUST 4, SATURDAY A hot dry day. Mr Hardy came home even 2, Slept last night at Ay«l»sham, Mr Smith of Clay came home with him & dind here. I poorly with dimness in my Eyes.

AUGUST 5, SUNDAY A hot dry day. No service at our Church. Mr Hardy, I & MA rid to Holt Church Afternoon in L Cart, came home to tea . . .

AUGUST 9, THURSDAY Excesive hot dry day. Mr Hardy & W^m at home all day. The Girls walk'd to Holt afternoon, drank tea at Miss Johnsons, home eve 8 . . .

AUGUST 14, TUESDAY A hot day. Mr Hardy & W^m at home all day. M^rs & Miss Forster, M^r & Mrs Temple & Mr Smith of Cley drank tea here.

AUGUST 15, WEDNESDAY A hot day. Mr Hardy & W^m at home all day. F Gidney began to wash 4 weeks linnen. M^r & Mrs Ellis of Cley, Mrs Flower of Sheringham & M^rs F Wymer drank tea here . . .

AUGUST 18, SATURDAY A Wet day. Mr Hardy went to Holt Mark^t afternoon, came home eveng 9. M & A Raven & Deb Johnson drank tea here. Robt Raven came Even 9 . . .

AUGUST 20, MONDAY A fine day. Mr Hardy & W^m at home all day. I & MA walkd up to Holt afternoon, she drank tea at Mr Johnsons, I drank tea at Mr Bartells. A Wet Night . . .

AUGUST 22, WEDNESDAY A Showry day. Mr Hardy went to Cromer morn 11, came home eveng 9. MA very Ill. 2 Miss Johnsons, 2 Miss Ravens & Miss Jinnis [Jennis] drank tea here, W^m supt at Mr Johnsons, Holt.

AUGUST 23, THURSDAY A Showry day. Mr Hardy & I went to Sheringham to meet a party, Dind & drank tea there, came home eve 9.

AUGUST 24, FRIDAY A fine day. W^m at home all day. Mr Hardy & MA went with M^r & Mrs Moore to Mr Kendles of Sherington [Sharrington], drank tea there, came home even 10.

AUGUST 25, SATURDAY A fine day. I & MA walkd up to Holt afternoon, I drank tea at Mr Davys, MA drank tea at Mrs Jennis's. Mr Hardy walkd up to Holt after tea. Mr Stoddard of Norwich Slept here.

AUGUST 26, SUNDAY A Showry day. I, MA & Henry went to our Church foornoon, Mr Burrell preachd. Mr Hardy & H went to Holt Church afternoon, drank tea at Mr Bakers. W^m went to Thornage Church afternoon, came home to tea. Mr Stoddard went away foornoon . . .

SEPTEMBER 5, WEDNESDAY A close dry day. W^m at home all day. Mr Hardy, I & MA walkd to Bayfield afternoon, drank tea at Mr Forsters . . .

SEPTEMBER 9, SUNDAY A fine day. Our service foornoon, none of us there except Nanny [Ann Starling]. W^m & Henry went to Holt Church afternoon, drank tea at Mr Bartells, M^r B came home with him . . .

SEPTEMBER 12, WEDNESDAY A very Wet day. Mr Davy & Son John, a Mr Parker & Mr Urling [? Earling] Din'd & drank tea here. W^m went home with them & Supt, came home eveng 11. Mr Hardy at home all day . . .

SEPTEMBER 16, SUNDAY A very fine day. No service at our Church. We all went to Holt Church afternoon except W^m, he expected J Kendle. M^r & Mrs Seales came home with us to tea . . .

SEPTEMBER 20, THURSDAY A fine morn, showry «? afternoon». We Irond our Linnen. Mr Hardy walkd to Holt afternoon, drank tea at Mr Bartells, came home eve 10 . . .

SEPTEMBER 25, TUESDAY A dry morn, showry afternoon. Mr Hardy walkd up to Holt aftern, drank tea at Mr Bakers, came home eveng 10. W^m at home all day.

SEPTEMBER 26, WEDNESDAY A dry day. Mr Hardy & W^m at home all day .

SEPTEMBER 27, THURSDAY A fine day. Mr Hardy at home all day. M^r & Mrs Mendham calld afternoon, did not stay to tea. MA went to Mrs Johnsons afternoon to go to Childrens Ball, W^m & H Goggs [? Raven] went even 8. MA slept at Mr Johnsons, W^m & H Rav^n came home Morn 4.

SEPTEMBER 28, FRIDAY A Wet day. Mr Hardy & W^m at home all day, sent L Cart for MA to Holt afternoon.

SEPTEMBER 29, SATURDAY A close day, began to rain even 6. A wet night. We all walkd to Holt petty sessions afternoon. I & MA drank tea at Mr Bartells, came home in L Cart even 9.

SEPTEMBER 30, SUNDAY A dry day. Robt Raven came Morn 9, went away even 6. We all went to our Church Afternoon exept Mr Hardy, Mr Burrell preach'd & then preachd at Holt. Mr Hardy went to Holt Church . . .

OCTOBER 2, TUESDAY A cold dry day. Mr Hardy at home all day. W^m went to Briston & Edgefield afternoon, came home even 8. Robt Starling from London & Bett Davy came to speak to us afternoon, I & MA rid up to Holt with them & drank tea at Mr Davys.

OCTOBER 3, WEDNESDAY A dry windy day. W^m at home all day. Mr Hardy walkd to Holt afternoon after the Hay, came home even past 6 . . .

OCTOBER 6, SATURDAY A dry windy day. Mr Hardy walkd up to Holt foornoon, came home even 12. W^m went up after tea, came home with his Father. Mathew Davy came to Holt. Robt Raven came even 7, Henry Raven went home foornoon.

OCTOBER 7, SUNDAY A fine day. I & MA at our Church foornoon, a Sacrament. Robt Raven went away Morn 11. Mr Hardy & W^m went to Thornage Church afternoon, T Temple came home with them, drank tea & Supt here. Miss Leak & Miss Dewing drank tea here . . .

OCTOBER 11, THURSDAY A Wet day. W^m at home all day.

OCTOBER 12, FRIDAY A dry chearly day. W^m at home all Day. I & MA walkd up to Holt aftern, drank tea at Mr Davys. Recd a Letter from Mr Hardy from London.

OCTOBER 13, SATURDAY A tolerable day. I & MA walkd up to Holt Mark^t afternoon, drank tea at Mr Davys, W^m walkd up in eveng. Raind in eveng till 8 oClock. We came home eveng 9.

OCTOBER 14, SUNDAY A Wet Morn, fine afternoon. I & MA at our Church foornoon, Mr Burrell preach'd. W^m went to Holt Church afternoon, Mr Burrell preachd there. Adam Baker came to tea . . .

OCTOBER 16, TUESDAY A fine Morng, Wet afternoon. Maids & Neb Ram washd 4 Weeks Linn«en». W^m at home all day. Mrs Davy, Matt, Bett & Mary drank tea here.

OCTOBER 17, WEDNESDAY A fine Morng, Wet afternoon. W^m at home all day. Recd a Letter from Mr Hardy from London . . .

OCTOBER 21, SUNDAY A Showry day. Mr Hardy poorly. I & W^m went to our Church afternoon, Mr Attwood of Saxlinham preachd . . .

OCTOBER 28, SUNDAY A Close foggy day. No service at our Church. Mr Hardy very poorly. W^m went to Holt Church afternoon, Wm Bell came home with him to tea.

OCTOBER 29, MONDAY A fine day. Mr Hardy much as yesterday. W^m at home all day. M^r & Mrs Bartell drank tea here . . .

NOVEMBER 2, FRIDAY A fine day. Mr Hardy finely, rid up in L Cart as far as Wades at Holt afternoon. Mr Bartell drank tea here Afternoon. W^m rid to Cley afternoon to look at his new purchase, came home even 7.

NOVEMBER 3, SATURDAY A very fine day. Mr Hardy finely. W^m went to Holt Markt even 4, came home even 9.

NOVEMBER 4, SUNDAY A fine day. I went to our Church foornoon, Mr Burrell preach'd. W^m went to Thornage Church afternoon, came home to tea. Mr Baker & Mr Moore drank tea here. Mr Hardy better . . .

NOVEMBER 6, TUESDAY A fine day. Mr Hardy finely. W^m at home all day.

NOVEMBER 7, WEDNESDAY A close dry day. Mr Hardy at home all day. W^m rid to Weyborn aftern, settled an acct with Mr Temple & came home even 6 . . .

NOVEMBER 13, TUESDAY A fine day. Maids & M Loades washd 4 weeks linnen. Mr Hardy & W^m at home all day. T Temple of Thornage drank tea & Supt here.

NOVEMBER 14, WEDNESDAY A very showry day. Mr Hardy & W^m at home all day.

NOVEMBER 15, THURSDAY A showry day. Mr Hardy & W^m at home all day . . .

NOVEMBER 17, SATURDAY A cold day. Mr Hardy rid up to Holt Mark^t afternoon, drank tea at Mr Davys, came home even 8. W^m rid up after tea, home 8.

NOVEMBER 18, SUNDAY A cold windy day. I went to our Church foornoon, Mr Burrell preachd. W^m went to Holt Church Afternoon, drank tea at Mr Bartells, home before 8 . . .

NOVEMBER 21, WEDNESDAY A Wet morn, close afternoon, raind very heavy between 4 & 5 oClock. Mr Hardy & W^m rid to Cley afternoon, came home even 5. Mr Smith of Cley calld, drank tea here & staid till even 8.

NOVEMBER 22, THURSDAY A fine day. Mr Hardy & W^m at home all day.

NOVEMBER 23, FRIDAY A very wet morn, showry afternoon. Mr Hardy & I went to Fakenham Morn 9, dind & drank tea at Mr Custance, brought MA home with us even past 9.

NOVEMBER 24, SATURDAY A close dry day. Mr Hardy, I & MA walk'd up to Holt Markt afternoon, drank tea at Mr Seales, Wm came up after tea in L Cart.

NOVEMBER 25, SUNDAY A Wet day. I & MA went to our Church foornoon, Mr Burrell preachd. Wm went to Holt Church afternoon, came home to tea. Robt Raven came even past 7 . . .

NOVEMBER 30, FRIDAY A close dry day. Wm drank tea at Mr Kendles of Thornage, came home even 8. Mr, Mrs & Miss Baker drank tea here. Mr Hardy came home eveng 8 . . .

DECEMBER 2, SUNDAY A close dry day. I, Wm & MA went to our Church even 7, Mr Burrell preachd. Mrs Forster drank tea here. Wm went to Holt Church afternoon & drank tea at Mr Bartells.

DECEMBER 3, MONDAY A close dry day. Wm set of for Norwich & Brooke with Mr Bartell mong [morning] 7 to visit Mr Edmd Bartell, Mr Hardy at home all Day. Miss Debr Johnson drank tea here . . .

DECEMBER 6, THURSDAY A drisly close day. MA came home from Holt foornoon, Robt Raven went away abt Noon. Mr Hardy at home all day . . .

DECEMBER 8, SATURDAY A chearly day. Mr Hardy, Wm & MA walkd up to Holt Markt, MA & Wm drank tea at Mr Davys, sent the L Cart for them even 8.

DECEMBER 9, SUNDAY A close drisley day. I & MA went to our Church foornoon, Mr Burrell preachd. Wm went to Holt Church afternoon, drank tea at Mr Bakers.

DECEMBER 10, MONDAY A dry day, Wind high. Mr Hardy & Wm at home all day. Gardener at Work . . .

DECEMBER 14, FRIDAY A fine chearly day, wind rough. Wm & MA rid to Sheringham Morng 11, calld at Mr Flowers, dind at lower Sheringham, came home even 6. Mr Hardy at home all Day. Carpenters at work. Young Mendham drank tea here.

DECEMBER 15, SATURDAY A Wet day. Mr Hardy walkd to Holt Markt afternoon, drank tea at Mr Bartell. Wm rid up after tea, both came home even 10. Mrs Moore buried at Cley this Morng Aged 24.

DECEMBER 16, SUNDAY A close mild day. I, Wm & MA went to our Church foornoon, Mr Burrell preach'd. Mr Hardy & Wm went to Holt Church Afternoon, Mr Burrell preachd there. Adam Baker drank tea here . . .

DECEMBER 18, TUESDAY A close windy day. Mr Hardy & Wm at home all day. Wet windy night.

DECEMBER 19, WEDNESDAY A fine chearly day. Miss Stannard & Miss Baker here in foornoon. Mr Hardy, I & MA rid up to Holt in L Cart, drank tea at Mr Bartells, home even 9 . . .

DECEMBER 22, SATURDAY A Wet foornoon, fine afternoon. Mr Hardy walk'd to Holt foornoon, dind at Mr Moores, drank tea at Mr Davys, came home even 9. I & MA walk'd up Afternoon, drank tea at Mr Davys, Wm came up to tea, came home even 9 in L Cart. Wind very high all Night . . .

DECEMBER 29, SATURDAY A rainy day. Mr Hardy rid to Cley foornoon, dind at Mr Smiths, went from thence to Holt Markt, came home even 10. Wm rid to Holt Markt, came home at the same time.

DECEMBER 30, SUNDAY Wet Morng, chearly day. I & MA went to our Church foornoon, A Communion, no Sermon. Wm went to Holt Church Afternoon, came home to tea.

DECEMBER 31, MONDAY A fine day, froze towards eveng. Mr Hardy & Wm rid to Weborn Mor 10 [to Weybourne moring 10] to the Sale of a Ship Wreck on that beach, is [it] was not to be sold till to morrow, from thence they went to Sheringham & came home even 5. We all spent the eveng at Mr Bartells, met Mr & Mrs Forster, Mr & Mrs Temple . . .

1793

JANUARY 3, THURSDAY A small frost. Mr Hardy & Wm at home all day. Mr & Mrs Forster, Mr & Mrs Temple, Mr & Mrs Bartell & Mr Ellis spent the Eveng here. Brot Raven & little Nathl Raven «came» even 5.

JANUARY 4, FRIDAY A sharp frost, very fine day. Brot Raven & Wm walkd up to Holt foornoon, came back to dinner. Bett Davy came to Dinner, Mrs Davy came to tea. Miss Stannard came.

JANUARY 5, SATURDAY A sharp frost, snowd great part of the day. Mr Raven & Nathl went away after dinner. Mr Hardy & Wm walkd up to Holt Markt even 3, came home even 10. Thawd & raind in eveng then froze again.

JANUARY 6, SUNDAY A very sharp frost foornoon, thawd afternoon, raind in eveng & froze again towards Morng. MA, Wm, Miss Stannard & Miss Bartell went to our Church afternoon, Mr Burrell preach'd. I did not go to Church being very poorly with abad Cold . . .

JANUARY 9, WEDNESDAY A sharp rime frost. Mr Hardy & Wm at home all day. Thawd & raind.

JANUARY 10, THURSDAY A close day. Mr Hardy & Wm at home all day. John Baker came afternoon & reckond for Mr Man of Clay . . .

JANUARY 13, SUNDAY A very fine day. I & MA at our Church afternoon, Mr Burrell preachd & then went to Holt. Wm went to Holt Church afternoon, Miss & Adam Baker & Miss Stannard came home with him to tea . . .

JANUARY 15, TUESDAY A Wind frost. Mr Hardy went to Blakny Morn 10, came home even 12, Wm at home all day. Maids & Mrs Thompson Wash'd 5 weeks linnen.

JANUARY 16, WEDNESDAY A Wind frost. Mr Hardy & Wm at home all day. Mr Page of Holt came in even & reckond.

JANUARY 17, THURSDAY A moist morng, fine day. Mr Hardy walkd up to Holt afternoon, drank tea at Mr Bakers. Wm rid up & drank tea & Supt at Mr Bartells with Mr Wade.

JANUARY 18, FRIDAY A Close dry day. Christopher Buxton & Sarah Mays was Married [both of Letheringsett]. Mr Hardy drank tea at M^r T Temples of Thornage. W^m at home all day . . .

JANUARY 20, SUNDAY A sharp rime frost. I & MA went to our Church foornoon, Mr Burrell preach'd. Mr Hardy & W^m went to Holt Church afternoon, came home to tea. The Revd Mr Thomas of Holt was Married to Miss Winn of same place . . .

JANUARY 22, TUESDAY A dry close day, no frost. Mr Hardy walk'd out with M^r T Temple & drank tea there, W^m at home all day.

JANUARY 23, WEDNESDAY A frost, chearly day. Mr Hardy & W^m at home all day. Mary & Sarah Davy drank tea here. M^rs [Miss Mary Ann] Wilson from Holt was buried.

JANUARY 24, THURSDAY A small rain all day. Mr Hardy went to the quarter Sessions at Holt Morn 11, W^m went after dinner, both came home even 8. M^r T Temple Supt here.

JANUARY 25, FRIDAY A frost. Mr Hardy & W^m at home all day. M^r & Mrs Bartell drank tea & Supt here . . .

JANUARY 27, SUNDAY A fine day, no frost. I, W^m & MA went to our Church foornoon, Mr Burrell preach'd. Mr Hardy & W^m went to Holt Church afternoon . . .

JANUARY 30, WEDNESDAY A fine day. Mr Hardy at home all day. MA rid up to Holt aftern to Mr Davys to go to the Ball. W^m went to the Ball after tea, came home Morn past 2. Mr Smith drank tea here . . .

FEBRUARY 1, FRIDAY A very fine day. Mr Hardy walk^d up to Holt Aftern, drank tea at Mr Bakers, W^m walk^d up & drank tea at Mr Davys, they came home even past 8.

FEBRUARY 2, SATURDAY A fine Morng, Wet afternoon & even. MA went up to Holt foornoon, dind, drank tea, Slept at Mr Davys. Mr Hardy & W^m went to Mark^t afternoon, drank tea at Mr Bartells, went to the Play at 3 Acct [3rd act], came home past 11.

FEBRUARY 3, SUNDAY A fine day. MA came from Holt foornoon. Mr Moore of Holt dind here. I, W^m & MA went to our Church Afternoon, Mr Burrell preachd & then preachd at Holt.

FEBRUARY 4, MONDAY A fine day. Mr Hardy went to S^r [Sir] George Chads, from thence to Gunthorp & came home eveng 7 . . .

FEBRUARY 7, THURSDAY A fine day. W^m & MA & their 2 Cousins rid to Sherringham foornoon, came back to dinner. W^m & Nathl Raven drank tea at Mr Johnsons at Holt & went to the Play, came home even past 11. Mr Hardy at home all day.

FEBRUARY 8, FRIDAY A Showry day. Mr Hardy at home all day. Nathl & H Raven walk^d up to Holt foornoon, came back to dinner & went away after dinner. Mr Hardy at home all day. Amy Green Died.

FEBRUARY 9, SATURDAY A Showry day. W^m went to Fakenham foornoon, dind at Mr Custances, came home even 5, drank tea & went to Holt Markt, went to the Play at the 3^d Acct. Mr Hardy went to Mark^t & went to the Play. A very bad Night of Wind & rain . . .

FEBRUARY 12, TUESDAY A Close dry day. Mr Hardy & W^m rid to Salthouse afternoon, came home eve 8. Henry Raven came foornoon . . .

FEBRUARY 14, THURSDAY A very wet morng, dry close aftern. Mr Hardy went to Mr Girdlestones of Kelling, dind & Supt there, came home even 12.

FEBRUARY 15, FRIDAY A close cold day. Mr Hardy & W^m at home all day. Jo^s Davy drank tea here . . .

FEBRUARY 17, SUNDAY A very fine day. All went to our Church foornoon, Mr Burrell preachd. W^m went to Holt Church afternoon. Miss Baker & Adam, Miss Stannard & Miss Man, Miss Bartell & Robt drank tea here.

FEBRUARY 18, MONDAY A wet Morn, dry afternoon. Mr Hardy at home all day. W^m went to Gunthorp foornoon, came home even 3. M^r & Mrs Burrell & 2 Miss Leakes drank tea here. Mr Bartell came to see me, had 1 Bottle & one Pill.

FEBRUARY 19, TUESDAY A rime frost, very fine day. Mr Hardy & W^m at home all day. I Poorly. Mr Bartell came to see me, had one Bottle of Phisic. Eliz Loades went to Whisonsett . . .

FEBRUARY 21, THURSDAY A lowring Morng, fine day. Mr Hardy & W^m went to Gunthorp foornoon, came home eveng 7. Sent to Mr Bartell for a bottle of Phisic . . .

FEBRUARY 23, SATURDAY A close dry day. Mr Hardy walkd up to Holt Mark^t afternoon, drank tea at Mr Bartells, went to the Play. I & W^m & MA rid up to Holt aftern in L Cart. MA drank tea at Miss Alpes, I & W^m drank tea at Mr Bartells.

FEBRUARY 24, SUNDAY A very fine day. All went to our Church Afternoon, Mr Burrell preach^d . . .

FEBRUARY 26, TUESDAY A fine day. Mr Hardy & W^m at home all day. W^m went to the Play in eveng, home pst 11 . . .

FEBRUARY 28, THURSDAY A very fine day. W^m rid to Mr Girdlestons of Kelling foornoon, came home to dinner. Mrs Lewis, Mrs Davy & 2 Daught^rs drank tea here. Mr Hardy came home Morng 2 . . .

MARCH 2, SATURDAY A Close day & began to rain even 4 & wind rose very high in eveng & continued all Night. Mr Hardy, W^m & MA walk^d up to Holt Mark^t. Mr Hardy drank tea at Mr Bartells & came home even 8. W^m & MA drank tea at the Widow Fishers, went to the Play & came home even 12.

MARCH 3, SUNDAY A Cold Windy dry day. All went to our Church foornoon, Mr Burrell preachd. Mr Hardy & W^m went to Holt Church After. M^r H drank tea at Mr Moores, came home past 6. W^m drank tea at Mr Bartells, came home past 8.

MARCH 4, MONDAY A fine day. W^m went to Gunthorp foornoon, came home even 3, Mr Hardy at home all day. Mr Moore of Holt drank tea here.

MARCH 5, TUESDAY A dry close day. Mr Hardy & W^m at home all day. M^r & M^rs & Miss Baker drank tea here . . .

MARCH 8, FRIDAY A fine day. Mr Hardy & W^m at home all day.

MARCH 9, SATURDAY A close dry windy cold day. Mr Hardy went to Holt Mark^t, supa [supped] with M^r

Moore & went to the {y} Play at 3d Accts, came home even past 11. W^m at home all day.

MARCH 10, SUNDAY A cold windy day. W^m set of for Whisonset morng ten. Mr Hardy, I & MA went to our Church foornoon, Mr Burrell preachd. Mr Hardy went to Holt Church aftern & drank tea at Mr Bakers, came home ev 7.

MARCH 11, MONDAY A Cold dry day, wind high. Mr Hardy at home all day . . .

MARCH 14, THURSDAY A fine day. W^m & Robt Raven walkd up to Holt foornoon, Robt went away after dinner. M^r T Temple dind here, we all drank tea at Mr Burrells.

MARCH 15, FRIDAY A beautiful day. Mr Hardy & W^m at home all day. Mr Bartell, Charlot & Robt, Miss Baker & a Mrs Forster from Lennard [Lenwade] Bridge & a Miss Ward from Dereham walkd down from Holt foornoon, they all except Miss Baker drank tea here aftern. Mrs Bartell, Mr Wade the Miller & a Mr Hindes the Player drank tea here.

MARCH 16, SATURDAY A close cold day. Mr Hardy, W^m & MA went to Holt Mark^t afternoon & went to the Play, drank tea & supt at Mr Bartells, came home even 12 in L Cart. A Wet eveng from 6 to ten o Clock.

MARCH 17, SUNDAY A cold dry day. All went to our Church except W^m who went to Holt Church afternoon & drank tea at Mr Bartells . . .

MARCH 19, TUESDAY A very fine day. We washd 4 weeks linn«en». Mr Hardy & W^m at home all day.

MARCH 20, WEDNESDAY A Wet day. Mr Hardy & W^m at home all day.

MARCH 21, THURSDAY A Wet morng, drisly afternoon. Mr Hardy at home all day. M^r P Miles came even 6. W^m went to Gunthorp & came home even 4, MA & he went to the Play, came home eve past 11.

MARCH 22, FRIDAY A dry calm day. Mr Hardy & W^m at home all day.

MARCH 23, SATURDAY A fine day. We all walk^d up to Holt Mark^t afternoon. I & MA drank tea at Mr Davys & came home in L Cart even past 8. Mr Hardy & W^m went to the Play, Supt at Mr Bartells, came home Morn 1.

MARCH 24, SUNDAY A cold wet day. I & MA went to our Church foornoon, Mr Burrell preachd. W^m went to Thornage Church aftern, drank tea at Mr Kendles, home even 7.

MARCH 25, MONDAY A Cold windy day. Mr Hardy & W^m at home all day . . .

MARCH 28, THURSDAY A chearly day but cold. Mr Hardy drank tea at Mr Temples afternoon. W^m rid to Briston & Edgefield Aftern, came back by Holt, drank tea & Supt at Mr Wades, came home even past 8. A sharp rime frost . . .

MARCH 30, SATURDAY A tolerable day. Mr Hardy walk^d to Holt Mark^t afternoon, drank tea at Mr Davys, MA drank tea at Mr Johnsons, they walk'd home even 8. W^m went to Cromer & Beckhithe Morn 10, came back to Holt even 7, went to the Play at 3^d Acct, sup [supped] at Mr Johnsons & came home even past 12.

MARCH 31, *Easter Sunday* A fine day but cold. M^r & Mrs Baker & Family came to our Church afternoon & drank tea here.

APRIL 1, MONDAY A cold wet day. Mr Hardy at home all day. W^m went to Holt afternoon, drank tea at Mr Seales & «spent» the eveng at Mr Bartells, came home even past 9.

APRIL 2, TUESDAY A cold dry close day. Mr Hardy & W^m at home all day . . .

APRIL 5, FRIDAY A dry cold day. Mr Hardy & W^m at home all day.

APRIL 6, SATURDAY A cold chearly day, wind high. We all went to Holt Afternoon, drank tea at Mr Bakers, I & M^r H walkd home Eveng 7. W^m & MA went to the Play, came home in L Cart even 12 . . .

The visit to Whissonsett
8–13 April 1793

APRIL 8, MONDAY A cold chearly day. Mr Hardy & I set of for Whisonset Morn 10, got to Brother Ravens before 2, dind, drank tea & Supt there.

APRIL 9, TUESDAY A cold chearly day. At Bro^t Ravens all day. M^r & Mrs Moy & Rose, Robt & Phillis Raven drank tea there.

APRIL 10, WEDNESDAY A Close cold day. Dind, drank tea & Supt at Mr Goggs, slept at Bro Ravens.

APRIL 11, THURSDAY A Wet Morng, close cold day. We dind, drank tea & supt at Sister Ravens at the Hall.

APRIL 12, FRIDAY A close morng, fine afternoon. Mr Hardy & Bro^t Raven went to Gresenhall foornoon, dind & drank tea at Mr Ben Croffts, came home even 8. Sister Goggs & Sister Raven dind & drank tea at Brother Rav^n.

APRIL 13, SATURDAY A cold close day. Mr Hardy walkd up to the Hall foornoon. We dind at Mr Goggs & sett of for home even past 3, got home alittle after 6.

[LETHERINGSETT]

APRIL 14, SUNDAY A very cold day. All went to our Church afternoon, Mr Burrell preach'd. W^m went up to Holt after Church, drank tea at Mr Bakers . . .

APRIL 16, TUESDAY A Wet morng, stormy afternoon, wind high. Mr Hardy walkd up to Holt Afternoon to meet M^r & Mrs Wymer of Scottow at Mr Bartells, drank tea & supt there, came home even past 11. W^m at home all day . . .

APRIL 18, THURSDAY A wet cold morng, dry close afternoon. Mr Hardy walkd up to Holt aftern, drank tea at Mr Bartells, came home even 9.

APRIL 20, SATURDAY A chearly day but cold. Mr Hardy, I & MA walkd up to Holt Mark^t afternoon. I & MA drank tea at Miss Leakes, M^r H drank tea at Mr Davys, W^m walk'd up after tea, we all walkd home even past 8.

APRIL 21, SUNDAY A cold chearly day. All went to our Church afternoon, Mr Burrell preach^d. W^m walkd up to Holt after Church, drank tea at Mr Bartells. M^r & Mrs Bartell walkd down with him after tea . . .

APRIL 23, TUESDAY A dry chearly day. W^m went to Hildonveston with Mr Moore to look at some Timber, they came back to dinner. We all walk'd up to Holt foornoon, came home to dinner. Bro^t Raven & Mr Croffts went away even past 4, M [Mary] Raven went to Holt in the eveng with Miss A Johnson.

APRIL 24, WEDNESDAY A close cold day. Mr Hardy & W^m at home all day. Mrs Forster drank tea here.

APRIL 25, THURSDAY A close cold morng, wet afternoon. Mr Hardy walk'd up to Holt fair foornoon, dind at Mr Bartells, drank tea at Mr Davys, came home eveng 8. Robt & Nathl Raven came to dinner. W^m & MA went to Holt with them afternoon, drank tea at Miss Johnsons, came home in L Cart eveng 9 . . .

APRIL 27, SATURDAY A close cold day. Mr Hardy, I, W^m & MA walk'd up to Holt afternoon, drank tea at Mr Bartells, W^m drank tea at Mr Davys, walkd home eveng 8.

APRIL 28, SUNDAY Chearly day but cold. No service at our Church, Mr Hardy & W^m went to Holt Church Afternoon. Jo^s Davy drank tea here, John Neve of Coltishal calld here in eveng.

APRIL 29, MONDAY A cold day. Mr Hardy walkd up to Holt afternoon, drank tea at Mr Bartells . . .

MAY 3, FRIDAY A fine day but cold. Mary Raven & Deb^r Johnson drank tea here. Mr Hardy & W^m at home all day.

MAY 4, SATURDAY A fine morn, close cold afternoon. Mr Hardy, I & MA rid to Holt in L Cart, W^m rid up on Minor, we all drank tea at Mr Davys, came home even 8.

MAY 5, SUNDAY A cold Showry day. All went to our Church afternoon, Mr Thomas preachd.

MAY 6, MONDAY A fine morng, close cold afternoon. Mr Hardy, I & W^m rid to Sheringham aftern, drank tea there, came home evng 8. M^r & Mrs Bartell, M Raven & Deb^r Johnson drank tea here with MA . . .

MAY 9, THURSDAY A showry day. M Raven & Deb Johnson dind & drank tea here, M^r & Mrs Temple drank tea here. Mr Hardy & W^m at home all day.

MAY 10, FRIDAY A chearly day. Mr Hardy & W^m at home all day. I & MA walk'd up to Holt aftern, drank tea at Mr Bakers.

MAY 11, SATURDAY A fine day. We all walkd up to Holt afternoon. I & MA & W^m drank tea at Mr Bartells, Mr Hardy drank tea at Mr Bakers. I poorly with dimness in my Eyes . . .

MAY 13, MONDAY A very fine day. Mr Hardy & W^m rid to Bale foornoon, came home to dinner. M Raven came to dinner & drank tea here . . .

MAY 18, SATURDAY A cold dry day. Mr Hardy walk'd up to Holt Mark^t aftern, I, W^m & MA rid up in L Cart. I drank tea at Mr Davys, M^r H & W^m at Mr Bartells, MA at Mrs Jenes's [Jennis's] . . .

MAY 20, MONDAY A chearly day but cold. Mr Hardy at home all day, W^m at home all day. Hannah Boone came from Glandford. Mr Wade drank tea & Supt here, M Raven & Deb^r Johnson supt here.

MAY 21, TUESDAY A very cold windy day. Mr Hardy at home all day. W^m went to Blakey [Blakeney] afternoon, Mr Wade came home with him to Supper.

MAY 22, WEDNESDAY A close cold day. Mr Hardy & W^m at home all day. Hannah Boone went away. M Raven came in eveng. Mrs Vickery of Holt died.

MAY 23, THURSDAY A cold dry day. Mr Hardy at home all day. Bro^t Raven came to dinner, he & W^m walkd up to Holt afternoon, came back to tea. M Raven & Deb Johnson came afternoon, Slept here. Mrs Davy, Bett & Susan drank tea here.

MAY 24, FRIDAY A cold dry day. Bro^t Raven went away after tea. M^rs & Miss Baker drank tea here . . .

MAY 26, SUNDAY A cold windy day. All went to our Church foornoon except Mr Hardy, Mr Burrell preach^d. Miss M Johnson drank tea here. M^r & Mrs Forster, Mr Baker & Son, Mr Wade & Miss A Johnson calld in after tea . . .

MAY 30, THURSDAY A cold dry day. I very poorly. Mr Hardy at home all day. W^m, Robt & M Rav^n walkd up to Holt foornoon. Robt went away after tea, took Minon [Minor] home with him. W^m & MR took a ride to Bale in eveng . . .

JUNE 3, MONDAY A fine warm day. Mr Hardy & I rid in L Cart to Mr Temples after tea. MR & MA walkd up to Holt after tea.

JUNE 4, TUESDAY A warm dry day. Mr Hardy at home all day . . .

JUNE 6, THURSDAY A dry hot day. Ann & Nathl Raven from Whisonsett came morng 11. MA, M & Ann Raven drank tea at Miss Johnsons, Holt. A Showr of rain eveng 5. Mr Hardy at home all day.

JUNE 7, FRIDAY A hot dry day. Mr Hardy at home all day. The Girls & N Rav^n & Henry Raven rid to Weybon foornoon, came home to dinner. 2 Miss Jennes^s & Deb Johnson drank tea here . . .

JUNE 14, FRIDAY A very cold day. Mr Hardy & MR walkd up to Holt aftern. H Raven went to Dereham & from thence to Whisonsett.

JUNE 15, SATURDAY A fine morng, showry afternoon & eveng. I, MR & MA rid up to Holt afternoon, drank tea at Mr Seales, came home even 8. Mr Hardy walkd up, drank tea at Mr Davys & Supt at Mr Moores, came home eveng past 11.

JUNE 16, SUNDAY A Showry day. All went to our Church foornoon, Mr Burrell preach'd. MA sett of for Norwich [[[by Mary Ann] for the Guild]] with M^rs & Miss Forster in Mrs Sheppards post Chaise even 3. MR drank tea at Mr Burrells . . .

JUNE 19, WEDNESDAY A small rain foornoon & cold close afternoon. Mr Hardy at home all day. M^r & Mrs Burrell & the 2 Miss Leeks drank tea here . . .

JUNE 21, FRIDAY A fine day. M Raven walkd up to Holt foornoon with B Leek, came home to dinner & went home eveng 6. Mr Moore dind & drank tea here. Albro [Aldborough] Fair.

JUNE 22, SATURDAY A cold windy day. Mr Hardy walkd to Holt Mark^t Afternoon, came home even 9. Wind high in the night . . .

JUNE 29, SATURDAY A fine day. R Raven went away after dinner. W^m came from N Walsham to Holt & dind at Mr Moores, Mr Hardy drank tea «at Mr» Davys. I & MA drank tea at Miss Leakes, walkd home eveng 8. A heavy showr eveng 5.

JUNE 30, SUNDAY A very fine day. W^m & H Raven went to Holt Church afternoon & came home to tea. Mr Hardy, I & MA went to our Church ¼ before 5, Mr Burrell preachd. Mr Bartell & 2 Childr^n calld here after tea. Mr Moore Supt here . . .

JULY 2, TUESDAY A Showry day. Mrs Moy from Horningtoft calld to speak to us from Holt foornoon. Mr Hardy walkd up to Holt afternoon to speak to Mr Moy, came home even 9. W^m at home all day. We wash'd some small linnen.

JULY 3, WEDNESDAY A very fine day. Mr Hardy walkd up to Holt afternoon, drank tea at Mr Moores. W^m rid out after tea. Mrs Buckle & Mrs Herring from Norwich came eveng 7 to Mr Forsters . . .

JULY 5, FRIDAY A very hot dry day. Mr Hardy went to Hildonveston with Mr Moore to measure Timber morng 10, came home eveng 9. MA walkd up to Holt afternoon, drank tea at Mrs Jennes^s. M^r & Mrs Temple & M^r J Kendle of Thornage drank tea here, Mr Moore & T Temple supt here . . .

JULY 7, SUNDAY Extreme hot day. All went to our Church foornoon, Mr Burrell preach'd. W^m & H went to Holt Church afternoon, came home to tea. Mr Tooby, Mr Moore & 2 Childr^n, Mr Baker, M^r & Mrs Burrell here in eveng . . .

JULY 9, TUESDAY A foggy morng, warm afternoon. Sisters Goggs & Raven & H Goggs came half after 9. Mr Hardy at home all day. H Goggs went away after tea. Rich'd Johnson of Holt Married to Miss Lacy of Norwich.

JULY 10, WEDNESDAY A warm dry day. Mr Hardy & W^m at home all day. M^r & Mrs Baker of Holt drank tea here.

JULY 11, THURSDAY A warm dry day. Mr Hardy, I, Sisters & MA drank tea at Mr Bakers, W^m at home all day.

JULY 12, FRIDAY A very fine day. We all went to Sheringham Afternoon, Sisters & MA in Howards Post Chaise, M^r H & I in our L Cart, W^m with Mr Moore in his Whiskey, drank tea at Sandersons, came home Eveng 10.

JULY 13, SATURDAY A fine day. H Goggs came for his Mother 8, they went away even 6. Mr Hardy & W^m at home all day.

JULY 14, SUNDAY A very fine dry day. All went to our Church Afternoon, Mr Burrell preachd . . .

JULY 16, TUESDAY A very hot dry day. We washd 5 Weeks linnen. Mr Hardy & W^m at home all day.

JULY 17, WEDNESDAY A dry day, not altogether so hot a«s» yesterday. Mr Hardy, I & MA dind, drank tea & Supt at Mr Bartells, met M^r & Mrs Geo^r Wymer from Norwich there.

JULY 18, THURSDAY A dry morng, a small rain all the Afternoon. M^r & Mrs Wymer, M^r & Mrs Bartell & Mr Wade dind & drank tea here.

JULY 19, FRIDAY A fine dry day. Cley fair. Mr Hardy & W^m at home all day. M^r & Mrs Wymer went away from Mr Bartells.

JULY 20, SATURDAY A fine day. All walkd to Holt Market afternoon, drank tea at Mr Davys.

JULY 21, SUNDAY A fine day. All went to our Church foornoon, Mr Burrell preach'd. Mr Moore supt here . . .

JULY 24, WEDNESDAY A dry day. W^m at home all day . . .

JULY 26, FRIDAY A fine day. W^m at home all day. Mr Hardy & Mr Moore came home eveng past 11, they came by Dereham & Gresenhall.

JULY 27, SATURDAY A drisly day. Mr Hardy walk'd to Holt Mark^t afternoon. I & W^m rid up in L Cart after tea, came home eveng 9.

JULY 28, SUNDAY A very cold close day, shows for rain but had none. No service at our Church, Mr Hardy, W^m & Henry went to Holt Church afternoon, came back to tea. Mr Wade & young Kendle drank tea here . . .

JULY 31, WEDNESDAY A Wet foornoon, dry afternoon. Mr Hardy at home all day . . .

AUGUST 2, FRIDAY A fine dry day. Mr Hardy at home all day.

AUGUST 3, SATURDAY A dry day & windy. Mr Hardy walk^d to Holt Mark^t afternoon, came home eveng past 8.

AUGUST 4, SUNDAY A Showry foornoon, dry afternoon. All went to our Church foornoon, Mr Burrell preachd. Henry went to Holt Church afternoon . . .

AUGUST 6, TUESDAY A dry day. Mr Hardy at home all day. Expected W^m & MA from Yarmouth but they did not come.

AUGUST 7, WEDNESDAY A dry hot day, great shows for rain in the eveng, had but a very small shower with Lightning. Expected W^m & MA home, did not come . . .

AUGUST 9, FRIDAY A heavy showr abt 2 oclock, wind high all day. Expected W^m & MA home, did not come. Mr Hardy at home all day . . .

[Mary Hardy fell seriously ill on 16 August and did not write her diary again until 17 October 1793]

above Letheringsett Church, Easter 2011—the bicentenary year of the death of William Hardy [*photograph Margaret Bird 2011*]

1793

Manuscript ledger 4 (cont.)
21 July 1790–7 May 1800

[LETHERINGSETT]

OCTOBER 18, FRIDAY A Close foggy day. Bro^t & Daughtr went away after dinner, W^m went with them. Mr Hardy & I rid a little way with them.

OCTOBER 19, SATURDAY A Close foggy day. I & Mr Hardy rid to fir Closes [Furze Closes] after dinner then M^r H went to Holt Mark^t, came «home» even 8.

OCTOBER 20, SUNDAY A Close day. Our Service at even 5, Mr Hardy & MA there. W^m came home eveng 9 . . .

OCTOBER 23, WEDNESDAY Close day. Wm Brewd. M^r H & I took a ride afternoon . . .

OCTOBER 27, SUNDAY A fine day. All went to our Church foornoon, Mr Burrell preach'd. W^m & H [Henry Raven] went to Holt Church after«noon». M^r & Miss Bartell, Miss & Adam Baker & Miss Stannard drank tea here & Mr Moore drank tea here.

The visit to Whissonsett
28 October–2 November 1793

OCTOBER 28, MONDAY A fine day. Mr Hardy & I sett of for Whisonsett in Mr Moores Whisky morn past 10, got to Brother Ravens even 2, dind, drank tea & slept here.

OCTOBER 29, TUESDAY A cold dry windy day. I & M [Mary] Raven rid to Fakenham foornoon, came back to Bro Ravens to dinner. Mr Hardy & Bro^t Raven took a walk foornoon. M^r & Mrs Goggs, Mrs Raven [of the Hall] drank tea at Bro^t Ravens. A very wet night.

OCTOBER 30, WEDNESDAY A fine day. We took a ride to Mr Moys of Horningtoft then went to Mr Goggs to dinner. I Slept there, Mr Hardy went to Bro^t Ravens to Sleep.

OCTOBER 31, THURSDAY A rime frost. Mr Hardy & Bro^t took a ride to Brisley foornoon. We dind at Bro^t Ravens, M^r & Mrs Goggs dind & drank tea there.

NOVEMBER 1, FRIDAY A Showry day. We dind & drank tea at Sister Ravens at the Hall. Mrs Prior from Yarmouth came.

NOVEMBER 2, SATURDAY A fine day but cold. We sett of [off] for home morng past 10, got home eveng 3. I was very poorly. Mr Hardy went to Holt Mark^t, came home eveng 9. A Wet night.

[LETHERINGSETT]

NOVEMBER 3, SUNDAY A Showry day. MA, W^m & H Raven went to our Church foornoon, W^m & HR went to Holt Church aftern. I very poorly.

NOVEMBER 4, MONDAY A dry foornoon, Showry afternoon. Mr Hardy walkd up to Holt foornoon, came home to dinner. Mr Moore dind & drank tea here . . .

NOVEMBER 7, THURSDAY A Showry day. Mr Hardy & W^m at home all day. Mr Mason dind here, his Wagon came for the Bark.

NOVEMBER 8, FRIDAY A Close dry day but wet Night. Mr Hardy at home all day. W^m rid to Edgefield with Mr Moore, dind at Mr Moores, came home to tea . . .

NOVEMBER 10, SUNDAY A very wet Morng, fine afternoon. Mr Hardy, W^m, MA & HR went to our Church foornoon, Mr Burrell preachd. W^m went to Holt Church afternoon, drank tea at Mr Wades, came home eve 8 . . .

NOVEMBER 12, TUESDAY A fine day. Mr Hardy at home all day. Mr Geo^r Custance came, dind here. W^m & MA went with him to Holt, drank tea & supt at Mr Bakers, came home eveng 11. A very wet night. M^r & M^rs & Miss Bartell drank tea here . . .

NOVEMBER 14, THURSDAY A very fine day. Mr Hardy at home all day, W^m at home . . .

NOVEMBER 16, SATURDAY A Close day. Mr Hardy, W^m & MA walkd up to Holt Market Afternoon, drank tea at Mr Bartells, came home eveng 9.

NOVEMBER 17, SUNDAY A fine day. No service at our Church, Mr Hardy went to Holt Church Afternoon. Mr Moore came home with him, drank tea & supt here. Robt Raven came to dinner, staid all Night . . .

NOVEMBER 19, TUESDAY A fine Morng, foggy afternoon. Mrs Flower calld here. Mr Hardy & W^m dind at Mr Wades at Holt, came home eveng 10. Bett & Susan Davy drank tea here.

NOVEMBER 20, WEDNESDAY A Close foggy day. Wm Brewd, Mr Hardy at home all day.

NOVEMBER 21, THURSDAY A Close foggy day. Mr Hardy at home all day. W^m & MA rid up to Holt afternoon, drank tea at Mr Davys, came home even 10 . . .

NOVEMBER 24, SUNDAY A close dry day. All went to our Church foornoon, Mr Burrell preachd. W^m drank tea at Mr Kendles of Thornage . . .

NOVEMBER 26, TUESDAY A Close mild day. Mr Hardy at home all day. W^m drank tea & Supt at Mr Thomas^s at Holt, came home even 12 . . .

NOVEMBER 29, FRIDAY A close day. Mr Hardy at home all day. W^m brewd.

NOVEMBER 30, SATURDAY A very fine day. Mr Hardy & MA walkd up to Holt Market aftern, MA drank tea at Mr Davys, Mr Hardy at Mr Bartells. W^m rid up in L [little] Cart after tea, came home eveng past 9.

DECEMBER 1, SUNDAY A close mild day. All went to our Church foornoon, Mr Burrell preachd. W^m & Henry went to Holt Church Afternoon.

DECEMBER 2, MONDAY A dry mild day. Mr Hardy at home all day. W^m walkd up to Holt aftern, drank tea at Mrs Fishers, came home eveng 8.

DECEMBER 3, TUESDAY A Close day. Mr Hardy at home all day, Wm Brewd . . .

DECEMBER 6, FRIDAY A fine bright day. Mr Hardy & W^m at home all day. H Raven went to Sheringham afternoon with Mr Flowr [Flower's] Whisky & brought home our Cart.

DECEMBER 7, SATURDAY A Close dry day. Mr Hardy & W^m went to Holt Market, came home eveng 10.

DECEMBER 8, SUNDAY A drisly day. All went to our Church except myself foornoon, Mr Burrell preach'd . . .

DECEMBER 11, WEDNESDAY A rainy day. W^m set of for Whisonsett morng 7, Mr Hardy at home all day.

DECEMBER 12, THURSDAY A very fine day. Miss Wymer from Norwich calld here foornoon. Mr Hardy & MA rid to Mr Bartell, drank tea & Supt there, came home even past 11 . . .

DECEMBER 14, SATURDAY A fine day. Mrs Sanderson went away after breakfast, Henry Goggs went away after dinner. Mr Hardy walk^d up to Market aftern. MA & the 2 young Ladies went in L Cart, W^m on Horseback, drank tea at Mr Bakers, came home eveng 9.

DECEMBER 15, SUNDAY A Close foggy day. All went to our Church foornoon, Mr Burrell preachd. Miss Fisher, Miss Leeds & Mr Wade drank tea here. Mrs Bransby [Elizabeth, née Lighten] was buried. Mr Burrell read a Lecture in the eveng. A very wet night.

DECEMBER 16, MONDAY A wet morng, close foggy day. W^m brew'd. Mr Hardy at home all day, Mr Chaplin here in eveng.

DECEMBER 17, TUESDAY A very fine day. We wash^d 3 weeks linnen. Mr Hardy at home all day. W^m went to Holt morng 11 with Miss Wymer & Miss Bartell, dind & drank tea at Mr Bartells, came home eveng 9. Mr Moore drank tea here.

DECEMBER 18, WEDNESDAY A Wet day. Mr Hardy at home all Day. Mrs Flower & M^r S Flower dind here & drank tea & went to the assembly at Holt with W^m & MA, came home Morng past 4 & slept here.

DECEMBER 19, THURSDAY A very fine day. Mr Hardy & W^m at home all day. M^r & Mrs Flower went home eveng 6, Miss Wymer dind & drank tea here.

DECEMBER 20, FRIDAY A rime frost, fine day. Mr Hardy & W^m at home all day, Mr Moore dind & drank tea here.

DECEMBER 21, SATURDAY A rime frost, chearly day. MA walkd up to Holt foornoon, dind & drank tea at Mr Bartells. Mr Hardy & W^m at Market after, came home even 10 . . .

DECEMBER 23, MONDAY A fine day. Wm Brew'd, Mr Hardy at home all day.

DECEMBER 24, TUESDAY A Close day. W^m at home all day. Mr Hardy walk'd to Holt afternoon, came home eveng 10 . . .

DECEMBER 26, THURSDAY A close day, raind a little aftern. Mr Hardy & W^m at home all day. Miss Custance, Anne Raven & Nathl Raven came to Dinner.

DECEMBER 27, FRIDAY A close dry day. Mr Hardy & W^m at home all day, Adam Baker drank tea & Supt here.

DECEMBER 28, SATURDAY A close day. Mr Hardy walkd up to Holt Mark^t afternoon. W^m & the Girls rid up Holt in L Cart, drank tea at Mr Bakers, came home even 9, M^r H came home ½ after 9.

DECEMBER 29, SUNDAY A fine day. No service at our Church, Mr Hardy & the Girls rid to Holt Church afternoon. Mr Wade drank tea here. W^m poorly.

DECEMBER 30, MONDAY A rime frost, fine day. Mr Hardy at home all day. W^m, MA & 2 Girls went to a Ball at Holt, came home Morng 3.

DECEMBER 31, TUESDAY A fine day. Mr Hardy & W^m at home all day. M^r T Temple & Mr Moore drank tea & Supt here.

1794

JANUARY 1, WEDNESDAY A Sharp rime frost. Mr Hardy & W^m at home all day. M^r & Mrs Temple, Miss M Johnson, Miss Hanault & Miss Bartell drank tea here. Robt & Nathl Raven came to tea.

JANUARY 2, THURSDAY A very sharp rime frost. Mr Hardy at home all day. The young people walkd to Mr Temples foornoon, came back to dinner. I & Miss Custance went to speak to Mrs Burrell foornoon. The young people walkd to Holt Afternoon, drank tea at Miss Johnsons, came home eveng past 9 . . .

JANUARY 4, SATURDAY A sharp frost, close day. Mr Hardy walk'd up to Holt Mark^t afternoon, drank tea at Mr Bartells, came home eveng past 10. The Girls & W^m walk'd up & drank tea at Mr Sheldrakes, came home eveng past 9.

JANUARY 5, SUNDAY A Sharp frost, close day. All went to our Church foornoon, Mr Burrell preachd. Mr Custance from Fakenham & Mr Baker Dind here, went away eveng 4 . . .

JANUARY 7, TUESDAY Frost, bright day. Mr Hardy at home all day. The Girls & W^m walkd up to Holt Afternoon, drank tea at Mrs Jennes's, came home in Malt Cart.

JANUARY 8, WEDNESDAY A Frost, close day. Mr Hardy, W^m & the Girls at home all day.

JANUARY 9, THURSDAY A frost, bright day. Miss Custance, Ann Raven & W^m walk'd up to Holt foornoon, came back to dinner. Mrs Davy, Jo^s, Bett & Susan, M^r & Mrs Sheldrake & Miss Alpe drank tea here.

JANUARY 10, FRIDAY A Sharp rime frost. Mr Hardy at home all day. I walkd to speak to Mrs Burrell foornoon, found her poorly. The Girls & W^m walkd up to Holt Afternoon, drank tea at Mr Johnsons, came home eve 10.

JANUARY 11, SATURDAY Thawd, close day. Mr Hardy walk'd up to Holt foornoon, dind at Mr Moores, came home eveng 10. W^m & the Girls walkd up afternoon, drank tea at Miss Alpes, came home eveng past 9 in L Cart . . .

JANUARY 13, MONDAY A rime frost, chearly day. Mr Hardy at home all day, Wm Brew'd. Mr Moore dind here. The Girls walkd up to Holt aftern, drank tea at Mr Bakers, W^m went for them eveng past 8. Miss Custance staid at Mr Bakers.

JANUARY 14, TUESDAY A fine day. We washd 4 weeks linnen. Mr Hardy & W^m at home all day.

JANUARY 15, WEDNESDAY A Close foggy day, raind toward eveng. Mr Hardy & W^m at home all day.

JANUARY 16, THURSDAY A frost, fine day. Mr Hardy & W^m at home all day, Mr Wade drank tea here & Supt . . .

JANUARY 18, SATURDAY A frost, fine day. Mr Hardy walk'd up to Holt Mark^t aftern, drank tea at Mr Moores, came home eveng 10. Mrs Forster & Wm Herring drank tea here.

JANUARY 19, SUNDAY A frost, fine day. All went to our Church foornoon, Mr Burrell preach'd. W^m & the 2 Girls went to Holt Church Afternoon, came home to tea . . .

JANUARY 22, WEDNESDAY A fine day. Mr Hardy at home all day, I & W^m rid to Kelling foornoon in Mr Branfords Whiskey. W^m & the Girls drank tea at Mr Wades, Holt.

JANUARY 23, THURSDAY A drisly morning, dry afternoon. Mr Hardy walkd up to Holt quarter Sessions Morng 11, dind at Mr Bartells, drank tea at Mr Bakers. W^m went up afternoon, drank tea at Mr Bakers, came home even'g. Robt, Mary & Ann Raven went away after dinner.

From the newspaper
The anti-war vote 1794
[[JANUARY 24, FRIDAY . . . [by William Hardy]
Peers
Albemarl, Bedford, Chedworth, Cholmondely, Derby, Guilford, Lansdown, Lawtherdale [Lauderdale], Egmont, Norfolk, St John, Stanhope
Commons
Wm Adams, W L Antonie, Sir J Aubrey, ——Bouverie, J R Burch, G Bing, J B Church, T W Coke, E Coke, Wm Colhoun, J Courtenay, T C Crespigny, T Erskine, Sir H Featherstone, R^t Hon R Fitzpatrick, Sir H Fletcher, Hon T Foley, R^t Hon. C. J. Fox, Ph Francis, Chas Grey, Ja^s Hare, J Hercourt, Film^n Honeywood, H Howard, D Howell, W Hussey, R S Milnes, Cunliffe Shaw, Jos Jeckyll, Sir Wm Lemon, N Mackleod, Hon F Maitland, Sir Wm Milner, Dud^y North, Wm Plumer, ——Powlett, Sir M W Ridley, Ld Wm Russell, W C Shawe, R B SHERIDAN, W Smith, H Sleed, C Sturt, And St John, L^d R Spencer, B Tarlton, M A Taylor, T Thomson, L^d J Townshend, Sir E Vane, B N Vaughan, R Viner, J Walwynn, C C Western, J Wharton, S Whitbread Junr, T Whitmore, R Wilbreham, Sir E Wonnington, R Milbank, J Crew, Lord Wycombe
Tellers W Adams, Chas Grey . . .]]

[LETHERINGSETT]
JANUARY 26, SUNDAY A Sharp frost, chearly day. All went to our Church Aftern, Mr Burrell preach'd.

JANUARY 27, MONDAY A very sharp frost, chearly day. Wm Brew'd. Mr Hardy walk'd up to Holt afternoon, drank tea at Mr Seales's then went to Mr Bakers were [where] was some Company, came home eveng 10.

JANUARY 28, TUESDAY Sharp frost, chearly morng, Snowd hard afternoon about one hour then cleard up & frose again. Miss Custance & Miss Jennis here foornoon. Mr Hardy at home all day. W^m drank tea & Supt at Mr Thomas's, Holt, came home eveng 12.

JANUARY 29, WEDNESDAY A Sharp frost. Mr Hardy at home all day, I went foorn to speak to Mrs Burrell, W^m at home all day. Snowd again in eveng & then frose sharp again.

JANUARY 30, THURSDAY A Sharp frost. Mr Hardy & W^m at home all day. Frost went away this night . . .

FEBRUARY 1, SATURDAY A fine day. Mr Hardy & W^m at home all day. Robt Raven from Whisonsett came eveng 4 . . .

FEBRUARY 3, MONDAY A very fine day. Mr Hardy & I rid to Mr Temples of Thornage afternoon to speak to Mrs Temple, came home to tea. MA walkd up to Holt afternoon to se«e» Miss Custance at Mr Bakers, she being unwell, drank tea there. Henry went for her eveng 7.

FEBRUARY 4, TUESDAY A small rime frost, fine day. W^m & Henry went to Gunthorp in Turnip Cart foornoon, came home eve 3. Miss Custance, 2 Miss Jennis^s, Miss D Johnson, Miss Bartell & Adam Baker drank tea here.

FEBRUARY 5, WEDNESDAY A fine dry day. Mr Hardy poorly with the Gout. W^m at home all day, Mr Thomas & Mr Moore from Holt dind here . . .

FEBRUARY 8, SATURDAY A very fine day. Mr Hardy much as Yesterday. W^m & MA & Miss Custance walk'd up to Holt afternoon, drank tea at Mr Bakers, came home eveng past 9 . . .

FEBRUARY 10, MONDAY A chearly day, Wind high & Cold. Mr Hardy better foornoon & worse in afternoon. M^r & M^{rs} & Miss Bartell drank tea here. Wm Brew'd.

FEBRUARY 11, TUESDAY A dry Morng, wet afternoon. Mr Hardy somthing better in Morng, worse again in eveng. W^m drank tea & Supt at Mr Bartells, came home after 12, met M^r & Mrs Cutting & Mr Ward from Sheringham. Washd 4 weeks linnen . . .

FEBRUARY 13, THURSDAY A fine morng, close windy aftern. Mr Hardy very lame in both feet. W^m sett of for Fakenham & Whisensett morng 10. Miss Baker & Miss Custance came foornoon for a walk . . .

FEBRUARY 15, SATURDAY A fine day but windy. Mr Hardy somthing better but very lame, cant walk at all. Mr Moore dind here. W^m went to Holt Mark^t eveng 4, came home eveng 9.

FEBRUARY 16, SUNDAY A Wet Day. Mr Hardy much as yesterday. I, MA & H Raven went to our Church foornoon, Mr Burrell preach'd. Mr House [Howes] from Cromer din'd here. W^m went to Holt Church Afternoon, came home to tea . . .

FEBRUARY 18, TUESDAY A Close dry day. Mr Hardy very bad with the Gout in his knee. Mrs Flower went away eving [evening] 7. Miss Custance, M^r & Mrs Baker, Miss Rouse & Miss Bartell, Mr Moore & Mr Davy drank tea here.

FEBRUARY 19, WEDNESDAY A close dry day. Mr Hardy very poorly with the Gout in his knee. W^m at [and] N Raven dind at Mr Bakers. M^r G Custan«c»e & Miss C calld here afternoon going home from Holt.

FEBRUARY 20, THURSDAY A close dry day. Mr Hardy something better. W^m at home all day, Mr Ellis call«ed» here in the eveng.

FEBRUARY 21, FRIDAY A Wet morng, dry afternoon. Mr Hardy much as Yesterday. W^m at home all day, Mr Baker drank tea here.

FEBRUARY 22, SATURDAY A dry windy day. Mr Hardy something better. W^m & MA rid up to Holt Market eveng, drank tea at Mr Bartells, W^m drank tea at Mr Davys, came home even 8.

FEBRUARY 23, SUNDAY A close windy day. Mr Hardy something better. All went to our Church afternoon except M^r H, Mr Burrell preach'd. M^r & Mrs Forster came to our Church & drank tea here . . .

MARCH 1, SATURDAY A fine day. Mr Hardy & I rid up to Holt foornoon to Mr Moores, came home to Dinner. W^m & MA walkd up to Holt Markt afternoon, came home eveng 8.

MARCH 2, SUNDAY A very wet day. All went to our Church foornoon, Mr Burrell preach^d . . .

MARCH 4, TUESDAY A very wet foornoon, fine Aftern. Mr Hardy much as yesterday. W^m at home all day, T Temple drank tea here . . .

MARCH 6, THURSDAY A fine Morng, drisly afternoon. Mr Hardy something better. W^m at home all day. Bro^t Raven & Wife came eveng past 2.

MARCH 7, FRIDAY A very fine day. Sister Raven very ill. Bro^t Raven, I & W^m rid up to Holt foornoon in Brothers Chaise, came home to dinner, Bro^t & Mr Hardy rid out afternoon. M^r & Mrs Sheldrake drank tea & Supt here.

MARCH 8, SATURDAY A very fine morng, cold windy close afternoon. Mr Hardy much as yesterday. W^m & MA rid up to Holt in L Cart Afternoon. MA drank tea at Mrs Jennis^s, W^m at Mrs Fishers, came home e [evening] 8. Bro & Sister Raven went away abt Noon, Sister very poorly.

MARCH 9, SUNDAY A fine day. Mr Hardy much as yesterday. All went to our Church afternoon except M^r H, Mr Burrell preachd. Mr Wade drank tea & Supt here.

MARCH 10, MONDAY A fine day. W^m sett of for Norwich Morng 6 with Mr Wade, came home eveng 7.

MARCH 11, TUESDAY A very wet Morng, fine windy dry afternoon. Mr Hardy finely. Wm Brewd. Maids & Eliz Loades washd 4 Weeks Linnen, got dry & foulded. M^r H, I & MA drank tea at Mr Burrells, M^r & Mrs Sheldrake there . . .

MARCH 13, THURSDAY A fine morng, raind aftern. Mr Hardy much as yesterday. W^m at home all day.

MARCH 14, FRIDAY A windy close day. Mr Hardy much as yesterday. W^m at home all day. Robt Raven came to dinner, went home after tea. M^r & Mrs Temple & R Temple drank tea here, Mr Moore supt here. 2 Soldiers at work in Garden Aftr . . .

MARCH 16, SUNDAY A very fine day. All went to our Church foornoon, Mr Burrell preach'd. W^m & MA walkd to Holt Church afternoon, came home to tea.

MARCH 17, MONDAY A very fine day. Wm Brew'd, Mr Hardy finely. 2 Soldiers at work in Garden Afternoon, Skivens [Skiffins] cutting trees in Garden all day. Miss Wymer & Miss Bartell came foornoon. MA drank tea & Supt at Mr Bartells, met Mrs Raven of Norwich & M^r & Mrs Cutting there, came home even past 10. Mrs Chrismas brought to Bed with a Girl.

MARCH 18, TUESDAY A wet morng, showry day. 2 Soldiers at work in Garden ¾ of a day . . .

MARCH 20, THURSDAY A Wet morng, fine afternoon. 2 Soldiers at work in Garden Afternoon. Mr Hardy & W^m at home all day. M^r & Mrs Smith «of» Clay, J^os Davy, Mr Kendle, Thos Johnson drank tea here.

MARCH 21, FRIDAY A very fine day. Mr Hardy went to Mr Moores at Holt to draw out a Pipe of Wine, dind at the Lion, came home eveng past 6. W^m & MA rid «to» Mr Flowers at Sheringham, dind & drank tea there, came home eveng past 10. Skivens at Garden cutting trees.

MARCH 22, SATURDAY A very fine day. 2 Soldiers at work all day. Mr Hardy finely. W^m went to Holt Mark^t eveng 6, came home past 10.

MARCH 23, SUNDAY A very fine day till even 4 then turnd hasy. Henry Raven went to Whisonsett & came home eveng past 8. We all went to our Church afternoon, Mr Burrell preach'd. Mr Moore drank tea here . . .

MARCH 27, THURSDAY A very fine day. Mr Hardy & W^m at home all day . . .

MARCH 29, SATURDAY A fine morng, wet afternoon. Mr Hardy at home all day. W^m went to Market after the workmen left work.

MARCH 30, SUNDAY A fine day. All went to our Church foornoon, Mr Burrell preach'd. W^m walk'd up to Holt afternoon, was too late for Church, came home to tea. Mr Wade drank tea & Supt here.

MARCH 31, MONDAY A fine day. Wm Brew'd, Mr Hardy at home all day. Mr Moore drank tea & Supt here. Atwood & Skivens at work in Garden all day. Raind in eveng.

APRIL 1, TUESDAY A very fine day. Mr Hardy & W^m at home all day. Atwood & Skivens at work in Garden all day. Wm Supt at Mr Burrells, came home eveng 9.

APRIL 2, WEDNESDAY Fine Morng, wet afternoon. Mr Hardy & W^m at home all day. Atwood at work in Garden foornoon . . .

APRIL 4, FRIDAY Wind very high & Stormy. Mr Hardy & W^m at home all day.

APRIL 6, SUNDAY A Showry day. All went to our Church Afternoon, Mr Burrell preachd . . .

APRIL 9, WEDNESDAY A fine day. M^r H, MA & I went to our Church foornoon. W^m rid to Blakney afternoon, drank tea at Mrs Drosiers, came home eveng 7. M^r, M^rs & Miss Bartell & Mr Wade drank tea here . . .

APRIL 11, FRIDAY A fine day. Atwood in Garden aftern. Mr Hardy & W^m at home all day. A good deal of rain in the Night.

APRIL 12, SATURDAY A Showry day. Mr Hardy at home all day. W^m went to Holt Mark^t Afternoon, came home eveng 10. Henry Raven went to Whisonsett after tea.

APRIL 13, SUNDAY A Cold windy day. All went to our Church foornoon. Mrs Forster drank tea here, Robt Staff dind & Supt here. Henry came home & Robt Raven with him.

APRIL 14, MONDAY A fine warm day. Wm Brewd Porter. Mr Hardy at home all day. Robt Raven went home after tea . . .

APRIL 16, WEDNESDAY A very fine dry day. Mr Hardy at home all day. W^m rid to Edgefield afternoon, came back to Holt & drank tea at Mr Bartells, home eveng past 7 . . .

APRIL 18, *Good Friday* A fine day. All went to our Church foornoon except W^m, Mr Burrell preachd.

APRIL 19, SATURDAY A fine Morng, A Thunder Storm afternoon. Mr Hardy at home all day. W^m & MA rid up to Holt Market after tea, came home eveng past 9.

APRIL 20, *Easter Sunday* A fine day. All went to our Church Afternoon, Mr Burrell preachd . . .

APRIL 22, TUESDAY A very warm dry day. Mr Hardy & W^m at home all day. Atwood at work in Garden . . .

APRIL 25, FRIDAY A very fine warm day. W^m & MA rid up to Holt Fair Afternoon, drank tea at Mr Bartells, came home even 8. Mr Hardy at home all day . . .

APRIL 30, WEDNESDAY A dry cold windy day. Mr Hardy & W^m at home all day . . .

MAY 2, FRIDAY A fine day. Mr Hardy & W^m at home all day . . .

MAY 4, SUNDAY A fine day. All went to our Church Afternoon, Mr Burrell preach'd, Mr Burrell here after tea.

MAY 5, MONDAY A Close cold day. Mr Hardy at home all day, Wm Brew'd.

MAY 6, TUESDAY A close windy day. Mr Hardy & W^m at home all day. Maids & Betty Loades wash'd 4 Weeks «linen». I went to speak to Mrs Burrell after tea.

MAY 7, WEDNESDAY A Showry cold day, wind high. Mr Hardy & W^m at home all day . . .

MAY 10, SATURDAY A very fine morng but cold, a very Showry afternoon. Wm Brew'd. Mr Hardy, I & MA rid up to Holt Mark^t afternoon, drank tea at Mr Sheldrakes, Mr Burrell there.

MAY 11, SUNDAY A dry day but cold. All went to our Church foornoon, Mr Burrell preachd. W^m & Henry went to Holt Church after, came home to tea. W^m rid to Mr Birds of Thornage after tea.

MAY 12, MONDAY A Showry day. Mr Hardy & W^m at home all day.

MAY 13, TUESDAY A fine morng, Showry afternoon. Mr Hardy at home all day. W^m & MA rid to Sheringham, din'd & drank tea at Mr Flowers, came home even past 8.

MAY 14, WEDNESDAY A very fine warm day. Wm Brewd. Mr Hardy at home all day. M^r & Mrs Flower of Sheringham dind & drank tea here . . .

MAY 17, SATURDAY A fine day. Mr Hardy at home all day. I, MA & R [Rose] Raven walk'd up to Holt after tea.

MAY 18, SUNDAY A close day but very little rain. All went to our Church afternoon. M^r & Miss Symonds came from Yarmouth to tea, M^r & Mrs Forster calld after tea. M^r H Chaplin of Blakney Died this morng.

MAY 19, MONDAY A fine day. Mrs Davy, Bett & Susan drank tea here. W^m came home eve 10.

MAY 20, TUESDAY A cold Showry day. Wm Brewd. Mr Hardy, Mr Symonds, Miss S [Symonds], Rose R [Raven] & MA went to Sheringham afternoon, drank tea there, came home even 9, M^r & Mrs Bartell there.

MAY 21, WEDNESDAY A cold close day. Mr Hardy at home all day. Mr Symonds went away after breakfast. W^m & R Raven took a ride after tea. M^r & Mrs Sheldrake drank tea here.

MAY 22, THURSDAY A cold showry day. Mr Hardy at home all day. W^m walk'd up to Holt afternoon, came home to tea. Mr Moore & Mr Wade drank tea & Supt here . . .

MAY 26, MONDAY A chearly day but cold. Mr Hardy at home all day. We all walkd up to Holt afternoon, drank tea at Mr Davys, W^m came for us in L Cart . . .

MAY 30, FRIDAY A cold close day. Mr Hardy & W^m at home all day. Miss Symonds poorly after tea. Skivens at work in Garden.

MAY 31, SATURDAY A very cold Close day. Mr Hardy, I & Miss Symonds rid up to Holt in L Cart, W^m, MA & R Raven walkd, we all drank tea at Mr Bartells. Robt & Phillis Raven came even 6.

JUNE 1, SUNDAY A Cold day. All went to our Church afternoon, Mr Burrell preachd. Miss Symonds was taken with fitts at tea time. Robt & R Raven went away after tea, Henry went with them as far as Fakenham . . .

JUNE 3, TUESDAY A close cold day, an appearance for rain. Mr Hardy at home all day. Maids & Eliz Loades Wash'd 4 weeks linnen. W^m brewd & went up to Holt aftern.

JUNE 4, WEDNESDAY A Close cold day. Mr Hardy & W^m at home all day.

JUNE 5, THURSDAY A close cold day. Mr Hardy & W^m at home all day. Miss Symonds taken with fitts eveng 9 . . .

JUNE 7, SATURDAY A close showry day. W^m brewd. Mr Hardy walkd to Holt Market afternoon, came home eve past 10.

JUNE 8, SUNDAY A fine day. All went to our Church foornoon, Mr Burrell preachd. Miss Symonds poorly. W^m walkd up to Holt afternoon, came home to tea.

The visit to Whissonsett
9–14 June 1794

JUNE 9, TUESDAY A cool dry day. I & W^m sett of for Whisonsett morng 11, took up our Lodging at Mr Goggs.

JUNE 10, TUESDAY A warm dry day. Took a walk to Bro^t Ravens foornoon. Sister Goggs, I & W^m rid to Fakenham afternoon, drank tea at Mr Custances, went home eveng 8 . . .

JUNE 12, THURSDAY A hot dry day. Sister Goggs & I took a ride in the Chaise to Mr Norris s at Stanfield, came back by Horningtoft & spoke to M^r & Mrs Moy.

JUNE 13, FRIDAY A very hot dry day. We dind, drank tea & Supt at Mrs Ravens at the Hall.

JUNE 14, SATURDAY A Showry [shower] in the morng, very hot foornoon, cool afternoon. Took a walk to Bro^t Ravens foornoon, dind & drank tea at Sister Goggs, sett of for home eveng past 5, got home alittle after 8. A very great showr here afternoon did not reach farther then [than] Sherington. N Raven came home with us.

[LETHERINGSETT]

JUNE 15, SUNDAY A fine day but not hot. Mr Symonds came for his daughter eveng 2. All went to our Church afternoon, Mr Burrell preach'd . . .

JUNE 17, TUESDAY A cold dry day. Mr Hardy at home all day. W^m, MA & P [Phillis] Raven rid to Guestwick

afternoon, drank tea at Mr Keelers, came home eveng
10 . . .

JUNE 19, THURSDAY A fine day. Mr Hardy at home all
day. W^m went «to» Sheringham & Albro [Aldborough]
morng past 10, came home eveng 11.

JUNE 20, FRIDAY A dry morng, a fine Showr at noontime.
Mr Hardy at home all day. W^m went up to Holt afternoon, drank tea at Mr Bartells.

JUNE 21, SATURDAY A very fine day. Mr Hardy at home
all day. W^m rid up to Holt Markt, drank tea at Mr Bartells, I & MA walkd up after tea. Nathl Raven came for
his Sister Phillis morng 7, they went away after dinner,
Henry went with them. Mr Wade supt here.

JUNE 22, SUNDAY A hot dry day. We all went to our
Church foornoon, Mr Burrell preachd. Mr Geo^r Wymer
from Norwich, M^r & M^{rs} & Miss Bartell drank tea &
Supt here . . .

JUNE 24, TUESDAY A fine morng, Showry day. Mr Hardy
& I rid to Sheringham in Chaise, W^m & MA on Hors-
back, dind & drank tea at Mr Flowers, came home
eveng past 9.

JUNE 25, WEDNESDAY A fine day. Mr Hardy at home all
day. W^m rid to Hempstead afternoon & came back to
Holt & drank tea at Mr Bartells, came home eveng past
8. Mr Ellis of Cley Supt here.

JUNE 26, THURSDAY A fine day. Mr Hardy at home all day.
W^m went to Holt afternoon, came home to tea . . .

JUNE 28, SATURDAY A fine day. I something better, M^r
Bartell came to see me. Mr Hardy walkd to Holt Mark^t,
came home eveng 9. W^m rid up after tea, came home
eve 9.

JUNE 29, SUNDAY A fine day. MA poorly with a Cold. All
went to our Church Afternoon, Mr Burrell preachd . . .

JULY 1, TUESDAY A Hot day. Mr Hardy & W^m at home
«all» day. Mr Wade supt here.

JULY 2, WEDNESDAY A Hot dry day. Mr Hardy & W^m at
home all day. Mrs Sheldrake drank tea here . . .

JULY 6, SUNDAY A very hot dry day. All went to our
Church foornoon, Mr Burrell preachd, had a Lecture
in eveng. Robt Raven came to dinner, went home evng
8. Mr Wade drank tea & Supt here . . .

JULY 10, THURSDAY A Hot dry day. Mr Hardy poorly
with pain in his side & a Cold. W^m & MA rid up to
Holt in L Cart after tea . . .

JULY 13, SUNDAY An Excesive Hot day. All went to our
Church eveng 6, Mr Burrell preach'd . . .

JULY 15, TUESDAY A very hot dry day. W^m rid to Wells
morng 10, came home eve'g 8. Mr Hardy, I & MA dind
& drank tea at Mr Bakers, Mrs Custance & Mrs Raven
there, came home 9.

JULY 16, WEDNESDAY A very hot day, a small shower
afternoon. Mr Hardy & W^m went to Hildonveston
[Hindolveston] afternoon.

JULY 17, THURSDAY A Hot day. Mr Bakers Family, M^{rs}
Custance, Mrs Raven dind & drank tea here. Sister
Raven, Nathl & Mary came afternoon. Mr Burrell &
Family drank tea here.

JULY 18, FRIDAY A very sultry Morng, Wet afternoon
with Thunder. Mrs Forster & Mrs Herring drank tea

here. Mr Forster & W Herring came eveng 8 from Holt,
went away eveng 10 . . .

JULY 20, SUNDAY A very hot day. All went to our Church
foornoon, Mr Burrell preachd. W^m went to Holt Church
Afternoon, came home to tea . . .

JULY 22, TUESDAY A fine day. Mr Hardy at home all day.
W^m went to Cley afternoon, drank tea at Mr Ellis's,
came home eve 10. M^r, M^{rs} & Miss Hatfield drank tea
here.

JULY 23, WEDNESDAY A fine day. Mr Hardy at home all
day, W^m at home all day. Jo^s Davy drank tea here. I &
MA walkd up to Holt after tea.

JULY 24, THURSDAY A very Showry day. Mr Hardy at
home all day, W^m rid up to Holt after tea. Mr Ellis of
Cley drank tea here . . .

JULY 29, TUESDAY A fine day. Mr Hardy & W^m at home
all day. Mr Burrell had our Chaise to Fulmerston [Ful-
modeston]. We Irond . . .

AUGUST 1, FRIDAY A Close day. Mr Hardy & W^m at home
all day.

AUGUST 2, SATURDAY A Showry foornoon, fine afternoon.
Mr Hardy rid up to Holt foornoon to speak to Marget-
son, came home to dinner. I, W^m & MA walk'd up to
Holt Mark^t, drank tea at Mr Bartells. Mr Sheldrake had
our Cart to Fakenham . . .

AUGUST 5, TUESDAY A fine day. Mr Hardy & W^m at home
all day. I better. Men fetching Coales from Blakney all
day . . .

AUGUST 7, THURSDAY A fine Morng, wet afternoon. Miss
Johnson & a Miss Gills from Thetford calld here foornoon. Mr Moy of Horningtoft at Holt. Mr Hardy & W^m
at home all day.

AUGUST 8, FRIDAY A Cold wet day. MA sett of for Norwich in a returnd Post Chaise with Miss Bartell Morn
past 11. Nathl Raven of Whisonsett & a Mr Watson
of Mileham came morng past 12, dind here, went up
to Holt afternoon. Watson was admitted to «a» small
Estate in Mileham & went home even 6, the others
came home to tea . . .

AUGUST 10, SUNDAY A Cold dry day. We all went to
our Church eveng 6, Mr Burrell preach'd. Mr Macks
Daught^r of Holt was buried.

AUGUST 11, MONDAY A fine dry day. We began Harvest.
Mr Hardy & W^m at home all day. M^r & Mrs Bartell
drank tea here . . .

AUGUST 19, TUESDAY A fine dry day. Mr Hardy & W^m at
home all day. Mr Man of Cley was buried . . .

AUGUST 21, THURSDAY A hot dry day. Mr Hardy & W^m
at home all day.

AUGUST 22, FRIDAY A hot dry day. Mr Hardy at home all
day. W^m rid to Mr Flowers of Sheringham, dind there, rid
to lower Sheringham afternoon, came home eveng 8 . . .

AUGUST 24, SUNDAY A very fine day. M^r & Mrs Seales
came afternoon & went to Church with us & drank tea
here. M^r & Mrs Bartell & Childr^n, M^r & Mrs Forster of
Bayfield came after tea.

AUGUST 25, MONDAY Dry morng, began raining Morng
8, continued Showry all day with Thunder. W^m brewd,
Mr Hardy at home all day . . .

AUGUST 29, FRIDAY A fine day. W^m at home all day. Mr Hardy, I & MA rid up to Holt Afternoon, drank tea at Mr Bartells.

AUGUST 30, SATURDAY A Wet day. Mr Hardy walkd up to Holt Mark^t, drank tea at Mr Davys, came home even 8. W^m rid up to Holt, drank tea at Mr Bartells, came home eveng 10 . . .

SEPTEMBER 1, MONDAY A fine day. Mr Hardy at home all day, W^m brewd.

SEPTEMBER 2, TUESDAY A Showry close Morng, very wet Aftern & Windy. Mr Hardy & W^m at home all day. M^r & Mrs Burrell drank tea here.

SEPTEMBER 3, WEDNESDAY A fine day, wind reather Cold. W^m dind at the Turtle Feast at the Shire House at Holt. Mr Hardy, I & MA walkd up to Holt afternoon, drank tea at Mr Bakers. We all came home eveng 8 . . .

SEPTEMBER 7, SUNDAY A fine day. All went to our Church afternoon, Mr Burrell preachd. W^m walk'd up to Holt after tea to take leave of Math^w Davy, supt there & came home eveng 10.

SEPTEMBER 8, MONDAY A very Stormy day, wind high. Wm Brew'd. Mr Hardy at home all day. Henry Goggs came eveng 5, Slept here.

SEPTEMBER 9, TUESDAY A Cold wet day. Mr Hardy & W^m at home all day. Henry Goggs went away after tea.

SEPTEMBER 10, WEDNESDAY A fine dry day. Mr Hardy, I & MA drank tea at T Temples of Thornage, W^m came to us after tea, Mr Bartells Family there.

SEPTEMBER 11, THURSDAY A fine morng, close afternoon. Mr Hardy & W^m at home all day. M^r & M^rs & Miss Bartell & a Miss Wigg & M^r & Mrs Temple drank tea here.

SEPTEMBER 12, FRIDAY A dry close day. We all drank tea at Mr Bartells of Holt, Wm Supt there, met M^r & Mrs Temple there . . .

SEPTEMBER 14, SUNDAY A fine day. All went to our Church Afternoon, Mr Burrell preach'd & read a Lecture in the eveng. W^m went to Holt Church afternoon, drank tea at Mr Bakers, home past 6 . . .

SEPTEMBER 16, TUESDAY A Cold windy day. Mr Hardy & W^m dind & drank tea at Mr Bartells, came home eveng 7, M^r H eveng 8. Hannah Boone came Morng 10 . . .

SEPTEMBER 18, THURSDAY A very windy day. Mr Hardy & W^m at home all day . . .

SEPTEMBER 21, SUNDAY A very fine day. Robt Raven came to dinner, went home after tea. We all went to our Church Afternoon, Mr Burrcll preach'd.

SEPTEMBER 22, MONDAY A Showry day. Wm Brew'd, Mr Hardy at home all day. T Boyce & J Ram at work in Garden.

SEPTEMBER 23, TUESDAY A very Showry day. Mr Hardy & W^m at home in Morn. T Boyce & J Ram in Garden. M^r H & W^m rid to Gunthorp Afternoon in the Chaise.

SEPTEMBER 24, WEDNESDAY A very Showry day. Mr Hardy sett of for Reepham with M^r & Mrs Bartel in Howards post Chaise Morng half past 6, came home eveng 8. Mr Wade dind here. T Boyce in Garden.

SEPTEMBER 25, THURSDAY A Showry cold day. Mr Hardy & W^m at home all day. T Boyce in Garden.

SEPTEMBER 26, FRIDAY A Cold Showry day. Mr Hardy & W^m at home all day. T Boyce in Garden.

SEPTEMBER 27, SATURDAY A very Showry day. Mr Hardy walkd to Holt Market afternoon. W^m & MA rid up in Chaise, drank tea at Mrs Fishers, came home Eveng 10.

SEPTEMBER 28, SUNDAY A dry day but cold. All went to our Church Afternoon. Mr Burrell preach'd & read a Lecture in the eveng.

SEPTEMBER 29, MONDAY A very fine day. Mr Hardy & I rid to Cley to Manns Sale, din'd at Mr Ellis, came home eveng 8 . . .

OCTOBER 4, SATURDAY A fine Morng but began to rain ab^t 11 & Continued all day. Mr Hardy & W^m rid to Cley foornoon to send home the Goods bought at the Sale, dind at Mr Ellis^s, came to Holt Mark^t aftern, drank tea & Supt at Mr Bartells, came home eveng 11, Edm^d Bartell from Brook.

OCTOBER 5, SUNDAY A fine day but wet eveng. M^r & M^rs & Robt & Mr Edm^d Bartell [junior], Peter & S [Sally] Rouse drank tea, Bartell family Supt here. I, MA & the Ladies went to our Church Afternoon, Mr Burrell preach'd . . .

OCTOBER 7, TUESDAY A Cold chearly day. M^r & Mrs Flower from Sheringham came Morng 10, W^m & MA rid in our Chaise with them to Holkham to see the Hall & Gardens, came home eveng 9, MA very poorly. M^r & Mrs Flower Slept here. Mr Hardy at home all day. A Wet Night.

OCTOBER 8, WEDNESDAY A Chearly day but cold. Mr Hardy & W^m at home all day. M^r & Mrs Flower went away after tea . . .

OCTOBER 12, SUNDAY A fine day. All went to our Church foornoon, Mr Burrell preach'd. W^m came home from Whisonsett Eveng 8 . . .

OCTOBER 14, TUESDAY A mild Showry day. Mr Hardy at home all day. W^m went {went} to Mr Davys of Holt in eveng to speak to John Davy from London . . .

OCTOBER 18, SATURDAY A fine day. Mr Hardy at home all day. 2 Bricklayers at work in Kitchen. W^m & MA rid to Holt Mark^t in Chaise, drank tea at Mr Sheldrakes, came home eveng 9.

OCTOBER 19, SUNDAY A fine day. All went to our Church Afternoon, Mr Burrell preach'd. Mrs Bartell went with Mrs Rouse to Mr Bucks of Sherford [Shereford].

OCTOBER 20, MONDAY A fine day. Mr Hardy & W^m at home all day. 2 Bricklayers at work in Kitchen.

OCTOBER 21, TUESDAY A fine day. Mr Hardy rid to Bayfield to see Mr Forster, he was taken Ill on Sunday, came home to dinner. 2 Bricklayers at work in Kitchen. Thos Johnson Died . . .

OCTOBER 24, FRIDAY A Close day. Mr Hardy at home all day. W^m rid up to Holt afternoon, drank tea at Mr Bartells, came home eveng 8 . . .

OCTOBER 27, MONDAY A very Wet day. W^m rid to Mr Flowers at Sheringham Morn 11, dind & drank tea there, came home eveng 8. Mr Hardy rid to Mr Temples of Thornage, drank tea there . . .

OCTOBER 29, WEDNESDAY A very fine day. Mr Hardy & W^m at home all day, Wm Brewd.

OCTOBER 30, THURSDAY A Wet Morng, dry Afternoon. Mr Hardy & W^m at home all day.

OCTOBER 31, FRIDAY A fine Morng, foggy afternoon. Mr Hardy at home all day. W^m rid to Holt afternoon, drank tea at Mr Bartells, home eveng 7.

NOVEMBER 1, SATURDAY A fine Morng, Rain towards eveng. W^m & MA rid up to Holt Mark^t afternoon, came home eveng 10, they drank tea & Supt at Mr Bartell . . .

NOVEMBER 3, MONDAY A fine Morng, very wet afternoon. Bro^t & Sister Raven came to Dinner, we had engadgd [engaged] to go to Mr Forsters but could not go.

NOVEMBER 4, TUESDAY A fine Morng, very wet afternoon. Bro^t & Sister & MA rid up to Holt foornoon, came back to dinner. Mr Hardy at home all day, Wm Brew'd. Mr Sheldrake drank tea & Supt here. {Wm Brew'd.}

NOVEMBER 5, WEDNESDAY Excesive wet day. Had engadgd to go to Mr Flowers at Sheringham, could not go. Mr Hardy & W^m at home all day, Mr Burrell drank tea here . . .

NOVEMBER 7, FRIDAY A fine day. Bro^t & Sister Raven went away after breakfast. Mr Hardy & W^m at home all day. Raind towards eveng.

NOVEMBER 8, SATURDAY Fine morng, close afternoon. Mr Hardy & I rid up to Holt Mark^t in L Cart. I drank tea at Mr Davys, Mr Hardy & W^m drank tea at Mr Bartells, home eveng 8 . . .

NOVEMBER 11, TUESDAY A fine day. Mr Hardy, I, W^m, MA, M^r & Miss Bartell drank tea at Mr Forsters at Bayfield, home eveng 10.

NOVEMBER 12, WEDNESDAY A very fine day. Mr Hardy & W^m at home all day. M^r & Miss Bartell & Miss Baker drank tea here.

NOVEMBER 13, THURSDAY A very cold day, Wind high, small Storms of Sleet. W^m & MA set of for Whisonset abt Noon in our Chaise, H Rav^n went with them as far as Snoring.

NOVEMBER 14, THURSDAY A close mild day. Mr Hardy at home all day. T Boyce in Garden.

NOVEMBER 15, SATURDAY A fine dry day. Mr Hardy walkd to Holt Mark^t afternoon. W^m & Mary Raven from Whisonsett came home eveng 4, W^m walkd to Holt & came home eveng 8.

NOVEMBER 16, SUNDAY A fine dry day. Mrs Forster came & went to Church with us eveng 4, did not stay to tea.

NOVEMBER 17, MONDAY A Close dry day. Wm Brew^d, Mr Hardy at home all day. T Boyce in Garden . . .

NOVEMBER 19, WEDNESDAY A very dry sharp windy day. Mr Hardy at home all day, went to Mr Burrell in the Eveng, home 8. W^m rid to Weybon [Weybourne] to look at some repairs doing there, from thence to Mr Flowers at Sheringham, drank tea there & came home Eveng past 9. T Boyce in Garden.

NOVEMBER 20, THURSDAY A very Cold dry windy day. Mr Hardy & W^m at home all day. Boyce in Garden.

NOVEMBER 21, FRIDAY A Close mild day. Mr Hardy at home all day. W^m rid to Mr Forsters, drank tea & Supt there, came home eveng past 11.

NOVEMBER 22, SATURDAY A fine dry day. We all walk'd up to Holt afternoon, drank tea at Mr Bartells, came home eveng past 8 in L Cart.

NOVEMBER 23, SUNDAY A foggy day. All went to our Church foornoon, Mr Burrell preach'd. Robt Bartell came afternoon, staid all Night on act of the rain. All went to hear the Lecture in eveng. A deal of rain in the Night.

NOVEMBER 24, MONDAY A wet morng, close foggy aftern. Mr Hardy rid up to Holt aftern, drank tea & Supt with Mr Bartell . . .

NOVEMBER 27, THURSDAY A very fine day. Mr Hardy & W^m at home all day. We Ironed. Mr Chrismas^s Child Christn^d at Holt [Eliza Holley Christmas, publicly].

NOVEMBER 28, FRIDAY A Wet morng, dry day. Mr Hardy & W^m at home all day.

NOVEMBER 29, SATURDAY A fine day. Mr Hardy & W^m walkd up to Holt Mark^t afternoon, came home eveng 9 . . .

DECEMBER 3, WEDNESDAY A Blustering Morng, fine after. Mr Hardy & I rid up to Holt in L Cart after dinner, went to the Sale a little while, came home eveng 4. M^r & M^r [Mrs] & Miss Bartell, M^r, Mrs Sheldrake & Child drank tea & Supt here. Mr Smith of Cley drank tea here.

DECEMBER 4, THURSDAY A very fine day. Mr Hardy at home all day, W^m brewd.

DECEMBER 5, FRIDAY A fine day. Carpenter at work in Kitchen. Mr Hardy at home all day. W^m & M Raven sett of for Whisonsett eveng 1, H Raven went with them as far as Snoring.

DECEMBER 6, SATURDAY A fine day. Mr Hardy rid to Holt Mark^t afternoon, drank tea at Mr Bakers, came home eveng 11.

DECEMBER 7, SUNDAY A very fine day. Mr Hardy, I & H Rav^n went to our Church foornoon, Mr Burrell preach'd. W^m, MA & R [Robert] Raven came home from Whisonsett even 4 . . .

DECEMBER 9, TUESDAY A Wet morng, dry afternoon. W^m at home all day. Mr Ellis of Cley dind here. Mr Hardy rid to Holt with him to a Sale of some Land of the late M^r J Mans, came home eveng past 9.

DECEMBER 10, WEDNESDAY A very fine day. Mr Hardy & W^m rid to Clay to draw of a Pipe of Wine, we had 1 8th [one eighth], came home even past 9.

[[DECEMBER 11, THURSDAY [by Mary Ann Hardy] A fine frosty day. Mr Hardy at home all day, W^m brewed.

DECEMBER 12, FRIDAY A frosty day. Mr Hardy at home all day. W^m rode up to Holt after dinner, drank Tea at Mr Bartells, came home even'g 9 . . .]]

DECEMBER 14, SUNDAY A Close rainy day. We all went to our Church Eveng 4, Mr Burrell preachd . . .

DECEMBER 17, WEDNESDAY A frost, fine day. Mr Hardy at home all day. W^m & MA & Nathl rid to Sheringham, dind & drank «tea» at Mr Flowers, came home half after 8 . . .

DECEMBER 19, FRIDAY A Sharp rime frost, fine day. We all drank tea at Mr Temples of Thornage.

DECEMBER 20, SATURDAY A very sharp rime frost, fine day. H Goggs came to Dinner, went to Holt Mark^t with Mr Hardy, came back to tea, Slept here.

DECEMBER 21, SUNDAY A very sharp frost, fine day. H Goggs went away ab^t Morn 9. We all went to our Church foornoon, Mr Burrell preachd.

DECEMBER 22, MONDAY A fine day but very cold. Mr Hardy & W^m at home all day . . .

DECEMBER 27, SATURDAY A Close drisly day. Mrs Flower went away ab^t Noon. Mr Hardy rid up to Holt foornoon, W^m went to Market afternoon, both came home eveng {eveng} 10.

DECEMBER 28, SUNDAY A fine day. All went to our Church foornoon, a Communion, no Sermon. W^m went to Holt Church Afternoon, drank tea at Mr Bakers, came home eveng 7. H & Nathl Raven went to Whisonsett morn 8 . . .

1795

JANUARY 2, FRIDAY A very sharp rime frost. Mr Hardy at home all day. I poorly, I & W^m rid out for an Airing foornoon. Mrs Burrell came to speak to me in Morn, M^r & Mrs Burrell drank tea here afternoon. Our Men got home some furze from Mr Jodrells.

JANUARY 3, SATURDAY A very sharp frost, fine day. Mr Hardy & W^m walkd to Holt Market, came home eveng 10. I poorly with dimness in my Eyes E7. . .

JANUARY 6, TUESDAY A Sharp frost. Mr Hardy came home Eveng 7, W^m & MA came home from Sheringham Eveng past 8.

JANUARY 7, WEDNESDAY A Close raw day. W^m brewd. Mr Hardy rid up to Holt afternoon to settle Howard«'s» affairs, came home eveng 10. M^r & Mrs Sheldrake drank tea & Supt here.

JANUARY 8, THURSDAY A Close dark day. Mr Hardy at home all day. W^m rid up to Holt in eveng, came home eveng 9 . . .

JANUARY 11, SUNDAY A frost, fine day. No service at our Church. I & H Raven rid to the Meeting at Briston Afternoon. Mr Hardy & W^m walkd to Holt Church, all came home to tea.

JANUARY 12, MONDAY A Sharp frost, close day. Mr Hardy went to Mr Burrells Audit to dinner, came home Morng past 2. W^m & MA drank tea at Mr Johnsons at Holt, came home eveng past 9. Thawd.

JANUARY 13, TUESDAY A Close cold day, no frost. Mr Hardy at home all day. W^m rid to [   ] & from thence to Sheringham, drank tea at Mr Flowers, home eve 9. Kild a large Hogg . . .

JANUARY 15, THURSDAY A Sharp frost. Mr Hardy & W^m at home all day. Miss Ann & Deb^r [Deborah] Johnson,

Miss Jennis & a Miss Dowson dind & drank tea here. Mrs Burrell taken Ill.

JANUARY 16, FRIDAY A severe day, sharp frost & Storms of Sleet. Mr Hardy & W^m at home all day . . .

JANUARY 21, WEDNESDAY Extreme sharp frost, snowd almost all day. Mr Hardy & W^m at home all day. Mary Woodcock was buried.

JANUARY 23, FRIDAY Extreme sharp frost & snowd great part of the day. Mr Hardy & W^m at home all day . . .

JANUARY 25, SUNDAY Sharp frost, bright day. All went to our Church afternoon, Mr Burrell preach'd.

JANUARY 26, MONDAY Very sharp frost, Windy. Mr Hardy & W^m at home all day, Wm Brew^d . . .

JANUARY 28, WEDNESDAY A Sharp frost, snowd all day, extreme bad day. Mr Hardy at home all day, Wm Brew'd.

JANUARY 29, THURSDAY A severe frost. Mr Hardy, I, MA & W^m drank tea & Supt at Mr Bartells, came home past Midnight . . .

FEBRUARY 1, SUNDAY A very sharp frost, snowd great part of the Day. All went to our Church foornoon, Mr Burrell preachd. Roades very Slippery indeed.

FEBRUARY 2, MONDAY A slow thaw, a small Snow almost all day. Mr Hardy at home all day, Wm Brewd. Froze again at Night. Hannah [   ] . . .

FEBRUARY 7, SATURDAY A very sharp frost, close day. Mr Hardy & W^m walkd to Holt Mark^t afternoon, came home eveng 12.

FEBRUARY 8, SUNDAY A fine thaw, the roades very slippery. All went to our Church afternoon, Mr Burrell preachd.

FEBRUARY 9, MONDAY The thaw still continue. Mr Hardy at home all day, Wm Brewd . . .

FEBRUARY 12, THURSDAY A Close reather drisly day. Mr Hardy at home all day. W^m set of for Gunthorp, Fakenham & Whisonsett Morng 11 . . .

The visit to Whissonsett
15–23 February 1795

FEBRUARY 19, THURSDAY Exstreme sharp frost, Wind high. M & A [Mary and Ann] Raven came to Sister Goggs to tea.

FEBRUARY 20, FRIDAY Exstreme sharp frost, wind high & Snowd the greatest part of the day. Mr Goggs rid to Fakenham foornoon, came home to dinner. Mr Hardy drank tea at Bro^t Ravens.

FEBRUARY 21, SATURDAY Exstreme sharp frost, a little snow fell. Mr Hardy & I drank tea at Bro^t Ravens. Cow Calvd . . .

[LETHERINGSETT]

FEBRUARY 26, THURSDAY A Close day. Mr Hardy & MA went to Mr Forsters in our Chaise and New Horse, drank tea there, came home even 10. Wm Brew'd.

FEBRUARY 27, FRIDAY A Close day, wind very cold. Mr Hardy & W^m at home all day.

FEBRUARY 28, SATURDAY A close morng & cold, began to snow before Noon & continued all day. Mr Hardy at home all day. W^m & MA rid to Holt Mark^t aftern in Chaise, drank tea at Mr Sheldrakes, came home eveng 9.

MARCH 1, SUNDAY A fine chearly day. All went to our Church foornoon, Mr Burrell preach'd. I & HR rid to Briston afternoon to the Meeting. W^m walkd up to Holt Church Afternoon, drank tea at Mr Bartells, home eveng 8. Froze sharp at Night.

MARCH 2, MONDAY A close cold day. Mr Hardy drank tea at Mr Burrells, Mrs Forster drank tea here. W^m at home all day . . .

MARCH 5, THURSDAY A Close cold windy day. Mr Hardy & W^m at home all day.

MARCH 6, FRIDAY A drisly Morng, dry afternoon, wind reather high. Mr Hardy at home all day, W^m brew'd. M^r & M^{rs} & Miss Bartell, M^r & Mrs Sheldrake & Child drank tea here. A wet eveng.

MARCH 7, SATURDAY A very cold drisly day. W^m & MA rid to Holt Market, drank tea at Mr Bakers, came home eveng past 8. Mr Hardy at home all day.

MARCH 8, SUNDAY A Chearly day but very cold. I & H Raven rid to Briston afternoon, came home to tea. Mr Hardy, W^m & MA went to our Church Afternoon, Mr Burrell preach'd . . .

MARCH 11, WEDNESDAY A fine Morng, showry afternoon. Mr Hardy at home all day removing Trees in Garden. Mr Edm^d Bartell call^d. W^m & MA drank tea & Supt at Mr Bartells, came home Morn 1.

MARCH 12, THURSDAY A close cold windy day. Mr Hardy & W^m at home all day. I & MA went & spoke to Mrs Burrell, she is better. Snow fell in the Night. I & MA at our Church foornoon.

MARCH 13, FRIDAY A Sharp day. Mr Hardy & W^m at home all day. Mr Seales drank tea here & recon'd. MA very poorly. Snowd in eveng . . .

MARCH 15, SUNDAY Snow deep, thawd, reather chearly Afternoon. All went to our Church foornoon except W^m, Mr Burrell preach'd. W^m & HR went to Holt Church afternoon, came home to tea . . .

MARCH 17, TUESDAY A very cold stormy day. Mr Hardy & W^m at home all day. Robt Staffe came eveng . . .

MARCH 20, FRIDAY A dry chearly day, wind cold. Mr Hardy & W^m at home all day.

MARCH 21, SATURDAY A chearly day. Mr Hardy walkd up to Holt Market afternoon, drank tea at Mr Bartells, came home eveng 11. W^m rid up, drank tea at Mr Bartell, went to the Play, supt at Mrs Fishers, came home eveng 12.

MARCH 22, SUNDAY A very fine day till eveng 3 then turnd hasy & cold. I & H Raven went to Briston Afternoon to meeting, home eveng past 5. Mr Hardy, W^m & MA went to our Church afternoon, Mr Burrell preach'd.

MARCH 23, MONDAY A Close day. Wm Brewd. Mr Hardy at home all day. T Boyce cutting a drain cross [across] the Garden . . .

MARCH 25, WEDNESDAY A close Morng, fine afternoon. Bro^t Raven, Ann, W^m & MA walkd up to Holt foornoon, came home to dinner. Mr Wade din'd & supt here, w«e» all took a ride to Cley afternoon, came home to tea Eveng 7. Mr Hardy poorly.

MARCH 26, THURSDAY A close cold Morng, fine aftern. Bro^t Raven, Daughtr, Nathl Raven went away after dinner, W^m went with them. Mr Hardy poorly.

MARCH 27, FRIDAY A fine day but cold. Mr Hardy rode up to Holt afternoon. I & MA walkd & drank tea at Mr Bakers, came home eveng 7. Mr Secker the Quaker of Holt was buried this foornoon.

MARCH 28, SATURDAY A fine day, wind Cold. Mr Hardy rid «to» Holt Market afternoon, came home eveng 8. I & MA walkd up afternoon, came home to tea. W^m came home eveng past 7.

MARCH 29, SUNDAY A very fine day. All went to our Church afternoon, Mr Burrell preachd. M^r & Mrs Forster came to Church & drank tea here.

MARCH 30, MONDAY A foggy morng, fine day, foggy eveng. Mr Hardy at home all day, W^m brew'd . . .

APRIL 2, THURSDAY A foggy morng, fine day. M Raven went home. Mr Hardy & W^m at home all day.

APRIL 3, FRIDAY A fine day but cold. All went to our Church foornoon, Mr Burrell preachd. W^m & MA rid to Study afternoon before tea . . .

APRIL 8, WEDNESDAY A moist morng, close foggy day. Mr Hardy rid up to Holt foornoon to meet the Justices, came home eveng 2, W^m at home all day. M^r & Mrs Temple, M^r & M^{rs} & Miss Bartell drank tea & Supt here . . .

APRIL 10, FRIDAY A Close Morng, chearly day. Mr Hardy & W^m at home all day, M^r & Mrs Sheldrake drank tea here. Rain fell in the Night. Wm Brew'd . . .

APRIL 13, MONDAY A foggy cold day. Maids & Eliz Woods washd 5 weeks linnen. Mr Hardy, I & MA drank tea at Mr Burrells, M^r & Mrs Robt Garret there. W^m went to Holt afternoon, drank tea at Mr Seales & came to Mr Burrells in eveng.

APRIL 14, TUESDAY A very fine day. Mr Hardy & W^m at home all day.

APRIL 15, WEDNESDAY A fine day. Mr Hardy & W^m at home all day . . .

APRIL 17, FRIDAY A fine day. Mr Hardy & W^m at home all day.

APRIL 18, SATURDAY A Cold windy day. Mr Hardy walkd up to Holt foornoon to the Justice sitting, dind at the Feathers & came home eveng past 9. W^m & MA rid up afternoon in Chaise, drank tea at Mr Davys, came home eveng past 9 . . .

APRIL 20, MONDAY Some small Showers foornoon, fine afternoon. Mr Hardy at home all day, Wm Brew'd.

APRIL 21, TUESDAY A fine day. Mr Hardy & W^m at home all day. M^{rs} & Mary & Susan Davy drank tea here. A small Shower in the eveng . . .

APRIL 23, THURSDAY Fine Morn, some small showers aftern. Mr Hardy & W^m at home all day . . .

APRIL 26, SUNDAY A Windy day & some short storms of rain. All went to our Church foornoon, Mr Burrell preach'd. I went to Briston Meeting aftern, Thos Boyce went with me. W^m went to Holt Church afternoon, drank tea at Mr Seales's . . .

APRIL 28, TUESDAY A Windy day & some Showers. Mr Hardy & W^m at home all day. N Raven & H Rav^n went to the Play at Holt, W^m went to them at 3^d Acct.

APRIL 29, WEDNESDAY Wind high, some showers foornoon, fine afternoon. I & MA drank tea at Mr Forsters,

Henry Raven came for us with the Chaise. N Raven went home after tea. Mr Hardy at home all day, Wm Brew'd.

APRIL 30, THURSDAY A Windy day. Mr Hardy & W^m at home all day.

MAY 1, FRIDAY A Windy day. Mr Hardy & W^m at home all day . . .

MAY 3, SUNDAY A fine day, wind cold. All went to our Church Afternoon, Mr Burrell preach'd. Miss Deb Johnson & 2 Miss Jennis's [Jennises] drank tea here.

MAY 4, MONDAY A fine warm day. Mr Hardy & W^m up to Holt foornoon, came home to dinner. M^r & Mrs Flower of Sheringham dind & drank tea here . . .

MAY 6, WEDNESDAY A very Hot day. Wm Brew'd, Mr Hardy at home all day . . .

MAY 9, SATURDAY A dry cold windy day . . .

MAY 11, MONDAY A very cold windy day. Mr Hardy rid to N Walsham Morn 9, came home eveng past 8, Wm Brewd. MA & M Raven drank tea at Mr Bartells at Holt.

MAY 12, TUESDAY A Cold windy day. Mr Hardy at home all day. W^m, MA & M Raven rid to lower Sherringham, came home eveng 8 . . .

MAY 14, THURSDAY A Cold windy day. Mr Hardy at home all day. MA & MR walkd to Holt afternoon, drank tea at Mr Sheldrakes.

MAY 15, FRIDAY A Cold close day, some small Showers. Mr Hardy & Sister Goggs rid to Mr Forsters in our Chaise, I, M Raven & MA walk'd, drank tea at Mr Forsters . . .

MAY 17, SUNDAY A bright day, wind fresh. I & H Raven went to Briston Meeting afternoon, came back in time & went to Church, Mr Burrell preach'd. Mrs Forster & Wm Herring drank tea here.

MAY 18, MONDAY A dry warm day. W^m went to Southreps foornoon, came back to Mr Flowers of Sheringham to tea, came home eveng 10 . . .

MAY 23, SATURDAY A very hot day & very dry & dusty. We all walk'd to Holt Mark^t afternoon. I & MA drank tea at Mr Davys, Mr Hardy at Mr Bakers. Turnd very Cold in eveng.

MAY 24, *Whit Sunday* A dry cold windy day. I & H Raven went to Briston meeting afternoon, all went to our Church Eveng 6. W^m went to Holt Church afternoon.

MAY 25, MONDAY A very cold windy dry day. Wm Brewd, Mr Hardy at home all day. M & S Davy drank tea here Afternoon.

MAY 26, TUESDAY A very cold dry windy day. W^m & MA set of for Whisonsett Morng past 9, Mr Hardy at home all day. Mr Forster drank tea & Supt here.

MAY 27, WEDNESDAY A very cold day, wind high. Mr Hardy at home all day.

MAY 28, THURSDAY Very cold wind high, small Showers. Mr Hardy at home all day. W^m came home from Whisonett eveng past 8, left MA at Mr Goggs.

MAY 29, FRIDAY A Wet day but very cold & Windy. Wm Brew'd, Mr Hardy at home all day.

MAY 30, SATURDAY A cold dry day. Mr Hardy & W^m walkd to Holt Mark^t Afternoon, came home eveng past 9.

MAY 31, SUNDAY A Windy day, great shows for rain, had only a small Showr ab^t 8 at Night. I & H Raven went to Briston Meeting Afternoon. Mr Hardy & W^m at our Church afternoon, Mr Burrell preachd . . .

JUNE 2, TUESDAY A fine day. W^m at home all day, Mr Hardy drank tea at Mr Burrells.

JUNE 3, WEDNESDAY A dry day, reather cool. Mr Hardy & W^m at home all day, Wm Brew'd.

JUNE 4, THURSDAY A very hot dry day. Mr Hardy & W^m at home all day . . .

JUNE 7, SUNDAY A Close day, wind North & Cold afterno [afternoon]. All went to our Church foornoon, HR & I rid to Briston afternoon to Meeting, came home to tea . . .

JUNE 15, MONDAY A Cold foggy day. Mr Hardy & W^m at home all day. Mr Burrell, Mr Todhunter & Mr Sheldrake drank tea here.

JUNE 16, TUESDAY A bright warm day. We washd 4 Weeks Linnen. Mr Hardy & W^m at home all day . . .

JUNE 25, THURSDAY A fine day. Mr Hardy at home all day. W^m dind & drank tea at Mr Colyers at Gunthorp, came home eveng past 9. A good deal of rain fell in the Night . . .

JUNE 27, SATURDAY A fine day. Mr Hardy walkd to Holt Mark^t Afternoon, drank tea at Mr Bartells, came home eveng pst 11. W^m rid up to Mark^t after tea, came home eveng 9.

JUNE 28, SUNDAY A fine Morng, began to rain Eveng 5, a very wet Eveng. Mr Hardy, MA & W^m went to our Church afternoon, Mr Burrell preachd. I & H Raven went to Briston meeting afternoon, he went to Whisonsett in the Eveng.

JUNE 29, MONDAY A Showry day. W^m at home all day. Mr Hardy walkd up to Holt Aftern, drank tea at Mr Moores, came home Eveng past 8 . . .

JULY 1, WEDNESDAY A fine day till eveng 5 then turnd hasy. Mr Hardy at home all day, Wm Brew'd. Mr Moore & Mr Banyard of Holt dind & drank tea here.

JULY 2, THURSDAY A very fine day. Mr Hardy at home all day. W^m rid to Gunthorp aftern after the Timber, came home eveng 7. I & MA walkd to Bayfield Afternoon, drank tea at Mr Forsters.

JULY 3, FRIDAY A fine day till eveng 6 then raind. Mr Hardy & W^m at home all day, M^r & Mrs Bartell drank tea & Supt here.

JULY 4, SATURDAY A Close cold day. Mr Hardy at home all day. W^m & MA rid up to Holt Mark^t after tea, J Davy & his new Wife at Mr Davys . . .

JULY 7, TUESDAY A dry cold day. Mr Hardy & W^m at home all day. Mr Goggs & his Servt [servant] came Eveng past 9, Slept here . . .

JULY 9, THURSDAY A very cold close windy day. Mr Hardy at home all day. W^m & MA dind & drank tea at Mr Bartells, they expected Mr Edm'd Bartell but he did not come . . .

JULY 11, SATURDAY A Cold Windy close day, very small drisly rain at times. Mr Hardy at home all day, MA dind & drank tea at Mr Davys. I poorly with a Cold.

JULY 12, SUNDAY A Close reather drisley day. I & H Raven went to Briston Meeting afternoon, W^m went to Holt Church afternoon. Mr Hardy & MA went to our Church afterno«o»n, Mr Burrell preachd. Mrs Forster drank tea here . . .

JULY 15, WEDNESDAY A Cold day, raind a little foorn. Mr Hardy & W^m at home all day. Bro^t & Sister Raven, W^m & MA walkd to Holt after tea. I very poorly with A Cold . . .

JULY 17, FRIDAY A drisly Morng, tolerable afternoon. Mr Hardy & W^m at home all day, Bro^t & Sister Raven went away after tea.

JULY 18, SATURDAY A Close cold drisly day. Mr Hardy & W^m went to Holt Market afternoon, came home eveng 9.

JULY 19, SUNDAY A tolerable day. All went to our Church foornoon, Mr Burrell preachd. I & HR went to Briston Meeting Afternoon. Mr Hardy went to Holt Church Afternoon, came home to tea.

JULY 20, MONDAY A very fine «day». Mr Hardy at home all day. Mrs Smith of Cley, Miss Baker, M^r & Miss Man from Holt & Miss Cole drank tea here. W^m rid to Southreps, came home eveng past 9 . . .

JULY 22, WEDNESDAY A Cold Showry day. Wm Brew'd, Mr Hardy at home all day.

JULY 23, THURSDAY A Cold showry day. Mr Hardy & W^m at home all day . . .

JULY 26, SUNDAY A very colose [close] cold day. All went to our Church afternoon, Mr Burrell preachd. Mr Hardy & W^m went to Holt Church afternoon . . .

AUGUST 4, TUESDAY A fine warm day. Mr Hardy & W^m at home all day.

AUGUST 5, WEDNESDAY A very fine day. Our Men fetchd some Hay from Edgefield. M^r & Mrs Forster & Mrs Herring from Norwich drank tea here. Mr Hardy at home all day, W^m rid to Edgefield foornoon & afternoon.

AUGUST 6, THURSDAY A very fine day. Wm Brewd. Mr Hardy rid to Cley Afternoon, came home eveng 6. M^r & Mrs Sheldrake & Mr Smith of Cley drank tea here.

AUGUST 7, FRIDAY A fine day. Mr Hardy, I, W^m & MA drank tea at Mr Forsters of Bayfield.

AUGUST 8, SATURDAY A fine day. MA poorly. Mr Hardy & W^m went to Holt Market, home Eveng 9.

AUGUST 9, SUNDAY A very fine day. I went to Briston Meeting afternoon, took the Boy with me. Mr Hardy, W^m & MA at our Church Afternoon. H Raven went to Whisonsett . . .

AUGUST 11, TUESDAY A Hot dry day. Mr Hardy at home all day. W^m, Nathl & the Girls rid up to Holt after tea . . .

AUGUST 13, THURSDAY A very Hot day. Mr Hardy at home all day, Wm Brew'd . . .

AUGUST 15, SATURDAY A Wet foornoon, dry aftern. Mr Hardy at home all day. Mrs Herring & Mrs Forster drank tea here. W^m & MA rid up to Holt Market afternoon, drank tea [   ].

AUGUST 16, SUNDAY A very fine day. All went to our Church foornoon, Mr Burrell preach'd. I & H Raven

went to Briston afternoon. W^m went to Holt Church afternoon, drank tea at Mr Bartells.

The visit to Whissonsett
17–22 August 1795

AUGUST 17, MONDAY A Close morng, raind ab^t 11 oClock. W^m went to Southreps Morn 6, came home eveng 3. Mr Hardy & I set of for Whisonsett eveng 5, got there Eveng 8, slept at Bro^t Raven . . .

AUGUST 19, WEDNESDAY A fine day. Mr Hardy & Bro^t rid to Mileham & Litcham. I went «to» Sister Goggs foornoon, dind at Bro^t Ravens . . .

AUGUST 22, SATURDAY Fine Morng, showry day. Mr Hardy & I set of for Letheringsett Morng 10, got home Eveng 1. W^m went to Holt Mark^t, came home eveng 8. Raind in eveng . . .

[LETHERINGSETT]

AUGUST 24, MONDAY A Hot day. Bro^t Raven & Mr Fox came to breakfast. M^r & Mrs Crofts, Bro^t, Mr Fox, M^r H, W^m & MA rid to the Camp foornoon, came home eveng past 4, dind, drank tea, Supt & Slept here.

AUGUST 25, TUESDAY A Hot dry day. M^r H, Mr Fox, Bro^t & W^m rid to Blakney foorn, M^r & Mrs Crofts rid to Holt, dind, drank tea & went home Eveng 6.

AUGUST 26, WEDNESDAY A very fine day. Wm Brewd, Mr Hardy at home all day. Maids & Eliz Woods washd 5 Weekes Linnen . . .

AUGUST 28, FRIDAY A fine day. Mr Hardy & W^m at home all day, Mr Faucet dind here . . .

AUGUST 30, SUNDAY A fine day. All went to our Church foornoon, Mr Burrell preachd. I & H Raven went to Briston Meeting afternoon. W^m went to Holt Church afternoon, came home to tea.

AUGUST 31, MONDAY A very fine day. We began Harvest. Mr Hardy, I & MA went in Mr Banyards Chaise to Mr Flowers to dinner & tea, came home eveng past 9. W^m went by Cley & from thence to Sheringham to Dinner.

SEPTEMBER 1, TUESDAY A fine Hot day. Mr Hardy at home all day. W^m went to Southreps, came home eveng 9 . . .

SEPTEMBER 13, SUNDAY A very fine day. All went to our Church foornoon, Mr Burrell preachd. Sister Goggs, I & H Raven rid to Briston afternoon, came home to tea. W^m went to Holt Church afternoon, drank tea at Mr Bartells.

SEPTEMBER 14, MONDAY A fine day. Mr Hardy & W^m at home all day.

SEPTEMBER 15, TUESDAY A very fine day. Mr Hardy & W^m at home all day.

SEPTEMBER 16, WEDNESDAY A very fine day. Mr Hardy at home all day, Wm Brew'd. M^r & Mrs Sheldrake drank tea here.

SEPTEMBER 17, THURSDAY A very fine day. Our Men got up a Stack of Barly. Mr Hardy, I, Sister Goggs & MA went to Bayfield, drank tea at Mr Forsters.

SEPTEMBER 18, FRIDAY A Hot dry day. Mr Hardy & Sister Goggs rid to the Camp afternoon, met MA & I at Mr Bakers at Holt, we drank tea there. W^m at home all day . . .

SEPTEMBER 20, SUNDAY A Hot dry day. Sister Goggs, I & H Raven went to Briston aftern. Mr Hardy & MA went to our Church afternoon, Mr Burrell preachd. W^m went to Holt Church afternoon, young Man [Isaac Mann] drank tea here . . .

SEPTEMBER 22, TUESDAY A Hot dry day. Wm Brewd. Mr Hardy, Sister Goggs, I & MA drank tea at Mr Davys of Holt . . .

SEPTEMBER 24, THURSDAY A fine morng, raind a little Afternoon. W^m & MA went to Sheringham in our Chaise with the Davys, dind & drank tea there, came home eveng past 8. Sister Goggs went away Eveng past 2. Mrs Forster of Bayfield, Mr Jo^n Hering & a Miss Riches drank tea here.

SEPTEMBER 25, FRIDAY A very fine day. Mr Hardy went to Mr Keelers of Gestick [Guestwick] Morng 9, dind & drank tea there, came home Eveng 10.

SEPTEMBER 26, SATURDAY A small Showr foornoon, fine afternoon. Mr Hardy walkd to Holt Mark^t aftern, drank tea at Mr Sheldrakes. W^m rid up & drank tea at Mr Davys, came home Eve 9.

SEPTEMBER 27, SUNDAY A very fine day. All went to our Church foornoon, Mr Burrell preachd. I & H Raven went to Briston.

SEPTEMBER 28, MONDAY A fine day. Wm Brewd, Mr Hardy at home all day . . .

SEPTEMBER 30, WEDNESDAY A fine day. Mr Hardy at home all day. W^m rid to Clay afternoon, came back by Holt, drank tea at Mr Davys.

OCTOBER 1, THURSDAY A dry morng, alittle rain aftern. W^m at home all day. Mr Hardy rid to Cley afternoon to speak to Mr Smith, came home Eveng past 6.

OCTOBER 2, FRIDAY A fine day. Mr Hardy at home all day, Wm Brew'd . . .

OCTOBER 4, SUNDAY A very wet day. All went to our Church afternoon, Mr Burrell preachd.

OCTOBER 5, MONDAY A fine day. W^m sett of for Whisonset Morng 9. Mr Hardy rid to Cley afternoon, drank tea at Mr Smiths, came home eveng 7. Raind in eveng . . .

OCTOBER 8, THURSDAY A close dry morng, very wet Afternoon. W^m at home all day, expected Mr Hardy, did not come.

OCTOBER 9, FRIDAY A fine Morng, very wet afternoon. W^m at home all day. Mr Hardy & MA came home from Norwich eveng past 5 . . .

OCTOBER 11, SUNDAY A very fine day. All went to our Church foornoon, Mr Burrell preach^d. W^m & H Raven went to Holt Church afternoon, W^m came home to tea.

OCTOBER 12, MONDAY A fine day. Mr Hardy & W^m at home all day. Mr John Davy drank tea here.

OCTOBER 13, TUESDAY A very wet day. W^m brewd, Mr Hardy at home all day. M^r & Mrs Sheldrake drank tea here.

OCTOBER 14, WEDNESDAY A showr in the morng, fine day. Mr Hardy at home all day. W^m went to Southreps Morng 6, M^r J Davy went with him, drank tea & Supt at Mr Davys, came home Eveng past 10. A good deal of rain with Thunder in the Night . . .

OCTOBER 16, FRIDAY A Showry day, wind high. Mr Hardy & W^m at home all day.

OCTOBER 17, SATURDAY A very fine day. Mr Hardy at home all day. H Raven went to Whisonset Eveng 6. Gatherd Apples. W^m went to Holt Market . . .

OCTOBER 18, SUNDAY A very wet foornoon, fine aftern. All went to our Church afternoon, Mr Burrell preach'd. M^r & Mrs Forster drank tea here & Miss Richards.

OCTOBER 19, MONDAY A fine morng, close damp afternoon. Mr Hardy & W^m at home all day. M^r & Mrs John Davy & M Davy drank tea here, W^m went home with them & Supt there . . .

OCTOBER 21, WEDNESDAY A fine Morng, close aftern, a Showr of rain abt 5 o Clock. W^m at home all day. Mr Hardy, I & MA walkd up to Holt, drank tea at Mr Bakers, rid home in Chaise . . .

OCTOBER 23, FRIDAY A Wet morng, dry afternoon. Mr Hardy & W^m at home all day.

OCTOBER 24, SATURDAY A very windy & Stormy day. W^m rid to Cley foornoon, went from thence to Holt Mark^t, came home eveng 9. Mr Hardy walkd to Mark^t afternoon, came home eveng 8.

OCTOBER 25, SUNDAY A very fine day. All went to our Church foornoon, Mr Burrell preachd. H Raven & I went to Briston aftern.

OCTOBER 26, MONDAY A fine day. Wm Brewd, Mr Hardy at home all day.

OCTOBER 27, TUESDAY A fine Morng, windy & showry afternoon. Mr Hardy & W^m at home all day . . .

OCTOBER 30, FRIDAY A Windy day. Mr Hardy at home all day. W^m rid to Cley Afternoon, came home to tea . . .

NOVEMBER 1, SUNDAY A dry Windy Morng, Showry Afternoon. All went to our Church afternoon, Mr Burrell preachd. Robt Bartell dind & drank tea here.

NOVEMBER 2, MONDAY A Windy Stormy day. Mr Hardy at home all day. Wm Brew'd . . .

NOVEMBER 4, WEDNESDAY A Showry day. Mr Hardy at home all day.

NOVEMBER 5, THURSDAY A Wet morng, fine day. Mr Hardy at home all day. Gunton Thompson was Married to Ann Starling. Expected W^m home from Norwich, did not come. A great deal of rain in the Night, Wind prodegious high . . .

NOVEMBER 7, SATURDAY A fine day. Mr Hardy at home all day. W^m rid to Holt Market afternoon, came home eveng 10 . . .

NOVEMBER 9, MONDAY A Wet Morng, fine afternoon. Mr Hardy at home all day & poorly. W^m rid to Sheringham foornoon, dind there, came home Even 9.

NOVEMBER 10, TUESDAY A Close day. Mr Woods rider from London here foornoon. Mr Hardy very poorly with the Gout, W^m at home all day . . .

NOVEMBER 12, THURSDAY A Close day. Mr Hardy much as yesterday. W^m & Nathl walkd out foornoon, came home to dinner, rid to Sheringham Afternoon, came home Eveng 9.

NOVEMBER 13, FRIDAY A fine day. Mr Hardy something better. Miss Richards from Mr Forsters dind here, M^r & Mrs Forster drank tea here. M^r & Mrs Sheldrake drank tea & Supt here. N Raven went away after dinner.

NOVEMBER 14, SATURDAY A Close day. Mr Hardy much as yesterday. W^m & MA rid to Holt Mark^t afternoon, MA drank tea at Miss Johnsons, came home eve 9 . . .

NOVEMBER 17, TUESDAY A fine day. Mr Hardy better. MA walk'd up to Holt afternoon, drank tea at Mr Sheldrakes, W^m went for her after tea . . .

NOVEMBER 19, THURSDAY A Wet foornoon, fine afternoon. Mr Hardy at home all day. W^m rid to Sheringham foornoon, came home to dinner. M Raven & Miss Bartell dind, drank tea & Supt here, Deb Johnson drank tea & Supt.

NOVEMBER 20, FRIDAY A frost. Mr Hardy & W^m at home all day. MA walkd to Bayfield foornoon, dind & drank tea at Mr Forsters, HR went for her in Eveng. W^m brew'd . . .

NOVEMBER 22, SUNDAY A Close day, reather Windy. No service at our Church, H Raven & I went to the meeting at Cley afternoon. Raind in Eveng.

NOVEMBER 23, MONDAY A fine day. Mr Hardy at home all day, W^m at home all day.

NOVEMBER 24, TUESDAY A Wet foornoon, a fine afternoon. Wm Brew'd. MA rid up to Holt afternoon, drank tea at Mrs Jennisis. Bro^t & Sister Raven came to tea.

NOVEMBER 25, WEDNESDAY A Close Morng, wet afternoon. W^m & Bro^t Raven went to Holt Fair foornoon, came home to dinner. Mrs Flower from Sheringham dind & drank tea here . . .

NOVEMBER 27, FRIDAY A rime frost. Bro^t & Sister Raven went away aftern [after] dinner, M Raven went to Holt before tea. W^m rid to Sheringham aftern, came home eveng 9. Mr Hardy at home all day.

NOVEMBER 28, SATURDAY A Close foornoon, raind towards night, cleard up & froze in the Night. Mr Hardy at home all day. W^m went to Holt Mark^t afternoon, came home Even past 8 . . .

NOVEMBER 30, MONDAY A Wet day. Mr Hardy at home all day. W^m rid to Cley foornoon, came home to dinner, went up to Holt after tea.

DECEMBER 1, TUESDAY A mild chearly day. Mr Hardy at home all day. W^m rid to Sheringham foornoon, came home eveng 9. Mr Burrell drank tea here.

DECEMBER 2, WEDNESDAY A fild [mild] day & fine. Mr Hardy at home all day, W^m at home all day. Mr John Davy dind here. W^m went with him to Blakney afternoon, W^m came home to tea . . .

DECEMBER 4, FRIDAY A fine day. Wm Brewd, Mr Hardy at home all day.

DECEMBER 5, SATURDAY A drisley Morng, dry afternoon. Mr Hardy walkd up to Holt foornoon, dind at Mr Moores, drank tea at Mr Bartells, came home Eveng 9. W^m, MA & M Raven rid up to Holt Mark^t, drank tea at Mr Davys, came home eveng 9 . . .

DECEMBER 10, THURSDAY A fine dry day. Mr Hardy & W^m at home all day. M^r & Mrs Sheldrake & Child drank tea here.

DECEMBER 11, FRIDAY A fine Morng, hasy afternoon. Mr Hardy at home all day. W^m, MA & M Raven went to Mr Flowers at Sheringham eveng 3.

DECEMBER 12, SATURDAY A drisly Morng, tolerable afternoon. Mr Hardy walkd to Holt Mark^t afternoon, drank tea at Mr Seales's. W^m, MA & M Raven came from Sheringham to Holt aftern, drank tea at Mr Bartells. All came home together Eveng 9 . . .

DECEMBER 14, MONDAY A Wet day. Mr Hardy & W^m at home. We all excep W^m drank tea at Mr Burrells . . .

DECEMBER 26, SATURDAY A very fine day. I & MA walkd up to Holt foornoon, came home to dinner. W^m went to Albro [Aldborough] & Southreps morng 7, came back to Holt Markt even 4. H Raven went to Whissonsett Eveng 6.

DECEMBER 27, SUNDAY A very fine day. I went to Cley afternoon, T Boyce went with me, home to tea. W^m went to Holt Church afternoon, came home to tea. All went to our Church Eveng 6, Mr Burrell preachd. M^r [William] Coe of Holt was buried at Dalling . . .

DECEMBER 29, TUESDAY A fine day. Mr Hardy & W^m at home all day.

DECEMBER 30, WEDNESDAY A very fine day. Mr Hardy at home all day. W^m went to Holt aftern, drank tea at Mr Bakers, came home Eveng past 8.

DECEMBER 31, THURSDAY A Cold Windy day. Mr Hardy at home all Day, Wm Brewd. A Wet Eveng.

1796

JANUARY 1, FRIDAY A fine day. Mr Hardy at home all day, Wm Brewd . . .

JANUARY 4, MONDAY A fine day. Mr Hardy & W^m at home all day. W^m went up to Holt in Eveng . . .

The visit to Whissonsett
4–9 January 1796

JANUARY 6, WEDNESDAY A Wet morng, fine afternoon. Spent the day at Sister Goggs, Bro^t & Sister Raven dind, drank tea & Supt there.

JANUARY 7, THURSDAY A fine day. Dind, drank tea, Supt & slept at Bro^t Ravens . . .

[LETHERINGSETT]

JANUARY 11, MONDAY Fine morng, Wet afternoon. Mr Hardy & W^m at home all day. Miss Wymer & Miss Dewson dind, drank tea, Supt & Slept here.

JANUARY 12, TUESDAY A fine day, Windy. Mr Hardy at home all day, Wm Brew'd. Maids & Betty Milegan Wash«ed» 5 weeks Linnen. Miss Wymer went away after Breakfast.

JANUARY 13, WEDNESDAY A Wet dark day. Mr Hardy & W^m at home all day.

JANUARY 14, THURSDAY A fine day. Mr Hardy at home all day. W^m went to Cromer Morn 10, came home even past 6.

JANUARY 15, FRIDAY A fine day. Mr Hardy at home all day. W^m & MA walkd up to Holt foornoon, came home to dinner. Mr Bartell, Miss Wymer & Miss Dowson drank tea here . . .

JANUARY 18, MONDAY A fine day. Wm Brew'd, Mr Hardy at home all day . . .

JANUARY 20, WEDNESDAY A very fine day. Miss Richard from Mr Forsters dind here. We all drank tea & supt at Mr Bartells at Holt.

JANUARY 21, THURSDAY A fine day, wind high. H Raven went with MA in the Chaise to Mr Custances of Fakenham, he came home eveng past 7. The Quarter Sessions at Holt, W^m upon the Grand Jury, came home eveng past 8. Mr Hardy at Holt untill eveng 5.

JANUARY 22, FRIDAY A fine day. Mr Hardy & W^m at home all day . . .

JANUARY 25, MONDAY A Stormy morng, fine afternoon. Mr Hardy walkd up to Holt foornoon, came home to dinner. Wm Brew'd . . .

JANUARY 29, FRIDAY A very Stormy day. Mr Hardy very lame with the Gout. Miss Wymer & Miss Dewson drank tea here, W^m went to Holt with them in the Chaise after tea.

JANUARY 30, SATURDAY A very fine day. Mr Hardy much as yesterday. W^m went to Holt Mark^t eveng 4, came home even 8 . . .

FEBRUARY 4, THURSDAY A very fine day. Mr Hardy much as yesterday, W^m at home all day. M^r & Mrs Sheldrake drank tea here.

FEBRUARY 5, FRIDAY A Wet morng, fine afternoon. Mr Hardy finely, W^m at home all day.

FEBRUARY 6, SATURDAY A Wet morng, close afternoon. Mr Hardy finely. W^m went to Holt Mark^t afternoon, came home eveng 9 . . .

FEBRUARY 8, MONDAY A very fine day. Mr Hardy very poorly in the Morng, finely afternoon. M^{rs} & Miss Bartell, Miss Wymer & Miss Dewson drank tea here. Wm Brew'd.

FEBRUARY 9, TUESDAY A Close morng, Wet afternoon. Mr Hardy finely, W^m at home all day. Maids & Eliz Milegan washd 4 Weeks Linnen.

FEBRUARY 10, WEDNESDAY A Windy day, some storms of rain. Mr Hardy finely, at home all day, W^m at home all day . . .

FEBRUARY 16, TUESDAY A fine day. Mr Hardy at home all day, W^m came home from Whisonett eveng 7.

FEBRUARY 17, WEDNESDAY A fine day. W^m brew'd, Mr Hardy at home all day. T Boyce in Garden . . .

FEBRUARY 19, FRIDAY A fine foornoon, Wet afternoon. Mr Hardy at home all day. W^m rid to Cromer & Sheringham morng 9, came home even 8. T Boyce in Garden . . .

FEBRUARY 23, TUESDAY A fine day. The Girls & W^m walkd up to Holt foornoon, came home to dinner. Mr Hardy at home all day.

FEBRUARY 24, WEDNESDAY A very fine day, wind Cold. We all drank tea at Mr Bartells, home eve past 8.

FEBRUARY 25, THURSDAY A fine day. Mr Hardy at home all day. W^m & the Girls walkd up to Holt foornoon, came back to dinner. Nathl Raven went away after dinner . . .

FEBRUARY 27, SATURDAY A very cold stormy day. Mrs Flower went away after dinner. Mr Hardy, MA & Miss Custance went to Holt Mark^t, drank tea at Mr Bakers, came home eveng past 8. Storms of Snow in eveng.

FEBRUARY 28, SUNDAY A cold windy day. I, Miss Custance & J Thompson went to Cley meeting afternoon, came home eveng past 5. Snowd in eveng.

FEBRUARY 29, MONDAY A very sharp, frosty, cold, Windy, stormy day. Mr Hardy & W^m at home all day. Snowd in the eveng.

MARCH 1, TUESDAY A sharp frost. Mr Hardy & W^m at home all day.

MARCH 2, WEDNESDAY A Cold stormy day. Mr Hardy & W^m at home all day. Wm Brew'd . . .

MARCH 4, FRIDAY A frost, fine day. Mr Hardy & W^m at home all day. The Girls & W^m walk'd to Mr Temples of Thornage, came home to dinner. Miss Leeke drank tea here . . .

MARCH 12, SATURDAY A fine mild day. Mr Hardy at home all day. Miss Custance dind here, MA walk'd up to «Holt» with her afternoon, drank tea at Mr Bakers . . .

MARCH 14, MONDAY A very fine day. Mr Hardy at home all day. W^m dind & drank tea at Mr Colyers, came home eveng 8. Miss Custance & Miss Baker drank tea here.

MARCH 15, TUESDAY A very fine day. Wm Brew'd, Mr Hardy at home all day . . .

MARCH 17, THURSDAY A very fine warm day. Mr Hardy at home all day. W^m went to N Walsham & Southreps Morng 6, came home even 5. Bro^t Raven & Daughtr Mary came even 6.

MARCH 18, FRIDAY A very fine day. Mr Hardy, W^m, MA, Bro^t Raven & daughtr walkd up to Holt foornoon, came home to dinner, we all except M^r H took a little ride afternoon. Mrs Forster Supt here.

MARCH 19, SATURDAY A very fine day. Bro^t Raven & Daughtr went away after dinner. Wm Brew'd, Mr Hardy at home all day . . .

MARCH 24, THURSDAY A Cold dry day. Carpenters & Bricklayers at work. Mr Bartell & Edm'd Bartell call'd here afternoon. Mr Hardy, W^m & MA went home with them, drank tea & Supt there . . .

MARCH 28, MONDAY A very cold stormy day. Bricklayers & Carpenters at work. Mr Hardy & W^m at home all day . . .

MARCH 31, THURSDAY A fine day. Mr Hardy came home eveng 8, W^m at home all day. Bricklayers & Carpenters at work.

APRIL 1, FRIDAY A very fine day. Wm Brew'd, Mr Hardy at home all day. Bricklayers & Carpenters at work . . .

APRIL 4, MONDAY A very fine mild day. W^m at home all day, Mr Hardy at home all day. Carpenters at work.

APRIL 5, TUESDAY A fine day. Wm Brew'd, Mr Hardy at home all day. Deb Johnson, Miss Bartell, Ann & Rose Raven Dind & drank tea here. Mr Moore dind here, Wm Supt at Mr Moores . . .

APRIL 7, THURSDAY A Cold dry day. Mr Hardy & W^m at home all day. M^r & Mrs Bartell drank tea here.

APRIL 8, FRIDAY A very Cold day. Mr Hardy & W^m at home all day . . .

APRIL 12, TUESDAY A Close Morng, fine afternoon. We washd 5 Weeks Linnen. Wm Brewd, Mr Hardy came home Eveng past 6 . . .

APRIL 16, SATURDAY A very fine day. Wm Brewd Porter & went to Holt Mark^t after tea. Mr Hardy went to Mark^t afternoon, they came home eveng 10. Ann & Rose Raven dind here, MA walkd up to Holt with them, they came home before 8 . . .

APRIL 18, MONDAY A very fine dry day. Bricklayers & Carpenters at work. Mr Hardy & W^m at home all day. I poorly with dimness in my Eyes . . .

APRIL 21, THURSDAY A dry windy day. Mr Hardy & W^m at home all day. M^r & Mrs Baker drank tea here. Ann & Rose Raven came from Holt eveng 7 to stay here.

APRIL 22, FRIDAY A very dry day. Mr Hardy at home all day. I, W^m & MA & R & A Raven walkd to Mr Forsters at Bayfield to tea.

APRIL 23, SATURDAY A very dry warm day. Mr Hardy, W^m & the Girls walkd up to Holt Mark^t afternoon, drank tea at Mr Bartells . . .

APRIL 27, WEDNESDAY A fine day but very dry. Mr Hardy at home all day. W^m & the Girls went to Mr Flowers at Sheringham foornoon, dind & drank tea there, came home Ev 9.

APRIL 28, THURSDAY A very fine day. We walkd to Mr Forsters at Bayfield foornoon, Mrs Forster was not at home. M^r & Mrs Bartell drank tea here.

APRIL 29, FRIDAY A fine day. Mr Hardy & W^m at home all day. M^{rs} & Mary Davy, Miss Bartell, Miss Jennis, Miss Baker, Mr Roxby & a young Gentleman with him drank tea here.

APRIL 30, SATURDAY A dry windy day. Nathl, Ann & Rose Raven went away after dinner. Mr Hardy & W^m walk'd to Holt Market afternoon, came home eveng past 9. A fine rain in the Night.

MAY 1, SUNDAY A fine day. I & JT [John Thompson] went to Cley meeting afternoon. Mr Hardy, W^m & MA went to Holt Church aftern, Old M^r [Revd Bransby] Francis preach'd there. Service at our Church afternoon.

MAY 2, MONDAY A Cold drisly day. Mr Hardy at home all day, Wm Brew'd. M^r & Mrs Forster, M^{rs} & M^r J Herring drank tea here.

MAY 3, TUESDAY A Cold windy day. Mr Hardy & W^m at home all day.

MAY 4, WEDNESDAY A Cold windy day. Mr Hardy & W^m at home all day. Mr Banyard of Holt came in the Eveng. Mr Hardy & W^m went with him to Dobsons, came home even 10.

MAY 5, THURSDAY *Assention day* A Cold dry day, Wind North. Mr Hardy & W^m at home all day.

MAY 6, FRIDAY Reather milder then lately, wind South. Mr Hardy at home all day, W^m walk'd up to Holt after tea.

MAY 7, SATURDAY A Close cold day. We all walk'd up to Holt afternoon. I & MA drank tea at Mr Bakers, came home eveng 8. W^m drank tea at Mr Davy & came home past 9. A Wet Night . . .

MAY 10, TUESDAY A very Showry foornoon, fine aftern. Maids & Eliz Melegan Wash'd 4 Weeks Linnen. Mr Hardy at home all day, W^m drank tea with Miss Leakes at Mr Burrells.

MAY 11, WEDNESDAY A Cold Stormy day. Mr Hardy & W^m at home all day. We Irond.

MAY 12, THURSDAY A Cold stormy day. Mr Hardy & W^m at home all day . . .

MAY 15, *Whit Sunday* A Showry foornoon, fine afternoon. I & J Thompson went to Cley meeting. Mr Hardy, W^m & MA went to our Church afternoon, Mr Burrell preach^d.

MAY 16, MONDAY A fine day but cold. Mr Hardy at home all day. Wm Brewd & walkd up to Holt after tea . . .

MAY 18, WEDNESDAY A fine day but windy. Mr Hardy at home all day. W^m & MA sett of for Whisonsett Morng 10 . . .

The visit to Whissonsett
24–28 May 1796

MAY 25, WEDNESDAY A fine day. All day at Mr Goggs. Brother & Sister Raven dind, drank tea & Supt there.

MAY 26, THURSDAY A fine day. We all dind & drank tea at Bro^t Ravens, we Slept there . . .

[LETHERINGSETT]

JUNE 8, WEDNESDAY A fine day. I somthing better then yesterday. Mr Hardy, W^m & MA rid up to Holt after tea.

JUNE 9, THURSDAY A fine day. Mr Hardy & W^m at home all day.

JUNE 10, FRIDAY A Close day, reather Cold. Mr Hardy & W^m at home all day. I & MA drank tea with Miss Leake at Mr Burrells . . .

JUNE 14, TUESDAY A Close Windy day, A Showr from Even 4 to eveng 7. Mr Hardy & W^m at home all day. Maids & Eliz Melegan Washd 5 Weeks Linnen.

JUNE 15, WEDNESDAY A fine Morng, raind afternoon. Mr Hardy walkd up to Holt after Dinner to se the Artillerary come into Town, drank tea at Mr Bartells. W^m went up foornoon, dind at Mr Davys, drank tea at Mr Bakers. They came home Eveng 8.

JUNE 16, THURSDAY A fine Morng, raind alittle aftern. Mr Hardy & W^m went to Cley foornoon, came home Eveng 4 . . .

JUNE 18, SATURDAY A very fine day. Mr Richd Temple from Basham [Barmer] dind here. Mr Hardy, W^m & MA walkd to Holt Mark^t. MA drank tea at Mr Davys & came home eveng past 8, M^r H & W^m came home eveng 10. Plattons Wife Died ab^t 5 oClock this afternoon.

JUNE 19, SUNDAY A Pleasant day. We all went to our Church foornoon, Mr Burrell preach'd. I & J Thompson went to Cley meeting, came home eveng 6.

JUNE 20, MONDAY A fine day, a Showr afternoon. Wm Brewd. Mr Hardy, I & MA drank tea at Mr Forsters at Bayfield . . .

JUNE 22, WEDNESDAY A drisly Morng, fine day. W^m went to Bramton morng past 8, came home eveng past 9, Mr Hardy at home all day.

JUNE 23, THURSDAY A Close Morng, very fine day. Mr Hardy & W^m at home all day. M^r & Mrs Flower & Miss Golty [Goulty] dind & drank tea here, went home half past 9. Mr Coke of Holkham call«ed» here in eveng . . .

JUNE 26, SUNDAY A Hot day. I & J Thompson went to Cley meeting afternoon. M^r H & MA went to our Church afternoon, Mr Burrell preachd. W^m went to Holt Church, came home to tea . . .

JUNE 29, WEDNESDAY A very fine day. Bro^t Raven & his Daught^r M [Mary] & Mrs Cozens from Norwich came Morng 10. We all went with them afternoon to the Camp at Weyborn & from thence to Lower Sheringham, drank tea there & came home eve 10 . . .

JULY 4, MONDAY A fine day. Mr Hardy after the Hay all day, Wm Brew'd. Mr Sheldrake dind & Supt here, Miss Leake drank tea & Supt here . . .

JULY 6, WEDNESDAY A very Showry day. Mr Hardy at home all day. W^m went to Edgefield foornoon to look after the Hay, dind at Mr Mins's, came home even 2. MA walk'd to Mr Temples of Thornage with Miss Baker & Miss Mack, drank tea there.

JULY 7, THURSDAY A Showry day. Robt & Nathl, Rose & Phillis & M Raven & a Miss Rowdan [Julia Rowden] came to dinner, they walkd up to Holt after tea.

JULY 8, FRIDAY A fine Morng, very Showry afternoon. The young people rid to the Camp & Lower Sheringham foornoon, came home even 2. Mrs Sheldrake, Miss Baker & Miss Mack drank tea here. The young people went home after tea.

JULY 9, SATURDAY A very showry day. Mr Hardy & W^m walk'd to Holt Mark^t afternoon, came home eveng 10.

JULY 10, SUNDAY A Showry day. I & JT went to Cley meeting afternoon, came home to tea. M^r H, MA & H Raven went to our Church afternoon, Mr Burrell preachd.

JULY 11, MONDAY A Showry Morng, fine afternoon. M^r & Mrs Bartell drank tea here. Mr Hardy went after the Hay afternoon, drank tea at Mr Forsters . . .

JULY 13, WEDNESDAY A Wet morng, dry day. W^m at home all day. We Irond & finishd . . .

JULY 16, SATURDAY A hot day. Mr Hardy, I & MA rid up to Holt afternoon, W^m walkd up, we all drank tea at Mr Bartells. I & MA walkd home eveg 8, M^r H & Wm came home eveng 10 . . .

JULY 19, TUESDAY A very Showry day. Mr Hardy & W^m at home all day. Sister Goggs & Son came Eveng 2, Mr Goggs went away after tea.

JULY 20, WEDNESDAY A fine day. Our people stacking Hay at [all] day, Mr Hardy & W^m at home all day.

[JULY 21, THURSDAY *Entry omitted, according to marginal annotation by Mary Ann*] . . .

JULY 23, SATURDAY A Showry day. Mr Hardy & W^m walkd to Holt Mark^t afternoon, came home eveng past 9.

JULY 24, SUNDAY A Wet Morng, fine afternoon. Sister Goggs & I went to Cley meeting aftern, came home to tea. Mrs Smith of Cley sett of for London. Mr Hardy & MA went to our Church afternoon, Mr Burrell preachd. W^m went to Holt Church afternoon, came home to tea.

JULY 25, MONDAY Showry Morng then got out very fine & a very Showry afternoon. H Goggs & a Mr Cook from London came Morng 10. Mr Hardy, I & Sister went with them to the Seaside at Salthouse foornoon, came home to Dinner, they went away after tea.

JULY 26, TUESDAY A fine day. Mr Hardy & W^m at home all day.

JULY 27, WEDNESDAY A fine day. Mr Hardy & W^m at home all day.

JULY 28, THURSDAY A fine day. Mr Hardy & W^m at home all day . . .

JULY 30, SATURDAY A fine day. Mr Hardy & W^m went to Holt Mark^t afternoon, came home eveng past 9 . . .

AUGUST 1, MONDAY A fine day. M^r H poorly. I & Sister & MA drank tea at Mr Bartells of Holt, W^m went up in the eveng & Supt there. Edmd Bartell from Brook there . . .

AUGUST 3, WEDNESDAY A fine morng, showry afternoon. Mr Hardy & W^m at home all day.

AUGUST 4, THURSDAY A Wet morng, fine afternoon. Mr Hardy & W^m at home all day . . .

AUGUST 6, SATURDAY A fine day. Mr Hardy, MA & W^m walkd up to Holt Mark^t afternoon. MA came home eveng 8, they came home eve 10.

AUGUST 7, SUNDAY A fine day. Mr Hardy & MA at our Church afternoon, Mr Burrell preachd. W^m went to Holt Church afternoon, came home to tea. I went to Cley meeting afternoon, came home to tea.

AUGUST 8, MONDAY A Hot dry day. Mr Hardy at home all day, Wm Brew'd. Mrs Temple & a Young Lady & Gentleman came after tea . . .

AUGUST 12, FRIDAY A fine day. Mr Hardy & W^m at home all day. Mary, Sarah & Susan Davy drank tea here.

AUGUST 13, SATURDAY A fine day. Mr Hardy, I & MA rid up to Holt afternoon, drank tea at Mr Davys, came home eveng 8. W^m walk'd up after tea, home eveng 9 . . .

AUGUST 17, WEDNESDAY A fine day. Mr Hardy & W^m at home all day. MA very poorly . . .

AUGUST 20, SATURDAY A very hot day. Mr Hardy & W^m walkd to Holt Mark^t afternoon, came home even 9. MA walkd up after tea, came home even 8 . . .

AUGUST 22, MONDAY A fogg«y» day. Mr Hardy & W^m at home all day. Young Mr Balls dined, drank tea & Supt here.

AUGUST 23, TUESDAY A hot day. Mr Hardy & W^m at home all day. Mrs Sheldrake drank tea here.

AUGUST 24, WEDNESDAY A bright hot day. Mr Hardy dind & drank tea at Mr Bartells. I, W^m & MA drank tea there, Wm Supt there. M^r & Mrs Wymer from Norwich there.

AUGUST 25, THURSDAY A bright hot day. Mr Hardy & W^m at home all day. M^r & Mrs Wymer, M^r & M^rs & Miss Bartell dind & drank tea here. I Poorly with dimness in my Eyes.

AUGUST 26, FRIDAY Fine morng, a Shower afternoon. Mr Hardy & W^m at home all day.

AUGUST 27, SATURDAY A Showry day. Mr Hardy at home all day. W^m went to Holt Mark^t afternoon, came home eveng 9.

AUGUST 28, SUNDAY A very cold windy Showry day. I & JT went to Cley meeting aftern. M^r [Hardy], I, MA & W^m went to our Church foornoon, Mr Burrell preach'd. Mr Hardy poorly, W^m went to Holt Church afternoon. H Raven went to Whisonsett, came home eveng 10 . . .

SEPTEMBER 3, SATURDAY A fine day, our people got in alittle Wheat. Mr Hardy at home all day. W^m went to Holt Mark^t afternoon, drank tea at Mr Bartells, came home eveg 9 . . .

SEPTEMBER 5, MONDAY A fine day, our people got in some Pease. Mr Hardy & W^m at home all «day».

SEPTEMBER 6, TUESDAY A Close dry foornoon, began to rain Eveng 3, A Wet Night. Our people cutting Wheat foornoon & finish'd. Mr Hardy at home all day. W^m went to Holt afternoon with some Bills, came home eveng past 8.

SEPTEMBER 7, WEDNESDAY A fine day. Wm Brewd, Mr Hardy at home all day . . .

SEPTEMBER 14, WEDNESDAY A very fine Harvest day. Mr Hardy & W^m at home all day, I something better then Yesterday . . .

SEPTEMBER 20, TUESDAY A Wet morng, showry afternoon. Maids & Eliz Milegan washd 5 Weeks Linnen. Mr Hardy & W^m at home all day . . .

SEPTEMBER 22, THURSDAY A hasy day. Mr Hardy at home all day, Wm Brewd. Miss Leake drank tea & Supt here. I Bathd.

SEPTEMBER 23, FRIDAY A fine Morng, hasy afternoon. Mr Hardy at home all day. W^m went to Mr Balls, Saxlingham, afternoon, drank tea & Supt there. I Bathd . . .

SEPTEMBER 25, SATURDAY A fine day. Mr Hardy, W^m & MA walkd to Holt Mark^t afternoon. H Raven went for her in the Chaise & Colt, came home eveng 8 . . .

SEPTEMBER 28, WEDNESDAY A fine day. Mr Hardy & W^m at home all day. M^r & Mrs Forster, Mrs Richards & 2 Daughters, M^r & Mrs Baker drank tea here. Wm Brew'd. I Bath'd . . .

OCTOBER 3, MONDAY A fine Morng, close afternoon, raind at Night. W^m rid to Sheringham foornoon, came home eveng 7. Mr Hardy at home all day. I Bathd.

OCTOBER 4, TUESDAY A Close Wet day. Mr Hardy & W^m at home all day. I Bathd.

OCTOBER 5, WEDNESDAY A fine day. Wm Brew'd, Mr Hardy at home all day. M^r & Miss Bartell & Miss Dowson drank tea here. A Wet Night. I Bathd . . .

OCTOBER 8, SATURDAY A Cold close day. Mr Hardy went to Sale foornoon, came home even 3. W^m poorly, walkd to Holt Mark^t afternoon, came home eveng 8. I Bathd.

OCTOBER 9, SUNDAY A Wet Morng, cleard up morn 11 then raind again Eveng 3 till near 5 then cleard up again & was a dry Night. We all went to our Church foornoon, Mr Burrell preachd. I & J Thompson went to Cley meeting afternoon. Bell Leeke drank tea & Supt here . . .

OCTOBER 11, TUESDAY A fine Morng, a Shower ab^t 1 oClock, dry all the rest of the Day. Mr Hardy went to L [Lower] Sheringham foornoon to meet Mr Smith, came home eveng 8. Wm Brew'd. I & MA walkd to Holt Afternoon, drank tea at Mr Sheldrakes, met M^r & Mrs Burrell there. Wm Thackwray went a Shooting with Mr Kendle & dind there. I Bathd.

OCTOBER 12, WEDNESDAY A fine Morng, a Shower ab^t 2 oClock then fine the rest of the Day. W^m rid to Salthouse & Cley afternoon, came home eveng 9. I Bath^d . . .

OCTOBER 15, SATURDAY A very fine day. Mr Hardy & W^m at Holt Mark^t afternoon, came home Eveng 9, Mr Ellis Supt here. I Bathd . . .

OCTOBER 17, MONDAY A very fine day. W^m set of for Wells Morng 9, came home eveng near 9. Mr Hardy at home all day. A good deal of rain in the Night. I Bathd . . .

OCTOBER 19, WEDNESDAY A Showry day. Mr Hardy at home all day, Wm Brewd. I Bathd.

OCTOBER 20, THURSDAY A Wet Morng, fine afternoon. W^m & MA in Chaise & Wm Thack^w set of for Whisonsett Morng 10. Mr Smith of Cley dind here. I Bathd.

OCTOBER 21, FRIDAY A Close dry day. Mr Hardy at home all day poorly with a touch of the Gout. Mr Crafer of Holt here in the afternoon. I Bathd.

OCTOBER 22, SATURDAY A Showry morn, dry day. Mr Hardy rid to Holt Mark^t afternoon, came home eve 6. W^m & Wm Thackwray came home from Whisonset eveng half past 4. I Bathd . . .

OCTOBER 24, MONDAY A very Stormy day. Mr Hardy at home all day. Miss King of Holt was Married to a Mr Powell of Thurning. W^m went to Hildonveston foornoon, from thence to Crowson [Fulmodeston with Croxton] to speak to the Miss Leekes, dind at Mr Sanderfords [Revd Dr Peter Sandiford's], came home eveng 6. I Bathd . . .

OCTOBER 26, WEDNESDAY A stormy Morng, fine day. Mr Hardy at home all day, Wm Brew'd. Mr Moore Supt here. I Bathd.

OCTOBER 27, THURSDAY A very fine day. Mr Hardy & W^m at home all day. M^r T Balls drank tea & Supt here . . .

OCTOBER 29, SATURDAY A Close dry day. Mr Hardy walkd to Holt Mark^t afternoon, came home eveng 7. I & MA walkd up & came home to Tea. W^m came home even^g 5 & walk'd to Holt, came home eve 8 . . .

NOVEMBER 1, TUESDAY Omitted, nothing particular, a Wet Day . . .

The visit to Whissonsett
2–7 November 1796

NOVEMBER 4, FRIDAY A fine day. Sister Goggs better. Sister Raven came & drank tea with us.

NOVEMBER 5, SATURDAY Showry day. Sister Goggs much as Yesterday. M Raven drank tea with us . . .

NOVEMBER 7, MONDAY A very fine day. Bro^t Raven & I sett of for Letheringsett Morng past 10, stopt at Fakenham near an hour & got home eveng past 2. 2 Miss Leakes drank tea here. Mr Hardy at home all day, W^m at home.

[LETHERINGSETT]

NOVEMBER 8, TUESDAY A fine day. Bro^t Raven, W^m & the Girls walkd up to Holt foornoon, came home to dinner. M^r & M^{rs} & M Sheldrake drank tea & Supt here. I Bathd . . .

NOVEMBER 11, FRIDAY A Mild foggy day. Mr Hardy at home all day, W^m at home all day. I Bathd. Henry Raven came home from Whisonsett in the Chaise, left MA there. I Bathd.

NOVEMBER 12, SATURDAY A close dry day. Mr Hardy & I rid up to Holt Mark^t in the Chaise. W^m rid to Salthouse & from thence to Holt Mark^t after^n, we drank tea at the Miss Leakes, came home eveng 8. I Bathd . . .

NOVEMBER 16, WEDNESDAY A Sharp rime frosty Morng, very wet afternoon. Mr Hardy & W^m at home all day.

NOVEMBER 17, THURSDAY A fine morng, very Wet afternoon & night. Mr Hardy & W^m at home all day . . .

NOVEMBER 19, SATURDAY A Showry day. Mr Hardy at home all day. W^m rid to Holt Markt aftern, came home eveng 8.

NOVEMBER 20, SUNDAY A very Wet morng, tolerable aftern. We all went to our Church foornoon, Mr Burrell preach'd. I & Wm Thackwray went to Cley meeting afternoon . . .

NOVEMBER 23, WEDNESDAY A fine morng, close afternoon. Mr Hardy at home all day, Wm Brew'd. I Bathd.

NOVEMBER 24, THURSDAY A fine morng, close afternoon. Mr Hardy at home all day. W^m rid to Sasingham [Saxlingham] aftern, drank tea & Supt at Mr Balls, came home Eveng past 10. I Bathd.

NOVEMBER 25, FRIDAY *Holt fair* A Close day. Mr Hardy & W^m walkd up to Holt foornoon, came home to dinner. Miss Leekes dind, drank tea & Supt here. M^r T Balls dind & supt here, W^m & he walkd up to Holt afternoon, drank tea at Mr Bartells. I Bathd.

NOVEMBER 26, SATURDAY A Close day. Mr Hardy walkd to Holt Mark^t afternoon, came home even 9. W^m dind at Mr Savorys at Bayfield, went from thence to Holt mark^t eveng 4, came home eveng 9. I Bathd.

NOVEMBER 27, SUNDAY A drisly day. I & Wm Thackwray went to Cley meeting foornoon. No service at our Church. Mrs Gay from Hayden [Heydon] was buried at Stody . . .

NOVEMBER 29, TUESDAY A very fine bright day but Cold. Maids & Eliz Milegan Washd 5 weeks Linnen. Mr Hardy went to Blakney with T Temple of Thornage afternoon, drank tea & Supt at Mr Temples, came home past 12. Raind in eveng, Wind high at North, snowd towards morng.

NOVEMBER 30, WEDNESDAY Wind high at North, snowd great part of the day. Mr Hardy at home all day. W^m went to Holt in eveng, came home to supper.

DECEMBER 1, THURSDAY A frost & snowd great part of the day. Mr Hardy & W^m at home all day . . .

DECEMBER 3, SATURDAY A very sharp frost. Mr Hardy & W^m walkd to Holt Mark^t afternoon, came home eveng 9 . . .

DECEMBER 6, TUESDAY A Sharp frost, bright day. Mr Hardy, I & W^m drank tea at Mr Sheldrakes, met M^r & Mrs Bartell there. A sharp night . . .

DECEMBER 8, THURSDAY A sharp frost & snowd great part of the day. Mr Hardy at home all day . . .

DECEMBER 10, SATURDAY A very sharp frost. Mr Hardy & W^m walkd up to Holt Mark^t Afternoon, M^r H came home eveng 7, W^m came home even 9.

DECEMBER 11, SUNDAY A very sharp frosty morng, began to thaw ab^t 11, continued all day & all night. I & JT went to Cley meeting foornoon. Mr Hardy went to our Church afternoon, Mr Burrell preachd. W^m went to Holt Church afternoon, drank tea at Mr Seales. Thos Balls drank tea here . . .

DECEMBER 15, THURSDAY A fine Morng, drisly day. Mr Hardy at home all day. W^m walk'd up to the Heath farm foornoon, came back to dinner . . .

DECEMBER 17, SATURDAY A Close dry day. Mr Hardy walk'd up to Holt Mark^t afternoon, drank tea at Mr Bartells, came home even 7. W^m rid up to Mark^t, drank tea at the Miss Leekes, came home even 9.

DECEMBER 18, SUNDAY A frosty Morng, very close, a very wet afternoon. I, MA, W^m & Wm Thackwray went to our Church foornoon, Mr Burrell preach'd. Mr Hardy poorly with the Gout.

DECEMBER 19, MONDAY A Wet day. Mr Hardy & W^m at home all day . . .

DECEMBER 26, MONDAY A very sharp wind frost. Old Mrs Cobon [Alice, widow of John] from Burnham was buried in this Churchyard. Mr Hardy & W^m sett of for Wells in the Chaise Morng near 10, got home eveng 8.

DECEMBER 27, TUESDAY A very sharp frost, Wind high. Maids & Eliz Milegan washd 4 Weeks Linnen. Mr Hardy & W^m at home all day.

DECEMBER 28, WEDNESDAY A very severe Morng, raind & froze as it came down, in the afternoon turnd to a real thaw. Mr Temple of Thornage drank tea & Supt here . . .

DECEMBER 30, FRIDAY A very mild day, raind foornoon, dry afternoon. Mr Hardy, I, W^m & MA drank tea & Supt at Mr Bartells, came home even 12 . . .

1797

JANUARY 2, MONDAY A dry mild day. Mr Hardy at home all day. W^m rid to Edgefield afternoon with Mr Savory to buy some Lan [?], came home to tea . . .

JANUARY 4, WEDNESDAY A Mild foggy day. Mr Hardy & I rid to the Bullin Farm afternoon. W^m drank tea & Supt at Mr Balls of Saxlingham, came home eveng past 10.

JANUARY 5, THURSDAY A Mild foggy day. Mr Hardy & W^m at home all day.

JANUARY 6, FRIDAY A cold drisly day. Mr Hardy & W^m at home all day. M^rs & S Davy, Miss Howard & Miss Savory from Bayfield drank tea here.

JANUARY 7, SATURDAY A Close dry day. Mr Hardy walkd to Holt Mark^t afternoon, drank tea at Mr Bartells, came home eveng 8. W^m walkd to Holt, drank tea at Miss Leekes, came home eveng 9. A little snow fell in the Eveng.

JANUARY 8, SUNDAY A very cold dry day. I & J Thompson went to Cley meeting foornoon. I, Mr Hardy & W^m went to our Church afternoon. MA very poorly, could not go to Church.

JANUARY 9, MONDAY A sharp frost, close day. Mr Hardy & W^m at home all day. M^r & Mrs Sheldrake drank tea & Supt here . . .

JANUARY 11, WEDNESDAY A Sharp frost, close day. Mr Hardy & W^m at home all day . . .

JANUARY 15, SUNDAY A close dry day. All went to our Church foornoon, Mr Burrell preachd. W^m went to Holt Church afternoon . . .

JANUARY 18, WEDNESDAY A Close drisly day. Mr Hardy & W^m at home all day. M^r & M^rs & Miss Bartell, Mrs Temple, James & Dorithy drank tea & Supt here . . .

JANUARY 20, FRIDAY A Close day. Mr Hardy & W^m at home all day. M^r & Mrs Savory, Miss Howard & Miss Savory drank tea here.

JANUARY 21, SATURDAY A Close day. Mr Hardy & W^m went to Holt Mark^t afternoon, came home eveng 9 . . .

JANUARY 23, MONDAY A Close dry day. W^m sett of Morng 10 for Sheringham, Runton & Cromer were [where] he slept. Mr Hardy at home all day.

JANUARY 24, TUESDAY A Close day, drisly afternoon. MA rid up to Holt & drank tea at Mr Sheldrakes, came home eveng 9. Mr Hardy at home all day.

JANUARY 25, WEDNESDAY A sharp rime frost, very fine day. Mr Hardy at home all day.

JANUARY 26, THURSDAY A rime frost in the morng, thawd all day & close & froze again at Night. Mr Hardy at home all day. W^m came home from Coltishall Eveng past 5 . . .

JANUARY 28, SATURDAY A Close dry foornoon, very wet afternoon. Mr Hardy walkd up to Holt foornoon, drank tea at Mr Davy, came home eveng past 9. W^m rid to Holt Mark^t afternoon, came home eveng past 9.

JANUARY 29, SUNDAY A Wet morng, very fine afternoon. All went to our Church foornoon, Mr Burrell preach'd. I & JT went to Cley meeting afternoon.

JANUARY 30, MONDAY A dark Windy day. Mr Hardy & W^m at home all day.

JANUARY 31, TUESDAY A very stormy morng, wind high, but afterward brightned up to a fine aftern. Mr Hardy & W^m at home all day. Maids & Eliz Milegan washd 5 weeks Linnen.

FEBRUARY 1, WEDNESDAY A close hasy morng, fine aftern. Mr Hardy at home all day. W^m went to Mr Balls, Saxlinham, afternoon, drank tea & Supt there.

FEBRUARY 2, THURSDAY A very fine day. Wm Brew'd. M^r T Balls & Sister & 2 young Ladies came here foornoon. Miss Howard & Miss Savory came here afternoon, did not stay to tea. Mr Hardy at home all day . . .

FEBRUARY 4, SATURDAY A beautiful day. Mr Hardy, I, MA & W^m walkd up to Holt Mark^t aftern, drank tea at Mr Bakers, W^m drank tea at Mr Davys.

FEBRUARY 5, SUNDAY A Close foggy day. I & J Thompson went to Cley meeting foornoon. All went to our Church afternoon, Mr Burrell preach'd. W^m went to Mr Savorys at Bayfield after Church, drank tea & Supt there, came home eve 10.

FEBRUARY 6, MONDAY A Close foggy day. Mr Hardy walkd to Bayfield afternoon, drank tea at Mr Savorys, W^m at home all day. T Balls Junr dind, drank tea & supt here . . .

FEBRUARY 9, THURSDAY A beautifull day. Mr Hardy very poorly. Miss B Leeke, 2 Miss Davys, Miss Howard & Miss Savory from Bayfield drank tea here.

FEBRUARY 10, FRIDAY A Close foggy day. Mr Hardy very poorly. I & MA drank tea at Mr Bakers, met M^r & Mrs Savory, M^r & Mrs Temple, 2 Mrs Custance. W^m came with the Chaise for us . . .

FEBRUARY 13, MONDAY A small rain foornoon, fine afternoon. Mr Hardy at home all day & better. W^m rid to Cley afternoon, came home Eveng 4, he & MA went to Mr Temples of Thornage to tea, met M^r & Mrs Savory.

FEBRUARY 14, TUESDAY A frosty morng, stormy afternoon. Mr Hardy & W^m at home all day. M^r T Balls drank tea & Supt here . . .

FEBRUARY 17, FRIDAY A rime frost, fine day. Mr Hardy & W^m at home all day. Mr Temple drank tea here.

FEBRUARY 18, SATURDAY A very fine day. Mr Hardy rid to Holt afternoon, came home eveng 9. W^m walk'd to Holt afternoon, came home eve 9.

FEBRUARY 19, SUNDAY A very fine day. I & JT went to Cley meeting forenoon, MA & W^m went to our Church afternoon. Mr Hardy poorly with the Gout in his hand. M^r & Mrs Bartell here foornoon . . .

FEBRUARY 21, TUESDAY A rime frost, very fine day. W^m at home all day. Bro^t & Sister & we took a walk afternoon, M^r & Mrs Sheldrake drank tea & supt here. Mr Hardy came home eveng past 9.

FEBRUARY 22, WEDNESDAY A rime frost, very fine day. Wm Brew'd. Bro^t & Sister Raven, Mr Hardy, I & MA drank tea at Mr Sheldrakes. W^m at home all day . . .

FEBRUARY 24, FRIDAY A rime frost, very fine day. Mr Hardy & W^m at home all day. Bro^t & Sister Raven went away after dinner . . .

FEBRUARY 26, SUNDAY A very close foggy day. All went to our Church foornoon, Mr Burrell preachd. I & JT went to Cley meeting.

FEBRUARY 27, MONDAY A rime frost, fine day. Mr Hardy at home all day & poorly, W^m at home all day. M^r & Miss Bartell, Miss Savory & Miss Davy drank tea here . . .

MARCH 3, FRIDAY A very fine day. Mr Hardy at home all day. I & MA walk'd up to Holt afternoon, drank tea at Mr Bartells. W^m walkd up for us & drank tea at Mr Davys, home eveng 7 . . .

MARCH 6, MONDAY A frosty Morng, fine day. Mr Hardy & W^m at home all day. Maids began to Wash 5 Weeks Linnen.

MARCH 7, TUESDAY A frosty morng, very fine day. Maids & Eliz Milegan Wash'd. Mr Hardy & W^m at home all day, W^m very poorly. Mr Bignold & Mr Edwards dind here. Raind in the Night . . .

MARCH 9, THURSDAY A Close cold day. Mr Hardy at home all day. Nathl Raven came to dinner, he & W^m walk'd up to Holt afternoon, came back to tea . . .

MARCH 12, SUNDAY A very cold windy day. All went to our Church foornoon, Mr Burrell preachd. H Raven came home from Whisonsett Eveng 9 . . .

The visit to Whissonsett
13–18 March 1797

MARCH 14, TUESDAY A dry chearly day. I walkd to Mr Goggs foornoon, Sister Goggs dind with us at B [Brother] Ravens. Mr Hardy & Bro^t took a Walk foornoon.

MARCH 15, WEDNESDAY A dry chearly day. We went to Church foornoon & dind, drank tea & supt there [? at Brother Raven's] . . .

MARCH 18, SATURDAY A dry chearly day. I & MR [Mary Raven] walkd to Sister Goggs foornoon, dind at Bro^t Ravens & sett of for home eveng 2, calld at Mr Custances at Fakenham & ariv'd at home eveng 5. N Raven the Younger [from Whissonsett Hall] came home with us . . .

[LETHERINGSETT]

MARCH 21, TUESDAY A dry chearly day. Mr Hardy rid up to Holt Heath afternoon, came home to tea. W^m at home all day . . .

MARCH 25, SATURDAY A Windy day, Wet afternoon. Mr Hardy & W^m at home all day. Bricklayers & Carpenters at Work . . .

MARCH 28, TUESDAY Some small Showers in the Morng, very fine day. I poorly with dimness in my Eyes. W^m & MA sett of for Whisonsett morng past 10, Mr Balls went away. Mr Hardy rid up to Holt Heath Farm after dinner, staid all the Afternoon . . .

MARCH 31, FRIDAY A fine morng, some small showers in the day & a very fine eveng. Mr Hardy went to M^r T Temples at Thornage afternoon to tea, met some Company there, came home even 8. W^m & MA came home from Whisonsett even pst 8.

APRIL 1, SATURDAY A Showry day. Mr Hardy & W^m rid up to Fur Closes foornoon & rid to Holt Farm aftern & came back to Holt Mark^t, came home Eve 8 . . .

APRIL 5, WEDNESDAY A Wet Morng, dry a few hours in the middle of the day & then raind again. Mr Hardy at home all day. W^m finely & went to Bayfield to tea . . .

APRIL 8, SATURDAY A close cold windy day. Mr Hardy & W^m rid up to Holt Farm afternoon & returnd to Holt Mark^t, drank tea at Mr Bartells. I & MA walkd to Holt afternoon, drank tea at Miss Leakes.

APRIL 9, SUNDAY A very Cold close Windy day. We all went to our Church foornoon, no Sermon. M^r & M^{rs} & Miss Forster came to dinner & Slept here.

APRIL 10, MONDAY A Cold close windy day. M^r & M^{rs} & Miss Forster went away about 12 oClock. M [Mr] Hardy at home all day. W^m drank tea at Mr Bartells, met T Balls there . . .

APRIL 15, SATURDAY A Close showry day. Mr Hardy & W^m rid up to Holt Farm & Market & came home Eveng past 9 . . .

APRIL 17, MONDAY A very fine day. Mr Hardy & W^m at home all day. M^r & M^{rs} & M Davy drank tea here . . .

APRIL 19, WEDNESDAY A very Wne day. MA & Wm rid up to Holt foornoon. Mr Hardy at home all day, Mr & Mrs Baker drank tea here . . .

APRIL 21, FRIDAY A very fine day. W^m & MA went to Mr Balls, Saxlinham, to tea. Mr Hardy at home all day.

APRIL 22, SATURDAY A very fine day. Mr Hardy went to Holt foornoon, dind at the Feathers, drank tea at Mr Bartells, came home even past 6. W^m & MA rid up to Holt afternoon, drank tea at Mrs Jennis's, came home even 8 . . .

APRIL 25, TUESDAY A Beautiful day. Mr Hardy & W^m went up to Holt Fair foornoon, came home to dinner, Mr Hardy walkd up again after dinner. M^r T Temple of Blakney dind & drank tea here. I, W^m & MA walkd up to Holt after tea, came home before 8, M^r H came home eveng 8.

APRIL 26, WEDNESDAY A close morng, Wet afternoon & Night. Mr Hardy at home all day. W^m rid to Holt afternoon, drank tea at Mr Bartells, came home eveng 8 . . .

APRIL 28, FRIDAY A fine day. Mr Hardy rid up to Holt farm afternoon & went to Mr Moores, came home eveng 8. W^m rid to fur Closes afternoon & drank tea at Mr Savorys, came home 9 . . .

APRIL 29, SATURDAY A Showry day. Mr Hardy & W^m went to Holt Mark^t after tea, came home Even [ ] . . .

MAY 5, FRIDAY A very Showry foornoon, a fine Afternoon. M^r & Mrs Savory, 2 Miss Howards & a M^r & Mrs Hawkins from Lynn drank tea here. I Bathd.

MAY 6, SATURDAY A Showry morng, fine afternoon. Mr Hardy & W^m rid to Markt aftern in the Cart . . .

MAY 10, WEDNESDAY A very wet foornoon, close hasy aftern. Mr Hardy at home all day . . .

MAY 12, FRIDAY A fine day. Mr Hardy at home all day. Mr Temple of Blakeny drank tea here.

MAY 13, SATURDAY A very fine day. Mr Hardy rid to Holt Mark^t afternoon, came home Eve 9. W^m & MA came home from Mr Forsters Eveng 5. W^m walkd to Holt after tea, came home even 9. I Bathd . . .

MAY 16, TUESDAY A Beautiful day. Maids & Eliz Milegan Washd 6 Weeks Linnen. Mr Hardy & W^m at home all day . . .

MAY 18, THURSDAY A very fine day. Mr Hardy & W^m at home all day, M^r & M^rs & Miss Sheldrake drank tea here . . .

MAY 20, SATURDAY A very fine day, not so hot as yesterday. Mr Hardy at home all day. W^m & MA rid up to Holt Mark^t aftern, drank tea at Mr Davys, home past 8. I Bathd . . .

MAY 22, MONDAY A very fine day. W^m at home all day. Mr Hardy rid to Holt Farm afternoon, M^r T Balls drank tea here. I Bathd . . .

MAY 24, WEDNESDAY A very fine day. Mr Hardy & W^m at home all day. M^r & Mrs Burrell, M^r N Burrell, M^r & Mrs Moy, Mrs Johnson, M^r & Miss Sheldrake drank tea here . . .

MAY 26, FRIDAY A fine day but windy. I Bathd. Mr Hardy & W^m rid up to Holt Farm foornoon, came home to dinner . . .

MAY 28, SUNDAY A very fine day. I & J Thompson went to Cley meeting foornoon. Mr Hardy & MA went to our Church afternoon, Mr Burrell preach'd. W^m went to Holt Church afternoon, came home to tea . . .

MAY 31, WEDNESDAY A fine morng, some very small showers in the day. Mr Hardy at home all day, M^r T Balls here a little while in the Eveng. W^m came home from Whisonsett eveng past 8 . . .

JUNE 3, SATURDAY A very wet day. Mr Hardy at home all day. W^m went to Holt Mark^t afternoon, came home eveng 9 . . .

JUNE 7, WEDNESDAY A fine morng, showry afternoon. Mr Hardy & W^m dind at Mr Bartells. M^r & M^rs & Miss Bartell, M^r & Mrs Wood from London drank tea & Supt here, Mr Smith from Cley drank tea here . . .

JUNE 12, MONDAY A very showry day. Mr Hardy at home all day. W^m sett of for Whissonsett after tea for his Sister. I Bathd.

JUNE 13, TUESDAY A very fine day. Mr Hardy at home all day. W^m & MA came home from Whissonsett eveng 9 . . .

JUNE 15, THURSDAY A close dry day. Mr Hardy at home all day. W^m went to Mr Kendles of Sherinton [Sharrington] afternoon, came home eveng 8. Maids & Eliz Milegan washd 4 Weeks linnen.

JUNE 16, FRIDAY A very fine day. Mr Hardy & W^m went to Sheringham Afternoon, came home even 8. We Irond & finishd.

JUNE 17, SATURDAY A fine day. Mr Hardy at home all day. W^m went to Holt Mark^t afternoon, came home eveng past 9 . . .

JUNE 20, TUESDAY A Showry Morng, close, dry afternoon. Mr Hardy & W^m [   ]. Our Company went away Eveng 6 . . .

JUNE 22, THURSDAY A fine day. Mr Hardy at home all day. W^m & MA drank tea & Supt at Mr Davys, Holt. A very wet Eveng. M^r T Forster of Holt House [at Leziate] & 2 young Herrings from Norwich dind here . . .

JUNE 24, SATURDAY A Showry day. Mr Hardy at home all day. W^m went to Holt Market afternoon, came home eveng 9.

JUNE 25, SUNDAY A Showry day. I & J Thompson went to Cley Meeting foornoon. Mr Hardy, MA & W^m went to our Church afternoon. H Raven came home from Whisonsett eveng past 10 . . .

JUNE 28, WEDNESDAY A fine day till eveng 7 then a heavy Shower. Mr Hardy & W^m at home all day. M [Mary] Sheldrake dind & drank tea here. I Bathd . . .

JUNE 30, FRIDAY A fine day. Mr Hardy & W^m at home all day . . .

JULY 2, SUNDAY A very fine day. I & MA went to our Church foornoon, Mr Burrell preach'd. I & JT went to Cley meeting afternoon, W^m went to Holt Church afternoon, came home to tea. Wm Raven dind here, went to Johnsons, Holt, to tea, supt & Slept here . . .

JULY 5, WEDNESDAY Wet Morng, Showry day. Mr Hardy at home all day. W^m walk'd up to Holt afternoon, drank tea at Miss Leakes. I Bathd . . .

JULY 7, FRIDAY A Showry Morng, dry clos«e» afternoon. Mr Hardy & W^m at home all day. M^r & Miss, M^r & Mrs Edmd Bartell, Mr Moore & his 2 Childr^n dind & drank tea here. I Bathd . . .

JULY 11, TUESDAY A Showry day. Mr Hardy at home all day. W^m went to Mr Bartells afternoon, drank tea there, met Mr Edm^d Bartell.

JULY 12, WEDNESDAY A Showry day. Mr Hardy & W^m at home all day. Mr Sheldrake dind & Supt here . . .

JULY 14, FRIDAY A Hot day. Mr Hardy & W^m makin Hay. M^r & Mrs Sheldrake drank tea here, Mr Ellis of Cley drank tea & Supt here. I Bathd . . .

JULY 16, SUNDAY A very Hot dry day. All went to our Church foornoon, Mr Burrell preachd. I & JT went to Cley meeting afternoon. W^m went to Holt Church afternoon, came home to tea. I Bathd . . .

The visit to Whissonsett
18–22 July 1797

JULY 19, WEDNESDAY A very fine day. Mr Hardy & I walkd up to the Hall foornoon, walkd to Mr Goggs after dinner, came back to Brothers to tea then walkd to Mr Goggs in the Eveng. Mrs Cozens & M Rav^n went to Mr Birds at Rudham to dinner, Mr Cozens came in the Eveng . . .

JULY 21, FRIDAY A very fine day. M^r & Mrs Cozens went away Morng 11. Sister Raven & I walkd to Horningtoft foornoon to speak to Mrs Moy, we drank tea at Sister Ravens at the Hall.

JULY 22, SATURDAY A very fine day. M^r H & I went to speak to Sister Goggs foornoon, dind at Bro^t Ravens, sett of for home even 3, got home eveng 6.

[LETHERINGSETT]

JULY 23, SUNDAY A fine day. I & JT went to Cley meeting foornoon. Mr Hardy, W^m & MA went to our Church afternoon. W^m went to Seaside to bathe.

JULY 24, MONDAY A fine day. Mr Hardy & W^m at home all day. I Bathd . . .

JULY 26, WEDNESDAY A fine day, Hot. I Bathd. Mr Hardy & W^m at home all day . . .

JULY 28, FRIDAY A fine day, not so hot as yesterday. I Bathd. Mr Hardy & W^m went up to the Holt Farm afternoon, came home eveng 7.

JULY 29, SATURDAY A fine day. W^m went to the seaside to bathe. Mr Hardy & W^m rid to Holt Farm & to Mark^t afternoon. I & MA walkd up to Holt & drank tea at Mr Sheldrakes, M^r T Temple & W^m drank tea there.

JULY 30, SUNDAY A very heavy Showr of rain with Thunder & Lightning morng 7 to past 8, a small shower afternoon. We all went to our Church foornoon, Mr Burrell preach'd. I & J Thompson went to Briston meeting afternoon . . .

AUGUST 1, TUESDAY Very heavy Showers accompanyd with Thunder all day. Mr Hardy & W^m at home all day. I Bathd. A dry Night . . .

AUGUST 3, THURSDAY A Showry day. Mr Hardy at home all day & W^m at home all day . . .

AUGUST 9, WEDNESDAY A windy day, some small showers. Mr Hardy & W^m at home all day. I Bathd. Mr Bird of Rudham, M & N Raven from Whisonsett came to tea.

AUGUST 10, THURSDAY A fine day. Mr Hardy at home all day. W^m & MA, Mr Bird, M & N & H Raven went to Sheringham afternoon, came home even 9. M^r C Kendle Supt here.

AUGUST 11, FRIDAY A Showry foornoon. Mr Hardy & W^m at home all day. M^r B [Bird], M & N Raven, W^m & MA rid up to Holt foornoon, they went away after tea. I Bathd . . .

AUGUST 15, TUESDAY A very fine day. M^r G [Goggs] & M^r C [Cook] & W^m took arid [a ride] foornoon, they went away Eveng 3. Mr Hardy at home all day . . .

AUGUST 17, THURSDAY A fine day. W^m went to Sea side to bathe, Mr Hardy at home all day. M^r & Mrs Flower of Sheringham dind & drank tea here, M^r and Mrs Davy drank tea here . . .

AUGUST 19, SATURDAY A Showry day. Mr Hardy walkd up to Holt foornoon, dind at Mr Moores, came home eveng 8. W^m walkd up aftern, came home even 9. I Bathd, W^m went to Sea side to Bathe . . .

AUGUST 21, MONDAY A Showry day. W^m went to Seaside to Bathe, Mr Hardy at home all day. I Bathd.

AUGUST 22, TUESDAY A Showry morng, fine day. Mr Hardy & W^m at home all day. Maids & Eliz Milegan Washd 4 Weeks Linnen.

AUGUST 23, WEDNESDAY A fine day. W^m went to Seaside to Bathe. Mr Hardy & W^m at home all day . . .

AUGUST 26, SATURDAY A fine day. Mr Hardy at home all day. W^m & MA rid to Holt Mark^t afternoon, drank tea at Mr Davys. I Bathd . . .

AUGUST 28, MONDAY Showry day. Mr Hardy & W^m at home. I Bathd . . .

SEPTEMBER 2, SATURDAY A Showry morning, Wind very high, dry afternoon. Mr Hardy at home all day. I Bathd. W^m went to Holt Mark^t afternoon, came home eveng 8 . . .

SEPTEMBER 4, MONDAY A very fine day. Our Men Stack'd the Wheat & some pease, Mr Sheldrake & Thos Youngman at work here. Mr Hardy & W^m at home all day, the Miss Leekes drank tea & Supt here. I Bathd . . .

SEPTEMBER 6, WEDNESDAY A Showry Morng, dry Close afternoon. Men Caring [carrying] Barley aftern. Mr Hardy & W^m at home all day, Mr Mendham repairing the Organ. I Bathd.

SEPTEMBER 7, THURSDAY A fine day. Mr Mindham here. Men carying Barly, Mr Hardy at home all day . . .

SEPTEMBER 11, MONDAY A Wet day. Mr Hardy & W^m at home all day . . .

SEPTEMBER 14, THURSDAY A dry foornoon, Wet afternoon. Mr Hardy at home all day, I Bathd. W^m went to Holt afternoon, drank tea at Mr Bartells, met Edm^d Bartell there. {I Bathd.}

SEPTEMBER 15, FRIDAY Showr ab^t Noon. Mr Hardy rid up to Holt Farm afternoon, W^m at home all day. Raind in the Night . . .

SEPTEMBER 17, SUNDAY A Wet morng, dry day. I & JT went to Cley meeting foornoon. Mr Hardy, W^m & MA went to our Church afternoon, Mr Burrell preachd. Miss Howard drank tea here . . .

SEPTEMBER 20, WEDNESDAY A fine Morng, showry afternoon. Mr Hardy & W^m at home all day. [[[by Mary Ann Hardy] Masons & Carpenters at work.]] I Bathd . . .

SEPTEMBER 22, FRIDAY A very fine day. Mr Hardy up to Holt Farm afternoon, W^m at home all day. 2 Bricklayers & Carpenter at work. I Bathd.

SEPTEMBER 23, SATURDAY A very fine day. Mr Hardy up to Holt Farm afternoon. I & MA went up to Holt Afternoon, drank tea at Mr Bartells . . .

SEPTEMBER 26, TUESDAY A very Wet day. Maids & Eliz Milegan washd 5 Weeks Linnen. Mr Hardy & W^m at home all day.

SEPTEMBER 27, WEDNESDAY A foggy Morng, fine day. Miss Richard went away abt Noon. Mr Hardy & W^m rid up to Holt after dinner to see a Horse race, came home to tea. I Bathd.

SEPTEMBER 28, THURSDAY A fine day. Mr Hardy & W^m at home all day. Bro^t Raven came from Whisonsett eveng past 7 . . .

OCTOBER 3, TUESDAY A fine day. Mr Hardy, I, W^m & MA drank tea at Mr Seales at Holt.

OCTOBER 4, WEDNESDAY A fine day. Mr Hardy & W^m at home all day. I Bath^d . . .

OCTOBER 6, FRIDAY A beautiful day. Mr Hardy & H Raven sett of for Southreps & Cromer Morng past 7, W^m at home all day. I & MA walk'd to speak to Mrs Savory afternoon, came home to tea.

OCTOBER 7, SATURDAY A fine day. Mr Hardy returnd from Cromer Eveng 4, stopt at Holt Mark^t till even 7. W^m walkd up to Holt after tea, came home eveng 9. I Bathd.

OCTOBER 8, SUNDAY A foggy morng, close aftern. All went to our Church foorn, Mr Burrell preach'd. I & MA & J Thompson went to Briston meeting afternoon. W^m went to Holt Church afternoon, drank tea with the Miss Leekes. I Bathd.

OCTOBER 9, MONDAY A fine day. Mr Hardy at home all day, W^m at home. I & MA walkd up to Holt aftern, came home to tea . . .

OCTOBER 11, WEDNESDAY A fine day. Mr Hardy & W^m at home all day . . .

OCTOBER 14, SATURDAY A Windy stormy day. Mr Hardy at home all day. W^m went to Holt Mark^t aftern, came home even 9. I Bathd.

OCTOBER 15, SUNDAY A fine day. I & Lad went to Cley meeting foornoon, Mr Hardy & MA went to our Church afternoon. W^m went to Holt Church afternoon & drank tea at Mr Davy, came home eveng 7.

OCTOBER 16, MONDAY A Close day. Mr Hardy & W^m at home all day. Mr Ellis of Cley drank tea & Supt here. I Bath'd.

OCTOBER 17, TUESDAY A Close day. Mr Hardy & W^m at home all day. I Bathd.

OCTOBER 18, WEDNESDAY A close drisly morng, fine aftern. Mr Hardy & W^m at home all day. I Bathd.

OCTOBER 19, THURSDAY A fine day. Mr Hardy at home all day. W^m went to Holt afternoon to settle some accts [accounts], came home to tea. M^r & Mrs Bartell drank tea here . . .

OCTOBER 21, SATURDAY A very Cold windy day. Mr Hardy at home all day. W^m went to lowr [Lower] Sheringham foornoon, dind at Mr Flowers & came to Holt Mark^t, came home even 8. I Bathd . . .

OCTOBER 23, MONDAY A fine day. Mr Hardy {and} at home all day. W^m rid to Corpusty & Briston, came home even 4. M^r & Mrs Sheldrake & P Raven drank tea here. I Bath'd.

OCTOBER 24, TUESDAY A Wet Morng, showry Day. Maids & Eliz Milegan washd 4 weeks linnen, Mr Hardy & W^m at home all day. Miss Baker & Miss Bartell drank tea here, Mr Myles Custance drank tea here . . .

right A page from Mary Hardy's diary, showing the narrow-columned layout imposed by the use of a commercial ledger for all five MS volumes; the entries cover the period 23–29 Oct. 1797. After a slow process of recovery following her illness of 1793 the diarist has regained her vitality, taking to attending Wesleyan Methodist meetings on Sundays and once more bathing in the garden. Her husband's gout is so debilitating that on 29 Oct. he resolves to cancel his trip to London, Mary Ann taking the seat he had booked in the coach   [*Cozens-Hardy Collection*]

1797

Manuscript ledger 4 (cont.)
21 July 1790–7 May 1800

[LETHERINGSETT]

OCTOBER 31, TUESDAY A very cold windy day. Mr Hardy very poorly with the Gout. I Bathd . . .

NOVEMBER 7, TUESDAY A very foggy day. Mr Hardy much as yesterday . . .

NOVEMBER 9, THURSDAY A very Wne Morng, foggy afternoon. Mr Hardy very bad & full of pain in his foot & knee.

NOVEMBER 10, FRIDAY A beautiful day. Mr Hardy better than yesterday. M^r & Mrs Temple of Thornage drank tea here. I Bathd.

NOVEMBER 11, SATURDAY Mr Hardy worse than yesterday. A beautiful day. I Bathd.

NOVEMBER 12, SUNDAY Mr Hardy continue very poorly, had a bad Night. A very foggy day. I & the Lad went to Cley meeting foornoon.

NOVEMBER 13, MONDAY A very fine day. Mr Hardy somthin [something] better than yesterd«ay». I Bathd . . .

NOVEMBER 16, THURSDAY A beautifull day. Mr Hardy better then yesterd. M^r & Mrs Davy drank tea here . . .

NOVEMBER 18, SATURDAY A very stormy windy day. I Bathd. Mr Hardy much as yesterday. W^m went to Holt Mark^t afternoon, came home even 9. A very stormy night . . .

NOVEMBER 21, TUESDAY A rough wind, some small Storms of rain. Maids & Eliz Milegan washd 4 weeks Linnen. W^m at home all day. Mr Hardy much as yesterday. I Bathd.

NOVEMBER 22, WEDNESDAY A Cold windy Stormy «day». Mr Hardy much as yesterday. W^m went to Mr Savory to tea, Supt there. Wind very high in the Night.

NOVEMBER 23, THURSDAY A good deal of snow fell in the morng, cleard up & frose. Mr Hardy much as yesterday. W^m at home all day.

NOVEMBER 24, FRIDAY A very sharp rime frost. Mr Hardy much as yesterday. W^m at home all Day.

NOVEMBER 25, SATURDAY A Sharp frost, very bright day. Mr Hardy much as yesterday. W^m at Market. Sister Raven from the Hall came to dinner, the Man went home again afternoon. Thawd in the even, a very Wet windy Night . . .

NOVEMBER 28, TUESDAY A Close mild day. Mr Hardy very poorly. Sister Raven & Robt [Raven] went away Morng 11. I Bathd. W^m & MA drank tea at Mr Bakers, came home even 9.

NOVEMBER 29, WEDNESDAY A small rime frost in the morng, Snowd all day & part of the Night. Mr Hardy very bad both feet & both Knees.

NOVEMBER 30, THURSDAY Snow very deep, thaw'd all day. Mr Hardy somthing better than yesterday. W^m at home all day . . .

DECEMBER 3, SUNDAY A sharp rime frost, very fine day. Mr Hardy much better then yesterday. MA went to our Church foornoon, Mr Burrell preachd. W^m & H Raven went to Holt Church afternoon, I & the Boy went to Briston meeting afternoon . . .

DECEMBER 7, THURSDAY A small rime frost, fine day. I Bathd. Mr Hardy finely. Mr Bartell came about Noon to meet Mr Geo^r [George] Wymer of Reepham, he did not come, M^r B dind here. W^m at home all day . . .

DECEMBER 9, SATURDAY A Frosty morng, fine day. Mr Hardy much as yesterday. W^m & MA rid to Holt Markt afternoon, drank tea at Mr Sheldrakes, came home even 9.

DECEMBER 10, SUNDAY A Fosty [frosty] morng, began to snow ½ after 9, continued about 2 hours then thaw'd. I & J Thompson went to Cley meeting in the Morng. MA & W^m went to our Church aftern, Mr Burrell preach'd. Mr Hardy much as yesterday.

DECEMBER 11, MONDAY A small rime frost. Mr Hardy finely. W^m at home all day. Raind afternoon & eveng.

DECEMBER 12, TUESDAY A frosty morng, turn'd to a wet day. Mr Hardy poorly. W^m at home all day.

DECEMBER 13, WEDNESDAY A Sharp frosty morng, thaw'd in the day. Mr Hardy somthing better than yesterday. W^m went to Mr Savorys to tea & supt there . . .

DECEMBER 15, FRIDAY A fine morng, very wet afternoon. Sister Ravens Man came for Phillis, they went away after dinner. W^m drank tea at Mr Bartells, came home even 9. I Bathd.

DECEMBER 16, SATURDAY A Close day, rather windy. Mr Hardy finely. I Bath'd. W^m went to Holt Mark^t, drank tea at Mr Bartells, met Mr Edmd Bartell there, came home even 9 . . .

DECEMBER 18, MONDAY A Close drisly day. Mr Hardy much as yesterday, I poorly . . .

DECEMBER 20, WEDNESDAY A Close day. Mr Hardy finely. W^m at home all day. Bro^t Raven came after 2. I Bathd.

DECEMBER 21, THURSDAY A close day. Mr Hardy finely. W^m at home all day. Bro^t Raven went away after dinner . . .

DECEMBER 23, SATURDAY A Close day. Mr Hardy finely. W^m & MA went to Holt Mark^t afternoon, drank tea at Mrs Jennis's. I Bathd.

DECEMBER 24, SUNDAY A very fine day. I & Boy went to Cley meeting foornoon. MA went to our Church afterno«o»n, Mr Burrell preach'd. W^m went to Holt Church afternoon, came home to tea . . .

DECEMBER 27, WEDNESDAY A fine mild day. Mr Hardy finely. W^m & MA drank tea & Supt at Mr Bartells.

DECEMBER 28, THURSDAY A small rime frost, very fine day. I Bathd. Mr Hardy finely, W^m at home all day. Thos Boyce in Garden . . .

DECEMBER 30, SATURDAY A very fine day. Mr Hardy finely. W^m & MA walk'd up to Holt Mark^t afternoon, drank tea at Mr Davys, Mr Wade came home with them & Slept here. Thos Boyce in Garden. I Bath'd . . .

1798

JANUARY 3, WEDNESDAY A sharp rime frost, very beautiful day. Mr Hardy finely, walkd into Brewhouse & Garden. W^m at home all day.

JANUARY 4, THURSDAY A Close mild day. Mr Hardy finely. I Bath'd. W^m at home all day. MA walk'd to Mr Savorys at Bayfield, drank tea there, W^m went for her in the eveng in the L Cart.

JANUARY 5, FRIDAY A fine mild day. Mr Hardy finely. I Bathd. W^m at home all day . . .

JANUARY 8, MONDAY A Sharp frost, close day. Mr Hardy finely, MA Ill with pain in her teeth & face. W^m at home all day.

JANUARY 9, TUESDAY A black frost, close day. Mr Hardy finely, MA something better. W^m at home all day. Henry Raven came home eveng past 8.

JANUARY 10, WEDNESDAY A Black frost, close day. Mr Hardy finely. W^m at home all day . . .

JANUARY 12, FRIDAY Thawd all day. Mr Hardy finely. W^m rid to Blakney afternoon, came back to Mr Savorys & drank tea there, came home even 8 . . .

JANUARY 22, MONDAY A mild close day. I poorly. Mr Hardy at home all day, W^m at home all day . . .

JANUARY 25, THURSDAY A very fine day. Mr Hardy at home all day. M^r & Mrs Davy & Miss A Howard drank tea here. I Bathd.

JANUARY 26, FRIDAY A sharp rime frost. Mr Hardy at home all day. Thawd towards eveng & raind in the Night.

JANUARY 27, SATURDAY A drisly morng, fine day. Mr Hardy rid to Holt Farm foornoon. W^m & MA came home from Whisons^t to dinner. W^m went to Holt Mark^t afternoon, came home eveng 9. I Bathd . . .

JANUARY 29, MONDAY A Close windy day. Mr Hardy at home all Day. W^m walk'd up to Holt afternoon, drank tea at Mr Davys, came home eveng past 9, M^r & M^{rs} & M Sheldrake drank tea & supt there. I Bathd . . .

JANUARY 31, WEDNESDAY A fine morng, stormy day. I Bathd. Mr Hardy at [and] W^m at home all day.

FEBRUARY 1, THURSDAY A very beautiful day. I & Mr Hardy went to Cley, din'd & drank tea & recond with Mr Smith, came home eveng past 9, W^m at home all day. M^r & M^{rs} & Miss Temple of Thornage drank tea here.

FEBRUARY 2, FRIDAY A fine morng, drisly afternoon. Mr Hardy & W^m at home all day. I Bathd.

FEBRUARY 3, SATURDAY A fine mild day. Mr Hardy at home all day. W^m, MA & P Raven walk'd to Holt Mark^t afterno, drank tea at Mr Bakers, came home even 9 . . .

FEBRUARY 5, MONDAY A rime frost, fine day. Mr Hardy & W^m at home all day. M^r & M^{rs} & Miss Baker & Miss Howard drank tea here . . .

FEBRUARY 8, THURSDAY A rime frost, a beautifull day. I Bathd. Mr Hardy at home all day. MA & PR walkd to Holt afternoon, W^m went for them after tea.

FEBRUARY 9, FRIDAY A rime frost. Mr Hardy & W^m at home all day . . .

FEBRUARY 15, THURSDAY A fine morng, raind alittle afternon. Bro^t & Mr Goggs went to the Sale foornoon, Bro^t came back to dinner, Mr Goggs staid till eveng 5.

FEBRUARY 16, FRIDAY A small frost, a storm or 2 of hail & Snow fell afternoon. M [Mr] Goggs went to Sale foornoon, came home to dinner. Bro^t Ravn, MA, P Rav^n [Phillis Raven] & Miss Cook went to Sale foornoon, came home to dinner, they all went up afternoon, the Sale was over, came home to tea. I Bathd.

FEBRUARY 17, SATURDAY A sharp frost, a squal of snow morn 9. Our friends went away Morn 10 except Miss Cook. Mr Hardy at home all day. W^m went to Holt Mark^t eveng 3, came home eve 8 . . .

FEBRUARY 19, MONDAY A fine day, the snow wasted a good deal. Mr Hardy & W^m at home all day. I Bathd.

FEBRUARY 20, TUESDAY A sharp rime frost. Maids & Eliz Milegan wash'd 5 Weeks Linnen. Mr Hardy & W^m at home all day.

FEBRUARY 21, WEDNESDAY A frost, very fine day. Mr Hardy & W^m at home all day.

FEBRUARY 22, THURSDAY A fine day, no frost. Mr Hardy at home all day. W^m rid to Mr Williams at Thornage after tea in eveng. I Bathd . . .

FEBRUARY 27, TUESDAY A sharp rime frost. Mr Hardy & W^m at home all day. Miss Sarah & Susan Davy drank tea here.

FEBRUARY 28, WEDNESDAY A sharp rime frost, very fine day. Mr Hardy at home all day. W^m went to albro [Aldborough] with Mr Williams of Thornage, came home to tea. Mr Fox & Nathl Raven went to Hempstead to Mr Crafers, came back to Holt in the eveng & slept there.

MARCH 1, THURSDAY A sharp frost, fine day. Mr Hardy & Mr Fox rid to Holt heath Farm afternoon. W^m & N Raven walk'd up to Holt in eveng to Mr Bartells.

MARCH 2, FRIDAY A small rime frost, very fine day. I Bath'd. W^m & Mr Fox & N Raven went to Sheringham foornoon, came home to dinner, Mr Hardy at home all day . . .

MARCH 5, MONDAY A very mild moist morng. I Bathd. Mr Hardy & W^m at home all day . . .

MARCH 8, THURSDAY A very fine mild day. W^m & Mr Goggs walk'd to Mr Savorys at Bayfield foornoon, Mr Goggs & Miss Cook went away eveng 2. Mr Hardy at home all day. I Bathd.

MARCH 9, FRIDAY A beautiful day. Mr Hardy & W^m at home all day. T Boyce in Garden.

MARCH 10, SATURDAY A fine morng, Wet afternoon & Night. Mr Hardy at home all day. I Bath'd. W^m walk'd to Holt Mark^t afternoon, came home eveng 9.

MARCH 11, SUNDAY A cold stormy day. All went to our Church foornoon, Mr Burrell preach'd. I & P Raven & Boy went to Briston meeting afternoon, W^m went to Holt Church afternoon.

MARCH 12, MONDAY A dry chearly day but cold. W^m & P Raven sett of for Whisonsett morng past 9, Mr Hardy at home all day. I & MA walkd to Holt afternoon, drank tea at Miss Leakes . . .

MARCH 16, FRIDAY A fine day, a small frost. Mr Hardy & W^m at home all day.

MARCH 17, SATURDAY A Stormy day. Mr Hardy at home all day. W^m walkd to Holt Mark^t aftern, came home eveng 11. I Bathd. MA very Ill. H Raven went to Whisonsett eveng past 6 . . .

MARCH 20, TUESDAY A cold day. Mr Hardy & W^m at home all day. M & S Davy drank tea here . . .

MARCH 22, THURSDAY A sharp frost. Mr Hardy at home all day. W^m rid [rode] to Barningham [Briningham] foornoon to speak to Mr Bisill, he was not at home, W^m came home to dinner. Mr Hardy & T Boyce in Garden cutting down trees in shrubery.

MARCH 23, FRIDAY A stormy day & very cold. Mr Hardy & T Boyce in Garden. W^m at home all day. I Bathd.

MARCH 24, SATURDAY A cold day, raind afternoon & eveng. I Bathd. Mr Hardy at home all day. W^m walk'd to Holt Mark^t afternoon, drank tea at Mr Bartells & came home eveng 9 . . .

MARCH 27, TUESDAY A cold stormy morng, fine day. Maids & Eliz Milegan washd 5 weeks Linnen . . .

MARCH 29, THURSDAY Reathe [Rather] Stormy day. Mr Hardy at home all day. W^m went to Mr Savorys, drank tea & Supt there.

MARCH 30, FRIDAY A sharp frost, cold day. Mr Hardy at home all day. T Boyce in Garden. W^m, MA & P Rav^n went to Mr Flowers of Sheringham to din«n»er, came home even past 8 . . .

APRIL 3, TUESDAY A Wet morng, dry afternoon. I Bath'd. Mr Hardy & W^m at home.

APRIL 4, WEDNESDAY A Wet foornoon, High wind afternoon. W^m & P Raven went to Cromer Morng pst 8, came home Eveng past 8. Mr Hardy rid to Holt afternoon to speak to Mr Smith of Cley, he was not there, drank tea at Mr Bakers & came home eveng past 8.

APRIL 5, THURSDAY A cold day. Mr Hardy & W^m at home all day. I Bathd . . .

APRIL 7, SATURDAY A fine mild morng, very wet afternoon. Mr Hardy & W^m at home all day. I Bathd . . .

The visit to Whissonsett
10–18 April 1798

APRIL 13, FRIDAY A fine day. M^r H & I, M^r & M^{rs} & Sister Goggs dind, drank tea & Supt at Brot Ravens. Mrs Buskill [Buscall] came to Mr Goggs. M^r & Mrs Temple of Blakney drank tea here [? at Letheringsett], Miss Leakes & T Balls [   ].

APRIL 14, SATURDAY A Windy cold day. I & Mrs Goggs, Mary & Nathl Raven rid to Fakenham foornoon to speak to Mrs Skrimshire & Mrs Custance, came back to dinner. Mrs Raven at the Hall drank tea at Mr Goggs. Mr Eastaugh came in the eveng, slept there . . .

[LETHERINGSETT]

APRIL 19, THURSDAY A fine morng, raind alittle afternoon. Mr Hardy & W^m at home all day. I Bathd. M^r & M^{rs} & Miss Temple drank tea here.

APRIL 20, FRIDAY Cold close windy day. Mr Hardy & I rid to Mr Savorys afternoon, drank tea there. W^m at home all day.

APRIL 21, SATURDAY A Cold day. Mr Hardy & W^m rid to Holt Mark^t afternoon, came home eveng 8. I Bath'd . . .

APRIL 24, TUESDAY A very fine day. Mr Hardy at home all day. M^{rs} & Miss Bartell drank tea here. I Bath'd . . .

APRIL 26, THURSDAY A very fine day. Mr Hardy, I & MA rid up to Holt afternoon. M^r H went to Heath farm, I & MA walk«ed» round by the fairstead & came home to tea. M^r & Mrs Savory calld in the eveng.

APRIL 27, FRIDAY A dry day. Mr Hardy & W^m at home all day. I Bathd.

APRIL 28, SATURDAY A fine day but very dry. W^m & MA walkd up to Holt, drank tea at Mrs Jennis's. Mr Wade came home with them eveng 8, Supt here. I Bath'd . . .

APRIL 30, MONDAY A Close dry day. Maids & Eliz Milegan wash'd 5 Weeks Linnen. Mr Goggs from Whissonsett came foornoon, dind & drank tea here, went away half past 7. MA drank tea & Supt at Miss Leakes, Holt, Wm Supt there. M^r H at home all day . . .

MAY 4, FRIDAY A Close cold day, shows for rain but went of [off]. Mr Hardy at home all day, W^m & MA rid to Mr Savorys to tea. I Bathd M12.

MAY 5, SATURDAY A Cold dry day. Mr Hardy at home all day. W^m walk'd up to Holt Mark^t after tea, came home eveng 9. I Bathd.

MAY 6, SUNDAY A cold day [? dry] day. All went to our Church foornoon, Mr Burrell preachd. I & MA & Boy went to Briston meeting afternoon. A very fine Shower in the eveng. Robt Bartell dind & drank tea here . . .

MAY 8, TUESDAY A fine day. Mr Hardy & W^m at home all day. I Bathd.

MAY 9, WEDNESDAY A fine Morng, 2 little Showers afternoon. Mr Hardy & W^m at home all day . . .

MAY 11, FRIDAY Some small Showers & cold. Mr Hardy & W^m at home all day. T Boyce in Garden. I Bathd.

MAY 12, SATURDAY A Showry day. Mr Hardy at home all day. W^m & MA rid up to Holt Mark^t afternoon, came home even Even past 9. I Bathd. Thos Boyce in Garden . . .

The visit to Whissonsett
15–17 May 1798

MAY 16, WEDNESDAY A Very Showry day. I very poorly with dimness in my Eyes. We drank tea at Bro Raven [Brother Raven's].

MAY 17, THURSDAY A Very Windy day. We went to Whisonsett Church foornoon, M^r [George] Norris read Prayers. Mr Hardy & I sett of for home even 3, calld at Mr Custances & got home eveng 6 . . .

[LETHERINGSETT]

MAY 18, FRIDAY A very fine day. Mr Hardy at home all day. W^m went to Sheringham afternoon, drank tea at Mr Pages, came home even 9. Mr Smith, Cley, drank tea here. Mr Estaugh of Hempton came even 8 & supt & Slept here. I Bathd.

MAY 19, SATURDAY A fine day. Mr Estaugh went away M11. Mr Hardy & MA rid to Holt afternoon, came home even 9. W^m walkd up after tea, came home eveng 9. I Bath'd.

MAY 20, SUNDAY A very fine day. All went to our Church foornoon, Mr Burrell preach'd. I & MA & Boy went to Briston meeting afternoon, W^m went to Holt Church aftern.

MAY 21, MONDAY A fine day. Mr Hardy rid to Cley afternoon to speak to Mr Smith, he was not at home. I & MA walkd up to Holt afternoon, drank tea at Miss Leakes. W^m at home all day. I Bathd.

MAY 22, TUESDAY A very fine day. M^r, I & MA drank tea at Mr Temples at Thornage, Miss Davys there. W^m drank tea at Mr Balls, Saxlinham . . .

MAY 25, FRIDAY A fine day. Mr Hardy & W^m at home all day. I Bathd.

MAY 26, SATURDAY A fine day. Mr Hardy at home all day. I Bathd. Mr Smith of Cley & Mr Ellis came to breakfast. W^m went to Holt Market afternoon, home eve 9 . . .

MAY 31, THURSDAY A Cold day, raind a little towards eveng. Mr Hardy at home all day. I poorly.

JUNE 1, FRIDAY A Cold close day. Mr Hardy at home all day. I very poorly. W^m & MA came home even past 8.

JUNE 2, SATURDAY A fine day. I better then yesterday. Mr Hardy at home all day. W^m went Holt Markt afternoon, came home eveng 9. MA walkd to Holt after tea.

JUNE 3, SUNDAY A very fine day. All went to our Church foornoon, Mr Burrell preachd. W^m went to Holt Church afternoon, came home to tea.

JUNE 4, MONDAY A very warm day. Mr Hardy & W^m at home all day . . .

JUNE 6, WEDNESDAY A fine day, a small showr in the foornoon. Mr Hardy & W^m at home all day.

JUNE 7, THURSDAY A very cool dry day. Mr Hardy & W^m at home all day. I Bathd . . .

JUNE 11, MONDAY A fine day. Mr Hardy & W^m at home all day. Bro^t & Sister Raven from Whisonsett came Eveng 7. I Bathd.

JUNE 12, TUESDAY A fine day. Bro^t & Sister went to speak to Mr Burrell, M^r & Mrs Burrell drank tea here. W^m at home all day . . .

JUNE 14, THURSDAY A very fine day. Bro^t & Sister Raven, Mr Hardy, I & W^m went to Sherringham morng past 9, dind & drank tea there, came home even past 10 . . .

JUNE 20, WEDNESDAY A fine day. M^r & Mrs Moy, M^r & M^{rs} & Widdow & Ann Johnson, M^r & Mrs Burrell paid us a Morning visit. M^r & Mrs Moy went home afternoon. W^m & MA rid to Blakney afternoon, drank tea at Mr Temples & Supt there on acct of a heavy Showr of rain in the eveng, came home even 11. Mr Hardy at home all day. M^r T Balls & Mr Smith drank tea here . . .

JUNE 23, SATURDAY A very fine day. Mr Hardy at home all day. W^m walk'd to Holt Mark^t afternoon, came home eveng past 9. MA & Boy rid to Fakenham morng past 9, dind & drank tea at Mr Skrimshires, came home eveng 10. I poorly with dimness in my Eyes & pain in my Head.

JUNE 24, SUNDAY A very fine day. I & MA went to Cley meeting foornoon. Mr Hardy, MA & W^m went to our Church afternoon, Mr Burrell preach'd . . .

JUNE 29, FRIDAY Extreme Sultry day. A fine Showr afternoon with Thunder not very near. I Bathd. Mr Hardy & W^m at home all day. M^r & Mrs Burrell, Miss A & Miss D Johnson & Miss Nesbit drank tea here . . .

JULY 3, TUESDAY A very fine day. Mr Hardy & W^m at home all day. Ann Raven poorly. {M^r Hardy & W^m at home all day.}

JULY 4, WEDNESDAY A fine day. Mr Hardy & Sister Goggs rid to Holt farm foornoon. W^m & the Girls rid to Mr Savorys afternoon in the Malt Cart, drank tea there. I Bathd.

JULY 5, THURSDAY A Showry day. W^m & the Girls rid to Sheringham afternoon, M^r & Mrs Savory went with them, they come eveng 9, raind very hard in eveng. M^r H at home. I Bathd . . .

JULY 7, SATURDAY A Windy day, Mr Hardy rid to Holt Mark^t aftern. W^m & the Girls walk'd up & drank tea at Mr Davys, came home eveng 9 . . .

JULY 9, MONDAY A Showry day. Mr Hardy at home all day. W^m & MA drank tea & Supt at Mr Burrells, the Girls came here foornoon.

JULY 10, TUESDAY A Showry foornoon, fine afternoon. Maids & Eliz Milegan Washd 5 Weeks linnen. Mr Hardy & W^m at home all day.

JULY 11, WEDNESDAY A Showry day. W^m sett of for Norwich Morng 6, got as far as Edgefield, came back eveng 11 on acct of the rain. M^r H at home all day . . .

JULY 13, FRIDAY A Showry foornoon, fine afternoon. Mr Hardy at home all day. M & A Raven drank tea here, W^m came home eveng 10.

JULY 14, SATURDAY A very wet foornoon, showry afternoon. H Goggs came to dinner. M, A & N Raven went away Eveng 3. Mr Goggs & Mr Hardy rid up to Holt afternoon, came home even 8. W^m walkd up after tea, came home eveng 9 . . .

JULY 17, TUESDAY A fine day. Mr Hardy & W^m at home all day.

JULY 18, WEDNESDAY A fine day. Mr Hardy & W^m at home all day. Mrs Flower of Sheringham & Miss Kettle from Norwich dind & drank tea here, M^{rs} & Miss Bartell drank tea here . . .

JULY 21, SATURDAY A fine day. Mr Hardy & W^m rid to Holt farm & Market afternoon, came home even 8. I Bathd . . .

JULY 23, MONDAY A fine day. Mr Hardy & W^m at home all Day. I Bathd.

JULY 24, TUESDAY A Showry day. Mr Hardy & W^m at home all day . . .

JULY 26, THURSDAY A fine morng, Showry afternoon. Mr Hardy, I & MA rid up to Holt afternoon, drank tea at Miss Leekes. W^m at home all day . . .

JULY 28, SATURDAY A Showry day. Mr Hardy & W^m rid up to Holt Farm & Market after tea, came home eveng 8. Mr Temple of Blakney drank tea here . . .

JULY 31, TUESDAY A very hot dry day. Mr Hardy & W^m at home all day. Miss Jennis drank tea here. I Bathd . . .

AUGUST 3, FRIDAY A fine day. W^m at home all day, Mr Hardy rid up to Holt farm after dinner. M^r & Mrs Savory of Sisted [?Sustead, ?Syderstone (Sistern)] & M^r J Savory of Bayfield drank tea here.

AUGUST 4, SATURDAY A Showry day. Mr Hardy & W^m rid up to Holt farm afternoon & from thence to Holt Mark^t, came home eveng past 8. I Bath'd. Very heavy showers in the Night . . .

AUGUST 9, THURSDAY A fine Morng, a small Shower aftern. Mr Hardy at home all day, W^m at home all day. MA walkd up to Holt after tea, I went to meeting in the Eveng . . .

AUGUST 18, SATURDAY A very fine day. Mr Hardy at home all day. W^m went to Holt Mark^t after tea, came home eveng 9.

AUGUST 19, SUNDAY A very fine day. I & Boy went to Cley meeting foornoon. Mr Goggs from Whisonsett came to Dinner, went home & W^m with him after tea. We all went to our Church afternoon, Mr Burrell preach'd. I poorly with dimness in my Eyes afternoon.

AUGUST 20, MONDAY A very fine day. Mr Hardy at home all day. I but poorly, rid up to fur [Furze] Closes afternoon . . .

AUGUST 24, FRIDAY A very windy dry day. Men got up the rakins [rakings] of 6 Acres [the Six Acres]. W^m & MA drank tea at Mr Savorys of Bayfield. I Bathd.

AUGUST 25, SATURDAY A Stormy Morng, wind very high all day. Mr Hardy at home all day. W^m went to Holt Mark^t afternoon, came home even 9. Mrs Hooper & M^r & Mrs Roberson [Robinson] came to Mr Davys from London . . .

AUGUST 27, MONDAY A fine day. Mr Hardy & W^m at home all day. The Miss Leakes dind, drank tea & Supt here.

AUGUST 28, TUESDAY A fine day. Mr Hardy at home all day. W^m & MA went to Mr Savorys to tea to meet the Davys. I Bathd.

AUGUST 29, WEDNESDAY A very fine day. Mr Hardy & W^m at home all day. M^r & Mrs Roberson, Mrs Hooper, Miss Howard from Bayfield, M^r & S Davy of Holt dind & drank tea here. I Taken poorly with dimness in my Eyes after tea . . .

AUGUST 31, FRIDAY A very fine day. Mr Hardy & I rid up to Holt farm afternoon, Mrs Bartell came home with us, drank tea here, Miss Bartell drank tea here. I Bathd . . .

SEPTEMBER 2, SUNDAY A very fine day. I & Boy went to Cley meeting foornoon. Mr Hardy, W^m & MA went to our Church afternoon . . .

The visit to Whissonsett
3–8 September 1798

SEPTEMBER 4, TUESDAY A Close windy day. Sister Goggs dined & drank tea with us at Bro^t Ravens.

SEPTEMBER 5, WEDNESDAY A dry Windy day. Mr Hardy & Bro^t Raven rode to Sidersone [Syderstone] in the morn^g, returnd to tea, we all drank tea at Mr Goggses . . .

[LETHERINGSETT]

SEPTEMBER 10, MONDAY A Showry day. Mr Hardy & W^m at home all day. Maids began to wash 4 weeks linnen . . .

SEPTEMBER 12, WEDNESDAY Some small Showers foornoon, fine afternoon. Mr Hardy & W^m at home all day. I Bath'd.

SEPTEMBER 13, THURSDAY A Very showry day. Mr Hardy & W^m at home all day. I poorly with pain in my Stomach.

SEPTEMBER 14, FRIDAY A close dry day. Mr Hardy & W^m at home all day. M^r & M^rs & Miss Temple & Mrs Booth from Norwich drank tea here.

SEPTEMBER 15, SATURDAY A Wet foornoon, fine towards Eveng. I Bath'd. Mr Hardy at home all day. W^m went to Holt Mark^t afternoon, came home even 8.

SEPTEMBER 16, SUNDAY A very fine day. MA very Ill, I could not go to Cley meeting foornoon. Mr Hardy, I & W^m went to our Church afternoon, Mr Burrell preach'd.

SEPTEMBER 17, MONDAY A fine day. Mr Hardy & W^m at home all day. MA something better. I Bath'd.

SEPTEMBER 18, TUESDAY A very fine morng, close afternoon. Mr Hardy & W^m at home all day. M^r & Miss Bartell drank tea here.

SEPTEMBER 19, WEDNESDAY A fine morng, close rather moist afternoon. Mr Hardy at home all day. W^m & MA sett of for Whissonsett Morng 10, got there to dinner, drank tea, Supt & Slept there . . .

SEPTEMBER 21, FRIDAY A fine day. Mr Hardy & W^m at home all day.

SEPTEMBER 22, SATURDAY A fine day. Mr Hardy at home all day. W^m went to Holt Mark^t afternoon, came home eveng 9. I Bathd . . .

SEPTEMBER 26, WEDNESDAY A Close cold day. Mr Hardy & W^m at home all day. I Bathd.

SEPTEMBER 27, THURSDAY A drisly Morng, very Wet afternoon & Eveng. Mr Hardy & W^m at home all day . . .

SEPTEMBER 29, SATURDAY A Wet foornoon, showry afternoon. Mr Hardy at home all day. W^m went to Holt Mark^t after tea, came home Eveng 9.

SEPTEMBER 30, SUNDAY A fine day. I & Boy went to Cley meeting foornoon. Mr Hardy & I went to our Church afternoon, Mr Burrell preachd. W^m went to Holt Church afternoon . . .

OCTOBER 2, TUESDAY A fine day. Maids & Eliz Milegan washd 3 Weeks Linnen. Mr Hardy & W^m at home all day . . .

OCTOBER 8, MONDAY A fine day. Mr Hardy & W^m at home all day. I Bath'd . . .

OCTOBER 14, SUNDAY A very fine day. I & Thos Boyce went to Cley meeting foornoon. All went to our Church aftern, Mr Burrell preach'd . . .

OCTOBER 16, TUESDAY A fine day. Mr Hardy at [and] W^m at home all day. S [Susanna] Winn was Buried. Raind afternoon . . .

OCTOBER 19, FRIDAY A fine day. Mr Hardy & W^m at home all day.

OCTOBER 20, SATURDAY A fine day. Mr Hardy at home all day. W^m went to Holt Mark^t afternoon, came home eveng 8. I Bath'd.

OCTOBER 21, SUNDAY A moist morng, fine day. Mr Hardy, I & MA went to our Church foornoon, Mr Burrell preach'd. I & MA & T Boyce went to Briston meeting afternoon, Bell Leeke drank tea here. Miss Leeke & Miss Kirby came to Church in the Eveng, Supt here . . .

OCTOBER 23, TUESDAY A very fine day. Mr Hardy at home all day. W^m came home by Sisderston [Syderstone] & drank tea at Mr Skrimshires at Fakenh«am» & came home eveng 9 . . .

OCTOBER 26, FRIDAY A fine day. Mr Hardy at home all day. W^m drank tea at Mr Balls, Saxlingham, came home eveng 8. I Bathd.

OCTOBER 27, SATURDAY A fine Morng, Wet afternoon. Mr Hardy at home all day. W^m walkd to Holt Market afternoon, came home eveng past 10, Supt at Mr Bartells. A very wet afternoon & eveng till ten at Night then abated. I Bathd.

OCTOBER 28, SUNDAY A very heavy rain in morng preventd me from going to Cley meeting, very Showry all day. Mr Hardy & I went to our Church afternoon, Mr Burrell preachd. W^m went to Holt Church afternoon, came home to tea . . .

NOVEMBER 6, TUESDAY A fine day. Mr Hardy & W^m at home all day. Mr Hardy rid up to Holt farm aftern, M^r & Miss Bartell drank tea here.

NOVEMBER 7, WEDNESDAY A very wet day. Mr Hardy at home all day. W^m went to Mr Bartells to tea, met M^r & Mrs Balls of Saxlingham there. I very poorly.

NOVEMBER 8, THURSDAY A Wet morng, dry afternoon. Mr Hardy & W^m at home all day . . .

NOVEMBER 10, SATURDAY A very fine day. W^m went to Holt Market afternoon, came home eveng 10.

NOVEMBER 11, SUNDAY A very fine day. I & Boy went to Cley meeting foornoon. W^m went to Holt Church afternoon, came home to tea.

NOVEMBER 12, MONDAY A fine day. W^m at home all day. Mr Hardy & MA came eveng 6, they dind at Mr Skrimshires at Fakenham. Raind in the Night . . .

NOVEMBER 16, FRIDAY A Cold Stormy day. Mr Hardy & W^m at home all day.

NOVEMBER 17, SATURDAY A fine day, arime frost. Mr Hardy walkd up to Holt foornoon, dind at Mr Bartells, came home to tea. W^m went to Mark^t afternoon, drank tea at Mr Bartells, came home eve 9.

NOVEMBER 18, SUNDAY A sharp rime frost, fine day. All went to our Church foornoon, Mr Burrell preach'd. I, MA & Boy went to Briston meeting afternoon. W^m went to Holt Church afternoon, came home to tea. M^r H, I & MA went to Church in eveng, M^r B read a Lecture.

NOVEMBER 19, MONDAY A sharp morng, fine day. Mr Hardy at home all day. W^m rid to Cley afternoon, drank tea at Mr Smiths, came home eveng 8 . . .

NOVEMBER 23, FRIDAY A fine day. Mr Hardy at home all day . . .

NOVEMBER 30, FRIDAY A fine day. I taken poorly with dimness in my Eyes early in the Morng. Mr Hardy & W^m at home all day.

DECEMBER 1, SATURDAY A fine day. I poorly with dimness in my Eyes foornoon. Mr Hardy at home all day. W^m rid to Holt Mark^t afternoon, came home eveng 8 . . .

DECEMBER 3, MONDAY A fine morng, wet afternoon. Mr Hardy & W^m at home all day.

DECEMBER 4, TUESDAY A frosty morng, fine day. Mr Hardy & W^m at home all day, M^r T Balls drank tea here.

DECEMBER 5, WEDNESDAY A close foggy day. Mr Hardy at home all day. W^m rid to Mr Savory afternoon, drank tea & Supt there, came home even 9 . . .

DECEMBER 7, FRIDAY A Close foggy day. Mr Hardy at home all day. W^m came home from Whisonsett eveng 5.

DECEMBER 8, SATURDAY A Close day. Mr Hardy at home all day. W^m went to Holt Mark^t afternoon, came home eveng 8 . . .

DECEMBER 10, MONDAY A sharp frost. Mr Hardy & W^m at home all «day».

DECEMBER 11, TUESDAY A sharp frost. Mr Hardy & W^m at home all day. Bro^t Raven & Daughtr Mary came eveng 2.

DECEMBER 12, WEDNESDAY A sharp frost. W^m, Bro^t, M Raven & MA walkd to Holt foornoon, came home to dinner. Mr Hardy at home all day.

DECEMBER 13, THURSDAY A very sharp wind frost. Bro^t Raven & M [Mary] went away ab^t Noon. Mr Hardy & W^m at home all day.

DECEMBER 14, FRIDAY A very sharp frost. Miss B Leeke came foornoon, dind, drank tea & Supt here. Miss Leeke drank tea & Supt here.

DECEMBER 15, SATURDAY Thaw'd, foggy day. Mr Hardy & W^m rid up to Holt Mark^t afternoon, came home eveng past 7 . . .

DECEMBER 17, MONDAY A mild foggy day. Mr Hardy & W^m rid up to Holt Farm afternoon.

DECEMBER 18, TUESDAY Foggy day. We washd. Mr Hardy at home . . .

DECEMBER 21, FRIDAY A Close dry day. Mr Hardy & W^m at home all day, Edmd Bartell dind here. Mr Bartell of Holt came after dinner, did not stay to tea . . .

DECEMBER 23, SUNDAY A fine mild morng, turnd cold afternoon. I & Billy pinchin went to Cley meeting foornoon. We all went to our Church Afternoon, Mr Burrell preachd . . .

DECEMBER 26, WEDNESDAY A very sharp frost & snowd the greatest part of the «?day». Mr Hardy & W^m at home all day . . .

DECEMBER 31, MONDAY A frosty day. M^r «Hardy and» W^m at home all day. M^r & Mrs Temple of Thornage & M^r & Mrs Savory drank tea here . . .

1799

JANUARY 2, WEDNESDAY A Close day, thawd a little in the day & froze again at Night. Mr Hardy & Wm at home all day. Miss & Mr John Baker [jnr] drank tea here . . .

JANUARY 4, FRIDAY The Weather much as yesterday & froze again at Night. Mr Hardy & Wm at home all day. Mr Mindham here all day & Slept here.

JANUARY 5, SATURDAY The Weather much as yesterday. Mr Hardy at home all day. Mr Goggs came to dinner, he & Wm walkd to Holt Markt afternoon, came home to tea . . .

JANUARY 12, SATURDAY A very sharp rime frost. Mr Hardy at home all day. Wm & MA walkd to Holt Market afternoon, drank tea at Mr Bakers . . .

JANUARY 14, MONDAY Thawd slow. Mr Hardy at home all day. Wm & MA went to Mr Davys to tea, came home eveng 9. Mr Emmanuel came to dinner & slept here. Maids began to wash 4 weeks Linnen . . .

JANUARY 17, THURSDAY A sharp frost. MA rid up to Holt foornoon, came home to dinner. Mr Hardy at home all day. Wm went to Holt afternoon, came home even 8 . . .

JANUARY 19, SATURDAY A Close foggy day. Mr Hardy at home all day. Mr Forster dind here, Wm went up to Holt Markt with him eveng 4, came home eveng 9. Froze at Night.

JANUARY 20, SUNDAY A sharp frost in morng, thawd afternoon & raind alittle in the eveng. I & Boy went to Cley meeting in the morng. Mr Hardy went to our Church afternoon, Mr Burrell preachd. Mr Thos Sheppard dind here.

JANUARY 21, MONDAY A frosty morng, close day. Mr Hardy & Wm at home all day . . .

JANUARY 23, WEDNESDAY A Showry day. Mr Hardy at home all day. Wm came home from Fakenham eveng 5 . . .

JANUARY 25, FRIDAY A very fine bright day. Mr Hardy at home all day. Wm went to Holt afternoon to recon with Mr Moore, drank tea at Miss Leekes, came home even 8.

JANUARY 26, SATURDAY A Close mild day. Mr Hardy at home all day. Wm went to Holt Markt afternoon, drank tea at Mr Bartells, came home even 9 . . .

JANUARY 28, MONDAY A frost, fine day. Mr Hardy at home all day. Wm went to Mr Savorys afternoon, drank tea & Supt there . . .

JANUARY 31, THURSDAY An extreme sharp frost, began to Snow afternoon & continued all night, Wind being very high the Snow was very much drifted . . .

Whissonsett: a funeral and snow
1–22 February 1799

FEBRUARY 6, WEDNESDAY Snow'd a little all day, cold & close. Sister Goggs very poorly. Mr & Mrs Goggs, Mr Hardy & I went to Sister Ravens afternoon, drank tea there, Slept at Mr Goggs . . .

FEBRUARY 8, FRIDAY Thaw'd alittle in the day & froze again at Night. Mr Hardy walkd to S [Sister] Ravens foornoon, came back to dinner. Snow'd a deal in the Night, wind very high. S [Sister] Goggs better.

FEBRUARY 9, SATURDAY A Terible coarse morng, thawd all day & froze again at Night. Mr Hardy & I drank tea at Sister Ravens at the Shop. S Goggs poorly . . .

FEBRUARY 13, WEDNESDAY A very Stormy morng, thawd a little in the day. Mr Hardy & I walkd to Shop (found Sister Raven very poorly with an Inflamation in her Eyes), went back to Mr Goggs to tea. Froze at Night.

FEBRUARY 14, THURSDAY A Sharp frost in morng, thawd afternoon. Mr Goggs went to Fakenham Markt afternoon, came home eveng 8. Mr Eastaugh came to Mr Goggs to tea & Slept there. Raind in the eveng & Night . . .

FEBRUARY 16, SATURDAY A fine chearly day, thawd slowly. Mr Hardy & Mr Goggs rid to Shop foornoon, came back to dinner. I & Mrs Goggs walk'd to Shop afternoon, drank tea there. Some snow fell in the Night.

FEBRUARY 17, SUNDAY A very Close day, frosty morng & Snowd great part of the afternoon. Mr Hardy & Mr Goggs went to Church foornoon. Froze sharp again at Night.

FEBRUARY 18, MONDAY Thaw'd & raind all day. We should have gone to S Ravens at the Shop but could not . . .

[LETHERINGSETT]

FEBRUARY 26, TUESDAY A fine day. Mr Hardy better. Wm at home all day . . .

MARCH 1, FRIDAY A fine day. Mr Hardy at home all day. MA walkd up to Holt after«noon» to Mr Francis Sale, drank tea at Mr Bakers. Wm walkd up to MA after tea, came home even 9.

MARCH 2, SATURDAY A very fine day. Mr Hardy at home all day. Wm walk'd up to Holt Market aftern, came home Eveng past 8. Mr Smith of Cley came eveng 7, Slept here . . .

MARCH 4, MONDAY A Sharp rime frost, very fine day. Mr Hardy at home all day. Wm & MA walkd to Mr Savorys at Bayfield to tea, came home eveng past 8 . . .

MARCH 6, WEDNESDAY A very cold close day, alittle Snow & Sleet fell foornoon. Mr Hardy at home all day. Wm & MA went to Mr Kendles of Sherington [Sharrington] to tea with Mr & Mrs Savory, came home half past 7. Mr Emanuel came even'g 8 . . .

MARCH 9, SATURDAY A sharp frost in morng, began to snow abt 8 oClock & continued all day & great part of the night following. Mr Hardy at home all day. Wm rid to Holt Markt afternoon, drank tea at Mr Bakers, came home even 9. Thawd in the day & froze again towards Morng.

MARCH 10, SUNDAY A bright day, the Snow wasted very much. I was taken with dimness in my Eyes morn 8. Mr Hardy, Wm & MA went to our Church foornoon, Mr Burrell preach'd. H Raven went to Whisonsett Morng past 9.

MARCH 11, MONDAY A Close morng, fine day but cold. Mr Hardy & Wm at home all day. H Raven came home foornoon.

MARCH 12, TUESDAY A Chearly day, wind Cold. Wm rid to Blakney foornoon, came home to dinner. Mr Hardy at home all day. H Raven went to Mr Kendles, Sherington, afternoon, drank tea & Supt there . . .

MARCH 15, FRIDAY A dry chearly day. Staffe went away Morn 8. Mr Hardy at home all day. Wm walkd up to Holt afternoon, drank tea at Mr Bartells, home eveng 8.

MARCH 16, SATURDAY A fine day but cold. Mr Hardy at home all day. Mr Skrimshire from Fakenham din'd & drank tea here. Wm went to Holt Markt afternoon, came home to tea.

MARCH 17, SUNDAY Fine chearly day, wind cold. I & Boy went to Cley meeting foornoon. I poorly with dimness in my Eyes afternoon. Mr Hardy, Wm & MA went to our Church afternoon, Mr Burrell preach'd.

MARCH 18, MONDAY A chearly day, wind cold, raind towards eveng. Mr Hardy & Wm at home all day. I poorly with dimness in my Eyes & head ach. MA walk'd to Holt afternoon, came home to tea.

MARCH 19, TUESDAY A Bright morng, close cold afternoon. Mr Hardy & Wm at home all day. I but poorly.

MARCH 20, WEDNESDAY A bright morng, close afternoon. Mr Hardy & Wm at home all day. I very poorly in morng with dimness in my Eyes. Mrs Bartell, Mr & Miss Baker drank tea here. Mr Imm[
] . . .

MARCH 23, SATURDAY A Close cold day. Mr Hardy at home all day. Wm went to Holt Markt afternoon, came home eveng 8 . . .

MARCH 28, THURSDAY A Close day. H Raven went with Mrs Skrimshire to Fakenham foornoon, came home eveng 9. Mr Hardy & Wm at home all day. A deal of Snow fell in the eveng & Night . . .

MARCH 30, SATURDAY A sharp frost, close day, wind high towards Eveng. Mr Hardy at home all day. Wm went to Holt Markt afternoon, drank tea at Mr Bartells, came home eveng 9 . . .

APRIL 1, MONDAY A very sharp frost, wind high. Mr Hardy & Wm at home all day . . .

APRIL 3, WEDNESDAY A very sharp frost. Mr Hardy & Wm at home all day. Wind East. Mr Bartell calld . . .

APRIL 5, FRIDAY A Cold day but no frost, Snow'd all the foornoon & raind afternoon. Mr Hardy & Wm at home all day.

APRIL 6, SATURDAY A Close cold day. Mr Hardy at home all day. Wm went to Holt Markt afternoon, drank tea at Mr Seales, came home eveng 9. MA walkd up, drank tea at Miss Leakes, came home even 7 with Mrs Temple . . .

APRIL 8, MONDAY A Wet foornoon, clear'd up abt 4 OClock. Mr Hardy & Wm at home all day . . .

APRIL 13, SATURDAY A dry day but cold. Mr Hardy at home all day. Wm went to Holt Markt afternoon, drank tea at Mr Bakers, came home Eve 8.

APRIL 14, SUNDAY A Close cold Morng, reather chearly afternoon, Wind high at East. I & Boy went to Cley meeting foornoon. Mr H, MA & Wm went to our Church afternoon, Mr Burrell preach'd, Mr & Mrs Savory came to our Church.

APRIL 16, TUESDAY A Close mild day, some very small Showers. Mr Hardy walkd to the fir Closes afternoon. Mrs Lebon & Children & Miss S Burcham calld afternoon. The Miss Leekes drank tea & Supt here . . .

APRIL 20, SATURDAY A close showry day. Mr Hardy at home all day. Wm went to Holt Markt afternoon, came home Eveng 9 . . .

APRIL 22, MONDAY A Cold Showry day. Mr Hardy at home all day. Wm & MA & Miss Bartell went to Mr Flowers, Sheringham, to dinner. Wm rid to L [Lower] Sheringham afternoon to look «at» some repairs doing at the Jetty, came home eveng 9.

APRIL 23, TUESDAY A Cold close day. Mr Hardy & Wm at home all day. MA walk'd up to Holt afternoon, drank tea at Mr Bartells.

APRIL 25, THURSDAY A very cold close day, raind towards eveng. Wm walkd up to Holt Fair foornoon, came home to dinner, Mr Hardy at home all day . . .

APRIL 30, TUESDAY A reather chearly day but wind very cold at North. Wm rid to Sherringham foornoon & came back to dinner. Pump Men at Work & finishd foornoon. Mr Hardy at home all day. The 2 Miss Leakes calld here in the Eveng.

MAY 1, WEDNESDAY A mild day, not much Sunshine. Mr Hardy & Wm at home all day. Mr Immanuel came in eveng, Slept here.

MAY 2, THURSDAY Very cold, Wind north again, a small drisly rain foornoon, close all day. Wm & MA sett of for Whisonsett Morng 11 in our Chaise. Mr Hardy at home all day, Mrs Dobson drank tea here.

MAY 3, FRIDAY A Close day. Mr Hardy at home all day.

MAY 4, SATURDAY A drisly foornoon, close afternoon. Mr Hardy at home all day. Wm & MA came home from Whisonsett eveng 8 . . .

MAY 6, MONDAY A drisly morng, very close foggy afternoon. Mr Hardy at home all day. Wm rid to Mr Savorys at Bayfield to tea . . .

MAY 10, FRIDAY A drisly close morng, began to rain hard abt 10 oClock & continued all day with small intermisions {all day}. Mr Hardy & Wm at home all day.

MAY 11, SATURDAY A fine day but reather cold. Mr Hardy at home all day. Wm went to Holt Markt after tea, came home eveng past 9.

MAY 12, *Whit Sunday* A Close foggy morng, fine afternoon. I & Boy went to Cley meeting foornoon. Mr Hardy, I & MA went to our Church afternoon, Mr Burrell preach'd. Wm went to Holt Church afternoon, came home to tea, the 2 Miss Leakes drank tea here.

MAY 13, MONDAY A Cold dry day. Mr Hardy at home all day. Wm rid to Melton afternoon, came home to tea. The 2 Miss Leakes drank tea & Supt here. Mrs Lebon & Miss Dix calld after tea, left John here . . .

MAY 17, FRIDAY A very close cold windy day. Mr Hardy & Wm at home all day. Mr & Mrs Goggs, Wm & MA walkd to Holt after tea . . .

MAY 22, WEDNESDAY A fine day. Mr Hardy & Wm at home all day, Witwood at work in the Garden. Mr Immenuel came eveng past 9.

MAY 23, THURSDAY A cold close day, Wind high. Mr Hardy & Wm at home all day. Mr Immanuel went away M11. Witwood at work in Garden . . .

MAY 25, SATURDAY A fine day. Mr Goggs came morng 11, dind & drank tea here & went home in Eveng. Wm went to Holt Market after tea, came home eveng 10. Mr Hardy at home all day.

MAY 26, SUNDAY A fine day, wind cold. I & Boy went to Cley meeting foornoon, all went to our Church afternoon . . .

MAY 28, TUESDAY A fine dry day. Mr Hardy & Wm at home all day . . .

JUNE 1, SATURDAY A Showry day. Mr Hardy at home all day . . .

JUNE 4, TUESDAY A very stormy day, wind very high. Mr Hardy at home all day. Mr Bartell drank tea here. We should have gone to Mr Temples of Thornage but the weather prevented us. Wm Lamb very bad.

JUNE 5, WEDNESDAY A showry morng, fine afternoon. Mr Hardy, I & MA drank tea at Mr Temples of Thornage. Lamb very bad.

JUNE 6, THURSDAY A fine dry day. Mr Hardy at home all day. Lamb a little better . . .

JUNE 8, SATURDAY A very warm day. Mr Hardy at home all day. Lamb much as Yesterday . . .

JUNE 10, MONDAY A dry cold windy day. Mr Hardy at home all day. I & MA walkd to Holt afternoon, drank tea at Mr Bakers.

JUNE 11, TUESDAY A Cold windy day. Mr Hardy at home all day. MA walkd up to Holt afternoon, drank tea at Miss Kirbys. Maids & Eliz Loades Washd 5 weeks Linnen. Lamb very bad . . .

JUNE 14, FRIDAY A Cold chearly day. Mr Hardy at home all day . . .

JUNE 19, WEDNESDAY A Close cold day. Mr Hardy at home all day. Wm rid up to Holt afternoon & round by Mr Savorys, drank tea there, home even 9. Mr Roberson [Robinson] came to Mr Davys from London.

JUNE 20, THURSDAY A Cold close day, a very thick fogg in eveng. Mr Hardy & Wm at home all day . . .

JUNE 22, SATURDAY A very fine warm day. Mr Hardy at home all day. Wm went to Holt Market afternoon, drank tea at Mr Bartells. Mr Roberson went from Mr Davys this morning for London, took his little Girl & Susan Davy with him.

JUNE 23, SUNDAY A Close warm morng, raind about 2 hours afternoon. I & Boy went to Cley meeting foornoon, Mrs Smith gone to Yarmouth. Mr Hardy, MA & Wm went to our Church afternoon, Mr Burrell preach'd.

JUNE 24, MONDAY [

                                                    ] . . .

JUNE 27, THURSDAY [at Whissonsett] A very dry hot day. Took a walk to Horningtoft & round by Mr Goggs & back to dinner. Mr & Sister Goggs & some young people from Colkirk drank tea there . . .

JULY 3, WEDNESDAY [at Letheringsett] A very hot dry day, some appearance of rain towards eveng but had none. Mr Hardy & Wm at home all day.

JULY 4, THURSDAY A very hot day, a very small Shower in the eveng. Mr Hardy at [and] Wm at home all day.

JULY 5, FRIDAY A very hot day. Mr Hardy at home all day. Wm & MA walk'd to Mr Temples of Thornage to tea, met Mr & Mrs Bloom of Wells there & some other company.

JULY 6, SATURDAY A very hot day. Mr Hardy at home all day. Wm went to Holt Markt afternoon, came home eveng 9 . . .

JULY 8, MONDAY A Hot day, raind a fine Shower in the eveng, a dry Night. Mr Hardy & Wm at home all day . . .

JULY 10, WEDNESDAY A fine day. Mr Hardy & Wm at home all day . . .

JULY 15, MONDAY A Showry day, wind high. Mr Hardy at [and] Wm «at» home all day. H Raven & Sister Goggs came to dinner.

JULY 19, FRIDAY A Close reather drisly day. Mr Hardy & Wm at home all day. Mr & Mrs Burrell, Miss Ann & Deborah Johnson & Miss Baker drank tea here.

JULY 20, SATURDAY A fine day. Wm & Nathl went to the Sea to bathe in Morng after breakfast, they took a ride to Blakney, came back to dinner. Mr Hardy walkd to the fir Closes afternoon. Wm & Nathl walkd to Holt Market after tea, came home eveng 9, the Girls walkd to Holt after tea . . .

JULY 23, TUESDAY A drisly morng, fine afternoon. Mr Hardy at home all day. Wm & Nathl, MA & Ann Raven walkd to Holt, drank tea at Mr Bakers. Mrs Bartell drank tea here . . .

JULY 25, THURSDAY A Showry day. Wm & Nathl set of for Whisonsett Morng past 9. Mr Hardy at home all day . . .

JULY 29, MONDAY A Close day. Mr Hardy & Wm at home all day. Wm & Nathl Raven went to speak to Mrs Savory at Bayfield foornoon . . .

JULY 31, WEDNESDAY A very showry day. Wm & Nathl Raven went to Seaside to Bathe. Mr Hardy & Wm at home all day . . .

AUGUST 2, FRIDAY A fine morng, began to rain Eveng 1 & continued almost all the afternoon. We all except MA & Wm attempted to go to Sheringham afternoon but went no further then Holt on account of the rain & returnd back again. Mr Cook & Sons & Mr Goggs went away after tea.

AUGUST 3, SATURDAY A fine day except some small Showers in the Morng. Mr Hardy at home all day. Wm went to Holt Markt afternoon, came home eveng 8 . . .

AUGUST 5, MONDAY A Showry day. Mr Hardy at [and] Wm at home all day.

AUGUST 6, TUESDAY A fine morng, drisly afternoon, Wet eveng. Maids & Eliz Loades Wash'd 4 Weeks linnen. Mr Hardy, I & Wm drank tea at Mr Savorys of Bayfield.

AUGUST 7, WEDNESDAY A Showry foornoon, fine afternoon. Mr Hardy & Wm at home all day. The Miss Leakes & Miss Kirby drank tea here.

AUGUST 8, THURSDAY A dry day till eveng 5, from that time Wet all Night. Mr Hardy, Sister Goggs, I, Wm & MA drank tea at Mr Seales's.

AUGUST 9, FRIDAY A Wet morng, fine afternoon. Mr Hardy at home all day. Wm drank tea & Supt at Mr T Balls, Saxlingham.

AUGUST 10, SATURDAY A Wet morng, fine afternoon. Mr Hardy at home all day. Wm went to Holt Markt after tea, Mr T Balls drank tea here . . .

AUGUST 14, WEDNESDAY A very fine day. Wm at home all day. Mr Hardy, Sister Goggs, I & MA drank tea at Mr Bartells.

AUGUST 15, THURSDAY Dry day, wind very high. Mr Hardy, Sister Goggs & I drank tea at Mr Temples at Thornage, Mrs Bartell met us there.

AUGUST 16, FRIDAY A Stormy windy day. Mr Hardy & Wm at home all day.

AUGUST 17, SATURDAY A Windy day, some small Showers. Mr Hardy at home all day. Wm rid to Markt afternoon, came home eveng 9 . . .

AUGUST 22, THURSDAY A Close morng, began to rain morng 10, continued all day. Mr Hardy & Wm at home all day.

AUGUST 23, FRIDAY A fine day. Mr Hardy & Wm at home all day. Mr Goggs came to dinner, went away after tea. Mr Baker of Holt drank tea here . . .

AUGUST 25, SUNDAY A Very fine day. We all went to our Church foornoon, Mr Burrell preachd. I, MA & Boy went to Briston meeting afternoon. MA went to Lecture in eveng . . .

AUGUST 30, FRIDAY A Close windy day. Mr Hardy at home all day. Wm & MA din'd & drank tea at Mr Flowers at Sheringham. Gardner Witwood at work . . .

SEPTEMBER 4, WEDNESDAY A Very fine day. Mr Hardy at home all day. Wm rid to L Sheringham foornoon, came home to tea. Mr & Mrs Davy & Mrs Roberson, Mr & Mrs & Miss Temple & Miss Savory drank tea here. Mr Emmanuel came eveng past 7.

SEPTEMBER 5, THURSDAY A Beautiful day. Mr Hardy & Wm at home all day . . .

SEPTEMBER 10, TUESDAY A Very fine day. Mr Hardy at home all day. Wm walkd to Holt afternoon, came home to tea . . .

SEPTEMBER 14, SATURDAY A Very showry day. Mr Hardy at home all day. Wm went to Holt Markt afternoon, came home eveng past 9 . . .

SEPTEMBER 17, TUESDAY A Close drisly morng, very wet eveng. Mr Hardy at home all day. Wm rid to Mr Savorys afternoon, drank tea & Supt there . . .

SEPTEMBER 19, THURSDAY A Very showry day. Mr Hardy & Wm at home all day. Mr Myles Custance & Wife, Old Mrs & Thos Custance & Mr Baker dind here, they went to Mr Bakers to tea. Wm & MA drank tea & Supt there . . .

SEPTEMBER 21, SATURDAY A Showry morng, fine afternoon. Mr Hardy at home all day. Wm went to Holt Markt after tea, came home eveng 9 . . .

SEPTEMBER 23, MONDAY A Very Wet morng, fine afternoon. Mr Go{o}ggs went away after tea. Mr Hardy & Wm at home all day . . .

SEPTEMBER 26, THURSDAY A small shower in the morng, cleard up to a bright foornoon but changd again abt 2 o Clock & raind at times all night. Mr & Mrs Seales, Mr & Miss Baker, Mrs Bartell & Mr Williams of Thornage drank tea here . . .

SEPTEMBER 29, SUNDAY A Very fine morng, close in before Noon & raind all the afternoon. I & Boy went to Cley meeting foornoon. Mr Hardy & Wm went to our Church afternoon, Mr Burrell preach'd.

SEPTEMBER 30, MONDAY A very fine day. Mr Hardy & Wm at home all day. Mr & Mrs Moy from Litcham came to Mr Burrells, they went up to Holt afternoon . . .

OCTOBER 2, WEDNESDAY A Very fine day. Mr Hardy & Wm at home all day. Maids & Molly Mays Wash'd 4 Weeks Linnen.

OCTOBER 3, THURSDAY A fine day till eveng 5 then raind. Mr Hardy & Wm at home all day. Mr P Myles went away after dinner.

OCTOBER 4, FRIDAY A Very stormy day. Mr Hardy & Wm at home all day. Mr & Mrs Moy, Mr & Mrs Burrell & the Widow T Johnson [?Mrs William Tower Johnson] dind, drank tea & Supt here . . .

OCTOBER 7, MONDAY A close morng, Wet afternoon. Mr Hardy & Wm at home all day.

OCTOBER 8, TUESDAY A fine day till eveng 5 then raind. Mr Hardy & Wm at home all day.

OCTOBER 9, WEDNESDAY A fine day. Mr Hardy at home all day. Wm & Mr Seales rid to Fakenham foornoon, dind at Mr Peckovers, came home eveng 7. Mr Seales drank tea here . . .

OCTOBER 11, FRIDAY A Very fine day. Mr Hardy & Wm at home all day.

OCTOBER 12, SATURDAY A fine morng, showry afternoon. Mr Hardy at home all day. Wm went to Holt Markt afternoon, drank tea at Miss Leakes, came home even 9.

OCTOBER 13, SUNDAY A Wet morng, fine day. I & Henry Raven went to Cley meeting in the morng. Mr Hardy, Wm & MA went to our Church afternoon, Mr Burrell preachd.

OCTOBER 14, MONDAY A fine day. Mr Hardy & Wm at home all day.

OCTOBER 15, TUESDAY A Very fine day. Mr Hardy & Wm at home all day . . .

OCTOBER 19, SATURDAY A Close drisly day. Wm walkd up to Holt foornoon, came home to dinner & went again afternoon, drank tea at Mr Bartells, came home eveng 9 . . .

OCTOBER 24, THURSDAY A Wet day. Mr Hardy & Wm at home all day.

OCTOBER 25, FRIDAY A Very wet day. Mr Hardy & Wm at home all day. I was taken very Ill in the night . . .

OCTOBER 30, WEDNESDAY A fine day. Mr Hardy at home all day. Sister Raven & Daughter, Wm & MA drank tea at Mr Burrells.

OCTOBER 31, THURSDAY A dry close day. Mr Hardy & W^m at home all day. Sister Raven & Daughtr & MA rid up to Holt afternoon, drank tea at Mrs Johnsons. MA came home eveng past 8, Sister & Daughtr slept there . . .

NOVEMBER 5, TUESDAY A Very fine Morng, began to rain about 11, continued all day. Maids & Susan Lamb Washd 5 Weeks Linnen. Mr Hardy at home all day. W^m walk'd up to Holt foornoon, came home to dinner, rid to Saxlinham afternoon.

NOVEMBER 6, WEDNESDAY A Very showry day. Mr Hardy at home all day. W^m went to Mr Savorys afternoon, drank tea & Supt there.

NOVEMBER 7, THURSDAY A fine day but Windy. Mr Hardy & W^m at home all day. H Raven went to Fakenham foornoon, came home eveng 11 . . .

NOVEMBER 12, TUESDAY A Cold stormy day, wind high. Mr Hardy at home all day. W^m went up to Holt in the Eveng, came home even past 8 . . .

NOVEMBER 14, THURSDAY A Close dry day. Mr Immanuel went to Holt Morng 11, came again even 8, slept here. Mr Hardy at home all day. W^m dind, drank tea & Supt at Mr Seales, Holt, came home even 11.

NOVEMBER 15, FRIDAY A Wet day. Mr Hardy & W^m at home all day.

NOVEMBER 16, SATURDAY A fine day. Mr Hardy at home all day. W^m went to Holt Market Afternoon, came home Eveng 9.

NOVEMBER 17, SUNDAY A frost, very fine day. Mr Hardy, I & MA went to our Church foornoon, Mr Burrell preachd. I & MA & Boy went to Briston meeting afternoon. W^m went to Holt Church afternoon, came home to tea . . .

NOVEMBER 19, TUESDAY A drisly morng, close day. Mr Hardy at home all day, W^m at home all day.

NOVEMBER 20, WEDNESDAY A Very fine day. The 2 Miss Leekes came foornoon, dind & drank tea here. Mr Immanuel came afternoon, gave MA a Lesson then went to Holt, came again even 7, Slept here . . .

NOVEMBER 23, SATURDAY A Very close foggy day. Mr Hardy at home all day. W^m & MA came home from Whisonsett Eveng 2. W^m went to Holt Mark^t, came home eveng 9.

NOVEMBER 24, SUNDAY A Close foggy day. I & Boy went to Cley meeting foornoon. Mr Hardy & MA went to our Church afternoon, Mr Burrell preach'd. W^m went to Holt Church afternoon, drank tea at Mr Bartells, came home eveng 6 . . .

NOVEMBER 26, TUESDAY A very fine day. W^m & MA walkd up to Holt foornoon, came home to dinner. Mr Hardy at home all day . . .

NOVEMBER 28, THURSDAY A Very fine day. Mr Barrs went away after breakfast, Mr Hardy at home all day. W^m & MA went to Mr Savorys at Bayfield to tea . . .

NOVEMBER 30, SATURDAY A fine day. Mr Hardy & W^m went to Holt Market afternoon, came home eveng 8. . .

DECEMBER 3, TUESDAY A Close foggy day. Susan Lamb & Betty Loades Washd 4 Weeks Linnen, Molly came again. Mr Hardy & W^m at home all day . . .

DECEMBER 6, FRIDAY A Close moist day. Mr Hardy & W^m at home all day.

DECEMBER 7, SATURDAY A tolerable dry day. M^r & Mrs Goggs & Mrs Raven from Whisonsett came to Dinner. Mr Hardy & W^m, M^r & Mrs Goggs, Mrs Raven & MA went up Holt afternoon, came home to tea . . .

DECEMBER 9, MONDAY A fine day. Mr Hardy & W^m at home all day, M^r & Mrs Goggs & Mrs Raven went away Eveng 2. The 2 Miss Leekes drank tea here.

DECEMBER 10, TUESDAY A fine day. Mr Hardy & W^m at home all day . . .

DECEMBER 12, THURSDAY A Very fine day. Mr Hardy & W^m at home all day. Mr Immanuel here foornoon. The 2 Miss Leekes dind & drank tea here, Miss Savory drank tea here . . .

DECEMBER 15, SUNDAY A Cold close dry day. Mr Hardy, I & MA went to our Church foornoon. M^r & M^{rs} & Miss Savory came to our Church foornoon, Mr Burrell preach'd. I & Mrs Youngman went to Briston meeting afternoon. W^m went to Holt Church afternoon, came home to tea. H Raven drank tea & Supt at Mr Kendles, Brinton . . .

DECEMBER 17, TUESDAY A Wind frost & very cold. Mr Hardy at home all day. W^m walkd up to Holt foornoon, dind at Mr Bartels.

DECEMBER 18, WEDNESDAY A Sharp wind frost, Storms of Hail & Snow. Mr Hardy & W^m at home all day. Mr Immanuel came afternoon, Slept here.

DECEMBER 19, THURSDAY Wind high, very sharp frost, frequent Storms of Snow. Mr Hardy & W^m at home all day. Immanuel went away eveng 1.

DECEMBER 20, FRIDAY Very sharp frost & storms of Snow & Hail. Mr Hardy at home all day. Mr Immanuel went away after dinner. W^m went to Mr Colliers at Gunthorp, dind, drank tea & Supt there. A Very sharp Night.

DECEMBER 21, SATURDAY A Very sharp frost, no storms till eveng. Mr Hardy at home all day. I & MA walkd up to Holt afternoon, came home to tea. W^m walkd to Holt Mark^t, drank tea at Mr Bartells, came home eveg [evening] 9.

DECEMBER 22, SUNDAY A Sharp frost, fine day. I & Boy went to Cley meeting foornoon. We all went to our Church afternoon, Mr Burrell preach'd. M^r & Mrs Savory at our Church afternoon . . .

DECEMBER 24, TUESDAY A Sharp frost, small showers of snow. Mr Hardy & W^m at home all day . . .

DECEMBER 27, FRIDAY A sharp frost, snowd great part of the foornoon. Immanuel went away morng 11. W^m went to Mr Temples of Blakney to dinner, came home eveng 11. Mr Hardy came home eveng past 5.

DECEMBER 28, SATURDAY A Sharp frost, fine day. Mr Hardy at home all day. W^m went to Holt Mark^t afternoon, came home eveng 9. Some snow fell in the night . . .

DECEMBER 30, MONDAY A Very sharp frost. Mr Hardy & W^m at home all day . . .

1800

JANUARY 2, THURSDAY Snow deep, snowd great part of foorn & turnd to a thaw. Mr Hardy & W^m at home all day. M^r & Mrs Temple of Blakney & a Miss King drank tea here. Thaw continued all night.

JANUARY 3, FRIDAY Thaw still continue. Mr Hardy & W^m at home all day, W^m drank tea at Mr Burrells . . .

JANUARY 5, SUNDAY A Close morng, fine mild day. I «and» Boy went to Cley meeting foornoon. We all went to our Church afternoon, Mr Burrell preachd. M^r & Mrs Savory came to our Church & drank tea at Mr Burrells . . .

JANUARY 9, THURSDAY A Very close foggy day. W^m walkd up to Holt foornoon, came home to dinner, rid to Saxlingham, drank tea & Supt at Mr Balls s, came home eveng 10.

JANUARY 10, FRIDAY A Very close foggy day. W^m rid to Blakney foornoon, came home to dinner. Mr Hardy at home all day.

JANUARY 11, SATURDAY A Very close foggy day. Mr Hardy at home all day. W^m went to Holt Mark^t afternoon, came home eveng past 9. MA very poorly.

JANUARY 12, SUNDAY A Close foggy day. I & Mr Hardy went to our Church foornoon, MA very poorly. W^m went to Holt Church Afternoon, came home to tea.

JANUARY 13, MONDAY A Close foggy day. Mr Hardy at home all day, W^m at home all day. MA very poorly . . .

JANUARY 15, WEDNESDAY A very close foggy day. Mr Hardy & W^m at home all day. M^r & Mrs Savory drank tea & Supt here.

JANUARY 16, THURSDAY A Close foggy day. Mr Hardy at home all day. W^m rid to Blakney afternoon, drank tea at Mr Temples, came home eveng 8 . . .

JANUARY 18, SATURDAY A Close drisly day. Mr Hardy at home all day. W^m went to Holt Mark^t afternoon, came home eveng 9.

JANUARY 19, SUNDAY A Close drisly day. I & Boy went to Cley meeting foornoon. MA much as yesterday. Mr Hardy & W^m went to our Church afternoon, Mr Burrell preach'd . . .

JANUARY 21, TUESDAY A Sharp rime frost, very bright day. Mr Hardy at home all day . . .

JANUARY 23, THURSDAY A Very sharp frost, wind high & very cold close day, snowd & raind in Eveng then froze again towards morng. Mr Hardy & W^m at home all day. Quarter Sessions at Holt.

JANUARY 24, FRIDAY A sharp frost, fine day. Mr Hardy & W^m at home all day . . .

FEBRUARY 1, SATURDAY Thawd & snow'd foornoon, close afternoon. Mr Hardy at home all day. W^m went to Holt Mark^t afternoon, drank tea at Mr Bartells, came home eveng 9.

FEBRUARY 2, SUNDAY A frost in the morng, fine foornoon, close afternoon. I & Boy went to Cley meeting foornoon. Mr Hardy, Ann Raven & W^m went to our Church afternoon.

FEBRUARY 3, MONDAY A fine day, wind reather cold. Mr Hardy & W^m at home all day . . .

FEBRUARY 6, THURSDAY A frost, very fine day. W^m rid to Cley foornoon, came home to dinner. Mr Hardy at home all day. Mrs Flower & Miss Bartell dind & drank tea here, Mr Bartell & M^r T Balls of Saxlingham drank tea here.

FEBRUARY 7, FRIDAY A sharp frost, fine day. Mr Hardy at home all day. W^m, MA & Ann Raven dind & drank tea at Mr Bartells.

FEBRUARY 8, SATURDAY A sharp frost, close day. Mr Hardy at home all day. W^m, MA & Ann Raven walkd up to Holt Mark^t, drank tea at Mrs Johnsons, came home even 9 . . .

FEBRUARY 12, WEDNESDAY A Sharp frost, fine day. Mr Hardy at home all day. W^m rid to Sherington afternoon to speak to M^r [   ], came back to Mr Temples of Thornage, drank tea & Supt there. Mr Immanuel came in the Eveng.

FEBRUARY 13, THURSDAY A sharp frost, windy & very close all day. W^m at home all day. Mr Hardy walkd up to Holt afternoon to speak to Mr Seales, came home to tea . . .

FEBRUARY 15, SATURDAY A Wind frost, close day. Mr Hardy at {at} home all day. W^m went to Holt Mark^t afternoon, came home even 9 . . .

FEBRUARY 21, FRIDAY A Very fine day. Mr Hardy & W^m at home all day. Mrs Lebon drank tea here, Mr Balls drank tea & Supt here.

FEBRUARY 22, SATURDAY A Very fine day. Mr Hardy at home all day. W^m went to Holt Mark^t afternoon, drank tea at Mr Bartells, came home eveng 9 . . .

FEBRUARY 24, MONDAY A Very cold close day. Mr Hardy at home all day. W^m went to Blakney afternoon, drank tea at Mr Temples, came home Eveng 10.

FEBRUARY 25, TUESDAY A Cold hasy day. Mr Hardy at home all day. W^m went to Holt afternoon, drank tea at Mr Seales & supt at Mr Bartells, came home eveng 10. Maids & Susan Lamb washd 4 weeks linnen . . .

FEBRUARY 27, THURSDAY A Very sharp wind frost, wind high. Mr Hardy & W^m at home all day . . .

MARCH 2, SUNDAY A little Snow fell in the morng, fine Day. I & Boy went to Cley meeting. Mr Hardy, I, W^m & MA went to our Church aftern, Mr Burrell preach'd.

MARCH 3, MONDAY A Very sharp rime frost, fine Day. Mr Hardy poorly with a Cough. W^m at home all Day.

MARCH 4, TUESDAY A Sharp frost, frequent storms of Snow. Mr Hardy at home all day very poorly with a Cough. W^m at home all Day . . .

MARCH 8, SATURDAY A Very sharp frost. Mr Hardy at home all day. W^m went to Holt Mark^t Afternoon, came home eveng 9.

MARCH 9, SUNDAY A frost but very fine day. I & MA went to our Church foornoon, Mr Burrell preach'd. I & MA went to Briston Meeting afternoon. W^m went to Holt Church afternoon, drank tea at Mr Bartells.

MARCH 10, MONDAY A Very sharp wind frost. Mr Hardy & W^m at home all day. Thawd afternoon . . .

MARCH 12, WEDNESDAY A Close cold day, drisly afternoon. A Publick Fast by Proclamation, Mr Burrell preachd foornoon. M^r & Mrs Savory came to Church foornoon. M^r J Baker Junr & Robt Bartell dind & drank tea here, Mr Savory drank tea here. Dennis Howard came in the Eveng. I poorly with dimness in my Eyes . . .

MARCH 14, FRIDAY A chearly day but cold. Mr Hardy & W^m at home all day. Mrs Flower, Miss Bartell, A Mr Siles, Mr Ja^s Temple & Sister Mary came here foornoon.

MARCH 15, SATURDAY A Close cold day. Mr Hardy at home all day. W^m went to Holt Mark^t afternoon, came home eveng 9.

MARCH 16, SUNDAY A fine morng, cold hasy afternoon. I & Boy went to Cley meeting foornoon. Mr Hardy went to our Church Afternoon, Mr Burrell preachd. W^m went to Holt Church afternoon, came home to tea. Mrs Lebon drank tea here . . .

MARCH 18, TUESDAY A cold chearly day. Mr Hardy & W^m at home all day.

MARCH 20, THURSDAY A Close cold day. Mr Hardy at home all day. W^m drank tea & Supt at Mr Savory of Bayfield.

MARCH 21, FRIDAY A Close cold day. Mr Hardy at home all day. W^m rid to Cley & Blakney foornoon, came home eveng 4.

MARCH 22, SATURDAY A Close cold day. Mr Hardy at home all day. W^m went to Holt Mark^t after tea, came home eveng near 10 . . .

MARCH 24, MONDAY A Very fine mild day. Mr Hardy & W^m at home all day. The Miss Leakes drank tea here . . .

MARCH 26, WEDNESDAY A fine day. Mr Hardy & W^m at home all day.

MARCH 27, THURSDAY A Very fine day. Mr Hardy & W^m at home all day. M^r N Raven from Whisonsett & Miss Custance from Fakenham came to dinner. MA & Miss C rid up to Holt afternoon, Miss Baker came back with them to tea, Miss C went to Holt with Miss Baker.

MARCH 28, FRIDAY A close day, raind alittle afternoon. Mr Hardy at home all day. W^m & N Raven rid to Sherington foornoon, came home to dinner. Mr Raven went away eveng 4. A good deal of rain in the Night.

MARCH 29, SATURDAY A Close drisly morng, tolerable afternoon. Mr Hardy at home all day. W^m went to Holt Markt afternoon, drank tea at Mr Bakers, came home eveng past 9.

MARCH 30, SUNDAY A fine day. I & Boy went to Cley meeting foornoon. Mr Hardy, I, W^m & MA went to our Church Afternoon, Mr Burrell preachd. H Raven went to Whisonsett last night, came home eveng 10. Raind in the Night.

MARCH 31, MONDAY A Close foornoon, Wet Afternoon & Night. Mr Hardy & W^m at home all day.

APRIL 1, TUESDAY A fine bright morng, very Wet afternoon. Mr Hardy at home all day. W^m & MA dind & drank tea at Mr Bakers at Holt.

APRIL 2, WEDNESDAY A dry morng, Wet afternoon. Mr Hardy & Wm at home all day. Mr & Miss Baker & Miss Custance came here foornoon.

APRIL 3, THURSDAY A mild dry day. Mr Hardy & W^m at home all day . . .

APRIL 5, SATURDAY A dry day, Wind high. Mr Hardy at home all day. W^m went to Holt Mark^t afternoon.

APRIL 6, SUNDAY A Very fine dry day. Mr Hardy, I & MA went to our Church foornoon, Mr Burrell preach'd. I & MA & Boy went to Briston meeting afternoon, W^m went to Holt Church afternoon. Mr Bartell & Robt walkd down after tea . . .

APRIL 16, WEDNESDAY A dry windy day. I somthing better then yesterday, Mr Bartell calld to se me.

APRIL 17, THURSDAY Raind early in the morng, windy day. I better. We were at home all day.

APRIL 18, FRIDAY A fine day. Expected Mr Hardy & W^m home, did not come. MA & Miss Custance walkd to Mr Temples, Thornage, afternoon, drank tea there, met a large party . . .

APRIL 21, MONDAY A Close dry morng, began to rain eveng 4, Continued all the eveng. Mr Hardy at home all day. W^m, MA & Miss Custance rid to Bodham afternoon, drank tea at Mrs Custances, came home eveng 8 . . .

APRIL 23, WEDNESDAY A fine bright morng but began to rain ab^t 9 & continued all day. Maids & Susan Lamb washd 4 Weeks Linnen . . .

APRIL 26, SATURDAY A fine day till eveng 6 then a fogg fell. Mr Goggs came eveng past 3, he & W^m went to Holt Mark^t after tea, came home eveng 8. Mr Hardy at home all day.

APRIL 27, SUNDAY A Close foggy morng, raind from noon till 3 oclock then a close eveng. We all went to our Church afternoon, Mr Burrell preachd. M^r & Mrs Goggs went home after tea.

APRIL 28, MONDAY A fine day. Mr Hardy & W^m at home all day. A fogg fell in the eveng . . .

APRIL 30, WEDNESDAY A Very [?] day. Mr Hardy & W^m at home all day, the 2 Miss Leakes dind & drank tea here.

MAY 1, THURSDAY A fine day. Mr Hardy & W^m at home all day . . .

MAY 3, SATURDAY A Very fine day. Mr Hardy at home all day. W^m went to Holt Mark^t aftern, came home eveng 8 . . .

MAY 5, MONDAY A Very fine day but not so Hot as yesterday. Mr Hardy & W^m at home all day. M^r & Mrs Bartell drank tea here. I poorly with dimness in my Eyes . . .

[Then follows the visit to Cambridge, Hertfordshire and London, transcribed in full in Diary 4]

Manuscript ledger 5
8 May 1800–21 March 1809

JUNE 21, SATURDAY A very fine day. Mr Hardy at home all day, W^m went to Holt Markt after tea. I Taken with dimness in my Eyes.

JUNE 22, SUNDAY Some very small showers foornoon, fine aftern. I & M [Mary] Raven & the Boy went to Cley meeting foornoon. We all went to our Church afternoon, Mr Burrell preach'd . . .

JUNE 25, WEDNESDAY A Very warm dry day. Mr Hardy & W^m at home all day. Mr Goggs very poorly . . .

JUNE 28, SATURDAY A fine day. Mr Hardy much as Yesterday. W^m went to Holt Mark^t afternoon, came home eveng 9.

JUNE 29, SUNDAY A very small drisly rain foornoon, dry afternoon. Mr Hardy much as Yesterday. I & MA went to our Church foornoon, Mr Burrell preachd. Miss Harold & 3 other Ladies at Mr Burrells. W^m went to Holt Church afternoon, Mr Man [Isaac Mann] preachd there . . .

JULY 2, WEDNESDAY A Warm dry day. Mr Hardy somthing better then yesterday. Nathl & Ann Raven went away after tea . . .

JULY 4, FRIDAY A Very warm dry day. Mr Hardy finely, W^m at home all day. I poorly with dimness in my Eyes in the eveng.

JULY 5, SATURDAY A dry windy day. Mr Hardy finely. W^m went to Holt Mark^t Afternoon, came home eveng 9.

JULY 6, SUNDAY A fine dry day. I, LY [Lydia Youngman] & Boy went to Cley meeting in the Morng. Mr Hardy much as Yesterday. W^m & MA went to our Church Afternoon, Mr Burrell preachd . . .

JULY 8, TUESDAY A Very hot day. Mr Hardy & W^m at home all day. Mr Immanuel came foornoon, Slept here. Began to rain eveng 8, continued all Night . . .

JULY 11, FRIDAY A Warm dry day. Mr Hardy & W^m at home all day. Miss Stannard, Miss Bartell, Miss Rouse & Miss Baldro [?Baldero] Dind & drank tea here. M^r & Mrs Davy & Mrs Bartell drank tea here . . .

JULY 17, THURSDAY A fine day. Mr Immanuel went away after tea, Mr Hardy & W^m at home all day. M Hagon at work . . .

JULY 19, SATURDAY A fine day. Mr Hardy at home all Day. W^m went to Holt Mark^t after tea, came home eveng past 9.

JULY 20, SUNDAY A fine day. I & Wm Lamb went to Cley meeting foornoon. Mr Hardy & MA went to our Church Afternoon, Mr Burrell preach^d. W^m went to Holt Church afternoon . . .

JULY 22, TUESDAY A Hot dry day. Mr Hardy & W^m at home all day.

JULY 23, WEDNESDAY A Hot dry day. Mr Hardy & W^m at home all day . . .

JULY 26, SATURDAY A dry day but not so hot as Yesterd. Mr Hardy at home all day. Sister Raven & Daughtr & MA rid to Holt afternoon, drank tea at Mrs Johnsons. W^m went to Mark^t after tea . . .

JULY 29, TUESDAY A Cool close day. Mr Hardy & W^m at home all day. Miss Ann Johnson & Miss Nisbit, M^r & Mrs Burrell drank tea here.

JULY 30, WEDNESDAY Excessive Hot day. W^m at home all day. Mr Hardy, I, Sister Raven & M Raven rid to Mr Sturlys of Thornage to tea.

JULY 31, THURSDAY Excessive Hot day. Mr Fox came to dinner. Mr Hardy & W^m at home all day. I poorly with dimness in my Eyes.

AUGUST 1, FRIDAY Excesive Hot day. Mr Hardy & W^m at home all day . . .

AUGUST 4, MONDAY A Cool windy day. W^m at home all day. MA dind & drank tea at Mr Bakers at Holt, met M^r & Mrs Parsons Custance & Mrs Custance there. Mr Hardy drank tea there . . .

AUGUST 6, WEDNESDAY A small shower in the Morng, dry windy day. Mr Hardy & W^m at home all day. Maids & M Mays washd 5 weeks Linnen. Mr Immanuel [
        ] . . .

AUGUST 12, TUESDAY A dry day but not so hot as Yesterday. Mr Hardy & W^m at home all day. The Miss Leekes came after tea, Henry Raven came home eveng past 9.

AUGUST 13, WEDNESDAY A Very warm dry day. Mr Hardy & W^m at home all day. N Raven from Whisonsett came eveng 3, Slept here. Mr Immanuel came eveng 8, Slept here . . .

AUGUST 16, SATURDAY A dry warm day, Thermometer 72. Mr Hardy at home all day. Mrs Stannard, W^m & MA walk'd up to Holt after tea. M^r T Temple brought MA home in his Whiskey, W^m walkd home eveng 9. I poorly with dimness in my Eyes Morn 5.

AUGUST 17, SUNDAY A dry Hot day, Thermometer 76 even 4. I & Boy went to Cley meeting foornoon. M^r H, I & MA went to our Church afternoon, Mr Burrell preach'd. W^m went to Holt Church afternoon, came home to tea. Mr Temple & Mr Watson of Blakney came after tea, staid above an hour . . .

AUGUST 19, TUESDAY A shower in the morng & again at Eveng. Mr Hardy & W^m at home all day. I poorly with dimness in my Eyes in the Night.

AUGUST 21, THURSDAY A Very Showry day. Immanuel here all day, W^m & he walkd to Holt after tea. Mr Hardy at home all day. Mr Bartell & Mrs Stannard drank tea here, Mr Immanuel Slept here. I poorly with dimness in my Eyes in the Night.

AUGUST 22, FRIDAY A Very showry day. Mr Hardy & W^m at home all day. Mrs Stannard & Miss Bartell came to dinner, Slept here.

AUGUST 23, SATURDAY A tolerable dry day. Mr Hardy at home all day. Mrs Stannard, Miss Bartell, W^m & MA walkd up to Holt afternoon, drank tea at Mr Bartells, W^m & MA came home eveng 8 . . .

AUGUST 26, TUESDAY A Very wet day. Mr Hardy at home all day. W^m went to Mr Savorys to tea, Supt there, Mr Hardy at home all day. A Very Wet Night.

AUGUST 27, WEDNESDAY A Very wet foornoon then Cleard up till Eveng 4 then raind again. Mr Hardy at home all day. W^m walkd up to Holt afternoon, drank tea at M^r

Bakers, came home even 8. Mr Immanuel came eveng 8, Slept here.

AUGUST 28, THURSDAY A Drisly morng, fine day. I poorly with dimness in my Eyes ab^t Noon. Mr Hardy at home all day. Mr Immanuel went away Eveng 2, W^m walk'd up to Holt afternoon . . .

AUGUST 31, SUNDAY A very fine day. I & Boy & LY [Lydia Youngman] went to Cley meeting foornoon. I poorly. Mr Hardy & MA went to our Church Afternoon, Mr Burrell preach'd. W^m went to Holt Church afternoon, came home to tea . . .

SEPTEMBER 2, TUESDAY A dry windy day, a prospect for rain but did not, raind in the Night. Mr Hardy & W^m at home all day. Maids & Susan Lamb washd 4 Weeks Linnen . . .

SEPTEMBER 5, FRIDAY A Very wet day. Mr Hardy & W^m at home all day.

SEPTEMBER 6, SATURDAY A fine day. Mr Hardy at home all Day. W^m went to Holt Mark^t afternoon, drank tea at Mr Seales s [Sales's], came home eve 9 . . .

SEPTEMBER 8, MONDAY A Showry day. Mr Hardy at home all day. W^m went up Holt Afternoon, drank tea at Mr Banyards, came home Eveng past 8 . . .

SEPTEMBER 12, FRIDAY A Very fine warm day. M^r & M^{rs} [John] Cozens went away after dinner. Mr Hardy at home all day. M^r & Mrs Smith of Cley came to dinner & drank tea here. W^m went to Mr Williams s of Thornage to meet Mr Roberson [Robinson] afternoon, came home eveng 11, Supt there.

SEPTEMBER 14, SUNDAY A Very fine day. I & Boy went to Cley meeting in the Morng. Mr Hardy & MA went to our Church Afternoon, Mr Burrell preachd. W^m went to Holt Church Afternoon, came home to tea.

SEPTEMBER 15, MONDAY A Very fine Hot day. I taken poorly with dimness in my Eyes foornoon. Mr Hardy & I rid up to Holt farm aftern, W^m at home all day. Mr Kendle of Brinton, 3 Sons & 2 Daughters, drank tea here. Mr Immanuel came, Slept here.

SEPTEMBER 16, TUESDAY A Very warm day. Mr Hardy at home all day. W^m & MA went to Mr Kendles of Brinton to tea. Mr Goggs from Whissonsett came eveng 8, Slept here . . .

SEPTEMBER 18, THURSDAY A Very fine day. Mr Hardy at home all day. W^m & MA sett of for Fakenham & Whissonsett after dinner, Mrs Lebon drank tea here.

SEPTEMBER 19, FRIDAY A fine day till eveng 6 then raind a small Shower. Mr Hardy at home all day . . .

SEPTEMBER 22, MONDAY A fine Morng, showry Afternoon. Mr Hardy rid up to Holt afternoon with a Mr Selby from London, drank tea at Mr Bartells, came home eveng 7. I poorly with dimness in my Eyes in the Eveng.

SEPTEMBER 23, TUESDAY A fine day. Mr Hardy at home all Day. W^m went to Holt After tea, spent the Eveng with Mr Selby at the Feathers, came home eveng 11 . . .

SEPTEMBER 26, FRIDAY A fine day. The Miss Leekes drank tea here. Mr Hardy & W^m rid up to Holt after tea to meet Mr Selby at Mr Bartells, Supt there & came home eveng 11 . . .

SEPTEMBER 29, MONDAY A fine morng, Showry Afternoon. Mr Hardy & W^m at home all day.

SEPTEMBER 30, TUESDAY A fine morng, Showry day. Maids & S Lamb washd 4 Weeks Linnen. Mr Hardy & W^m at home all day . . .

OCTOBER 3, FRIDAY A fine day. Mr Hardy & W^m at home all day. Mr Parslee drank tea here.

OCTOBER 4, SATURDAY A fine morning, a Shower ab^t Noon, close afternoon. Mr Hardy at home all day. I & MA went to speak to Mrs Burrell foornoon. M^r T Balls drank tea here. W^m went to Holt Mark^t after tea, came home eveng 9 . . .

OCTOBER 7, TUESDAY A fine morng, a very heavy Shower Afternoon then cleard up to a fine eveng. Mr Hardy & W^m at home all day. I taken with dimness in my Eyes morng 5. The 2 Miss Leakes dind & drank tea here, Mr Bartell drank tea & Supt here.

OCTOBER 8, WEDNESDAY A fine day. Mr Hardy at home all day. I taken poorly with dimness in my Eyes foornoon twice. W^m & MA went to Mr Savory to tea, Mr Savory was not at home.

OCTOBER 9, THURSDAY A Windy stormy day. Mr Hardy at home all day. W^m went to M^r T Balls afternoon, drank tea & Supt there, came home even 11.

OCTOBER 10, FRIDAY A Showry day. Mr Hardy at [and] W^m at home all day . . .

OCTOBER 12, SUNDAY A Windy close day. I taken with dimness in my Eyes Morng, very poorly with pain in my Head all day. Nathl Raven Junr [? from the Hall] came to dinner, Slept here. Mr Hardy, I & MA went to our Church afternoon, Mr Burrell preach'd.

OCTOBER 13, MONDAY A fine day. Mr Hardy at home all day. MA walkd to Holt Afternoon, drank tea at Mr Bakers, came home Eveng past 6.

OCTOBER 14, TUESDAY A Close cold Windy day. Mr Hardy & W^m at home all day.

OCTOBER 15, WEDNESDAY A fine day. Mr Hardy & W^m at home all day . . .

OCTOBER 17, FRIDAY A fine morng, close afternoon. Mr Hardy & W^m at home all day. Mrs Lebon came for John & drank tea here . . .

OCTOBER 20, MONDAY A Close cold day. Mr Hardy & W^m at home all day.

OCTOBER 21, TUESDAY A Close windy day. Mr Hardy & W^m at home all day. I taken with dimness in my Eyes Morng 8 . . .

OCTOBER 24, FRIDAY A Close mild Day. Mr Hardy & W^m at home all day . . .

OCTOBER 26, SUNDAY A Showry day till eveng 4 then prov'd fine. I & Boy went to Cley meeting foornoon. Mr Hardy & MA went to our Church Afternoon, Mr Burrell preach'd. W^m went to Holt Church afternoon, came home to tea.

OCTOBER 27, MONDAY A Very wet day. Mr Hardy & W^m at home all day.

OCTOBER 28, TUESDAY A fine foornoon, very wet aftern. Mr Hardy & W^m at home all day, Mr Williams of Thornage drank tea here.

OCTOBER 31, FRIDAY A Very fine day. Mr Hardy at home all day. W^m came home from Whisonsett Eveng past 8.

NOVEMBER 1, SATURDAY A Very fine day. Mr Hardy at home all day. W^m went to Holt Mark^t afternoon, drank tea at Mr Seales, came home eveng 9 . . .

NOVEMBER 3, MONDAY A fine morng, drisly afternoon. Mr Hardy at home all day, W^m at home all day.

NOVEMBER 4, TUESDAY A fine day. Mr Hardy at home all day. MA walkd up to Holt afternoon, drank tea at Mr Bartells. W^m drank tea at M [Mr] Williams, Thornage, came home even 9.

NOVEMBER 5, WEDNESDAY A fine Morng, Wet eveng. Mr Immanuel came to dinner then went to Holt & came back eveng 8, Slept here. Mr Hardy at home all day. W^m rid to Cley afternoon, drank tea at Mr Colebys, came home Eveng past 8.

NOVEMBER 6, THURSDAY A Wet day. Mr Hardy & W^m at home all day. Mr Immanuel went away Afternoon.

NOVEMBER 7, FRIDAY A Close dry day. Mr Hardy at home all day. W^m & MA went to Mr Temples of Thornage, came home even 9. Rain'd a little in the Eveng . . .

NOVEMBER 12, WEDNESDAY A Very fine dry day. Mr Hardy & W^m at home all day.

NOVEMBER 13, THURSDAY A fine dry day. Mr Hardy & W^m at home all day . . .

The visit to Whissonsett
17–27 November 1800

NOVEMBER 18, TUESDAY A Close dry day. Sent our Lad home with the Horses after breakfast, spent the day at the Shop. Sister Goggs dind & drank tea with us.

NOVEMBER 19, WEDNESDAY A Close day. We dind, drank tea & Supt at Mr Goggs . . .

NOVEMBER 24, MONDAY A Very Wet day, we staid within all day.

NOVEMBER 25, TUESDAY A Very Wet foornoon, cleard up at Eveng. Mr Hardy & I, M^r & Mrs Goggs drank tea at the Shop . . .

[LETHERINGSETT]

NOVEMBER 28, FRIDAY A Wet morng, fine day. Mr Hardy & W^m home all day. M^r & Mrs Goggs came eveng 5. A Snow fell in the Night.

NOVEMBER 29, SATURDAY A fine day. Mr Hardy at home all day. W^m & Mr Goggs walkd to Holt Mark^t. Mrs Goggs & MA & Boy rid up to Holt afternoon, they all came home to tea.

NOVEMBER 30, SUNDAY A Wet foornoon, tolerable afternoon. We all went to our Church foornoon, Mr Burrell preach'd. Ann Raven & Deb Johnson came to Mr Burrells to tea . . .

DECEMBER 4, THURSDAY A Sharp rime frost. Mr Hardy & W^m at home all day. Mr Immanuel came foornoon, staid all night. A very wet eveng. Ann Raven & Deb Johnson calld foornoon.

DECEMBER 5, FRIDAY A fine day. Mr Immanuel went away after breakfast. Mr Hardy & W^m at home all day. Wet eveng . . .

DECEMBER 7, SUNDAY A small frost in morng, fine day. I & Boy went to Cley meeting foornoon. Mr Hardy & MA went to our Church Afternoon, Mr Burrell preach'd. W^m went to Holt Church afternoon, Ann Raven came home with him to stay some time . . .

DECEMBER 10, WEDNESDAY A Close foggy day. Mr Hardy & W^m took a walk onto the Hall Farm Hills afternoon . . .

DECEMBER 12, FRIDAY A Very thick foggy day. Mr Hardy & I took a walk onto the Hall Farm Hills Afternoon, MA & Ann Raven took a short walk Afternoon. W^m went to Mr Balls s, Saxlingham, drank tea & Supt there.

DECEMBER 13, SATURDAY A Very thick foggy day. Mr Hardy at home all day. W^m went to Holt Mark^t afternoon, came home eveng 9 . . .

DECEMBER 15, MONDAY A beautiful day. Mr Hardy & W^m at home all day. The Miss Leekes from Hunworth came to dinner, slept here, Immanuel slept here.

DECEMBER 16, TUESDAY A Close day. Mr Hardy at home all day. W^m & A Raven went to Lower Sheringham foornoon, came home even 3. Miss Leakes here all day & slept here, Immanuel here all day & slep«t» here . . .

DECEMBER 20, SATURDAY A Close day. Mr Hardy at home all day. W^m went to Holt Mark^t Afternoon, came home eveng 9. Mr Wade of Stibard came to tea & Slept here.

DECEMBER 21, SUNDAY A fine day. I & Lad went to Cley Meeting foornoon. Mr Hardy & MA went to our Church Afternoon, Mr Burrell preach'd. N Raven came to dinner, he & W^m & Ann Raven went to Holt Church Afternoon, came home to tea.

DECEMBER 22, MONDAY A Very fine day. Mr Hardy at home all day. Nathl & A Raven went away Morng 11. W^m went to Holt Afternoon. Maids & M Mays Washd 4 weeks Linnen.

DECEMBER 24, WEDNESDAY A Close mild day. Mr Hardy at home all day. W^m went to Saxlingham Afternoon, drank tea & Supt at Mr Balls s, came home even 11 . . .

DECEMBER 26, FRIDAY A fine day till eving 4 then turnd very Foggy. W^m at home all day. Mr Hardy & I drank tea at Mr Burrells, Mr Balls drank tea here . . .

DECEMBER 28, SUNDAY A fine day. Mr Hardy, I & MA went to our Church foornoon, Mr Burrell preach'd. I, MA & Boy went to Briston meeting Afternoon. W^m went to Holt Church afternoon, M^r [?Christopher] Stannard preachd there. Froze in the Night.

DECEMBER 29, MONDAY Thawd. A deal of Snow fell in foornoon. Mr Hardy at home all day. W^m & MA dind & drank tea at Mr Bartells, Holt, came hom«e» even 9.

DECEMBER 30, TUESDAY A Sharp frost, chearly day. Mr Hardy & W^m at home all day. M^r & Miss Bartell & Mr Stannard dind, drank tea & Supt here . . .

1801

JANUARY 2, FRIDAY A fine day. W^m something better, MA very poorly. Mr Hardy at home all day. Mr Mendham [Mindham] hanging the Chamber. Mr Stannard & Miss Bartell drank tea here. I poorly with dimness in my Eyes.

JANUARY 3, SATURDAY A fine mild day. Mr Mendham went away after breakfast. Mr Hardy at home all day. MA very poorly. W^m finely, went to Holt Mark^t afternoon.

JANUARY 4, SUNDAY A Very fine day. I & Boy went to Cley meeting foornoon, Mr Hardy went to our Church afternoon. W^m went to Holt Church Afternoon, came home to tea. MA Very poorly with A Cold.

JANUARY 5, MONDAY A fine day. Mr Hardy & W^m at home all day. Mr Stannard & Mr Bartell drank tea here. Mr Immanuel came in Eveng, Slept here.

JANUARY 6, TUESDAY A Very fine day. Mr Hardy & W^m at home all day. Mr Immanuel «?came» & Slept here . . .

JANUARY 10, SATURDAY A Close mild day. Mr Hardy at home all day. W^m went to Holt Mark^t Afternoon, drank tea at Mr Davys, came home Eveng past 9.

JANUARY 11, SUNDAY A Close mild day. Mr Hardy, I & MA went to our Church foornoon, Mr Burrel preach'd. Mr Goggs & Mr Coock [Cook] from London came to dinner, Slep«t» here.

JANUARY 12, MONDAY A Close mild day. Mr Hardy & W^m at home all day. Mr Goggs & Mr Cook here all day & Slept here again. M^r & Mrs Balls, M^r & Mrs Mendham drank tea here . . .

JANUARY 18, SUNDAY A Very fine day. I & Boy went to Cley meeting foornoon. Mr Hardy, W^m, MA & Mr Miles [Myles] went to our Church afternoon, Mr Burrell preach'd.

JANUARY 19, MONDAY A beautifull day. Mr Hardy & P Miles took a walk into Holt Farm, I & MA took A walk afternoon. W^m at home all day.

JANUARY 20, TUESDAY A Wet morng, fine day. Maids & M Mays Washd 4 Weeks Linnen. Mr Wm Custance dind & staid all Night. Miss Baker dind & drank tea here, Mr Baker drank tea here. Mr Hardy & W^m at home all day . . .

JANUARY 25, SUNDAY A Sharp fine day. Mr Hardy, I & MA went to our Church foornoon, Mr Burrell preach'd. I, MA & Boy went to Briston meeting afternoon. W^m went to Holt Church afternoon, came home to tea. Mrs Bell from Holt was caried thro Town this morng to be Buried Aged 89 Years.

JANUARY 26, MONDAY A sharp frosty Morng & snowd a little then turnd to a thaw, dry day. W^m at home all day. Mr Hardy, I & MA walkd to Mr Savorys at Bayfield to tea, came home eveng 9 . . .

JANUARY 28, WEDNESDAY A Close mild day. Mr Hardy & W^m at home all day. Mr Miles here . . .

FEBRUARY 1, SUNDAY A fine day. I & Boy went to Cley meeting foornoon, Mr Immanuel went away about Noon. Mr Hardy & MA went to our Church Afternoon. W^m went to Holt Church Afternoon, came home to tea.

FEBRUARY 2, MONDAY A fine mild day. Mr Hardy & W^m at home all day. I poorly with dimness in my Eyes foornoon.

FEBRUARY 3, TUESDAY A Close mild day. Mr Hardy & W^m at home all day.

FEBRUARY 4, WEDNESDAY A dry windy day but very mild. Mr Hardy & W^m at home all day. I & MA walk'd up to Holt Afternoon, came back to tea. The 2 Miss Leakes calld foornoon from Holt. Mr Immanuel came to tea, Slept here . . .

FEBRUARY 7, SATURDAY A Close day. The Miss Leekes went away after breakfast. Mr Hardy & W^m at home all day. I & MA walkd up to the fur Closes afternoon.

FEBRUARY 8, SUNDAY A Close mild day. Mr Hardy, I & MA went to our Church foornoon, Mr Burrell preachd. I, MA & Boy went to Briston meeting Afternoon. W^m went to Holt Church afternoon, came home to tea . . .

FEBRUARY 11, WEDNESDAY A Wind«y» day, frequent Storms of Snow. Mr Hardy at home all day. W^m rid to Cley afternoon & from thence to Mr Savorys, Bayfield, drank tea & Supt there. Mr Immanuel came in the Eveng . . .

FEBRUARY 14, SATURDAY A Sharp frost, frequent storms of Snow. W^m went to Holt Mark^t afternoon, drank tea at Mr Bakers, came home eveng 9. Mr Hardy at home all day . . .

FEBRUARY 18, WEDNESDAY A Very fine day. Mr Hardy at home all day. I taken poorly with dimness in my Eyes. Mr Immanuel came to tea & Slept here. W^m walkd up to Holt Afternoon, came home eveng 10.

FEBRUARY 19, THURSDAY A Close cold day. W^m sett of for Whisonsett morng ten, Mr Thos Balls went with him. Mr Hardy at home all day, I poorly. A Very coarse eveng, a great deal of Snow fell & wind high. Mr Immanuel went away eveng 6.

FEBRUARY 20, FRIDAY A Cold slopy [sloppy] day, snow wasted apace. Mr Hardy at home all day, I poorly. W^m came home from Whisonsett even 8.

FEBRUARY 21, SATURDAY A Wet day. Mr Hardy at home all day. W^m went to Mark^t afternoon, drank tea at Wid^w [Widow] Fishers, came home even 8 . . .

FEBRUARY 23, MONDAY A Very fine day. Mr Hardy at home all day. W^m came home from Norwich Eveng ½ past 6.

FEBRUARY 24, TUESDAY A Very fine day. Mr Hardy at home all day. I & MA walk'd up to Holt Afternoon, drank tea at Mr Bartells, W^m came to tea.

FEBRUARY 25, WEDNESDAY A Wet day. Mr Hardy & W^m at home all day. Mr Immanuel came eveng 6, Slept here . . .

FEBRUARY 28, SATURDAY A Close day. Mr Hardy and W^m went to Holt Mark^t afternoon, drank tea at Mr Davys, came home eveng 9. A Stormy Night . . .

MARCH 4, WEDNESDAY A Very fine day. W^m & Mr Hardy at home all day. Mr Immanuel came after dinner, slept here. I poorly with dimness in my Eyes foorn. Mr Glover Supt & Slept here . . .

MARCH 6, FRIDAY A Wet day. Mr Hardy & W^m at home all day. Mr Immanuel went away after Breakfast . . .

MARCH 9, MONDAY A Close morng, wet afternoon. Mr Hardy took awalk into Hall Farm afternoon, got wet. W^m walkd to Bayfield, drank tea at Mr Savorys, he was not at home. Mr Glover came in the Eveng, Slept here.

MARCH 10, TUESDAY A dry day but cold. Mr Hardy at home all day. W^m went to Saxlingham Afternoon, drank tea & Supt at Mr Balls's, came home eveng 11 . . .

MARCH 15, SUNDAY A Cold Stormy Morng, wind high, fine Afternoon. Mr Hardy, I & MA went to our Church Afternoon, Mr Burrell preachd. W^m went to Holt Church Afternoon, drank tea at Mr Seales.

MARCH 16, MONDAY A close windy day. Mr Hardy & W^m at home all day. Witwood at work in the Garden . . .

MARCH 18, WEDNESDAY A fine day but Cold. Mr Hardy at home all day . . .

MARCH 20, FRIDAY A fine morng. Wind got up very high towards Noon, Very wet Afternoon. Mr Hardy at home all day. Mr Mendham came foornoon to finish the Bedstead, Slept here.

MARCH 21, SATURDAY A Close windy day. Mr Hardy at home all day. Mr Glover dind & drank tea here & went to Holt in the eveng. W^m went to Holt Mark^t afternoon, came home eveng 8 . . .

MARCH 23, MONDAY A Close day. Mr Hardy & W^m at home all day. Mr Glover went away before breakfast. Mrs Temple & Family drank tea here.

MARCH 24, TUESDAY A Close day, raind towards eveng. Mr Hardy & W^m at home all day. Mr Croffts from Fakenham came eveng 3, went home after tea. M^r & Mrs Temple & Family came to tea, M^r & Mrs Burrell, Miss Nesbit & Miss A Johnson drank tea here . . .

MARCH 27, FRIDAY A fine day. Mr Hardy & W^m at home all day. I & MA walk'd up to Holt Afternoon, drank tea at Mr Davys. Henry Raven in Town . . .

MARCH 31, TUESDAY A Very fine day. Mr Hardy at home all day. I & MA took awalk afternoon to the Fur Closes.

APRIL 1, WEDNESDAY A Very beautiful day. Mr Hardy at home all day.

APRIL 2, THURSDAY A Very fine warm day. Mr Hardy at home all day. M^r [   ] Wood from London drank tea here . . .

APRIL 4, SATURDAY A Very warm bright day. Mr Hardy rid up to Holt Farm afternoon & stopt at Mark^t coming back. MA walkd up to Holt after tea, they came home eveng 8 . . .

APRIL 6, MONDAY A Cold dry day. Mr Hardy at home all day. MA & Boy & Miss Baker went to Fakenham Morng 9, Dind & drank tea at Mr Custances (Mrs Bennit & Mrs John Custance there), came home eveng 8.

APRIL 7, TUESDAY Wind high, Showry afternoon. Mr Hardy at home all day. Mr Glover here ashort time after tea . . .

APRIL 9, THURSDAY A Cold day, wind high at West. Mr Hardy at home all day. MA rid up to Holt Afternoon, drank tea at Mr Bartells, walkd home. Rec'd a Letter from W^m at London. Mr Immanuel came Even 8, Slept here . . .

APRIL 11, SATURDAY A Cold windy Stormy day. Mr Hardy rid up to Holt Mark^t Afternoon, drank tea at Mr Davys, walkd home Eveng past 8.

APRIL 12, SUNDAY Very cold, wind high, frequent Storms of Hail & Snow. I & Sarah Goodman & Boy went to Cley meeting foornoon. Mr Hardy & MA went to our Church Aftern, Mr Burrell preach'd.

APRIL 13, MONDAY A Cold windy day. Mr Hardy at home all day . . .

APRIL 17, FRIDAY A Very fine day. Mr Hardy & W^m at home all day.

APRIL 18, SATURDAY A fine day. Mr Hardy at home all day. W^m went to Holt Market afternoon, supt at Mr Parslees, came home even 11.

APRIL 19, SUNDAY A Very fine day. Mr Hardy, I & MA went to our Church foornoon, Mr Burrell preachd. M^r & Mrs Goggs came to dinner.

APRIL 20, MONDAY A Very fine day. Mr Hardy, Mr Goggs, I & Mrs Goggs took awalk onto the Hall Farm foornoon.

APRIL 21, TUESDAY A dry day but cold. M^r & Mrs Goggs went to Mr Buskalls at Wiverton foornoon. Mr Hardy at home all day. W^m & MA walkd to Bayfield Aftern, drank tea at Mr Savorys . . .

APRIL 23, THURSDAY A fine day. Mr Hardy at home all day. W^m & MA drank «tea» at Mr Savorys, Bayfield.

APRIL 24, FRIDAY A fine day. I very poorly with pain in my Stomack. M^r & Miss Bartell drank tea here.

APRIL 25, SATURDAY A fine day. Mr Hardy at home all day. W^m went to Holt Mark^t afternoon, drank tea at Mr Bartells, came home eveng 8.

APRIL 26, SUNDAY A Very fine day. I & Girling went to Cley meeting foornoon. Mr Hardy & MA went to our Church Afternoon, Mr Burrell preachd. W^m went to Holt Church Afternoon, came home to tea . . .

MAY 2, SATURDAY A Cold Windy day. Mr Hardy at home all day. W^m rid to Cley foornoon, came home to dinner, went to Holt Mark^t after tea, came home eveng 8.

MAY 3, SUNDAY A Cold morng, a Wet afternoon. M^r H, I & MA went to our Church foornoon, Mr Burrell preach'd, M^r & Mrs Savory at Church. W^m went to Holt Church Afternoon, came home to tea . . .

MAY 6, WEDNESDAY A Cold dry day. Mr Hardy & I rid up to Holt to Hipkins Sale afternoon, drank tea at Mr Bartells. W^m at home all day.

MAY 7, THURSDAY A Close cold day. I & W^m walkd to Holt to Hipkins Sale, dind at Mr Bartells. I drank tea at Mrs Chases, W^m came home to tea. Miss Ann & Deb Johnson, Miss Bartell & J Baker drank tea with W^m . . .

MAY 9, SATURDAY A Cold dry day. I walkd up to Holt foornoon to the Sale, drank tea at Mr Bartells. Mr Hardy rid up to Holt Farm Afternoon, he drank tea at Mr Bartells, we walkd home even 7. W^m walkd to Mark^t Afternoon, came home even 8.

MAY 10, SUNDAY A fine dry day. I & Girling went to Cley meeting foornoon. Mr Hardy went to our Church Afternoon, Mr Burrell preachd. W^m went to Holt Church Afternoon, drank tea at Mr Bartells, home Eveng 6 . . .

MAY 12, TUESDAY A Close morng & reather drisly at times. W^m went to Sheringham foornoon, came home eveng 8. I & Mr Hardy & the Miss Leekes walkd to Holt Afternoon to the Sale. They went home, M^r H & I drank tea at Mr Bakers . . .

MAY 15, FRIDAY A Very wet foornoon, clear'd up towards Eveng. Mr Hardy & W^m at home all Day . . .

MAY 19, TUESDAY A Hasy morng, fine afternoon. Mr Hardy at home all day. W^m walk'd up to Holt after tea, came home even 9. Mr Hase finishd mending the Copper . . .

MAY 21, THURSDAY A Very fine day, reather hot. Mr Hardy took a walk afternoon into Hall Farm, W^m at home all day. Mrs Chase & Mrs Bartell drank tea here . . .

MAY 24, SUNDAY A Very fine warm day. I & Girling went to Cley meeting foornoon. Mr Hardy went to our Church Aftern, Mr Burrell preach'd. W^m went to Holt Church afternoon, drank tea at Mr Seales, did not git home till Even 9.

MAY 25, MONDAY A Very fine warm day. Mr Hardy & W^m at home all day. Mr Temple of Blakney dind & drank tea here.

MAY 30, SATURDAY A Cold close day. Mr Hardy at home all day. W^m went to Holt Mark^t afternoon, drank tea at Mr Bartells, came home Eve 9 . . .

JUNE 2, TUESDAY A Close cold day. Mr Hardy at home all day. W^m & MA rid to T Balls Afternoon to tea . . .

JUNE 4, THURSDAY A Wet Morng, close cold afternoon. Mr Hardy & W^m at home all day. Imanuel came, slept here . . .

The visit to Whissonsett
5–16 June 1801

JUNE 6, SATURDAY A fine day. Took a walk to the Shop foornoon, at home afternoon . . .

JUNE 8, MONDAY A Very warm day. Mr Eastaugh came to tea & slept there.

JUNE 9, TUESDAY A Very hot day. M^r & M^rs & Miss Wright & a young Gentleman came to Mr Goggs to dinner, they stayd & Supt . . .

JUNE 11, THURSDAY A fine day. Mr Hardy & I, M^r & Mrs Goggs rid to Fakenham afternoon, drank tea at Mr Eastaughs.

JUNE 12, FRIDAY A Cold close day, raind a little ab^t 6 oClock. Mr Hardy & Mr Goggs rid to Dereham foornoon, dind at Mr Wright at Howe [Hoe], came home eveng 10, Supt at Mr Ravens. Sister & Mrs Goggs, Miss Cook & I dind, drank tea & Supt at Mr Ravens . . .

JUNE 14, SUNDAY A fine day but cool. I went to Fakenham with Mr Goggs foornoon, went to the Chapel foornoon & Afternoon, dind at Mr Custances. Mrs Goggs came for me Afternoon, we got home to tea.

JUNE 15, MONDAY A Cold dry day. Mr Hardy, I & Mrs Goggs walk'd to Horningtoft foornoon to speak to Mrs Jennis, she was not at home, we came back to dinner. . .

[LETHERINGSETT]

JUNE 17, WEDNESDAY A fine day but cold. Mr Hardy & W^m at home all day. M^r & Mrs Savory, old Mrs Savory & Mrs Poutage drank tea here. The 2 Miss Leekes dind & drank tea here.

JUNE 18, THURSDAY A dry day. Mr Hardy & W^m at home all day, I & MA walk'd to Holt after tea.

JUNE 19, FRIDAY A dry day. Mr Hardy at home all day. W^m din'd & drank tea at Mr Williams, came home eveng 9.

JUNE 20, SATURDAY A Close dry day. Mr Hardy at home all day. W^m went to Holt Mark^t Aftern, drank tea at Mr Bartells. I & MA walkd up after tea . . .

JUNE 22, MONDAY A Dry day. Mr Hardy & W^m at home all day.

JUNE 23, TUESDAY A dry cool day. Mr Hardy, I, W^m & MA walk'd to Bayfield, drank tea at Mr Savorys, walk'd home by Mr Jodrils . . .

JUNE 25, THURSDAY A dry day, reather warm. Mr Hard«y» at home all day. W^m & MA rid up to Holt Afternoon, drank tea at Mr Bartells.

JUNE 26, FRIDAY A Very warm dry day. Mr Hardy at home all day. W^m & MA drank tea at Mr Temples at Thornage.

JUNE 27, SATURDAY A Very warm dry day. Mr Hardy at home all day. W^m went to Mark^t aftern, came home eveng 9.

JUNE 28, SUNDAY A Very warm dry day. Mr Hardy, I & MA went to our Church foornoon, Mr Burrel preach'd. I & MA & Girling went to Briston meeting afternoon. W^m went to Holt Church, came home to tea . . .

JULY 2, THURSDAY A fine morng, began to rain ab^t 11 oclock, continued till eveng 3 then I [a] dry eveng. Mr Hardy at home all day. W^m & MA & Girling sett of for Fakenham morng 10, they din'd & drank tea at Mr Custances. W^m intended to go to Whisonsett but changd his mind & came home even 9, brought Mrs John Custance home with them . . .

JULY 4, SATURDAY A fine day. Mr Hardy at home all day. George Phillipo went away after dinner. I poorly with dimness in my Eyes & a Cold. W^m went to Holt Mark^t afternoon, drank tea at Mr Bartells, came home even 9.

JULY 5, SUNDAY A drisly morng, fine day. I & Mrs Custance & Girling rid to Cley meeting foornoon. W^m went to Holt Church afternoon, came home to tea. Mr Hardy & MA went to our Church Afternoon, Mr Burrell preachd . . .

JULY 9, THURSDAY A Cold stormy day. Mr Hardy poorly with the Gout. W^m came home from Whisonsett Eveng 9, Sister Goggs & Miss Cook came home with him.

JULY 10, FRIDAY A Cold dry day. Mr Hardy very bad with the Gout in both Feet. W^m at home all day.

JULY 11, SATURDAY A fine day. Mr Hardy reather better then yesterday. Mr John Custance came to breakfast, dind here. W^m & he walkd to Holt Mark^t Afternoon, came home to tea . . .

JULY 15, WEDNESDAY A Wet morng, showry day. Mr Hardy much as yesterday, W^m at home all day.

JULY 16, THURSDAY A fine morng, very heavy showers with Thunder Afternoon. Mr Hardy something better then Yesterday, W^m at home all Day . . .

JULY 18, SATURDAY A Very fine day. Mr Hardy rid out after dinner with W^m onto Hall Farm. W^m went to Holt

Mark^t Afternoon, came home eveng past 9. MA & Miss Cook walkd up to Holt after tea.

JULY 19, SUNDAY A Very fine day. I & Miss Cook went to Cley meeting foornoon. Sister Goggs, Miss Cook & MA went to our Church Afternoon, Mr Burrell preach'd. W^m went to Holt Church Aftern. M^r & Mrs Cozens from Norwich came half past 8.

JULY 20, MONDAY A fine day. Mr Hardy better. W^m, MA, Miss Cook & M^r & Mrs Cozens rid to Sheringham Afternoon, came home Eveng 9. A Very great Fogg in Eveng . . .

JULY 23, THURSDAY A fine day. Mr Hardy something better. W^m at home all day. Expected Mrs Chase, she did not come.

JULY 25, SATURDAY A Very fine day. Mr Hardy much as yesterday. Mr Eastaugh came to dinner & drank tea here. W^m went to Holt Mark^t afternoon . . .

JULY 27, MONDAY A Very Hot day. Mr Hardy & W^m at home all day. M^r H Goggs came Eveng past 6.

JULY 28, TUESDAY A fine day, Wind reather rough. Mr Hardy & W^m at home all day. MA & Girling sett of for Whisonsett in the Gigg half past 9, Girling came home ½ past 8. Mrs Bartell drank tea here . . .

JULY 30, THURSDAY A fine day. Mr Hardy & W^m at home all day . . .

AUGUST 3, MONDAY A Very warm dry day. Mr Cook from London came from Whisonsett to breakfast. Mr Hardy & Mr Cook rid to Cley through the Hall Farm Afternoon, came back to tea. Molly wash'd the small Linnen.

AUGUST 4, TUESDAY A dry Hot day. Mr Goggs came to breakfast. Mr Hardy, Mr Cook & Mr Goggs rid to Sheringham Afternoon, came home eveng past 8. Maids & Eliz Bullock wash^d . . .

AUGUST 6, THURSDAY A dry Hot day. Mr Hardy at home all day. Mrs Chase drank tea here.

AUGUST 7, FRIDAY A Hot dry day. Mr Hardy at home all day.

AUGUST 8, SATURDAY A Hot dry day. Mr Hardy rid to Holt Farm after tea . . .

AUGUST 18, TUESDAY A Hot dry day. Mr Hardy & W^m at home all day. M^r & Mrs Moy, M^r & Mrs Burrell came to speak to us foornoon, M^r & Mrs Moy on A Visit at Mr Burrells. Mr Williams drank tea here afternoon . . .

AUGUST 23, SUNDAY A dry Hot day. I & MA went to our Church foornoon, Mr Burrell preach'd. I, MA & Girling went to Briston meeting Afternoon. Mr Creed drank tea here. W^m went to Holt Church foornoon & Afternoon. Mr Burrell had A Lecture in the Even. M^r & Mrs Moy came in the Eveng to take their leave of us, they intending to go away from Mr Burrells in the morn . . .

SEPTEMBER 6, SUNDAY A Very Wet foornoon, dry afternoon from 2 oClock. Mr Hardy, I, W^m & MA went to our Church foornoon, A Sacrament, no Sermon. Mr Creed drank tea & Supt here.

SEPTEMBER 7, MONDAY A Very heavy rain all the foornoon, a dry afternoon, the Water very high in the River. The Maids Washd 4 Weeks large Linnen. Mr Hardy & W^m at home all day . . .

SEPTEMBER 9, WEDNESDAY A fine day. Mr Hardy at home all day. W^m went to Mr Savorys Aftern, drank tea & Supt there . . .

SEPTEMBER 13, SUNDAY A Very fine day. I & Wm Girling went to Cley Meeting foornoon. We all except W^m went to our Church Afternoon, W^m went to Holt Church Afternoon.

SEPTEMBER 14, MONDAY A Close dry day. Mr Hardy at home all day. W^m walkd up to Holt foornoon with J Hardy & Ladies, he Dind & drank tea at Mr Wm Williams at Thornage, came home eveng 9 . . .

SEPTEMBER 16, WEDNESDAY [at Whissonsett] A foggy morng, fine warm day. Took a walk to the Hall foornoon, drank tea at Shop, Supt & Slept at Mr Goggs. M^r & Mrs Moy there . . .

SEPTEMBER 24, THURSDAY [at Letheringsett] Showry day. Mr Hardy [duplicate entry erased]. W^m at home all day. Mr Hardy, I, M^r & Mrs Jo^s Hardy & M^r [?Mrs] Coulson drank tea at Mr Burrell. M^r & M^rs & Miss Goggs from Colkirk dind here, went away eveng 2 . . .

SEPTEMBER 26, SATURDAY A fine day. Mr Hardy at home all day. W^m went to Holt Mark^t afternoon, came home eveng 9. A Wet Night. I poorly with dimness in my Eyes in the Morng . . .

SEPTEMBER 28, MONDAY A fine morng, Showry Afternoon. Mr Hardy at home all day. W^m went to A Sale at Melton after dinner, from thence to Mr Coopers at Briston to tea, came home eveng past 9. Maids Washd part of 4 weeks Linnen. I poorly with dimness in my Eyes in the Eveng . . .

SEPTEMBER 30, WEDNESDAY A fine Morng, Close day. Mr Hardy at [and] W^m at home all day.

OCTOBER 1, THURSDAY A fine day. Mr Hardy at home all day. Mr Wm Williams of Thornage drank tea & Supt here . . .

OCTOBER 3, SATURDAY A fine day. Mr Hardy at home all Day. W^m went to Holt Mark^t Afternoon, came home eveng 9.

OCTOBER 4, SUNDAY A fine day except a shower ab^t 2 oClock. Mr Hardy, I & MA went to our Church foornoon, A Sacrament. I & MA & Wm Girling went to Briston Meeting Afternoon. Mr Creed drank tea here . . .

OCTOBER 16, FRIDAY A fine day. Mr Hardy at home all day. W^m walkd up to Holt Afternoon, came home Eveng 9 . . .

OCTOBER 18, SUNDAY A fine day. Mr Hardy, I & MA went to our Church foornoon, Mr Burrell preachd, had A Lecture in the Eveng. I & MA & Wm Girling went to Briston meeting Afternoon. W^m went to Holt Church Afternoon, came home to tea. I poorly in the Night with dimness in my Eyes . . .

OCTOBER 22, THURSDAY A Cold dry Morng, showry afternoon. Mr Hardy at home all day. W^m rid to Cley afternoon, from thence to Mr Savorys, drank tea & Supt there, came home Eveng 10.

OCTOBER 23, FRIDAY A Very fine day. Mr Hardy at home all day. I & MA rid up to Holt Afternoon, drank tea at Mr Bartells, met M^r & Mrs Seales there. W^m came for us in the Eveng, walk'd home . . .

OCTOBER 25, SUNDAY A fine day. My Stomack much better. Mr Hardy went to our Church Afternoon. W^m went to Holt Church Afternoon, came home to tea. Mrs Chase calld to speak to me After Church . . .

OCTOBER 27, TUESDAY A Close cold day. W^m & MA sett of for Whisonsett morng 10, Mr Hardy at home all day. Mrs Dobson drank tea here . . .

OCTOBER 29, THURSDAY A Close cold day. Mr Hardy & W^m at home all day . . .

NOVEMBER 3, TUESDAY A Very fine day. Maids wash'd 2 Weeks Linnen. Mr Hardy at home all day, W^m walk'd up to Holt in the eveng.

NOVEMBER 4, WEDNESDAY A Wet Windy day. Mr Hardy & W^m at home all day. Mr Immanuel came eveng 8, went back to Holt Eveng 11. I taken very bad with pain in my Stomack Eveng 9. Wind very high in the Night with Storms of Snow &c . . .

NOVEMBER 6, FRIDAY A fine day. Mr Hardy & W^m at home all day. I very poorly with pain in my Stomack & dimness in my Eyes foornoon, Mr Bartell came to see me.

NOVEMBER 7, SATURDAY A fine day. I very poorly with pain in my Stomack, Mr Bartell calld to se me. Mr Hardy at home all day. W^m went to Holt Mark^t afternoon & Mr Goggs with him, came home eveng 8.

NOVEMBER 8, SUNDAY A frost, very fine day. I very poorly. Service at our Church Afternoon, our Servants went. W^m went to Holt Church Afternoon, came home to tea.

NOVEMBER 9, MONDAY A frost, very fine day. Mr Hardy & W^m at home all day. I much better. Ge^o Phelippo supt here.

NOVEMBER 10, TUESDAY A Mild foggy day. Mr Hardy & W^m at home all day.

NOVEMBER 11, WEDNESDAY A fine day. Mr Hardy & W^m at home all day.

NOVEMBER 12, THURSDAY A fine day. Mr Hardy & W^m at home all day. Mrs Chase, M^{rs} & Miss Bartell drank tea here, sent them home in our Gigg. Mr Immanuel [ ] . . .

NOVEMBER 14, SATURDAY A Close foggy day. Mr Hardy at home all day. Mr Immanuel here all day & slept here at Night. W^m went to Holt Mark^t afternoon, came home eveng 9. Mr Smith of Cley din'd here . . .

NOVEMBER 19, THURSDAY A Stormy day. Mr Hardy at home all day. W^m came home from Whisonset Eveng 8. Mr Immanuel came to tea, Slept here.

NOVEMBER 20, FRIDAY A Cold Stormy Day. Mr Hardy & W^m at home all day. Mr Immanuel here all day & Slept here.

NOVEMBER 21, SATURDAY A Very cold chearly day. Mr Hardy at home all day. W^m went to Holt Mark^t afternoon, came home eveng 8. Mr Immanuel here all day & slept here. A Very windy Cold [ ] . . .

NOVEMBER 25, WEDNESDAY A tolerable day, Wet windy Eveng. Mr Hardy at home all day. W^m & Mr Goggs walkd to Holt Fair foornoon, came back to dinner. Miss Ravens & MA walkd to Holt foornoon, the Ravens went away after dinner. Mr Goggs went to Wiveton to Mr Buskals afternoon, came back Eveng 8, Slept here. W^m up to Holt afternoon, came back to tea.

NOVEMBER 26, THURSDAY A fine morng, close afternoon. Mr Goggs went away Morng 11, Immanuel left us foornoon. Mr Hardy & W^m at home all day.

NOVEMBER 27, FRIDAY A Close windy day. Mr Hardy & W^m at home all day. Sarah Collins taken Ill . . .

DECEMBER 1, TUESDAY A Close drisly day. Mr Hardy & W^m at home all day. Maid & Betty Loades Wash'd 2 Weeks Linnen.

DECEMBER 2, WEDNESDAY A Sharp frost the first of the Morng, raind before Noon. Mr Hardy at home all day. W^m went to Hempsted with Mat^h Leake, Holt, drank tea with Mr Oliver, came home even 9 . . .

DECEMBER 6, SUNDAY A fine day. I & Wm Girling went to Cley meeting foornoon. Mr Hardy went to our Church Afternoon, Mr Burrell preach'd. W^m went to Holt Church Afternoon.

DECEMBER 7, MONDAY A Very fine day, afrost. Mr Hardy & W^m at home all day. Mr Goggs came to dinner, we all took awalk onto Hall Farm afternoon.

DECEMBER 8, TUESDAY A Sharp frosty morng, close day & thawd & raind in the Night. Mr Hardy & W^m at home all day. Mr Goggs went away Eveng past 3 . . .

DECEMBER 11, FRIDAY A frost, chearly day. Mr Hardy & W^m at home all day. I, MA & Wm Girling rid up to Holt in Gigg, came back to dinner.

DECEMBER 12, SATURDAY A Very sharp frost, Wind high at West, alittle Snow fell foornoon. Mr Hardy & W^m walkd up to Holt afternoon, came home eveng 9.

DECEMBER 13, SUNDAY A Sharp frost, bright day. Mr Hardy, I & MA went to our Church foornoon, Mr Burrell preachd. W^m went to Holt Church afternoon, I, MA & Wm Girling went to Briston Meeting Afternoon. Mr Creed drank tea here.

DECEMBER 14, MONDAY A Sharp frosty Morng & close day & thawd. Mr Hardy & W^m at home all day.

DECEMBER 15, TUESDAY A Sharp frosty Morng, close day & thawd alittle & froze again at Night. W^m & Mr Seales went «to» Fakenham in our Gigg, dind at Mr Peckovers, came home eveng ½ past 7. The 2 Miss Leakes din'd & drank tea here . . .

DECEMBER 18, FRIDAY A Sharp frost. Mr Hardy at [and] W^m at home all day. Mr Williams drank tea & Supt here, Mr Immanuel came to tea & Slept here.

DECEMBER 19, SATURDAY A Sharp frost, fine day. Mr Hardy at home all day. W^m went to Holt Mark^t aftern, came home eveng past 9. Mr Immanuel went to Holt foornoon, came back in eveng & Slept here.

DECEMBER 20, SUNDAY A Sharp frost. I & Wm Girling went to Cley meeting foornoon. W^m went to our Church Afternoon, Mr Burrell preachd. Mr Immanuel went away foornoon. Began to thaw eveng 4, continued all Night . . .

DECEMBER 22, TUESDAY A small frost, fine day. Mr Hardy & W^m at home all day. Mr Immanuel here all day & Slept here. {M^r Immanuel here all day & slept here.}

DECEMBER 23, WEDNESDAY A Very Wet day. Mr Hardy & W^m at home all day. Mr Mendham drank tea & Supt here. Expected M^r & Mrs Balls from Saxlingham, they did not come on Acct of the weather. Immanuel here all «day» & slept here . . .

DECEMBER 26, SATURDAY A small frost, fine day, raind in Eveng, wind high. Mr Hardy at home all day. W^m went to Holt Mark^t afternoon, came home eveng past 9 . . .

DECEMBER 28, MONDAY A fine day. Mr Hardy & W^m at home all day . . .

DECEMBER 30, WEDNESDAY A frosty morng, snowd alittle foorn, close afternoon. Mr Hardy & W^m at home all day.

DECEMBER 31, THURSDAY A frost, wind high North, frequent Storms of Hail & Snow. Mr Hardy at home all day. W^m & MA sett of for Whisonsett Morng past 11.

1802

JANUARY 1, FRIDAY Wind high & frequent Storms of Snow foornoon, fine afternoon, sharp frost. Mr Hardy at home all day . . .

JANUARY 4, MONDAY A sharp frost, close day. Mr Hardy & W^m at home all day. Snow'd in the Night.

JANUARY 5, TUESDAY Thawd slowly all day. Mr Hardy at home all day. W^m drank tea & Supt at Mr Savorys, Bayfield, came home even 10. Snowd in eveng & great part of the Night.

JANUARY 6, WEDNESDAY A Close day, reather thawd & froze again at Night. Mr Hardy & W^m at home all day.

JANUARY 7, THURSDAY A Slow thaw all day. Mr Hardy & W^m at home all day.

JANUARY 8, FRIDAY A slow thaw all day. Mr Hardy & W^m at home all day. Mr Savory drank tea here, M^r & M^{rs} T Balls drank tea & Supt here.

JANUARY 9, SATURDAY A thaw. Mr Hardy went up to Holt Afternoon, drank tea at Mr Bartells. MA & W^m drank tea at Mr Bakers, came home eveng 9 . . .

JANUARY 11, MONDAY A sharp frost & some Storms of Snow. Mr Hardy & W^m at home all day. Maids Wash'd 2 Weeks Linnen.

JANUARY 12, TUESDAY A sharp frost, bright day. Mr Hardy at home all day. W^m drank tea & Supt at M^r T Balls, Saxlingham, came home Eveng 11. A great deal of Snow fell in the Night . . .

JANUARY 14, THURSDAY Sharp frost, wind high & frequent Storms of Snow, the Snow very much drifted. Mr Hardy & W^m at home all day.

JANUARY 15, FRIDAY A Very sharp frost, bright day. Mr Hardy at home all day. W^m went to Mr Colliers, dind & drank tea there, came home eveng 9.

JANUARY 16, SATURDAY A Very sharp rime frost in the morng, began to thaw very slowly afternoon. Mr Hardy at home all day. W^m went to Holt Mark^t Afternoon, came home Eveng 10.

JANUARY 17, SUNDAY A slow thaw, fine day. I & Wm Girling went to Cley meeting foornoon. Mr Goggs came to dinner & slept here. Mr Hardy, Mr Goggs & W^m went to our Church aftern, Mr Burrell preachd.

JANUARY 18, MONDAY A thaw, fine day. Mr Goggs went away at Noon. Mr Hardy at home all day. W^m & MA rid up to Holt afternoon, drank tea at Mr Bartells, came home even 9 . . .

JANUARY 20, WEDNESDAY A Close day. Mr Hardy & W^m at home all day.

JANUARY 21, THURSDAY Wind very high & Stormy. Mr Hardy & W^m at home all day. Ann Fryer at work here . . .

JANUARY 23, SATURDAY A frosty morng, close afternoon. Mr Hardy at home all day. W^m went to Mark^t afternoon, drank tea at Mr Seales, Supt at Mr Mendhams, came home eveng past 11 . . .

JANUARY 25, MONDAY A fine day. Mr Hardy at home all day. W^m dind & drank tea at Mr Williams at Thornage, came home eveng past 10 . . .

JANUARY 29, FRIDAY A fine day. Mr Hardy & W^m at home all day. Eliz Wortly much as yesterday.

JANUARY 30, SATURDAY A rime frosty morng, close afternoon. Mr Hardy at home all day. W^m went to Holt Mark^t afternoon, came home eveng past 9 . . .

FEBRUARY 2, TUESDAY A Very fine day. Mr Hardy at home all day. Miss Leeke dind & drank tea here. W^m came home eveng past 8.

FEBRUARY 3, WEDNESDAY A fine day. Mr Hardy & W^m at home all day. Immanuel came eveng 8, slept here, Mr Creed Slept here. Raind in the Night.

FEBRUARY 4, THURSDAY A fine day. Mr Hardy & W^m at home all day . . .

FEBRUARY 6, SATURDAY A Close drisly day. Mr Hardy at home all day. W^m went to Holt Mark^t afternoon, came home eveng past 9. A very stormy Night.

FEBRUARY 7, SUNDAY A stormy day. Mr Hardy, I & MA went to our Church foornoon, Mr Burrell preachd. I & MA & Wm Girling went to Briston meeting Afternoon. W^m went to Holt Church Afternoon, came home to tea.

FEBRUARY 8, MONDAY A rime frosty Morng, very wet windy Afternoon. Mr Hardy & W^m at home all day . . .

FEBRUARY 10, WEDNESDAY A fine day. Mr Hardy & W^m at home all day. M^r & Mrs Goggs from Whisonsett & Mr Cook from London came to dinner, Slept here, T Balls drank tea here. Alittle Snow fell in the Night.

FEBRUARY 11, THURSDAY A Chearly day. M^r & Mrs Goggs & Mr Cook went away morng 11. Mr Hardy & W^m at home all day.

FEBRUARY 12, FRIDAY A frosty morng, reather stormy, tolerable day. Mr Hardy & W^m at home all day. Mr Williams & Sister of Thornage dind & drank tea here, Mr Savory of Bayfield drank tea & Supt here.

FEBRUARY 13, SATURDAY A Close day. Mr Hardy at home all day. W^m went to Holt Mark^t eveng 3, came home Eveng 9. Snowd in the Eveng.

FEBRUARY 14, SUNDAY A frosty morng & close. I & Wm Girling went to Cley meeting foornoon. I, MA & Wm Girling went to Briston meeting Afternoon. Mr Hardy went to our Church Afternoon, Mr Burrell preach'd. W^m went to Holt Church Afternoon, came home to tea. Frequent Storms of Snow Afternoon & Eveng.

FEBRUARY 15, MONDAY A frosty morng, close afternoon. Mr Hardy & W^m at home all day.

FEBRUARY 16, TUESDAY A sharp frost, snowd even 4 & froz very sharp in eveng. Mr Hardy & W^m at home all day. Mr John Baker [junior] drank tea here.

FEBRUARY 17, WEDNESDAY A Close day. Mr Hardy at home all day. W^m & MA drank tea at Mr Bartells, Holt. I poorly with A Cold.

FEBRUARY 18, THURSDAY A Close damp day. Mr Hardy & W^m at home all day . . .

FEBRUARY 20, SATURDAY A fine day. Mr Hardy at home all day. W^m went to Holt Mark^t afternoon, drank tea at Mr Yorks, came home eveng past 8. I very poorly with A Cold . . .

FEBRUARY 22, MONDAY A drisly foornoon, close afternoon. Mr Hardy at home all day. W^m went to T Balls, Saxlingham, afternoon with Mr Mendham, drank tea & Supt there, came home eveng [   ]. I very bad with A Cold.

FEBRUARY 23, TUESDAY A Close foggy day. Mr Hardy & W^m at home all day. I very bad with a Cold. L Youngman drank tea here . . .

FEBRUARY 26, FRIDAY A Cold close day. Mr Hardy at home all day. I much as Yesterday . . .

FEBRUARY 28, SUNDAY A Close mild day. I & MA & Wm Girling went to Briston meeting Afternoon. W^m went to Holt Church afternoon, came home to tea. Mr Hardy went to our Church Afternoon, Mr Burrell preachd. M^r & Mrs Savory came to our Church.

MARCH 1, MONDAY A Close day. Mr Hardy & W^m at home all day . . .

MARCH 3, *Ash Wednesday* A fine day. Mr Hardy at home all day. W^m went to Mr Williams at Thornage to tea, came home eveng 9. Mr Immanuel came to dinner, went to Holt Eveng 3.

MARCH 4, THURSDAY A fine chearly day, wind Cold at North. Mr Hardy & W^m at home all day. Mrs Bartell, Miss S Davy & Mr Temple, Thornage, drank tea here . . .

MARCH 6, SATURDAY A Sharp rime frost, fine day. Mr Hardy at home all day. W^m went to Holt Mark^t afternoon, drank tea at Mr Bakers, came home eveng past 9 . . .

MARCH 11, THURSDAY A Very fine mild day. Mr Hardy & W^m at home all day. M^r & Miss Bartell here foornoon, Mr Immanuel dind here . . .

MARCH 14, SUNDAY A Very stormy day, wind very high at North. I poorly with dimness in my Eyes foornoon. MA & Wm Girling went to Briston meeting afternoon. W^m went to Holt Church Afternoon, came home to tea. Mr Hardy & the Maids went to our Church Afternoon . . .

MARCH 17, WEDNESDAY A Very fine day. Mr Hardy, I & MA walkd to Bayfield Afternoon, drank tea at Mr Savorys. W^m came to us after tea . . .

MARCH 20, SATURDAY A Cold Windy day. Mr Hardy at home all day. W^m went to Holt Mark^t afternoon, came home eveng past 9 . . .

MARCH 23, TUESDAY A fine dry day. Mr Hardy at home all day. W^m went to Wells foornoon, came home eveng 8. M^r & Miss Baker & Miss Leake drank tea here. Maids Wash'd 2 Weeks Linnen. I poorly with dimness in my Eyes in the Night . . .

MARCH 25, THURSDAY A Very fine day. Mr Hardy & W^m at home all day. Miss Bartell drank tea here. I taken with dimness in my Eyes in Eveng . . .

MARCH 27, SATURDAY A Very fine day. Mr Hardy at home all day. W^m went to Holt Mark^t Afternoon, came home eveng 9.

MARCH 28, SUNDAY A Very fine day. I & MA & Wm Girling went to Cley Meeting foornoon & to Briston Meeting Afternoon. W^m went to Holt Church afternoon, came home to tea. Mr Hardy went to our Church Afternoon . . .

APRIL 1, THURSDAY A Very fine day. Mr Hardy walkd up to the Sale at Holt Afternoon, came home to tea Eveng 6. Mr Meakin & M^r & Mrs Bartell drank tea here.

APRIL 2, FRIDAY A Very fine day. Mr Hardy at home all day. Mr Creed drank tea here.

APRIL 3, SATURDAY A fine day. Mr Hardy walkd to Holt Mark^t Afternoon, drank tea at Mr Bartells, came home eveng 7 . . .

APRIL 7, WEDNESDAY A Very fine day. Mr Hardy at home all day. I taken with dimness in my Eyes Aftern.

APRIL 8, THURSDAY A fine day. Mr Hardy at home all day. I taken with dimness in my Eyes going to Bed. A fine Shower in the Eveng.

APRIL 9, FRIDAY A fine dry day. Mr Hardy at home all day. Dimness in my Eyes Even 6 . . .

APRIL 11, SUNDAY A Cold Windy day. I & MA & W Girling went to Briston Meeting Afternoon alf [?], Mr Hardy went to our Church Afternoon. Mr Meakin drank tea here.

APRIL 12, MONDAY A Cold stormy windy day. Mr Hardy at home all day . . .

APRIL 14, WEDNESDAY A Wet Morng, tolerable fine Afternoon. Mr Hardy & W^m at home all day. Mr Smith of Cley drank tea here . . .

APRIL 17, SATURDAY A fine day. Mr Hardy at home all day. W^m went to Holt Mark^t Afternoon, drank tea at Mr Bartells, came home eveng 8. I, MA & A Ravn walkd up to Holt After tea . . .

The visit to Whissonsett
20–29 April 1802

APRIL 21, WEDNESDAY A fine day. Walkd to Shop foornoon. 2 Mrs Ravens drank tea at Mr Goggs.

APRIL 22, THURSDAY A fine day. I very poorly. We drank tea at Sister Ravens [at the shop].

APRIL 23, FRIDAY A Close cold day. We drank tea at the Hall.

APRIL 24, SATURDAY A Close day. M^r R Goggs & Wife drank tea & Supt at Mr Goggs . . .

APRIL 28, WEDNESDAY A fine day but Cold. Sister G & M^r & M^{rs} G drank tea at Sister Ravens . . .

[LETHERINGSETT]

APRIL 30, FRIDAY A Cold Windy day. Mr Hardy, I, MA & Ann Raven drank tea at Mr Burrells. W^m dind & drank tea at Mr Williams at Thornage, came home Eveng 9 . . .

MAY 4, TUESDAY A Cold Windy day. Mr Hardy, I, MA & A Raven drank tea at Mr Temples of Thornage. W^m & AR rid to Sheringham foornoon, came back to dinner. Maids Washd . . .

MAY 7, FRIDAY A fine chearly day, wind cold. Mr Hardy & W^m at home all day.

MAY 8, SATURDAY A Very fine day. Mr Hardy at home all day. W^m, I, MA & AR walkd up to Holt after tea . . .

MAY 10, MONDAY A fine dry day, Wind Cold. Mr Hardy & W^m at home all day . . .

MAY 12, WEDNESDAY A dry day, wind Cold. Mr Hardy at home all day. I, W^m, MA & A Raven went to Mr Savorys Afternoon to tea . . .

MAY 14, FRIDAY A Dry cold day. W^m, MA, N & A Raven walk'd up to Holt foornoon, came home to dinner. N & A Raven went away Eveng past 3. Mr Hardy at home all day.

MAY 15, SATURDAY A fine day, wind Cold. Mr Hardy at home all day. W^m went to Holt Mark^t Afternoon, came home eveng past 9.

MAY 16, SUNDAY Some small showers foornoon, Wind cold at N East. Mr Hardy, I & MA went to our Church foornoon, A Sacrament. I & MA & Wm Girling went to Briston Meeting Afternoon. W^m went to Holt Church Afternoon, came home to tea.

MAY 18, TUESDAY Stormy Morng, fine day but very cold. W^m sett of for Norwich with Mr Williams of Thornage Morng 7. Mr Hardy at home all day.

MAY 19, WEDNESDAY A Very Wet foornoon & Cold close afternoon. Mr Hardy at home all day.

MAY 20, THURSDAY Fine Morng, a Showr ab^t 2 oClock, cold Close afternoon. Mr Hardy at home all day. W^m came home from Norwich Even 8.

MAY 21, FRIDAY A Very fine warm day. Mr Hardy & W^m at home all day. M^r & M^{rs} & Miss Mendham [Mindham], Miss Woodrow & Miss Sarah Davy drank tea here . . .

MAY 24, MONDAY A Dry day, wind Cold. Mr Hardy & W^m at home all day.

MAY 25, TUESDAY A fine day, wind rather rough. Mr Hardy at home all day. W^m rid to Mr Savory at Bayfield Afternoon, came home to tea. Miss Leeke Dind & drank tea here, M^r & M^{rs} & Susan Davy drank tea here . . .

MAY 27, THURSDAY A fine warm day. Mr Hardy at home all day. W^m rid to Thornage after tea, Mr Williams was not at home, from thence to Holt, came home Eveng past 9.

MAY 28, FRIDAY A fine warm day. Mr Hardy at home all day. W^m rid to Mr Williams, Thornage, Afternoon, drank tea there, came home Eveng past 9. I & MA took a walk to little Thornage after tea . . .

MAY 30, SUNDAY A Cold day, showers afternoon. Mr Hardy, I & MA went to our Church foornoon, M^r

Burrell preachd. I, MA & Wm Girling went to Briston Meeting afternoon. M^r H & W^m went to Holt Church Afternoon, Mr Meakin preach'd.

MAY 31, MONDAY A close morng, fine afternoon but cold. Mr Hardy & W^m at home all day. Maids wash'd . . .

JUNE 3, THURSDAY A fine warm day. Mr Hardy & W^m at home all day. Raind a good deal in the night.

JUNE 4, FRIDAY A Very warm day. Mr Hardy & W^m at home all day. Mr Savory & a Mrs Isaacks drank tea here. Raind in the Night.

JUNE 5, SATURDAY A fine day, a Shower in the Eveng. Mr Hardy at home all day. W^m went to Holt Mark^t Afternoon, came home eveng 10 . . .

JUNE 7, MONDAY A Showry day & Cold. Mr Hardy at home all day. W^m rid to Cley afternoon, drank tea at M^r [Revd John] Ravens, Cley, came home Eveng 8. A great deal of rain fell in the Night.

JUNE 8, TUESDAY A Very wet morng, tolerable aftern. Mr Hardy at home all day. W^m rid to Blakney foornoon, came home to dinner. Mr Temple of Blakney, Mr Williams of Thornage & his Brother Bird [? brother-in-law] Dind, drank tea & Supt here . . .

JUNE 11, FRIDAY A Very fine day. Mr Hardy at home all day. Miss Leake & Miss Bartell calld after tea . . .

JUNE 13, SUNDAY A Very fine day. Mr Hardy, I & MA went to our Church foornoon, A Sacrament, no Sermon. I & MA & WG went to Briston meeting. Mr Hardy & W^m went to Holt Church aftern, came home to tea . . .

JUNE 15, TUESDAY A Very fine day. Mr Hardy & W^m at home all day. Maids washd 2 Weeks Linnen. Mr Meakin drank tea here . . .

JUNE 19, SATURDAY A Very fine day. Mr Hardy at home all day. W^m went to Holt Mark^t after tea. Wm Girling went to Cromer afternoon for MA & Ann Raven, they came home eveng 8.

JUNE 20, SUNDAY A Very fine day. I & W^m G went to Cley meeting foornoon. We all went to Holt Church Afternoon except Mr Hardy who went to our Church Afternoon, Mr Burrell preach'd.

JUNE 21, MONDAY A Very warm dry day. Wm Girling went to Cromer with MA & AR morng past 8, came home eveng 2. Sister Raven & I drank tea at Mrs Johnsons, Holt. Mr Hardy & W^m at home all day.

JUNE 22, TUESDAY A fine day. Mr Hardy & W^m at home all day, we all drank tea at Mr Burrells . . .

JUNE 25, FRIDAY A fine day Day, a small shower in the Eveng. W^m at home all day. Mr Hardy & I went to Mr Sturlys to tea, Sister Raven came home with us . . .

JUNE 27, SUNDAY A fine day. Mr Hardy, I & MA went to our Church foornoon, no Sermon. M^r H went again to Church in Eveng, Mr Burrell preachd. I & MA & W^m G went to Briston Meeting Afternoon, W^m went to Holt Church Aftern . . .

JUNE 29, TUESDAY A Very showry day & windy. MA & WG went to Cromer foornoon, Sister Raven came back with him Eveng 3. Mr Hardy & W^m at home all day . . .

JULY 2, FRIDAY A Showry day & Cold. Mr Hardy & W^m at home all day. M^rs & Miss Lydia Sturly drank tea here.

JULY 3, SATURDAY A fine morng, wind high and Cold, a very heavy Showr eveng 6. Mr Hardy at home all day. Wm Girling went to Cromer Afternoon for MA & AR, they came home eveng 8. W^m went to Holt Mark^t afternoon, came home eveng 10.

JULY 4, SUNDAY A fine day but Cold. I & W^m G went to Cley meeting foornoon. I, W^m, MA & A Raven went to Holt Church Afternoon . . .

JULY 6, TUESDAY A Windy dry day. Mr Hardy & W^m at home all day. M^r & Mrs Moy, M^r & Mrs Burrell, M^r & «?Mrs» Marsh & Sister, a Mrs Black & 2 Children from Norwich drank tea here.

JULY 7, WEDNESDAY A Very fine day. Mr Hardy & W^m at home all day. Mrs Chase & Mrs Bartell dind & drank tea here . . .

JULY 9, FRIDAY A fine day. Mr Hardy at home all day. Sister Raven & I walk'd up to Holt Afternoon, drank tea at Mrs Chases. W^m walkd up to Holt after tea.

JULY 10, SATURDAY A Very Wet day untill Eveng 4. Mr Hardy at home all day. Wm Girling went to Cromer for MA & A Raven, came home eveng 9. W^m went to Holt Mark^t afternoon, came home eveng 10 . . .

JULY 14, WEDNESDAY A fine day but rather cold. Expected Mr Hardy & W^m home, did not come . . .

JULY 16, FRIDAY A fine day. Mr Hardy at home all day. W^m walk'd up to Holt after tea, came back eveng past 9 . . .

JULY 19, MONDAY A Showry day. Mr Hardy & W^m at home all day. Mr Goggs came for Mrs Cook & Children Morng 11, they went away after tea . . .

JULY 23, FRIDAY A Showry cold day. Mr Hardy & W^m at home all day . . .

JULY 25, SUNDAY A fine day. We all went to our Church foornoon, Mr Burrell preach'd. I & MA & Wm Girling went to Briston meeting afternoon. I poorly with dimness in my Eyes after I came home. Mr Hardy & W^m went to Holt Church afternoon, came home to tea.

JULY 26, MONDAY A Dry day, raind in the Eveng. Mr Hardy at home all day. W^m went to Mr Bartells to dinner, drank tea & Supt there, came home even 11.

JULY 27, TUESDAY A Close foornoon, rather drisly aftern. Maids washd 2 weeks Linnen. Mr Hardy at home all day. M^r & Mrs Latham from Cromer came foornoon & Miss Bartell. W [William] went to Mr Colebys Sale at Cley aftern.

JULY 28, WEDNESDAY A drisly morng, very wet afternoon. Mr Hardy & W^m at home all day.

JULY 29, THURSDAY A Showry day. Mr Hardy & W^m at home all day . . .

JULY 31, SATURDAY A Very Showry day. Mr Goggs came to dinner, went away after tea. W^m went to Holt Mark^t after tea, came home even 10 . . .

AUGUST 7, SATURDAY A Very hot day. Mr Hardy at home all day. W^m, MA & M Raven walkd up to Holt after tea, came home eveng 9 . . .

AUGUST 10, TUESDAY A Hot day. Maids washd 2 weeks Linnen. Mr Hardy at home all day. W^m went to Saxlingham afternoon, drank tea at M^rT Balls, came home Eveng 9. M^r & Mrs Bartell calld after tea.

AUGUST 11, WEDNESDAY Hot day. Mr Hardy at home all day. I, W^m & MA drank tea at Mr Bartells, M Raven poorly.

AUGUST 12, THURSDAY A Hot morng, a Shower of rain eveng 2 then cleard up to a fine afternoon & even. W^m, MA & M Raven went to Sheringham afternoon, came home Eveng 9.

AUGUST 13, FRIDAY A Hot day. Mr Hardy & W^m at home all day.

AUGUST 14, SATURDAY A Hot dry day. Mr Hardy at home all day. W^m went to Holt Mark^t after tea, came home eveng past 10 . . .

AUGUST 22, SUNDAY A Very fine day. Mr Hardy, I & MA & M Raven went to our Church foornoon, Mr Burrell preach'd. I & MA & Wm Girling went to Briston meeting Afternoon. M^r H, W^m & MR went to Holt Church aftern . . .

AUGUST 29, SUNDAY A Very Hot day. I & W^m G went to Cley meeting foornoon. We all went to Holt Church afternoon. Wm Girling went to Beckham afternoon . . .

SEPTEMBER 12, SUNDAY A Very fine day. I & Wm Girling went to Cley Meeting foornoon. We all went to Holt Church Afternoon, Mr Meakin preachd, he came alittle while in the Eveng.

SEPTEMBER 13, MONDAY A Cool dry day. Mr Hardy at home all day. W^m rid to Cley afternoon, drank tea at Mr Smiths, came home eveng 7. Mr Meakin drank tea here . . .

SEPTEMBER 15, WEDNESDAY A Very fine warm day. Mr Hardy & W^m at home all day. M & Nathl Ravn from the Shop, Whisonsett, came to dinner.

SEPTEMBER 16, THURSDAY A Very fine Hot day. Mr Hardy & W^m at home all day. Nathl Raven went away Eveng 3. We expected M^r & Mrs York but they did not come.

SEPTEMBER 17, FRIDAY A fine Hot day. Mr Hardy at home all day. MA & M Raven drank tea at Mr Bartells, Holt, W^m went for them after tea.

SEPTEMBER 18, SATURDAY A Very fine Hot day. Mr Hardy at home all day. I, MA & M Raven drank tea at Mr Bakers at Holt, W^m drank tea & Supt there, the Custances from Cromer met us there . . .

SEPTEMBER 20, MONDAY A Very warm dry day. Mr Hardy & W^m at home all day. Mr Ja^s Moore din'd & drank tea here. The 2 Miss Leekes dind & drank tea here . . .

SEPTEMBER 25, SATURDAY A Very fine day. W^m & G Philipo sett of for Norwich Morng ½ past 4, came home Eveng 9. Mr Hardy at home all day.

SEPTEMBER 26, SUNDAY A fine day. We all went to Holt Church Afternoon, Mr Meakin preach'd.

SEPTEMBER 27, MONDAY A Close cold day. Mr Hardy & W^m at home all day. M^r T Fox came to dinner, Slept here. Miss Bartell, Miss Alders, Miss Green, Miss Baker, 2 Miss Temples & Miss Bird drank tea here . . .

The visit to Whissonsett
28 September–2 October 1802

SEPTEMBER 30, THURSDAY A Hot dry day. We spent the day at the Shop, Sister Goggs drank tea with us.

OCTOBER 1, FRIDAY A Hot dry day. We dind, drank tea & Supt at Mr Goggs . . .

[LETHERINGSETT]

OCTOBER 3, SUNDAY A Very warm dry day. I & Wm Girling went to Cley meeting foornoon, MA went with me to Briston meeting Afternoon. Mr Hardy & MA went to our Church foornoon, a Sacrament, no Sermon. M^r H & W^m went to Holt Church Afternoon.

OCTOBER 4, MONDAY A Very windy day, small showr in Morn. Mr Hardy & W^m went to Sheringham foorn, came home eveng 3.

OCTOBER 5, TUESDAY A Windy dry day. Maids washd 2 Weeks Linnen. M^{rs} & Mr Edm^d Bartell & Mr Meakin drank tea here. Mr Hardy & W^m at home all day . . .

OCTOBER 8, FRIDAY A dry blustering day. Mr Hardy at home all day. W^m rid to Fakenham foornoon, came home eveng 8. Rain in the Night.

OCTOBER 9, SATURDAY A Close drisly day. Mr Hardy at home all day. W^m went to Holt Mark^t afternoon, came home Eveng past 9.

OCTOBER 10, SUNDAY A fine day but Cold. We all went to Holt Church Afternoon, Mr Meakin preachd. A Mr Gilder [? Guelder/Geldart] from Hull drank tea here . . .

OCTOBER 16, SATURDAY A Sharp rime frost, very fine day. Mr Hardy at home all day. W^m went to Holt Mark^t afternoon, came home eveng 9.

OCTOBER 17, SUNDAY A sharp rime frost, very fine day. I & Wm Girling went to Cley meeting foornoon. I & MA & Wm Girling went to Briston meeting Afternoon, Mr Hardy & W^m went to Holt Church Afternoon. Mr Immanuel drank tea here . . .

OCTOBER 21, THURSDAY A Close windy day. Mr Hardy & W^m at home all day . . .

OCTOBER 24, SUNDAY A Very wet morng. We all went to Holt Church Afternoon, G Philipo drank tea here.

OCTOBER 25, MONDAY A Very fine day. Mr Hardy & W^m at home all day. Mr Goggs from Whisonsett came eveng 3, Slept here. Raind in the Eveng . . .

OCTOBER 28, THURSDAY A Very fine day. Mr Hardy & W^m at home all day, M^r H poorly with the Gout.

OCTOBER 29, FRIDAY A fine day. Mr Hardy very poorly with the Gout . . .

OCTOBER 31, SUNDAY A rime frost, fine day. I & Wm Girling went to Cley meeting foornoon. I, MA & W^m G went to Briston Meeting Afternoon. W^m went to Holt Church Afternoon, came home to tea. Mr Hardy much as Yesterday.

NOVEMBER 1, MONDAY A Wet day. Mr Hardy & W^m at home all day . . .

NOVEMBER 3, WEDNESDAY A fine day. Mr Hardy much as Yesterday. W^m went to Mr Williams of Thornage Afternoon, came home eveng 9. Mr Immanuel came Eveng 2, Slept here.

NOVEMBER 4, THURSDAY A fine day. Mr Hardy much as Yesterday, W^m at home all day. Mr Immanuel went to Holt foornoon, came back to tea, Slept here . . .

NOVEMBER 6, SATURDAY A fine day. Mr Hardy something better. W^m & MA went to Holt Mark^t Afternoon, drank tea at Mr Mendhams, came home Even 9. M^r R Everit, Mr Ladle & Mr Mendham [Mindham] of Holt din'd here . . .

NOVEMBER 9, TUESDAY A Very fine day. Mr Hardy much as Yesterday. W^m went to Mr Williams of Thornage to tea, came home even 9.

NOVEMBER 10, WEDNESDAY A fine day. Mr Hardy much as Yesterday. I, W^m & MA walkd up to Holt Afternoon to Mr Parslees Sale, drank tea at Mr Seales . . .

NOVEMBER 12, FRIDAY A Close stormy day. Mr Hardy something better. W^m at home all day.

NOVEMBER 13, SATURDAY A Cold stormy day. Mr Hardy much as Yesterday. MA went up to Holt Afternoon, drank tea at Mr Bartells. W^m went to Mr Williams of Thornage to dinner, met a party there, came home between 11 & 12 o Clock.

NOVEMBER 14, SUNDAY A Close foggy day. I & W^m G went to Cley meeting foornoon. I, MA & W^m G went to Briston Meeting Afternoon. Mr Hardy much as Yesterday . . .

NOVEMBER 17, WEDNESDAY A Close day. Mr Hardy finely. W^m came home eveng 9 . . .

NOVEMBER 20, SATURDAY A Wet day. Mr Hardy finely. W^m went to Holt Mark^t afternoon, drank tea at Mr Bartells, came home eveng 9.

NOVEMBER 21, SUNDAY A Close mild day. I & W^m G went to Briston meeting Afternoon, W^m & MA went to Holt Church Afternoon. Mr Hardy very finely.

NOVEMBER 22, MONDAY A Very fine mild day. I & MA walkd up to Holt foornoon, came home to dinner. Mr Hardy & W^m at home all day.

NOVEMBER 23, TUESDAY A Close Stormy day. Mr Hardy & W^m at home all day. Phillis Raven & Miss Sturly came to tea, PR staid all Night.

NOVEMBER 24, WEDNESDAY A Very close showry day. Mr Hardy & W^m at home all day . . .

NOVEMBER 26, FRIDAY A Sharp rime frost. Mr Hardy & W^m at homc all day.

NOVEMBER 27, SATURDAY A Frost, fine day. Mr Hardy at home all day. MA & P Raven walkd up to Holt Aftern, came home to tea. W^m went to Holt Mark^t afternoon, came home even 10.

NOVEMBER 29, MONDAY A Wet day. Robt Raven came for Phillis foornoon, went away Eveng past 3. Mr Hardy & W^m at home all day.

NOVEMBER 30, TUESDAY A Close showry day. Maids washd 2 weeks Linnen. Mr Hardy & W^m at home all day.

DECEMBER 1, WEDNESDAY A Showry day. Mr Hardy & W^m at home all day. Mr Sturly, Mr Williams of Thornage, Mr Cook, Thornage, & Mr Savory of Bayfield drank tea here.

DECEMBER 2, THURSDAY A Sharp frost. Mr Hardy at home all day. W^m rid to Mr Collyers to dine with him but he was not at home, came home Eveng 5.

DECEMBER 3, FRIDAY A Close windy morng, Wet Afternoon. Mr Hardy & Wm at home all day. I was taken with dimness in my Eyes at tea time & again Morng 5.

DECEMBER 4, SATURDAY A Rime frost, fine day. Mr Hardy at home all day. Wm went to Holt Markt Afternoon, came home eveng 10 . . .

DECEMBER 6, MONDAY A fine day, frost. Mr Hardy & Wm at home all day. Mr T Temple of Blakney drank tea & Supt here.

DECEMBER 7, TUESDAY A frost, very fine day. Mr Hardy at home all day. I & Wm rid to Cley Afternoon, drank tea at Mr Smiths, came home eveng 9.

DECEMBER 8, WEDNESDAY A Sharp frosty Morn, thawd Afternoon & raind in the Eveng & a deal of rain in the Night. Mr Hardy & Wm at home all day. Mr & Mrs Bartell drank tea here . . .

DECEMBER 11, SATURDAY A Very windy day. Mr Hardy at home all day. Wm went to Holt Markt afternoon, came home eveng 9. Windy Night . . .

DECEMBER 13, MONDAY A Close day. Mr Hardy at home all day, Wm at home all day . . .

DECEMBER 15, WEDNESDAY A Mild close day. Mr Hardy & Wm at home all day.

DECEMBER 16, THURSDAY A fine day, wind cold. Mr Hardy & Wm at home all day.

DECEMBER 17, FRIDAY A Very cold Windy day. Mr Hardy & Wm at home all day.

DECEMBER 18, SATURDAY A Very fine day. Mr Hardy at home all day. Wm went to Holt Markt Aftern, drank tea at Mr Bakers, came home eveng past 9.

DECEMBER 19, SUNDAY A Close drisly day. We all went to Holt Church Afternoon, Mr Meakin preach«ed».

DECEMBER 20, MONDAY A fine day. Mr Hardy [
                    ]. Wm rid to Blakney foornoon, came home eveng 3, went to Mr Savorys at Bayfield, drank tea & Supt there, came home eveng past 10.

DECEMBER 21, TUESDAY A fine day. Mr Hardy at home all day. It was to day Wm went to Bayfield, not yesterday . . .

DECEMBER 26, SUNDAY A fine day. I & Wm G went to Cley meeting foornoon & to Briston meeting Afternoon, MA went with me Afternoon. Mr Hardy & Wm went to Holt Church Afternoon, Mr H & MA went to our Church foornoon . . .

1803

JANUARY 1, SATURDAY A fine day. Mr Hardy at home all day. Wm went to Holt Markt afternoon, came home Eveng past 8. Raind in the Night.

JANUARY 2, SUNDAY A very fine day. We all went to Holt Church afternoon, Mr Meakin Preach'd.

JANUARY 3, MONDAY A fine day. Mr Hardy at home all day. Wm went to Sheringham Morng 9, came back to Holt & spent the Eveng at Holt, came home Eveng past 9 . . .

JANUARY 8, SATURDAY Very Wet day. Mr Hardy at home all day, Wm came home from Norwich Even 8 . . .

JANUARY 12, WEDNESDAY A Very Sharp frost, fine day. Mr Hardy at home all day. Wm & Mr Goggs went to Mr Balls «at» Saxlingham Afternoon, drank tea & Supt there, came home even 11. Miss B Leeke dind, drank tea & Supt here, Mrs Norgate drank tea & Supt here . . .

JANUARY 14, FRIDAY A Sharp frost, fine day. Mr Hardy at home all day. Wm & MA came home from Whisonsett Eveng past 6. Wm went to spend the Eveng at Mr Bartells, Holt, came home eveng past 11 . . .

JANUARY 19, WEDNESDAY A frost, close day. Mr Hardy & Wm at home all day. Mr & Mrs Davy of Holt drank tea here.

JANUARY 20, THURSDAY A sharp frost, close day. Mr Hardy & Wm at home all day.

JANUARY 21, FRIDAY A frost, alittle Snow fell in the morng then thawd slowly all day. Mr Hardy walk'd to Holt Quarter Session foornoon, came home eveng 5, Wm at home all day. Raind alittle in the Night.

JANUARY 22, SATURDAY A Close rather drisly day. Mr Hardy at home all day. Wm went to Holt Markt afternoon, came home even past 9 . . .

JANUARY 24, MONDAY A fine day but windy. Mr Hardy & Wm at home all day. Froz again very sharp at Night.

JANUARY 25, TUESDAY An Extreme sharp frost. Mr Hardy & Wm at home all day. Maids Wash'd 2 Weeks Linnen. Mr Meakin drank tea here . . .

JANUARY 27, THURSDAY A Very sharp frost. Mr Hardy & Wm at home all day.

JANUARY 28, FRIDAY A Sharp frost, alittle Snow fell in the Morng, Chearly day. Mr Hardy & Wm at home all day.

JANUARY 29, SATURDAY A Sharp frost. Mr Hardy at home all day. Wm went to Holt Markt Afternoon, came home Eveng past 8. Some snow fell in the eveng . . .

FEBRUARY 1, TUESDAY A Sharp frost. Mr Hardy at home all day. Wm went to Cley afternoon, came home Eveng 7 . . .

FEBRUARY 6, SUNDAY A sharp frost, frequent Squarls of Snow. No service at our Church, Mr Burrell being bad with A Cough. I & Wm Girling went to Briston Meeting Afternoon. Mr Hardy, Wm, MA, Mr & Mrs Goggs went to Holt Church Afternoon, Mr Meakin preach'd . . .

FEBRUARY 9, WEDNESDAY A Sharp frost. Mr Hardy at home all day. W^m set of for Cromer Morng 10, staid all Night, Slept at Mr Edm^d Bartles.

FEBRUARY 10, THURSDAY A very sharp frost, bright day. Mr Hardy at home all day, W^m came home from Cromer Eveng 5.

FEBRUARY 11, FRIDAY A sharp frost, bright day. Mr Hardy & W^m at home all day.

FEBRUARY 12, SATURDAY A Sharp frost, very close day. Mr Hardy at home all day. W^m went to Holt Mark^t afternoon, drank tea at Mr Seales, came home eveng past 10.

FEBRUARY 13, SUNDAY A rapid thaw, raind from morng untill eveng past 3 then cleard up to a fine eveng. Mr Hardy & I rid, W^m & MA walkd, to Holt Church afternoon, Mr Meakin preach'd. Mrs Chase was buried this Morng about 11 oclock. Frose again in the Night.

FEBRUARY 14, MONDAY A thaw, fine day. Mr Hardy & Wm at home all day . . .

FEBRUARY 16, WEDNESDAY A Close open day. Mr Hardy & W^m at home all day . . .

FEBRUARY 18, FRIDAY A fine day. Mr Hardy at home all day. Mr Moore drank tea & Supt here, W^m came from Wells even 7.

FEBRUARY 19, SATURDAY A Very fine day. Mr Hardy at home all day. W^m went to Holt Mark^t afternoon, drank tea at Mr Bartells, came home eveng 9. Sarah Goodman came Afternoon.

FEBRUARY 20, SUNDAY A fine day. I & Wm Girling went to Cley meeting foornoon, MA went with us Afternoon to Briston Meeting. Mr Hardy & W^m went to Holt Church Afternoon.

FEBRUARY 21, MONDAY A fine Morng, very foggy Afternoon. Mr Hardy at home all day. W^m & MA went to Mr Cooks of Thornage to tea, came home eveng 9.

FEBRUARY 22, TUESDAY A fine day. Mr Hardy & W^m at home all day. Maids Wash'd 2 Weeks Linnen.

FEBRUARY 23, WEDNESDAY A fine day. Mr Hardy at home all day. W^m walk'd up to Holt Afternoon, came home to tea . . .

FEBRUARY 25, FRIDAY A Very fine day. Mr Hardy at home all day. I & MA walkd up to Holt Afternoon, Mr Meakin came home with us to tea. W^m came home from Whisonsett Even 7.

FEBRUARY 26, SATURDAY A fine day. Mr Hardy at home all day. W^m went to Holt Mark^t Afternoon, came home Eveng 9. Raind in the Eveng, Wind high at West . . .

MARCH 5, SATURDAY A Chearly day & froze. Mr Hardy at home all day. W^m went to Holt Mark^t aftern, came home Eveng past 9 . . .

MARCH 7, MONDAY A Sharp wind frost. Mr Hardy [
].

The visit to Whissonsett
8–16 March 1803

MARCH 9, WEDNESDAY A Sharp frost, Wind high & Stormy. At Mr Goggs all day . . .

MARCH 12, SATURDAY A Cold chearly day. M^rs & M & A Raven drank tea & Supt at Mr Goggs . . .

MARCH 17, THURSDAY A drisly morng, fine afternoon. Mr Hardy at home all day.

MARCH 18, FRIDAY A fine day. Mr Hardy at home all day. W^m walk'd up to Holt after tea, came home to Supper.

MARCH 19, SATURDAY A dry day, wind South but Cold. Mr Hardy at home all day. W^m went to Holt Mark^t Afternoon, came home Eveng past 9.

MARCH 20, SUNDAY A fine day. I & Wm Girling went to Cley meeting foornoon & to Briston Meeting Afternoon, MA went to Briston with us Afternoon. Mr Hardy & W^m went to Holt Church Aftern.

MARCH 21, MONDAY A Showry day. Mr Hardy & W^m at home all day. Mr Meakin & M^r T Balls drank tea here.

MARCH 22, TUESDAY A Very fine day. W^m rid to Edgefield foornoon, came home to dinner, Mr Hardy at home all day. W^m drank tea «at» M^r J Savorys. Maids washd 2 Weeks Linnen. Miss Baker & Miss Thompson drank tea here.

MARCH 23, WEDNESDAY A Very fine warm day. Mr Hardy at home all day. I & MA walkd up to Holt Afternoon, drank tea at Mr Davys. W^m walkd up to Holt Afternoon, drank tea at Mr Meakins, came home eveng 8 . . .

MARCH 28, MONDAY A Very fine warm day. Mr Hardy & W^m at home all day.

MARCH 29, TUESDAY A fine day. W^m & MA set of for Norwich ½ past 9, Mr Hardy at home all day. Ann Fryer at work upon the Carpet. A Mr Mellish calld here in the Eveng from Norwich.

MARCH 30, WEDNESDAY A Very fine day. Mr Hardy at home all day.

MARCH 31, THURSDAY A Very fine day. Mr Hardy at home all day. W^m & MA came home eveng past 8 . . .

APRIL 2, SATURDAY A fine day. Mr Hardy at home all day. W^m went to Holt Mark^t Afternoon, came home Eve 9.

APRIL 3, SUNDAY A Small Showr ab^t Noon, fine day. I & W^m went to Cley foornoon, W^m left me there & came home to dinner & went to Holt Church Afternoon & came for me in the Eveng. Mr Hardy, W^m & MA went to Holt Church Afternoon . . .

APRIL 5, TUESDAY A Very fine day. Mr Hardy & W^m at home all day. Maids Wash'd 2 Weeks Linnen.

APRIL 6, WEDNESDAY A Very fine day. Mr Hardy & W^m at home all day.

APRIL 7, THURSDAY A Wet foornoon, fine Afternoon. Mr Hardy at home all day. W^m went to Mr Williams of Thornage, drank tea & Supt there, came home Eveng 11 . . .

APRIL 9, SATURDAY A Very fine day. Mr Hardy at home all day. W^m went to Holt Mark^t afternoon, came home Eveng past 9 . . .

APRIL 14, THURSDAY A fine day. Mr Hardy & W^m at home all day.

APRIL 15, FRIDAY A fine Warm day. Mr Hardy at home all day. W^m drank tea & Supt at M^r T Temples of Thornage, came home Eveng 11.

APRIL 16, SATURDAY A Very warm day. Mr Hardy at home all day. W^m went to Holt Mark^t Afternoon, came home Even 10.

APRIL 17, SUNDAY A small showr morng 9. I & Wm Girling went to Cley meeting foornoon & MA went with us to Briston Meeting Afternoon. Mr Hardy & W^m went to Holt Church Afternoon.

APRIL 18, MONDAY Some small Showers & reather Cold. Mr Hardy & W^m at home all day.

APRIL 19, TUESDAY A Windy day, some small Showers foornoon. Maids Wash'd. Miss Bartell drank tea here.

APRIL 20, WEDNESDAY A Wet day, wind high. Mr Hardy & W^m at home all day, came home eveng 9 [?].

APRIL 21, THURSDAY A Cold stormy day, wind high. Mr Hardy at home all day. W^m dind & drank tea at Mr Williams of Thornage.

APRIL 22, FRIDAY A Cold stormy day. Mr Hardy & W^m at home all day. Mr Marsh of Salthouse & Mat Leak of Holt drank tea here.

APRIL 23, SATURDAY A fine day. Mr Hardy at home all day. I & MA walk'd up to Holt Afternoon, drank tea at Mr Davys. W^m walkd to Mark^t, drank tea at the Wid^w Fishers, came home Even 10.

APRIL 24, SUNDAY A Very showry day. I & Wm Girling went to Briston Meeting Afternoon. Mr Hardy, W^m & MA went to Holt Church Afternoon.

APRIL 25, MONDAY A fine day except a Shower ab^t 4 oClock Afternoon. Mr Hardy walkd up to Holt Afternoon, drank tea at Mr Moores, came home eveng 7. W^m walkd up Afternoon, drank tea & Supt at Mr Bartells, came home Eveng 10. Mr Gibbon Junr dind & drank tea here. Mr Goggs of Whisonsett came eveng past 4, Slept here.

APRIL 26, TUESDAY A dry day but cold. Mr Hardy & W^m at home all day. Mr Goggs went away Even 6 . . .

APRIL 30, SATURDAY A fine day. Mr Hardy at home all day. W^m went to Holt Mark^t Afternoon, came home Eveng 9 . . .

MAY 2, MONDAY A Cold stormy day, wind high. Mr Hardy at home all day. W^m went to Sheringham Afternoon, came home even 9. M^rs & Susan Davy & Miss Bartell drank tea here. A Thunder Storm with large Hail Even 5.

MAY 3, TUESDAY A Windy showry day. Mr Hardy & W^m at home all day. Maids Wash'd . . .

MAY 5, THURSDAY A fine day. Mr Hardy & W^m at home all day.

MAY 6, FRIDAY A Very fine day. Mr Hardy & W^m at home all day, Mrs Savory drank tea here.

MAY 7, SATURDAY A fine day. Mr Hardy at home all day. W^m went to Holt Mark^t Afternoon, came home Eveng 10. I & MA & M Raven walkd up to Holt Aftern, drank tea at Mr Bakers, came home eveng 8.

MAY 8, SUNDAY A fine day. Service at our Church Afternoon. Mr Hardy & W^m went to Holt Church Afternoon. M Raven went to our Church Afternoon, Mr Burrell preach'd. I & MA & Wm Girling went to Briston meeting Aftern . . .

[Then follows the visit to Lincoln, Hull and York, transcribed in full in Diary 4]

JUNE 13, MONDAY A fine day except a Shower Afternoon. Mr Hardy & W^m at home all day. The 2 Mr Bakers & the Custances dind & drank tea here, Mrs Bennet Slept here . . .

JUNE 15, WEDNESDAY A fine morng, Wet afternoon. Mr Hardy & W^m at home all day. MA very poorly with pain in her Face and teeth.

JUNE 16, THURSDAY A Very fine warm day. Mr Hardy & W^m at home all day, M^r & Mrs Bartell drank tea here. MA very poorly with pain in her teeth and Face.

JUNE 17, FRIDAY A Windy dry day. Mr Hardy at home all day. W^m & MR rid to Sheringham Afternoon, came home eveng 8.

JUNE 18, SATURDAY A fine day. Mr Hardy at home all day. W^m & M Raven went to Holt Mark^t Afternoon, drank tea at Mr Davys, came home Eveng 9.

JUNE 20, MONDAY A fine day, a small drisling rain in the Eveng. Mr Hardy at home all day & poorly with the tooth Ake. W^m dind & drank tea at Mr Savorys at Bayfield. MA & M Raven drank tea there, met a large party there.

JUNE 21, TUESDAY A fine morng, very showry Afternoon. Mr Hardy & W^m at home all day. Maids & S Boyce washd 2 Weeks Linnen. M Raven drank tea at Miss Bakers, Holt.

JUNE 22, WEDNESDAY A Wet Cold day. Betty Wortly very poorly all day. Mr Hardy & W^m at home all day.

JUNE 23, THURSDAY A dry day but very Cold. M Raven went away to Mr Sturlys foornoon. W^m & MA went to Fakenham in the Gigg, dind & drank tea at Mr Custances, came home ½ past 9. Mr Hardy at home all day. . .

JUNE 26, SUNDAY A Very fine day. I & Wm Girling went to Cley meeting foornoon, MA went with us to Briston meeting Afternoon. Mr Hardy & W^m went to Holt Church Afternoon, no service at our Church . . .

JUNE 30, THURSDAY A fine day. Mr Hardy & W^m at home all day.

JULY 1, FRIDAY A Very fine day. Mr Hardy & W^m at home all day.

JULY 2, SATURDAY A Very Hot day. Mr Hardy at home all day. Mr Meakin & A Mr Bingle came to speak to us foornoon, Mr Bingle din'd & drank tea here. W^m went to Holt Mark^t afternoon, came home Eveng past 9 . . .

JULY 5, TUESDAY A small showr in the morng, fine day. Mr Hardy & W^m at home all day. Maids Washd 2 weeks Linnen.

JULY 6, WEDNESDAY A Very fine day. Mr Hardy at home all Day. W^m & Jo^s Cook rid to Sheringham Afternoon, came home eveng 9.

JULY 7, THURSDAY A Very fine day. Mr Hardy at home all day. W^m & Jo^s Cook set of for Fakenham Morng 10, Mr Smith of Cley went with them. I & MA walkd up to Holt Afternoon, drank tea at Mr Davys . . .

JULY 11, MONDAY A Very hot day. Mr Hardy & W^m at home all day. Ann Raven came to stay with us a few days . . .

JULY 14, THURSDAY A Cold windy day. Mr Hardy at home all day, W^m rid to Hunworth after tea. MA &

A Raven walkd to Holt Afternoon, drank tea at Miss Nesbits.

JULY 15, FRIDAY A Close cold day. Mr Hardy & W^m at home all Day.

JULY 16, SATURDAY A Very hot dry day. Mr Hardy at home all day. W^m went to Holt Mark^t afternoon, came home Eveng 9. M^r & Mrs Goggs came eveng 7, slept here.

JULY 17, SUNDAY A close moderate day. M^r & Mrs Goggs, Ann Ravn, Mr Hardy, W^m & MA went to Holt Church Afternoon, Mr Meakin preachd. I & W^m [Girling] went to Briston meeting Afternoon. M^r & Mrs Goggs went away after tea.

JULY 18, MONDAY A Very hot day. Mr Hardy & W^m at home all day.

JULY 19, TUESDAY A Hot dry day. Maids Washd 2 weeks Linnen. Mr Hardy & W^m at home all day.

JULY 20, WEDNESDAY A Hot day, asmall showr towards Eveng. Mr Hardy & W^m at home all day.

JULY 21, THURSDAY A Very fine day. Mr Hardy at home all day. W^m & Ann Raven rid to Briston Afternoon, came home half past 8.

JULY 22, FRIDAY A Very hot day. Mr Hardy, I, Sister Goggs, MA & A Raven went to Holt Afternoon, drank tea at Mr Bartells.

JULY 23, SATURDAY A Very hot day. Mr Hardy at home all day. W^m went to Holt Mark^t Afternoon, came home Eveng 9 . . .

JULY 28, THURSDAY A Hot dry day. Mr Hardy at home all day, W^m went up to Holt in the Eveng.

JULY 29, FRIDAY A Hot dry Morng, raind a heavy shower Aftern. Mr Hardy & W^m at home all day . . .

AUGUST 3, WEDNESDAY A Hot windy day. Mr Hardy at home all day. I & MA walkd up to Holt Afternoon, drank tea at Mr Davys. W^m came t{o}o us after tea. Asmall drisly rain in the eveng . . .

AUGUST 5, FRIDAY A fine day. Mr Hardy at home all day. W^m set of for Whisonsett with Sister Goggs, slept there.

AUGUST 6, SATURDAY A Showry day. Mr Hardy at home all day. W^m came home Eveng 6, brought Miss Cook. Mr Cook & Mr Goggs came, slept here . . .

The visit to Whissonsett
9–12 August 1803

AUGUST 9, TUESDAY A Hot dry day. Mr Hardy & I set of for Whisonsett Morng 10, got there Eveng 1, Wm Girlin came back in the Eveng with the Horses. We dind & drank tea & Supt & slept at Sister Ravens at the Malt House. I poorly with dimness in my Eyes in the Night. A large party at Mr Goggs to Day.

AUGUST 10, WEDNESDAY A Close day, reather raind at times. At Sister Ravens all day. A party drank tea there.

AUGUST 11, THURSDAY A little rain in the morng, fine day. We took a walk to Mr Goggs foornoon, drank tea at Mr Nathl Ravens Afternoon [at the shop].

AUGUST 12, FRIDAY A fine day. We took awalk to Mr Goggs foornoon. Wm Girling came with the Horses Morng 8, we sett of for home Eveng were we arivd Even 6 . . .

AUGUST 16, TUESDAY A Very Hot day. Maids & Sarah Boyce wash'd 2 Weeks Linnen. Mr Hardy at home all day. W^m went to Mr Savory to tea Afternoon, came home Eve 8.

AUGUST 17, WEDNESDAY A Very hot day. Mr Hardy & W^m at home all day . . .

AUGUST 21, SUNDAY A Very cool dry day. I & Miss Cook & Wm Girling went to Cley Meeting foornoon, MA went with me to Briston Meeting Afternoon. Mr Hardy, Miss Cook & W^m went to Holt Church Afternoon . . .

AUGUST 27, SATURDAY A fine day. Mr Hardy at home all day. W^m went to Holt foornoon, came home to dinner, went to Mark^t after tea, came home Eveng 9.

AUGUST 28, SUNDAY A fine day. I & Miss Cook & Wm Girling went to Briston Meeting Afternoon. Mr Hardy, W^m & MA went to Holt Church Afternoon, Mr Hardy drank tea at Mr Bartells . . .

AUGUST 30, TUESDAY A Wet Morng, a very small drisly rain atimes all day. Maids & S Lamb washd 2 Weeks Linnen. Mr Hardy at home all day, W^m walkd up to Holt after tea . . .

SEPTEMBER 2, FRIDAY A fine day. Mr Hardy & W^m at home all day . . .

SEPTEMBER 13, TUESDAY A fine day. Mr Hardy & W^m at home all day. I, MA & Sister Raven walkd up to Holt Afternoon, drank tea at Mr Meakins.

SEPTEMBER 14, WEDNESDAY A fine day. Mr Hardy & W^m at home all day.

SEPTEMBER 15, THURSDAY A fine day. Mr Hardy & W^m at home all Day. I, MA & Sister Raven drank tea at Mrs Johnsons . . .

SEPTEMBER 17, SATURDAY {A} some very small Showers of rain. Mr Hardy at home all day. W^m rid to Blakny foornoon, came home to dinner, went to Holt Mark^t Afternoon, came home Even 9 . . .

SEPTEMBER 19, MONDAY A fine day. Mr Hardy & W^m at home all day.

SEPTEMBER 20, TUESDAY A fine Morng, showry afternoon. Maids & S Boyce wash'd 3 Weeks Linnen. Mr Hardy & W^m at home all day . . .

SEPTEMBER 22, THURSDAY A fine day. Mr Hardy at home all day. W^m rid to Kelling & Holt Afternoon, drank tea at Mr Meakins, came home Eveng 8.

SEPTEMBER 23, FRIDAY A fine day. Mr Hardy & W^m at home all day. Sister Raven, M^r A [and Mary Ann] rid to Thornage, drank tea at Mr Sturlys, SR [Sister Raven] Slept there.

SEPTEMBER 24, SATURDAY A fine day. Mr Hardy at home all day. Mr Thos Gibbons [junior] came Morng 8 a Shooting, Breakfst«ed» & dind here. W^m & he went to Holt Mark^t Afternoon, came home eveng 9, «he» supt here & went home to Wells . . .

SEPTEMBER 26, MONDAY A Very fine day. Mr Hardy & W^m at home all day. I, MA & Sister Raven walk'd up to Holt Afternoon, drank tea at Mr Bartells.

SEPTEMBER 27, TUESDAY A fine day. We all drank tea at Mr Burrells, met M^r & Mrs Savory there.

SEPTEMBER 28, WEDNESDAY A fine day. Mr Hardy, I, Sister Raven & MA & W^m drank tea at Mr Temples.

SEPTEMBER 29, THURSDAY A fine day. Mr Hardy & W^m at home all day. Mr Oxenborough of Wells & Immanuel din'd here. Mr Bingle dind, Supt & Slept here.

SEPTEMBER 30, FRIDAY A fine day till Eveng 5 then raind but did not Continue long. Mr Bingle went away after tea. Mr Meakin, Mrs Davy & Sarah drank tea here. Mr Hardy at home all day, W^m dind & drank tea at Mr John Savorys.

OCTOBER 1, SATURDAY A fine day. Mr Hardy at home all day. W^m went to Holt Mark^t afternoon, came home Even 9.

OCTOBER 2, SUNDAY A fine day, reather Cold. I & Sister Rav^n & Wm Girling went to Cley Meeting foornoon, MA went with us to Briston Afternoon. Mr Hardy, W^m & Sister Rav^n went to Holt Church Afternoon.

OCTOBER 3, MONDAY A fine day untill Eving 6 then raind. Mr Hardy & W^m at home all day.

OCTOBER 4, TUESDAY A Wet morng, frequent showers in the Day. Mr Hardy at home all day. W^m went to Aylsham foornoon to an Auction of Mr Coopers of Briston, came home Eveng past 8.

OCTOBER 5, WEDNESDAY A fine day. Mr Hardy & W^m at home all day . . .

OCTOBER 9, SUNDAY A Very showry day, Wind high. I, MA & WG went to Briston Meeting Afternoon, Mr Hardy & W^m went to Holt Church Aftern.

OCTOBER 10, MONDAY A Showry day. Mr Hardy & W^m at home all day . . .

OCTOBER 16, SUNDAY A fine day. I & Ja^s Stapleton went to Cley Meeting foornoon, I & W^m went to Briston Meeting Afternoon. M^r & Mrs Goggs came to dinner & Slept here, they with Mr Hardy & MA went to Holt Church.

OCTOBER 17, MONDAY A fine day. Mr Hardy at home all day. W^m went to Mr Balls, Saxlingham, Afternoon, came home [   ]. M^r & Mrs Goggs went away after dinner . . .

OCTOBER 21, FRIDAY A Close Mild day. Mr Hardy & W^m at home all day.

OCTOBER 22, SATURDAY A fine day. Mr Hardy at home all day. W^m walk'd up to Holt foornoon, came back to dinner, went to Holt Mark^t afternoon, came home Even 9.

OCTOBER 23, SUNDAY A Very fine day. I & MA & Boy went to Briston meeting Afternoon. Mr Hardy & W^m went to Holt Church Afternoon, Mr Meakin preach'd.

OCTOBER 24, MONDAY A Very fine day. Mr Hardy & W^m at home all day. Miss Bell Leake dind & drank tea here.

OCTOBER 25, TUESDAY A Very Close foggy day. Mr Hardy & W^m at home all day.

OCTOBER 26, WEDNESDAY A foggy day. Mr Hardy & W^m at home all day.

OCTOBER 27, THURSDAY A foggy Morng, fine day. Mr Hardy & W^m at home all day. Mr Immanuel came to tea, Slept here.

OCTOBER 28, FRIDAY A frost, very fine day. Mr Hardy & W^m at home all day . . .

OCTOBER 31, MONDAY A Cold windy day. Mr Hardy & W^m at home all day.

NOVEMBER 1, TUESDAY A drisly Morng, dry Windy day. Maids Wash'd. Mr Hardy at home all day. W^m went to Mr Williams of Thornage in the Eveng to meet A Mr Brown, came home Eveng 11 . . .

NOVEMBER 3, THURSDAY A Cold dry day. Mr Hardy & W^m at home all day.

NOVEMBER 4, FRIDAY A Cold dry day. Mr Hardy & W^m at home all day. Mr Williams & Mr Brown here an hour or 2 in the foornoon. M^r & Mrs Savory & Miss Atthill drank tea here.

NOVEMBER 5, SATURDAY A Very Close Cold day. Mr Hardy at home all day. W^m walkd up to Holt foornoon, came home to dinner, went to Holt Mark^t Afternoon, came home Eveng.

NOVEMBER 6, SUNDAY A Close dry foornoon, raind Afternoon. We all went to Holt Church Afternoon, Mr Meakin preach'd.

NOVEMBER 7, MONDAY A Close dry day. Mr Hardy at home all day. W^m & MA went to Mr Savorys of Bayfield to tea. I poorly with dimness in my Eyes Morng 9 & Again Eveng 9 . . .

NOVEMBER 13, SUNDAY A fine day. I & Wm Girling went to Cley meeting foornoon. I, MA & Ja^s Stapleton went to Briston Meeting Afternoon, A Sacrament . . .

NOVEMBER 16, WEDNESDAY A Very Wet day. Mr Hardy at home all day. I poorly with dimness in my Eyes Morn 6.

NOVEMBER 17, THURSDAY A Wet foornoon, fine afternoon. Mr Hardy at home all day. M^r & Mrs Philippo & Mr Ellis dind here.

NOVEMBER 18, FRIDAY A fine day. Mr Hardy at home all day.

NOVEMBER 19, SATURDAY A fine day. Mr Hardy went to Holt Mark^t Afternoon, drank tea at Mr Bartells, came Even 8.

NOVEMBER 20, SUNDAY A fine day. I & MA & Ja^s Stapleton went to Briston meeting Afternoon. Mr Hardy went to our Church Afternoon, Mr Burrell preach'd.

NOVEMBER 22, TUESDAY A Very Wet Day. Mr Hardy at home all day.

NOVEMBER 23, WEDNESDAY A Showry day. Mr Hardy at home all day.

NOVEMBER 24, THURSDAY A fine day. Mr Hardy at home all Day, Immanuel came in the Eveng & Slept here.

NOVEMBER 25, FRIDAY *Holt Fair* Immanuel went away after dinner, Mr Hardy at home all Day . . .

NOVEMBER 27, SUNDAY A Sharp frosty morng, raind alittle towards Eveng. I & Wm Girling went to Cley meeting foornoon. I, MA & Thos Wakefield went to Briston Meeting Afternoon. Mr Hardy at Holt Church Afternoon.

NOVEMBER 28, MONDAY A fine day. Mr Hardy at home all day.

NOVEMBER 29, TUESDAY A Wet foornoon, dry windy Afternoon. Mr Hardy at home all day. Maids Washd 2 Weeks Linnen.

NOVEMBER 30, WEDNESDAY A fine Morng, Storms of Sleet Afternoon. Mr Hardy at home all day.

DECEMBER 1, THURSDAY A Showry day. Mr Hardy at home all day.

DECEMBER 2, FRIDAY A fine Morng, Wet Afternoon. Mr Hardy at home all Day . . .

DECEMBER 5, MONDAY A frost. Mr Hardy at home all day. A little Snow fell in the Night.

DECEMBER 6, TUESDAY A Sharp frost. Mr Hardy at home all day. I & MA walkd up to Holt & came back to dinner. Mr Bartell & Mr Stannard walkd down foornoon. Rec'd a letter from W^m . . .

DECEMBER 12, MONDAY A frosty Morng, Thawd in the Day time. Mr Goggs went away ½ past 1. Mr Hardy & W^m at home all day.

DECEMBER 13, TUESDAY A Close drisly day. Maids Washd 2 weeks Linnen. Mr Hardy & W^m at home all Day . . .

DECEMBER 15, THURSDAY A Close Windy day. Mr Hardy at home all day. W^m went to the School Feast at Holt, dind at the Feathers, drank tea at Mr Bartells, came home Eveng past 10.

DECEMBER 16, FRIDAY A Close foggy day. Mr Hardy at home all day. W^m drank tea & Supt at Mr Bartells.

DECEMBER 17, SATURDAY A Very Close foggy day. Mr Hardy at home all day. W^m went to Holt Mark^t Afternoon, came home eveng past 9.

DECEMBER 18, SUNDAY A Close drisly day. Mr Hardy went to our Church Afternoon, Mr Burrell preach'd. W^m & MA went to Holt Church Afternoon, Mr Meakin preach'd. I was but poorly, did not go out.

DECEMBER 19, MONDAY A Very Wet day. W^m & MA dind, drank tea & Supt at Mr Burrells. Mr Hardy & I drank tea & Supt there, expected to meet M^r & Mrs Skrimshire there, they did not come on acct of the Weather.

DECEMBER 20, TUESDAY A Close dry day. M^r & Mrs Skrimshire from Fakenham came to Dinner, Slept here. M^r & Mrs Burrell & Miss Deb Johnson & Mr Williams of Thornage dind, drank tea & Slept here . . .

DECEMBER 23, FRIDAY A Close mild day. Mr Hardy & W^m at home all day. Raind a good deal in the night . . .

DECEMBER 26, MONDAY A fine day. Mr Hardy & W^m at home all day.

DECEMBER 27, TUESDAY A Close drisly day. Mr Hardy & W^m at home all day. M^r & M^{rs}, Ja^s & Do^l [?Dorothy] Temple & Mr Williams drank tea here. Maids Wash'd 2 Weeks Linnen.

DECEMBER 28, WEDNESDAY A Very wet day. Mr Hardy & W^m at home all day . . .

DECEMBER 30, FRIDAY A Wet Morng, dry Afternoon & very Wet Eveng. Mr Hardy at home all day, went to Mr Burrells after tea, Supt there, came home past 10.

DECEMBER 31, SATURDAY A Mild dry day, Very Wet Eveng & Night. Mr Hardy at home all day. W^m went to Holt Market Afternoon, came home past 9 . . .

1804

JANUARY 2, MONDAY A fine day. Mr Hardy at home all day. Mr Moore & his 2 Daughters dind here, M^r & Miss Susan Davy drank tea here. W^m dind & drank tea at Mr Williams of Thornage.

JANUARY 3, TUESDAY A sharp rime frost. Mr Hardy at home all day.

JANUARY 5, THURSDAY A Sharp rime frost, began to snow ab^t 8oCl, continued all the foornoon, the«n» thawd. I poorly with dimness in my Eyes ab^t Noon. Mr Hardy & W^m at home all day. Hase here at Dinner & slept here. . .

JANUARY 7, SATURDAY A Chearly day, reather frosty. I poorly with dimness in my Eyes Morng 10. Mr Hardy at home all day. W^m went to Holt Mark^t Afternoon, came home Eveng 10 . . .

JANUARY 10, TUESDAY A Close foggy day. Mr Hardy & W^m at home all day, Maids Wash'd 2 Weeks Linnen.

JANUARY 11, WEDNESDAY A dry day. Mr Hardy & W^m at home all day.

JANUARY 12, THURSDAY A Close open day. Mr Hardy & W^m at home all day. I poorly.

JANUARY 13, FRIDAY A Dry morng, stormy Afternoon. I better. Mr Hardy & W^m at home all day.

JANUARY 14, SATURDAY A Close mild day. Mr Hardy at home all day. W^m went to Holt Mark^t Aftern, came home Eveng 10.

JANUARY 15, SUNDAY A Very Wet day till Eveng 3 then cleard up to A fine Night. Mr Hardy went to our Church Afternoon, Mr Burrell preachd. W^m went to Holt Church Afternoon, Mr Loyd [Lloyd] preach'd. I & MA did not go out, the Weather being so very bad.

JANUARY 16, MONDAY A Close mild day. Mr Hardy & W^m at home all day. Mr Gibbons Junr from Wells call'd here in the Eveng.

JANUARY 17, TUESDAY A Close mild day. Mr Hardy at home all day. W^m walk'd up to Holt Afternoon to collect some Bills, drank tea at Mr Davys, came home even 9 . . .

JANUARY 19, THURSDAY A Close dry day. Mr Hardy at home all day. W^m drank tea & Supt at Mr Williams at Thornage. A Very Wet Eveng . . .

JANUARY 21, SATURDAY A dry mild day. Mr Hardy at home all day. W^m went to Holt Mark^t Afternoon, came home Eveng 10 . . .

JANUARY 23, MONDAY A fine mild day. Mr Goggs & Mr Cook went away Eveng 4. W^m went with them, they drank tea at Mr Skrimshires at Fakenham, got to Whisonsett abt 8. Mr Hardy at home all day.

JANUARY 24, TUESDAY A fine mild day. Maids washd 2 Weeks Linnen. W^m came home from Whisonsett Eveng 8 . . .

JANUARY 27, FRIDAY A fine day. Mr Hardy at home all day. W^m rid to Thursford foornoon, came home Eveng 8.

JANUARY 28, SATURDAY A Showry foornoon, Wet Afternoon. Mr Hardy at home all day. W^m went to Holt Mark^t Afternoon, came home Eveng past 9.

JANUARY 29, SUNDAY A fine day but Windy. I, MA & Boy went to Briston Meeting Afternoon, took the new Mare. Mr Hardy & W^m went to Holt Church Afternoon, Mr Meakin preach'd . . .

JANUARY 31, TUESDAY A Dry Morng, drisly Afternoon. Mr Hardy & W^m at home all day. Mr Immanuel came in the Eveng, Slept here . . .

FEBRUARY 3, FRIDAY A Very fine mild day, raind in the Even. Mr Hardy & W^m at home all day . . .

FEBRUARY 6, MONDAY A Very sharp Stormy day. Mr Hardy & W^m at home all day.

FEBRUARY 7, TUESDAY A sharp frosty day, frequent Storms of Snow & Hail Afternoon. Mr Hardy & W^m at home all day.

FEBRUARY 8, WEDNESDAY A sharp frosty Morng, thaw'd Afternoon. Maids Wash'd 2 Weeks Linnen. Mr Hardy & W^m at home all day.

FEBRUARY 9, THURSDAY A fine open day. Mr Hardy & W^m at home all day.

FEBRUARY 10, FRIDAY A fine day but stormy Night. Mr Hardy & W^m at home all day . . .

FEBRUARY 20, MONDAY A Cold dry day. Mr Hardy & W^m at home all day.

FEBRUARY 21, TUESDAY A fine day. Mr Hardy & W^m at home all day . . .

FEBRUARY 23, THURSDAY A Cold Stormy day. Mr Hardy & W^m at home all day.

FEBRUARY 24, FRIDAY Wind high at West, frequent Storms of Hail & snow. Mr Hardy & W^m at home all day . . .

FEBRUARY 28, TUESDAY A Very Cold stormy day. Mr Hardy at home all day. W^m went to Mr Williams at Thornage to tea, came home even 9. Mr Immanuel came to dinner, Slept here. A dreadful Night of Storms of Wind & Snow, Wind very high in the Night, Snow much drifted.

FEBRUARY 29, WEDNESDAY Very Cold & Windy, frequent Storms of Hail & Snow. Mr Hardy at home all day. Mr Immanuel & W^m walkd to Holt Afternoon, came back Even 8, Immanuel Slept here. Snowd in the Night.

MARCH 1, THURSDAY A Sharp frost in the Morng, thawd as the Day got up. Mr Immanuel went away Morng 8. Mr Hardy at home all day. W^m rid to Cley Aftern, drank tea at Mr Marsh^s, came home near Even 11.

MARCH 2, FRIDAY Frosty morng, thawd in the Day, Wind very Cold. Mr Hardy & W^m at home all day. Froze again at Night.

MARCH 3, SATURDAY A Close foornoon, Snowd very hard all the Afternoon & Night. Mr Hardy at home all day. W^m went to Holt Mark^t Afternoon, came home eveng past 9 . . .

MARCH 5, MONDAY A Cold thaw. Mr Hardy & W^m at home all day. Mr Williams of Thornage drank tea & Supt here . . .

MARCH 8, THURSDAY A dry Cold day. Mr Hardy & W^m at home all day.

MARCH 9, FRIDAY A Close cold day, drisly Afternoon & Eveng. Mr Hardy & W^m at home all day. Mr Immanuel came to tea & Slept here.

MARCH 10, SATURDAY A Very fine mild day. Mr Hardy at home all day. W^m went to Holt Mark^t Afternoon, came home Eveng 10.

MARCH 11, SUNDAY A Chearly day, Wind Cold. I poorly with dimness in my Eyes morng 9. I & MA went to Briston meeting Afternoon. W^m went to Holt Church Afternoon, Mr Meakin preach'd. Mr Hardy went to our Church Afternoon, Mr Burrell preach'd.

MARCH 12, MONDAY A Very fine day. Mr Hardy & W^m at home all day. I poorly with dimness in my Eyes ab^t Noon. M^r & Mrs Bartell, M^r & Miss Baker drank tea here . . .

MARCH 15, THURSDAY A fine day. Mr Hardy much as Yesterday, W^m at home all day . . .

MARCH 17, SATURDAY A Close Cold day. Mr Hardy much as Yesterday. W^m went to Holt Mark^t Afternoon, came home eveng 10 . . .

MARCH 20, TUESDAY A Very sharp frost, Wind high. Mr Hardy much a [as] Yesterday. Maids Washd 2 Weeks Linnen.

MARCH 21, WEDNESDAY A sharp frost, wind high. Mr Hardy much as Yesterday. W^m went to Mr Savorys at Bayfield to tea, met Mr Chas Savory there, came home Eveng 10 . . .

MARCH 23, FRIDAY A Sharp frost, Cold day. Mr Hardy somthing better, W^m at home all day . . .

MARCH 28, WEDNESDAY A Cold dry day. Mr Hardy much as Yesterday, W^m at home all day.

MARCH 29, THURSDAY A Cold dry day. Mr Hardy much as Yesterday. W^m finely, at home all day. Mr Williams of Thornage Supt here.

MARCH 30, *Good Friday* A fine dry day but Cold. Mr Hardy much as Yesterday. I & MA walk'd up to Holt Church Afternoon, Mr Meakin preachd. W^m walk'd up to Holt Afternoon, was too late for Church, drank tea at Mr Bartells, came home Eveng 7. Service at our Church foornoon, Mr Burrell preach'd. Raind a good deal in the Even & Night . . .

APRIL 2, MONDAY A Cold dry day. Mr Hardy better. W^m at home all day . . .

APRIL 5, THURSDAY A Cold Stormy day. Mr Hardy finely. Mr Meakin calld Afternoon but did not stop long. W^m came home from Whisonsett Eveng 8 . . .

APRIL 7, SATURDAY A Cold dry day. Mr Hardy much as Yesterd. W^m went to Holt Mark^t afternoon, came home Eve 10.

APRIL 8, SUNDAY A fine day. Mr Hardy but poorly. I & MA & Boy went to Briston Meeting Afternoon. W^m went to Holt Church Afternoon, Mr Meakin preach'd. Mr Meakin began preaching at Dawling [Field Dalling] this Morng.

APRIL 9, MONDAY A Very Cold Windy day. Mr Hardy somthing better then Yesterday. W^m at home all day . . .

APRIL 11, WEDNESDAY A Cold Windy day. Mr Hardy much as Yesterday. W^m rid up to Holt Afternoon & from thence to Mr Williams, Thornage, drank tea there, came home Eveng 10. Mr Goggs brought Jane Skinner to Geo^r Philipos, drank tea there, came home Even 7, Supt & Slept here.

APRIL 12, THURSDAY A Cold Windy day. Mr Hardy poorly. W^m at home all day, M^r T Balls drank tea & Supt here . . .

APRIL 14, SATURDAY A Close Cold day. Mr Hardy much as Yesterday. W^m went to Mark^t Afternoon, came home Even near 10, Mr Williams came home with him to supper. I poorly with dimness in my Eyes Eveng 2 . . .

APRIL 16, MONDAY A Very Cold close windy day. Mr Hardy finely. W^m at home all day, {W^m at home} . . .

APRIL 19, THURSDAY A Very Cold day, frequent Storms of Snow. Mr Hardy at home all day, W^m walkd up to Holt after tea. A good deal of Snow fell in the Night.

APRIL 20, FRIDAY A Very Cold Stormy day. Mr Hardy & W^m at home all day.

APRIL 21, SATURDAY A Sharp frost, chearly day, Wind high Aftern. Mr Hardy at home all day. W^m went to Holt Mark^t Afternoon, came home Even 10, Mr Williams came home with him & Supt here.

APRIL 24, TUESDAY A Very Wet Morng, dry windy Afternoon. Mr Hardy at home all day. W^m came home from Norwich Eveng 8 . . .

APRIL 27, FRIDAY A Showry mild day. Mr Hardy at home all day. W^m went to Mr Williams, Thornage, after tea, came home to supper.

APRIL 28, SATURDAY A Showry Mild day. Mr Hardy at home all day. W^m went to Holt Mark^t afternoon, came home Eveng past 9.

APRIL 29, SUNDAY A Very fine Warm day. Mr Hardy at home all day. I but poorly in the Morng, could not go to Cley. I, W^m & MA went to Briston Meeting Afternoon, Mr Breden [Breeden] preachd there.

APRIL 30, MONDAY A Very fine warm day. Mr Hardy at home all day. W^m went with Mr Williams to Mr Reeves, Weighton [Wighton], din'd & drank tea there, came home Even 11 . . .

MAY 2, WEDNESDAY A Very fine warm day. Mr Hardy & W^m at home all day.

MAY 3, THURSDAY A Very fine warm day. Mr Hardy & W^m at home all day . . .

MAY 5, SATURDAY A fine Warm day. Mr Hardy at home all day. W^m went to Holt Mark^t Afternoon, came home Eveng 10 . . .

MAY 7, MONDAY A fine day, not so warm as Yesterday. Mr Hardy & W^m at home all day. M^r & Mrs Eastaugh came to dinner & Slept here.

MAY 8, TUESDAY A Close cold day. Mr Hardy & W^m at home all day. M^r & Mrs Eastaugh rid up to Holt foornoon, came back to dinner, Slept here. Mr Immanuel dind, drank tea & Supt here . . .

MAY 12, SATURDAY A Cold dry day. Mr Hardy walkd up to Holt foornoon, came home Eveng 2. W^m went to Holt Mark^t afternoon, came home Eveng past 9, M^r

Williams came with him & Supt here. W^m came home from Whisonsett Morn 11, Sister Goggs came home with him . . .

MAY 15, TUESDAY A Very fine day. Mr Hardy at home all day. W^m went to Geo^r Savorys after tea, came home Eveng 11.

MAY 16, WEDNESDAY A Very fine warm day. Mr Hardy & W^m at home all day, W^m poorly afternoon. Mr Williams of Thornage Supt here.

MAY 18, FRIDAY A Very fine day. Mr Hardy & W^m at home all day.

MAY 19, SATURDAY A fine day, turnd cold towards Night. Mr Hardy at home all day.

MAY 21, MONDAY A Very fine day. Mr Hardy went up to Holt foornoon, came home to dinner, W^m at home all day. Mr Savory & Mr Williams of Thornage Dind & drank tea here. Expected Mr Reeve of Weaton [Wighton], he did not come . . .

MAY 23, WEDNESDAY A Very fine day. Mr Hardy & W^m at home all day. Mr Reeve of Weiton Dind here, Mr Williams of Thornage dind & Supt here.

MAY 24, THURSDAY A Windy day & some small Showers of rain. Mr Hardy & W^m at home all day . . .

MAY 26, SATURDAY A dry day & Windy. Mr Hardy at home all day. W^m went to Holt Mark^t after tea, came home soon after 9. Mr Goggs went away after tea . . .

MAY 28, MONDAY A fine day, reather Windy. Mr Hardy went up to Holt foornoon, came home to dinner. W^m at home all day, Mr Meakin drank tea here.

MAY 29, TUESDAY A dry Windy day. Mr Hardy & W^m at home all day. Maids Wash'd 2 weeks Linnen. Ann Fryer here at work. A Showr Afternoon. M^r & M^{rs} N Raven came from Sturlys to speak to us after tea.

MAY 30, WEDNESDAY A dry windy day. Mr Hardy & W^m at home all day.

MAY 31, THURSDAY A dry windy day. Mr Hardy & W^m at home all day. Mr Meakin came to breakfast, M^r & Mrs Davy & M^r T Balls drank tea here.

JUNE 1, FRIDAY A dry Windy day. Mr Hardy & W^m at home all day. Mr Moore dind & drank tea here. Ann Fryer at work.

JUNE 2, SATURDAY A fine dry day. Mr Hardy at home all day. W^m went to Holt Mark^t afternoon, came home Eveng past 9 . . .

JUNE 5, TUESDAY A Very Hot day, A Very fine Showr in the Eveng. Mr Hardy & W^m at home all day. Ann Fryer at work.

JUNE 6, WEDNESDAY A Hot dry day untill Even 6 then raind A fine Shower. Mr Hardy & W^m at home all day. Rec'd a Letter from MA at Whisonsett. Ann Fryer at work.

JUNE 7, THURSDAY A Windy day. W^m & Sister Goggs set of for Whisonsett Morng half past 9, Mr Hardy at home all day. Ann Fryer at work . . .

JUNE 9, SATURDAY A fine cool day. Mr Hardy at home all day. Ann Fryer at work. M^r T Balls drank tea here. W^m went to Holt Mark^t after tea, came home Eveng past 9 . . .

JUNE 11, MONDAY A fine day. Mr Hardy at home all day. W^m drank tea at Mr Williams at Thornage, came home Eveng 9 . . .

JUNE 13, WEDNESDAY A Very fine day. Mr Hardy & W^m at home all day . . .

JUNE 16, SATURDAY A fine day. Mr Hardy at home all day. W^m went to Holt Mark^t after tea, came home Eveng 9 . . .

JUNE 19, TUESDAY A fine day. Mr Hardy & W^m at home all day. I, MA & M Raven drank tea at M^r J Savorys at Bayfield, W^m came to us after tea . . .

JUNE 23, SATURDAY A fine day. Mr Hardy at home all day. W^m, MA & M Raven went to Holt Mark^t after tea, came home Even 9 . . .

JUNE 26, TUESDAY [at Whissonsett] A fine day, not so hot as Yesterday. We were at Mr Goggs all day . . .

JULY 3, TUESDAY [at Letheringsett] A fine morng, drisly Eveng. Mr Hardy & W^m at home all day. M & Susan Davy came foornoon . . .

JULY 7, SATURDAY A Very Wet foornoon, dry afternoon. Mr Hardy at home all day. W^m went to Holt Mark^t Afternoon, came home Eveng 9 . . .

JULY 9, MONDAY A Cold chearly day, raind in the night. Mr Hardy & W^m at home all day . . .

JULY 11, WEDNESDAY A Cold Windy day. Mr Hardy & W^m at home all day. M^r T Balls drank tea & Supt here.

JULY 12, THURSDAY A Chearly day, wind reather Cold. Mr Hardy at home all day. W^m & MA & M Raven rid to Cromer, dind & drank tea at Mr Bartells, came home Eveng past 10 . . .

JULY 14, SATURDAY A Very fine day. Mr Hardy at home all day. W^m & M Raven walkd up to Holt after tea, came home Eveng past 9.

JULY 15, SUNDAY A Hot dry day. Mr Hardy & MR went to our Church foornoon, Mr Burrell preach'd. I & MA & D Mays went to Briston meeting Afternoon. W^m went to Briningham Church Aftern, Mr Loyd preach'd.

JULY 16, MONDAY A Very Hot dry day. I taken poorly with dimness in my Eyes M [morning] 8. Mr Hardy & W^m at home all day. M^r & M^{rs} & Miss Bartell drank tea here, M^r & Mrs Savory came in the Eveng . . .

JULY 21, SATURDAY A Very Cold Windy Stormy day. Mr Hardy at home all day. W^m went to Holt Mark^t afternoon, came home Eveng 10, Mr Williams of Thornage came home with him to Supper . . .

JULY 27, FRIDAY A fine day. Sister Raven & I rid to Thornage foornoon, Phillis no better then she was Yesterday, Mrs Raven & Mrs Skrimshire there. Mr Hardy & W^m at home all day, MA walkd up to Holt after tea. M^r & Miss Bartell came in the Eveng. Mrs Seales, M^r & Mrs Kendle from Yarmouth here foornoon . . .

JULY 29, SUNDAY A fine day. Mr Hardy & Sister Raven went to our Church foornoon, Mr Burrell preachd. I, MA & D Mays went to Briston Meeting Afternoon. W^m went to Barningham [Briningham] Church Afternoon, Mr Loyd preach'd . . .

AUGUST 1, WEDNESDAY A Hot morng, coll [? cold, ? cool] close afternoon. Mr Hardy & W^m at home all day. M^r & Mrs Breerton [Brereton] drank tea here. I taken sick in the Night.

AUGUST 2, THURSDAY A Cool day. Mr Hardy at home all day. W^m went to Mr Balls, Saxlingham, drank tea & Supt there. A Tempest in the Night.

AUGUST 3, FRIDAY A Close Hot day. Mr Hardy at home all day. W^m dind & drank tea at Mr Temples at Blakney, came home Eveng past 10.

AUGUST 4, SATURDAY A Very foggy Sultry day foornoon, A heavy Showry Afternoon with Thunder. Mr Hardy at home all day. W^m went to Holt Mark't Afternoon, came home Even p [past] 8. Mr Williams supt here . . .

AUGUST 8, WEDNESDAY A Very showry day. Mr Hardy & W^m at home all day. M^r & Mrs Meakin & a Mrs Carr from London drank tea here . . .

AUGUST 10, FRIDAY A Windy day. Mr Hardy & W^m at home all day. M^r & M^{rs} & Ann Raven walkd up to Holt foorn & went home after tea.

AUGUST 11, SATURDAY A fine day. Mr Hardy at home all day. W^m went to Holt Mark^t Afternoon, came home Eveng 9, Mr Williams Supt here. Sister Raven walkd to Holt Afternoon, drank tea at Old Mrs Johnsons . . .

AUGUST 14, TUESDAY A fine day. Mr Hardy & W^m at home all day . . .

AUGUST 17, FRIDAY A Showry day. Mr Hardy at home all day. M^r & Mrs Cook, M^r & Mrs Goggs, I & W^m rid to Sheringham Afternoon, drank tea there, came home Eveng 9.

AUGUST 18, SATURDAY A Very Showry day. Mr Hardy at home all day. W^m went up to Holt foorno, came home to dinner Eveng 2. M^r & Mrs Cook, M^r & Mrs Goggs went away Eveng past 3. W^m went to Holt Mark^t Eveng 4, came home even 9 . . .

AUGUST 22, WEDNESDAY A fine dry day till Eveng 6 then raind. Mr Hardy & W^m at home all day. Mrs Robinson & Child, M^r & Mrs Bartell from Cromer, Miss Bartell [? of Cromer], Mr Stannard & Miss Bartell [? of Holt], Missrs [Misses] Mary & Sarah Davy dind & drank tea here, M^r & Mrs Bartell [of Holt] came to tea. M^r T Fox came Eveng 9 for Sister Raven, slept here.

AUGUST 23, THURSDAY A little shower in the Morng, dry windy day. Mr Hardy & W^m at home all day. Mr Fox & Sister Raven went away after dinner.

AUGUST 24, FRIDAY A fine day. Mr Hardy at home all day. Mrs Smith of Cley & her Sister & A Miss C[   ] drank tea here. W^m met Mr Bartell & a party at M^r T Temples of Thornage.

AUGUST 25, SATURDAY A fine day. Mr Hardy at home all day. W^m went to Holt Mark^t afternoon, drank tea «at» Mr Bartells. MA walkd up afternoon, drank tea at Mr Davys, met Mrs Robinson there.

AUGUST 26, SUNDAY A Very fine day. I, MA & Wm Girling went to Briston Meeting Afternoon. W^m rid to Barningham [Briningham] Church Afternoon, Mr Loyd [Lloyd] preachd. Mr Hardy at home all day . . .

SEPTEMBER 2, SUNDAY A fine day. Mr Hardy poorly, did not go to Church service in the afternoon, Mr Burrell preachd. I & D Mays went to Cley meeting foornoon. W^m, I & MA went to Briston meeting Afternoon.

SEPTEMBER 3, MONDAY A fine Hot day. Mr Hardy & W^m at home all day . . .

SEPTEMBER 7, FRIDAY A Very Hot dry day. Mr Hardy at home all day. W^m went to Mr Williams to tea Afternoon, came home eveng 9 . . .

SEPTEMBER 9, SUNDAY A Very fine dry day. Service at our Church foornoon, Mr Hardy did not go. I, MA & Wm Girling went to Briston meeting Afternoon. W^m went to Briningham Church Afternoon.

SEPTEMBER 10, MONDAY A Very Hot day, close afternoon. Mr Hardy at home all day. W^m & MA walkd to Mr Savorys to tea afternoon, Mrs Davy drank tea here . . .

SEPTEMBER 14, FRIDAY Not quite so sultry as Yesterday but very hot. Mr Hardy & W^m at home all day. Mrs Balding & S Davy drank tea here.

SEPTEMBER 15, SATURDAY A Very Hot day. Mr Hardy at home all day. W^m went to Holt Mark^t aftern, came home eveng past 8. Mr Williams supt here . . .

SEPTEMBER 22, SATURDAY A Cold day, Wind high. Mr Hardy at home all day. W^m went to Holt Mark^t afternoon, came home Eveng 8 . . .

SEPTEMBER 25, TUESDAY A fine day. Mr Hardy & W^m at home all day. I & MA walkd up to Holt Afternoon, drank tea at Mr Davys . . .

SEPTEMBER 27, THURSDAY A Cold drisly day. Mr Hardy at home all day. W^m rid to Mr Williams after tea, came home Eveng 10.

SEPTEMBER 28, FRIDAY A Close day, frequent very small drisling Showers. Mr Hardy & W^m at home all day. I taken with dimness in my Eyes Eveng 2 & otherwise very poorly all day & Night . . .

OCTOBER 4, THURSDAY A fine day. Mr Hardy at home all day & W^m at home all day. I poorly. Mr Custance went away after Breakfast . . .

OCTOBER 6, SATURDAY A Very fine day. Mr Hardy at home all day. W^m walkd up to Holt foornoon, did not return to dinner, dind at Mrs Fishers, came home even 8 . . .

OCTOBER 15, MONDAY A fine day. Mr Hardy & W^m at home all day. I very poorly foornoon with dimness in my Eyes . . .

OCTOBER 17, WEDNESDAY A Very Wet morng, fine afternoon. Mr Myles Custance & Mr Bennet came A Shooting, dind & drank tea here. Mr Hardy & W^m at home all day.

OCTOBER 18, THURSDAY A Very Wet day. Mr Hardy & W^m at home all day . . .

OCTOBER 20, SATURDAY A fine day. Mr Hardy at home all day. W^m went to Holt Mark^t afternoon, came home Eveng 9.

OCTOBER 21, SUNDAY A fine day. Service at our Church foornoon. Mr Hardy at home all day. I, MA & Wm Girling went to Briston meeting afternoon, W^m went to Barningham [Briningham] Church Afternoon . . .

OCTOBER 24, WEDNESDAY A fine day. Mr Hardy at home all day. I much better then Yesterday.

OCTOBER 25, THURSDAY A fine day. Mr Hardy at home all day . . .

OCTOBER 27, SATURDAY A fine Morng, began to rain Morng 11 & continued Showry all day. Mr Hardy rid to Holt Mark^t Afternoon, drank tea at Mr Bartells, Supt at the Feathers & came home Even 12 . . .

OCTOBER 29, MONDAY A Close dry day. Mr Hardy, I & M Raven drank tea at Mr Burrell. Recd a Letter from W^m from London.

OCTOBER 30, TUESDAY A fine day. Mr Hardy at home all day. Maids Wash'd 2 Weeks Linnen.

OCTOBER 31, WEDNESDAY A fine day. Mr Hardy at home all day. Raind a deal in the Night . . .

NOVEMBER 2, FRIDAY A Mild Showry day. Mr Hardy at home all day. M^r & Mrs Burrell drank tea here . . .

NOVEMBER 6, TUESDAY A Very fine day but cold & Windy. Mr Hardy at home all day. I & M Raven walkd up to Holt Afternoon, came home to tea . . .

NOVEMBER 8, THURSDAY A fine day. Mr Hardy, I & M Raven took a walk Afternoon . . .

NOVEMBER 10, SATURDAY A Very Wet day. Mr Hardy at home all day. W^m went to Holt Mark^t afternoon, came home Eveng 9.

NOVEMBER 11, SUNDAY A Close dry day. I & M [Matthew] Philipo went to Cley meeting foornoon, MA & Wm Girling went with me to Briston Meeting Afternoon. Mr Hardy & M Raven went to our Church Afternoon, Mr Burrell preach'd.

NOVEMBER 12, MONDAY A Wet day. Mr Hardy & W^m at home all day.

NOVEMBER 13, TUESDAY A Wet day. Mr Hardy & W^m at home all day. Maids Wash'd 2 Weeks Linnen.

NOVEMBER 14, WEDNESDAY A Wet day. Mr Hardy & W^m at home all day.

NOVEMBER 15, THURSDAY A Close foggy day. Mr Hardy & W^m at home all day, Mr Williams of Thornage drank tea & Supt here . . .

NOVEMBER 17, SATURDAY A Close dry day. Mr Hardy at home all day. W^m went to Holt Mark^t Afternoon, came home Even 9.

NOVEMBER 18, SUNDAY A fine day. Mr Hardy at home all day. W^m went to Briningham Church afternoon, Mr Loyd preach'd. I, MA & Wm Girling went to Briston Meeting Afternoon . . .

NOVEMBER 21, WEDNESDAY A Dry day. Mr Hardy at home all day, W^m at home all day.

NOVEMBER 22, THURSDAY A fine day. Mr Hardy at home all day. MA walkd up to Holt foornoon, came home to dinner. W^m went to Mr Williams at Thornage to tea, came home Even past 9.

NOVEMBER 23, FRIDAY A Wet foggy day. Mr Hardy & W^m at home all day . . .

NOVEMBER 27, TUESDAY A dry Windy day. Mr Hardy & W^m at home all day. Maids Washd 2 weeks Lin [linen]. I poorly with dimness in my Eyes Morn 11 . . .

NOVEMBER 29, THURSDAY A fine morng, showers of rain foornoon. Mr Hardy at home all day. W^m went up to Holt after tea, Supt at Mr Bartells, came home eveng 10 . . .

DECEMBER 3, MONDAY A fine day. Mr Hardy went up to Holt foornoon, came home Eveng 2. W^m went to Albro [Aldborough] foornoon in Gig, came home Eveng 6. Mr Bingle came foornoon, dind, drank tea & Supt & Slept here. Paul Myles came in Even.

DECEMBER 4, TUESDAY A fine day. Mr Hardy & W^m at home all day. Mr Bingle went away foornoon, Mr Williams drank tea & Supt here.

DECEMBER 5, WEDNESDAY A Close drisly day. Mr Hardy at home all day. W^m drank tea & Supt at Mr Savorys at Bayfield, came home Even 10 . . .

DECEMBER 7, FRIDAY A foggy day. Mr Hardy & W^m at home all day.

DECEMBER 8, SATURDAY A Close foggy day. Mr Hardy at home all day. W^m went to Holt Mark^t afternoon, came home Eveng 9 . . .

DECEMBER 10, MONDAY A Close dry day. Mr Hardy at home all day. W^m went to Mr Colyers to dinner, drank tea & Supt there, came home Even past 11.

DECEMBER 11, TUESDAY A fine Morng, a Shower ab^t 11 o Clock, a fine Afternoon. Mr Hardy & W^m at home all day. M^r & M^rs & Miss Temple drank tea here. Maids Washd 2 Weeks Linnen . . .

DECEMBER 13, THURSDAY A Close dry day. Mr Hardy & W^m at home all day.

DECEMBER 14, FRIDAY A fine day. Mr Hardy at home all day, W^m at home all day.

DECEMBER 15, SATURDAY A fine day. Mr Hardy at home all day. W^m went to Holt Mark^t afternoon, drank tea at Mr Bartells, came home Eveng 9.

DECEMBER 16, SUNDAY A Cold stormy day. Mr Hardy at home all day. I, MA & Wm Girling went to Briston meeting Afternoon, W^m went to Barningham Church Aftern. Storms of Snow & Hail in the Night.

DECEMBER 17, MONDAY Wind high & froze, frequent Storms of Snow & Hail all day. Mr Hardy at home all day. W^m went with Williams to Mr Pauls of Stody to tea, came home Eveng 10 . . .

DECEMBER 19, WEDNESDAY A Sharp Wind frost, very Stormy day. Mr Hardy & W^m at home all day. A Sharp Night . . .

DECEMBER 21, FRIDAY A Sharp frosty Morng, thawd slowly as the day got up. Mr Hardy & W^m at home all day. Froze again in the Night, Wind rough.

DECEMBER 22, SATURDAY A Sharp wind frost. Mr Hardy at home all day. W^m went to Holt Mark^t Afternoon, came home Eveng 10.

DECEMBER 23, SUNDAY A Sharp frosty Morng, began to thaw ab^t 10 o Clock & continued all day. I & Math Philipo went to Cley meeting foornoon. I, MA & Wm Girling went to Briston meeting Afterno, Mr Breeden dind here. Mr Hardy went to our Church Afternoon, Mr Burrell preachd . . .

DECEMBER 26, WEDNESDAY Thawd slowly all day, very close, small Snow fell almost all day. W^m went to Mr Breertons at Blakney to Dinner, came home Morng 3 . . .

DECEMBER 29, SATURDAY A Sharp Wind frost. Mr Hardy at home all day. W^m went to Holt Mark^t Afternoon, came home Even 9 . . .

DECEMBER 31, MONDAY A Sharp frost. Mr Hardy & W^m at home all day. M^r & Miss Bartell drank tea here.

1805

JANUARY 1, TUESDAY A Sharp frost, fine day. Mr Hardy at home all day, W^m sett of for Whisonsett abt 12 o Clock.

JANUARY 2, WEDNESDAY A Slow thaw all day. Mr Hardy at home all day.

JANUARY 3, THURSDAY A Close foggy day. Mr Hardy at home all day, W^m came home from Whisonsett Eveng past 8 . . .

JANUARY 6, SUNDAY A Close foggy day. I & M Philipo went to Cley meeting foornoon, Mr Simmons dind here. I, MA & Wm Girling went to Briston Meeting Afternoon. Mr Hardy went to our Church Afternoon, Mr Burrell preach'd . . .

JANUARY 8, TUESDAY A rime frost. Mr Hardy & W^m at home all day . . .

JANUARY 11, FRIDAY I poorly this morng with dimness in my Eyes. A Sharp frosty morng, thawd in the Day. Mr Hardy at home all day, W^m came home from Whisonsett Even past 8. Washd 2 Weeks Linnen.

JANUARY 12, SATURDAY A Sharp frost all day. Mr Hardy at home all day. W^m went to Holt Mark^t Afternoon, came home [   ].

JANUARY 13, SUNDAY A fine day, reather windy. Mr Hardy at home all day. I, MA & Wm Girling went to Briston meeting Afternoon, W^m went to Briningham Church Afternoon. I poorly with dimness in my Eyes Eveng 8.

JANUARY 14, MONDAY A fine day. Mr Hardy at home all day. W^m walk'd up to Holt Afternoon, came home Eveng past 8 . . .

JANUARY 19, SATURDAY A Sharp rime frost. Mr Hardy at home all day. W^m went to Holt Mark^t Afternoon, drank tea at Mr Banks, came home Eveng 8. A Very coarse Windy snowy Night.

JANUARY 20, SUNDAY A Cold coarse Wet morng, dark drisly day. I could not go to Cley this Morng. I, MA & W^m went to Briston meeting Afternoon, Mr Breden preachd. Mr Hardy went to our Church Aftern, Mr Burrell preachd. A rainy Eveng . . .

JANUARY 22, TUESDAY A Very Cold coarse day, asmall Snow & Sleet all day. Mr Hardy at home all day. Wm Dind & drank tea at Mr Banks, Holt, came home Eveng 11. A Snowy windy Night.

JANUARY 23, WEDNESDAY A Cold stormy day. Mr Hardy at home all day. W^m went to Mr Williams of Thornage to tea, came home Even 9.

JANUARY 24, THURSDAY A Sharp wind frost. Mr Hardy & W^m at home all day. M^r T Balls drank tea & Supt here . . .

JANUARY 28, MONDAY A Sharp frost. Mr Hardy & W^m at home all day. Mr Smith of Cley calld here in the Morng . . .

JANUARY 30, WEDNESDAY Thaw'd, A small Snow, very close day. Mr Hardy & W^m at home all day . . .

FEBRUARY 1, FRIDAY A Sharp frost. Mr Hardy at home all Day. W^m dind, drank tea & Supt at Mr Williams at Thornage, came home Even 11.

FEBRUARY 2, SATURDAY A Sharp frosty Morng, thawd in the Day. A little Snow fell in the Eveng, froze again at Night. Mr Hardy at home all day. W^m went to Holt Mark^t afternoon, came home alittle after 8.

FEBRUARY 3, SUNDAY A Sharp frost, Snowd a good deal foornoon, fine Afternoon. I & M Philipo went to Cley meeting foornoon, Mr Simmond dind here. I, W^m & MA went to Briston Meeting Aftern. Mr Hardy went to our Church Afternoon, Mr Burrell preach'd.

FEBRUARY 4, MONDAY Began to thaw in the Morng, raind all day. Mr Hardy & W^m at home all day . . .

FEBRUARY 7, THURSDAY A sharp frosty Morng, thawd Afternoon. Mr Hardy at home all day. I & MA walkd up to Holt Afternoon, drank tea at Mr Davys. W^m rid to M^r T Balls, Saxlingham, drank tea & Supt there, came home Eveng past 10.

FEBRUARY 8, FRIDAY A fine Morng, Close afternoon, raind towards Eveng. Mr Hardy & W^m at home all day, M^r & Mrs Davy drank tea here.

FEBRUARY 9, SATURDAY A fine day but very damp. W^m went up to Holt with Mr Burrell about Noon, came home again Eveng 3, came home a little before 9 [?] . . .

FEBRUARY 11, MONDAY A Mild day. Mr Hardy & W^m at home all day . . .

FEBRUARY 13, WEDNESDAY A fine day. Mr Hardy & W^m at home all day. Mr Williams dind, drank tea & Supt here . . .

FEBRUARY 16, SATURDAY A fine day, no frost. Mrs Smith of Cley dind here, I & MA walk'd up with her to the Auction Afternoon. M^r & Mrs Smith came home with us to tea, Supt & Slept here. W^m went to Holt Mark^t afternoon, came home ½ past 9.

FEBRUARY 17, SUNDAY A frosty Morng, very fine day. M^r & Mrs Smith, I & Ma^t Philipo went to Cley meetin, Mr Breden din'd here. I, W^m & MA went to Briston Meeting Afternoon.

FEBRUARY 18, MONDAY A fine day. Mr Hardy & W^m at home all day. M^r J Baker & the two Miss Davys drank tea here.

FEBRUARY 19, TUESDAY A Sharp frost, fine day. Mr Hardy & W^m at home all day. Maids & S Boyce wash'd 3 Weeks Linnen . . .

FEBRUARY 22, FRIDAY A fine day. Mr Hardy at home all day, W^m at home all day. Mr More dind here . . .

FEBRUARY 26, TUESDAY A fine dry day. Mr Hardy & W^m at home all day . . .

FEBRUARY 28, THURSDAY A Cold Windy day. Mr Hardy & W^m at home all day . . .

MARCH 2, SATURDAY A Chearly day but cold & Windy. Mr Hardy at home all day. Mr Bingle, I & MA walkd as far as Mr Jodrils Plantations Afternoon, came back to tea. W^m went to Holt Mark^t Afternoon, came home Eveng 9 . . .

MARCH 4, MONDAY A fine day. Mr Hardy & W^m at home all day. 2 Miss Davys calld in the Morng . . .

MARCH 6, WEDNESDAY A Cold dry Windy day. Mr Hardy at home all day. W^m & MA walkd to Holt Afternoon, drank tea at Mr Bakers. Ann Fryer at work here Afternoon.

MARCH 7, THURSDAY A dry close cold day. Mr Hardy & W^m at home all day.

MARCH 8, FRIDAY A fine day but Cold. Mr Hardy & W^m at home all day.

MARCH 9, SATURDAY A Close Cold windy day. Mr Hardy at home all day. W^m & MA walk'd up to Holt Mark^t Afternoon, drank tea at Mr Davys, came home 9 . . .

MARCH 12, TUESDAY A small Showr in the Morng, dry windy day. M^r & Mrs Goggs, Mr Cook & Son went away after tea. M^r & Wm Hardy at home all day.

MARCH 13, WEDNESDAY A Very fine mild day. Mr Hardy & W^m at home all day. Maids & S Boyce wash'd 3 Weeks Linnen. Mr Balls drank tea here . . .

MARCH 16, SATURDAY A fine day. Mr Hardy at home all day. W^m went to Holt Mark^t Afternoon, came home Eveng 9.

MARCH 17, SUNDAY A Very fine day but Windy. I, Sister Raven & Wm Lamb went to Cley meeting foornoon, Mr Breeden dind here. I, W^m & MA went to Briston Meeting Afternoon. Mr Hardy & Sister Raven went to our Church Afternoon . . .

MARCH 19, TUESDAY A dry day, reather Cold. Mr Hardy & W^m at home all day.

MARCH 20, WEDNESDAY A Close Cold dry day. Mr Hardy at home all day. W^m & T Balls rid to Wells in our Gigg on business Morng 8, came home Eveng near 10.

MARCH 21, THURSDAY A Cold dry day. Mr Hardy & W^m at home all day.

MARCH 22, FRIDAY A dry Cold day. Mr Hardy & W^m at home all day, M^r T Temple of Thornage drank tea & Supt here . . .

MARCH 25, MONDAY A Sharp rime frost in the Morng, fine day. Mr Hardy at home all day. I, Sister Raven & MA walk'd up to Holt Afternoon, drank tea at Mr Davys, W^m came for us in the Eveng.

MARCH 26, TUESDAY A dry Cold day. Mr Hardy & W^m at home all day. 2 Miss Fishers, 2 Miss Davys & Miss Baker drank tea here.

MARCH 27, WEDNESDAY A dry Cold day. Mr Hardy & W^m at home all day.

MARCH 28, THURSDAY A dry Cold day. W^m at home all day. Sister Raven, I & MA walk'd to Mr Temples at Thornage to tea, Mr Hardy rid there.

MARCH 29, FRIDAY A Sharp frosty Morng, Snowd alittle foornoon, chang'd to asmall rain Afternoon & Even'g. Mr Hardy & W^m at home all day.

MARCH 30, SATURDAY A Close drisly day. Mr Hardy at home all day. W^m went to Holt Mark^t afternoon, came home Even 9.

MARCH 31, SUNDAY A Wet Morng, fine Mild day. I & Wm Lamb went to Cley meeting foornoon, Mr Symmonds din'd here. I, MA & Wm Girling went to Briston Meeting Afternoon, W^m went to Dawling Church Afternoon. Mr Hardy & Sister Raven went to our Church Afternoon, Mr Burrell preach'd.

APRIL 1, MONDAY A Wet Morng, fine day. Mr Hardy at home all day, W^m at home all day.

APRIL 2, TUESDAY A Wet Morng, fine day. Mr Hardy at home. Maids & S Boyce Wash'd 3 Weeks Linnen. I, Sister Raven & W^m rid to Mr Sturlys Aftern to tea, S Raven Slept there.

APRIL 3, WEDNESDAY A drisly Morng, fine day. Mr Hardy at home all day. W^m drank tea at Mr Savorys, came home Eveng 9. Wm Lamb went to Mr Sturlys for Sister Raven.

APRIL 4, THURSDAY A Showry day. Mr Hardy & W^m at home all day. Mr Goggs & Mr Nathl Raven came Even 9, Slept here . . .

APRIL 6, SATURDAY A Close cold day. Mr Hardy at home all day. W^m went to Holt Mark^t Afternoon, came home eveng 9. Mrs Raven poorly . . .

APRIL 8, MONDAY A Very fine day. Mr Hardy & W^m at home all day. Sister Raven better. I & MA walkd up to Holt Afternoon, came home to tea.

APRIL 9, TUESDAY A Very fine day. Mr Hardy & W^m at home all day. I poorly with dimness in my Eyes Eveng 3.

APRIL 10, WEDNESDAY A Very fine day. Mr Hardy & W^m at home all day. I poorly with dimness in my Eyes Eveng 11 . . .

APRIL 13, SATURDAY A Very Warm dry day. Mr Hardy at home all day. W^m [   ] . . .

APRIL 21, SUNDAY A Close morng, fine day but cold. I, MA & Wm Girling went to Briston meeting Afternoon. W^m went to Briningham Church Afternoon. Mr Hardy & Sister Raven went to our Church Afternoon, Mr Burrell preach'd.

APRIL 22, MONDAY A fine day. Mr Hardy & W^m at home all day . . .

APRIL 24, WEDNESDAY A drisly Morng, fine day. Mr Hardy & W^m at home all day . . .

MAY 2, THURSDAY A chearly day but rather Cold. Mr Hardy at home all day. W^m rid to Mr Breertons on business foornoon, came home to dinner. Mr Williams drank tea & Supt here.

MAY 3, FRIDAY A fine day but cold. Mr Hardy & W^m at home all day. I very poorly afternoon. M^r T Balls drank tea & Supt here.

MAY 4, SATURDAY A fine Warm foornoon, A showr about 2 o Clock. Mr Hardy at home all day. M^rs & Miss Sturly drank tea here. W^m went up to Holt foornoon on business, came home to dinner & went to Holt Mark^t after tea, came home Eveng 9 . . .

MAY 6, MONDAY A fine morng, showry Afternoon. W^m at home all day. Mr Hardy walkd up to Holt Afternoon, drank tea at Mr Davys. Mr Moore dind & drank tea here . . .

MAY 9, THURSDAY Showers in the Morn, Cold Windy Aftern. Mr Hardy at home all day. W^m & M Raven walk'd up «to» Holt after tea.

MAY 10, FRIDAY A Very Showry day. Sent Lamb to Norwich in the Gigg for MA, they came home Even past 8. Mr Hardy, W^m, I & Sister Raven drank tea at Mr Burrells, Mr Moy there.

MAY 11, SATURDAY A Cold Stormy Windy day. Mr Moy & M Raven went away after Breakfast. Mr Hardy at home all day. W^m went to Holt Mark^t after tea, came home Even 9, Mr Williams Supt here . . .

MAY 14, TUESDAY A fine day but cold. Maids & S Boyce washd 3 Weeks Linnen. Mr Hardy & W^m at home all day.

MAY 15, WEDNESDAY A Very wet day. Mr Hardy at home all day. W^m drove Mrs Lathem & Miss Bartell to Cromer in our Gigg foornoon, dind & drank tea at Edmd Bartells, came home Eveng past 9 . . .

MAY 17, FRIDAY A Very fine warm day. Mr Hardy & W^m at home all day.

MAY 18, SATURDAY A Cold Windy day. Mr Hardy at home all day. M^r T Fox came Morng 10 for Mrs Raven, they went away Eveng 4. W^m went to Holt Mark^t Afternoon, came home Eveng 9 . . .

MAY 23, THURSDAY A Very Cold high Windy day. Mr Hardy & W^m at home all day . . .

MAY 26, SUNDAY A Very fine day. I poorly in the Morng, did not go to Cley. Mr Hardy, I, MA & W^m went to Briston Meeting Afternoon, Mr Simmonds din'd here . . .

MAY 28, TUESDAY A Very fine day. Mr Hardy & W^m at home all day. D Turner painting foornoon.

MAY 30, THURSDAY A fine day. Mr Hardy & W^m at home all day. M^r & Mrs Davy drank tea here. Mr Moore came afternoon & new potted the Shrubs, drank tea & Supt here. D Turner paintin.

MAY 31, FRIDAY A Very Cold windy day. Mr Hardy at home all day. W^m drank tea at M^r T Temples, Thornage, met M^r & Mrs Lake [?Leak], M^r & Mrs Bartell, Holt, there . . .

JUNE 4, TUESDAY A dry day. Mr Hardy at home all day, W^m at home all Day. Mr Cozens went away Eveng 2.

JUNE 5, WEDNESDAY A Cold dry day. Mr Hardy at home all day. W^m dind, drank tea & Supt at Mr Bartells, Holt, met M^r & Mrs Bartell of Cromer & M^r & Mrs Latham there. Maids & S Boyce wash«ed» 3 Weeks Linnen.

JUNE 6, THURSDAY A Cold Morng, A Shower afternoon & Eveng. Mr Hardy & W^m at home all day. M^r & Miss Bartell & Mrs Bartell, Cromer, & Mr Latham drank tea here.

JUNE 7, FRIDAY A fine dry day. Mr Hardy at home all day. W^m drank tea at Mr Williams, Thornage, came home Eveng past 10.

JUNE 8, SATURDAY A [   ] Day. Mr Hardy at home all day. W^m & MA walk'd to Holt Afternoon, drank tea at Mr Bartells, came home Even past 9 . . .

JUNE 10, MONDAY A Very wet day. Mr Hardy & W^m at home all day. Mr Smith of Cley came to meet a Mr Lee on business, drank tea here . . .

JUNE 14, FRIDAY A Very Wet day. Mr Hardy & W^m at home all day.

JUNE 15, SATURDAY A Very wet Morng, fine day. Mr Hardy at home all day & poorly with the Gout. W^m went to Holt Mark^t afternoon, came home Eveng 10.

JUNE 16, SUNDAY A tolerable day, a few small Showers about. I, MA & Wm Girling went to Briston Meeting Afternoon. W^m went to Briningham Afternoon, Mr Loyd preachd . . .

JUNE 18, TUESDAY A Showry day. Mr Hardy at home all day. W^m walkd up to Holt foornoon, came home to dinner.

JUNE 19, WEDNESDAY A fine day. Mr Hardy at home all day. W^m & MA sett of for Whisonsett Morng past 10 oClock. L Youngman drank tea here . . .

JUNE 24, MONDAY A Very fine Warm day. Mr Hardy at home all day, Mr Simmonds went away Eveng 4.

JUNE 25, TUESDAY A Very showry day. Mr Hardy & W^m at home all day. Maids & Sarah Boyce Wash'd 3 Weeks Linnen.

JUNE 26, WEDNESDAY A fine day. Mr Hardy, I & W^m & M Raven drank tea at Mr Bartells.

JUNE 27, THURSDAY A fine Morng, Showers from Eveng 5 great part of the Night. Mr Hardy & W^m at home all day. M^r & M^rs & Miss Bartell & A Miss M A Raven from Dereham drank tea here.

JUNE 28, FRIDAY A Close cold day. Mr Hardy & W^m at home all day . . .

JUNE 30, SUNDAY A Very fine warm day. I & Wm Girling went to Briston Meeting afternoon. W^m went to Dawling [Field Dalling] Church Afternoon, no Service there, no Service at our Church.

JULY 1, MONDAY A Very Warm day. Mr Hardy & W^m at home all day. M^r T Temple of Blakney drank tea & Supt here, Mr Williams Supt here.

JULY 2, TUESDAY A Close drisly day. Mr Hardy & W^m at home all day . . .

JULY 5, FRIDAY A Close warm day. Mr Hardy & W^m at home all day. M^r & Miss Bartell walkd down in the Eveng.

JULY 6, SATURDAY A fine day. Mr Hardy at home all day. W^m went to Holt Mark^t after tea, came home Eveng 9 . . .

JULY 11, THURSDAY A Very Close cool day, 2 or 3 small showers. Mr Hardy at home all day. I & MA walkd up to Holt afternoon to Baldwins [Balding's] Sale, bought nothing, drank tea at Mr Bartells. W^m came for us after tea.

JULY 12, FRIDAY A Close Cold day. Mr Hardy & W^m at home all day.

JULY 13, SATURDAY A fine day, wind Cold. Mr Hardy at home all day. W^m went to Holt Mark^t Afternoon, came home [   ].

JULY 14, SUNDAY A Close cold day. Mr Hardy at home all day. Mr Cozens came to Breakfast, went with I, W^m & MA to Briston Meeting Afternoon.

JULY 15, MONDAY A fine day but cold. Mr Hardy & W^m at home all day. Mr Cozens went away before tea.

JULY 16, TUESDAY A Showry Cold day. Mr Hardy at home all day. Maids & S Boyce washd 3 Weeks Linnen. W^m went to Mr Balls, Saxlingham, Afternoon, drank tea & Supt there, came home Eveng 11.

JULY 17, WEDNESDAY A Close day. Mr Hardy & W^m at home all day. M^r & Mrs Thomlison [?John Winn and Frances Thomlinson] calld here afternoon. M^r & M^rs & Miss Bartell drank tea here . . .

JULY 19, FRIDAY A Very fine Hay day. Mr Hardy & W^m at home all day. Widd^w [Widow] Fisher & Judah Fisher drank tea here.

JULY 20, SATURDAY A Hott day. Mr Hardy at home all day. W^m & MA walkd up to Holt Mark^t after tea, came home Even past 9. Mr Williams Supt here . . .

JULY 24, WEDNESDAY A Dry fine day. Mr Hardy at home all day. Mr Hardy, Mr Goggs & R [Robert] Raven went away Eveng 3. W^m went to Mr Savorys to tea, came home Eveng 9.

JULY 25, THURSDAY A fine day. Mr Hardy & W^m at home all day . . .

JULY 27, SATURDAY A fine day. Mr Hardy at home all day. W^m went to Holt Mark^t after tea, came home Eveng past 9. Mr Williams of Thornage Supt here . . .

JULY 29, MONDAY A fine day except a small showr or 2. Mr Hardy & W^m at home all day. M^r & Mrs Davy drank tea here . . .

AUGUST 5, MONDAY A Shower morng early, fine day. Mr Goggs, M^r Jo^s & Miss Cook from London came to dinner, slept here. Mr Hardy & W^m at home all day. Mr Cozens went away after tea . . .

AUGUST 9, FRIDAY A Very hot day. Mr Hardy and W^m at home all day. Paul Myles here . . .

AUGUST 13, TUESDAY A fine day. M^r & Mrs Petchell went away foornoon, Mr Wilks & Mr Cozens went away after dinner. Mr Hardy & W^m at home all day.

AUGUST 14, WEDNESDAY A fine day. Mr Hardy at home all day. W^m set of for Whisonsett after dinner.

AUGUST 15, THURSDAY A fine day. Mr Hardy at home all day. W^m came home from Whisonsett Eveng 9, brought Sister Raven home with him, they drank tea at Mr Custances, Fakenham. M^r & Miss Bartell drank tea here.

AUGUST 16, FRIDAY A fine day [?dry] day. Mr Hardy & W^m at home all day.

AUGUST 17, SATURDAY A fine day. Mr Hardy at home all day. W^m went to Holt Mark^t afternoon, came home Eveng 9. I poorly with dimness in my Eyes ab^t Noon & again Even 8 . . .

AUGUST 20, TUESDAY A Close Windy day. Mr Hardy & W^m at home all day.

AUGUST 21, WEDNESDAY A Wet morng, dry day. Mr Hardy & W^m at home all day. M Raven & Betsy Hawkins came to dinner, Slept here.

AUGUST 22, THURSDAY A Close day. Mr Hardy at home all day. W^m & the Girls walkd up to Holt foornoon, M Raven & B Hawkins went away Eveng 5. Mr Cozens & MA came home from Norwich Eveng 6.

AUGUST 23, FRIDAY A fine day. Mr Hardy at home all day. W^m rid to Saxlingham with intent to drink tea at Mr Balls, he was not at home, came home Eveng 8.

AUGUST 24, SATURDAY A fine day. Mr Hardy at home all «day». W^m went to Holt Mark^t Afternoon, came home Eveng 9.

AUGUST 25, SUNDAY A fine day. Mr Hardy at home all day. I, W^m & MA went to Briston Meeting Afternoon, Mr Eastaugh preachd there. Sister Raven went to our Church foornoon, Mr Burrell preach'd.

AUGUST 26, MONDAY A fine day. Mr Hardy & W^m at home all day.

AUGUST 27, TUESDAY A fine day. Maids & S Boyce washd 3 Weeks Linnen. Mr Hardy at home all day. W^m drank tea & supt at M^r T Balls, Saxlingham . . .

SEPTEMBER 5, THURSDAY A fine day. Mr Hardy & W^m at home all day.

SEPTEMBER 6, FRIDAY A Very fine day. Mr Hardy & W^m at home all day . . .

SEPTEMBER 9, MONDAY A fine day. Mr Hardy at home all day. Mrs Wm Custance calld here Afternoon going from Cromer to Fakenham [   ]. W^m went to Hildonveston Morng 9 on business, came home Even 8 . . .

SEPTEMBER 12, THURSDAY A Wet foornoon, close foggy Afternoon. Mr Hardy & W^m at home all day.

SEPTEMBER 13, FRIDAY A fine day. Mr Hardy & W^m at home all day. Mrs Smith calld in the Morng.

SEPTEMBER 14, SATURDAY A Very fine day. Mr Hardy at home all day. W^m & M Rav^n walkd to Holt afternoon, drank tea at Mr Bakers, came home Even 9 . . .

SEPTEMBER 16, MONDAY A Very fine day. Mr Hardy & I rid to Cley afternoon, drank tea at Mr Smiths. W^m at home all day. Sarah & Susan Davy dind & drank tea here . . .

SEPTEMBER 20, FRIDAY A Close Morng, fine day. Mr Hardy at home all day. W^m & M Rav^n walkd to Thornage Aftern, drank tea at Mr Sturlys. John Baker drank tea here . . .

SEPTEMBER 22, SUNDAY A Wet day. M Raven went to our Church foornoon, Mr Burrell preachd. We did not go out on Acc^t of the rain.

SEPTEMBER 23, MONDAY A Close Morng, fine afternoon. Mr Hardy & W^m at home all day. Mr Cozens went away Morn 10.

SEPTEMBER 24, TUESDAY A Showry foornoon, dry Afternoon. Mr Hardy at home all day. Maids & S Boyce washd 4 Weeks Linnen.

SEPTEMBER 25, WEDNESDAY A fine day. Mr Hardy at home all day, W^m drank tea at Mr Savorys.

SEPTEMBER 26, THURSDAY A Cold Showry day. Mr Hardy & W^m at home all day.

SEPTEMBER 27, FRIDAY A fine day. W^m & MA set of for Whisonsett Morng 10, Mr Hardy at home all day.

SEPTEMBER 28, SATURDAY A fine day. Mr Hardy at home all day. W^m & MA came home from Whisonsett Eveng ½ past 6. W^m went to Holt Mark^t, came home Eveng 9. Wm Williams came & Supt here . . .

OCTOBER 3, THURSDAY A fine day. Mr Hardy & W^m at home all day.

OCTOBER 4, FRIDAY A Very fine day. Mr Hardy & W^m at home all day . . .

OCTOBER 9, WEDNESDAY A Very fine day. I poorly in the Morng with dimness in my Eyes. H Raven & Wife went away before dinner, Mr Hardy & W^m at home all day.

OCTOBER 10, THURSDAY A fine morng, cold windy afternoon. Mr Hardy at home all day. W & MA & M Rav^n walk'd up to Holt Afternoon, drank tea at Mr Davys, came home Even 8 . . .

OCTOBER 12, SATURDAY A Very fine day. Mr Hardy at home all day. W^m & M Raven walkd up to Holt Mark^t afternoon, drank tea at Mr Davys, came home eveng 9.

OCTOBER 13, SUNDAY Showry day. I & M Rav^n & J Thompson went to Cley meeting foornoon. Mr Hardy «and» I went to Briston Meeting Afternoon. Mr Cozens came to dinner, he & MA went with us to Briston Afternoon.

OCTOBER 14, MONDAY A fine day. Mr Cozens went away after dinner. Mr Hardy & W^m at home all day.

OCTOBER 15, TUESDAY A Wet foornoon, fine afternoon. Mr Hardy & W^m at home all day.

OCTOBER 16, WEDNESDAY A Showry day. Mr Hardy & W^m at home all day. A Very Wet Night . . .

OCTOBER 18, FRIDAY A Very fine day. Mr Hardy at home all day, W^m did not come home.

OCTOBER 19, SATURDAY A [   ] day. Mr Hardy at home all day. W^m came home from Norwich Eveng 7, stopt at Holt Mark^t, came home Even 9 . . .

OCTOBER 22, TUESDAY A fine day, Mr Hardy & W^m at home all day . . .

OCTOBER 24, THURSDAY A Wet Morng, close dry day. Mr Hardy & W^m at home all day. M^r & Mrs Banks & Miss Sharp drank tea here.

OCTOBER 25, FRIDAY A Wet day. Mr Hardy & W^m at home all day.

OCTOBER 26, SATURDAY A Close Cold Showry day. Mr Hardy at home all day. W^m walkd up to Holt foornoon on business, came home to dinner, went to Mark^t afternoon, came home Even 10.

OCTOBER 27, SUNDAY A Cold close showry day. No preaching at Cley. I, W^m & MA went to Briston Meeting Afternoon. Mr Cozens came to dinner & Slept here. M^r H, M^r C & M Rav^n went to our Church Afternoon, Mr Burrell preach'd.

OCTOBER 28, MONDAY A Very fine day. Mr Hardy at home all day. W^m & M Raven sett of for Whisonsett Morng 10, Mr Cozens went away foornoon. Miss Baker & Miss Bartell drank tea here.

OCTOBER 29, TUESDAY A Close day. Mr Hardy at home all day. Maids & S Boyce wash'd 3 Weeks Linnen. I taken poorly with dimness in my Eyes.

OCTOBER 30, WEDNESDAY A fine day. Mr Hardy & W^m at home all day.

OCTOBER 31, THURSDAY A fine day. Mr Hardy & W^m at home all day.

NOVEMBER 1, FRIDAY A fine day. Mr Hardy & W^m at home all day . . .

NOVEMBER 4, MONDAY A fine Day, frost. Mr Hardy at home all day, W^m at home all Day.

NOVEMBER 5, TUESDAY A Very fine day. Mr Hardy at home all day. I, MA, W^m & M Raven walkd up to Holt Afternoon, drank tea at Mr Bartells.

NOVEMBER 6, WEDNESDAY A Very close foggy day. Mr Hardy & W^m at home all day . . .

NOVEMBER 8, FRIDAY A Close foggy day. Mr Hardy & W^m at home all «day».

NOVEMBER 9, SATURDAY A fine bright day. Mr Hardy at home all day. W^m & M Raven went to Holt Mark^t afternoon, she drank tea at Mrs Johnsons, came home Eveng past 9 . . .

[*Mary Ann Hardy married Jeremiah Cozens on 12 November and moved to his Sprowston farm, becoming 'Mrs C'*]

NOVEMBER 20, WEDNESDAY A Very fine day. Mr Hardy & W^m at home all day.

NOVEMBER 21, THURSDAY A fine day. Mr Hardy & W^m at home all day . . .

NOVEMBER 23, SATURDAY A frost, very fine day. Mr Hardy at home all day. I poorly with dimness in my Eyes after dinner. W^m went to Holt Mark^t afternoon . . .

The visit to Sprowston
30 November–11 December 1805

DECEMBER 3, TUESDAY A Close foornoon, very Wet afternoon. Mr Wilks spent the Eveng with us.

DECEMBER 4, WEDNESDAY A Dry day. Mr Wilks came in the Eveng . . .

DECEMBER 8, SUNDAY A fine day. M^r & M^rs C & I went to the Methodist Meeting foornoon, came back to dinner. M^r C & I went to Mr Wilks meeting afternoon, came back to tea. M^rs C staid at home with her Father Afternoon, he being poorly. M^r & Mrs Goggs went to Norwich foornoon & staid all day, came back Eveng 9. Mr Wilks came in the Eveng.

DECEMBER 9, MONDAY A Very stormy day. Mr Hardy poorly. M^r & Mrs Goggs could not go away on account of the Weather. Mr Wilks came in the Even.

DECEMBER 10, TUESDAY A fine day. M^r & Mrs Goggs went away after breakfast. Mr Hardy poorly. M^r & Mrs Wilks came & Supt with us . . .

[LETHERINGSETT]

DECEMBER 12, THURSDAY A Cold Stormy day. Mr Hardy very Lame. W^m at home all day. A deal of Snow fell in the Night, wind high.

DECEMBER 13, FRIDAY A Very Snowy Day & froze. Mr Hardy very lame & poorly. W [William] rid to Thos Balls^s, Saxlingham, drank tea & Supt there. Mr Wm Cook of Thornage drank tea here. A Very Cold Stormy Night.

DECEMBER 14, SATURDAY A Very coarse day, thawd afternoon. Mr Hardy very poorly, I poorly with dimness in my Eyes M10. W^m went to Holt Mark^t afternoon, came home Eveng near 10. A Deal of Snow fell in the Night . . .

DECEMBER 16, MONDAY A Sharp frost, stormy day. Mr Hardy & W^m at home all day . . .

DECEMBER 18, WEDNESDAY A Slow thaw all day. Mr Hardy something better. W^m at home all day. Adam & Miss Baker drank tea here.

DECEMBER 19, THURSDAY A frosty morng, Thawd Afternoon. Mr Hardy very poorly with the Gout. W^m sett of for Whisonsett after Dinner.

DECEMBER 20, FRIDAY A slow thaw. Mr Hardy much as Yesterd. W^m did not come home.

DECEMBER 21, SATURDAY A fine morng, a Very Wet day. Mr Hardy very poorly. W^m came home to dinner & went to Holt Mark^t afternoon, came home Eveng past 9. Mr Smith of Cley dind here . . .

DECEMBER 23, MONDAY A frosty day. Mr Hardy something better. W^m at home all day. Sister Raven walkd up to Holt foornoon.

DECEMBER 24, TUESDAY A Sharp frosty morng, thawd & raind before Noon. Mr Hardy finely. W^m at home all day, Mr Sneling [Snelling] dind here . . .

DECEMBER 26, THURSDAY A Very Wet day. Mr Hardy finely.

DECEMBER 27, FRIDAY A fine day. Mr Hardy finely . . .

DECEMBER 31, TUESDAY A Close mild day. Mr Hardy finely. W^m & Mrs Cozens walkd up to Holt foorn, came home to dinner. M^r & Mrs Woodcock drank tea here . . .

1806

JANUARY 2, THURSDAY A Squarly [squally] foornoon, fine day. Mr Hardy but poorly. W^m at home all day. M^r & M^rs & Miss Bartell & Miss Clemence [Clements] & Miss Baker drank tea here, W^m went for them in Cart & Caried them home again. Froze sharp in the Night.

JANUARY 3, FRIDAY A fine day. Mr Hardy poorly. I, W^m & Mrs Cozens, M^r & Mrs Burrell drank tea at Mr Rouses.

JANUARY 4, SATURDAY A Close dry foornoon, a wet afternoon. Mr Hardy very poorly. W^m went to Holt Mark^t afternoon, came home Eveng 9.

JANUARY 5, SUNDAY A fine day. I & James went to Cley meeting foornoon, Mr Revel dind here. I, W^m & Mrs Coz went to Briston Meeting Afternoon. Mr Hardy finely . . .

JANUARY 7, TUESDAY A fine day. Mr Hardy finely. I, W^m, M^r & Mrs Cozens & Mrs Rav^n walkd up to Holt foornoon. Mr Foster [? Forster] & young Thos Foster dind & drank tea here. Mrs Ravn poorly.

JANUARY 8, WEDNESDAY A fine morng, a very stormy day. Mr Hardy finely. W^m at home all day. M^r & Mrs Cozens should have gone home but the Weather prevented them . . .

JANUARY 10, FRIDAY A Very Stormy day, wind high & Cold. Mr Hardy finely. W^m at home all day. A Very bad night with frequent Storms of Hail & Snow, Wind very high . . .

JANUARY 13, MONDAY A frosty morng, fine day. Mr Hardy finely. W^m at home all day. Mr Goggs & Son & Ann Raven came to Dinner, Slept here.

JANUARY 14, TUESDAY A Wet windy morng, fine aftern. Mr Goggs & Son went away ab^t Noon. Mr Hardy & W^m at home all day.

JANUARY 15, WEDNESDAY A good deal of Rain fell in the morng, a dry Windy day. Mr Hardy at home all day. W^m rid to Swanton Aftern & Sheronton [Sharrington], drank tea at Mr Coplands, came home Eveng 8. A Very windy Stormy night. Maids & Eliz Loades washd 4 Weeks Linnen.

JANUARY 16, THURSDAY Wind very high & Stormy all day. Mr Hardy & W^m at home all day.

JANUARY 17, FRIDAY A fine day. Mr Hardy & W^m at home all day. M^r & Mrs Mendham drank tea & Supt here.

JANUARY 18, SATURDAY Fine morng, Very Stormy afternoon & Night. W^m went to Holt Mark^t Aftern, came home Eveng past 9.

JANUARY 19, SUNDAY A fine day. I & S Rav^n & Boy went to Cley Meeting foornoon, Mr Burley Dind here. I, W^m & Ann Raven went to Briston Meeting Afternoon.

JANUARY 20, MONDAY A Wet day. Mr Hardy & W^m at home all day.

JANUARY 21, TUESDAY A fine day. Mr Hardy & W^m at home all day.

JANUARY 22, WEDNESDAY A fine day. Mr Hardy & W^m at home all day. Rain in the Night . . .

JANUARY 25, SATURDAY A fine day. Mr Eastaugh went away before breakfast. Mr Hardy at home all Day. W^m went to Holt Mark^t afternoon, came home eveng 9.

JANUARY 26, SUNDAY A rime frost in the Morng, a very fine day. S Rav^n went to our Church foornoon. Mr Hardy at home all day. I, W^m & A Rav^n went to Briston Meeting Afternoon, no preacher there.

JANUARY 27, MONDAY A Wet day. Mr Hardy & W^m at home all day . . .

JANUARY 31, FRIDAY A frosty morng, fine day. Mr Hardy at home all day. W^m dind & drank tea at Mr Temple, Thornage, came home Even 10. I poorly with dimness in my Eyes.

FEBRUARY 1, SATURDAY A Tolerable day. Mr Hardy at home all day. W^m went to Holt Mark^t afternoon, drank tea at M^r [John Custance] Leakes, came home Even 9.

FEBRUARY 2, SUNDAY A frost, Very fine foornoon, some storms «of» Snow afternoon. I, Sister Rav^n & Boy went to Cley foornoon, Mr Revel dind here. I & W^m went to Briston Meeting afternoon. A little Snow fell in the Night . . .

FEBRUARY 4, TUESDAY A Sharp frosty morng, thawd in the Day. Mr Hardy & W^m at home all day. Mrs Girling went away . . .

FEBRUARY 13, THURSDAY A Chearly day but cold. Mr Cozens & Mr Hawkins went away ab^t Noon. Mr Hardy at home all day. Wm Dind & drank tea at Mr Leakes, Holt, came home Eveng past 10.

FEBRUARY 14, FRIDAY A fine Morng, raind a good deal Aftern. Mr Hardy at home all day. W^m went with Mr Leake, Holt, to Mr Robt Breerton, Blakney, to dinner Eveng 4, came home Eveng 12.

FEBRUARY 15, SATURDAY A Close day. Mr Hardy at home all day. W^m went to Holt Mark^t Afternoon.

FEBRUARY 16, SUNDAY A Close foggy day. I & S Rav^n & Boy went to Cley Meeting foornoon, Mr Burly dind here. W^m & I went to Briston Meeting Afternoon. Raind in the Eveng & Night.

FEBRUARY 17, MONDAY A fine day. Mr Hardy at home all day. Sister Raven, I & W^m drank tea at Mrs Davys . . .

FEBRUARY 20, THURSDAY A fine day. Mr Hardy at home all day. W^m & Sister Raven sett of for Fakenham & Whisonsett Eveng ½ past 1.

FEBRUARY 21, FRIDAY A dry close day. Mr Hardy at home all day. W^m came home from Whisonsett Eveng 8. Mary very Ill. A Wet Night.

FEBRUARY 22, SATURDAY A Close dry day. Mr Hardy at home all day. W^m went to Holt Mark^t Aftern, came home Eveng past 9 . . .

FEBRUARY 24, MONDAY A Very fine day. Mr Hardy & W^m at home all day. M^r & Mrs Cozens came to tea.

FEBRUARY 25, TUESDAY A fine day. Mr Hardy, I, Mrs Cozens & W^m went to Mr Temples to tea. Mr Cozens went to Toffts to Mr Cases, dind & drank tea there & calld at Mr Temples as he came back . . .

MARCH 1, SATURDAY A Cold Windy day. Mr Hardy at home all day. I poorly with dimness in my Eyes ab^t Noon & again ab^t Midnight. W^m went to Holt Mark^t afternoon, came home Eveng past 9.

MARCH 2, SUNDAY A fine day, reather Cold. I poorly, could not go to Cley foornoon. I, W^m & Mrs Cozens went to Briston meeting Afternoon.

MARCH 3, MONDAY A fine day. Mr Hardy, I & Mrs Cozens rid up to Holt Afternoon, drank tea at Mr Bartells, W^m came to tea . . .

MARCH 7, FRIDAY A Very Close mild day. Mr Hardy & W^m at home all day. M^r & Mrs Cozens went away Eveng 2.

MARCH 8, SATURDAY A fine day, close. Mr Hardy at home all day. W^m went to Holt Mark^t afternoon, came home Eveng 10.

MARCH 9, SUNDAY A fine Morng, Very cold day, frequent Storms of Snow & Sleet. Mr Hardy at home all day. I & W^m went to Breningham Church Afternoon, Mr Upjohn preachd. G Philipo & Wm Girling went to Whisonsett Morng 7, came home Eveng 8 . . .

MARCH 11, TUESDAY A Cold frosty morng, thawd in the day, Snowd in the Afternoon & Eveng. Mr Goggs & Mr Hawkins went away Even 3. Mr Hardy & W^m at home all day. A good deal of Snow fell in the Night & froze.

MARCH 12, WEDNESDAY A Sharp frosty morng, thawd in the day. Mr Hardy at home all day, W^m rid to Blakney foornoon. M^r & Mrs Temple & Son & Daughter drank tea here.

MARCH 13, THURSDAY A Sharp frosty morng, a deal of Snow, thawd in the Day. Mr Hardy at home all day. W^m went to Mr Walls afternoon, drank tea there, came home Even 9.

MARCH 14, FRIDAY A Very sharp frosty morng, Thawd & Snowd foornoon. Mr Hardy at home all day. Wm went to Mr Banks, Holt, to dinner Eveng 4, came home Eveng [   ].

MARCH 15, SATURDAY A Sharp frost, dry day. Mr Hardy at home all day. Wm went to Holt Markt Afternoon, came home Eveng past 9 . . .

MARCH 17, MONDAY A Tolerable dry Morng, very wet Afternoon. I poorly with dimness in my Eyes Morng 8. Wm set of for Toffts [Toftrees] & Whisonsett Morng 10. Mr Hardy at home all day.

MARCH 18, TUESDAY A Close dry morng, Wet afternoon & Eveng. Mr Hardy at home all day. Wm did not come home.

MARCH 19, WEDNESDAY A Close foggy day. Wm came home from Whisonsett abt Noon. Mr Hardy at home all day.

MARCH 21, FRIDAY A Close dry day. Mr Hardy & Wm at home all day.

MARCH 22, SATURDAY A dry day. Mr Hardy at home all day. Wm went to Holt Markt afterno«on», came home Eveng past 9.

MARCH 23, SUNDAY A dry Windy day. Mr Hardy at hom«e» all day. I & Wm went to Briston meeting Afternoon, Mr Eastaugh preach'd . . .

MARCH 25, TUESDAY A Close foggy day. Mr Hardy at [and] Wm at home all day . . .

MARCH 28, FRIDAY A Close cold day. Mr Hardy & Wm at home all day. The 2 Miss Davys drank tea here.

MARCH 29, SATURDAY A Cold close day. Mr Hardy at home all day . . .

MARCH 31, MONDAY A Cold Close day. Mr Hardy at home all day.

APRIL 1, TUESDAY A Cold dry day. Mr Hardy at home all day . . .

APRIL 5, SATURDAY A Cold dry day. Mr Hardy at home all day. Wm went to Holt Markt afternoon, came home Eveng past 9 . . .

APRIL 11, FRIDAY A Very cold windy day. Mr Hardy very poorly with the Gout in his Hand. Wm at home all day. I poorly with dimness in my Eyes Even 8.

APRIL 12, SATURDAY A Very cold dry day. Mr Hardy poorly with Gout & Cough. Wm went to Holt Markt afternoon, came home Eveng 9. A good deal of Snow fell in the Night, wind high.

APRIL 13, SUNDAY A Very Cold Stormy day, could not go to Cley nor Briston on acct of the weather. Mr Hardy very poorly. Mr Burly dind here, Wm Girling went to Briston meeting afternoon . . .

APRIL 15, TUESDAY A Cold close day. Mr Hardy very poorly, Wm at home all day.

APRIL 16, WEDNESDAY A Chearly day, wind cold. Mr Hardy very poorly. Wm rid to Cley foornoon with Mr Love in his Whiskey, came home to dinner, went to Mr Williams after tea, came hom«e» to Supper.

APRIL 17, THURSDAY A Close cold day. Mr Hardy much as yester, Wm at home all day.

APRIL 18, FRIDAY A bright morng, Close day. Mr Hardy much as Yesterday, Wm at home all day. Raind a good deal in the Night . . .

APRIL 21, MONDAY A Close drisly day. Mr Hardy better, Wm at home all day . . .

APRIL 24, THURSDAY A Cold windy day. Mr Hardy finely, Wm at home all day . . .

APRIL 26, SATURDAY A Very sharp Windy day. Mr Hardy finely . . .

APRIL 28, MONDAY A Cold Windy Stormy day. Mr Hardy finely. Wm & Mr Mendham [Mindham] came home from Sprowston Eveng 8 . . .

MAY 1, THURSDAY A Mild dry day. Mr Hardy & Wm at home all day.

MAY 2, FRIDAY A Very fine mild day. Mr Hardy & Wm at home all day.

MAY 3, SATURDAY A Very Cold windy Stormy day. Mr Hardy at home all day. Wm went to Holt Markt Afternoon, came home Eveng 9 . . .

MAY 5, MONDAY A dry day, wind cold. Mr Hardy at home all day. Wm walkd up to Holt foornoon, came home to dinner, set of for Whisonsett Eveng 4 in the Gigg for Mrs Raven.

MAY 6, TUESDAY A Very Warm day. Mr Hardy at home all day. Wm & Sister Raven came home Even 8.

MAY 7, WEDNESDAY A fine dry day, not so warm as yesterda«y». Mr Hardy & Wm at home all day.

MAY 8, THURSDAY A dry day but rather cold. Mr Hardy & Wm at home all «day». Mr & Mrs Bartell drank tea here.

MAY 9, FRIDAY A fine warm day. Mr Hardy & Wm at home all day. I & Sister Raven walkd up to Holt after tea . . .

MAY 13, TUESDAY A Close cold day. Mr Hardy very poorly. Wm came home Even 7 . . .

MAY 16, FRIDAY A fine day, Wind Cold. Mr Hardy & Wm at home all day. 2 Miss Davys & Mr Balls drank tea here.

MAY 17, SATURDAY A fine day. Mr Hardy at home all day. Wm went to Holt Markt aftern . . .

MAY 22, THURSDAY A dry cold day, Wind NE. Mr Hardy & Wm at home all day.

MAY 23, FRIDAY A Cold windy day. Mr Hardy & Wm at home all day. Mr & Mrs John Breerton drank tea here, Mr & Mrs Wall of Bayfield calld in the Eveng.

MAY 24, SATURDAY A Cold Windy day. Mr Hardy at home all day. Wm went to Holt Markt Afternoon, came home Even 9 . . .

MAY 27, TUESDAY A Very warm day. Mr Hardy & Wm at home all day. I & Sister Raven walkd up to Holt after tea . . .

JUNE 6, FRIDAY A Very warm day. Mr Hardy at home all day. S Raven poorly with an Inflamation in her Eye. I & Mrs Cozens walkd up to Holt, drank tea at Mrs Davys, met a party there.

JUNE 7, SATURDAY A Very Warm day. Mr Hardy at home all day. Wm «and» Mrs Cozens walkd up to Holt, drank tea at Miss Clements, came home Eve 9.

JUNE 8, SUNDAY A Very warm day. Mr Hardy at home all day. No service at our Church. I & Mrs C & Boy went to Cley meeting foorn, Mr Burly preach'd & dind here. Wm, Mrs C & I went to Briston Meeting Afternoon.

JUNE 9, MONDAY A hot day. Mr Hardy at home all day. W^m & Mrs Cozens went to Mr Bartells to tea, came home Even 9 . . .

JUNE 13, FRIDAY A Hot dry day. Mr Hardy at home all day. W^m & Mrs Cozens set of for Sprowson Eveng 5. M^r & Mrs Goggs, M^r & Mrs Cook sett of for Whisonsett at the same time.

JUNE 14, SATURDAY A hot day. Mr Hardy at home all day . . .

JUNE 16, MONDAY A Hot dry day. Mr Hardy at home all day. W^m came home from Sprowston Even 9.

JUNE 17, TUESDAY A dry Cool day. Mr Hardy at [and] W^m at home all day. Maids & Betty Loades Washd 4 Weeks Linnen . . .

JUNE 19, THURSDAY A dry day. Mr Hardy & W^m at home all day.

JUNE 20, FRIDAY A dry fine day, not hot. Mr Hardy at home all day. Mr Banks drank tea & supt here. I very poorly.

JUNE 21, SATURDAY A dry Windy Morng, asmall shower abt Noon. I Very poorly with a Cold. Mr Hardy at home all day. W^m went to Holt Mark^t afternoon, came home Eveng 10 . . .

JUNE 24, TUESDAY A Cold dry day. M^r & Mrs Cozens & Mrs Raven & W^m rid to Bayfield Hall afternoon, came back to tea. I very poorly . . .

JUNE 30, MONDAY A Wet foornoon, dry Afternoon. Mr Hardy & W^m at home all day. Mr Bartell calld to see me afternoon, drank tea here. I somthing better.

JULY 1, TUESDAY A dry day, a Showr in the Eveng. Mr Hardy at home all day, W^m at home all day. I very poorly.

JULY 2, WEDNESDAY A Cool day. Mr Hardy & W^m at home a [all] Day. I something better, Mr Bartell came to {to} see me . . .

JULY 4, FRIDAY A fine day, not hot. Mr Hardy at home all day, Mr Moore dind here. W^m dind at Mr Williams, Thornage, came home Even 11.

JULY 5, SATURDAY A fine day. Mr Hardy at home all day. Sister Raven walkd up to Holt Afternoon, drank tea at old Mrs Johnsons, came home even p 8. W^m went to Holt Mark^t after tea, came home Eveng past 9. I poorly with dimness in my Eyes Eveng 8.

JULY 6, SUNDAY A Showry morng, fine day. I, SR & Boy went to Cley meeting foornoon, Mr Reven [Revell] dind here. I & W^m went to Briston meeting afternoon, Wm Girling went. Mr Bartell calld foornoon to speak to me, I was not at home.

JULY 7, MONDAY A dry morng, some small showers aftern & a very heavy Showr Eveng 8. Mr Hardy & W^m at home all day . . .

JULY 14, MONDAY A fine day. Mr Hardy & W^m at home all day.

JULY 15, TUESDAY A fine foornoon, showry Afternoon. M^r & M^{rs} & M [Mary] Cozens came to dinner, slept here . . .

JULY 17, THURSDAY A fine morng, A Heavy showr ab^t 11 oClock, fine Afternoon. Mr Hardy & W^m at home all day. M^r & Mrs Cozens went away eveng past 5.

JULY 18, FRIDAY A fine morng, showry afternoon. Mr Hardy & W^m at home all day. M^r & M^{rs} & Miss Leales [?Leaks/Sales], Miss Dean & Miss Baker drank tea here.

JULY 19, SATURDAY A Wet morng, fine afternoon. Mr Hardy at home all day. W^m went to Holt Mark^t Afternoon, came home eveng 9. Wm Girling went to Sprowston Even past 6.

JULY 20, SUNDAY A fine foornoon, ashowr Eveng 4. I, S Raven & Boy went to Cley meeting foornoon, Mr Burly dind here. I & W^m went to Briston meeting Afternoon, Mr Hardy & S Raven went to our Church Afternoon. Wm Girling came home eveng 12.

JULY 21, MONDAY A Showry day. Mr Hardy at home all day. W^m & S Raven rid to Mr Wm Cooks, Thornage, to tea.

JULY 22, TUESDAY A Very fine day. Mr Hardy at home all day. W^m rid to Saxthorp Afternoon, came home Even past 8. I & S Raven walkd up to Holt after tea.

JULY 23, WEDNESDAY A fine morng, Wet afternoon. Mr Hardy & W^m at home all day. M^r & Mrs Sturly drank tea here, Mr Williams drank tea & Supt here . . .

JULY 26, SATURDAY A Very Wet foornoon, close dry afternoon. Mr Hardy at home all day. W^m went to Holt Mark^t afternoon, came home even 9 . . .

AUGUST 2, SATURDAY A Very heavy showr with Thunder Eve 2. Mr Hardy at home all day. W^m went to Holt Mark^t after tea, came home Eveng 9 . . .

AUGUST 5, TUESDAY A fine day. Mr Hardy & W^m at home all day. I & S Raven & Phillis Raven rid up to Holt after tea in L [little] Cart, came home walking.

AUGUST 6, WEDNESDAY A fine day. Mr Hardy at home all Day, W^m [   ] . . .

The visit to Sprowston
7–19 August 1806

AUGUST 8, FRIDAY A Hot day. We were at home all day. Mr Breeden, Mr Niwton [Newton] & a Miss Neal drank tea with us.

AUGUST 9, SATURDAY A Hot day. I & Mrs Cozens & Boy rid to Norwich Afternoon, came back to tea . . .

AUGUST 11, MONDAY A fine day. At home all day . . .

AUGUST 16, SATURDAY A fine day. Mr Hardy, I & Mrs Cozens went to Norwich foornoon, dind & drank tea at Mr Ja^s Cozens . . .

[LETHERINGSETT]

AUGUST 20, WEDNESDAY A Showry day. Mr Hardy & W^m at home all day.

AUGUST 21, THURSDAY A fine day. Mr Hardy & W^m at home all day.

AUGUST 22, FRIDAY A fine day. Mr Hardy & W^m at home all day . . .

AUGUST 24, SUNDAY A fine day except asmall showr eveng 4. Mr Hardy at home all day. I, Mrs Cozens & Phillis Raven went to Briston meeting Afternoon. W^m went to Briningham Church Aftern, Mr Upjohn preachd . . .

AUGUST 26, TUESDAY A Close foornoon, raind part of the aftern. Mr Hardy & W^m at home all day . . .

AUGUST 30, SATURDAY A fine day. Mr Hardy at home all day. W^m went to Holt Mark^t after tea, came home eveng 9 . . .

SEPTEMBER 4, THURSDAY A raind a good deal the midle of the day. Mr Hardy & W^m at home all day.

SEPTEMBER 5, FRIDAY A Very fine day. Mr Hardy & W^m at home all day.

SEPTEMBER 6, SATURDAY A Very fine day. Mr Hardy at home all day. W^m went to Holt Mark^t afternoon, came home Eveng 8.

SEPTEMBER 7, SUNDAY A Very fine day. Mr Hardy & S Raven went to our Church foornoon, Mr Burrell preachd. I, SR & Wm Girling went to Briston meeting Afternoon. W^m went to Briningham Church Afternoon, Mr Upjohn preachd . . .

SEPTEMBER 13, SATURDAY A [   ] day. Mr Hardy at home all day. W^m went to Holt Mark^t afternoon, came home Eveng past 9.

SEPTEMBER 14, SUNDAY A Very fine day. I & S Raven & Boy went to Cley meeting foornoon, Mr Revel dind here. I & W^m went to Briston Meeting Afternoon. Mr Hardy & SR went to our Church Afternoon, Mr Burrell preachd . . .

SEPTEMBER 26, FRIDAY A Very fine day. Mr Hardy & W^m at home all day. S Raven walkd up to Holt after tea . . .

OCTOBER 3, FRIDAY A Wet morng, close drisly day. Mr Hardy & W^m at home all day.

OCTOBER 4, SATURDAY A tolerable fine day but raind in the Eveng. Mr Hardy at home all day. W^m went to Holt Mark^t afternoon, came home Eveng past 9.

OCTOBER 5, SUNDAY A fine day. Mr Hardy & S Raven went to our Church foornoon, Mr Burrell preach'd. I, S Rav^n & Wm Girling went to Briston meetin Afternoon . . .

OCTOBER 7, TUESDAY A Close mild day. Mr Hardy & W^m at home all day. I poorly with dimness in my Eyes ab^t Noon & again Even 8 . . .

OCTOBER 10, FRIDAY A fine day. Mr Hardy at home all day. W^m drank tea at Mr Pauls, Stody, came home Eveng 10 . . .

OCTOBER 12, SUNDAY A Very fine day. I & S Raven & Wm Girling went to Cley meeting foornoon, Mr Julian dind here. I & W^m went to Briston meeting Afternoon. A frosty Night . . .

OCTOBER 18, SATURDAY A Very fine day. Mr Hardy at home all day. W^m sett of for Sprowston Eveng . . .

OCTOBER 20, MONDAY A Very fine day. Mr Hardy at home all day, M^r & Miss Bartell drank tea here. W^m came home from Sprowston Even 8 . . .

OCTOBER 22, WEDNESDAY A drisly dark day. Mr Goggs & Mr Hawkins went away after Breakfast, Mr Hardy & W^m at home all day.

OCTOBER 23, THURSDAY A fine Morng, drisly day. Mr Hardy & W^m ahome all day . . .

OCTOBER 25, SATURDAY A Very cold Windy day. Mr Hardy at home all day. W^m went to Holt Market afternoon, came home Even near 10. Mr Breden went away foornoon.

OCTOBER 26, SUNDAY A fine mild day. I & Boy went to Cley meeting foornoon. W^m & I went to Briston meeting Afternoon, A Sacrament there. Mr Hardy went to our Church Aftern, Mr Burrell preach'd . . .

OCTOBER 31, FRIDAY A fine day. Mr Hardy at home all day.

NOVEMBER 1, SATURDAY A fine day. Mr Hardy at home all day . . .

NOVEMBER 4, TUESDAY A Close foornoon, Wet afternoon. Mr Hardy at home all day. Maids & Betty Loades Washd 4 Weeks Linnen . . .

NOVEMBER 6, THURSDAY A fine day. Mr Hardy at home all day. I poorly with dimness in my Eyes Eveng 2.

NOVEMBER 7, FRIDAY A fine day. Mr Hardy at home all day. Recd a Letter from W^m.

NOVEMBER 8, SATURDAY A fine day. Mr Hardy at home all day . . .

NOVEMBER 11, TUESDAY A rime frost, fine day. Mr Hardy at home all day . . .

NOVEMBER 14, FRIDAY A Close mild day. Mr Hardy at home all day . . .

NOVEMBER 23, SUNDAY A fine morn, rime frost. I & T Boyce went to Cley Meeting foornoon, M [Marmaduke] Revel din'd here. A Very Wet Afternoon, did not go to Briston on acct of the rain.

NOVEMBER 24, MONDAY A dry foornoon, Wet afternoon. Mr Hardy at home all day. W^m went to Mr Walls, Bayfield, Afternoon, drank tea & Supt there, came home Eveng 10 . . .

NOVEMBER 26, WEDNESDAY A fine Morng, Very Wet aftern & Eveng. Mr Hardy & W^m at home all day.

NOVEMBER 27, THURSDAY A dry morng, Very Wet Night. Mr Hardy & W^m at home all day . . .

NOVEMBER 29, SATURDAY A Rainy foornoon & a very great Storm attended with Lightning Even 5. Mr Hardy at home all day. W^m went to Holt Afternoon, came home Even 9.

NOVEMBER 30, SUNDAY A fine day. Mr Hardy at home all day. Sister Raven went to our Church foornoon, Mr Burrell preach'd. I & W^m & SR went to Briston meeting Afternoon, Mr Tilney preachd . . .

Sprowston: Mary Ann's lying-in
4–23 December 1806

DECEMBER 8, MONDAY A fine day, raind in the Night. Mrs Cozens finely.

DECEMBER 9, TUESDAY A Very showry day. M^rs C finely. M^r C & Mrs Davy [Davey] & Mr Wilks drank tea here.

DECEMBER 10, WEDNESDAY A dry morn, Wet afternoon. M^r C went to Norwich afternoon, drank tea at Mr Ja^s Cozens, came home Eveng 8 . . .

DECEMBER 12, FRIDAY A Wet Windy day. M^rs C finely. A very Stormy Night.

DECEMBER 13, SATURDAY A Wet Windy day. M^r C went to Norwich foornoon, came home to tea . . .

DECEMBER 17, WEDNESDAY A dry close day. Mr Balls went away before breakfast. W^m went to Norwich foorn, dind at Mr John Cozens, M^r & M^rs C came back with him to tea.

DECEMBER 18, THURSDAY A Very Wet foornoon, close dry aftern. W^m went away after dinner. A Wet night.

DECEMBER 19, FRIDAY A Stormy day, fine Eveng . . .

DECEMBER 22, MONDAY A Wet foornoon, close afternoon. M^{rs} C finely. A Stormy night . . .

[LETHERINGSETT]

DECEMBER 24, WEDNESDAY A Wet foornoon, dry afternoon. Mr Hardy & W^m at home all day . . .

DECEMBER 30, TUESDAY A Close morng, Very Wet afternoon. Mr Hardy & W^m at home all day. Maids & Eliz Loades Washd 4 weeks Linn.

DECEMBER 31, WEDNESDAY A fine day. Mr Hardy at home all day. W^m dind & drank tea at Mr Williams, Thornage, came home Eve 9.

1807

JANUARY 1, THURSDAY A fine day. Mr Hardy & W^m at home all day . . .

JANUARY 3, SATURDAY A fine day. Mr Hardy at home all day. W^m went to Holt Mark^t afternoon, drank tea at Mr Bakers, came home Even 9 . . .

JANUARY 5, MONDAY A rime frost. Mr Hardy & W [William] at home all day . . .

JANUARY 7, WEDNESDAY A fine day. Mr Hardy & W^m at home all day.

JANUARY 8, THURSDAY A frost, fine day. Mr Hardy & W^m at home all day. Sarah Davy & a young Mr Field came in the afternoon, did not stay to tea.

JANUARY 9, FRIDAY A Close foggy day. Mr Hardy at home all day. W^m drank tea at Mr Walls at Bayfield.

JANUARY 10, SATURDAY A frosty morng, fine day. Mr Hardy at home all day. W^m went to Holt Mark^t afternoon, came home eveng 11 . . .

JANUARY 12, MONDAY A fine day. Mr Hardy & W^m at home all day.

JANUARY 13, TUESDAY A Very fine frosty foornoon, Stormy afternoon. Mr Hardy at home all day. W^m sett of on Horseback for Fakenham & Whisingsett Morng 11. I taken poorly With dimness in my Eyes Even 1. A sharp frosty Night.

JANUARY 14, WEDNESDAY A sharp frost, fine day. Mr Hardy at home all day. I poorly with dimness in my Eyes Eveng 4. A sharp frosty Night.

JANUARY 15, THURSDAY A Sharp frost, began to Hail & rain, Wind high Eveng 5, continued untill Eveng 9 then cleard up. Mr Hardy at home all day. W^m came home from Fakenham Eveng 9.

JANUARY 16, FRIDAY A fine mild day. Mr Hardy a [and] W^m at home all day. Miss Baker calld foornoon.

JANUARY 17, SATURDAY A frost, fine day. Mr Hardy at home all day. W^m went to Holt Mark^t afternoon, came home Eveng past 9.

JANUARY 18, SUNDAY A fine day. I & Ned went to Cley meetin foornoon. W^m & I went to Briston meeting Afternoon, Mr Revel preachd . . .

JANUARY 20, TUESDAY A fine day. Mr Hardy at home all day. W^m went to Mr Williams to tea, came home Eveng 9.

JANUARY 21, WEDNESDAY A frosty morning, fine day, Eveng past 4 a Sharp Showr of Sleet. Mr Hardy at home all day. W^m went to Cromer foornoon, did not come home.

JANUARY 22, THURSDAY A sharp frosty morng, thawd in day & raind at night. Mr Hardy at home all day. W^m came home eveng 9 . . .

JANUARY 24, SATURDAY A fine day. Mr Hardy at home all day. W^m went to Holt Mark^t afternoon, came home Eveng past 9.

JANUARY 25, SUNDAY A fine day. Mr Hardy at home all day. Service at our Church foornoon. I & W^m went to Briston meeting Afternoon.

JANUARY 26, MONDAY A Close day. Mr Hardy & W^m at home all day . . .

JANUARY 29, THURSDAY A fine day. Mr Hardy & W^m at home all day . . .

FEBRUARY 5, THURSDAY Snowd in morng & a frost, thawd in the day & froze again at Night. Mr Hardy & W^m at home all day . . .

FEBRUARY 7, SATURDAY A Sharp frost. Mr Hardy at home all day. W^m & P Myles went to Holt Mark^t Afternoon, came home eveng 10.

FEBRUARY 8, SUNDAY A Close morng, Very Wet afternoon. We were all at home all day on acct of the Weather.

FEBRUARY 9, MONDAY A Wet foornoon, fine afternoon but Windy. Mr Hardy at home all day. W^m walkd up to Holt after tea, came home Eveng 9 . . .

FEBRUARY 11, WEDNESDAY A Close windy day. Mr Hardy at home all day. W^m sett of for Whisonset in the Gigg for Mrs Raven Morng ½ past 11.

FEBRUARY 12, THURSDAY A fine mild day. Mr Hardy at home all day. W^m & Sister Raven came home Eveng 9 . . .

FEBRUARY 14, SATURDAY A Very fine day. Mr Hardy at home all day. W^m went to Holt Mark^t aftern, drank tea at Mr Bartells, came home Eveng ½ past 8.

FEBRUARY 15, SUNDAY A Very fine mild day. I & S Raven & Servt went to Cley meeting foornoon, Mr Revel dind here. I & W^m & Mrs Raven went to Briston meeting Afternoon.

FEBRUARY 16, MONDAY A Very fine day. Mr Hardy, I & Sister Raven drank tea at Mr Burrells. W^m dind & drank tea at Mr Walls, Bayfield, came home Eveng 12 . . .

Sprowston: the county election
18 February–7 March 1807

FEBRUARY 20, FRIDAY A frost & Stormy. All at home all day. Mr Wilks drank tea with us.

FEBRUARY 21, SATURDAY A Cold Stormy day. M^r C went to Norwich foornoon, came home Eveng 5 . . .

FEBRUARY 25, WEDNESDAY A Stormy day. M^r & M^{rs} Jo^n [John] C came to tea & staid & supt on acct of the rain, being a very wet night.

FEBRUARY 26, THURSDAY A tolerable day but froze at Night & some Snow fell. All at home all day.

FEBRUARY 27, FRIDAY A Sharp frost, frequent Storms of Snow. M^r & Mrs Wilks supt with us.

FEBRUARY 28, SATURDAY A Very cold Stormy day. Nothing particular.

MARCH 1, SUNDAY A Cold dry day. M^r H, I, M^r & M^{rs} C went to M [Mark] Wilks meeting foornoon. M^r & M^{rs} C & I went to Cherry Lane meeting afternoon . . .

MARCH 3, TUESDAY A Close dry day. All at home. Mr Breeden & a Mr Hill came to tea & Supt. Mr Wm Cozens came to tea & slept there, Wm Hardy came to tea & Slept there . . .

[LETHERINGSETT]

MARCH 9, MONDAY A Very cold stormy day. Mr Hardy at home all day. W^m went to Mr Walls to tea & Supt there, came home eveng past 10. I poorly in the Night with dimness in my Eyes.

MARCH 10, TUESDAY A Sharp frost. Mr Hardy & W^m at home «all» day.

MARCH 11, WEDNESDAY A Sharp frost, very cold all day. Mr Hardy at home all day. W^m rid to Salthouse & Kelling Afternoon, drank tea at M^r [Z.] Girdlestones, came home Eveng 8.

MARCH 12, THURSDAY A Cold dry day. Mr Hardy & W^m at home all day. Mrs Goggs of Whisonsett came Even past 9 in a Post Chaise with 2 Gentlemen going to Holt.

MARCH 13, FRIDAY A Close cold day. Mr Hardy & W^m at home all day.

MARCH 14, SATURDAY A Close cold day. Mr Hardy at home all day. W^m went to Holt Mark^t afternoon, came home Eveng 9.

MARCH 15, SUNDAY A Very cold day, frequent Storms of Snow, very sharp wind almost North. I & Sister Raven went to Cley meeting foorn, Mr Revel dind here. Mr Hardy at our Church Afternoon, Mr Burrell preachd. Mrs Cozens at home all «day» something better of her cold. I, S Raven & W^m went to Briston meeting Afternoon. A great deal of Snow fell in the Night.

MARCH 16, MONDAY A frosty morng, extreme bad afternoon with Snow, Hail & Wind. Mr Hardy at home all day. W^m went to M^r T Temples of Thornage afternoon, drank tea there.

MARCH 17, TUESDAY A Cold Windy day. Mr Hardy at home all day, W^m at home all day. A deal of Snow fell in the Night.

MARCH 18, WEDNESDAY A frosty Morng, thawd in the day. A Very sheavy [heavy] Showr of rain Eveng 3 then cleard up to a fine Eveng. Mr Hardy at home all day. W^m went with Sister Raven to Fakenham Morng & left her at Mr Skrimshires, dind & drank tea there, came home Even 9.

MARCH 19, THURSDAY A dry cold windy day. Mr Hary [Hardy] & W^m at home all day, Mrs Davy drank tea here.

MARCH 20, FRIDAY A dry cold day. Mr Hardy at home all day. I & Mrs Cozens rid up to Holt afternoon, drank tea at M^r [?Matthew] Davys. W^m came up to tea, we walkd home.

MARCH 21, SATURDAY A dry day but cold. Mr Hardy at home all day. I, W^m & Mrs Cozens rid up to Holt aftern, drank tea at Mr Bartells, walkd home.

MARCH 22, SUNDAY A Close cold day. I, W^m & Mrs Cozens went to Briston Meeting Afternoon. Mr Cozens came Eveng 6.

MARCH 23, MONDAY A fine chearly day but cold. Mr Hardy & W^m at home all day. Mrs Smith, Cley, dind & drank tea here, Mr Smith came to tea. Mr Bartell drank tea here . . .

MARCH 26, THURSDAY A Very cold hasy day. Mr Hardy at home all day. W^m rid to Saxthorp aftern, came home to tea . . .

MARCH 28, SATURDAY A cold day, Wind the same as yesterday. Mr Hardy at home all day. W^m went to Holt Mark^t afternoon, cam«e» [   ] . . .

MARCH 30, MONDAY A Cold dry day. Mr Hardy & W^m at home all day. M^r & Mrs Smith calld in afternoon. I poorly with a Cold & Cough.

APRIL 1, WEDNESDAY A Very Cold day, storms of Snow aftern. Mr Hardy & W^m at home all day. A good deal of Snow fell in the Night.

APRIL 2, THURSDAY The ground cover'd with Snow, the day che«a»rly but cold. W^m sett of for Sprowston Morng past 9. Mr Hardy at home all day.

APRIL 3, FRIDAY The Ground cover'd with Snow in the Morn & a frost, fine day but Cold. Mr Hardy at home all day.

APRIL 4, SATURDAY A Sharp frosty morng, fine day. Mr Hardy at home all day. W^m returnd from Sprowston Eveng 5, sent Ned up to Holt for his Horse. W^m stopt at Holt Mark^t, came home Eveng 9.

APRIL 5, SUNDAY A Cold dry day. Mr Hardy at home all {all} day. Service at our Church foornoon, a Sacrament. I & Wm Girling went to Briston meeting afternoon, W^m went to Baningham [Briningham] Church Afternoon . . .

APRIL 8, WEDNESDAY A Very fine day. Mr Hardy & W^m at home all day. I poorly with a Cold & Cough.

APRIL 9, THURSDAY A fine day. Mr Hardy & W^m at home all day. I very poorly with a Cold & Cough . . .

APRIL 12, SUNDAY A Very Windy day. I so poorly could not go to meeting. Mr Hardy went to our Church afternoon, W^m went to Dawlin Church Afternoon. Mr Revel dind here, Wm Girling went to Briston Meeting Afternoon.

APRIL 13, MONDAY A fine day. Mr Hardy at home all day. W^m rid to Mr Breertons, Brinton, Afternoon, drank tea there, came home Eveng past 7. [[[*by William Hardy*] I [ie Mary Hardy] very poorly.]]

APRIL 14, TUESDAY A fine day. Mr Hardy & W^m at home all day. I very poorly with a Cold . . .

APRIL 19, SUNDAY A Cold stormy day. I much as yesterday. Mr Hardy at home all day. W^m rid to Briningham Church Afternoon, Wm Girling at Briston meeting afternoon . . .

APRIL 23, THURSDAY A fine day, Wind reather Cold. Mr Hardy & W^m at home all day.

APRIL 24, FRIDAY A fince [fine] day. Mr Hardy at home all day. John Davy from London & S Davy came in forenoon. W^m went to Mrs Davys to tea, came home eveng 9. I much as Yesterday.

APRIL 25, SATURDAY A fine day. Mr Hardy at home all day. W^m went to Holt Mark^t afternoon, came home Eveng 9. I much as yesterday.

APRIL 26, SUNDAY A Very fine day. I was not well enough to go to Cley meeting foornoon, I was taken poorly with dimness in my Eyes morn past 9. Mr Juliar dind here, I & W^m went to Briston Meeting Afternoon . . .

APRIL 30, THURSDAY A very fine warm day. Mr Hardy at home all day. W^m went foornoon to [?North] Barningham in Gigg foornoon with Mrs Leeke [Leak] & Miss Baldro [?Baldero], dind & drank tea at Old Mr Leakes, came home eveng past 9 . . .

MAY 2, SATURDAY A Very fine day. I better. Mr Hardy at home all day. W^m went to Holt Mark^t afternoon, came home Eveng past 9 . . .

MAY 5, TUESDAY A Close mild day. Mr Hardy & W^m at home all day. I somthing better than Yesterday. A Very fine showr in the Eveng.

MAY 6, WEDNESDAY A dry cool day. Mr Hardy & W^m at home all day . . .

MAY 8, FRIDAY A Very fine day. Mr Hardy at home all day. W^m rid to Cley afternoon, came home Eveng 7 . . .

MAY 13, WEDNESDAY [at Sprowston] A tolerable dry day untill Even 4 & then raind again the greatest part of the Eveng. I, W^m & Mrs Cozens went to Norwich Afternoon & returnd to tea . . .

MAY 15, FRIDAY [at Letheringsett] A fine day. Mr Hardy & W^m at home all day. I poorly with dimness in my Eyes ab^t Noon.

MAY 16, SATURDAY A fine dry day. Mr Hardy at home all day. W^m went to Holt Mark^t afternoon, came home Eveng 9 . . .

MAY 20, WEDNESDAY A Cold dry day. Mr Hardy & W^m at home all day . . .

MAY 22, FRIDAY A fine day but wind cold. Mr Hardy & W^m at home all day.

MAY 23, SATURDAY A fine day. Mr Hardy at home all day. W^m went to Holt Mark^t Afternoon, came home Even 9. Miss Baker went away after tea.

MAY 24, SUNDAY A Very fine day. I & Edwd went to Cley Meeting foornoon, Mr Juliar preachd & dind here. I & W^m went to Briston Meeting Afternoon.

MAY 26, TUESDAY A fine morng, A fine Showr Aftern. Mr Hardy & W^m at home all day. M^r & M^rs & Miss Bartell drank tea here. A fine Showr in the Night . . .

MAY 30, SATURDAY A Cold windy foornoon, Very Wet Afternoon. Mr Hardy at home all day. W^m went to Holt Mark^t afternoon, came home Even 9 . . .

JUNE 1, MONDAY A Showry Cold day. Mr Hardy & W^m at home all day . . .

JUNE 3, WEDNESDAY A Close cold day. W^m rid to Borrough [Burgh Parva] and Melton foornoon, came home Even 3. We all drank tea at Mr Burrells. I poorly with dimness in my Eyes even 5 . . .

JUNE 6, SATURDAY A Cold dry morng, Very Wet afternoon. Mr Hardy at home all day. W^m went to Holt Mark^t afternoon, came home Even 9 . . .

JUNE 10, WEDNESDAY A dry day untill Even 5 then raind all the Eveng. M^r & Mrs Cozens went away Eveng 3.

JUNE 11, THURSDAY A fine day. Mr Hardy & W^m at home all day. I somthing better . . .

JUNE 13, SATURDAY A fine day. Mr Hardy at home all day. Mr Bartell calld to se me, I was somthing better.

JUNE 14, SUNDAY A Very fine day. Mr Hardy went to our Church Eveng past 6, Mr Burrell preach'd. I & Wm Girling went to Briston meeting . . .

JUNE 16, TUESDAY A Very fine day, Hot. Mr Hardy & W^m at home all day. I, M^rs [Joseph] Hardy & Miss Watson walkd up to Holt Afternoon, drank tea at Mr Bartells, met Mrs Davy &c there. A small Showr ab^t 6 o Clock . . .

JUNE 19, FRIDAY A Very fine day. Mr Hardy at home all day. W^m went to Mr Williams at Thornage to tea, came home Eveng 9. I taken with dimness in my Eyes Eveng 9 . . .

JUNE 21, SUNDAY A fine day [dry] day. I & Edw'd went to Cley Meeting foornoon. I taken with dimness in my Eyes Morng ½ past 9. Mr Juliar dind here. I & W^m went to Briston meeting Afternoon. Mr Hardy & Mrs Hardy & Miss Watson went to our Church in Eveng. Mr Juliar came Eveng 9, Slept here.

JUNE 22, MONDAY A Very fine day. Mr Hardy at home all day, W^m at home all day. Mr Moore, Holt, Dind & drank tea here. Mr Juliar went away Eveng 3. I, Mrs Hardy & Miss Watson walkd up to Holt Afternoon, drank tea at Mrs Davys. I poorly with dimness in my Eyes before breakfast.

JUNE 23, TUESDAY A Very fine day. Maids & S Boyce Washd 4 weeks Linnen. Mr Hardy at home all day. I taken poorly with dimness in my Eyes Even 1. W^m dind, drank tea & Supt at Mr Temples, Blakney . . .

JUNE 26, FRIDAY A Very fine day. Mr Hardy & W^m at home all day . . .

JUNE 28, SUNDAY A Very dry day. Mr Hardy, Mrs Hardy & Miss Watson went to our Church foorn, Mr Burrell preach'd. I & W^m went to Briston meeting Afternoon. Wm Girling came home Even 7.

JUNE 29, MONDAY A Very dry day. Mr Hardy & W^m at home all day. I taken with dimness in my Eyes Eveng 9.

JULY 1, WEDNESDAY A fine day, Wind reather Cold. Mr Hardy & W^m at home all day . . .

JULY 5, SUNDAY A Very fine day. I & Edw'd went to Cley meeting foornoon, & I & W^m went «to» Briston meeting Afternoon. Mr Julian dind here. I taken with dimness in my Eyes in the Night . . .

JULY 7, TUESDAY A fine dry day. Mr Hardy at home all day. W^m went to Whisonsett Aftern, took Mr Burrell with him «in» the Gigg.

JULY 8, WEDNESDAY A Very Hot dry day. Mr Hardy at home all day. W^m came home Eveng 9.

JULY 9, THURSDAY A Very Hot dry [day]. Mr Hardy & W^m at home all day.

JULY 10, FRIDAY A Very Hot dry day. Mr Hardy & W^m at home all day.

JULY 11, SATURDAY A Very Hot day, A Thunder Storm Eveng 8. Mr Hardy at home all day. W^m went to Holt Mark^t Afternoon, drank tea at Mr Bartells, came home Eveng 9 . . .

JULY 13, MONDAY A Hot day, some small Showers Afternoon. Mr Hardy & W^m at home all day. Mrs Hooper & Miss Davy calld Afternoon . . .

JULY 17, FRIDAY A Very Hot day. Mr Hardy at home all day. I, W^m & Mrs Cozens drank tea at Mrs Davys, Holt . . .

JULY 19, SUNDAY A Very Hot dry day. I & Mrs Cozens & Wm Girling went to Cley meeting, Mr Juliar dind here. I & W^m & Mrs Cozens went to Briston meeting Aftern, Wm Girling went. Mr Hardy went to our Church Afternoon, Mr Burrell preachd.

JULY 20, MONDAY A Very Sultry day. Expected M^r & Mrs Goggs to dinner but they did not come. M^{rs} & Miss M Davy, Mrs Hooper & 2 Childrⁿ drank tea here . . .

JULY 22, WEDNESDAY A Very Hot day. Maids & S Boyce washd 4 weeks Linnen. Mr Sturly & Son & Mr Williams of Thornage drank tea here. Mr Hardy & W^m at home all day . . .

JULY 24, FRIDAY A Very Hot day. A fine Showr ab^t Noon with some Thunder, some small showers in the Afternoon. Mr Hardy & W^m at home all day.

JULY 25, SATURDAY Fine day. Mr Hardy at home all day. W^m went to Holt Mark^t Afternoon, came home Eveng 9.

JULY 26, SUNDAY A Very fine day. I & Wm Girling went to Briston meeting afternoon, W^m went to Breningham Church Afternoon . . .

Sprowston: the Summer Assizes
27 July–8 August 1807

JULY 29, WEDNESDAY A fine day, wind reather high. M^r & Mrs Boardman dind at Mr Cozens, went away eve 4. We were at home all day.

JULY 30, THURSDAY A fine day. We were all at home all day . . .

AUGUST 1, SATURDAY A fine day. Mr Hardy went to Norwich with Mr Cozens foornoon, came home to dinner Eveng 3. M^{rs} C & I at home all day . . .

AUGUST 4, TUESDAY A Very fine day. Mr Hardy, I, M^r & Mrs Cozens went to Norwich Afternoon, drank tea at Mr John Cozens & went to Mr Wilks meeting in Eveng.

AUGUST 5, WEDNESDAY A Close dry day. At home all day. Mr John Cozens drank tea with us . . .

AUGUST 7, FRIDAY A foggy Morng, raind Afternoon. Mrs Wilks drank tea with us . . .

[LETHERINGSETT]

AUGUST 9, SUNDAY A fine day. I & Wm Girling went to Briston meeting Afternoon, Mr Juliar preach'd. W^m went to Briningham Church Afternoon, Mr Upjohn preach'd. Mr Hardy at home all day. Service at our Church foornoon, Mr Burrell preach'd.

AUGUST 10, MONDAY A fine day. Mr Hardy & W^m at home all day . . .

AUGUST 21, FRIDAY A Very Hot day. Mr Hardy very poorly. W^m drank tea at Mr Walls . . .

AUGUST 23, SUNDAY A Very Hot day. S Raven, Ann & Miss Sheldrake went to our Church foornoon, Mr Burrell preach'd. I & W^m & Ann Raven went to Briston meeting meeting Afternoon. M^r [Miss] Sheldrake went away to Mrs Temples of Weybon [Weybourne] After dinner. Mr Hardy poorly.

AUGUST 24, MONDAY A Very Hot day. Mr Hardy very poorly. W^m & Ann Raven went to Sheringham Afternoon.

AUGUST 25, TUESDAY A fine day, Very hot. Mr Hardy very poorly, W^m at home all day. M^r & Mrs Bartell drank tea here . . .

AUGUST 28, FRIDAY A Very Hot Windy day, A small Showr foornoon. Mr Hardy much as Yesterday. W^m at home all day. Expected M^r & Mrs Wm Cozens to dinner, he [they] did not come.

AUGUST 29, SATURDAY A Very Hot dry day. Mr Hardy something better. Mr Wm Cozens came to breakfst, dind & drank tea here & went back to Toffts [Toftrees]. W^m went to Holt Mark^t after tea . . .

AUGUST 31, MONDAY A Cool Showry day. Mr Hardy better. W^m at home all day. M^r & Mrs John & M^r T Custance call«ed» here ab^t Noon in their way to Cromer.

SEPTEMBER 1, TUESDAY A Very fine day, not hot. Mr Hardy finely. W^m dind & drank tea at Mr Robt Breartons of Blakney, came home Eveng 8. Miss Sheldrake dind & drank tea at Mrs Davys, Holt.

SEPTEMBER 2, WEDNESDAY A fine day. Mr Hardy finely. W^m at home all day. M^{rs} & Miss Mary & Susan Davy drank tea here . . .

SEPTEMBER 6, SUNDAY A Very High Windy day. Mrs Raven & Ann went to our Church foorn, W^m went to Briningham Church Afternoon. Wm Girling went to Briston Meeting Afternoon, I could not go, the Wind was so boisterous. Mrs Simpson & Mrs Penrice calld in the Eveng to speak to Mrs Raven.

SEPTEMBER 7, MONDAY A fine day. Mr Hardy finely. W^m at home all day. Mr Custance, Fakenham, & a Mr Snukes, M^r & Mrs John & Mr Thos Custance & Mr John Baker dind & drank tea here. Our Harvest Men had their Supper at Dobsons.

SEPTEMBER 8, TUESDAY A fine «day». Mr Hardy finely. W^m & Sister & Ann Raven rid to Thornage on A Morng Visit to Mrs Penrice, W^m left them there to spend the

Day. W^m dind & drank tea at Mr Williams at Thornage, they all came home Eveng 9 . . .

SEPTEMBER 11, FRIDAY A Very fine day. Mr Hardy finely. W^m went to Mr Breertons, Blakney, to dinner, met a large party there, came home Eveng 11.

SEPTEMBER 12, SATURDAY Cold & showry Afternoon. Mr Hardy much as Usial. W^m went to Holt Mark^t Afternoon, came home Even 8 . . .

SEPTEMBER 14, MONDAY A Cold day, A few small Showers afternoon. Mr Hardy & W^m at home all day. Expected M^r & Mrs Cozens but they did not come.

SEPTEMBER 15, TUESDAY A fine day but cold. Mr Hardy & W^m at home all day. M^r & Mrs Cozens came Eveng 2.

SEPTEMBER 16, WEDNESDAY A Showry Morng, fine day. Mr Hardy finely. Mr Cozens went out A Shooting foornoon. We took a walk afternoon to Thornage, came home to tea . . .

SEPTEMBER 18, FRIDAY A fine day. Mr Hardy & W^m at home all day. M^r & Mrs Cozens went away Morng 10 . . .

SEPTEMBER 23, WEDNESDAY A fine morng, a Very heavy Showr from 2 to 3 o Clock & from 5 to 7 in the Eveng. I was very poorly with dimness in my Eyes about Noon. W^m came home from Sprowston Eveng past 9 . . .

SEPTEMBER 25, FRIDAY A fine day. Mr Hardy & W^m at home all day.

SEPTEMBER 26, SATURDAY A fine day. Mr Hardy at home all day. W^m went to Holt Mark^t afternoon, came home Eveng 9.

SEPTEMBER 27, SUNDAY A Wet Morng, cleard up ab^t 10 oclock, raind again A heavy Showr ab^t 2 o Clock & cleard up again. I & Edw'd went to Cley meeting foornoon, Mr Gilpin dind here. I & W^m went to Briston meeting Afternoon.

SEPTEMBER 28, MONDAY A dry Morng, Wet afternoon. Mr Hardy at home all day. W^m went to Mr Walls Afternoon to tea, came home Even 9.

SEPTEMBER 29, TUESDAY A dry Morng, Very Wet afternoon. Mr Hardy at home all day. W^m walkd up to Holt Afternoon, came home to tea. Maids & S Boyce washd 3 Weeks Linn«en» . . .

OCTOBER 1, THURSDAY A Close dry day. Mr Hardy & W^m at home all day. Raind a good deal in the Night.

OCTOBER 2, FRIDAY A Wet morng, fine Afterno. Mr Hardy & W^m at home all day.

OCTOBER 3, SATURDAY A Very beautifull day, quite Warm. Mr Hardy at home all day. W^m went to Holt Mark^t Afternoon, came home Eveng 9 . . .

OCTOBER 5, MONDAY A Very fine day. Mr Hardy & W^m at home all day. Mrs Seales & a Mrs Till & Miss Dean calld Afternoon.

OCTOBER 6, TUESDAY A Very fine day. Mr Hardy & W^m at home all day. S Boyce Washd A Weeks Linnen . . .

OCTOBER 8, THURSDAY A Close cold windy day. Mr Hardy drank tea at Mr Burrells. I & W^m rid to Fakenham Morng 10, dind & drank tea at Mr Custances, Mrs Bennet there, came home ½ past 9.

OCTOBER 9, FRIDAY A Close day. Mr Hardy at home all day. W^m dind at Mr Williams at Thornage, came home Eveng 9 . . .

OCTOBER 15, THURSDAY A Very fine day. Mr Hardy & W^m at home all day. Expected Mr Goggs, he did not come. I taken with dimness in my Eyes Eveng 10 . . .

OCTOBER 17, SATURDAY A Very fine day. Mr Hardy at home all day. I & W^m went to Holt Mark^t Afternoon, I drank tea at Mrs Davys, W^m drank tea at Mr Bartells.

OCTOBER 18, SUNDAY A fine day. Mr Hardy went to our Church foornoon, Mr Burrell preach'd. I & Wm Girling went to Briston meeting Afternoon, W^m went to Briningham Church . . .

OCTOBER 21, WEDNESDAY A Very fine day. Mr Hardy at home all day. W^m came home from Sprowston Eveng half past 9. I very poorly.

OCTOBER 22, THURSDAY A Wet morng, close day. Mr Hardy at home all day. W^m went to Hempstead with Mr Leake, Holt, Dind & drank tea at Old Mr Leakes, came home Even 9.

OCTOBER 23, FRIDAY A Close day, began to rain Even 4, continued untill even 8. Mr Hardy at home all day. W^m rid to Mr Girdlestons, Kelling, Aftern, drank tea there, came home even 9. M^rs & Susan Davy drank tea here, sent them home in the Malt Cart on acct of the rain.

OCTOBER 24, SATURDAY A fine day. Mr Hardy at home all day. I poorly. W^m went to Holt Mark^t afternoon, came home Even 9 . . .

OCTOBER 26, MONDAY A [   ], A Close drisly foornoon, fine aftern. Mr Hardy & W^m at home all day. M^r & Mrs Cozens & Child came ½ past 5.

OCTOBER 27, TUESDAY A Cold close day. Mr Hardy & W^m at home all day. Mr Cozens went out A Shooting.

OCTOBER 28, WEDNESDAY A fine day. Mr Hardy & W^m at home all day. Mr Cozens went away Eveng past 3. Mr Wall, M^r & Mrs Burrell drank tea here.

OCTOBER 29, THURSDAY A [I] poorly with dimness in my Eyes Morng 11. Mr Eastaugh came ab^t Noon, Slept here. Mr Hardy & W^m at home all day.

OCTOBER 30, FRIDAY A Wet Morng, dry afternoon. Mr Eastaugh went away after dinner. Mr Hardy & W^m at home all day.

OCTOBER 31, SATURDAY A fine day. Mr Hardy at home all day. W^m went to Holt Mark^t Afternoon, came home Eveng 9 . . .

NOVEMBER 3, TUESDAY A fine day. Mr Hardy, I & Mrs Cozens rid up to Holt Afternoon, drank tea at Mr Bartells, W^m walk'd up . . .

NOVEMBER 7, SATURDAY A fine day. Mr Hardy at home al [all] Day. W^m went to Holt Mark^t aftern, came home Eveng 9.

NOVEMBER 8, SUNDAY A fine day. I & Mrs Cozens & Ja^s went to Cley Meeting foornoon, Mr Bumstead dind here. I, W^m & M^rs C went to Briston meeting Afternoon. Mr Hardy went to our Church Afternoon, Mr Burrell preachd . . .

NOVEMBER 14, SATURDAY A Cold Stormy day. W^m came home from Fakenham Morng 11. I was something better than I was yesterday. Mr Hardy at home all day. W^m went to Holt Mark^t Afternoon, came home Eveng 9 . . .

NOVEMBER 16, MONDAY A Very cold blustering day. I very poorly. Mr Hardy & W^m at home all day . . .

NOVEMBER 20, FRIDAY A tolerable Morng, Very coarse Stormy Afternoon & Night. Mr Hardy at home all day. I Very poorly.

NOVEMBER 21, SATURDAY A Sharp rime frost. I very poorly, Mr Bartell calld to se me Afternoon. Mr Hardy at home all day. W^m walkd up to Holt & came home to Dinner & went to Holt Mark^t aftern, came home ½ past 9 . . .

NOVEMBER 29, SUNDAY A slow thaw, raind afternoon. I was very poorly, Mr Bartell calld ab^t Noon. Service at our Church foornoon. M^r & Mrs Cozens went to Briston Meeting Afternoon.

NOVEMBER 30, MONDAY A Close day. Mr Hardy & W^m at home all day. I very very poorly, Mr Bartell calld to see me. Susan Davy calld to see me afternoon. An Assembly at Holt.

DECEMBER 1, TUESDAY A rime frost in the Morng, foggy damp Day. I was very poorly all day. Maids & S Boyce washd 4 Weeks Linnen. Mr Bartell calld to see me.

DECEMBER 2, WEDNESDAY A fine day. I very poorly, Mr Hardy & W^m at home all day. Mr Bartell came . . .

[*Mary Hardy was seriously ill from 3 December and needed a full-time nurse; her daughter Mary Ann Cozens made the entries from 6 December. After a gap in the record from 19 December to 7 January William Hardy began making the entries on 8 January. Mary Hardy resumed on 18 January*]

=1808=

JANUARY 20, WEDNESDAY A fine day. Mr Hardy & W^m at home all day. I was much as Yesterda, recd A Letter from Mrs Cozens. Mr Unthank calld here foornoon . . .

JANUARY 24, SUNDAY A Very Chearly day, Thawd slowly. I much as yesterday. Mr Hardy at home all day. Mrs Raven went to our Church foornoon, Mr Burrell preachd. W^m went to Briningham Church Aftern, Wm Girling went to Bodham Aftern . . .

JANUARY 26, TUESDAY A fine chearly day, a frost. Mr Hardy at home all day. W^m went to Mr Walls to tea {tea}, expected to meet M^r & Mrs Rouse, mistook the Day . . .

JANUARY 28, THURSDAY A Cold windy day. Mr Hardy & W^m at home all day. I somthing better. Mr Upjohn came afternoon, drank tea here, Mr Colman came in the Eveng . . .

JANUARY 31, SUNDAY A Very fine chearly day. Mr Bumsted dind here. W^m & Girlin went to Briston meeting afternoon. Mr Burrell taken I [?Ill] from home, prevented him from preaching at Letheringsett. Mr Bartell cam to se me . . .

[[FEBRUARY 4, THURSDAY [*by William Hardy*] A very fine day. Wife a little better, took a Walk forenoon and Afternoon. At home all day. Men planting, W^m & Mr Cozens went in the forenoon to see them.

FEBRUARY 5, FRIDAY A Very fine day. Wife as Yesterday, Walked into Garden. M^r & Mrs Cozens set off for Sprowston past 1 OClock, W^m went with them as far as Saxthorp. Men planting.

FEBRUARY 6, SATURDAY A very fine day. Wife as Yesterd^y, Walked into Garden. Men planting. Wm Went to Market, came home E9.

FEBRUARY 7, SUNDAY A Dry fine day. Wife a little better, Walked into Garden. W^m & Mrs Raven went to Brinningham Church . . .]]

FEBRUARY 10, WEDNESDAY A frost, a little Snow on the ground. Mr Hardy & W^m at home all day. I much as Yesterday. W^m wrote to Sprowston to send by Mr Youngman to Morrow . . .

FEBRUARY 12, FRIDAY A Windy «day» & snowd a good deal. Mr Hardy & W^m at home all day. I much as yesterday.

FEBRUARY 13, SATURDAY A frosty day. Mr Hardy at home all day. W^m went to Holt Mark^t afternoon, came home Eveng past 9. Mr Bartell calld to see me foornoon. Old Mrs Temple was Buried at Blakney. Another fall of Snow in the Night . . .

FEBRUARY 15, MONDAY A frost, a great deal of Snow on the Ground. Mr Hardy & W^m at home all day. I was finely in the day but was taken very poorly in the Eveng, had a Very bad Night. I walkd into Garden.

FEBRUARY 16, TUESDAY A Very slow thaw. Mr Hardy & W^m at home all day. I poorly, walkd into Garden . . .

FEBRUARY 19, FRIDAY A White frost, Very fine day. Mr Hardy & W^m at home all day. I was poorly . . .

FEBRUARY 20, SATURDAY A White frost. Mr Hardy & W^m at home all day. Mr Sheppard from Warham calld & dind here. I poorly. Mr Hardy at home all day, W^m went to Holt Mark^t afternoon.

FEBRUARY 21, SUNDAY A frost, Very fine day. Mr Hardy & Mrs Raven went to our Church foorn. Sa^r [Sarah] Davy call'd foornoon. W^m went to Briningham Church Afternoon. Wm Girling went to Briston Meeting Afternoon, Mrs Hill of Briston very Ill . . .

MARCH 1, TUESDAY A Close morng, fine afternoon. Mr Hardy & W^m at home all day. M^r & Mrs Cozens came Even half past 5. I not so well as Yesterday.

MARCH 2, WEDNESDAY A Close Mild day. Mr Hardy & W^m at home all day. I was not so well as Yesterday, Mr Bartell call«ed» to se me.

MARCH 3, THURSDAY A remarkable fine day. M^r & Mrs Cozens went away Eveng 2. W^m drove me out in the Gigg Afternoon. I was very poorly, taken with dimness in my Eyes ab^t Noon & again Eveng 4. Mr Hardy at home all day. W^m rid to Edgefield after tea. M^r & Mrs Bartell & Mrs Raven from Dereham drank tea here.

MARCH 4, FRIDAY A Very fine day. I was very poorly all day, taken with dimness in my Eyes Even 4. Mr Eastaugh came to dinner, Slept here. Mr Hardy at home all day. W^m drank tea at Mr Bartells, came home Eveng past 9. Mr Bartell came to see me . . .

MARCH 6, SUNDAY A Beautifull day. I was finely. Mr Hardy at home all day. Sister Raven very poorly, did not go to Church foornoon. W^m went to Briningham Church Afternoon, Mr Upjohn preachd. Girling went to Briston Meeting Afternoon. Mr Bartell here foornoon . . .

[[MARCH 10, THURSDAY [*by William Hardy*] A Cold dry day. All at home allday. Wife very poorly but a little better towards evening. Mr Walker dined here. Workmen building Dobsons house . . .]]

MARCH 19, SATURDAY A Very Cold Windy day. I was but poorly. Mr Hardy at home all day. W^m went to Holt Mark^t Afternoon, came home a little after 9.

MARCH 20, SUNDAY A Very Cold Windy day. I was very poorly. Mr Hardy at home all day. Sister Raven went to our Church foornoon, Mr Burrell preachd. W^m & Girling went to Briston Meeting Afternoon . . .

MARCH 24, THURSDAY A Sharp frost & frequent Storms of Snow & Sleet. Mr Hardy and W^m at home all day. I finely. Snow in the Night.

MARCH 25, FRIDAY A Cold day. Mr Hardy at home all day. W^m went to Mr Temples of Blakny to dinner, came home Eveng 11. I was finely, I walkd into [   ].

MARCH 26, SATURDAY A Very Cold Windy day. Mr Hardy at home all day. W^m went to Holt Mark^t Afternoon, came home Eveng 10. I poorly.

MARCH 27, SUNDAY A Very Sharp Windy day. No service at our Church. Mr Gilpin calld & dind here, W^m & Girling went to Briston Meeting Afternoon. I something better then Yesterday . . .

MARCH 29, TUESDAY A bright day but Cold. Mr Hardy at home all day. W^m went to Cromer foornoon, dind & drank tea at Mr Bartels, came home Eveng 9. I was very poorly with pain in my Head.

MARCH 30, WEDNESDAY A Cold dry day. Mr Hardy & W^m at home all day. I was finely, Mr Bartell calld to see me foornoon. A Storm of Snow ab^t Sun Sett & more Storms in the Night . . .

APRIL 4, MONDAY A Windy Stormy day. Mr Hardy at home all day. I was very poorly, Mr Bartell calld to see me.

APRIL 5, TUESDAY A Very high Windy Stormy day. I was something better then yesterday. Mr Hardy at home all day. W^m & Mrs Cozens came home Even past 7 . . .

APRIL 7, THURSDAY A Milder day. Mr Hardy & W^m at home all day. I alittle better, Mr Bartell calld to see me.

APRIL 8, FRIDAY A dry day but Cold. Mr Hardy at home all day. W^m dind & drank tea at Mr Pauls of Study [Stody], came home Eveng 11 . . .

APRIL 10, SUNDAY A fine day. Mr Hardy at home all day. Mr Gilpin dind here. W^m, Mrs Cozens & Mrs Raven went to Briston Meeting Afternoon. I finely . . .

APRIL 12, TUESDAY A Wet morng, close cold day. Mr Hardy & W^m at home all day.

APRIL 13, WEDNESDAY A fine day. Mr Hardy at home all day, I finely. W^m & I & Mrs Cozens rid onto Farm foornoon, Mr Hardy at home all day. Sister Raven, Mrs Cozens & W^m drank tea at Mr Bartells.

APRIL 14, THURSDAY A Very fine warm day. I, W^m & Mrs Cozens took a ride foornoon to Bayfield & round by Saxlingham. Mr Hardy at [and] W^m at home all day. I poorly . . .

APRIL 16, SATURDAY A Cold Windy day, some small flights of Snow. Mr Hardy at home all day. W^m, I & Mrs Cozens rid out foornoon, I better then Yesterday. W^m went to Holt Mark^t, came home Eveng 9 . . .

APRIL 21, THURSDAY A Wet foornoon, Wind high & Cold, dry Cold Afternoon. I very poo«r»ly with Nervous Complaints all day. Mr Hardy & W^m at home all day . . .

APRIL 23, SATURDAY A Milder day then Yesterday. I something better then yesterday. W^m, I & Mrs Cozens took a ride out Aftern thro Hull Wood. W^m went Holt Mark^t Afternoon, came home. Mr Cozens came Eveng 8 . . .

APRIL 27, WEDNESDAY A Very Coarse Cold day. Mr Hardy & W^m at home all day . . .

APRIL 29, FRIDAY A fine day, Wind a little Cold. I was taken with dimness in my Eyes Morng 7 but was finely all day. I & W^m rid to Mr Sturlys, Thornage, foornoon. Mr Hardy at home all day. 2 Miss Davys drank tea here.

APRIL 30, SATURDAY A Cold day. Mr Hardy at home all day. I was very poorly all day, taken poorly with dimness in my Eyes Morn 6. W^m & I rid into Farm Afternoon & then «?he» went to Holt Mark^t, came home Eveng past 9 . . .

MAY 3, TUESDAY A Very warm day. Mr Hardy at home all day. I but poorly. W^m & I took a ride Afternoon through the Farm & round by Mr Walls. Mr Hardy at home all day, Mr Moore of Holt dind here.

MAY 4, WEDNESDAY A Very Warm day. I finely. I & Mr Hardy rid out foornoon. Mr Bartell call'd to see me foornoon. W^m at home all day.

MAY 5, THURSDAY A Very fine day. Mr Hardy at home all day. I & W^m rid out into the Farm Afternoon, & W^m drank tea at Mr Williams.

MAY 6, FRIDAY A Very Warm dry day. Mr Hardy at home all day. I was finely. I & W^m rid out foornoon into Farm & round by Glandford. M^r & Mrs Bartell, M^rs & Matt^h Davy, M^r & Mrs Rouse drank tea here.

MAY 7, SATURDAY A Very hot day. Mr Hardy at home all day. I was very poorly, did not ride out. Mr Gilpin calld an hour Afternoon going to Blakney. W^m went to Holt Mark^t afternoon, came home eveng 9. Rain in the Night.

MAY 8, SUNDAY A Very showry day. No service at our Church. Mr Gilpin dind here, W^m & Mrs Raven went to Briston meeting Aftern. I reather better then Yesterday.

MAY 9, MONDAY A Showry day. Mr Hardy walkd out Afternoon & got wet. W^m & I rid to Bayfield foornoon, I poorly . . .

MAY 11, WEDNESDAY A Windy day, a large Showr with Thunder Afternoon. Mr Hardy & W^m at home all day. I had a bad Night & rose by 5 o Clock this Morng & was poorly all day, Mr Bartell calld to se me.

MAY 12, THURSDAY A Wet day. Mr Hardy & W^m at home all day. I was poorly foorn & taken with dimness in my Eyes twice Afternoon . . .

MAY 15, SUNDAY A Very hot dry day. Service at our Church Eveng 6. Mr Hardy at home all day. W^m & S [Sister] Raven went to Briston meeting Afternoon . . .

MAY 17, TUESDAY A Cooler day then yesterday. I was very poorly. I, W^m & Mrs Cozens rid up to Holt Afternoon, came back to tea.

MAY 18, WEDNESDAY A dry day but Cold. Mr Hardy & W^m at home all day. M^r & Mrs Cozens went away Eveng 4. I & W^m rid onto Farm Afternoon, Mrs Seales & Miss Wall calld to speak to me in the Eveng.

MAY 19, THURSDAY A Cool day. Mr Hardy at home all day. W^m, I & Mrs Raven rid to Bayfield Afternoon.

MAY 20, FRIDAY A Cool day. Mr Hardy at home all Day. I, S Raven & W^m rid to Sandy Hills foornoon.

MAY 21, SATURDAY A Cold dry day. Mr Hardy at home all day. W^m went to Holt Mark^t Afternoon, came home eveng 9. I poorly.

MAY 22, SUNDAY A Showry cold day. I very poorly. Mr Bumstead dind here. W^m went to Briston Meeting Afternoon. Mr Hardy & S Raven went to our Church afternoon, Mr Burrell preachd. I poorly with dimness in my Eyes afternoon . . .

MAY 24, TUESDAY A fine day, wind brisk. I & W^m rid to Thornage foornoon. Mr Hardy at home all day. W^m met a party at Mr Rouses to tea, M^r & Mrs Bartell calld here Afternoon.

MAY 25, WEDNESDAY A fine day. I much as Yesterday. Mrs Seales, Miss Wall & Miss Dean came foornoon to walk in Garden. W^m rid to Melton afternoon . . .

MAY 27, FRIDAY A Very Wet day. Mr Hardy at home all day. W^m walkd up to Holt foorn, at home afternoon. I better then yesterday . . .

JUNE 4, SATURDAY A Wet Morng, dry afternoon. Mr Goggs & Son went away before dinner. Mr Hardy at home all day. W^m went to Holt Mark^t Afternoon, came home Eveng 9. I poorly. Mr Gilpin calld & took tea here . . .

JUNE 6, MONDAY Omitted.

JUNE 7, TUESDAY A fine day till Eveng 6 then raind. I poorly. Mr Hardy at home all day. W^m & Ann Raven walkd to Hunworth Wood after tea to Shoot Rooks. I & W^m & Ann Raven rid to Mr Sturlys foornoon, & I & S Raven rid up to Holt after tea, recd a Letter from London from Mrs Cozens.

JUNE 8, WEDNESDAY A Very Wet day. Mr Hardy at home all day. I finely. Wm Dind & drank tea at Mr Temples of Blakney . . .

JUNE 11, SATURDAY A Dry Cold day. I poorly. Mr Hardy at home all day. I took a ride with the Boy & Child in Dicky Cart. W^m came home eveng 5, went to Mark^t after tea & came home Eve 9.

JUNE 12, SUNDAY A Chearly day, wind Cold. Mr Hardy at home all day. I finely. I & W^m & Child rid out foornoon in Dicky Cart. W^m rid to Briningham Church afternoon. Service at our Church Even 6.

JUNE 13, MONDAY Omitted, nothing particular . . .

JUNE 22, WEDNESDAY A fine day. Mr Hardy & W^m at home all day. M^r [? Revd John] Glover & 3 Childr^n & 3 Miss Gays call«ed» here after tea, M^r & Mrs Hawkins & Mr Goggs calld in their way to Fakenham.

JUNE 23, THURSDAY A Close morng, a Show^r ab^t 3 oClock then a fine Eveng. Mr Hardy at home all day. I & W^m rid onto Farm after tea. I poorly.

JUNE 24, FRIDAY A fine day. I finely, Mr Hardy at home all day. W^m went to Mr Walls to tea, came home Eveng past 10. Mr Hardy at home all day, I rid up to Holt after tea.

JUNE 25, SATURDAY A Very fine day. W^m sett off for Sprowston & Norwich Morn ½ past 4, Mr Hardy at home all day. I rid up to Holt in the Eveng.

JUNE 26, SUNDAY A fine day. Mr Hardy at home all day. Service at our Church foornoon, Wm Girling went to Briston Meeting Afternoon. I poorly, taken with dimnes in my Eyes Eveng past 9 . . .

JUNE 28, TUESDAY A Close Cold day. Mr Hardy & W^m at home all day. I poorly . . .

JULY 1, FRIDAY A fine day but Cold. I had a bad Night but tolerable Day. Mr Hardy & W^m at home all day, I & W^m took a ride into Farm after tea.

JULY 2, SATURDAY A fine day, very dry. Mr Hardy at home all day. I & W^m took a ride foornoon as far as Bayfield. I taken with dimness in my Eyes ab^t Noon, very poorly all day & had a Bad night. W^m went to Holt Mark^t afternoon, came home Eveng 9.

JULY 3, SUNDAY A fine day, very dry. Mr Hardy at home all day. I very poorly, taken with disiness in my Head Eveng 1. Mr Gilpin dind here. W^m & Girling went to Briston Meeting afternoon. Service at our Church Afternoon. I had a tolerable Night.

JULY 4, MONDAY Some small Showers. I was taken with dimness in my Eyes last Night. Mr Hardy & W^m at home all day. Mr Goggs & Miss Cubit dind & drank tea here in their way from Cromer.

JULY 5, TUESDAY A fine day. Mr Hardy & W^m at home all day. I rid up to Holt in the Eveng, had a poor Night, taken with dimness in my Eyes early in the Morng.

JULY 6, WEDNESDAY A fine day. Mr Hardy & W^m ahome all day. I rid up to Holt afternoon for Susan Davy, she drank tea here. I poorly with dimness in my Eyes 2 or 3 times in the Eveng, had a good Night . . .

JULY 9, SATURDAY A Very fine day. I had dimness in my Eyes Morn 6 slightly. Mr Eastaugh went away after breakfast, Mr Hardy at home all day. W^m went to Holt Mark^t Afternoon, W^m came home Eveng past 9.

JULY 10, SUNDAY A Very Hot dry day. Mr Hardy at home all day. W^m went to Briningham Church, Girling went to Briston Meeting. I poorly . . .

JULY 14, THURSDAY A dry day, not so hot as Yesterday. Mr Hardy at home all day. W^m went to Mr Walls aftern, drank tea & Supt there. Maids & S Boyce washd 4 Weeks Linnen . . .

JULY 17, SUNDAY A Very Hot dry day. Service at our Church afternoon, Mr Burrell preachd. W^m went to Dalling Church afternoon, Mr Upjon preachd. I & W^m took a ride after tea to Holt & came back by our Farm.

JULY 18, MONDAY A Very Hot day. Mr Hardy at home all day, I finely. W^m at home all day.

JULY 19, TUESDAY A Very Hot day. Mr Hardy at home all day. Miss M & Susan Davy & 2 Miss Robensons drank tea here. I was but poorly.

JULY 20, WEDNESDAY A Very Hot dry day. Mr Hardy & W^m at home all day. I & Ja^s rid up to Holt Afternoon, came back to tea. I but poorly . . .

JULY 22, FRIDAY A Very Hot day. Mʳ Hardy at home all day. Wᵐ drank «tea» at Mʳ Temples, Thornage, came home Eveng 9. I rid up to Thornage in the Eveng.

JULY 23, SATURDAY A Very Hot day. Wᵐ went to Holt Markᵗ afternoon, came home Even 9. Mʳ Hardy at home all day. I poorly. A small Showr in the Eveng . . .

JULY 26, TUESDAY A Very Wet day. Mʳ Hardy & Wᵐ & Mʳ & Mʳˢ Cozens at at home all day. I very poorly with dimness in my Eyes severall times in the Day . . .

JULY 28, THURSDAY A Very Wet Morng, cleard up at Eveng 3. Mʳ Hardy & Wᵐ at home all day. M Wilks & Son & Daughtʳ went away half past 2. I better then yesterda.

JULY 29, FRIDAY A fine day. Mʳ Hardy at [and] Wᵐ at home all day . . .

AUGUST 4, THURSDAY A Very Hot day. Mʳ Hardy & Wᵐ at home all day. I poorly.

AUGUST 5, FRIDAY A Very Hot day. Mʳ Hardy at home all day. Wᵐ dind & drank tea at Mʳ Williams, Thornage, came home Eveng 10. I Very finely, I rid up to Holt after tea.

AUGUST 6, SATURDAY A Very Hot day. Mʳ Hardy at home all day. Taken with dimness in my Eyes Morng 5, poorly all day. Wᵐ went to Holt Markᵗ afternoon, came home Eveng past 9. I had a fine Night . . .

AUGUST 10, WEDNESDAY A Very fine day. I finely. Mʳ Hardy & Wᵐ at home all day, I rid up to Holt after tea.

AUGUST 11, THURSDAY A fine day. Mʳ Hardy at [and] Wᵐ at home all day. I finely.

AUGUST 12, FRIDAY A Hot dry day. Mʳ Hardy & Wᵐ at home all day. I & Wᵐ took a ride to Holt after tea, I finely . . .

The last visit to Sprowston
15 August–13 September 1808

AUGUST 18, THURSDAY A fine day. Mʳˢ Cozens & I rid to Catton after tea in Dickey Cart. I taken with dimness in my Eyes Eveng 8 . . .

AUGUST 22, MONDAY A hasy morng, fine day. Mʳ Hardy poorly. Mʳˢ S [?] from Norwich dind & drank tea at Mʳ Cozens . . .

AUGUST 26, FRIDAY A Very Hot day, A Showr abᵗ 6 o Clock. Mʳ & Mʳˢ John, Mʳ & Mʳˢ Jaˢ Cozens & Mʳ Hubbard drank tea at Mʳ Jere Cozens.

AUGUST 27, SATURDAY A foggy morng, turnd to a heavy rain Morng 8, continued all the foornoon, a dry Afternoon, fine eveng. I & Mʳˢ Cozens took a ride in Dickey Cart after tea round by Beeston Hall . . .

SEPTEMBER 4, SUNDAY A drisly Morng, fine «?day». I & Mʳ Hardy in Gig, Miss Leake & Mʳˢ Cozens in Dickey Cart, Mʳ C on Horseback went to Mʳ Wilks meeting foorn. I & BL [Bell Leak] & Mʳˢ C in Gig, Mʳ C on Horseback went to Cherry L [Lane] meeting aftern, Mʳ Revel preach'd. Mʳ Hardy at home afternoon.

SEPTEMBER 5, MONDAY A fine day till eveng 6 then a very heavy Shower. I & Bell Leake & Mʳˢ C rid up to Norwich afternoon in dicky Cart, drank tea at Mʳ Jⁿ Cozens then went to the Monthly meeting at Wilks Chappel. Mʳ C came for us in Gig.

SEPTEMBER 6, TUESDAY A Showry day, we were at home all day. Mʳ Cozens rid to Norwich after«noon» to meet his Broᵗ Wᵐ, drank tea at Mʳ Jⁿ Cozens, came home Even 9.

SEPTEMBER 7, WEDNESDAY Fine foornoon, raind again Even 5. Mʳ & Mʳˢ John, Mʳ & Mʳˢ Wᵐ, Mʳ & Mʳˢ Jaˢ Cozens & Mʳ Hubbard drank tea at Mʳ Cozens . . .

SEPTEMBER 9, FRIDAY A fine Morng, Showry afternoon. I & Mʳˢ Cozens rid to Norwich in Dickey Cart foornoo«n», came back to dinner. BL walkd to Catton & Norwich, came back even 3 . . .

[LETHERINGSETT]

SEPTEMBER 19, MONDAY A Very Wet day till eveng 3 then cleard up to a fine Eveng. Mʳ Hardy & Wᵐ at home all day. Mʳ & Mʳˢ Cozens came eveng 8 . . .

SEPTEMBER 22, THURSDAY A fine day. Mʳ Hardy & Wᵐ at home all day. Mʳ & Mʳˢ Cozens went away a little after 3. I poorly with dimness in my Eyes Eveng 4. Raind a good deal in the Even & Night.

SEPTEMBER 23, FRIDAY A Showry day. Mʳ Hardy at home all day. Wᵐ went to Mʳ Williams of Thornage a Shooting, came home Even past 9. I poorly . . .

SEPTEMBER 25, SUNDAY A Very fine day. Mʳ Gilpin dind here, I & Wᵐ went to Briston meeting Afternoon. Mʳ Hardy at home all day. I was finely . . .

SEPTEMBER 27, TUESDAY A Showry day. Mʳ Hardy at home all day. Wᵐ went to Mʳ Walls to tea, came home even 9. I finely.

SEPTEMBER 28, WEDNESDAY A Very Showry day. Mʳ Hardy at home all day, Wᵐ walkd up to Holt after tea. I taken with dimness in my Eyes Eveng 1 . . .

SEPTEMBER 30, FRIDAY A Stormy day. Mʳ Hardy & Wᵐ at home all day.

OCTOBER 1, SATURDAY A Wet Morn, dry aftern. Mʳ Hardy at home all day. Wᵐ went to Holt Markᵗ afternoon, came home Eveng 9 . . .

OCTOBER 4, TUESDAY A Close showry day. Mʳ Hardy & Wᵐ at home all day. I was finely. Maids & Eliz Spall [Spaul] washd 3 weeks Linnen. I was poorly . . .

OCTOBER 6, THURSDAY A fine day. Mʳ Hardy at home all day. Miss Deb Johnson & Mʳ Burrell & some young ladies calld in foornoon. Wᵐ went to Miss Fishers Sale Afternoon, came home Eveng 7.

OCTOBER 7, FRIDAY A fine day. Mʳ Hardy & Wᵐ at home all day. A Stormy eveng.

OCTOBER 8, SATURDAY A Stormy morn, very Wet afternoon. Mʳ Hardy at home all day. Wᵐ went to Holt Markᵗ afternoon, came home Eveng past 9. Mʳˢ Chissell [? Chiswell] died at Holt. Wind high in the Night.

OCTOBER 9, SUNDAY Wind very high & close foornoon, better towards eveng. Mʳ King dind here, I & Wᵐ went to Briston meeting Afternoon . . .

OCTOBER 13, THURSDAY A fine day. Mʳ Hardy at home all day. Wᵐ went to Mʳ Leakes at Holt to tea, came home Even 8. I finely.

OCTOBER 14, FRIDAY A Cold windy day. Mr Hardy at home all day. W^m walk'd up to Holt after tea, came home even 9. I poorly afternoon. Rain in the night.

OCTOBER 15, SATURDAY A Wet morng, dry afternoon. Mr Hardy at home all day. W^m went to Holt Mark^t afternoon, came home Eveng past 9.

OCTOBER 16, SUNDAY A Very Wet morng & Showry aftern. Mr Hardy at home all day. I taken poorly with dimness in my Eyes abt Noon. W^m & Girling went to Briston meeting in Gigg & great Mare. I could not go, being poorly, dimness in my Eyes in the Night . . .

OCTOBER 19, WEDNESDAY A Wet cold morn till 8 oClock then cleard up fine untill eveng 3 then began to rain again & Continued untill eveng 7 then cleard up, a dry Night. Mr Hardy at home all day. I finely all day . . .

OCTOBER 21, FRIDAY A dry cold day. Mr Hardy at home all day. I poorly . . .

OCTOBER 24, MONDAY A Wet morng, fine day. Mr Hardy at home all day. I but poorly in Eveng . . .

OCTOBER 28, FRIDAY A Wet morng, fine day. Mr Hardy at home all day. I finely all day. Rain in the Night . . .

OCTOBER 31, MONDAY A Close dry day. Mr Hardy at home all day. I but poorly . . .

NOVEMBER 2, WEDNESDAY A Very fine day. Mr Hardy at home all day. I better then yesterday.

NOVEMBER 3, THURSDAY A fine day. Mr Hardy at home all day. I but poorly.

NOVEMBER 4, FRIDAY A fine day. Mr Hardy took a walk into the Farm afternoon. Recd A Letter from W^m at London this eveng.

NOVEMBER 5, SATURDAY A fine day. Mr Hardy went to Holt Mark^t afternoon, came home Even 6. I finely . . .

NOVEMBER 11, FRIDAY A fine day but cold. Mr Hardy at home all day. I something better then yesterday . . .

NOVEMBER 14, MONDAY A Very fine day. Mr Hardy at home all day. W^m went to Holt Afternoon, drank tea at Mr Leakes, home eveng 9. I better then I was yesterday. M^r & Mrs Bartell drank tea here.

NOVEMBER 15, TUESDAY A dry day but cold. Mr Hardy & W^m at home all day. I finely.

NOVEMBER 16, WEDNESDAY A dry Windy day. Mr Hardy at home all day. W^m went to Holt afternoon, drank tea at Mrs Davys, came home eveng past 8. I finely.

NOVEMBER 17, THURSDAY A Dry windy day. Mr Hardy at home all day. W^m went to Holt Afternoon, drank tea at Mrs Davys, came home eveng past 8 . . .

NOVEMBER 19, SATURDAY A Fine day. Mr Hardy at home all day. W^m went to Holt Mark^t Afternoon, came home even 9. I taken poorly morng 9 with dimness in my Eyes.

NOVEMBER 20, SUNDAY A Very fine day. Mr Hardy went to our Church afternoon, Mr Burrell preachd. I taken with dimness in my Eyes ab^t Noon slightly. Mr Gilpin came to dinner, I & W^m went to Briston meeting afternoon.

NOVEMBER 21, MONDAY A Very fine day. Mr Hardy at home all day. {Mr Hardy at home all day.} W^m went to Holt foorn. M^r & Mrs Cozens & Child came Eveng 5 . . .

NOVEMBER 23, WEDNESDAY A fine day. Mr Hardy & W^m at {at} home all day. I poorly with dimness in my Eyes. Mr Cozens went out a Shooting foornoon.

NOVEMBER 24, THURSDAY A fine day. Mr Cozens went away after breakfast & left M^{rs} C & Child. Mr Hardy & W^m at home all day.

NOVEMBER 25, FRIDAY A Close foggy day. Holt Fair foornoon, «?William» came home to Dinner, went again after tea & came home after 9.

NOVEMBER 26, SATURDAY A Close reather drisly day. Mr Hardy at home all day. I but poorly. W^m went to Holt Mark^t afternoon, came home eveng past 9. A great deal of rain fell in the Night . . .

NOVEMBER 29, TUESDAY A tolerable day but very little dry. Mr Hardy & W^m at home all day. I poorly.

NOVEMBER 30, WEDNESDAY A fine day. Mr Hardy at home all day. W^m rid to Southreps aftern, slept at Mr Cubits. I finely.

DECEMBER 1, THURSDAY A fine day. Mr Hardy took a walk foornoon. W^m came home from Southreps Eveng 9. I finely.

DECEMBER 2, FRIDAY A fine day except a small Shower Afternoon. Mrs Cozens & Child & W^m sett of for Sprowston in our Gigg Morng near 11, Mr Hardy at home all day. I finely. A good deal of rain fell in the Night . . .

DECEMBER 5, MONDAY A fine day. Mr Hardy at home all day. I taken poorly with dimness in my Eyes Even 1.

DECEMBER 6, TUESDAY Fine morng, Close showry After. I better then yesterday, Mr Hardy poorly with a Cold. W^m came home from Sprowston eveng 7.

DECEMBER 7, WEDNESDAY A Very Cold windy day. Mr Hardy & I very poorly with Colds. W^m walkd to Holt Afternoon, came home Eveng past 9. A Very Windy Stormy Cold Night.

DECEMBER 8, THURSDAY A Cold close day. Mr Hardy poorly, I poorly with a Cough & Cold. W^m went to Mr Williams of Thornage to tea, came home eveng 9 . . .

DECEMBER 12, MONDAY A Very fine day. Mr Hardy at home all day. W^m went to Mr Walls to tea, came home even 9. I finely.

DECEMBER 13, TUESDAY A Very close damp Day. Mr Hardy at home all day. W^m went up to Holt Afternoon, came home Eveng 8. I finely.

DECEMBER 14, WEDNESDAY A Close foggy day. Mr Hardy at home all day. W^m rid to Saxlingham Afternoon, drank tea at Mr Balls, came home Even 9. I finely.

DECEMBER 15, THURSDAY A Close cold day. Mr Hardy at home all day, W^m at home all day. I finely.

DECEMBER 16, FRIDAY A rime frost, fine day. Mr Hardy at home all day, W^m at home all day. Mr Engall [? Thomas, of Belaugh] dind here, Mr Banks drank tea here. I finely . . .

DECEMBER 19, MONDAY A Sharp frost & frequent Storms of Snow. Mr Hardy at home all day, W^m at home all day. I poorly. Snow in the Night, Sharp frost.

DECEMBER 20, TUESDAY Snow little or much all day. Mr Hardy at home all day. W^m went to M^r T Temples afternoon to recon [reckon], took tea there, came home Eveng 9. I poorly. Sharp frost but calm.

DECEMBER 21, WEDNESDAY A Very sharp frost, Snow aftern & Eveng & drifted, wind reather high. Mr Hardy at home all day. W^m met aparty to tea at Mrs Davys, came home eveng past 9. I Very poorly.

DECEMBER 22, THURSDAY A Very Sharp frost & frequent Showers of Snow. Mr Hardy & W^m at home all day. I finely. Mr Wm Cook of Thornage drank tea here & rcond [reckoned] . . .

DECEMBER 28, WEDNESDAY A Thaw all day. Mr Hardy & W^m at home all day. The Boy went to Briston Afternoon with Mr Julean [Julian], he rid on Horseback, the Boy walkd. I something better.

DECEMBER 29, THURSDAY The thaw Continue. Mr Hardy & W^m at home all day. I much as yesterday.

DECEMBER 30, FRIDAY Still continue to thaw. Mr Hardy & W^m at home all day. I much as yesterday.

DECEMBER 31, SATURDAY A dry Cold close day. Mr Hardy at home all day. W^m went to Holt Mark^t afternoon, came home eveng near 10 o Clock. I much as Yesterday.

1809

JANUARY 1, SUNDAY A dry Cold day. Mr Hardy at home all day. No service at our Church. I taken with dimness in my Eyes Morng 11 slightly. W^m went Dawlin Church . . .

JANUARY 5, THURSDAY A Sharp frost. Mr Hardy & W^m at home all day. I poorly . . .

JANUARY 7, SATURDAY Continue thawing, roads very bad. Mr Hardy at home all day, Mr King went away Morng 11. I taken with dimness in my Eyes Even 5 slightly. W^m went to Holt Mark^t aftern, came home eveng past 9.

JANUARY 8, SUNDAY A Thaw & Wet afternoon. We were all at home all day, the roads being almost unpasible.

JANUARY 9, MONDAY Thaw continue. Mr Hardy & W^m at home all day. I tolerable.

JANUARY 10, TUESDAY A Close Cold day. Mr Hardy at home all day. W^m sett of on a journey with Mr Williams of Thornage to look at a Farm near Lynn foornoon.

JANUARY 11, WEDNESDAY A fine day but not much Sunshine. Mr Hardy at home all day, I but poorly.

JANUARY 12, THURSDAY A Close day, no frost. Mr Hardy at home all day. Starling Davy calld foornoon to speak to us. I but poorly.

JANUARY 13, FRIDAY A Snowy day. Mr Hardy at home all day. Expected W^m home but he did not come. A frost at Night & more Snow fell in the Night.

JANUARY 14, SATURDAY A frost. Mr Hardy at home all day. I poorly. W^m came home to dinner & went to Holt Mark^t afternoon, came home even past 9.

JANUARY 15, SUNDAY A sharp frost. Mr Hardy & I at home all day, I poorly. Mr Gilpin dind here, W^m & Girling went to Briston meeting Aftern.

JANUARY 16, MONDAY A Sharp frost, close day. Mr Hardy & W^m at home all day. Bell Leake drank tea here. I poorly.

JANUARY 17, TUESDAY A Sharp frost, bright day. Mr Hardy at home all day. W^m drank tea & Supt at Mr Math^h Davys, Holt, came home even [morning] past 2. I something better then yesterday.

JANUARY 18, WEDNESDAY A Sharp frost, bright day. Mr Hardy & W^m at home all day. I very poorly . . .

JANUARY 21, SATURDAY A frosty morng, thawd a little afternoon. Mr Gilpin went away before breakfast, Mr Hardy at home all day. W^m went to Holt Mark^t afternoon, came home Eveng 9 . . .

JANUARY 23, MONDAY A Sharp frost, snow deep & drifted. Mr Hardy & W^m at home all day. I finely.

JANUARY 24, TUESDAY A frost & Snowd great part of the day. Maids & Eliz Loades Washd 4 Weeks Linnen. Mr Hardy at home all day. W^m took tea & reckond with Mr Copland of Sherington, came home Even 9. I very poorly, bad Night. A very coarse Night with Snow & Hail & rain . . .

JANUARY 28, SATURDAY A reather finer day. Mr Hardy at home all day. W^m went to Holt Mark^t afternoon, came home Even 9. I poorly . . .

JANUARY 31, TUESDAY A Very fine day. Mr Hardy at home all day. W^m set of for Sprowston Eveng 2. I but poorly.

FEBRUARY 1, WEDNESDAY A fine day. Mr Hardy at home all day. I poorly . . .

FEBRUARY 4, SATURDAY A fine day. Mr Hardy at home all day. I & Mrs Cozens & Child rid as far at [as] Sherington Afternoon. W^m went to Holt Mark^t afternoon, came home eve 10. Mr Eastaugh came to tea, Slept here . . .

FEBRUARY 6, MONDAY A fine morng, raind afternoon. Mr Eastaugh went away Even 3. Mr Hardy at [and] W^m at home all day.

FEBRUARY 7, TUESDAY A Very Cold day, froze at Night. Mr Hardy & W^m at home all day. I poorly . . .

FEBRUARY 9, THURSDAY A Wet coarse windy day. Mr Hardy at home all day. W^m walkd up to Holt foornoon, dind at Mr Bartells, came home to tea . . .

FEBRUARY 11, SATURDAY A Close cold day. Mr Hardy at home all day. I & Mrs Cozens rid as far as Bayfield Hall aftern. W^m went to Holt Mark^t afternoon, came home Eveng past 9. I poorly.

FEBRUARY 12, SUNDAY A fine morng, Showry aftern. I very poorly. I & Wm Girling rid as far at [as] Hunworth by Holt foorn. Mr Gilpin dind here, W^m went to Briston Meeting afternoon. I poorly . . .

FEBRUARY 14, TUESDAY A fine day. Mr Hardy & W^m at home all day. Mr Jery Cozens came to tea. I poorly. I & M^rs C rid out afternoon.

FEBRUARY 15, WEDNESDAY A Coarse Stormy day. Mr Hardy at home all day. M^r C & W^m walkd to Bayfield to Mr Walls foornoon, at home Afternoon. I poorly. I & M^rs C rid out Afternoon . . .

FEBRUARY 18, SATURDAY A Coarse windy day. Mr Hardy at home all day. W^m went to Holt Mark^t afternoon, came home Even past 9. I poorly . . .

FEBRUARY 20, MONDAY A Cold close windy day. Mr Hardy & W^m at home all day.

FEBRUARY 21, TUESDAY A Cold blustering day. I poorly. Mr Hardy & W^m at home all day. Maids & S Boyce washd 4 Weeks Linnen . . .

FEBRUARY 24, FRIDAY A Cold Windy day. Mr Hardy at home all day. Mr Cozens went away Morn 9. W^m dind & drank tea at Mr Williams, Thornage, came home eveng 8.

FEBRUARY 25, SATURDAY A Cold Close day. Mr Hardy at home all day. W^m went to Holt Mark^t afternoon, came home even 10.

FEBRUARY 26, SUNDAY A Chearly day but cold. No service at our Church. Mr King dind here, Wm Girling went to Briston Meeting. I poorly, I taken with dimness in my Eyes in the Night.

FEBRUARY 27, MONDAY A Very fine day. Mr Hardy & W^m at home all day. I & S Raven rid part of the way to Holt foornoon, I taken with dimness in my Eyes & turnd back. M^r & Mrs Bartell & Mrs Davy drank tea here . . .

MARCH 1, WEDNESDAY A Cold calm day. Mr Hardy at home all day, W^m came home from Cromer Eveng 9. I & S Raven took aride foornoon round by Thornage. Mr Bartell calld afternoon, I something better.

MARCH 2, THURSDAY A fine day. Mr Hardy at home all day. W^m dind & drank tea at Mr Leakes, Holt. I & S Raven took a ride round by Bayfield & Saxlingham road foornoon . . .

MARCH 4, SATURDAY A Close drisly day. Mr King went away after dinner. W^m went to Holt Mark^t aftern, came home eveng 9 . . .

MARCH 6, MONDAY A Cold close day. Mr Hardy at home all day. W^m walkd up to Holt in eveng, home Even 9 . . .

MARCH 8, WEDNESDAY A Very fine day. W^m set of for Sprowston Morn 6, Mr Hardy at home all day. I & S Raven took aride to Sherington foornoon. Bell Leake & Susan Davy took tea here . . .

MARCH 11, SATURDAY A Very Cold windy day. Mr Hardy at home all day. W^m went to Holt Mark^t afternoon, came home Eveng 10.

MARCH 12, SUNDAY A Cold chearly day. Mr Hardy & S Raven went to our Church Afternoon, Mr Burrell preachd. I was poorly. Mr Gilpin dind here, W^m went to Briston meeting with him. Girling went to Cley meeting foornoon with Mr Colman.

MARCH 13, MONDAY A Very cold day. Mr Hardy at home all day, W^m at home all day. Mr Banks took tea here. I poorly.

MARCH 14, TUESDAY A Cold Windy day. Mr Hardy at [and] W^m at home all day. I poorly. M^r T Balls took tea here . . .

above The wheatfield. The view on the Whissonsett parish
border, looking south-west towards Tittleshall from the Raynham road. Following Mary Hardy's second near-fatal seizure
she took to open-air drives as a remedy in 1808–09. She would
have drawn strength from a love of the countryside fostered
during her childhood in this exhilarating landscape
[*photograph Margaret Bird 2011*]

facing page The family prospered. A silver button from the
coachman's 19th-century livery at Letheringsett Hall, with the
crest of Mary Hardy's grandson William H. Cozens-Hardy
[*Cozens-Hardy Collection*]

The full series of Mary Hardy volumes   by Margaret Bird, published by Burnham Press

The Diary of Mary Hardy   PUBLISHED 30 APRIL 2013

Diary 1 · 1773–1781 · Public house and waterway   ISBN 978–0–9573360–0–1
        The Coltishall years (full text)

Diary 2 · 1781–1793 · Beer supply, water power and a death   ISBN 978–0–9573360–1–8
        The early Letheringsett years (abridged text)

Diary 3 · 1793–1797 · Farm, maltings and brewery   ISBN 978–0–9573360–2–5
        The middle Letheringsett years (abridged text)
        with the diary of Henry Raven (full text)

Diary 4 · 1797–1809 · Shipwreck and meeting house   ISBN 978–0–9573360–3–2
        The last years at Letheringsett (abridged text)

*Each volume has an editorial introduction
and its own chronology, glossary, bibliography and index*

Set of four volumes   ISBN 978–0–9573360–4–9

The Remaining Diary of Mary Hardy   PUBLISHED 30 APRIL 2013
*Entries 1781–1809 not included in
the four-volume edition of the diary*   ISBN 978–0–9573360–5–6

Mary Hardy and her World   TO BE PUBLISHED
Volume 1 · A working family
Volume 2 · Barley, beer and the working year
Volume 3 · Spiritual and social forces
Volume 4 · Under sail and under arms

*Each volume has its own bibliography and index;
the chapters and appendices are listed opposite*

Set of four volumes

Sources: the original manuscripts   (held privately in the Cozens-Hardy Collection)

Diary of Mary Hardy
    Ledger 1 · 28 Nov. 1773–6 Jan. 1778
    Ledger 2 · 7 Jan. 1778–22 Sept. 1782
    Ledger 3 · 23 Sept. 1782–20 July 1790
    Ledger 4 · 21 July 1790–7 May 1800
    Ledger 5 · 8 May 1800–21 Mar. 1809

Diary of Henry Raven
    10 Oct. 1793–25 Oct. 1797

Mary Hardy and her World 1773–1809 by Margaret Bird
The nine books, containing 39 chapters, in this four-volume commentary

This analytical study is in course of preparation and will be published by Burnham Press.

The preface, foreword and acknowledgments appear at the beginning of volume 1 only.

The list of figures and tables in each of the nine books appears at the beginning of each book. Each volume has its own bibliography and index